Foster Care Independence Act/John H. Chafee Foster Care Indepen... (FCIA/Chafee) P.L. 106-169 (Replaced the former Title IV-E Independent Living Program)

- ❖ Provides flexible funding to states to develop and implement independent living services to all foster care children expected "to remain in foster care until age 18" irrespective of age
- ❖ Provides funding for "room and board" to youth who have left care and are less than 21 years old
- ❖ Allows Medicare coverage of former foster children through 21 years
- ❖ Encourages youth and community participation in programming

Juvenile Justice and Delinquency Prevention Act of 1974 (JJDPA) P.L. 93-415

- ❖ Diverts minor offenders
- ❖ Separates juvenile offenders from adult offenders in detention
- ❖ Places status offenders in secure detention facilities only if they have violated a court order and secure detention is found to be the only way to contain them
- ❖ Establishes the Office of Juvenile Justice and Delinquency Prevention
- ❖ Requires compliance as condition for states to receive federal funding for prevention and treatment services
- ❖ Mandates sharing of case information between child abuse and neglect and juvenile delinquency service systems

EIGHTH EDITION

Child Welfare and Family Services

Policies and Practice

Susan Whitelaw Downs
Wayne State University

Ernestine Moore
Wayne State University

Jean McFadden
Grand Valley State University

Boston ❖ New York ❖ San Francisco
Mexico City ❖ Montreal ❖ Toronto ❖ London ❖ Madrid ❖ Munich ❖ Paris
Hong Kong ❖ Singapore ❖ Tokyo ❖ Cape Town ❖ Sydney

Senior Acquisitions Editor: *Patricia Quinlin*
Editorial Assistant: *Carly Czech*
Marketing Manager: *Laura Lee Manley*
Production Supervisor: *Roberta Sherman*
Editorial Production Service: *Progressive Publishing Alternatives*
Composition Buyer: *Linda Cox*
Manufacturing Buyer: *Debbie Rossi*
Electronic Composition: *Progressive Publishing Alternatives*
Interior Design: *Progressive Publishing Alternatives*
Cover Administrator: *Joel Gendron*

For related titles and support materials, visit our online catalog at www.ablongman.com.

Between the time website information is gathered and then published, it is not unusual for some sites to have closed. Also, the transcription of URLs can result in typographical errors. The publisher would appreciate notification where these errors occur so that they may be corrected in subsequent editions.

Library of Congress Cataloging-in-Publication Data

Downs, Susan.
     Child welfare and family services: policies and practice. — 8th ed./Susan Whitelaw Downs,
Ernestine Moore, Jean McFadden.
        p.   cm
     Rev. ed. of: Child welfare and family services: policies and practice/Susan Whitelaw
Downs .... [et al.]. 7th ed.
     Includes bibliographical references and index.
     ISBN-13: 978-0-205-57190-1
     ISBN-10: 0-205-57190-5
        1. Child welfare—United States.   2. Family services—United States.
     I. Moore, Ernestine.   II. McFadden, Jean.   III. Child welfare and family services.   IV. Title.

HV741.C4995   2007
362.70973—dc22

                                                                        2007037615

Printed in the United States of America

10   9   8   7   6   5   4   3   2   RRD-VA   11   10   09   08

Dedication
To Lela B. Costin

We would like to acknowledge the contributions of the late Lela B. Costin, the primary author of this text for many years, and its heart and inspiration. The first edition, for which she was the sole author, was published in 1972. With each subsequent edition, her contribution to the education of future professional social workers grew. Wherever we travel, we meet people whose professional child welfare education was formed by her textbook and who continue to use it to guide their practice. Her firm belief that our society must do much better for its children, her keen ability to get to the heart of an issue, her research on child welfare history and policy, her tremendous energy for intellectual projects, and her encouraging mentoring of her coauthors are largely responsible for this book's success. She was a national leader of twentieth-century child welfare practice. We mourn her passing and celebrate her contributions to the field of social work and to the lives of children.

CONTENTS

Preface

Child Welfare and Family Services: Policies and Practice, Eighth Edition, presents concepts, policies, and practice in the broad field of child and family services. Material has been drawn from research findings, legislation, judicial decisions, professional literature, reports of social work practice, and interviews with practitioners. These sources inform the major subjects of the book: the needs of families and children, the major policies and programs of social services designed for them, and the policy issues that emerge for future planning. Our intent is to provide the student—undergraduate or graduate—with a substantive base of knowledge about policies and practice in family and child services.

The place of child and family services in the curricula of schools of social work has changed in response to broadened concepts of services for children and families within the human service community. In earlier years of social work education, child welfare was narrowly defined as a field of practice dealing mainly with children in the protective service system, in foster care, in institutions, or in the process of adoption. Correspondingly, child welfare courses were self-contained entities in a school's curriculum, combining policy and background knowledge with a large component of practice methods in this specialized field. Today, child welfare services have been redefined as child and family services and include knowledge of the traditional child welfare services as well as a wide range of programs to support families and children and to prevent the need for children's out-of-home care. Because this book addresses policies and programs directed at all children and families, the conceptual framework is appropriate not only for traditionally defined child welfare courses in which the instructor may choose to use the content selectively; it is also especially suitable in the curricula of schools of social work that offer "concentrations" or "specializations" more broadly defined as "services to families, children, and youth." Students in these concentrations are exposed to a range of social services to families and children, organized in a continuum from universal services, through preventive services of various kinds, to the traditional child welfare services. They may be assigned field placements in a variety of agencies serving families and children, including family service agencies, public and private child welfare agencies, child guidance clinics, the courts, and the schools. Students in related concentrations—for example, health and mental health services—for whom knowledge of public policy with respect to families is essential, often elect to enroll in family, child, and youth courses.

The text is designed for use in collaborative educational arrangements between public child welfare agencies and schools of social work. These partnerships evolved in the 1980s and 1990s, supported by state and federal funds to promote the reintegration of public agency practice into BSW and MSW programs. *Child Welfare and Family Services: Policies and Practice* is useful as a reliable reference for new personnel entering employment in child and family social agencies and as a tool for planned staff development programs. In some instances, it can be helpful to citizens in our highly technological society who want to influence the environment in which social services are carried out. Members of the global child welfare community find the text useful in understanding essential principles of child welfare practice, according to the American experience. This book is being used extensively abroad.

Our major objectives are to help the reader do the following:

1. Develop a vital concern for families and children and their potentialities; their cultural diversity; and their experiences in neighborhood and community.

2. Develop an overall orientation to the family as a unit of attention, and to the service concerns of family preservation, kinship care, services to children at risk, continuity of family relationships, and culturally appropriate services.

3. Identify problems necessitating family and child services, see how these problems are related to institutional gaps in the provision of appropriate services, and develop an appreciation for the need for collaboration and integration among service systems.

4. Become familiar with the policies, practices, and goals of current family and child welfare programs and acquire a basis for evaluating them.

5. Learn how services to families and children interact with the larger social and political structures, American cultural values, and global forces and trends, and the profound way these affect the goals and implementation of social policies.

6. Identify some of the salient aspects of social work history that arose in response to rather narrowly conceived social and family–child problems and that still influence family and child welfare programs in this country.

7. Distinguish between family and child welfare practices based on verified knowledge and those based mainly on custom and belief.

This book reflects our conviction that to be effective in today's turbulent world, it is essential that we avoid an overly narrow, categorical view of the welfare of children and their families. Services for children and families must be broadly defined. It would be inaccurate to portray child welfare as a narrow band of traditional services quite apart from the larger societal context in which it finds its energy, focus, and niche. It would be irresponsible to ignore the impact of public welfare and the courts as major influences on the status of children and families.

Full consideration is given to the basic core of child welfare services: services to protect children from neglect and abuse, family preservation services, foster care, adoption, and child advocacy. These topics are discussed with particular attention to continuity of family relationships, kinship care, and efforts to help children reach acceptable levels of health, safety, and educational achievement. We also have striven to highlight the cultural context within which children and families operate. We have been attentive to the need for cultural understanding and for the culturally competent organization of services. We have, thus, infused content on cultural and ethnic issues throughout the text.

In addition, the text includes the legal framework that governs the affairs of children and young persons (an aspect of the family and child welfare system whose importance has burgeoned) as reflected in laws of guardianship and recent United States Supreme Court decisions; the organization and functioning of the juvenile court and family courts; and the sociolegal issues that emerge in matters of poverty, unwed parenting, delinquency, child neglect and abuse, foster care, and adoption.

All the chapters in the eighth edition of *Child Welfare and Family Services: Policies and Practice* have been carefully revised and updated. The case material is drawn generally from our own experiences and that of other practitioners, but as presented here it is entirely fictitious. The chapters also include findings from recent research, important new court decisions and legislation affecting the child and the family, innovative demonstrations in recent practice with children and families, and content on global issues in child and family services.

NEW TO THIS EDITION

New to this edition are two chapters on child welfare practice, reflecting the need for child welfare caseworkers who can bring professional knowledge and judgment to the complex challenges of helping children and families involved in the public child welfare system. Chapter 4, Child Welfare Principles and Practice, provides a foundation for casework methods, processes and tasks in child welfare. This material is embedded in the historical and policy contexts of child welfare practice in the United States, which will help students integrate knowledge of social work methods with the particular constraints and mandates of practice in the child welfare policy environment. Chapter 9, Foster Care Practice and Issues, covers practice in foster care and other out-of-home settings for children. The material on foster care has been expanded from one to two chapters, to allow more coverage on practice methods. In addition to these chapters, content on child welfare practice has been infused throughout the text.

The order of the chapters reflects our preference for providing the student with a beginning understanding of families and of services to families, before moving to child welfare programs for specific populations of children and families. The first three chapters, An Introduction to Family and Child Services, Government Programs to Support Families and Children, and Services to Prevent Maltreatment and Support Families, provide a foundation for the study of family and child welfare. They present the historical background, an overview of services, the legal framework for the rights and responsibilities of children, parents, and the state, a discussion of federal policy and programs that affect families, and an introduction to preventive and developmental services that are, or should be, widely available to support families. Chapters 4 and 5 provide a foundation for child welfare practice in public and private agencies. Chapters 6 through 11 cover traditional child welfare services, including child protective services, family preservation services, foster care and adoption, and juvenile delinquency. Chapter 12 addresses the role of social workers in child advocacy and also professional issues in child welfare practice.

The chapters have also been written to stand alone so they can be ordered in a number of different ways to reflect the individual instructor's personal preferences in constructing a family and child services course and teaching outline. In our teaching, we have presented the chapters in differing order for different groups of students. This book is highly adaptable in organization.

At the end of each chapter are a chapter summary, questions for individual study and for class discussion, and a list of relevant Internet sites, reflecting the rapid increase in use of the World Wide Web. For additional exploration of ideas, the references at the end of each chapter provide a substantial bibliography of family and child services.

In the course of preparing eight editions of *Child Welfare and Family Services: Policies and Practice,* we have incurred many debts to numerous colleagues and academicians in other disciplines, and to administrators and staff members of public child welfare agencies and professional social workers in other settings, who carry out the demanding work in family and child services. They have directed us to new material and offered criticism and new insights that have been invaluable. We thank the reviewers of this edition: Emily Anderson, Borough Manhattan CC/CUNY; Richard Blake, Seton Hall University; Monique Busch, Indiana University; and Dale Weaver, California State University. We also thank our universities, Wayne State University and Grand Valley State University, for encouragement, resources, and support.

CHAPTER *1*

An Introduction to Family and Child Services

In the green years of childhood the young begin their irreversible march into the future with the resolution and sweet calmness of innocence.
The march of childhood goes on as long as the human race endures, an affirmation of new hope and the freshness of life that comes with every generation. The message proclaims another chance for mankind.

—*United Nations Children's Fund*

C hild and family welfare services reflect society's organized conviction about the worth of the child and the family, and the child's rights as a developing person and future citizen. Within the wide range of social welfare and social work, child welfare has a dual role: providing direct services to children and families when serious problems of children and youth are identified, and influencing public policy to improve the lives of all children. To strengthen family life for children is regarded as the primary purpose of child welfare.

The field of practice traditionally known as child welfare has been a dominant and influential force in the development of the social work profession. However, child welfare today as a specialized field of social work practice is vastly more complex than it was in the nineteenth and early twentieth centuries, when our ancestors confidently responded to problems of family functioning by "rescuing" children of poor or neglectful parents and placing them in institutions of one kind or another. Since then, for at least half a century, social changes have impelled child and family agencies to adapt and innovate services. Today's high public concern about the family, traditionally regarded as society's best institution for promoting stability, is showing more clearly the impact of social, industrial, and economic dislocation. Child and family welfare, as a specialized field of social work practice, is now facing challenges to its gradual but respected evolutionary growth as it confronts demands to move beyond the residual, outworn classification of child welfare services and to respond to new, complex family problems.

Some of the effects of rapid social change over the past decades are manifested in alternative family forms and child-rearing patterns, in the greatly accelerated entry of women with very young children into the labor force, in the unprecedented growth of female-headed families, and in increased official reporting of child abuse and neglect. Other developments have heightened concern among the public and professionals in the child welfare system—homelessness and immigration; and the heavy damage to parents, children, and adolescents caused by highly increased rates of drug use, especially by women.

Despite continuing reform efforts to preserve families and reduce the need for out-of-home placement for children, the number of children in foster care remains high. The public has become incensed at the shocking newspaper and television accounts of children who have been terribly abused sexually and physically, or neglected to the point of serious impairment or death, and the apparent inability of the child welfare system to prevent maltreatment or to protect children either in their own families or in substitute care. The anger at maltreating parents and apparent agency unresponsiveness has led to myriad calls for change, including congressional debate on bringing back orphanages for children of substance-abusing parents, class action and civil liability suits against agencies, and grassroots reform efforts to give children more legal standing in court to separate themselves from their parents. All these developments, as well as new federal and state legislation and judicial decisions, have served to give a new face to much of child welfare practice, and to make more urgent the need for competent personnel in the system of child and family social services.

This book, then, is about children. It is about their needs and their problems. It is about our society and its influence on children, and therefore it is also a book about families, governments, agencies, and professionals. It is about what we do *for* children, what we do *to* children, and what we do *with* children. It is also a book about how we can do better for the nation's children.

The welfare of children is dependent on the interaction between them and their environments. It is this focus that places the family at center stage because the family is the most dominant part of a child's environment. The family is the major instrument for providing for the welfare of children. It is the primary social institution in meeting social, educational, and health care needs. It is the family that negotiates with a larger environment to see that the child's needs are met. A larger society becomes involved when families are judged incapable of ensuring the child's welfare. This can occur because of the extraordinary needs of a special group of children, such as children with developmental disabilities, which can easily overwhelm family resources. Or it can occur because families, owing to lack of resources or major dysfunction, cannot meet even minimal standards of child care, as in the case of neglected or abused children.

Social work has had a uniquely important role in the connection between children, families, and organized social welfare. The earliest efforts of the profession were devoted to children and families. As Ann Hartman has described it:

> The profession has supported, replaced, taught, rehabilitated, treated, dismantled, abandoned, and embraced the family. To Mary Richmond [practitioner, teacher, and social work theoretician], the family was the central focus of social work's concern. The first professional practice journal was titled *The Family*. . . . The early child guidance workers focused their efforts on helping parents to be better parents, and the child-saving movement sought to rescue children by placing them with families. *(1981, p. 7)*

Traditionally, child welfare has been at the center of the social work profession. Today, that partnership between child welfare and social work is reflected in the philosophy that the best way to help children is to support, strengthen, and supplement the efforts of families. Laird has offered this precept for child and family welfare:

> Ecologically oriented child welfare practice attends to, nurtures, and supports the biological family. Further, when it is necessary to substitute for the biological family, such practice dictates that every effort be made to preserve and protect important kinship ties. Intervention in families must be done with great care to avoid actions which could weaken the natural family, sap its vitality and strength, or force it to make difficult costly adjustments. *(1985, p. 177)*

THE CHANGING AMERICAN FAMILY

Many observers claim that more changes have occurred in the American family over recent decades than ever before in our nation's history. The changes have led some to pronounce that the American family is breaking down and losing its preeminent position in American society. The more prevalent belief is that the American family is merely adapting to a very different world from the one it experienced earlier, and that the changes indicate American pluralism rather than breakdown. Regardless of the conclusions, few would argue that the past five decades have witnessed major changes in the family.

One major and continuing trend is the increase in the number of children in the United States. The number of children in the United States in 2003 was 73 million, above the peak of the baby boom in 1966 when the nation had 69.9 million children. This increase is fueled by immigration as much as by an increase in fertility. The "millennium generation," as the new baby boom is called, is more ethnically diverse than any previous one. Minority children (any group except non-Hispanic white) account for 44 percent of all children, compared to 26 percent in 1980. The biggest increase is in the percentage of Hispanic children, from 9 percent in 1980 to 19 percent today. They have overtaken African Americans, whose proportion of the child population has remained fairly stable at 16 percent. Asian and Pacific Islander children account for 4 percent of the child population, and Native American children continue to comprise about 1 percent (Federal Interagency Forum, 2005).

A recent and fast-growing trend is the increase in the number of children whose parents came to the United States from other countries, mainly Latin America and Asia. In 2004, 20 percent of children in the United States had at least one parent who was born abroad, up from 15 percent in 1994 (Federal Interagency Forum, 2005). These children face language and cultural barriers in addition to possible racial discrimination, and may need additional resources at school and at home.

Even though the number of children is increasing, they represent a smaller portion of the total population than they did in previous years. From a peak in 1966, when children under age 18 accounted for 36 percent of the population, children today account for only 25 percent, as other age groups increase more rapidly than the under-18 group (Federal Interagency Forum, 2005). This decreasing proportion may result in a loss to children of the government-provided services they need, such as schools, daycare, and health care, because there will be fewer households advocating for the needs of children.

American family structure is more diverse than it was thirty years ago. Today, about 32 percent of all American children live with a single parent, compared to 23 percent in 1980. This increase reflects the rise in the divorce rate and in the rate of births to unmarried mothers. Small but increasing percentages of children live with grandparents, other relatives, stepparents, adoptive parents, or parents' unmarried partners, with or without their own biological parent(s) in the home. About three million children live with neither parent (Federal Interagency Forum, 2002; 2005).

Related to the trend toward single-parent families is the increase in the percentage of children who are in child care arrangements because of their parents' employment. Today, over 60 percent of preschoolers and about half of grade school-aged children receive child care on a regular basis from someone other than a parent (Federal Interagency Forum, 2005). The movement of mothers of even very young children out of the home and into the workforce requires social policy to help families provide child care settings in which children can learn and thrive.

PROBLEMS OF CHILDREN AND YOUNG PERSONS

Among the nation's children are millions who are living and growing up under economic, social, or psychological conditions that hinder their development and future prospects.

Being Poor Means Being at Risk

Poverty is a condition that afflicts about 17 percent of American families with children (Federal Interagency Forum, 2005). The lack of sufficient means to live decently may grow out of parents' mental or physical illness or disability; low education levels or lack of marketable skills; or a lack of access to employment because of poor job skills; racial discrimination, or transportation difficulties.

Regardless of cause, for children, being poor means that the odds are stacked against them developmentally. Poor families almost always experience three associated ills: inadequate housing, poor schools, and insufficient health services. In addition, children in crowded inner cities usually have only the street as a place for play, where they are often at the mercy of the hostilities and violence that characterize much of street life in the inner city. Safe areas to play may be similarly lacking in some isolated rural areas.

> *He's scared and crying bad; stopped wanting to go to school 'cause of the shooting. (A mother in a dangerous neighborhood. The Ounce of Prevention Fund, 1993).*

Thousands of children experience the phenomenon of "homelessness," as their parents can no longer find nor sustain affordable housing. Many live in cars, shelters without privacy, rat-infested hotel rooms, or abandoned buildings. The effects on children and family life have been devastating. These families lack basic health care; the children develop chronic illnesses as a result of nutritional deficits and poor sanitation. Many of the children are deprived of regular school attendance. Homelessness has become a precipitating factor in foster care placements and a barrier to family reunification (Park, Metraux, Broadbar, & Culhane, 2004).

> *Davonte returned from the bathroom and slumped against his mother. "I'm cold," he murmured. "I want to go home."*
>
> *There was a pause. It was unclear where, exactly he meant: the apartment where they lived until October, whose contents . . . were in storage? The East River Family Center, their first and favorite placement, where they'd had a Christmas tree and opened presents before they'd been deemed ineligible and had to vacate the premises? Or some primal notion we all carry around in our minds of a comfortable place that is our own, where we can retreat to safety?*
>
> *"Are you sleepy?" [the mother] asked her son.*
>
> *"Yeah."*
>
> *"Well, we don't have a home," she said. "Isn't that sad?"*
>
> *(Egan, 2002, p. 32)*

Alienation, Violence, and Substance Abuse

As children age, they become susceptible to a variety of developmental risks to their health and to their social and intellectual development. Millions of youth confront a lack of opportunity to develop useful skills and find satisfying employment. Because as a nation we continue to isolate many young people in unstable, unrewarding, and dead-end jobs, it is not surprising that they do not feel that they have a stake in mainstream society.

The alienation of youth results from an accumulation of "risk factors," defined by Fraser, Kirby, and Smokowski (2004, p. 14) as "any influences that increase the chances for harm . . . or maintenance of a problem condition." In addition to personal and family influences, community and society conditions may also increase risk. For example, the public school may have failed to educate its pupils in ways that are relevant to the complexity of life today and to generate a level of competence vital to successful social functioning and individual well-being. For many school children, the result is a diminishing desire to learn; an inability to adapt to change; confusion about life goals; alienation from school and community; and antagonistic attitudes toward a society that has not solved its problems of war, poverty, unemployment, drugs, and racism. The mass media and entertainment industries expose youth to lifestyles that are not based on academic achievement, and glorify satisfaction of short-term pleasures over the self-discipline necessary to achieve long-term goals. The accumulation of risk factors increases the likelihood that young people will find that the avenue most open to them is delinquency, which is then compounded by the inadequate treatment and rehabilitative resources available.

Parents, teachers, social workers, and other professionals have also had to face a lack of knowledge about how to help youth with the serious problem of alcohol and drug usage. Young people throughout the population experiment with all kinds of available drugs. White and Hispanic youth report greater use of alcohol and drugs than do African American youth (Federal Interagency Forum, 2005; Snyder & Sickmund, 2006).

The AIDS (Acquired Immune Deficiency Syndrome) epidemic has tragically affected many children. Advances in medicine have reduced the risk that infants will get AIDS from their mothers. However, for teenagers, the risk is increasing. In 2003, about 450 children aged 13 or older became infected with the AIDS virus, the highest number ever recorded. Teenagers risk becoming infected through unprotected sex and through the injection of intravenous drugs. AIDS can also affect children by leaving them as orphans. Thousands of children are not infected themselves but are losing their mothers and fathers to disability or death from AIDS (Child Trends, no date).

With their parents at work and lacking opportunities for recreation or part-time work, many teenagers are left to fend for themselves after school, the period of greatest vulnerability for teenagers to commit delinquent acts or to become victims of crime (Snyder & Sickmund, 2006). Gang activities, drug and alcohol use, sexual activity, and other risky behaviors are likely to occur in the aimless hours between the end of the school day and the time when parents return home from work. Communities are challenged to provide better supervision and planned, productive activities for young people. Giving urgency to this issue of teen supervision is the increasing awareness of the dangers posed to young people from Internet sexual predators, who take advantage of the opportunity provided by electronic communication to exploit vulnerable youth (Wolak, Mitchell, & Finkelhor, 2006).

Youth suicide is a growing but under-recognized problem. American Indian youth are particularly vulnerable to death by suicide, reflecting the many challenges to healthy development that are found among some Indian populations (Snyder & Sickmund, 2006).

Children of Vulnerable Families

Among many families who seek help in behalf of their children, the presenting problem is centered on individual functioning or dysfunction in family interaction. Some parents are immature and overwhelmed with new or overdemanding responsibilities; others are poorly equipped with the knowledge needed today to give good care to children and maintain family balance. Despite greater availability of the means for birth control, many parents lack the help they want to plan the size of their families and use contraception effectively.

Some children's problems stem from their births to teenage parents who are themselves immature, highly vulnerable to loss of continued schooling, and lacking in knowledge of how to care for their children as well as the financial means to do so.

Children are frequently brought to the attention of social agencies because there are complaints that they are neglected or abused by their parents or other caregivers. The number of such reports is currently about three million per year (U.S. Department of Health and Human Services, 2006.) Federal funding and leadership have been inadequate to address the need of child protection. The solution to the problem of how to protect these children yet maintain the family continues to be elusive in too many cases. Some of these children must be enabled to live away from their own parents full time, with relatives, in foster homes, or in institutions.

Although most children live with their parents, who serve as their legal guardians, many children lack the protection of guardianship. These children are even more vulnerable to disregard of their individual rights. They are without an adult protector, guide, or advocate. For thousands of children who must live in institutions or experience other forms of substitute care, their duly appointed guardian is an officer of the state or an administrator of a large child care agency. This practice fixes responsibility for the child but denies the opportunity for an ongoing personal relationship with his or her guardian. Children of undocumented, foreign parents are an increasingly visible group who are particularly vulnerable to problems of guardianship in the child welfare system, and often do not have access to social and health services (Lincroft, Resner, & Leung, 2006).

All these problems directly affect the well-being of the nation's children and are appropriate for attention by family and child agencies. Yet, child welfare as a field of social work practice deals with only a small portion of the nation's children; the wider range of family and child service agencies addresses a large segment, mainly through offering various preventive and supportive services. In spite of these services, many children and families need help that is not available at all or that is insufficient to improve their situation.

RIGHTS AND RESPONSIBILITIES

All social services for children are based on certain assumptions about the relationships of a triad—*parent, child,* and *society* (see Figure 1.1). All the parts of the triad interact with a constant shifting of balance so that at certain times one part weighs more heavily than do the others in terms of influencing the behavior and welfare of children.

Each of these—parent, child, society—at any given time, has certain rights and responsibilities. Child welfare services are predicated on the conclusion that at certain times the well-being of the child may be insufficiently attended to because of conflict in the rights and roles of, or inadequacies of, or pressing demands on, any one of the parts of the triad.

Rights and Responsibilities of Children

An essential question in any formulation of family social policy is the extent to which children have their own rights and interests independent of parents, with a claim to their recognition and enforcement. The *rights* of children stem from their status—dependent, immature individuals who require care, protection, and guidance to survive and flourish. The child, then, *needs* certain forms of care in order to move gradually toward assumption of adult roles in society. But there are differences between children's needs and rights. Even though a child's needs may be known and established, they are not necessarily assured by rights.

Children's needs are defined by current knowledge about the physical, psychological, and social development of the child. Rights, however, are based on a legal definition carrying a claim, or an "entitlement," and therefore, enforceability. Statements of children's "needs" couched in language of "rights" are useful for defining goals in behalf of children, but they do not necessarily bring more enforceable rights.

The needs of children have been listed frequently and often with eloquence, and they have been attested to by impressive bodies of persons dedicated to the furtherance of the welfare of children. For example, in late 1989, the General Assembly of the United Nations, after ten years of negotiation, adopted an International Convention on the Rights of the Child (United Nations, 1989). Issues that slowed negotiations included abortion, adoption, child labor, and the minimum age for military combat. The Convention includes a child's right to a name, survival, education, and protection against exploitation and abuse, as well as safeguards against forcible separation

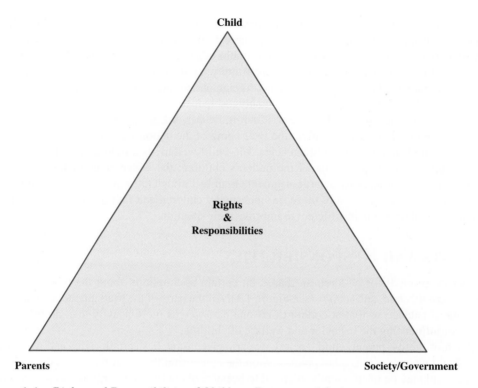

Figure 1.1   *Rights and Responsibilities of Children, Parents, and Society*

from the parents (U.N. Assembly, 1989). The United States has not signed the Convention, but insists that most of its core principles have been adopted in legislation and Supreme Court decisions (Hodgkin & Newell, 2002). These kinds of proclamations do not ensure enforceability, but they can be viewed as a constructive attempt to create international norms and inspire greater respect for children's rights.

In return for these commitments, children and young persons are expected to accept certain responsibilities to meet clear and consistent expectations of the adults responsible for them, to accept reasonable demands made on them, to develop a sense of personal accountability, to participate in voluntary work, and to take advantage of opportunities that help them develop their own sense of responsibility and capacity to alter society in constructive ways when they find it unacceptable.

In consideration of the legal rights of children and youth, Brieland and Lemmon (1985, p. 15) observed that "laws dealing with youths are characterized by paradoxes and inconsistencies." For example, young people can vote, join the military, and, in some states, marry without parental consent, by the age of eighteen, but still be too young to legally purchase alcohol or cigarettes.

The law has created certain "privileges and disabilities" for persons who are still minors. The intent is to protect children from the consequences of their own lack of judgment, or to prevent them from acting where they lack sufficient maturity to act advisedly. Examples of the first purpose are found in the child's privilege to disaffirm contracts, or special laws that protect children while using the Internet, such as the Child Online Privacy Protection Act (Public Law 105-277). An example of the second purpose is reflected in the child's inability to hold public office.

The U.S. Supreme Court has the final decision as to whether a particular law (federal, state, or local), as applied to a particular case, is constitutional or not. Therefore, Supreme Court decisions, and the reasoning behind them, provide a framework for understanding the nation's policies affecting children's rights. The Court's decisions are complex and at first glance contradictory, because they reflect the often conflicting needs and goals of parents, children, and society. Some of these cases are weighted in the direction of reinforcing the rights of parents in the upbringing of their children. Some clearly extend legal rights to minors; others limit rights they would have but for their status as minors. In all cases, the influences and interests of society are apparent.

Although the U.S. Constitution makes no reference to children per se, Supreme Court justices have clearly stated that the child, merely on account of his or her minority status, is not beyond the protection of the Constitution: "Whatever may be their precise impact, neither the Fourteenth Amendment nor the Bill of Rights is for adults alone" (*In re Gault,* 1967, p. 13). In some cases the Court has concluded that the child's right to due process is the same as that of an adult, particularly if the child risks being imprisoned (*In re Gault,* 1967; *Tinker v. Des Moines Independent Community School District,* 1969). But it has also rejected "the uncritical assumption that the constitutional rights of children are indistinguishable from those of adults," or that under the law children can never be treated differently from adults (*Bellotti v. Baird,* 1979, p. 633). The justices have offered three principles to explain why the constitutional rights of children cannot be unequivocally equated with those of adults: "the peculiar vulnerability of children; their inability to make critical decisions in an informed, mature manner; and the importance of the parental role in child-rearing" (*Bellotti v. Baird*, 1979, p. 623).

U.S. Supreme Court decisions, particularly since the mid-twentieth century, have gradually identified legally enforceable rights of minors. The Court's decisions accord children the protections enumerated in the First, Fourth, Fifth, Sixth, Eighth, and Fourteenth Amendments (Jacobs, 1995). The Court has been particularly active in delineating children's rights in criminal proceedings, starting with the landmark cases in the mid-twentieth century, *In re Gault* (1967) and *Kent v. United States* (1966).

A number of reproductive rights cases attempt to balance children's privacy rights with parents' rights to decide matters affecting their children. The Court's decisions have established that minors have the right to receive contraceptive services without parental permission (*Carey v. Population Services International, et al.,* 1977); that their parents may not have absolute veto power over their decision to have an abortion (*Bellotti v. Baird,* 1979); and that they have a right to an independent judicial determination whether they are mature enough to make a decision to have an abortion (*Hodgson v. Minnesota,* 1990). However, the Court has not precluded states from enacting legislation requiring or permitting notification to a parent of the minor's decision to have an abortion (*H.L. Matheson,* 1981; *Hodgson v. Minnesota,* 1990).

Current public policy on children's rights can be summarized as follows: Children are generally protected by the same constitutional guarantees as adults; society, through the legal system, can make adjustments to take account of children's vulnerability and the unique role of the family; and principles must be applied flexibly and sensitively to the special needs of children and parents. Those advocating for expanded and inclusive constitutional protections for children have perceived an ambivalence in the Court on rights bestowed and rights denied. Awareness of the principles and reasoning of the Court can make these seeming contradictions more understandable, if not fully acceptable, to child advocates.

Rights and Responsibilities of Parents

In our society, the primary right and responsibility of caring for children rests with the parents. As long as this care takes place in the child's own home and does not fall below a minimal standard demanded by a given community, then in most instances a wide range in quality and kind of care is tolerated. Differences are accepted and valued as part of our way of life, and the family is able to retain its privacy and independence.

The rights of parents and the ways in which they discharge the duties connected with these rights have crucial and far-reaching effects on the child. Parents have the rights of guardianship by the fact that the child was born to them. If the parents are unwed, the mother automatically assumes natural guardianship, but unmarried fathers may establish paternity and acquire rights (see below). Parents determine the living pattern and the standards of everyday conduct, which influence the developing personality of the child. They can determine religion and may affect basic ethical values of the child. They influence the type and extent of the child's education, the decision as to vocation, and the level of adult achievement. The quality of health care the child receives depends not only on the availability of health services in the community but also on the extent of the parents' knowledge and the choices made by them when medical care is needed. Even when guardianship is removed from parents, unless parental rights have been fully terminated by court action, certain rights (as well as the duty to support) remain; for example, the right of parents to receive notice of judicial proceedings involving the child and the right to give or withhold consent to the child's adoption.

Such far-reaching and well-entrenched rights of parents carry extensive responsibilities in relation to the child. Even though our society usually is willing to allow parents great latitude in the ways they meet their responsibilities, parental duties are demanding. In those instances in which the quality of parental care falls below the minimal level that a community will permit, usually the blame that is attached to parents is heavy. They will probably feel considerable censorship and rejection from the rest of the community.

The responsibilities of parenthood include (1) financial support—meeting the child's monetary needs in a society that looks with disfavor on economic dependency and the inability of parents to keep the family economically self-supporting; (2) the provision of physical care—keeping the child safe from harm and injury and giving attention to his or her physical condition and health demands; (3) emotional care—for many parents a nebulous and poorly defined concept, carrying connotations of responsibility without knowledge of ways to meet it; and (4) a range of other parental duties, such as giving guidance and supervision to the young child as well as to the adolescent, promoting the growth of self-discipline, and setting forth clear parental and societal expectations that are adapted to the individual child's pace and ability. In addition, the right of parents to make certain major decisions for the child—for example, consent to medical care, to enlistment in the armed forces, and to marriage—is also a serious responsibility.

Parental rights over various aspects of their children's lives have been reinforced in several Supreme Court decisions, which have established that parents have full right to choose to send their child to a public or a private school (*Pierce v. Society of Sisters*, 1925); to refuse to adhere to compulsory school attendance statutes when compliance violates their religious beliefs (*Wisconsin v. Yoder,* 1972); to institutionalize their child for mental health treatment provided that the child's condition is assessed, evaluated, and periodically reviewed (*Parham v. J.R.*, 1979); to have a clear and convincing standard of proof applied in proceedings to terminate their parental rights (*Santosky v. Kramer*, 1982); to have their decisions about third-party visitation with their child given weight in court (*Troxel v. Granville*, 2000); and to be free from warrantless or non-consensual drug screenings during pregnancy (*Ferguson v. City of Charleston*, 2001).

The Supreme Court has also issued decisions in which the rights of parents were limited. This line of cases recognizes that children have rights separate from their parents, and that the states have interests in protecting those rights. For example, in *Prince v. Massachusetts* (1944), the Court supported the states, allowing them greater authority than parents in the regulation of child labor.

In recent decades, the unwed father has gained legal recognition of some aspects of parental rights to his nonmarital child. A chain of U.S. Supreme Court cases (*Stanley v. Illinois*, 1972, *Quillon v. Walcott*, 1978, *Caban v. Mohammed*, 1979) has established that the father must have developed a significant and personal relationship with his nonmarital child to warrant constitutional protection in adoption proceedings. To date, the fact of biological relationship alone between father and nonmarital child does not merit protection. Unwed fathers must "grasp the opportunity" of their biological connection to their child to form an actual parenting relationship. Although uncertainty persists as to the scope of constitutional protections of the rights of the father regarding his nonmarital children, the Supreme Court decisions have established that fathers have the right to be notified and to be heard in adoption or termination of parental rights proceedings. If they have had a substantial relationship with their child, they have a right to a "determination of fitness" equal to that afforded married parents. Many states have statutes and procedural rules that further clarify the rights of unwed fathers.

There is increasing awareness of the heavy demands placed on adults in today's rapidly changing world, with recognition of the frequent limitations of parental strength in an industrialized, urban society. Clearly, the demands on modern-day families call for more attention to the types of aids and new services that all parents need to enable them to succeed in their responsibilities.

Rights and Responsibilities of Society

To promote children's welfare and to bring or maintain order in a modern way of life, society—through government—has the right and the responsibility to exercise authority to act in ways that benefit children.

One such power of the state is found it its use of *regulatory powers*. For the protection of children, generally, the state can set up regulations that govern all parents, such as in compulsory school attendance laws; it can impose regulations on third parties who employ children and young persons, or on doctors who may be required to screen children for lead poisoning, or on merchants who may be prohibited from selling alcohol or tobacco to minors. Regulations may also be applied to foster parents and social welfare agencies who wish to give care to children, consisting of prescribed standards of care and treatment. The intent in the state's use of its regulatory authority is to represent society's interest in all children through the application of broad powers to set standards applying to children generally, or all parents generally, or other adults acting in relation to children.

A second application of a state's right and responsibility to act in behalf of children is the principle of *parens patriae*, which translated literally means "father of the country." When parental care falls below a level allowed for by law, or when a child or young person engages in delinquent acts prohibited by law, the state has a responsibility to intervene, that is, to exercise the ancient law of *parens patriae*, under which the court, acting as a protector of the dependent and immature child, uses its power to require a better level of care or treatment for a particular child (*Chapsky v. Wood*, 1902; *Prince v. Massachusetts*, 1944; Nurcombe & Partlett, 1994).

With the authority of *parens patriae*, the government, through state and federal laws, plays significant roles in altering the parenting relationships.

- ❖ If the parents are unwed, state laws are invoked to establish paternity.
- ❖ If the parents separate or divorce, state child custody laws are invoked to determine custody, parenting time (visitation), and support.
- ❖ If the parents are temporarily unable to care for the child, state guardianship laws are invoked to provide for voluntary transfer of guardianship or state child abuse and neglect, or juvenile delinquency laws are invoked to provide for court wardship.
- ❖ If parents are found to be unable or unwilling to remedy the situation that necessitated court wardship, then state termination of parental rights or child emancipation laws are invoked to permanently terminate their rights and responsibilities.
- ❖ If new parents are found, state adoption laws are invoked to legally establish a new parenting relationship.

A third kind of power of the state to act for children is its *authority to legislate for the development of various child welfare services.* For example, at the federal level, the government can tax for programs so that if certain conditions are met states can receive federal money to aid in the development of their own plans of social services to children and their families. State governments have the power to adopt statutes that provide for the development and financing of a range of social services in behalf of children, including the establishment of foster care programs and services to families in their own homes. The importance of the state's authority to legislate and spend for the development of social services to children and their families cannot be overemphasized. How successfully children are helped often depends on the extent to which the statutes of a state reflect modern knowledge about children and their changing world, respect for their rights, and readiness to tax and appropriate money for professional services and facilities to meet the needs of children.

HISTORICAL HIGHLIGHTS OF SERVICES TO FAMILIES AND CHILDREN

The history of family and child welfare policy shows distinct, although sometimes overlapping, organized efforts to improve the welfare of children and the development of social services for them and their parents.

Indenture and "Outdoor Relief"

In the early years of this nation, individuals who could not maintain themselves or their families were considered the responsibility of the local township. Some children were mentally retarded; some were physically disabled. Some were orphaned by epidemics and other disasters. Some showed incorrigible behavior. The methods of treatment within a community, however, were simple. The youngest children who required support by the town were "farmed out" to the lowest bidder—a family that agreed to give care to the child for a small, regular sum of money or goods. Others were often sent to live in the dreary, unsanitary almshouses with the adult misfits of the town—the mentally ill, the mentally deficient, lawbreakers, and the aged and infirm.

Able bodied, older children were usually indentured; that is, placed under contract with a citizen of the town who agreed to maintain the child and teach him or her a trade or other gainful occupation in return for the profit from the child's labor. This was a favored practice, as everyone's labor was needed during the development of the new country. With the beginning of the Industrial Revolution, indenture became less feasible and by 1875 had almost completely disappeared (Folks, 1911). Despite some cases of cruel masters, indentured children, on the whole, were more fortunate than were children in almshouses. In that sense, indenture was seen as a forward step in child care (Thurston, 1930).

Another choice, termed *outdoor relief* and managed by the local poor law authority, was to give meager aid to dependent children in their own homes. This approach was poorly administered and the least accepted form of care (Abbott, 1938). Nevertheless, public outdoor relief provided aid to more dependent children than did all other special forms of protecting children. (A current form of outdoor relief is seen in today's Temporary Assistance for Needy Families program.)

Children's Institutions and the Growth of Voluntary Agencies

Gradually, society realized that children need a different type of care from adults and more "security" than was provided by a master under a contract of indenture. Many of the earliest institutions for children were sponsored not by government but by private child-caring agencies. To a large extent, these private or voluntary agencies had their beginnings in the desire of people to fulfill neighborly obligations. Orphanages were a response of the community to disasters that left children without parents (Downs & Sherraden, 1983). Concerned citizens would then undertake to organize a group of people to care for the children in need. Examples include the Ursuline Convent in New Orleans, which in 1729 undertook the care of ten girls who had been orphaned by Indian wars; an asylum for the care and education of destitute girls, established in Baltimore in 1799 by St. Paul's Church; and institutions in various states called Protestant Orphan Asylums, which came into being to care for children who were orphaned in the cholera epidemics of the 1830s. Many of these institutions later became child-placing agencies, extending their care of children into foster homes in the communities or taking on other community activities.

The latter half of the nineteenth century brought an era of "child-saving" activities. The intent was to save children from conditions of crime, vice, and poverty found in urban areas where slums were crowded with poor, European immigrants. The Children's Aid Societies, found first in the cities of the Eastern seaboard, took many children into care and placed them in free foster homes (Cook, 1995; Nelson, 1995). An example is the Children's Aid Society of New York City, founded in 1853 by the Reverend Charles Loring Brace, who organized a massive program that resettled nearly 100,000 children from eastern cities in free foster homes in midwestern and southern states.

In addition to the intent of the new voluntary agencies to protect harmless children orphaned by disaster or to save others from a life of crime and moral degradation, a third concern was protection of children from neglect and cruelty. While laws existed for the protection of children from cruelty and abuse, they were poorly enforced. The New York Society for the Prevention of Cruelty to Children—the first of its sort—was formed in 1875 to rescue children from cruelty and inhumane treatment and to bring about enforcement of existing laws and passage of new laws.

Still another kind of voluntary agency established in the nineteenth century pioneered in many kinds of service to families and children. Settlement houses such as Jane Addams's famous Hull House in Chicago and Lillian Wald's Henry Street Settlement in New York were notable examples. Founded with broad aims and open to all the inhabitants of the neighborhood, they focused on the needs of families and the preservation and enhancement of human dignity, skill, and values. They were attuned to the social forces that buffeted poor people, most of whom were immigrants of various nationalities and religions. These early settlement houses demonstrated new services for families and children and worked steadfastly for social reform and for strengthening local communities as environments for families.

African American Children. Slavery is a shocking and terrible part of American history. According to some estimates, between 1686 and 1786, approximately two million African people were forcibly taken from their homes; about 250,000 of them became slaves in America. Slavery as an institution was established to meet the need for cheap labor, particularly in the South. The economy of the North was also deeply implicated through its involvement in transporting slaves in its shipping industry. In addition to slaves, some Africans came to America during earliest colonial days as explorers and servants.

During the time of slavery and beyond, the family was the major and often only system of child welfare for African American children. In the North, African American children were excluded from most orphanages (Smith & Merkel-Holguin, 1995). A notable exception was the Philadelphia Association for the Care of Colored Children, a Quaker shelter for African American children founded in 1822. It was burned down by a white mob in 1838.

After the Civil War, limited progress was made in providing for needy African American children through the efforts of African Americans. They worked though mutual aid groups such as churches and benevolent organizations, some of which formed cooperative arrangements with white philanthropists and governmental sponsors. For example, the Virginia Industrial School for Colored Girls, founded in 1915, was maintained by the Virginian Federation of Colored Women's Clubs with an arrangement for interracial cooperation (Peebles-Wilkins, 1995). African American children were not fully integrated into the public child welfare system until after World War II (Billingsley & Giovannoni, 1972).

State Boards of Charities

During the latter part of the nineteenth century, states had begun to assume responsibility for certain classes of the poor—those the towns, parishes, and other local units of government were unwilling or unable to care for. Children, too, began to benefit from this assumption of responsibility by the state. Specialized state institutions were established: "reform" schools and training schools for children who were blind, deaf, or mentally deficient (Sherraden & Downs, 1984). This increased activity underscored the need for a central agency at the state level to coordinate the administration of the welfare programs that local governments had been unable to finance or administer. Massachusetts, in 1863, was the first state to establish such a central agency—the State Board of Charities—for the supervision of all state charities.

Federal Government Involvement

The federal government was long reluctant to become involved with child and family welfare because of concern that it would violate *states'* rights, as social welfare is considered primarily the domain of state and local government. Even more significant in the opposition to federal action was the fear of invasion of *parents'* rights. Traditionally, the right and the responsibility of raising children had been held by parents; the government's role was confined to local matters and protection. As one senator in 1919 framed the situation, "The homes of the country are best protected through the local government [and not by a] federal nursery that shall pass upon the wisdom of the mothers and fathers of the land" (Heyburn, 1919, p. 189). This emphasis on parents' rights, conceptualized as the essential, basic civil right to conceive and raise one's children without governmental interference, has continued to influence the development of federal policy (Bogenschneider, 2000).

Federal Policy on Native American Families. An exception to the general principle of nonintervention into family life was the role of the federal government in breaking up Native American families. During the early twentieth century, federal policy toward Native Americans was to encourage the dissolution of Indian culture and the incorporation of Indians into mainstream American life. As part of this policy, Native American children were removed from their families and placed in Indian boarding schools, where they were required to give up their language and culture, and where they lost ties to their families, who were far away on reservations. The Indian Child Welfare Act of 1978 has put safeguards in place to prevent the loss of Indian children to their culture.

Growth of Federal Programs

Despite the opposition to federal involvement in families, inequities among the states and the lives of children were apparent. Initial steps to address the problems nationally were indirect—the founding of the Children's Bureau and the first White House Conference of 1912. Significantly, these early endeavors were oriented toward wide dissemination of information, not the delivery of much-needed services to families. The Great Depression in the 1930s made it clear that government intervention was essential to help many persons and families cope with various overwhelming problems. Under the Social Security Act of 1935, the federal government established a financial assistance program for children (Aid for Dependent Children), the Social Security Insurance program, and child welfare programs (through Title IV-B of the Social Security Act), which introduced a major federal role in social welfare.

Federal spending on social policy increased during the three decades after World War II, as did federal regulation of these funds that would be spent at the state and local levels. Federal involvement increased at least in part because of growing skepticism that the states would allocate federal funds fairly and effectively. There was particular concern that southern states would discriminate against African Americans. However, it would be a mistake to overestimate the extent of federal power in social welfare policy during these decades. Most federal funds continued to be administered through state and local agencies.

Today, the federal government's influence in child welfare and juvenile justice continues through the states' acceptance of federal funds to implement programs. The acceptance of federal funds includes the commitment to implement federal statutory requirements or administrative guidelines with respect to the funding. Box 1.1 summarizes the most significant legislation and guidelines currently in effect in child welfare. The legislation reflects the great changes in child welfare policy and practice that occurred during the last half of the twentieth century, as the child welfare field became the focus of national concern. Major reforms occurred in foster care, adoption, child protection, and juvenile justice to make these programs more effective in protecting children, to move children through the system, and to ensure the rights of both parents and children while they were involved with child welfare agencies. The story of these changes and how current federal policy is being implemented at the state and local levels regarding specific child welfare programs is discussed in the chapters that follow.

Box 1.1

Major Federal Legislation for Child Welfare and Juvenile Justice Services as Amended through December 2006

Child Abuse Prevention and Treatment Act of 1974 (CAPTA) P.L. 93-247

❖ Defines child maltreatment
❖ Establishes National Center on Child Abuse and Neglect in HHS-ACYF to serve as clearinghouse for the development and transmittal of information on child protection research and demonstration programs; to provide technical assistance to states; to allocate federal funds for child abuse and neglect (CAN); and coordinate federal CAN activities.
❖ Authorizes grants to the states for child protection programming
❖ Ties receipt of funds by the states to the states' passing reporting laws with immunity provisions; mandated reporters; and public education initiatives

The Indian Child Welfare Act of 1978 (ICWA) P.L. 95-608

❖ Defines "Indian child"
❖ Provides that tribes have exclusive jurisdiction over child welfare issues involving an Indian child
❖ Provides specific procedures to ensure compliance by the states

Adoption and Safe Families Act of 1997 (ASFA) P.L. 105-89 (Amended significant provisions of the Adoption Assistance and Child Welfare Act of 1980 [AACWA])

❖ Clarifies that the health and safety of child is paramount
❖ Specifies certain offenses against the child or a sibling for which "reasonable efforts" to prevent removal was unnecessary
❖ Expands the required court oversight
❖ Requires permanency hearings within 12 months of out-of-home placement and initiation of termination of parental rights (TPR) proceeding where child is in care for 15 of last 22 months except if child is with relative, there is a compelling reason that TPR is not in best interests, or agency has not provided services in care plan.
❖ Sanctions concurrent planning, i.e., planning for return home and other permanent placement at same time
❖ Reaffirms reasonable efforts and reunification philosophy expressed under AACWA of 1980
❖ Promotes timely adoptions through provisions of incentives and funds post-adoption services
❖ Requires developments and implementation of performance standards
❖ In 2005 and 2006, four federal statutes were passed that reinforce ASFA's provisions for timely, safe, and permanent placements for children in the child welfare system: The Deficit Reduction Act of 2005 P.L. 109-171; The Safe and Timely Interstate Placement of Foster Children Act of 2006 P.L. 109-239; The Adam Walsh Child Protection and Safety Act of 2006 P.L. 109-248; and The Child and Family Services Improvement Act of 2006 P.L. 109-288.

Multiethnic Placement Act of 1994 P.L. 103-382 as amended by the Interethnic Placement Provisions of 1996

❖ Prohibits the delay or denial of foster home or adoption placement on the basis of the race, color, or national origin of the child or the potential foster or adoptive parent.

Box 1.1 (continued)

Foster Care Independence Act/John H. Chafee Foster Care Independence Program of 1999 (FCIA/Chafee) P.L. 106-169 (Replaced the former Title IV-E Independent Living Program)

❖ Provides flexible funding to states to develop and implement independent living services to all foster care children expected "to remain in foster care until age 18" irrespective of age

❖ Provides funding for "room and board" to youth who have left care and are less than 21 years old

❖ Allows Medicare coverage of former foster children through 21 years

❖ Encourages youth and community participation in programming

Juvenile Justice and Delinquency Prevention Act of 1974 (JJDPA) P.L. 93-415

❖ Diverts minor offenders

❖ Separates juvenile offenders from adult offenders in detention

❖ Places status offenders in secure detention facilities only if they have violated a court order and secure detention is found to be the only way to contain them

❖ Establishes the Office of Juvenile Justice and Delinquency Prevention

❖ Requires compliance as condition for states to receive federal funding for prevention and treatment services

❖ Mandates sharing of case information between child abuse and neglect and juvenile delinquency service systems

PUBLIC POLICIES FOR FAMILIES AND CHILDREN

The U.S. Constitution, in contrast to those of almost all other countries, has no mention of family. This omission reflects the American emphasis on the individual, liberty, rights, and freedom from governmental interference in personal life, in preference to communitarian values that emphasize the role of the individual in promoting the welfare of the family or other groups. Throughout the history of the United States, government involvement in social welfare gradually has increased, although often reluctantly, in response to problems that people recognized required a larger and more sustained effort than private charities could provide.

As used here, social policy refers to official decisions about social issues or a broad principle of operation for carrying out a specific aspect of the social welfare system. Policies define such matters as the nature of the services or aid, who shall receive service, what the standards of practice shall be, and specific principles and procedures for carrying out a social welfare program.

In the study of family and child welfare, we are primarily concerned with the impact of public social policy on the child and on family life developed by government through its judicial, legislative, and executive branches. Figure 1.2 shows these branches of government and the names of the governmental bodies in each branch at the federal, state, and local levels. Together these entities make up and implement most of the public social policy in the United States.

Family Policy

Family policy is a branch of social policy that deals with the relationship of government to families. It has been difficult to formulate family policy in the United States because family policy issues raise fears, unresolved reluctance, and serious division within a population that has been

BRANCH / LEVEL	LEGISLATIVE	EXECUTIVE	JUDICIAL
FEDERAL	U.S. Congress	President Department of Health and Human Services Other Departments	U.S. Supreme Court
STATE	State Legislature	Governor Department of Social Services Other Departments	State Supreme Court
LOCAL	City Council County Board of Commissioners School Board	Mayor County Executive School Superintendent	Family Court Juvenile Court District Circuit Court

Figure 1.2 *Sources of Policy by Level and Branch of Government*

wary of change in the relationships of the family and the state. To some extent, the reluctance of government to intervene in family life has given way to a perspective that encourages public involvement in certain areas of family life.

Family policy can be considered from a narrow or broad perspective. From a narrow perspective, policy analysts have identified four specific areas of family function that are the focus of family policy: (1) family creation, including marriage, pregnancy and childbirth, and adoption; (2) economic support; (3) childrearing; and (4) family caregiving (Bogenschneider, 2000). Evidence is growing that the government can play a positive role in helping families in these areas through such programs as Head Start, health insurance for children, welfare legislation, and child welfare legislation dealing with foster care and adoption.

A broader perspective on family policy takes into account the realization that virtually all governmental actions directly or indirectly affect families. Varying state and federal programs have an impact on family life even though family concerns were not a reason for the intervention or directly considered in the formulation of the policies (Ooms, 1990). For example, the globalization of the economy can affect drastically the ability of workers to find good-paying manufacturing jobs in the United States, and therefore also affects the well-being of families who depend on those workers for their livelihood. The Family Impact Seminars, organized at the University of Wisconsin, encourage state governments to evaluate legislation from a family perspective, whether or not it is specifically aimed at families. The seminars educate state legislators on the impact of legislation on "family well-being" (e.g., family stability, family relationships, and the family's ability to carry out its responsibilities) (Bogenschneider, 2000; The Policy Institute for Family Impact Seminars, no date).

Controversy surrounds many areas of family policy. The debate becomes most intense when it is focused, not in the abstract, but on a specific problem or proposal. For example, abortion and contraception, public policies regarding same-sex domestic partners, and the rights and responsibilities of unmarried fathers have developed proponents and opponents who can be equally vociferous. The lack of unanimity has contributed to the fragmented and erratic nature of American policy toward families in our pluralistic society.

CHILD AND FAMILY SERVICES

Principles of Child and Family Services

Child and family welfare practice and policy are guided by certain overarching principles. *A major principle of the field of child welfare and family services is that a safe and permanent home is the best environment for children.* Children are dependent, immature individuals who require care, protection, and guidance to survive and flourish. They need certain kinds of care in order to move gradually toward assumption of adult roles in society. The Casey Outcomes and Decision-Making Project (1998) has defined children's needs as "the opportunity to grow and develop in an environment which provides consistent nurture, support, and stimulation. Practice and research in child development have documented that families can usually best provide the consistent nurturing environment, and secure, uninterrupted relationships with caring adults, that are necessary for child well-being" (p. 4).

A second major principle concerns child safety. Children need to grow up in environments free of physical, sexual, and emotional abuse. They need to have the basic necessities of food, clothing, and shelter, and personal relationships with loving, attentive caregivers.

A major dilemma for the child welfare field is what to do when these two principles collide. Families enter the child welfare system because their ability to provide a safe environment for their children has been called into question. How can we as professionals take action that is congruent both with the principle that children do best when growing up in families and also with the principle that they need to be free from abuse and neglect?

One solution to this dilemma involves another principle of child and family services. *As the needs of children can best be met by families, a third major principle of family and child services is that they should work to strengthen and support family functioning.* Families deserve strong support from the community to help them provide an adequate environment for their children, including access to medical care, decent housing, and a minimally adequate income. Child and family services are offered to the family based on their needs and whether the family is voluntarily seeking help, is receiving child protective services, or has children in foster care. The term *wraparound services* refers to the effort to provide families who are struggling to provide a safe, nurturing environment with whatever community services they need to prevent separate placement of their children. These services are also provided to achieve family reunification if it has been necessary to remove the children from the home. Whether a child is at home or in foster care, the family is entitled to receive parent education, supportive counseling, help with housing and employment, drug or mental health treatment, and other services, depending on their needs. The provision of family support and preservation services is one way that child welfare and family services can reconcile the needs of children both for family life and for freedom from physical, sexual, and emotional abuse and from neglect.

A fourth major principle of family and child services is that placement decisions should respect the children's needs for family continuity. If children need to be separated from families, the focus should be on maintaining continuity of the children's emotional attachments to family (McFadden & Downs, 1995). Kinship networks can play an important part in maintaining this continuity. If safety concerns require that children be placed temporarily away from biological parents, the children are likely to feel more comfortable about the move if they are going to relatives they know, if they are moving with their siblings, or if they are remaining in their neighborhoods where they can stay in touch with friends, teachers, and relatives. Even for children who must be permanently separated from their parents, planning must focus on maintaining continuity of the child's attachments—for example, through permanent placement with relatives or foster parents already known to the child or through maintaining a connection to the biological parents in an "open adoption" arrangement.

These four principles guide the organization and delivery of all types of social services to families and children, and lead logically to the formation of program goals and desired outcomes of services. Types of child welfare services and their outcomes are discussed in the following sections.

Classification of Services

Services to families and children traditionally have been classified into four major groups: preventive and supportive, protective, foster care, and adoption services. These categories reflect the historical development of child and family services and their varying legal mandates.

❖ *Preventive and supportive services* are available to families to support and strengthen family life, to promote the healthy development of children and adults, to reduce risks to children, and to help families maintain connections with community institutions such as schools, welfare, and the workplace. Depending on the type of service offered, these services may be called therapeutic, preventive, or supportive. (See Chapters 2 and 3.)

❖ *Protective services* are for families who have fallen below a minimally sufficient level of childrearing and whose children therefore suffer from abuse or neglect. Services include investigation of the family's situation and help in improving family life so that the children can remain safely in the home. (See Chapters 5, 6, and 7.)

❖ *Foster care services* are for families who temporarily cannot maintain a minimally sufficient childrearing environment in the home. While children are in foster care, the focus is on helping parents to improve their life situation so that children can be returned to them safely. Children may be placed with relatives, called "kinship care," in a foster family, in a group home, or in a children's institution. They are helped to cope with the separation and to adjust to their new living situation. Arranging visitation to help family members maintain connection with one another and planning for reunifcation as early as possible are important aspects of foster care services. (See Chapters 8 and 9.)

❖ *Adoption services* are available to children in need of a new, permanent family because their biological parents have relinquished them for adoption or had their parental rights permanently terminated in court. Helping the child (if older) grieve for the loss of his or her biological family and adjust to the new family are key adoption services. Adoption services provide support to the adoptive family and the biological family. (See Chapter 10.)

Preventive and supportive services differ from the other three service categories—protective services, foster care, and adoption—in a number of ways. Protective services, foster care, and adoption are traditionally considered the elements making up the domain of child welfare services. Government, through regulation, funding, and the legal system, defines much of the framework within which these services are offered. Families usually do not seek out protective services and foster care services voluntarily; the agencies, through their legally established mandates, require the family's participation when its ability to maintain a minimally sufficient environment for children is in serious question. The families in these service systems come disproportionately from the poorest and most vulnerable segments of the population.

Preventive and supportive services, in contrast, are a loosely grouped category comprising a number of disparate programs and approaches offered in a variety of community settings. Their purposes are to prevent child maltreatment and strengthen families. (See Chapter 3.)

Pyramid of Services

The Pyramid of Services places services in a continuum of increasing intensity, reflecting the needs of the family (see Figure 1.3). Services needed by all families, such as schools, health care, and recreational facilities, are at the base of the pyramid, reflecting their status as widely available services. Families needing some extra support from time to time, often during family transitions such as divorce, birth, or death, or during other periods of stress, may need such services as a home visitor or parent education programs. Other families may also need a more specialized

Figure 1.3   *Pyramid of Services*

level of assistance, for such serious threats to family functioning as substance abuse, the physical or intellectual impairment of family members, or domestic violence. All of these services at the lower half of the pyramid are included in the category described earlier of preventive and supportive services and should be widely available in the community on a voluntary basis to families.

Services at the upper end of the pyramid include the traditional child welfare services of child protection, intensive family preservation, foster care, and adoption, for families who are in crisis and for families whose children cannot be protected and treated at home. They are needed by a relatively small number of families. They are of high intensity, in that the parents are expected to be highly involved in the treatment process, and require more professional time and other resources than do less intensive services.

RACE AND ETHNICITY IN CHILD WELFARE

The majority of the families involved with the formal child welfare system and the juvenile justice systems are members of cultural groups of color, particularly African Americans, Native Americans, and Hispanics or Latino Americans, even though these groups represent a relatively small proportion of the total population in the United States. This disparity between representation in the population and representation in the child welfare system is an example of "disproportionate representation." Research, policy analysis, and program and practice initiatives are addressing this topic of major concern: Why do children of some racial and ethnic groups stand a greater chance of being in the child welfare system than do other children?

"Disproportionate representation" is defined as the *under-* or *over*-representation of a specific population of interest. For example, the 2000 Census showed that African American children made up less than 15 percent of the overall child population, but in 2004 comprised 34 percent of the children in foster care (AFCARS Report, June, 2006). Conversely, Asian American children are under-represented in the child welfare system; they represent more than 3 percent of the overall child population yet account for less than 1 percent of the children in foster care.

What accounts for this disparity? Research has shown that the causes are multiple, complex, and interact with one another. Historical, social, and economic factors partly explain the disparity (Derezotes, Poertner, & Testa, 2005). The long history of oppression of African Americans through slavery and the Jim Crow laws created enormous strains on family life, prevented parents from earning a decent living, withheld education, and left entire communities in terror of organized, systematic violence against them. Native Americans suffered enormous losses during the conquest of North America by European cultures and underwent further cultural destruction by forced assimilation policies. Hispanic or Latino Americans have, as with the other groups, suffered overt and covert discrimination and racism, and have been hampered by language barriers and stresses of immigration and acculturation, all of which are exacerbated for those entering the country illegally.

Social services have also contributed to discrimination against children of certain ethnic and cultural groups. The majority of workers and administrators in the child welfare system are white, and the agencies and organizations within the child welfare system are based on models formulated by various European cultures. In past decades, service systems to families and children often were not culturally responsive and sometimes were actually destructive to the cultural values of various ethnic groups (McPhatter, 1997).

Examples of cultural bias, either intended or unintended, in child welfare include setting standards for foster and adoptive families that have the effect of excluding poor families, including many families of color; directing youth of color into the juvenile justice system while generally referring white youth to the mental health system; misinterpreting parents' behaviors and therefore erroneously assuming that they wish to harm or neglect their children; and failing to reach out in a cooperative and mutually respectful spirit to communities of color, leaving them excluded from planning and decision-making processes regarding agency policies and structures.

Findings from current research, which has examined the steps of the process through which children and families enter and move through the child welfare system, suggest that the interplay of race and the child welfare system is complex. For example, according to the Race Matters Consortium (2005, p. vii), community and family supports in communities of color can help compensate for the disadvantaged circumstances of children. These supportive networks, such as Head Start, might result in increased reporting of these children to protective services, whereas other children in more advantaged communities might not be reported because they do not participate in these programs. On the other hand, it has also been found that increased family support might actually result in shielding vulnerable children from the authorities, making them less likely to be reported for abuse and neglect. Research suggests that understanding the issue of racial disparity requires analysis at each stage of the child welfare decision-making process, from initial referral to child protective services, through the decision on whether to return a child to a family from foster care (Derezotes et al., 2005). Material in the following chapters will address the interplay of race and ethnicity with each stage of the child welfare process, and describe the complex interaction of system, economic, cultural, and family variables in creating the disproportionate representation of children of color in the system. Chapter 4 addresses practice issues in the provision of culturally competent social services.

THE ORGANIZATION OF SERVICES

Family and child services usually are provided under the auspices of a social welfare agency—a formal organization existing to serve children and their families and sanctioned by society. Some of the agencies offer a variety of services to families and children; others are specialized in that they offer fewer services or even only one.

Social welfare agencies providing services to children and their families are identified by various names, usually "child welfare agencies" or "family service agencies." Until recently, child welfare services and family services were conceptually and organizationally separate, despite their common professional knowledge and principles. According to Meyer (1985), the separation resulted in "a dysfunctional structure of services for both families and children" (p. 109). To understand how this separation came about, she cited the late nineteenth-century child-saving history of child welfare with its focus, not on maintaining intact families, but rather on child placement as a way to protect children from their parents, who were perceived by child-savers as inadequate or harmful. Another factor reinforcing separateness was the founding of two national organizations in the early twentieth century—the Child Welfare League of America and the Family Service Association of America—two bodies that traditionally have not found ways to join forces effectively. In addition, the fragmentation of federal funding in family and children's legislation worked to keep the fields of child welfare and family services apart. The current focus on family support to prevent abuse and neglect, and family preservation services to prevent foster care, now are resulting in a long-needed integration of child welfare services and family services. However, the transition to a fully integrated service system is not complete, and, in many communities, the work of family service agencies remains quite separate from that of child welfare agencies.

The organization offering the social services may be a "public" agency, or the services may be given under private auspices by a "voluntary" (nonprofit) agency or as a "proprietary" (for-profit) venture. Although both public and voluntary agencies are committed to broad, common goals in behalf of children, there are significant differences between the two forms of organization. Each has its separate legal base and means of financing its work; there are also differences in the underlying philosophy and in the groups of children served. Proprietary services for children differ considerably from both public and voluntary child welfare services.

Child welfare agencies come in all shapes and sizes. Some agencies may employ only two to five people and provide a specialized service, such as family treatment or adoption home placements. Some of the smaller agencies will have a few professionals and many volunteer or paraprofessionals, such as those in family support programs or in "big brother" and "big sister" programs.

Mental health centers, child guidance clinics, family service agencies, and youth service bureaus may all be midsize agencies. These types of agencies are more likely to provide several child welfare services. For example, mental health centers may provide psychological assessment, family therapy, individual counseling, groupwork, and perhaps consultation to schools and the juvenile court. Family service agencies may provide parenting education groupwork and a variety of treatment options. These agencies would typically employ between eight and fifty people.

At the most complex end of the continuum are the large state child welfare agencies. They may employ thousands of people who are responsible for providing a wide range of services, geographically dispersed throughout the state. The budgets of such organizations can reach hundreds of millions of dollars per year. These state agencies have been delegated public responsibility for the protection and care of children and authority over life-determining decisions for children and families who come under their mandate.

Public Child Welfare Services

The public child welfare agency is established by the passage of law—a particular statute that defines the agency's responsibilities for providing a welfare service for children and their families. Public welfare services for children and families are financed by taxation—federal, state, or local, or some combination of these sources. Most federal expenditures for children are made by or channeled through some unit of the Department of Health and Human Services. Federal funds provide a significant proportion of the total expenditures for children's programs, particularly in such programs as public assistance, Medicaid, Head Start, foster care, and maternal and child health services.

The primary responsibility for administering public child welfare services rests on the states and their regional and local subdivisions. The principle of local responsibility is well entrenched in the history of social welfare. Local and state influences have always been strong in child welfare programs because children and their families are closely linked to other concerns that traditionally have been regarded as the responsibility of the various states. For example, marriage, divorce, guardianship, custody, adoption, juvenile delinquency, and treatment of the mentally ill are all principally matters for legislation by the separate states.

Voluntary Family and Child Agencies

A voluntary (nonprofit) child and family welfare agency receives its authorization from a group of responsible citizens who undertake to assume responsibility for a defined and limited part of a community's social services for families and children. These agencies may form a corporate body and obtain a legal charter by showing that a need for a particular service exists and that a group of citizens is ready to support the activity. Some of these interested citizens are selected to serve as members of a board of directors with certain policy-making and advisory responsibilities in relation to a professional social work staff. The voluntary agency that provides out-of-home care of children is usually subject to the regulatory authority of the state and must establish its eligibility for a license certifying that it meets certain standards of child care. Voluntary agencies if they meet certain standards, may be accredited by national organizations such as the Council on Accreditation. As these agencies become connected to managed care systems, their operation is also subject to policy and oversight by managed care coordinating organizations.

In theory, voluntary welfare agencies are financed completely by voluntary contributions from citizens. However, the practice of channeling public tax monies to voluntary agencies has a long history. During the twentieth century, the practice grew of a public agency paying a private agency for services to children and families. Private agencies typically provide family preservation services, parent education and family support, foster care, and adoption services under purchase-of-service agreements with the state. Purchase-of-care arrangements raise complicated issues of agency autonomy in service planning and delivery, and in categories of clients served. If purchase of care is employed as a means of financing a community's social services for children, it should be carried out within a framework of community planning if it is to further the welfare of children and their families.

Faith-Based Initiatives. Many child and family agencies started under religious auspices, to serve the needs of new immigrant groups arriving in America. Immigration and its attendant problems of disease, poverty, and social isolation caused many families to split apart or cease to function as protective and nurturing environments for family members, leaving the children abused, neglected, orphaned, or abandoned. Churches and synagogues acted on the needs they saw around them by organizing service programs, such as orphanages, foster care programs, and food and shelter programs. The names of many voluntary agencies reflect their faith-based beginnings, even if they are no longer closely connected with a religious denomination; Protestant Children's Home, Jewish Family Services, Catholic Social Services, and St. Francis Home for Boys are just a few examples of names of agencies identifying their denominational roots. As indicated earlier, during the twentieth century, many, but not all, child welfare agencies begun under religious auspices formed partnerships with public child welfare agencies. In accepting governmental funding to provide services, these agencies also agreed to run secular programs and not use the money to convert people. In addition, they could not discriminate on the basis of religion in accepting clients for service or in hiring staff.

In the welfare reform legislation of the 1990s, Congress added "Charitable Choice" to the welfare bill, which gives religious congregations the right to compete with other charities for government funds without giving up their religious character. In 2002, President Bush initiated his program, Faith-Based and Community Initiatives, to support the work of faith-based social services (White House Faith-Based and Community Initiatives, 2002). This action has spurred debate on the advisability of providing federal funds directly to faith-based organizations. Proponents believe that the new initiative would simply level the playing field so that faith-based organizations could compete on equal footing with secular agencies for public dollars. They also believe that a religious or spiritual framework might enhance social services, at least in some areas, such as in hospice programs, substance abuse treatment centers, and teen pregnancy programs. Opponents fear erosion of the principle of the separation of church and state, and a return of the days when people could be denied basic services based on their religion, ethnicity, or race (Kramer, Finegold, DeVita, & Wherry, 2005). This debate has raised a host of issues on how government can reconcile, in its policies, two competing and compelling principles: nondiscrimination and equal access to needed services and programs, on the one hand, and respect for and support of ethnic (and religious) diversity, on the other (De Vita & Wilson, 2001).

Proprietary Child Welfare Services

Purchase of child welfare services is sometimes contracted between a public agency and a *proprietary for-profit* agency. For-profit contracting occurs mainly in the provision of child care for working parents. Very large numbers of other children have care arranged and carried out for them independently of any social welfare agency. Some families have found their own homemaker to bring into the home during periods of crisis and the mothers' absence. Some parents find a foster home and make arrangements for others to care for their children. Many children are placed in adoptive homes without the planning or supervision of a social welfare agency; this is very often arranged by an attorney for a fee or by other intermediaries.

Not enough is known about the quality of care and the experiences of children through these various independent arrangements. Some such children suffer poor quality of care, instability, and even abuse. However, some parents, particularly those with initiative, sound judgment, and financial resources, have been able to make satisfactory, independent arrangements for some aspects of their children's care.

Interagency Partnerships

A major barrier to more effective services to vulnerable families and children has been the way that social services are compartmentalized into separate organizations, each one responsible for providing only one service. For example, child welfare agencies traditionally have been responsible for investigating abuse and neglect and for placing children in out-of-home care; mental health agencies have provided inpatient and outpatient services to children with identified mental health problems; the juvenile justice system has provided correctional facilities and services; and the schools and the health care system have offered specific educational or health care services. Yet these organizations tend to serve the same children and families. The fragmentation of services is confusing for families, causes many to "fall through the cracks" and not get the service they need from any source, and is wasteful of resources. The following case shows a family in need of coordinated services.

> Mike is a fifth-grade boy, eleven years of age. He does not have a father at home. As far as is known, he has no contact with his father. Mike's mother is sickly and is generally homebound. He has an older sister who stays with him along with her boyfriend and a baby. Mike's older brother is in reform school. At the beginning of the year he was identified as a child who "gets into trouble and seldom finishes or does his homework." Mike responded by saying, "I don't care about school and my work is too hard." Mike follows peers who delight in disrupting classroom activities; he never smiles, and when things get too stressful, breaks into tears with no sound *(Bruner, 1991, p. 4)*

Mike's family needs economic assistance, social support, and psychological assistance, as well as educational help for Mike. However, our current service delivery system is structured into separate services with specific eligibility guidelines and bureaucratic regulations about what kinds of services it can offer and to whom. Mike and his family may get help but it is likely to be offered by different service providers working for different agencies and to be confusing for the family. Fragmented services to families such as Mike's can also be very expensive: reform school, psychological assessment and counseling for the brother, welfare assistance, and Medicaid for the family may cost the state tens of thousands of dollars annually but not result in an integrated plan to help the family.

Recognizing the problems caused by uncoordinated service systems, state governments and local communities are making efforts to increase the level of cooperation and collaboration among agencies.

Program Example: System of Care

Over the past twenty years, the System of Care Initiative has developed to provide a more integrated, effective level of service to children. Originally focused on middle- and high-school-aged children with learning disabilities and mental health problems, including substance abuse, the initiative has sought to coordinate services from education, mental health, juvenile justice, and child welfare. A successful pilot program in Ventura County, California, found that these systems serve many of the same families. The program learned that it could increase effectiveness, reduce strain on the family, and use resources more wisely by reducing fragmentation in service delivery (Knitzer & Yelton, 1990).

In 2004, a federal initiative provided funding to mental health services departments in states to develop coordinated service systems among all major agencies that serve children and adolescents. Services may include diagnostic and evaluation services, case management, intensive home-based services, day treatment, respite care, therapeutic foster care, and services that will help young people make the transition to adult systems of care. Involving parents as partners in the planning and implementation of treatment for their learning-disabled children, offering services in local communities, and cultural competence in serving families of minority ethnicity are important program components (Anderson & Mohr, 2003). According to preliminary results of an ongoing evaluation, children and adolescents participating in System of Care programs experience less institutionalization, fewer arrests, improved mental health, and better school performance, in comparison to their functioning prior to enrollment in the program (Community-based care, 2006).

Trends and Issues

Child Welfare in a Global Context

We are fast approaching the time when child welfare practice will take place in not only a national context but also a global one. As the boundaries separating nations become more permeable, due to rapidly improving technology, communications, and travel, information about children and children's services from every part of the globe becomes available to us here. This new perspective influences the way in which we understand our own service system, our assumptions about child rearing in families, and our ideas about the appropriate role of government in the lives of families and children. The preface to *Child Abuse: A Global Perspective* observes that as we "learn more about our counterparts in other countries, they become real to us, and our worldview cannot help but change. We will think of others as we think of those we know" (Schwartz-Kenney, McCauley, & Epstein, 2001).

We can no longer ignore children in faraway lands who are living in horrific conditions. We learn daily on our TV screens and in our newspapers of the hopeless plight of millions of children worldwide, their lives destroyed by war, poverty, famine, and disease, particularly HIV/AIDS. The sexual exploitation of children through pornography and sexual slavery, both here and abroad, has been made much easier by new communication technologies such as the World Wide Web, and seems almost impossible to deter. With the fall of the iron curtain in 1989, we discovered the plight of more than a million orphans languishing in institutions in Central and Eastern Europe. The late Princess Diana helped make the world aware that land mines claim the life and limbs of untold numbers of innocent children. Many people in the United States are also uncomfortably aware that the consumer products they buy may have been made by the labor of children in developing countries.

The increased movement of people across national boundaries has affected social workers in their own communities. Children and their families from many countries seek asylum from the traumas of their homeland, or simply more opportunity and a better life in the United States; as they settle in communities across the country, they become part of our personal and perhaps also our professional lives. Children of other cultures, many with limited English language skills, are arriving in our schools, health clinics, day care centers, and recreation programs, requiring staff to develop culturally competent service approaches (Pipher, 2002). The field of international adoption is expanding, as U.S. families adopt children from other countries in increasing numbers (Pasztor & McFadden, 2001). The child welfare community has been challenged to address the protection and guardianship of children who, although legal residents of the United States themselves, have parents who are here illegally or who have been deported.

Social workers and policy makers, as they learn more about child welfare practices and policies in other countries, are gaining new perspectives on policies and programs from abroad that hold promise for benefiting children here. The New Zealand Maori model of family decision making for the culturally sensitive protection of a family's children has been successfully exported to the United States. Information about the role of siblings in Africa in caring for AIDS orphans has helped us to "discover" siblings, often overlooked in child welfare services here, as a possible resource in maintaining family continuity for children who must be separated from their parents. In Canada, policies and practices have been developed to help immigrant children from war-ravaged countries find opportunities for healing and hope in a new homeland (Pasztor & McFadden, 2001).

Information on governmental policies and the condition of children in many other countries also is making us aware that we are doing a mediocre job, at best, on many measures of child well-being. Other countries have a very different understanding from ours on the role of government in providing to children basic social services, health care, and child care while their parents work. We are learning that strong supports for children's development will lead to better outcomes for children, thereby improving prospects for our nation's future (Child Trends, no date; Clearinghouse on International Developments in Child, Youth and Family Policies, 2001). The United States is also involved in international legal initiatives for the protection of children. The Hague Convention on Intercountry Adoption is an international treaty regulating the adoption of children across national boundaries. The United Nations Convention on the Rights of the Child is designed to protect and preserve the individual rights and basic human needs of children. The United States continues to be one of only two countries in the United Nations that has not ratified this treaty (the other is Somalia).

Information on children, families, and governments in other countries can give us new perspectives on service approaches and policies here, and renew our commitment to advocating for more resources to meet the needs of American children.

The Increasing Complexity of Child Welfare Practice

Since the early days of child welfare as a profession, society's expectations for child welfare have increased. New forces are impelling change. A number of legal reforms over the past four decades have increased accountability and reduced autonomy in agencies. Workers are required to work within a clear legal and policy framework. Efforts to contain costs of out-of-home care have led in some states to adoption of the health care model of "managed care," which further reduces the autonomy of individual agencies and workers. Society expects the child welfare system to protect children and also to preserve families. These sometimes competing goals have resulted in widely publicized reviews of agency decisions that have been proven by subsequent events to be bad judgments.

At the same time that child welfare has fallen under closer public scrutiny, the deteriorating condition of many children and families has presented new challenges to the system. The poverty, isolation, violence, substance abuse, and fractured family life experienced by many children have increased demands on the child welfare system. The erosion of educational, social, and health services and the lack of social cohesion in some urban and rural communities have meant that the child protection system is the only resort for a host of problems that might better have been addressed by other service systems or extended family networks, if they were available. The problems of families and children demand that the child welfare system broaden its scope and diversify its practice approaches into a wider arena of family and child services. The child welfare system must forge new relationships with families, with neighborhoods and communities, and with other organizations in the service delivery system.

In tandem with the increasing array of problems in child welfare and the services to address them, professional responsibilities also have become more complex in the past few decades. Issues of professional malpractice and liability and concerns about the scope and limits of confidentiality have influenced practice both directly and indirectly. New mandates increasingly require social workers to understand complicated protocols for risk management, to warn others of threats made about them, to conduct forensic investigations, and to testify competently in judicial proceedings. These heavy responsibilities and expectations have not been matched by sufficient training, leaving workers exposed to legal and other difficulties.

The social work profession and child welfare practice have a long, shared history. Social work has been the predominant discipline in the field of child welfare services. Starting in the 1970s, however, changes within the child welfare system weakened its status and the effectiveness of its services. The growth in the number of very difficult cases and the downgrading of positions by reclassifying them from professional to nonprofessional, accompanied by declining salaries, caused a decline in the number of professional staff (Kamerman & Kahn, 1989). Unfortunately, at the same time that child welfare was being perceived as less professional than other social work fields, the work was becoming increasingly complex, requiring higher levels of skill than ever before.

These developments encouraged renewed collaboration between public child welfare and social work education. Federal child welfare training monies have become available to finance special child welfare courses of study in schools of social work at both the BSW and MSW levels, for students who are current or future child welfare workers (Zlotnick, 1997; 2003). The program has grown significantly; in 2002, 49 states received an estimated $286 million in Title IV-E training reimbursements. However, states vary considerably in the extent to which they participate and therefore receive federal funding for child welfare training. In 2002, reimbursements ranged from an estimated low of approximately $10,000 in Alaska to a high of more than $79 million in California (NASW, 2004). A report from the U.S. General Accounting Office (2003) concluded that the partnership between public and private child welfare agencies and schools of social work is working to address the staffing crisis in child welfare, by improving both recruitment and retention.

Disaster Planning

In August 2005, Americans were stunned by the TV images of the effects of Hurricane Katrina on the city of New Orleans and the surrounding Gulf Coast. Thousands of people, mainly poor and African American, appeared stranded and destitute in the midst of rising flood waters and destroyed buildings. The appalling effect was made worse by the apparent bumbling and ineffective response of all levels of government, which left people without rescue or, after excruciating delays, placed them in unsanitary and dangerous shelters. Linked to images still fresh in our minds of New York City during the terrorist attack of 2001, a major impact of the disaster was to raise questions about the nation's readiness to cope with sudden, large-scale emergencies in our cities and rural areas.

A year after the hurricane hit, we began to understand the toll of the disaster and its aftermath on the children and families of the Gulf Coast and New Orleans. According to the National Center for Disaster Preparedness, the hurricane destroyed hundreds of thousands of homes and displaced more than one million people. School officials estimated that 125,000 children from Louisiana alone were forced to evacuate. Many of those hardest hit were living in poverty before the hurricane; afterward, they subsisted in tiny Federal Emergency Management Administration (FEMA) trailers in isolated fields far from services and community amenities or crowded in with relatives in new towns (Redlener, 2006; DeParle, 2006).

For children who lived in deprivation before the hurricane, the traumatic events of evacuation and the aftermath exacerbated their condition. For example, already behind in school, they suffered disruptions that put them further behind, and may now be in crowded classrooms in Houston or other cities that are not prepared for the influx of new pupils. Health care, to the extent that they had it, was also disrupted and records were lost. Mental health problems are also thought to be prevalent. Although children are often resilient in the face of disruption, those who lived in unstable families may find that their mental health problems have now increased (Golden, 2006). Some children, involved in worst-case scenarios, were separated from their families during the chaos of evacuation, and may not have known where their families were. Among those who suffered family disruption were the thousands of children in Louisiana's foster care system, who were evacuated to 19 states. Some lost track of their foster parents, their biological families, or both. Mental health experts believe that for children already at risk of poor developmental outcomes, the effects of additional trauma can increase that risk (Connolly, 2005).

Child and family advocates, government officials, and other concerned citizens are working to ensure that in the event of another large-scale disaster, children will be better protected from its effects. Golden (2006) recommends that special services be targeted to families with children that address comprehensively and in a coordinated fashion, the physical, educational, and psychosocial problems of these vulnerable families. The public child welfare system has a special responsibility for children who are separated from their families during evacuation and for children who are already in the child welfare system. A recent government report documented that state child welfare agencies need to improve disaster planning. Only twenty states reported that they had a written disaster plan, and most of these were incomplete. The report recommends that the federal government require states to include disaster planning in their state plans, and that the plans include provisions for preserving child welfare records, identifying children who may be dispersed, identifying new child welfare cases that emerge from the disaster, and coordinating services with other states and properly placing children evacuated from other states. (*Child Welfare*, 2006).

The terrorist attack of 2001 and the hurricane-related disasters of 2005 have raised awareness that the country is not prepared to protect its children in the event of a large-scale emergency. In addition to a greatly improved national and community emergency response system, it is important to pay particular attention to the needs of children who are caught up in chaotic situations.

CHAPTER SUMMARY

Child and family welfare services are provided in a framework of judicial and governmental policies and are strongly influenced by history, research, and current ideas about ways in which to help families and children. A grounding in child and family welfare services requires an understanding of all these influences. Child and family services are concerned with providing direct services to children and families in which serious problems are identified, and also with influencing public policy to improve the lives of all children. To strengthen family life for children is regarded as the primary purpose of child welfare.

In the United States, families have undergone great changes; today's families are more diverse than ever before, ethnically, racially, culturally, and in regard to family form, as families headed by married parents of the opposite sex is no longer the predominant form. Children in today's society face many risks to healthy growth and development, including poverty, a popular culture of alienation, violence, and glorification of risk-taking behavior, as well as a child welfare system that is inadequate to protect children and help families.

State and federal governments have provided funding and policies guiding child welfare practice for most of the nation's history; key federal legislation has emerged particularly since the 1970s. The courts also have a major role in shaping child welfare policy, particularly in the areas of delineating the rights and responsibilities of parents, children, and society/government. The Court clearly acknowledges that children are citizens who are entitled to the protections of the Constitution in their own right, but those protections need to be tempered on the basis of developmental capacities and childhood status within the family context.

Child and family services are guided by the principles emphasizing the need for children to live in families and also to be free from physical neglect and abuse. If children are not safe at home, child welfare services operate under the principle of supporting the family through intensive rehabilitation services; if the child must be removed for his or her own safety, family continuity is the principle guiding placement decisions, with relatives or others who have a relationship with the child given preference for placement. Child welfare agencies vary in size and auspices; common types are large, publicly financed state child welfare bureaucracies and smaller private agencies that undertake certain specialized functions. The complex problems of children and families often require the help of multiple service systems, including mental health organizations, schools, and substance abuse treatment programs. A persistent issue in child welfare organizations is the overrepresentation of children of minority ethnicity, reflecting conditions in society at large and also decision-making patterns within the child welfare system.

Child welfare as a field of social work practice continues to grow and change in response to social forces. We are becoming more aware of and interconnected to the global child welfare community, as advances in technology and communication reduce the boundaries between countries and cultures. Child welfare services are becoming increasingly complex; families and children coming into the system have more difficult and intractable problems than ever before. Federal policy mandates require that agencies work within strict guidelines to achieve outcomes, but are not given enough resources to do the job. An emerging challenge is planning for natural and other disasters, to ensure that children are not separated from their families and have their needs met during trying emergency conditions.

FOR STUDY AND DISCUSSION
STUDY AND DISCUSSION QUESTIONS

1. Learn about the background of a social agency in your area. When was it founded? Is it public or private? Was it started by a religious organization? If so, what are its links to that organization today? What are its funding sources? What are the main components and goals of its programs? Has the service mission changed over time?

2. Identify the problems that face children, youth, and families today. Delineate the services in your area that address these problems. Identify gaps and overlaps in services. Consider what new initiatives are needed, including better coordination among existing service systems.

3. Find out if some racial/ethnic groups are over- or underrepresented in your local child welfare system. Try to learn reasons for the disproportionate representation.

4. Find out the history of a local nonprofit child welfare agency in your area. In what ways does it reflect or differ from the history of child welfare described in the text?

5. Reconcile the Supreme Court's decisions on duties, rights, and limitations on parents in the care, custody, and control of their children.

6. Read in its entirety one of the U.S. Supreme Court decisions discussed in the text. Then, with other students, analyze the line of reasoning used by the majority and minority justices. How does such reasoning square with your own conception of a just balance in parent, child, and society rights and responsibilities?

Internet Sites

Annie E. Casey Foundation. Since 1948, the Annie E. Casey Foundation (AECF) has worked to build better futures for disadvantaged children and their families in the United States. The primary mission of the Foundation is to foster public policies, human service reforms, and community supports that more effectively meet the needs of today's vulnerable children and families. **www.aecf.org**

Child Trends. Child Trends is a nonpartisan research organization dedicated to improving the lives of children by conducting research and providing science-based information to improve the decisions, programs, and policies that affect children. **www.childtrends.org**

Child Welfare Information Gateway. Formerly the National Clearinghouse on Child Abuse and

Neglect Information and the National Adoption Information Clearinghouse, Child Welfare Information Gateway provides access to information and resources to help protect children and strengthen families. A service of the Children's Bureau, Administration for Children and Families, U.S. Department of Health and Human Services.
www.childwelfare.gov

Child Welfare League of America. The Child Welfare League of America (CWLA) is the nation's oldest and largest memebership-based child welfare organization. The web site lists the services offered to members and provides advocacy information for federal policy.
www.cwla.org

Children's Defense Fund. This advocacy organization is for children in the United States who cannot vote, lobby, or speak for themselves. It pays particular attention to the needs of poor and minority children and to those with disabilities.
www.childrensdefense.org

Clearinghouse on International Developments in Child, Youth and Family Policies. This organization provides information on international developments in child, youth, and family policies, including cross-national, comparative information on aspects of child welfare.
www.childpolicyintl.org

Federal Interagency Forum on Child and Family Statistics. This web site offers easy access to statistics and reports on children and families, including population and family characteristics, economic security, health, behavior and social environment, and education. The Forum fosters coordination, collaboration, and integration of Federal efforts to collect and report data on conditions and trends for children and families.
www.childstats.gov

The National Child Welfare Resource Center on Legal and Judicial Issues. This organization is dedicated to achieving safety, permanence, and well-being for abused and neglected children through improved laws and judicial decision-making.
www.abanet.org/child/rclji/

Race Matters Consortium. The Race Matters Consortium examines the disproportional representation of minority children in child welfare, discusses practices that will address the needs of children of color more appropriately, and collaborates with others who understand the need for attention to the issues in an effort to influence change in child welfare practice and policy.
www.racemattersconsortium.org

United States Supreme Court. This web site is maintained by the Administrative Office of the U.S. Courts. The purpose of this site is to function as a clearinghouse for information from and about the Judicial Branch of the U.S. Government.
www.uscourts.gov

References

Abbott, C. (1938). *The child and the state, vol. 1.* Chicago: University of Chicago Press.

AFCARS Report. (2006, June). *Administration for children, youth, and families.* U.S. Department of Health and Human Services. Available: www.acf.hhs.gov/programs/cb/stats_research/afcars/tar/report11.htm.

Anderson, J. A., & Mohr, W. K. (2003). A developmental ecological perspective in systems of care for children with emotional disturbances and their families. *Education and Treatment of Children, 26* (1), 52–74.

Bellotti v. Baird, 428 U.S. 132 (1979).

Bernstine, N. (1997). Housing and homelessness. *The state of America's children: Yearbook, 1997.* Washington, DC: Children's Defense Fund.

Billingsley, A., & Giovannoni, J. M. (1972). *Children of the storm: Black children and American child welfare.* New York: Harcourt Brace Jovanovich.

Bogenschneider, K. (2000, November). Has family policy come of age? A decade review of the state of U.S. family policy in the 1990s. *Journal of Marriage and the Family, 62*: 1136–1159.

Brieland, D., & Lemmon, J. (1985). *Social work and the law* (4th ed.). St. Paul, MN: West Publishing.

Bruner, C. (1991). *Thinking collaboratively: Ten questions and answers to help policy makers improve children's services.* Washington, DC: Education and Human Services Consortium.

Caban v. Mohammed, 441 U.S. 380 (1979).

Carey v. Population Services International, et al., 431 U.S. 678 (1977).

Casey Outcomes and Decision-Making Project. (1998). *Assessing outcomes in child welfare services: Principles, concepts, and a framework of core outcome indicators.* Englewood, CO: American Humane Association. Available: www.caseyoutcomes.org.

Chapsky v. Wood, 185 U.S. 373 (1902).

Child Trends. (no date). *Children newly diagnosed with AIDS.* Child Trends Data Bank. Available: www.childtrendsdatabank.orghttp://www.childtrendsdatabank.org/indicators/42ChildrenWithAIDS.cfm.

Child Trends. (no date). The Kids Count international data sheet. Available: www.childtrends.org.

Child Welfare: Federal Action Needed to Ensure States Have Plans to Safeguard Children in the Child Welfare System Displaced by Disasters (2006, July). United States Government Accountability Office. Washington, DC: U.S. Government Printing Office.

Clearinghouse on International Developments in Child, Youth and Family Policies. (2001). *New 12 country study neveals substantial gaps in U.S. early childhood education and care policies.* New York: Columbia University. Available: www.childpolicyintl.org.

Community-based care leads to meaningful improvement for children and youth with serious mental health needs. (2006, May 8). *News Release.* Washington, DC: Substance Abuse and Mental Health Services Administration web site. Available: http://systemsofcare.samhsa.gov/news/nr_index.aspx.

Connolly, C. (2005). Katrina's emotional damage lingers: Mental health experts say impact is far beyond what they've ever faced. *Washington Post,* p. A3.

Cook, J. F. (1995). A history of placing-out: The orphan trains. *Child Welfare, 74*(1), 181–200.

Council on Social Work Education. (1992). *Social work education and public human services: Developing partnerships.* Washington, DC: Council on Social Work Education.

DeParle, J. (2006). Orphaned. *The New York Times Magazine,* p. 26–43.

Derezotes, D. M., Poertner, J., & Testa, M. F. (Eds.). (2005). *Race matters in child welfare.* Washington, DC: Child Welfare League of America.

De Vita, C., & Wilson, S. (2001). *Faith-based initiatives: Sacred deeds and secular dollars. Emerging issues in philanthropy seminar series.* Washington, DC: The Urban Institute.

Downs, S. W., & Sherraden, M. (1983). The orphan asylum in the nineteenth century. *Social Service Review, 57*(2), 272–290.

Egan, J. (2002, March 24). To be young and homeless. *New York Times Magazine,* pp. 32–37 ff.

Federal Interagency Forum on Child and Family Statistics. (2002). *America's children: Key national indicators of well-being.* Washington, DC: U.S. Government Printing Office.

Federal Interagency Forum on Child and Family Statistics. (2005). *America's children: Key national indicators of well-being, 2005.* Federal Interagency Forum on Child and Family Statistics. Washington, DC: U.S. Government Printing Office.

Ferguson v. City of Charleston, 532 U.S. 67 (2001).

Folks, H. (1911). *The care of destitute, neglected, and delinquent children.* New York: Macmillan.

Fraser, M. W., Kirby, L. D., & Smokowski, P. R. (2004). Risk and resilience in childhood. In M. W. Fraser (Ed.), *Risk and resilience in childhood: An ecological perspective* (2nd ed., pp. 13–66). Washington, DC: NASW Press.

Golden, O. (2006). *Young children after Katrina.* Washington, DC: The Urban Institute.

Hagen, J. L., & Davis, L. V. (1977). Mothers' views on child care under the JOBS program and implications for welfare reform. In P. L. Ewalt, E. M. Freeman, S. A. Kirk, & D. L. Poole (Eds.), *Social policy: Reform, research and practice* (pp. 280–296). Washington, DC: NASW Press.

Hartman, A. (1981). The family: A central focus for practice. *Social Work, 26*(1).

Heyburn, I. (1919). *The congressional record* (Senate). Washington, DC: U.S. Government Printing Office, p. 189.

H. L. Matheson, 450 U.S. 398 (1981).

Hodgkin, R., & Newell, P. (2002). *Implementation handbook for the convention on the rights of the child.* New York: UNICEF.

Hodgson v. Minnesota, 497 U.S. 417 (1990).

In re Gault, 387 U.S. 1 (1967).

Jacobs, T. A. (1995, supp. 1997). *Children and the law: Rights and obligations.* St. Paul, MN: West Publishing.

Kamerman, S. B., & Kahn, A. J. (1989). *Social services for children, youth and families in the United States.* New York: Columbia University School of Social Work, Annie E. Casey Foundation.

Kent v. United States, 383 U.S. 541 (1966).

Knitzer, J., & Yelton, S. (1990). Collaborations between child welfare and mental health. *Public Welfare, 48*(2), 24–33.

Kramer, F., Finegold, K., De Vita, C., & Wherry, L. (2005). *Federal policy on the ground: Faith-based organizations delivering local services.* Washington, DC: The Urban Institute.

Laird, J. (1985). An ecological approach to child welfare. In C. Germaine (Ed.), *Social work practice: People and environments.* New York: Columbia University Press.

Lincroft, Y., Resner, J., & Leung, M. (2006). *Undercounted. Underserved. Immigrant and refugee families in the child welfare system.* Baltimore, MD: The Annie E. Casey Foundation.

McFadden, E. J., & Downs, S. W. (1995). Family continuity: The new paradigm in permanence planning. *Community Alternatives: International Journal of Family Care, 7*(1), 44.

McPhatter, A. R. (1997). Cultural competence in child welfare: What is it? How do we achieve it? What happens without it? *Child Welfare, 76*(1), 255–278.

Meyer, C. H. (1985). The institutional context of child welfare. In J. Laird & A. Hartman (Eds.), *Handbook of child welfare.* New York: Macmillan.

National Association of Social Workers (NASW). (2004). *Fact sheet: Title IV-E child welfare training program.* Available: http://www.socialworkers.org/advocacy.

Nelson, K. (1995). The child welfare response to youth violence and homelessness in the nineteenth century. *Child Welfare, 74*(1), 56–70.

Nurcombe, B., & Partlett, D. F. (1994). *Child mental health and the law.* New York: Free Press.

Ooms, T. (1990). Families and government: Implementing a family perspective in public policy. *Social Thought, 16,* 61–78.

Ounce of Prevention Fund. (1993). *Beethoven's Fifth: The first five years of the center for successful child development.* Chicago: Ounce of Prevention Fund.

Parham v. J.R., 442 U.S. 584 (1979).

Park, J. M., Metraux, S., Broadbar, G., & Culhane, D. (2004). Child welfare involvement among children in homeless families. *Child Welfare, 83*(5), 423–436.

Pasztor, E., & McFadden, J. (2001). Global perspectives on child welfare. *Child Welfare, 80*(5), 487–496.

Peebles-Wilkins, W. (1995). Janie Porter Barrett and the Virginia Industrial School for Colored Girls: Community response to the needs of African-American children. *Child Welfare, 74*(1), 143–161.

Pierce v. Society of Sisters, 268 U.S. 510 (1925).

Pipher, M. (2002). *The middle of everywhere: The world's refugees come to our town.* New York: Harcourt.

The Policy Institute for Family Impact Seminars. (no date). Available: http://familyimpactseminars.org/fampolicy.htm.

Prince v. Massachusetts, 321 U.S. 158 (1944).

Quillon v. Walcott, 434 U.S. 246 (1978).

The Race Matters Consortium. (2005). Introduction. *Race matters in child welfare.* D. M. Derezotes, J. Poertner, & M. F. Testa (Eds.). Washington, DC: Child Welfare League of America.

Redlener, I. (2006, May 9). Orphans of the storm. *The New York Times,* A27.

Santosky v. Kramer, 455 U.S. 745 (1982).

Schwartz-Kenney, B. M., McCauley, M., & Epstein, M. A. (Eds.). (2001). *Child abuse: A global view.* Westport, CT: Greenwood Press.

Sherraden, M., & Downs, S. W. (1984). Institutions for juvenile delinquency in historical perspective. *Children and Youth Services Review, 6*(3), 155–173.

Smith, E. P., & Merkel-Holguin, L. (1995). From family duty to family policy: The evolution of kinship care. *Child Welfare, 74*(1), 200–216.

Snyder, H., & Sickmund, M. (2006). *Juvenile offenders and victims: 2006 national report.* Washington, DC: U.S. Department of Justice, Office of Justice Programs, Office of Juvenile Justice and Delinquency Prevention.

Stanley v. Illinois, 405 U.S. 645 (1972).

Thurston, H. W. (1930). *The dependent child.* New York: Columbia University Press.

Tinker v. Des Moines Independent Community School District, 393 U.S. 503 (1969).

Troxel v. Granville, 530 U.S. 57 (2000).

U.N. Assembly approves doctrine to guard children's rights. (1989, November 21). *New York Times*, p. 9.

United Nations. (1989). *Convention on the rights of the child.* New York: United Nations.

U.S. Department of Health and Human Services, Administration on Children, Youth and Families. (2006). *Child maltreatment 2004.* Washington, DC: U.S. Government Printing Office.

U.S. General Accounting Office. (2003, March). *HHS could play a greater role in helping child welfare agencies recruit and retain staff* (GAO-03-357). Washington, DC: Author.

White House Faith-Based and Community Initiatives. (2002). *Guidance to faith-based and community organizations on partnering with the federal government.* Washington, DC: U.S. Government Printing Office. Available: www.fbci.gov/faith.

Wisconsin v. Yoder, 406 U.S. 205 (1972).

Wolak, J., Mitchell, K., & Finkelhor, D. (2006). *Online victimization of youth: Five years later.* Alexandria, VA: National Center for Missing and Exploited Children.

Zlotnick, J. L. (1997). *Preparing the workforce for family-centered practice: Social work education and public human services partnerships.* Alexandria, VA: Council on Social Work Education.

Zlotnik, J. L. (2003). The use of Title IV-E training funds for social work education: An historical perspective. *Journal of Human Behavior in the Social Environment, 7*(1/2), 5–20.

CHAPTER 2

Government Programs to Support Families and Children

In the midst of affluence, child poverty casts a lengthening shadow.

—*Children's Defense Fund*

CASE EXAMPLE:
Welfare Reform Creates Hard Choices for Mothers

Denise Jordan, a 34-year-old mother of three children, is a former welfare recipient who now has a government job in Washington, D.C., which she likes. Her oldest daughter is childless and in the Army. Her middle daughter, Kyisha, is 15 years old, with a sickly 9-month-old son, and pregnant again. Her youngest child is Kimberly, a bright 7-year-old, with an optimistic view of her future.

Denise Jordan is now faced with several major decisions, made more poignant given the changes in the federal welfare system. Before 1996, if a teenage girl became pregnant, she could establish her own household and begin collecting welfare benefits. Under the 1996 law, to collect welfare benefits, a teenage girl must live with her parents or guardians. If the family has too much income, then the girl gets no benefits. Denise Jordan makes too much for her family to receive benefits. Thus, Denise Jordan is faced with a dilemma—how to get child care assistance for Kyisha's babies.

Does she leave her full-time job, which she has gotten after years of being on welfare and working part-time jobs? If she does, then her family would be back on public assistance and qualify for benefits, including child care assistance for Kyisha's babies. Does she keep her job, but ask Kyisha to drop out of school and take care of her babies, thus saving the child care cost of about $800 a month, which would be half of Denise's take-home monthly salary?

Does Denise take a second job in the evenings to make the additional money necessary to cover child care costs? If she does, then she will not be available to help Kyisha take care of her babies in the evenings or help her 7-year-old when she comes home from school. In the neighborhood where Denise lives, she knows that keeping children occupied after school is extremely important.

> *I have felt myself a strong woman, but now I feel my spirit breaking.*
> *(Denise Jordan, in Boo, 1997)*

After not being able to talk Kyisha into an abortion or into putting the baby, once born, up for adoption or in foster care, Denise ponders other options for Kyisha. She could put her out on the street, but the child is too "slow" to make it on her own. She could encourage Kyisha and her boyfriend to marry, but she knows that is not likely given his limited resources. Even so, the boyfriend maintains an occasional presence in the family. In the end, after the second baby is born, Denise decides to keep her government job, not look for an additional evening job because the children need her presence more than the extra earnings, and ask Kyisha to drop out of school to take care of her babies. Denise hates to see Kyisha so trapped, but she hopes that life will be better for 7-year-old Kimberly (Boo, 1997).

This case study taken from a *Washington Post* article, conveys some of the private costs borne by those who leave welfare for work, and the dilemmas faced by the poor and the near-poor in the United States. This country has a history of dividing the poor into the deserving and the undeserving (Katz, 1986), with the undeserving seen as not worthy of assistance, whether from public or private sources. To be considered deserving, the poor must prove their worthiness, generally through the kinds of behaviors that they exhibit (e.g., being willing to work, being capable of maintaining strong families, and being willing to make short-term sacrifices for long-term gains).

Much of the current debate about welfare reform centers on how to get the poor to exhibit "proper" behaviors, with the assumption being that if they do so, they will no longer be poor. The federal welfare reform legislation passed in 1996, the Personal Responsibility and Work Opportunity Reconciliation Act (PRWORA), linked personal responsibility with work, and ended the country's sixty-year program that entitled poor people to public assistance.

FAMILY INCOME SECURITY

The fundamental relationship of family income security to child welfare was recognized in 1909 when the participants of the first White House Conference on the Care of Dependent Children stated the principle that the child's own home should not be broken up for reasons of poverty, and urged that monetary aid be given to maintain suitable homes for the rearing of children. Since that time, the link between child welfare and family income has become increasingly well understood; poverty is an important factor in child abuse and neglect, as well as in the placement of children in foster care. In addition, the life course of children is strongly influenced by the income of their family; higher levels of family income are associated with higher educational levels of children and other desirable developmental outcomes.

Yet, the nation has struggled to provide adequate income for children. Throughout our history, policies to provide adequate income to families with children have run into conflict with beliefs about the causes of poverty and government's role in providing for needy families. Policies that favor the deserving poor leave children vulnerable to extreme want in families in which the parents cannot or will not meet behavioral requirements for public assistance. Furthermore, policies that require parents to work may not adequately provide for the care of children during the parent's working hours.

After several decades of periodic attempts to reform the public welfare system, Congress passed and President Clinton signed into law the PRWORA of 1996. In this chapter, we will review the provisions of this attempt at welfare reform and evaluate its strengths and weaknesses for reducing poverty among children and their families. First, however, we will consider the nature of poverty among children and the principles and policies of governmental income maintenance programs (social insurance, public assistance, earned income tax credit, and child support enforcement). Because an understanding of the provisions of the new legislation is best arrived at from an awareness of a larger context, attention will be given to historical perspectives of the development of income maintenance programs in the United States.

NATURE OF POVERTY AMONG CHILDREN

Extent

The magnitude of poverty among families of children is evident from regularly issued reports of the Federal Interagency Forum on Child and Family Statistics, using data from the U.S. Census. The federal government's poverty-level index represents an attempt to classify families as being above or below an income level required to support an average family of a given composition, at the lowest level consistent with the standards of living prevailing in this country. The index currently in use was adopted in 1969 and is updated each year to reflect changes in the Consumer Price Index. The Index has been criticized for not adequately measuring poverty today, and various reforms to the measure are under consideration (Cassidy, 2006). In 2007, the poverty line threshold for a family that consists of a mother and two children was $17,170, meaning that a family with income below that level was considered poor, for research and program administration purposes (Federal Register, 2007).

Although poverty has declined for other population groups, notably the elderly, the United States has not been successful in reducing the poverty rate among children. Continuing losses in the battle against poverty are startlingly clear in census figures for 2004. From these data, the Children's Defense Fund derived these findings.

❖ Poverty in the United States is more prevalent now than in the early 1970s, having escalated rapidly since 2000.

❖ The number of American children living in poverty grew by 12.8 percent from 2000 to 2004. This means that 1.5 million more children were poor in 2004 than in 2000.

❖ For every five children who have fallen into poverty since 2000, more than three fell into "extreme poverty," meaning that their families lived at less than one-half of the poverty level. These families had to get by on about $7,500 a year.

❖ More than seven out of every ten poor children in 2004 lived in a family with at least one employed relative. Even if a parent works full time at the minimum wage, the family still lives in poverty (Children's Defense Fund, 2005, iv, p. 1).

In 2004, over thirteen million children were in families with income below the poverty level. The burden falls disproportionately on families that are headed by women, on children and young adults, and on minority groups. In 2003, 34 percent of African American children and 29 percent of Hispanic children lived in poverty, compared to 9 percent of non-Hispanic white children (Federal Interagency Forum 2005, p. 115).

Factors Contributing to Poverty

In the past thirty-five years, changes have occurred in the U.S. economy that make it difficult for many families to maintain a decent standard of living. One major change has been the stagnation in wages; in contrast to the quarter century following World War II, when wages increased rapidly, during the past thirty-five years they have risen much more slowly. Young, poorly educated men and women, who are just starting families have been hit hardest. These wage losses are related to fundamental changes in the U.S. economy:

❖ loss of manufacturing jobs due to foreign competition, automation, and the transfer of jobs by U.S. companies to overseas factories;

❖ growth of jobs in the service industry, which tend to pay less than manufacturing jobs, have fewer fringe benefits, and are less secure; and

❖ recent technological changes that affect the skill level needed by American workers and the stability of American firms.

Many Americans work but remain poor, often because they cannot find full-time work. A compounding factor is the eroded value of the minimum wage, currently set at $5.85 per hour, despite the continuing rise in the cost of living.

Certain characteristics make some people especially vulnerable to the threat of poverty. Furthermore, these characteristics tend to be found together, and when this is so, the risk of poverty is heavier. *Non-white status* increases the risk of poverty. Another factor is *large families.* A child who is growing up in a family with more than a few brothers and sisters is at greater risk of poverty, particularly if the family is vulnerable on some other count as well. *Single-parent families headed by a woman* bear an increased likelihood of poverty. Non-white families more often have a woman at the head, linking two situations, accompanied by a high risk of poverty. *Change in family composition*, particularly through divorce, is a significant factor underlying low economic status, given the history of difficulty in enforcement of child support by the noncustodial parent.

In families of the "working poor," the problem is *low earning power of the parents*. Sometimes they are unable to find or keep a job or have only irregular employment. Frequently, a poor family is headed by a parent who has worked steadily through the years, but still, his or her family lives in poverty. Often, the parent's work is unskilled, requires long hours, and has a low pay. And always, if the head of the family is under twenty-five years of age, and especially if or he she is African American, the likelihood of unemployment or underemployment is greater than for the middle-aged group.

Although the United States has always been a land of immigrants, immigration has increased rapidly in recent years. If current trends continue, the Urban Institute predicts that by 2010, children of immigrants will represent at least a quarter of all U.S. children (Beadle, 2006). *Children of families who are immigrating to the United States* are more likely to be poor than are native-born children, and are more likely to experience hunger and overcrowded housing. Many children of immigrants are U.S. citizens because they were born in this country, and are eligible for services. However, if their parents are undocumented, the family may be reluctant to seek help (Capps & Fortuny, 2006; Reardon-Anderson, Capps, & Fix, 2002).

Of special concern are the children of *migrant farm workers*, who occupy the lowest level of any major group in the U.S. economy. The estimated one to three million migrant farm workers are predominantly foreign-born, most coming to the United States from Mexico, over half of whom lack legal authorization to be in the United States. Half of farm workers earn less than $15,000 a year, well below the poverty line threshold for a family of four (U.S. Department of Labor, 2006). Children of migrant workers are likely to drop out of school, have untended health problems, and work in the fields with their parents. Agricultural farm labor is among the most dangerous occupations in the United States because of hard physical labor, pesticide exposure, and dangerous equipment. Children of migrant workers too often are trapped in a vicious circle of unending poverty and rootlessness (*Facts on Farmworkers*, 2001).

The relationship of *low levels of education* to unemployment and poverty is well known. The direct bearing of education on job potential becomes greater each year, with automated industry heightening the risk of a lifetime of poverty for youth who have insufficient education. Many young people who live in poor families do not finish high school and begin at age sixteen to swell the ranks of the unemployed. School dropouts tend to begin families early, thus stepping up the risk of enduring poverty.

The timing and circumstances of *marriage and childbearing* are of critical importance to future family income. The relationship of early marriage to low income is not just a circumstance of the first few years following marriage. As the size of the family grows and older children's needs expand, it becomes harder to match earnings with family needs. Early childbearing frequently forces the parents to make occupational decisions without sufficient education or real choice and is likely to supply a continual experience of poverty for the new family unit.

"A childhood spent in poverty can have negative impacts on an individual's entire life" (Children's Defense Fund, 2005, p. 2). The unfavorable influences of poverty begin early for children and continue for a long time—too often through all their lives. Although many children overcome material deprivation in childhood and lead satisfying and productive lives, many others are unable to compensate for the disadvantages of their early years. Childhood poverty is often among the causes of poor developmental outcomes for children, including early childrearing, crime and imprisonment, dropping out of school, and addictions and other self-defeating behaviors.

Public Assistance: Temporary Assistance for Needy Families

The term "public assistance" refers to tax-supported programs of financial aid for individuals and families based on established need. Temporary Assistance for Needy Families (TANF) is the largest public assistance program that serves families with children. TANF is a cooperative program between federal and state governments for the purpose of maintaining income to families in which children have been deprived of parental support for reasons such as the parent's death, continued absence from the home, mental or physical incapacity, and unemployment. The intent has been to provide financial assistance when a family has no income or insufficient income and to do so in ways that will enable children to remain in their own homes, where they can be reared by at least one of their parents or relatives. The program is financed by a sharing of costs between the federal and state governments. As a step toward achieving a valid basis for evaluation of the TANF program, a review of the background of the program and its original philosophy will be useful.

Background of the TANF Program

Mothers' Pensions

Activity on the part of social reformers of the early 1900s and resolutions of the first White House Conference on the Care of Dependent Children in 1909 highlighted concern about poor children who lost their own homes because of their parents' inability to support them. At this time, there was a new awareness of the importance of a child's own home and his or her need for family life experiences that found expression in the following resolution of the conference:

> Home life is the highest and finest product of civilization. It is the great molding force of mind and of character. Children should not be deprived of it except for urgent and compelling reasons. . . . Except in unusual circumstances, the home should not be broken up for reasons of poverty. (*Proceedings*, 1909, pp. 9–10)

Reaction against old methods of public outdoor relief (assistance to persons living in their own homes rather than in institutions) contributed to support for a new and special form of financial aid for mothers. Public relief, when it was given, reluctantly, consisted mostly of coal or grocery orders or emergency medical care. Another impetus to preserve the child's own home through the payment of public funds to mothers of dependent children was a reaction to the institutionalization of young children. Not only was there concern over children's loss of their home; public officials also realized that paying for children to live in an institution was costlier than furnishing a small amount of aid to them in their own home. The increasing legislation among states to prohibit or regulate child labor and the passage of compulsory school attendance laws were additional factors leading to the passage of mothers' pension laws. A child of 9 or 10 years of age was no longer free to quit school and go to work in factories and mines to help his or her widowed mother feed and care for younger brothers and sisters.

Mothers' pension laws were not passed without controversy, however. Much of the controversy was rooted in the fear that a family program of public assistance would not be restricted to "worthy" parents; mothers of "poor character" might also claim its help. Inherent in the controversy was a reluctance to enact any legislation that would appear to relieve fathers of responsibility for their children's support. It was feared that the substance of family life would be seriously weakened, and irresponsibility and immorality would be encouraged.

Nevertheless, there was support for the concept of the public responsibility for aid to needy children, popular distaste for the practice of removing children from their own homes for reasons of poverty, and belief that honest, efficient, and service-oriented public welfare could be created. Illinois passed the first statewide mother's pension law in 1911. Ten years later, forty states had enacted such laws.

In most locales, only mothers who were deemed "worthy" were eligible to receive assistance. Mothers were screened on the basis of their morality and whether they kept "suitable homes" for their children. Most of the recipients were widows. Less frequently, divorced, deserted, or separated mothers, or mothers whose husbands were incapacitated or physically disabled, were deemed eligible. Most questionable of all were unmarried mothers. In addition, mothers considered to be worthy and fit usually turned out to be white; only about 3 percent of recipients were African American.

The mothers' pension programs provided a model for a state-supported humanitarian effort on behalf of dependent children and reflected a growing commitment to the concept of public responsibility. But the program also left unresolved the complicated administrative problems of shared state and local responsibility, and complicating, ambivalent attitudes about suitable homes.

Aid to Families with Dependent Children. When the Social Security Act was passed in 1935, mothers' pensions were replaced by Aid to Dependent Children (ADC). The Act required that all states implement the program. As is clear from its name, ADC did not provide for mothers directly but only for their children. Coverage for mothers was introduced in 1950. In 1962, ADC was renamed Aid to Families with Dependent Children (AFDC) to reflect its new purpose of strengthening families. Initially, the program was limited to single parents, but in the 1960s it expanded in approximately half the states to include unemployed parents (AFDC-UP), thus providing aid to families with unemployed male heads.

The public increasingly viewed AFDC with suspicion and disappointment, and from time to time it came under bitter attack. Concerns were high that the existing AFDC program had an unintentional consequence of discouraging work by enabling recipients to subsist on welfare payments. Although at least half of all AFDC recipients remained on welfare only temporarily, others were caught in a pattern of continuing dependency, and the public perception was that their children too would grow up without the ability to become self-sufficient workers. Several states, in order to break the "cycle of dependency," created demonstration programs that encouraged or required work in return for welfare assistance. Studies showed a promising level of success, leading to the belief that such programs benefited welfare recipients and that the work supports that were offered by the states would eventually pay for themselves through reduced welfare payments (Stevens, 1988; Mathews, 1990). A social factor that contributed heavily to the new consensus that welfare should include work was that women had entered the workforce in large numbers for many years, and a new norm of family life was in place. Welfare mothers who stayed home with their children seemed out of step with the times.

In 1988, Congress passed the Family Support Act, with the intent to enable states to help poor families leave welfare and become self-sufficient. The Act required AFDC recipients to participate in education, job training, and work programs. The Family Support Act of 1988 reflected the country's shifting views of welfare and work. The Act incorporated the principle of parental responsibility by strengthening child support enforcement and by emphasizing work and employment training for parents. It also made AFDC available for two-parent families in every state. It offered work supports through the guarantee of child care and Medicaid for twelve months after the parent left welfare for work (Real welfare reform, 1988).

Provisions of TANF

In the years after the passage of the Family Support Act in 1988, momentum increased for further welfare reforms to link welfare benefits to approved parental behaviors of work and family responsibility. Despite earlier reforms, welfare still offered disincentives to work, since benefits were cut or terminated when parents began to earn income. Reformers believed that the whole welfare system needed to be transformed from a system that provided a low level of income to nonworking parents, to a program that provided a floor of assistance while helping people make the transition to work. The welfare program would offer financial assistance on an interim basis while recipients became established in the work force, and would also offer ongoing supports to families that would follow them even as they became earners. Donna Shalala, secretary of the Department of Health and Human Services (HHS), described the welfare reform strategy of the Clinton administration as "based on a simple point: welfare must be a temporary, transitional program that builds on core American values—work, family, opportunity, and responsibility" (Shalala, 1993, p. 5).

The nation's governors also lobbied to have more power devolved to the states. Devolution reflects the changing federal–state relationship in which the federal government gives greater flexibility to the states to determine social policies, and the states in turn assume more responsibility for the design and administration of social programs. An argument for increased state autonomy was that the state government was closer to the social and economic conditions that affect welfare use, and therefore could better design programs that would be effective locally. Furthermore, some states had already received exemptions to modify the federal AFDC program and had reported success in moving people from welfare to work in a cost-effective way that seemed to benefit, rather than harm, recipients. It was thought that the states could be "laboratories" to experiment with different programs, and from this variation would come good ideas that could be used by all. Therefore, Congress devolved much authority to the states when it dramatically transformed the social safety net for low-income families with the 1996 passage of the Personal Responsibility and Work Opportunity Reconciliation Act (PRWORA). PRWORA eliminated the sixty-one-year-old AFDC program and replaced it with a block grant to states to establish the TANF program.

The main features of TANF are (1) work requirements for nearly all adult recipients, (2) time limits for receiving assistance, and (3) great variability from state to state on many aspects of the program. Although the program remains very much as the PRWORA designed in 1996, both the states and the federal government have modified it over the years. Within broad federal guidelines, states are free to develop their own programs (Waller & Fremstad, 2006), and this variability makes it difficult to generalize about how TANF is implemented in the fifty states and District of Columbia. Some of the key features of TANF, with examples of variation among the states, are listed below. This list is based on the analysis of 2003 data by Gretchen Rowe and Linda Giannarelli (2006), for the New Federalism Initiative of the Urban Institute.

> *Virtually any statement about welfare is no longer universally true across the country.* —Rowe & Giannarelli, 2006

Eligibility. Applicants must have a monthly income that is low enough to meet the state's eligibility requirement. This amount varies widely—from $269 in Alabama, to $1,641 in Hawaii, in 2003—with a median income threshold requirement of $704 for all states. At the time of application, about half the states give the applicant a choice of receiving a one time *diversion* payment instead of entering the TANF program. The diversion payment is intended to help families whose main problem is a short-term emergency that is unlikely to be repeated get back on their feet quickly. The amount of the diversion payments also varies from state to state, with an average in 2003 of about $1,500.

In addition to low income, states may impose other eligibility requirements. If the applicant opts for the diversion payment, he or she is not eligible to enroll in the ongoing TANF program for a specified period. About one-third of all states require that applicants be *actively seeking employment* to qualify for assistance. Many states started TANF in 1996 with special, more stringent eligibility requirements for two-parent families, but most have removed them, finding that they could lead to the unfortunate consequence of family break-up.

Program Participation. Once enrolled in TANF, families must focus on finding and keeping a job. The federal government requires that recipients engage in *work activities* for 30 hours per week. States vary widely in what they consider to be work; differing, for example, on what types of training, education, or community volunteer activities count. In general, the emphasis is on getting a job immediately, rather than on job training or education. Most states have policies to exempt recipients from the work requirement in special situations, such as personal disability, heavy family caregiving responsibilities, or special economic circumstances in the community.

Once working, recipients are able to keep some or all of their assistance while earning an income. The purpose of this *income disregard* is to provide incentives for people to work without worrying that they will lose public assistance before they are well established in the workplace. As with other aspects of the program, states have very different policies regarding how much public assistance a recipient can receive in relation to their earnings.

Termination. *Time limits* for assistance are a key feature of TANF, making clear that TANF is temporary and that adults are expected to work on an ongoing basis. The federal law sets a lifetime time limit of 60 months (five years). However, states may impose shorter time limits or have intermittent time limits, such as imposing a period of ineligibility after a family has received benefits for one year. Most states provide for some kind of exception to time limits in special sit-uations, on a case-by-case basis. Families may also be terminated from TANF if they fail to meet program requirements. These *sanctions* vary considerably by state. For example, over half the states reduce a family's benefit by 25 percent or less for the first incident of noncompliance, while other states impose a larger reduction. If the family has been noncompliant many times, most states remove the family's entire benefit for a fixed period.

WORK AND FAMILY SUPPORTS

In addition to transforming the public assistance system, another key aspect of welfare reform in the 1990s was to develop and improve other, nonwelfare programs to help the working poor. As families moved off welfare and became (mainly) low-wage earners, they became eligible for an expanding array of income supports available to working poor families, whether or not they were on public assistance. Key income support programs are State Children's Health Insurance Program (SCHIP) and Medicaid, government health insurance programs for low-income families and children, the Earned Income Tax Credit, Child Support Enforcement, and food programs. The child care assistance program, another important work support program for families, is discussed in "Child Development Programs."

SCHIP and Medicaid

The federal program that is designed to address the health needs of the poor is Medicaid. Under the 1996 welfare reform act, states must provide Medicaid to persons who would have been eligi-ble for AFDC under the prior law. However, child advocates were concerned that the new welfare law would not protect children's health in homes where the parents left welfare for work, as they might no longer be eligible for Medicaid. In 1997, Congress addressed this gap in the safety net by establishing SCHIP, which provided funds to states to expand health insurance coverage to a larger group of uninsured children. SCHIP represented the largest single expansion of health cov-erage for children since Medicaid was established in the 1960s. States vary in how they organize their Medicaid and SCHIP programs, but generally, Medicaid is available for people who are re-ceiving public assistance and SCHIP serves children in families who are somewhat better off, with family income eligibility thresholds at or above twice the poverty line index.

SCHIP now serves about four million children in the United States. An evaluation of the pro-gram shows that, by and large, families do not see stigma in the program, and willingly enroll their children, once they are made aware of it. Furthermore, research has confirmed that most children on SCHIP would otherwise be uninsured, since their parents are typically in occupations with limited or no health coverage. Evidence shows that children benefit from SCHIP health cov-erage; they are more likely to get preventive care, and have fewer unmet dental and medical needs. Unfortunately, there are about nine million uninsured children in the United States, many of whom are eligible for Medicaid or SCHIP. There is a need for much more aggressive public infor-mation campaigns and targeted outreach to inform people of these programs (Kenney, 2006).

Food Programs

The Food Stamp program started in the 1930s and was extended broadly in 1974. It is the central program in the United States in alleviating hunger and helping low-income families obtain a more nutritious diet. Participants, who are usually below the poverty line index, receive a benefits card (replacing the old food coupons), which they use like a credit card at the grocery store. About ten million children live in households that receive food stamps, receiving on average a benefit of about 90 cents per meal. However, like SCHIP, only a fraction of eligible children are enrolled, particularly among poor families who do not participate in TANF. Much more effort is needed to reach these eligible households (Food Research and Action Center, no date: U.S. Department of Agriculture, 2005).

Another food program that targets pregnant mothers and children under age five, is the Women, Infants, and Children Program (WIC). Like Food Stamps, it is intended for low-income families, although eligibility for this program is more expansive, reaching families who are below 185 percent of the poverty line index. Nutritious foods are distributed to eligible families at a variety of local agencies, such as county health departments, migrant health centers, and Indian Health Service facilities, where participants are also usually able to receive health counseling and services such as prenatal care and well-child visits. In 2002, WIC served about seven million women and children each month (Food Research and Action Center, 2005).

Earned Income Tax Credit

The Earned Income Tax Credit (EITC) was passed by Congress in 1975 to offset the Social Security taxes paid by low-income families. The credit is available only to working poor people and is intended to encourage work by supplementing the income of low-wage earners. EITC is the fastest-growing antipoverty program in the country and has wide bipartisan support. It was a relatively small program until it was expanded in 1993, and is now the nation's largest antipoverty program for working families. In 2003, over nineteen million families received over thirty-four billion dollars from the credit (Holt, 2006.).

The EITC pays nothing if an individual does not work. As an individual's earnings increase, the EITC benefit also increases, up to a certain point. For workers who earn more, generally between $15,000 and $30,000, there is some concern that the EITC may not be as helpful, because, from that level of income onward, the amount of the benefit declines as earnings increase. The actual amount received depends on the number of children the family has, its earnings, and whether the tax filing is for a single parent or a married couple. To receive the EITC supplement, families must file a tax return, even if their incomes are so low that they do not owe income taxes. An important feature of the EITC is its refundability; the family will receive the full amount of the tax return for which they are eligible, even if that amount exceeds the amount of taxes the family paid.

The EITC has demonstrated its effectiveness in helping move families with children out of poverty. In a recent study, The Center on Budget and Policy Priorities found that in 2003, the EITC lifted 4.4 million people out of poverty, including 2.4 million children (Greenstein, 2005). The EITC also increases employment, since only people who work are eligible, and, for low-income workers, the size of the benefit increases as earnings increase, thus providing an incentive for more work. EITC is a cost-effective way for the government to support poor families. An indicator of its success is that eighteen states have now replicated the EITC on a state level, and other states are expected to follow.

The main criticism of the EITC is that it has a large overpayment rate, but research has not yet shown whether the overpayments are due primarily to negligence and fraud or to misunderstanding and misinterpretation. It appears that the error rate for the EITC is smaller than that of certain other areas of the income tax system. Overall, the EITC is a highly successful program to help poor working families. The Brookings Institution, in a recent comprehensive assessment of the program, concluded, "The EITC represents a tremendous resource both for the households that claim it and for the communities in which they live. It has surely earned the nation's continued attention and support" (Holt, 2006).

Child Support Enforcement

The Child Support Enforcement (CSE) program is a government program to increase child support by noncustodial parents. Recognizing that courts, who issue the orders, are not able to effectively enforce those orders in many cases, state and federal governments have accepted a major role in ensuring the efficient transfer of child support payments from the noncustodial parent to the child. Federal and state involvement in this area increased substantially in the 1990s, as part of the overhaul of the welfare system.

The program serves primarily low- and moderate-income families, including current and former TANF recipients, who in most cases are required to cooperate, and other families who request its help in enforcing child support orders. In addition to enforcing existing support orders, the program works to locate parents, establish paternity, and obtain child support orders from the courts. It also obtains health coverage for children through ensuring that the noncustodial parent's health insurance covers his or her children.

Although various levels of government have been involved in child support collection, particularly for families on welfare, for many years, legislation in the 1990s significantly increased the scope and effectiveness of the program. The effects of these reforms are evident in the program statistics for 2004: CSE collected 21.9 billion dollars in child support, including nearly 70 percent of the cases for which there was a court support order; established paternity for 1.6 million children; and obtained over 1 million court support orders for children who did not have them (Turetsky, 2005; Office of Child Support Enforcement, 2006).

Social Insurance

The term "social insurance" refers to programs that are established by law for the purpose of assuring financial benefits related to earlier compulsory contributions when an individual or family experiences loss of income due to specified risks. Social insurance is based on the idea of self-help and prevention of poverty and its resultant serious problems. In this country, our largest social insurance programs are provided for by the Social Security Act and its amendments. Let us consider first the old age, survivors, disability, and health insurance provisions (OASDHI) of this act, since these affect families and children.

OASDHI. Everyone in the country can and must participate in the OASDHI system if he or she works in "covered" occupations (almost all employed people are in "covered" work). If men and women work for specified periods during which they and their employers each contribute equally through the payment of taxes (a certain percentage of the employee's earnings), then they are insured against certain risks—specifically, the loss of income when they retire, become disabled, or die. They and their family members are eligible to receive benefits when such loss of income occurs. Substantial numbers of children receive benefits under the OASDHI program. In 2006, nearly four million children received monthly benefits averaging slightly under $500 for children whose parent had reached retirement age, $660 for children whose parent had died, and $300, for children whose parent was disabled (U.S. Social Security Administration, 2006).

Several other social insurance programs are contained in the Social Security Act. *Unemployment insurance* is intended to provide partial protection against loss of income due to unemployment of workers. *Worker's compensation*, or industrial accident insurance, is directed toward alleviating loss of income that arises from a worker's injuries on the job or death from fatal work-related injuries. As with unemployment insurance, it is financed primarily by employers and is administered by the states, resulting in large variation from state to state in types and amounts of benefits. *Veteran's benefits*, a system that has some general similarities to social insurance but some differences as well, encompasses a variety of programs for veterans of military service. Veterans may be able to obtain low-cost life insurance for the protection of their families, benefits to their surviving family members if they die in military service, disability benefits, medical care, and certain educational benefits. All these benefits are provided as a matter of earned right, based not so much on financial contribution as on a felt obligation that the American people have expressed in legislation.

Supplemental Security Income

Enacted in 1972, Supplemental Security Income (SSI) provides assistance to the elderly and to disabled children and adults who are below certain income levels. For the elderly, it supplements Social Security and pension income if the amount they receive in retirement benefits is insufficient. For those who are medically certified as physically or mentally unable to work, it provides a source of income. Because SSI is strict in its certification guidelines, only those who have considerable physical or mental disabilities can qualify for the program.

SSI is a federally designed program with a standard set of national benefits. SSI is only for low-income families; the family must have an income that does not exceed program requirements, and there is a ceiling on how much the child, if working, can earn and still be eligible. The child must have a physical or mental condition that results in "marked and severe functional limitations," and the condition must be long-lasting (Social Security, 2006). The SSI program for children has seen considerable growth in recent years. In 2005, over one million blind and disabled children under age 18 received SSI payments, compared with 107,000 children in 1975 (Social Security, 2006). The average monthly payment in 2005 to children was $518.

ASSESSMENT OF WELFARE REFORM

It has been ten years since PRWORA was enacted in 1996, which heralded a new era in how public assistance was provided to the nation's poorest families. Most analysts have hailed welfare reform as at least a moderate success. Welfare rolls dropped dramatically, from 12 million in 1996 to 4.5 million ten years later. About 60 percent of the mothers who left welfare found work, a figure far surpassing the predictions of many experts. Also contrary to some predictions, employers generally welcomed applications from recipients, and welfare "stigma" did not seem to follow mothers into the workforce (Clinton, 2006; Samuelson, 2006; Besharov, 2006). Child support payments increased dramatically. Welfare reform demonstrated that low-income parents were willing and able to work, but needed help in connecting with the workforce and in having access to income supports such as health insurance for children and child care assistance, which would continue even when their public assistance had ended. Some former welfare recipients perhaps also needed the personal motivation that comes from realizing that long-term assistance was no longer an option, as they faced a time limit for receiving welfare (Golden, 2005; *A decade of welfare reform*, 2006).

A deeper analysis reveals a more nuanced picture of the success of welfare reform. Welfare reform did not reduce poverty in single-mother families to any significant extent. Parents exchanged inadequate welfare income for inadequate earned income, but their overall condition did not change much. In the ten years since welfare reform began, it has become clearer that the poverty rate depends more on the overall state of the economy than on the specifics of welfare policy. When the economy is strong, as it was in the late 1990s, the poverty rate falls, and when the economy weakens, as it did in the first years of the twenty-first century, the poverty rate rises. A major conclusion of this finding is that effort must be directed at improving the earning power of families through both increased education and training of individuals and through effective economic policies (Seefeldt, 2004; McKernan & Ratcliffe, 2006; Pear & Eckholm, 2006).

Another important conclusion from the experiences of the past decade is that public assistance, in the form of direct cash payments to eligible families, is no longer the main welfare program for low-income families. Now that most welfare families are working, they have become a part of the larger group of the "working poor." Several antipoverty programs expanded their scope during the decade following the passage of PRWORA (Besharov, 2006). The EITC, child care assistance, child support enforcement, food programs, and publicly financed health insurance have demonstrated their effectiveness in helping poor families maintain functioning and provide suitable environments for their children (*Government work supports*, 2006). Unemployment Insurance has not been expanded as a result of welfare reform, but there are several proposals to increase benefits and ease eligibility to make it more of a resource for the working poor. Table 2.1 shows the expenditures for different family and income support programs for 2003, and illustrates the importance of these programs relative to cash payments to families. Medicaid, the EITC, and food stamps all had much higher expenditures than TANF (Burke, 2004).

Table 2.1 *Federal and State Outlays for Children and Their Families from Selected Major Income Support Programs, FY 2003*

Program	Federal Funds ($ in billions)	State/Local Funds ($ in billions)	Recipients (in millions)
TANF	7.7	6.2	5
EITC refunds	34.2	0	19
Child tax credit refunds	6.4	0	N/A
SSI, children only	5.6	0.2	0.95
Food Stamps	19.3	1.4	17.4
School lunches, etc.	9.6	n.a.	18.5
WIC	4.6	n.a.	7.6
Medicaid	40.6	30.6	39.3
SCHIP	4.4	1.7	6.2

Source: Burke, V. (October 28, 2004) *Welfare reform, an issue overview.* Congressional Research Service and The Library of Congress.

Although these programs have assisted families to get off and stay off welfare, they are lacking in coordination and cohesiveness. Many parents find it very difficult to learn about the programs, to understand whether they are eligible, and to navigate the different requirements and find time to visit all the different offices involved. They may not know, for example, about the EITC or how to get it (they must file a tax return, even if they owe no taxes). Families who are not on welfare may not know that they may be eligible for child health insurance or food stamps, wrongly assuming that these programs are only available through TANF. Even if parents do know the regulations of the programs, their work and family commitments may make it very difficult for them to find time to take advantage of the benefits theoretically available. Research of the Urban Institute (*Government work supports,* 2006) found that only seven percent of eligible families received all four of the main income supports: child care assistance, food assistance, health insurance, and the EITC. Some states are now beginning to coordinate and link together these work support programs so parents can apply for all of them at one office and get help from client advocates on the application process.

Another finding from research on the last ten years of welfare policy is that there is a group of low-income families whom current programs do not reach, estimated at between ten to fourteen percent of those leaving welfare. The parents in these families are likely to have mental health problems, physical disabilities, developmental disabilities, addictions, or caregiving responsibilities that have proved to be barriers to effective, consistent workforce participation. Many of these families have dropped out of or have been terminated from TANF, but did not leave TANF for a job. They are unemployed and their sources of income are not known. It is thought that children in these families are vulnerable to extreme want, as their families are worse off now than before welfare reform. These families have fallen through the holes in the safety net (Pear & Eckholm, 2006; Loprest & Zedlewski, 2006).

In the debate leading up to welfare reform in the 1990s, there was great concern that children would suffer from the loss of guaranteed benefits, and that they would be at greater risk for hunger, homelessness, and abuse and neglect. Fortunately, these concerns have not materialized. However, they remain at a disadvantage, along with other children of poor families, and are at risk of poor developmental outcomes and an unpromising start in life. There is some reason to believe that increased parental employment has negatively affected some children, particularly if good child care is lacking (Beadle, 2006; *A decade of welfare reform,* 2006). See the next section for a discussion of federal programs for low-income children.

It is important to recognize the reality of the lives of families who are struggling to make ends meet. Many parents work long hours at unsatisfying jobs. They may rightfully take pride in their self-sufficiency and accomplishments, but their success should not obscure the stressful and harsh conditions in which they are forced to operate. In the lives of many, there is little margin for unexpected emergencies. Low-paying jobs often do not allow parents time off for health and school appointments for their children. Jobs may be located far from home, and transportation difficulties can be overwhelming. The jobs themselves may be temporary or insecure, so the threat of loss of income is always hovering. Although children may be covered by SCHIP, the parents often have no health insurance and cannot afford medical care. Many poor families simply cannot put enough aside to start building assets, particularly home ownership and investments, that would lead to a brighter future. Child care, which will be discussed in a separate section of this chapter, is a huge problem for many families, as too often it is located inconveniently, is expensive, and is not developmentally appropriate for children. The safety net must continue to be strengthened to ease the undue burden on these families and to help their children take their future places as full contributing members of society (Golden, 2005; *Low income working families*, 2006).

SUPPORTING FAMILIES WITH DAY CARE AND CHILD DEVELOPMENT PROGRAMS

With most mothers at work some part of each day, the question of what happens to the children has become an issue of intense national interest. Highly publicized stories of children who are left in dangerous situations while their parents, oblivious of the problem, were at work, have received widespread coverage in the press. This concern reflects the anxiety parents feel about having to juggle home and work responsibilities, and their worries about whether, by working outside the home, they are shortchanging their children of the care they need, or even jeopardizing their safety (Vobejda & Davis, 1997; Lewin, 2002). The fact that day care is in the national spotlight indicates that, after decades of ignoring the reality that many children were being cared for by people other than their parents, the country is beginning to address the issue of what happens to children in a society organized around parental employment outside the home. "This fact of contemporary life represents a dramatic reapportioning of the care of young children from parents to others, starting in the first few months of life" (Phillips & Adams, 2001).

Unlike most industrialized countries, the United States has lagged in establishing government-assisted arrangements for the daytime care of children of working parents. Reasons for this long delay come from a host of conflicting values in U.S. society about the appropriate role of women as workers and mothers, and about the responsibility of government to participate in what many consider to be the "private sphere" of family life (Cherlin, 1998). During World War II, the United States experienced a brief interval of providing public support for good quality child care under the provisions of the Lanham Act of 1941. The Act provided federal funds to states to establish day care facilities for the children of working mothers in war-impacted communities until 1946, when the war ended and federal funds were withdrawn (Pedgeon, 1953; Farmer, 1969). The dismantling of the day care infrastructure built during the 1940s had long-term consequences. For the rest of the twentieth century, such considerations as the high cost of quality child care, the cultural diversity of U.S. families, and controversy over the effects of day care on children's growth and development inhibited the establishment of comprehensive federal policy on day care. "The gaps in caregiving do not exist because parents work or even because they work hard. The gaps are formed by social conditions that never adapted to the changes in where and how parents work" (Heymann, 2000).

Today, however, a variety of social forces have created a national consensus on the need for a more comprehensive approach to the nation's child care needs. Kamerman (2001, p. 259) has identified the following reasons for the increased national interest in child care. Research on brain development has underlined the importance of early childhood experiences in the development of the brain, and developmental psychologists have shown that early childhood programs can significantly benefit children and help them get ready to learn at school. Economists have pointed out that investing in children, who are "human capital" of the future, is sound economic policy.

> *The increase in funding for roads and bridges has been far greater than the increase in funding for kids. . . . Kids who enter school not ready to learn never catch up.* —Adele Simmons, of Metropolis 2020, Chicago. (Wobbly first steps, 2003)

The movement of women, including the mothers of young children, into the workforce now seems to be permanent. The percent of women with children under age six who are in the labor force increased from 47 percent in 1980 to 63 percent in 2004 (Children's Defense Fund, 2005, p. 62). For children aged 6 to 13, 78 percent have mothers working outside the home (Bachu & O'Connell, 2000). Welfare reform of 1996 has strongly affected public policy in day care. TANF requires even parents of very young children to work, and federal subsidies for child care were part of the PRWORA legislation.

Federal Legislation

Parents, businesses, and federal, state, and local governments all contribute to the payment for child care in the United States. The federal role in funding child care increased in the early 1990s, and then expanded again in 1996 as part of welfare reform. Between 1996 and 2003, federal and state child care spending almost doubled, but has leveled off since then. Besharov and Higney (2006) reported the following expenditures for the three largest federal child care programs.

❖ *Child Care Development Block Grant* provides funds to states for child care subsidies for low-income families, including those in welfare-to-work programs, and for improving the quality and supply of child care. Funding increased from 1997 to 2001 by 84 percent, and totaled over $9 billion in 2003, including both federal and state matching funds. About 1.75 million children per month receive child care through this subsidy program.

❖ *Head Start* is a federally and locally financed early childhood development program for low-income children, and is used as a child care service by many low-income working mothers. Head Start funding has also increased in recent years, to about 6.5 billion dollars in 2003, when it served over 1 million children. The increase was due mainly to quality improvements and to lengthening hours of operation.

❖ *Child and Dependent Care Tax Credit* helps families reduce their child care costs by allowing them to deduct up to $5,000 of these costs from their federal tax obligation. An important limitation of this program is that it helps only families who earn enough to pay federal taxes. In 2003, the federal cost of this program was $2.7 billion.

In addition to these programs, numerous smaller funding streams exist, such as those that funnel resources to children with disabilities and Native American children. All together, Besharov and Higney estimated that the total of government spending on child care in 2003 was over $20 billion. Despite increased spending, there continue to be too many gaps, shortages, coordination problems among programs, and poor-quality programs in the child care services arena.

The Family and Medical Leave Act

The Family and Medical Leave Act was signed into law by President Clinton in 1993, the culmination of seven years of lobbying by child advocacy groups. It addresses the needs of families for both job security and caregiving. The law requires employers of fifty or more workers to grant employees who work twenty-five or more hours per week up to twelve weeks of unpaid leave per year, for the birth or adoption of a child, for the care of a seriously ill child or other family member, or for a serious illness of their own. Although the leave is unpaid, employers do have to provide health benefits during the leave. Because part-time workers and workers in small businesses are exempt, only about half the nation's workers are covered by the law. Despite this limitation, the law is a milestone toward the goal of making work more compatible with family life for American workers and their children, and puts the United States in the company of other industrialized countries, most of which have provisions for leave following childbirth and for child care emergencies.

Day Care Regulation

Although varying in form, all states have statutory provisions for the regulation of day care for children. The intent of these regulations is to safeguard children from harm and prevent ills that might befall them from poor care and supervision. Licensing and regulatory standards are important strategies in assuring quality in day care, although the standards represent minimum baseline requirements, below which no program may operate. They do not provide a guarantee that day care will be of high quality. States, not the federal government, make and enforce regulations for day care (Gazan, 1998).

All states do require that day care centers be licensed, with some exceptions for religiously affiliated programs. Typically, regulations specify the amount of space that must be available to each child, child–adult ratios, and fire and other building safety requirements. Providers may be required to pass health examinations and criminal background checks, and have certain levels of education (Children's Foundation, 2002).

In contrast to day care centers, most private day care homes are not regulated at all, although homes caring for three or more nonrelative children and homes serving TANF families may need to comply with licensing laws. Even if licensing is required for day care homes, the requirement is largely unenforced (Galinsky, Howes, Kontos, & Shinn, 1994).

The lack of consistent, dependable state oversight of day care homes means that parents must be informed consumers of child care. Current TANF policy now provides parents with child care vouchers and allows them to find their own child care, rather than using only those from an approved agency list. Forming alliances with the day care staff, visiting on a drop-in basis, talking with the child about his or her day, and asking questions about confusing situations are important ways for parents to continually monitor their children's progress in day care.

Working Parents' Child Care Arrangements

The U.S. Census Bureau (2005) issues periodic reports on child care arrangements of American families. Child care providers can be broadly classified as either "relatives," including parents, siblings, and grandparents, or "nonrelatives," such as in-home babysitters and nannies, neighbors, and friends. Other categories of "nonrelatives" include family day care providers, who care for children outside the child's home, and organized child care facilities such as day care centers, preschools, Head Start programs, and prekindergarten programs in the schools. For school-aged children, the categories also include school-based programs, enrichment activities such as sports and art, and self-care. Figure 2.1 shows the distribution of children in these various arrangements in 2002.

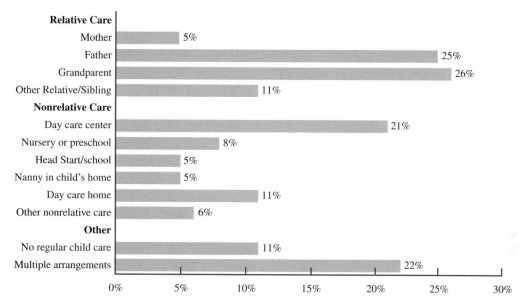

Figure 2.1 *Children Under Age 5 of Employed Mothers in Types of Child Care Arrangements, 2002*

Source: U.S. Census Bureau (2005, October). *Who's minding the kids?* Child care arrangement: Winter, 2002. Washington, DC: U.S. Department of Commerce, U.S. Census Bureau, p.4.

Note: Total does not equal 100% because children may be in multiple arrangements.

The type of arrangement parents make varies with the age of the child. In 2002, about 11.6 million preschoolers, or 63 percent of all children under age 5, were cared for in some type of regular child care arrangement. Preschoolers are more apt to be cared for by relatives than nonrelatives. About a quarter of all preschoolers are cared for in day care centers, with smaller percentages cared for in day care homes or at home by babysitters. Preschool-aged children of working mothers spend long hours in day care, with an average of 32 hours per week.

Once children reach school-age, the time spent in school accounts for much of their time while their parent is working. However, grade school-aged children also need supplementary care. In 2002, of the 24 million grade school-aged children whose mothers were working outside the home, nearly 70 percent were also in a supervised situation, including care by relatives, day care homes, enrichment activities, and school-based programs. As children get older, self-care during nonschool hours becomes more likely.

Head Start

A major assumption of public responsibility for children's daytime programs came about through Project Head Start (U.S. Office of Education and Office of Economic Opportunity, 1966). Head Start is intended to give preschool children from economically disadvantaged backgrounds child development services to prepare them to enter first grade ready to learn, with the social and cognitive skills needed to be successful in school (Zill et al., 1998). The Administration for Children,

Youth and Families (ACYF) in the U.S. Department of Health and Human Services administers Head Start. ACYF awards grants to local public and nonprofit agencies, Indian tribes, and school systems to operate Head Start programs. Two-thirds of Head Start children are of minority ethnicity, and about 13 percent have disabilities (Administration for Children and Families, 2002). Head Start is for three and four year olds. With current emphasis on the importance of early learning experiences in brain development, in 1994, ACYF started a supplementary program, called Early Head Start, for two and three year olds.

The comprehensive program places emphasis on working with all aspects of a child's environment, including the family and the community. It aims to improve children's physical health through medical assessment and remedial health programs; help with their emotional and social development by encouraging qualities such as self-confidence, expectation of success, spontaneity, curiosity and self-discipline; improve their mental processes, with particular attention to conceptual and verbal skills; and strengthen the child–parent relationship.

Parents are encouraged to participate in every phase of developing and administering the program. Many work as teachers' aides and in other nonprofessional capacities. Parenting education courses have taught parents how to improve the home environment and help young children "learn to learn" at home.

Does Head Start Have Lasting Effects?

Substantial research is now tracking the outcomes of children enrolled in Early Head Start and Head Start (U.S. Department of Health and Human Services, 2002; 2005). Preliminary findings are encouraging; by the end of kindergarten, former Head Start participants were found to be at "national norms in early reading and early writing and were close to meeting national norms in early math and vocabulary knowledge. . . . A higher proportion of [Head Start] parents read to their children more frequently than those parents of children who were not enrolled in [Head Start]." Other positive outcomes include "long term effects on grade repetition, special education, and graduation rates" (National Head Start Association, no date). A study in San Bernardino County, California, concluded that "society receives nearly $9 in benefits for every $1 invested in these [Head Start] children. These benefits include increased earnings, employment, and family stability, and decreased welfare dependency, crime costs, grade repetition, and special education. Properly trained [Head Start] parents can decrease Medicaid costs by $198 per family" (National Head Start Association, no date). Importantly, research has found that program quality is linked to child performance, reinforcing the need to find a way to pay for high-quality programs for children (Zill et al., 1998).

The Perry Preschool Project, a program similar in some ways to Head Start, has conducted a longitudinal investigation of the children it served in the 1960s to see how they have fared later in life. The results of this follow-up study have shown that the Perry graduates derived many benefits, including reduced grade retention, welfare usage, and crime, and increased school completion and employment rates. (Berreuta-Clement et al., 1984; Schweinhart, Barnes, & Weikart, 1993).

Early development programs cannot guarantee success in life. Although Perry Preschool Project graduates were likely to be more successful than their peers who did not attend preschool, they were less successful than children from middle- and upper-income families. A reasonable conclusion of the effects of early childhood programs is, "they cannot overpower the effects of poor living conditions, inadequate nutrition and health care, negative role models, and substandard schools. But good programs can prepare children for school and possibly help them develop better coping and adaptation skills that will enable better life outcomes, albeit not perfect ones" (Zigler & Styfco, 1994, p. 129). In addition to benefits to children, Head Start has helped numerous parents and has had a positive effect on their communities. Thousands of parents obtain training and jobs through Head Start each year and may go on to further their education and become employed.

Policy Issues in Child Care: Availability, Cost, and Quality

Despite of major increases in funding for child care as a result of welfare reform, day care is still underfunded and is not meeting the needs of many families. The Children's Defense Fund (2005, p. 61) has pinpointed the large gaps in service for America's poor families. "Only one out of seven children eligible for the Child Care and Development Block Grant (CCDBG), the federal child care assistance program, receives assistance. In about one-third of the states, a family of three earning $25,000 a year would not qualify for child care assistance. Twenty states had either waiting lists or frozen intake in 2005, with well over 450,000 children on these lists." Shortages also exist in the provision of Head Start programs. "More than three million children eligible for Head Start and Early Head Start were not served in 2004 . . . in 2003, about half of all eligible preschool-age children were served by Head Start . . . [and] less than three percent of eligible infants and toddlers were served by Early Head Start" (p. 61). With or without help from federal programs, parents very often find that they must work and must find some arrangement for their children. They can ill-afford the child care that they need to have, and the care of their children may be substandard.

The increase in the number of working parents and consequent need for child care has given rise to an intense debate on the effects of nonparental care on child development (Stolberg, 2001; Lewin, 2002; Waldfogel, Brooks-Gunn, & Han, 2002). The National Institute of Child Health and Human Development (NICHD) has released periodic reports from its ongoing research on the effects of nonparental care on children. Using an ethnically and demographically diverse sample of 1,000 children, the study has followed them from the time that they first entered child care as infants, as young as one-month-old, to the present, when the first cohorts are in middle school. These children spent an average of 27 hours per week in nonmaternal care over the first four and a half years of life. The first two years of life, most child care took place in the family homes with relatives or in child care homes; as the children got older, they were more likely to be in child care centers. The main findings from this research are that overall there is no difference in development between young children who are entirely in maternal care and those who spend some time in nonmaternal care. Early exposure to child care can foster children's cognitive and social learning or it can leave them behind in learning and at risk for troubled relationships. The outcome depends largely on the quality of the child care setting. The study identifies good-quality settings as those with responsive, warm caregivers who surround children with warmth, language, and a chance to learn. Unfortunately, the study also found that children whose families lack good incomes or government supports are most often exposed to poor quality care (Phillips & Adams, 2001; National Institute of Child Health and Human Development, 2006).

Another great shortage is in after-school programs for middle and high-school aged children in self-care. About 3.3 million children under age 13 are without adult supervision for part of the day (Vandivere et al., 2003). It is widely acknowledged that many school children aged 6 to 12 are only loosely supervised in a piecemeal pattern of care by older siblings, neighbors, relatives, and parents themselves, interspersed with periods of self-care. Children aged 13 and older are frequently left to fend for themselves, instead of being in enrichment and recreational programs. Research has shown that children left unsupervised are more likely to be involved in crime. The after-school hours from 3 PM to 6 PM are hours when children are most likely to be victims or perpetrators of violent crime, to be in car crashes, to experiment with drugs and cigarettes, to engage in sexual intercourse with resultant pregnancies, and to become hooked on violent video games, which are now thought to be a training ground for violent behavior (Newman et al., 2000). Children in low-income areas are most at risk for criminal behavior in after-school hours; these children stand to benefit most from well-designed after-school enrichment programs and are among the least likely to get them.

Even though both state and federal governments have increased their support of child care in recent years, there are still too many children who do not receive adequate child care. Shortages exist particularly in the provision of enough child care financing for low-income families, in the number of high-quality child care settings for children of all income levels, and in after-school programs for older children. Government, communities, foundations, and businesses must all play a larger role in helping parents find good-quality child care arrangements. The development of comprehensive child care policy has been hampered by its separation into two different areas: *work support* programs, such as the Child Care Block Grants, offered primarily to low-income parents to help them find child care so they can enter the workforce; and *education for young children,* such as Head Start, to help children in low-income families improve early childhood development. Edie (2006) argued that it no longer makes sense to have two different sets of policies and programs that are targeted to the same low-income families. Since learning occurs from birth onward, it would make better use of resources and make day care planning easier for families if these two areas were combined. In particular, funding for work support child care needs to take into account the lessons learned from Head Start on how to run developmentally appropriate programs.

MEASURING THE WELL-BEING OF AMERICA'S CHILDREN

The Interagency Forum on Child and Family Statistics is a cooperative effort of over twenty agencies in the federal government. The Forum's mission is to "improve the reporting and dissemination of information on the status of children to the policy community and the general public" (Federal Interagency Forum, 2005, p. iii). Every two years, the Forum issues a report on the most recent, reliable, official statistics that gives a profile of the strengths and difficulties confronting the nation's children. Nine contextual measures provide demographic and environmental information, and twenty-five key indicators represent a broad range of important aspects of children's lives. Comparisons of current statistics with those of earlier years show improvement or decline on a given indicator. These reports provide the best available profile of the overall well-being of children in the United States. They can be considered a "national scorecard" on how we are doing as a nation in creating a healthy and safe society for children, and allow international comparisons. They may also help policymakers establish priorities and track progress toward policy goals for children. Box 2.1 provides a list of the population and family characteristics and of the twenty-five indicators of children's well-being included in the most recent report.

Box 2.1

National Indicators of Child Well-Being

Population and Family Characteristics (contextual measures)
Child population
Children as a proportion of the population
Racial and ethnic composition
Children of at least one foreign-born parent
Difficulty speaking English
Family structure and children's living arrangements
Births to unmarried women
Child care
Children's environments

Indicators of Children's Well-Being

Economic Security Indicators
Child poverty and family income
Secure parental employment
Housing problems
Food security and diet quality
Access to health care

Health Indicators
General health status
Activity limitation
Overweight
Childhood immunization
Low birthweight
Infant mortality
Child mortality
Adolescent mortality
Adolescent births

Behavior and Social Environment Indicators
Regular cigarette smoking
Alcohol use
Illicit drug use
Youth victims and perpetrators of serious violent crimes

Education Indicators
Family reading to young children
Early childhood care and education
Mathematics and reading achievement
High school academic coursetaking
High school completion
Youth neither enrolled in school nor working
Higher education

Special Features (new to this report)
Asthma
Lead in the blood of children
Parental reports of emotional and behavioral difficulties

Overall, the trends point to some improvements in the lives of children since the early 1990s, but there are also areas of increased concern. The following is a sample of the findings from the 2005 report.

❖ Child poverty has fluctuated since the early 1980s, from a high of 22 percent in 1993 to a low of 16 percent in 2000. The current rate is 18 percent.

❖ The percent of children who are overweight has increased from 6 percent in 1976–1980 to 16 percent in 1999–2002.

❖ In 2003, 89 percent of American children were covered by health insurance. The percentage of children covered by private health insurance is dropping, while that of children covered by public insurance is increasing.

❖ Infant mortality declined significantly in the twentieth century, to a low of 6.8 births per thousand in 2001. Since then it has risen slightly, due primarily to the increase in the number of very low birthweight babies. Child mortality (children aged 1–17) dropped by half between 1980 and 2002.

❖ The birth rate for adolescents has declined to 22 births per thousand females aged 15–17, the lowest rate ever recorded. The decline cuts across all racial and ethnic groups.

❖ Serious violent crime among juveniles increased from 2003 to 2004, but is still lower than the peak rates in 1993.

❖ The average mathematics scale score for fourth and eighth graders was higher in 2003 than in all previous years since assessment began in 1990. Little change occurred in reading scores.

❖ In 2003, 5 percent of children aged 4–17 were reported by a parent to have definite emotional or behavioral difficulties. This is a new indicator added for the 2005 report, so there are no comparison data for previous years.

These trends, many of them positive, must be accepted with caution until longer-term trends can be tracked. It should be noted also that even with current improvements, some indicators show a still unacceptably low condition, such as the increasing obesity of children and the large numbers still living in poverty. The infant mortality rate, although low, is still higher than that of most other industrialized countries. Those concerned with the well-being of children will watch with interest and concern as these reports provide an increasingly comprehensive picture over time of changes in the condition of American children.

TRENDS AND ISSUES

Income Supports for Immigrant Families

In the past thirty-five years, the number of immigrants in the United States has tripled, as has the number of immigrant children. The foreign-born population passed 35 million in 2005. This total consists of roughly equal numbers of undocumented immigrants, legal immigrants, and naturalized citizens (about 30 percent each) and another 10 percent who are refugees or are here on a temporary basis, such as students (Passel, 2006). Unlike previous immigrations, who were largely from Europe and Africa, the current wave of immigrants come mainly from South America, Mexico, and Asia. Immigrants are concentrated in six states: California, New York, Texas,

Florida, Illinois, and New Jersey, but are rapidly dispersing throughout the Midwest and the Southeast (Capps & Fortuny, 2006).

In 1970, 6 percent of U.S. children had at least one immigrant parent; today over 20 percent do. Children of immigrants are those who have at least one foreign-born parent. About three-quarters of these children are U.S.-born citizens, even though most of their immigrant parents are not citizens of the United States and may be undocumented.

Many of our basic welfare programs took form before the wave of immigration of the last decades of the twentieth century, and were not designed for this population. Until welfare reform of 1996 (PRWORA), public assistance was structured primarily to help poor single-mother families without a working father in the home. But most poor immigrant families are headed by a married couple, at least one of whom is working. The problems of immigrant families consist of their immigration status, since many are undocumented, their lack of education or English language skills, and their employment in low-skill, poorly paid jobs. Despite working long hours, many immigrant families are poor and experience hardship such as hunger and lack of health care. Although the poverty rate for immigrants is lower than for African Americans, the rate of poverty among immigrants is increasing. Children in immigrant families are more likely than other children to experience food-related problems, crowded housing, and poor health (Capps & Fortuny, 2006).

Because of economic hardship, immigrant families have great need for public support. The benefits they need most are those associated with low-wage work: tax credits, housing, food assistance, health insurance, and child care subsidies, yet they are less likely to get them than are native-born Americans. One major factor in whether an immigrant family uses benefits is their immigration status; undocumented immigrants are ineligible for most public aid programs, including the EITC, TANF, food stamps, and Medicaid. Children in these families may be legal U.S. citizens, and therefore eligible for some public services, even if their parents are undocumented. But undocumented parents are very likely not to understand that their children are eligible for services, or they may be afraid that any contact with the government could result in their deportation.

The other major reason that immigrants are less likely than native-born Americans to use benefits has to do with the provisions of the PRWORA of 1996. The Act restricted TANF and Medicaid eligibility to those who had been in the country for at least five years, and to a few other special groups. Food stamp eligibility was limited to adults who had been working in the United States for at least ten years. Since 1996, some of these provisions have been softened, and states have used state funds to provide services to immigrants not available under federal programs. However, recent legal immigrants in most states remain ineligible for most of these programs. As a result of the provisions of PRWORA, the participation of immigrants in public income support programs dropped. Even those who are eligible to receive services may be afraid to apply, fearing that their citizenship application, or their application to sponsor relatives in the future, may be compromised.

Other barriers to participation include language problems, confusion about eligibility rules or application procedures, and various problems with documenting need. Many immigrants work in casual or temporary labor markets, and may not have employment and income documentation needed to apply. Furthermore, they may be asked to verify their sponsor's income as well as their own, which sponsors may be unwilling to provide.

Children of immigrants are at risk for lower cognitive and language development and poorer performance in school than children of natives. This gap is mainly due to poverty, low parent education, and limited English proficiency, all factors associated with school achievement. Immigrant children are missing out on many of the early childhood developmental programs, such as Head Start and good-quality child care centers, which can help children prepare for school and narrow gaps in performance with children of more educated and affluent backgrounds (Capps & Fortuny, 2006).

Currently, there is debate about how the nation should respond to the needs of immigrant families (Haskins, Greenberg, & Fremstad, 2004). Some believe that the current restrictions on benefits is the correct one. U.S. immigration policy has always included the expectation that immigrants should be able to support themselves, and that if they fall on hard times, their sponsors are expected to help them. In this view, the United States offers immigrants many benefits, including the freedom to live in a society governed by laws, individual liberty, and the prospect of joining one of the world's most prosperous economies. The nation is entitled to expected that immigrants, in their turn, should obey the law and avoid receiving public benefits until they become citizens.

> *What do we want for these children? Do we want them not to have access to health insurance and a regular source of health care? Is that the better social policy?*—*Michael Fix, Migration Policy Institute (Suchetka, 2006).*

An opposing view is that immigrants should be eligible for public services, with no distinction between citizens and noncitizens. The rationale for this view is that the children of immigrants are important to our nation's future prosperity, and the continued viability of our social insurance programs such as Social Security. It is in the nation's interest that immigrant children should receive a good education and health care so that they can help the nation in the future. To achieve this, the nation should offer their families the income, health, and child development supports they need to raise prosperous, contributing members of society. This debate is far from being resolved, as this country, like many other industrialized countries, tries to cope with the social and economic costs and benefits of vastly increased immigration. At the moment, there is a consensus building for expanding eligibility for certain types of income and work supports, such as possibly restoring food stamps and SSI benefits for certain immigrants, and extending State Child Health Insurance prenatal benefits to undocumented women, to help them have healthy pregnancies. There is also general support for expanded early childhood education opportunities, and more English language acquisition programs, (Haskins, Greenberg, & Fremstad, 2004). However, the nation has not yet found the common ground needed to devise suitable policies that meet the needs of today's families and are consistent with our values and history as a nation of immigrants.

Welfare Reform: Challenging Populations

In 1997, Pavetti, Olson, Nightingale, and Duke reported that 90 percent of welfare recipients experienced at least one of the following barriers to employment: low basic skills, substance abuse, depression, had a child with a chronic illness or disability, or had a physical health condition themselves. In 2002, Loprest found that of the recipients who left welfare between 1997 and 1999, 22 percent were back on the rolls. The long-term recipients, that is, those continuously on welfare for two years, and the returners, that is, those who had left welfare but returned, shared these characteristics: poor physical or mental health and less high school education. Early in the welfare reform process, it was recognized that poor physical or mental health of the child's parent would be a major barrier to sustained employment. Approximately 40 percent of the states' TANF recipients had multiple barriers to employment in 1997. States initially focused their attention on those with the fewest barriers to employment. Early on, caseloads were screened to determine whether any of those with physical or mental disabilities might qualify for Supplemental Security Income and, if so, to refer them for SSI. In 1999, approximately 40 percent of the TANF recipients had multiple barriers to employment, no change from 1997. However, of those persons receiving TANF support, 20 percent with multiple barriers were working some hours, up from 5 percent in 1997 (Weil, 2002).

Most states began to consider the more extensive support systems that would be required to transition persons with multiple barriers, with poor physical or mental health being one barrier, from welfare to work who did not qualify for SSI. These recipients require extensive coordination between mental health systems, vocational rehabilitation systems, and TANF systems. The significant increase in recipients with multiple barriers who are working but still eligible for welfare benefits is indicative that these populations can be gainfully employed. Given both their personal characteristics and the current economic environment, a modified policy may be more appropriate: namely, part-time employment with ongoing TANF benefits along with continuing mental and physical health supports (particularly continuing health insurance benefits for adults).

Persons with substance abuse issues are another group of recipients who initially offered challenges. Many states initiated drug screening programs for applicants and recipients to detect drug use/abuse and make referrals to drug abuse treatment services early in the TANF cycle. After some legal challenges, these policies were found legally acceptable so long as they were implemented to detect a service need and provide treatment and not to deny services. Another strategy was to carefully assess the impact of the parents' substance abuse on child safety. Many cases of parental substance abuse were referred to children's protective services. Some cases resulted in voluntary placement of the children with relatives. Others resulted in abuse and neglect petitions with placement of the children in foster care. Many TANF cases were closed to substance-using and -abusing parents and many child only cases were opened with relatives as grantees when the parents failed to participate in the required substance abuse treatment programming. Some advocates are concerned that these parents will be lost to the systems of service and continue their downward spirals. Insufficient substance abuse services are as much of a challenge for the TANF systems as they are for the child welfare system.

Persons in domestic violence situations are another group of recipients who offer unique challenges. Initially, some advocates argued that this group of recipients should be granted waivers or deferrals from the work requirements because of concerns about safety. However, others argued that they should not be categorically denied the opportunity to participate in programs that would increase their capacity for economic independence. Most states implemented employment protocols, including screening for domestic violence in all cases. Services were offered to those who had domestic violence issues. After assessment, victims of violence could obtain a temporary deferral if it were determined necessary for safety or they could be immediately referred for work activities. Joint decision-making in individual cases appears to be the most beneficial approach to these challenging cases because there is no uniform face to domestic violence and its impact on employability.

Perhaps the greatest challenge to welfare reform in the coming years is not the people and their characteristics, but the state of the economy.

CHAPTER SUMMARY

The United States has not solved the problem of persistent poverty among children. In 2004, over thirteen million children were poor. African American and Hispanic children are more likely than others to be poor, as are children in single-parent households. Poverty is caused in large measure by a number of changes in the U.S. economy that make it difficult for families to maintain a decent standard of living, including wage stagnation and a declining need for male workers with few skills and limited education.

Before the Great Depression of the 1930s, providing for the poor was mainly the responsibility of local and state governments. From 1935 until recently, the federal government, in partnership with the states, provided a safety net to eligible poor families with children through the Aid to Families with Dependent Children (AFDC) program. This program fell into disfavor, as concern grew that it discouraged work by enabling recipients to subsist on welfare payments, which were withdrawn if the recipient became employed.

In 1996, Congress passed the Personal Responsibility and Work Opportunity Reconciliation Act (PRWORA), which eliminated the AFDC program and replaced it with block grants to the states to establish Temporary Assistance for Needy Families (TANF) programs. TANF places emphasis on work and leaves states responsible for designing and implementing their welfare programs.

TANF provides temporary cash assistance for eligible families and also helps in finding and keeping work. The federal government also provides other kinds of assistance to families in need, including tax credits, food stamps, medical benefits, and social insurance. These programs are available to the "working poor" as well as welfare recipients.

Families in which parents work and children are in day care have become prevalent in American society. Today, about 60 percent of all preschoolers are in some form of day care or early childhood development program. Day care arrangements include care by relatives, family day care that is offered in the caregiver's home, in-home caregivers, and day care centers. Much day care is unregulated, particularly family day care. Most school-aged children are in school during the hours that their parents work, but many children spend time alone, without adult supervision, during the week.

Child development programs, such as Head Start, have as their primary goal the enhancement of preschool-aged children's development so that they will enter school ready to learn. These programs focus on the family, as well as the children, and see the parent as the child's first and most important teacher.

Care for children during the hours that their parents work has emerged as a major public policy issue. Recent research documenting the mediocre quality of many day care centers, combined with research showing the importance of high-quality day care for children's development, have given strong empirical support to efforts to improve conditions under which children are cared for during the day. Although federal and state support for day care has increased, greater government involvement is needed.

The United States now has a "national scorecard" to assess how well the public policies of the country are succeeding in improving the well-being of America's children. The Interagency Forum on Child and Family Statistics shows that America's children are improving on some measures of well-being, but poverty and access to health care remain largely unsolved problems.

Concern is increasing about the large number of children of immigrants who live in poverty and do not have access to educational and health care services. Even if the children were born in the United States and are citizens, their access to services is often linked to the immigration status of their parents, who may be undocumented. Public welfare policy is also concerned with the population of adults who are "falling through the cracks" of programs designed to get people off welfare through work; this population consists of adults who are mentally or physically ill or who abuse substances and are challenged to maintain employment that can sustain them.

FOR STUDY AND DISCUSSION
STUDY AND DISCUSSION QUESTIONS

1. Identify one or more nonprofit organizations in your community that provide resources to poor families. What kinds of resources do they provide? Where do their funds come from?

2. Review the historical development of our governmental income maintenance programs. Trace and evaluate recurring themes that are still evident in present-day policy and practice.

3. Identify two major employers in your community. Ask the employers about the kinds of entry-level jobs their companies provide. What skills and attitudes do they expect of entry-level employees? How much to they pay entry-level employees? What are the fringe benefits?

4. Propose a variety of arrangements that could be made to serve school-aged "self-care" children who need supervision and guidance outside school. Do such programs exist in your community?

5. Talk with a welfare worker and a representative of an immigrant support group about what kinds of public income supports and child care are available for immigrant families. Read policy and research papers on immigration. From the interviews and reading, take a position on what the U.S. policy should be regarding the provision of income benefits to legal immigrant families. What is your position on the provision of income benefits to undocumented immigrant families?

Internet Sites

Child Trends: Research in the Service of Children. Child Trends is a nonprofit, nonpartisan research organization dedicated to improving the lives of children by conducting and disseminating research to improve the decisions, programs, and policies that affect children and their families. **www.childtrends.org**

Child Welfare Information Gateway. The Gateway provides access to information and resources to help protect children and strengthen families. A service of the Children's Bureau, Administration for Children and Families, U.S. Department of Health and Human Services. **www.childwelfare.gov**

The Children's Defense Fund. This advocacy organization is for children in the United States who cannot vote, lobby, or speak for themselves. It pays particular attention to the needs of poor and minority children and those with disabilities. **www.childrensdefense.org**

Federal Interagency Forum on Child and Family Statistics. This web site offers easy access to statistics and reports on children and families, including population and family characteristics, economic security, health, behavior and social environment, and education. The Forum fosters coordination, collaboration, and integration of

Federal efforts to collect and report data on conditions and trends for children and families.
www.childstats.gov

Head Start Information and Publication Center. Head Start Information and Publication Center (HSIPC), a service of the Office of Head Start, supports the Head Start community and other organizations working in the interest of children and families by providing information products and services, conference and meeting support, publication distribution, and marketing and outreach efforts.
www.headstartinfo.org

Institute for Women Policy Research. The Institute for Women's Policy Research (IWPR) conducts rigorous research and disseminates its findings to address the needs of women, promote public dialogue, and strengthen families, communities, and societies. IWPR focuses on issues of poverty and welfare, employment and earnings, work and family issues, health and safety, and women's civic and political participation.
www.iwpr.org

National Center for Children in Poverty. The National Center for Children in Poverty (NCCP) is a leading public policy center that is dedicated to promoting the economic security, health, and well-being of America's low-income families and children. Using research to inform policy and practice, NCCP seeks to advance family oriented solutions and the strategic use of public resources at the state and national levels to ensure positive outcomes for the next generation.
www.nccp.org

National Head Start Association. The National Head Start Association is a private, not-for-profit membership organization dedicated exclusively to meeting the needs of Head Start children and their families. The Association provides support for the entire Head Start community by advocating for policies that strengthen services to Head Start children and their families; by providing extensive training and professional development to Head Start staff; and by developing and disseminating research, information, and resources that enrich Head Start program delivery.
www.nhsa.org

National Institute of Child Health and Human Development. The National Institute of Child Health and Human Development (NICHD) was initially established to investigate the broad aspects of human development as a means of understanding developmental disabilities, including mental retardation and the events that occur during pregnancy. Today, the Institute conducts and supports research on all stages of human development, from preconception to adulthood, to better understand the health of children, adults, families, and communities.
www.nichd. nih.gov

The Urban Institute. To promote sound social policy and public debate on national priorities, the Urban Institute gathers and analyzes data, conducts policy research, evaluates programs and services, and educates Americans on critical issues and trends.
www.urban.org

Zero to Three: National Center for Infants, Toddlers, and Families. Zero to Three's mission is to support the healthy development and well-being of infants, toddlers, and their families. It is a national nonprofit multidisciplinary organization that advances its mission by informing, educating, and supporting adults who influence the lives of infants and toddlers.
www.zerotothree.org

References

A decade of welfare reform: Facts and figures. (2006). Washington, DC: The Urban Institute.

Administration for Children and Families. (2002, September 4). *2002 Head Start fact sheet.* Washington, DC: U.S. Department of Health and Human Services. Available:www2.acf.dhhs.gov/programs/hsb/research/02_hsfs.htm

Bachu, A., & O'Connell, M. (2000, September). *Fertility of American women.* (Current Population Reports, P20-526. U.S. Department of Commerce, Census Bureau.) Washington, DC: U.S. Government Printing Office.

Beadle, M. (2006). *Children in low-income families. Summary of the Urban Institute and Child Trends Roundtable on children in low-income families.* The Urban Institute. Available: www.urban.org/url.cfm?ID=311354.

Berreuta-Clement, J. R., Schweinhart, L. J., Barnett, W. S., Epstein, A. S., & Weikart, D. P. (1984). *Changed lives: The effects of the Perry Preschool Program on youths through age 19.* Ypsilanti, MI: High/Scope Press.

Besharov, D. J., (2006, August 15). End welfare lite as we know it. *New York Times,* p. A23.

Besharov, D. J., & Higney, C. A. (2006). *Federal and state child care expenditures (1997–2003).* Washington, DC: Administration on Children, Youth and Families, U.S. Department of Health and Human Services.

Boo, K. (1997, October 19). Painful choices: Denise Jordan is off welfare and loves her job, but what about her daughter? *Washington Post,* p. A1.

Burke, V. (2004). *Welfare reform: An issue overview.* CRS issue brief for Congress. Washington, DC: Congressional Research Service.

Capps, R., & Fortuny, K. (2006) *Immigration and child and family police.* The Urban Institute. Available: www.urban.org/url.cfm?ID=311362.

Cassidy, J. (2006, April 3). Annals of economics, relatively deprived. How poor is poor? *The New Yorker,* pp. 42–47.

Cherlin, A. J. (1998, April 5). By the numbers. *New York Times Magazine,* pp. 39–41.

Children's Defense Fund. (2005). *The state of America's children: 2005.* Washington, DC: Children's Defense Fund.

Children's Foundation. (2002). *Family child care licensing study.* Washington, DC: Author.

Children's Foundation. (2002). *Family child care licensing study.* Washington, DC: Author.

Clinton, B. (2006, August 22). How we ended welfare, together. *New York Times,* p. A19.

Edie, D. (2006). *Toward a new child care policy.* Washington, DC: The Urban Institute.

Facts on farmworkers in the United States. (2001). Cornell University, Media and Technology Services. Available: www.farmworkers.cornell.edu/pdf/facts_on_farmworkers.pdf.

Farmer, J. (1969). *Senate hearings on Head Start Child Development Act* (Pt. 1, 91st Cong., 1st Sess.).

Federal Interagency Forum on Child and Family Statistics. (2005). *America's children: Key national indicators of well-being 2005.* Federal Interagency Forum on Child and Family Statistics. Washington, DC: U.S. Government Printing Office.

Federal Register. (2007, Jan. 24). The 2007 HHS poverty guidelines. *Federal Register, 24* (15), 3147–3148.

Food Research and Action Center. (no date). *Food Stamp Program.* Available: www.frac.org.

Food Research and Action Center. (2005). *WIC in the states: Thirty-one years of building a healthier America.* Washington, DC: Author.

Galinsky, E., Howes, C., Kontos, S., & Shinn, M. (1994). *The study of children in family child care and relative care: Highlights of findings.* New York: Families and Work Institute.

Gazan, H. S. (1998, April 3). *Regulation: An imperative for ensuring quality child care.* Paper presented at the Yale University Bush Center in Child Development and Social Policy. New York: Foundation for Child Development.

Golden, O. (2005). *Assessing the new federalism, eight years later.* Washington, DC: The Urban Institute.

Government work supports and low-income families: Facts and figures. (2006). Washington, DC: The Urban Institute.

Greenstein, R. (2005). *The earned income tax credit: Boosting employment, aiding the working poor.* Washington, DC: Center on Budget and Policy Priorities.

Haskins, R., Greenberg, M., Fremstad, S. (2004). *Federal policy for immigrant children: Room for common ground?* Future of Children Policy Brief. Washington, DC: The Brookings Institution.

Heymann, J. (2000). *The widening gap: Why America's working families are in jeopardy and what can be done about it?* New York: Basic Books.

Holt, S. (2006) *The earned income tax credit at age 30: What we know. Research Brief.* Washington, DC: The Brookings Institution.

Kamerman, S. B. (Ed.). (2001). *Early childhood education and care: International perspectives.* New York: Institute for Child and Family Policy at Columbia University.

Katz, M. B. (1986). *In the shadow of the poorhouse: A social history of welfare in America.* New York: Basic Books.

Kenney, G. (2006) *Five Questions for Genevieve Kenney.* Washington, DC: The Urban Institute. Available: www.urban.org/toolkit/fivequestions/GKenney.cfm.

Lewin, T. (2002, July 21). A child study is a peek. It's not the whole picture. *New York Times,* p. WK4.

Loprest, P., & Zedlewski, S. (2006). *Welfare reform must fix safety net.* Washington, DC: The Urban Institute. Available: www.urban.org/url.cfm?ID=000991.

Low income working families. (2006). Washington, DC: The Urban Institute. Available: www.urban.org/toolkit/issues/workingfamilies.cfm.

Mathews, J. (1990, May 18). Working off welfare: Study sees state treasuries as major beneficiaries. *Washington Post,* p. A4.

McKernan, S., & Ratcliffe, C. (2006). *Five questions for Signe-Mary McKernan and Caroline Ratcliffe.* Washington, DC: The Urban Institute. Available: www.urban.org/toolkit/fivequestions/Mckerman_Ratcliffe.cfm.

National Head Start Association. (no date). *Benefits of Head Start (HS) and Early Head Start (EHS) programs.* Alexandria, VA: Author.

National Institute of Child Health and Human Development. (2006). *The NICHD study of early child care and youth development: Findings for children up to age 4½; years.* NIH-Publication no: 05-4318. Washington, DC: Author.

Newman, S., Fox, J. A., Flynn, E. A., & Christeson, W. (2000). *America's after-school choice: The prime time for juvenile crime, or youth enrichment and achievement.* Fight Crime: Invest in Kids. Available: www.fightcrime.org.

Office of Child Support Enforcement. (2006). *Child support enforcement, FY 2005: Preliminary report.* Washington, DC: U.S. Department of Health and Human Services, Administration for Children and Families. Available: www.acf.hhs.gov/programs/cse/pubs/2006/reports.

Passel, J. (2006). *The size and characteristics of the unauthorized migrant population in the U.S.: Estimates based on the March 2005 Current Population Survey.* Research Report. Washington, DC: Pew Hispanic Center.

Pavetti, L., Olson, K., Nightingale, D., Duke, A., & Isaacs, J. (1997). *Welfare to work options for families facing personal and family challenges.* Washington, DC: The Urban Institute.

Pear, R., & Eckholm E. (2006, August 21). A decade after welfare overhaul, a fundamental shift in policy and perception. *New York Times,* p. A12.

Pedgeon, M. (1953). *Employed mothers and child care.* Bulletin 246. Washington, DC: Women's Bureau.

Phillips, D., & Adams, G. (2001, Spring–Summer). Caring for infants and toddlers. *The Future of Children,* 35–51.

Proceedings of the conference on the care of dependent children. (1909, January 25–26). 60th Cong., 2nd. Sess., S. Doc. No. 721. Washington, DC: U.S. Government Printing Office.

Real welfare reform at last. (1988, October 1). *New York Times,* p. 14.

Reardon-Andeson, J., Capps, R., & Fix, M. (2002). *The health and well-being of children in immigrant families.* The Urban Institute. Available: http://www.urban.org/publications/310584.html.

Rowe, G., & Giannarelli, L. (2006, July). *Getting on, staying on, and getting off welfare: The complexity of state-by-state policy choices.* Washington, DC: The Urban Institute.

Samuelson, R. J. (2006, August 22). Welfare to work: Unexpected benefits can include self-respect. *Plan Dealer,* p. B9.

Schweinhart, L. J., Barnes, H. V., & Weikart, D. P. (1993). *Significant benefits: The High/Scope Perry Preschool Study through age 27.* (Monographs of the High/Scope Educational Research Foundation, No. 10.) Ypsilanti, MI: High/Scope Press.

Seefeldt, K. (2004). *After PRWORA: Barriers to employment, work and well-being among current and former welfare recipients.* Ann Arbor,

MI: National Poverty Center, University of Michigan.

Shalala, D. (1993). Welfare reform: A priority for the Clinton administration. *Children Today, 27,* 4–6.

Stevens, W. K. (1988, June 22). Economics, politics and sociology converge to bring a historic change within reach. *New York Times,* p. 1.

Stolberg, S. G. (2001, April 22). Science, studies and motherhood. *New York Times,* p. WK3.

Suchetka, D. (2006, May 5). The battle over benefits for illegal immigrants. *Plain Dealer.* p. A1, A11.

Turetsky, V. (2005). *The child support enforcement program: A sound investment in improving children's chances in life.* Washington, DC: Center for Law and Social Policy.

U.S. Census Bureau. (2005, October). *Who's minding the kids? Child care arrangements: Winter, 2002.* Washington, DC: U.S. Department of Commerce, U.S. Census Bureau.

U.S. Department of Agriculture. (2005). *Characteristics of food stamp households: Fiscal year 2004, Summary.* Washington, DC: Food and Nutrition Service, Office of Analysis, Nutrition, and Evaluation. Available: www.fns.usda.gov/oane.

U.S. Department of Health and Human Services. (2002). *Making a difference in the lives of infants and toddlers and their families: The impacts of Early Head Start, Executive Summary.* Washington, DC: Author.

U.S. Department of Health and Human Services. (2005). *Executive summary, Head Start impact study first year findings.* Washington, DC: Author.

U.S. Department of Labor. (2006). *Findings from the National Agricultural Workers Survey, 2001–2002.* Available: http://www.doleta. gov/agworker/report9/summary.cfm.

U.S. Office of Education and the Office of Economic Opportunity. (1966). *Education: An answer to poverty.* Washington, DC: U.S. Government Printing Office.

U.S. Social Security Administration. (2006). *Children receiving SSI, 2005.* Washington,

DC: Social Security Administration, Office of Policy, Office of Research, Evaluation, and Statistics.Available: www.socialsecurity.gov/ policy/docs/statcomps/ssi_children/2005/ssi_ children05.pdf.

U.S. Social Security Administration. (August, 2006). Monthly Statistical Snapshot: Office of Policy: U.S. Social Security Administration. Available: www.ssa.gov/policy/docs/ quickfacts/stat_snapshot/index.html.

Vandivere, S., Tout, K., Zaslow, M., Calkins, J., & Capizzano, J. (2003). *Unsupervised time: Family and child factors associated with self-care.* Washington, DC: The Urban Institute.

Vobejda, B., & Davis, P. (1997, November). Keeping an eye on the hand that rocks the cradle. *Washington Post National Weekly Edition,* p. 30.

Waldfogel, J., Brooks-Gunn, J., & Han, W. (2002, March–April). Early maternal employment's effects on children. *Poverty Research News, 6*(2), The newsletter of the Northwestern University/University of Chicago Joint Center for Poverty Research.

Waller, M., & Fremstad, S. (2006). *New goals and outcomes for temporary assistance: State choices in the decade after enactment.* Washington, DC: The Brookings Institution.

Weil, A. (2002, May). Ten things everyone should know about welfare reform. *New Federalism.* Series A, no. A52. Washington, DC: The Urban Institute.

Wobbly first steps (2003, April 12). *The Economist,* p. 34.

Zigler, E., & Styfco, S. J. (1994). *Head Start and beyond: A national plan for extended childhood intervention.* New Haven: Yale University Press.

Zill, N., Resnick, G., McKey, R., Clark, C., & Connell, D. (1998). *Head Start program performance measures, Second progress report.* Research, Demonstration and Evaluation Branch and the Head Start Bureau, Administration on Children, Youth and Families. Washington, DC: U.S. Department of Health and Human Services.

CHAPTER 3

Services to Prevent Maltreatment and Support Families

The little world of childhood with its familiar surroundings is a model of the greater world. The more intensively the family has stamped its character upon the child, the more it will tend to feel and see its earlier miniature world again in the bigger world of adult life.

—Carl Gustav Jung

Mitakuye oyasin. (We are all related.)

—Oglala Lakota Sioux

CHAPTER OUTLINE

CASE EXAMPLE:
Reaching Out to a Family at Risk for Child Maltreatment

This case shows a family support worker in Hawaii's Healthy Start program reaching out to an overburdened mother just home from the hospital with a new baby.

Jane is a poor Hawaiian woman in her early thirties who lives in a community where the disparities between rich and poor are extreme. When the Healthy Start program first came into contact with Jane, she had just given birth to twins, leaving Jane with four children under the age of 3. Because Jane had no phone, Healthy Start home visitor Evelyn went to Jane's home to meet Jane, an introduction that took three months to complete.

Each week for twelve weeks, Evelyn stood outside Jane's door hoping to speak to her. While Evelyn waited patiently, a typical scene would ensue: Jane and her partner could be heard shouting and yelling, the older children sobbing, and the twin babies screaming, looking for attention amid the confusion. When the older children stared out the window at Evelyn, the fighting seemed to escalate. Evelyn worried about what to do, but stuck with a gut feeling that if she persisted with the family she could make contact.

When Jane finally did let Evelyn in, Evelyn learned something that surprised her about her earlier visits. Jane told her that although she was afraid to let this strange woman into her commotion-filled home, she also felt soothed by her presence.

This was the start of trust-building between Evelyn and Jane, which was necessary to begin work on Jane's many needs. Jane's family had no family doctor and no concept of preventive medicine. Evelyn soon discovered that Jane had used the drug "ice" (methamphetamine) while pregnant with her first two children and that extended family members sold the drug on the streets. Two months after giving birth to the twins, Jane was pregnant with a fifth child. In another ten months, she would become pregnant again.

Over a period of months, Evelyn and Jane set some initial goals for their work together: finding an acceptable means of birth control, developing an understanding and commitment to well-care (i.e., preventive health care) for her children, finding programs to help her become drug-free, and establishing a stable home.

In three years of work and weekly visits with Jane, Evelyn feels that the family has made important headway. The older children have been enrolled in kindergarten and Head Start; the twins have started in a special program for children with developmental delays; and the newest baby has received consistent medical care since birth and shows no signs of delay. Most importantly, Jane's approach to her children's health and development has changed. No longer are emergencies the only time her children come into contact with a doctor. All six of her children receive regular health checkups from a local physician. Jane actively seeks out programs and activities for them as well. Instead of sending her children to school alone, Jane now walks them there and even volunteers at her son's Head Start program.

Jane's attitude toward Evelyn has transformed as well. Jane calls Evelyn every other day from a pay phone and talks openly about her daily problems. Although Jane's situation isn't altogether rosy—she has recently lost her housing and lives in a hut on the beach— Jane and Evelyn continue to work at the problem one step at a time. Jane thinks differently now about what she can do to help her children get off to the right start.

(Adapted from Charles Bruner and Judy Langford Carter, *Family Support and Education: A Holistic Approach to School Readiness.* Denver and Washington, DC: National Conference of State Legislatures, 1991. Reprinted with the permission of National Conference of State Legislators.)

T wenty years ago this family might have been sent home from the hospital with no follow-up services, until, as seems likely, the parents' care of the children deteriorated to the point that someone made a referral to child protective services. The children probably would have been placed in foster care. The prevention services described in this chapter are an effort to intervene early in the lives of families, before the home situation becomes untenable, so that children can safely remain with their parents.

A description of the Hawaiian Healthy Start Program is located in this chapter, in the Family Support Services section.

NEED FOR PREVENTIVE AND FAMILY SUPPORT SERVICES

For most of the twentieth century, professionals in human services recognized the importance of strengthening families to prevent child abuse and neglect. Yet, efforts to conceptualize and develop social services to preserve, strengthen, and enhance family life and the quality of the child's environment have lagged. Society's reliance on the family for essential nurturance and guidance of the nation's children has not been accompanied by necessary changes in social and economic policies and preventive social provisions. As a result, social agencies tend to be overwhelmed with demands from families and children in crisis. (See Chapter 6.)

The negative consequences of child abuse and neglect are very great for children, families, and society. It is more humane and reasonable to prevent abuse before it occurs, than to attempt to alleviate the damage afterwards. Abused and neglected children suffer at the time of maltreatment, and may continue to suffer in their inability to adequately fulfill adult roles involving work, love, and parenthood. The costs to society of abuse and neglect are also great, including criminal prosecution of abusers, treatment of children, and managing child victims in the child welfare and juvenile justice systems.

Starting with the passage of the Family Preservation and Support Services Act of 1993, the U.S. Department of Health and Human Services has given increasing visibility to efforts to strengthen families and reduce maltreatment through such initiatives as the Child Abuse Prevention Initiative, the Healthy Marriage and Responsible Fatherhood Initiative, and various programs to prevent teen pregnancy. However, only a very small proportion of federal and state governments' expenditures on child maltreatment is directed toward prevention, and funding is highly vulnerable during periods of economic downturn.

Efforts to mobilize a national consensus on the need for preventive services have benefited from the success of preventive campaigns in other areas of life. Reductions in the number of deaths from traffic accidents involving alcohol, in the incidence of AIDS in the United States, in the number of pregnancies to teenagers, and in smoking among all sectors of the population have been attributed, in part, to the success of national campaigns to change consciousness on the acceptability of risky behaviors. These trends give hope for similar results from efforts to prevent child abuse and neglect (Thomas et al., 2003).

THE MANY FACES OF FAMILY LIFE

The "traditional" family form—two married parents caring for children born within their marriage, with the father as the essential wage earner and the mother the chief child caregiver in the home—was for many years considered the norm. Today, however, relatively few children live in a traditional family. Variety and diversity characterize current family forms; children may live with two parents, one parent, a parent and a stepparent or the parent's partner, or with grandparents and other relatives, with or without their own parents present. Some family forms carry additional demands or have needs and problems that become intensified, making access to supportive and preventive social services even more essential.

Single-Parent Families

One of the most remarkable demographic trends is the large increase in the number of American children living with one parent, usually the mother. Families headed by women do not constitute a new phenomenon, having been present throughout history. Nevertheless, the acceleration in the number of such families and awareness of the problems that many of them face have attracted national concern. The needs of single-parent families are not markedly different from those of all other families. At the same time, because of the responsibility of single parents to carry out the duties of child care and family decision making without a marital partner, and because of the high probability that family income will be limited, normal needs and problems may become harder to deal with (Schmitz, 1995; Jung, 1996; Jones, Forehand, Brody, & Armistead, 2002).

Children in divorced families may face a number of special challenges. A study by McLanahan and Sandefur (1994) found that, other things being equal, teenagers who spent part of their childhood apart from their biological father were twice as likely to drop out of high school, twice as likely to become parents themselves before age 20, and one and a half times as likely to be idle in their late teens and early twenties. One explanation for the difficulties of children of divorce has already been mentioned—the great drop in income often following divorce, which may require that a family move to a less desirable location and leave behind school friends and helpful neighbors. Children may find that parents have less time for them after divorce. Although many fathers do remain involved with their children, the reality for many families is a "disappearing father," one who absents himself from his children emotionally and financially (Furstenberg & Harris,

1990, p. 4). The remaining parent, usually the mother, although physically present, may have difficulty shouldering all the responsibilities of single parenthood. Children of divorced parents often have experienced parental conflict, and numerous studies have shown that conflict between parents affects children negatively. They may blame themselves for the deterioration in their parents' relationship (Amato, 1993). No single explanation is sufficient to explain the various adjustments children may make following divorce, and it seems likely that a combination of factors is at play, including both increased stress and loss of former supports and resources (Wallerstein & Blakeslee, 1996; Emery, 1999; Hetherington, 1999; Thompson & Amato, 1999; Wallerstein, 2005.)

A few children face the extreme risk of abduction, if they have become pawns in bitter quarrels between divorcing parents. The number of abductions is increasing, due to the higher rate of divorce and the greater ease of cross-country travel. The practice is pervasive and found among all social classes and racial groups. The need is very great for more professional services to parents considering divorce to help them understand the consequences and reach a custody decision that each can accept, one that is the best alternative for the child. In recent years, social workers in some family and child social agencies and in court services have been providing such help.

Families with Lesbian or Gay Parents

Although it has always existed, homosexuality has until recently been an unacknowledged phenomenon in our society. With increasing openness about sexual orientation, lesbian and gay families are slowly becoming more visible in the community. Caseworkers in child welfare are being called on more frequently than in the past for advice and guidance in relation to families headed by lesbian or gay parents, particularly in matters of child custody and in planning services for these families.

In a more socially tolerant climate that was brought about by changes in sex mores and in the rights of women, homosexuals' need for secrecy about themselves has been reduced, particularly in urban areas. Homosexual parents now find more support for their sexual identification. However, this support is often elusive. For example, some states now have laws stating that homosexuality cannot be used as a basis for custody decisions, but in other states parents who openly identify themselves as lesbian or gay are presumed to be unfit as parents (Patterson, 1992). (See Chapter 10.) Underlying these attitudes is a series of largely untested stereotyped beliefs: (1) The child reared in a homosexual home will lack traditional role models and will be more likely than others to become gay or lesbian; (2) the child will be harmed by the stigma that attaches to the parent and inevitably extends to the child; (3) the child is at risk of sexual abuse by the parent or the parent's friends; and (4) homosexuality will compete with and undermine the provision of parental care, thus impairing the child's overall growth and development (Patterson, 1992). Behind these fears is a view of homosexuality as indicative of an inherent pathology that would dominate all other aspects of family interaction.

Research over the past twenty years has failed to support any of these assumptions and has shown no differences overall between the adjustment and well-being of children in lesbian or gay families versus those in other types of families (Patterson; 1992; Wainright, Russell, & Patterson, 2004; Wainright & Patterson, 2006). The difficulties that lesbian and gay families face are not caused by homosexuality per se but rather by the stigma associated with homosexuality in U.S. society. The widespread view is, "it is good to be a mother, but it is bad to be a lesbian" (Levy, 1992, p. 23). One area of concern is the issue of disclosure of the parent's sexual orientation to the children. It is generally agreed that it is preferable to tell children at a young age of their parent's homosexuality. It is better for the child to hear the disclosure from a parent, who can explain the situation to the child in a caring and loving way, than for the child to hear of it first from relatives, neighbors, or schoolmates, who may have prejudicial interpretations (Gartrell et al., 2000; Morgan, 2000).

Although it is neither desirable nor practically feasible for the parent not to tell the child but remain in hiding to the world at large, there are potential negative consequences to leading an openly lesbian or gay existence, including discrimination in jobs, housing, and child custody decisions (Lott-Whitehead & Tully, 1993).

Social workers can play a significant role in helping lesbian and gay parents decide to come out, as they weigh the value of living without secrecy with concerns about losing child custody and discrimination. Social workers can also help these parents devise strategies for disclosing their sexual orientation to their children and their families of origin. Support groups for parents and children may be helpful in building self-esteem and creating mutual aid networks. Advocacy for all family members may be necessary with schools, the legal system, and other traditional service systems (O'Dell, 2000).

Early Childbearing and the Family

Historically, teenage pregnancy was a problem left to parents, schools, faith communities, and social service agencies. But starting in the 1970s, the old concern about unwed mothers expanded into an explosive controversy about teenage sexuality and teenage parenting. The issues involved—adolescent sexual intercourse, contraception, abortion, sexually transmitted diseases and HIV/AIDS, substance abuse, adoption, race, family structure, child support, and welfare dependency—evoke impassioned conflicts of value and ideology.

The enormous increase in systematic study of the subject since the 1970s is an outgrowth of a highly publicized belief that the nation is confronted with a dangerous "epidemic" of teenage pregnancies. It is curious that during most of the past forty years, while interest in the problem increased dramatically, births to teenagers were actually declining. A major cause for the increased public attention has been the *great increase in the percentage of teenage births to parents who are not married.*

There have been both positive and negative outcomes from this concern about a teenage pregnancy epidemic. Positively, it has increased public awareness and acceptance of the need for contraceptive services and education about sexuality for adolescents, and has stimulated federal funds for such services and for research. Negatively, however, the "crisis" approach has been sexist in its focus on the problem-laden, sexually active female; it has directed attention away from the more fundamental social and economic problems that warp the lives of so many teenagers, especially if they are black or come from low-income backgrounds.

In 2004, there were forty-one births per thousand teen girls aged 15 to 19. After a steady decline from 1950 to the mid-1980s, the teen birth rate rose by 24 percent from 1986 to 1991. From 1991 to 2001, it fell steadily with an overall decline of 26 percent, thus reversing the earlier increase. The largest decline since 1991 was for African American teenagers, which has fallen by 36 percent. Hispanic teen birth rates declined 14 percent between 1994 and 2001. However, the teen birth rates for African American and Hispanic young women are still higher than for other racial groups; Hispanic teens now have the highest birth rate (Teen Pregnancy, 2002). Explanations for this reduction include better access to sex education and other teenage pregnancy programs, abstinence, increased contraceptive use, fear of HIV/AIDS and other sexually transmitted diseases, and abortion. It should be noted that the abortion rate among teenagers has also declined, suggesting that abstinence and contraception are increasingly important factors.

Although the recent decline is encouraging, there are reasons to be concerned about the teen birth rate: (1) The United States has the highest rates of teen pregnancy and birth in the Western industrialized world. (2) More than four out of ten young women become pregnant at least once before they reach the age of 20—nearly one million a year. Most of these pregnancies are unintended and most are to unmarried teens. (3) The younger a teenager becomes sexually active, the more likely she is to have had unwanted or involuntary sex (Moore & Driscoll, 1997; Teen Pregnancy, 2002).

In considering the consequences of teenage parenting, it must be kept in mind that underlying factors that were present in the lives of these new parents prior to pregnancy, notably poverty, living in a single-parent family, and minority ethnicity, may also be present afterward. Nevertheless, many years of research have documented that the teenager who becomes a parent is vulnerable to a range of risks to herself and to her child as well. Teen mothers are less likely to complete school and more likely to need public assistance. The children of teen mothers are more likely to have lower birth weights, to perform poorly in school, and are at greater risk of abuse and neglect. Sons of teen mothers are more likely to end up in prison, and daughters of teen mothers are more likely to become teen mothers themselves (Butler, 1992; Maynard, 1996; O'Dell, 2001).

The welfare reform law, the Personal Responsibility and Work Opportunity Reconciliation Act of 1996, contains several provisions intended to discourage out-of-wedlock births and adolescent childbearing. Minor teen parents are required to live in an adult-supervised setting and to stay in school to receive benefits. States are required to submit plans for establishing pregnancy prevention programs and for educating the public on statutory rape. Bonuses are available to states that reduce out-of-wedlock births and abortion among the general population, and states may also get grants to provide abstinence education. States are encouraged to develop special voluntary paternity procedures for teens (Barkan, 1996; Mayden & Brooks, 1996). However, the relationship of welfare policies and the behavioral choices of teenagers is not clear; studies attempting to ascertain whether the availability of welfare contributes to teenage pregnancy have obtained inconclusive results (Allen & Pittman, 1986).

CULTURALLY DIVERSE FAMILIES

The effectiveness of family support services depends in large measure on the extent to which the services have been planned and offered within the context of a family's own cultural, racial, and ethnic identity. (See Chapter 10.) Family and child services focus on family functioning and childrearing practices. Any group's cultural or ethnic identity is most clearly reflected within the family. Whether the services offered are based on an understanding of ethnically determined behaviors and cultural differences will be a potent influence on whether they are used. Ethnicity is significant in determining how different groups define normality and social competence. The way in which a family addresses a particular situation reveals the practical strategies it has developed over time to manage many aspects of daily life. However, the usefulness of these strategies may not be readily understood by a caseworker who is charged with assessing family functioning but is unfamiliar with the culture (Cross, 1996; Schiele, 1996; Korbin, 2002).

As suggested by the National Association of Social Workers Standards for Cultural Competence in Social Work Practice (National Association of Social Workers, 2001), family support programs must address cultural issues at all levels of the organization. Individuals of the same race or ethnicity as the families being served should be included among the professional, paraprofessional, and volunteer participants in a family support program. This practice is essential to an accurate interpretation of community norms and of the ways ethnicity affects a family's lifestyle and childrearing practices. Having members of the service team who share the family's culture facilitates recruitment and empathetic communication and understanding, and gives credibility to the services being offered. Program materials such as flyers, handouts, crafts, and videos should reflect the ethnic background of participants. Decisions about the kinds of services to offer, scheduling, and overall approach will be more successful if they are made using knowledge from those closely connected to the community (Choi, 2001; Hurdle, 2002).

Immigrant Families

At the beginning of the twenty-first century, this country is experiencing another great wave of immigration, paralleling the former "era of immigration" that occurred in the early years of the twentieth century. During the 1990s, there were more immigrants in the United States than ever before in its history. The increase in immigration has been very rapid. In 1970, 10 million persons in the United States were foreign born, less than 5 percent of the population. By 2000, there were 30 million who were foreign born, comprising 11 percent of the population. This phenomenon has raised many questions: Can we accommodate all who are coming? How are the immigrants and their children faring? How will it change the country? (Fix & Passel, 2001).

Who are the immigrants? In 2001, there were over 1 million immigrants in the United States. They came from every continent on the globe: 38 percent from North and Central America and the Caribbean (19 percent from Mexico); 33 percent from Asia (particularly India, China, the Philippines, and Vietnam); 16 percent from Europe (currently many from Bosnia-Herzegovina or the former Soviet Republics); 5 percent from Africa; and nearly 7 percent from South America. Immigrants fall into various immigration status categories: In 2000, 30 percent were naturalized citizens, 30 percent were legal aliens, 28 percent were undocumented aliens, and 10 percent were in other categories (U.S. Department of Justice, 2003).

Immigrant families are found in every part of the United States although they are concentrated in six states: California, New York, Florida, Texas, Illinois, and New Jersey, with very large concentrations in New York City and Los Angeles (U.S. Department of Justice, 2003).

Children are a large part of the immigration population. Children of immigrants are the fastest-growing segment of the U.S. population under age 18; one in five children in this country is the child of an immigrant, and one in four poor children is the child of an immigrant. Most of these children were born in the United States and are U.S. natives. This gives rise to another important fact about immigrant families: Most noncitizen families are mixed, with at least one noncitizen parent and a citizen child (Fix & Passel, 2001).

The Urban Institute has reported on the well-being of children in immigrant families, including both children born abroad and in the United States. The study reported that even though children of immigrants are more likely to live in two-parent families than are children of native-born Americans, they are more likely to be poor. They are more likely than children of natives to have health problems and behavioral problems but are doing about as well in school as are children of native-born parents. They and their families tend to have less access to health and mental health services (Reardon-Anderson, Capps, & Fix, 2002).

Immigrant families are in a process of cultural transition regarding their language, religion, education, and lifestyle. A number of factors affect the way that they experience this process, including the reasons for immigration, the availability of support systems, the structure of the family, and the degree of harmony between the home culture and the new one (Landau, 1982). According to Landau (1982), these factors interact with one another to create situations that may require social service intervention; for example, a family that experienced a very stressful immigration and has very few supports in this country may become very isolated and possibly dysfunctional. One common area of stress is the differential rate of assimilation of different family members. Landau emphasized, "recognition of transitional conflict is the key to helping families in cultural transition" (p. 556). Sibling rivalry, marital stress, and particularly intergenerational conflicts can be understood as stemming from different adjustments to the culture of the host country (Costigan & Dokis, 2006; Updegraff et al., 2006).

Interventions with immigrant families require a high level of cultural competence and ideally are conducted by social workers who are of the same cultural background or who are immersed in its traditions and speak the language. See the description of a multiservice center for Chinese immigrant families, in this chapter, for one example of a culturally specific social service program. However, social workers in many settings, including those in the child welfare system, are likely to come into contact with immigrant children and their families, and will need to develop skills of cultural competency to intervene effectively.

African American Families

Among American families that are African American, great diversity exists. Country of origin, level of acculturation, religion, and socioeconomic status combine to create families that differ in lifestyle and values (Black, 1996; Boyd-Franklin, 2006). However, all black families in the United States share the experience of color discrimination. Racism and oppression too often have prevented African Americans from moving into the mainstream of American life. The strengths of black families are credited with helping those of African American descent to advance in education, income, and employment, despite the almost overwhelming obstacle of discrimination. As a group, African American families value kinship ties and mutual help, work, and educational attainment (Nobles, 1988; Billingsley, 1992; Hill, 1997).

> *If we are going to serve Black children and families, we have to understand how Blacks are simultaneously like every family in this country, like some other families, and like no other family at all. The professional helping person has to be able to assess at what point they are dealing with universalities and at what point they are dealing with unique issues. (Solomon, 1985, p. 10)*

Three aspects of black family and community life that have helped African Americans survive in the United States are role flexibility of family members, the extended family support system, and the church. Black parents are able to take on a range of roles within the family, regardless of gender; fathers and mothers both expect to work outside the home and to care for children and the home, although women do seem to assume more responsibility for childrearing. This flexibility helped black families to survive the undermining of the male role as family provider, caused by discriminatory employment practices (Hines & Boyd-Franklin, 1996).

The concept of role sharing extends to children as well as grandparents and other extended family members, who may take instrumental and affective roles in the family. Freeman (1990) cited the advantages and potential difficulties for children of role sharing in the family. "Such patterns tend to broaden each child's role network and teach him or her responsibility for others in the 'group'—those within the same cultural context. In assessment, however, distinctions must be made between these normative cultural expectations within black families, and dysfunctional circumstances involving child neglect" (p. 58).

Caseworkers and other professionals especially need an understanding of the extended family ties found in black communities. Here, the definition of "family" includes extended family members and perhaps also close family friends. Extended family networks operate informal exchange systems of mutual help, sharing resources of various kinds, such as material goods, transportation, and child care. Relatives often live near each other and help raise their nieces, nephews, and grandchildren. "Informal adoption" is not unusual, in which children are raised by close family members other than their parents (Billingsley, 1992). These arrangements take place outside the formal child welfare system; usually, the family turns to the public child protection system only after the resources of the extended family have attempted to resolve the problem. The child welfare system is a "last resort" for the family, if extended family strengths are insufficient to maintain an adequate level of protection for the child (Mosley-Howard & Evans, 2000; Barnes, 2001).

African American families are complex, and power in the family may reside with relatives such as grandparents, who are key decision-makers in issues that affect their children and grandchildren (Hunter, 1997). Caseworkers may find that these significant family members do not necessarily present themselves to the agency, yet ignoring them risks jeopardizing the planned interventions with the family. These influential family members are usually best identified and included in the treatment plan if sessions with the caseworker are held in the family home.

The black church has been the predominant cultural institution of Americans of African descent. During slavery and the Jim Crow era, the church was a source of strength, consolation, and community solidarity. In today's world, the church continues to be a strong source of cohesiveness in African American communities (Billingsley, 2002.) Churches offer social support in times of family crisis and offer age-related activities for all family members. Groups for the enhancement of personal and family development, day care centers, and support groups for people with various physical and psychological difficulties are offered through the churches. Innovative programs are being developed in many churches to help adolescent boys make the transition to manhood, through sports, recreation, opportunities for exchanges with adult role models, and group sessions devoted to health, spirituality, family life, and the special problems of black men (Haight, 1998).

Hispanic/Latino Families

The diverse groups in the United States who are known as "Hispanic" or "Latino" share a common link to Latin America, the Spanish language, and certain religious and cultural values. Within this unity of background, there is great variation. The majority is of Mexican or Chicano origin, many of whom are not immigrants but original settlers in lands later conquered by the United States and now comprising the southwestern portion of the nation. Smaller percentages of Hispanic/Latino persons in the United States are immigrants from Puerto Rico, Cuba, and Central and South America.

Hispanic Americans are the fastest-growing ethnic group in the United States, and, according to the 2000 census data, are now also the largest (O'Hare, 2001). The great increase in population is due largely to immigration, particularly from Mexico and among Central Americans fleeing economic and political turmoil (Ortiz, 1995).

Hispanic/Latino groups share a history of exploitation and oppression, conquest and defeat. In Latin America, as in the United States, white European groups held power and gained control of the land while oppressing indigenous populations. Although liberation movements have been successful in some parts of Latin America, the social and economic effects of civil war and ongoing oppression have caused many people from these countries to look to the United States as a place to achieve security and economic stability (Garcia-Preto, 1996).

However, once in the United States, Latin American immigrants frequently encounter prejudice and oppression based on their language, traditions, and color. They may see themselves as placed at the bottom of the social ladder. Recent proposed and enacted legislation penalizing illegal and, in some cases, legal immigrants have increased the sense of alienation among Hispanic groups. They may perceive the dominant Anglo culture as cold, competitive, and hostile to their own culture, which they see as warmer, more family oriented, and more respectful of individual dignity (Padilla, 1997).

Poverty is a way of life for many persons of Hispanic background, although most Hispanic families have an adult who is working or looking for work. A major factor in the pervasive poverty of Hispanic families, in spite of high levels of work, is the low level of educational attainment; other factors are recent immigration and the lack of English language ability (Zambrana, Silva-Palacios, & Powell, 1992; Aponte, 1993).

Social workers involved with Hispanic families need to learn about the specific cultural attributes of those families, because much diversity exists among those who are identified as Hispanic or Latino, depending on the country of origin. However, some commonalties have been identified for Hispanic/Latino families in general. Familism is a characteristic strongly emphasized in discussions of Latino family life—the family as a central source of emotional support through close bonds not only with immediate family members but also with grandparents, aunts, uncles, cousins, and family friends (Garcia-Preto, 1996). Grandparents are influential in the lives of children, less as authority figures than as sources of love and nurturance. Extended family networks offer much needed social support to Hispanic families, especially those who are recent immigrants and have left other supports behind. Many Hispanic families prefer to live close to extended family members. Support may take the form of economic or other instrumental help, and also of socioemotional interaction (Coohey, 2001; Halgunseth, Ispa, & Rudy, 2006).

Extended family systems include not only blood relatives but also other persons close to the family such as *compadres* (godparents) and *hijos de crianza* (adopted children, whose adoption may not have been legalized), as described by Garcia-Preto (1996). *Compadrazco* (godparenthood) is a system of ritual kinship with binding, mutual obligations for economic assistance, encouragement, and even personal correction. *Hijos de crianza* refers to the practice of transferring children from one nuclear family to another within the extended system in times of crisis. Relatives assume responsibility as if the children were their own and "do not view the practice as neglectful" (p. 151).

Although the concepts of *machismo* and *marianismo,* terms describing prescribed sex roles for men and women, may reflect a general organizing framework for relations between the sexes, the reality is much more complicated than these terms suggest. The mother in Mexican American family life is critically important in intrafamily relationships, despite the common characterization of the father as the unquestioned authority in the family. Family decision making is often either a joint process of both parents or primarily the job of the mother. Vega (1990) pointed to the flexibility and adaptability of Hispanic families to meet changing social conditions, with the result that families may differ greatly on how closely they adhere to traditional gender roles.

For Hispanic women, joining the labor force is not necessarily a sign of personal autonomy or liberation from the family. If the family is poor, the mother may work out of economic necessity and quit when the family has achieved economic stability. Thus, the status of being employed may reflect positively on men, but for women, it may reflect the family's vulnerability (Vega, 1990).

Hispanic families seen by caseworkers usually want help in improving their lives. They may have special concerns for the safety of their children, as the poor neighborhoods in which they often live are plagued by violence, disease, and low educational attainment. They may be grieving for losses associated with immigration, and, if here illegally, may have extremely serious problems in accessing needed health and social services. Adolescents may feel a conflict between values and expectations at home and the allure of popular culture. Garcia-Preto recommended that social workers help Hispanic families reflect on cultural contrasts and on the positives and negatives of each culture. "The metaphor of building bridges to connect the world they come from to the world they live in now helps them to take what is needed from both. Validating the positives in their culture is essential to help Latinos rid themselves of shame, regain their dignity, make connections, and have a sense of community" (Garcia-Preto, 1996, p. 153; Bean, Perry, & Bedell, 2001).

> *We are bilingual, bicultural, and by ourselves. How do we retain our assets, how do we contribute to society at large in a synergy that makes us all more?* —Mario J. Aranda

Native American Families

After centuries of decline, the population of Native Americans in the United States is again increasing. The introduction of modern medical services in rural areas has helped lower infant mortality rates, and improved adaptations to modern living have increased somewhat the longevity of adults.

The term *Indian* can be defined in many ways, such as having a certain percentage of Indian blood as established by the Federal Register of the United States, enrollment in a recognized tribe, community recognition, and self-declaration, the method used by the Census Bureau. Each Indian nation sets its own criteria for membership. Over half of those declaring themselves to be Indian live in urban areas. There is a wide range of cultural identification; at one end of the spectrum are those who claim Indian heritage because of an Indian ancestor; at the other end are those born on reservations who speak native languages as well as English (Sutton & Broken Nose, 1996). Native Americans differ from other ethnic "minority" groups in that the federal government and some state governments have specific legal rights and responsibilities toward them, including tribal recognition and issues of tribal sovereignty (Weaver, 1998).

Traditional Indian culture was diverse, with an estimated 200 different nations at the time of first European contact in the 1600s. In spite of much variation, it is broadly true that each nation provided natural systems to safeguard children and promote their healthy development. Children were raised in an extended family environment that included three or more generations; separate households of cousins, aunts, and uncles; and nonrelatives who became incorporated into the family. Aunts, uncles, and grandparents had specific roles and responsibilities regarding the family's children and were also ready to help if the parents became overburdened, incapacitated, or died. Children could form bonds to several parental figures who offered affection, education in proper behavior, and various role models (Sutton & Broken Nose, 1996). Spiritual beliefs reinforced the value of children as a special gift from the Creator (Cross, 1986).

The conquest of America by Western immigrants drastically altered tribal life. The loss of land separated families so that the extended family system could no longer provide a nurturing environment for children. Adults lost their traditional occupations and their ability to be role models as competent providers. Women's domestic skills made it easier for them than for Indian men to find work in the economy of the dominant culture, both on and off the reservation. The massive unemployment of Indian men has resulted in an increase of single-mother families. Alcohol, introduced by early explorers to Native American cultures with no social context to control its use, has plagued Indian families. For Indian and non-Indian families alike, alcoholism is associated with higher rates of family problems, child maltreatment, and developmental disabilities. Native Americans have a shared background of being a people subject to policies that had the effect of genocide, resulting in the devastation of an entire people and their civilization (DuBray & Sanders, 1999).

Native American families historically have been at great risk of family breakup because of government programs and policies. Indian boarding schools, established in the late nineteenth century by the Bureau of Indian Affairs, were designed to "separate a child from his reservation and family, strip him of his tribal lore and mores, force the complete abandonment of his native language, and prepare him in such a way that he would never return to his people" (*Indian Education,* 1969). Consequently, Indian children were often forcibly removed from their homes, given English names, required to speak English, and in many instances not allowed to return home. A devastating effect of this program was that young people grew up with no experience of family life and no parental role models to guide their own efforts in establishing families after they were grown and had left the schools (Tafoya & Del Vecchio, 1996). Some children suffered abuse in these institutions, which offered them only negative patterns of childrearing.

Through the years, Indian children continued to be at highest risk of out-of-home placement of children in any racial or cultural group in the country, with placement rates reported to be twenty times higher than that of white children (Johnson, 1981). Many non-Indian foster and adoptive families provided loving and caring homes, but the children were inevitably deprived of the opportunities needed to incorporate their cultural heritage into their personal identity. By the 1970s, it is estimated that a quarter of all Indian children were not living with their families but were in boarding schools or in foster or adoptive homes (Johnson, 1981). This great loss of Indian children to their cultural heritage gave impetus to the passage of the Indian Child Welfare Act of 1978, federal legislation intended to restore and preserve Indian families (Bending, 1997).

Despite adversity, Indian culture and Indian families endure. Present-day Indians are survivors who have learned to adapt to an alien culture. Many urban Indian families are coping and managing successfully. A study of Indian women in rural North Dakota who were affiliated with Head Start found that their family and personal relationships were characterized by mutual respect and helpfulness. The women were optimistic and courageous, and were "certain they could make plans work" (Light & Martin, 1986).

In recent years, the interest of government and industry has focused on certain tribes that own land that is rich in energy and other natural resources. Resource development and other entrepreneurial activity such as the development of casinos on Indian lands is changing social and economic conditions of life on reservations, and may result in greater economic and political power for Native American groups in relation to the dominant society.

FRAMEWORK FOR PREVENTIVE AND FAMILY SUPPORT SERVICES

Evidence has accumulated that in many cases the abuse and neglect of children might have been prevented if prompt and supportive services had been directed to the problems in the child's own family (MacLeod & Nelson, 2000). This awareness has led to an intensified interest in developing more and better services to protect children in their own homes from abuse and neglect (Daro & Donnelly, 2002; Thomas et al., 2003). *Preventive services* and *family support services* are terms covering a wide range of programs aimed at preventing abuse and neglect and strengthening family functioning. They comprise a very loosely defined category of services that may include a variety of approaches.

In this chapter, the term *preventive services* refers to any program that has as its main goal the prevention of child maltreatment. The term *family support services* refers to a type of preventive program specifically intended to support family functioning. Family support programs are a widely used and significant component of preventive services in the area of child protection.

Educational approaches are also useful in deterring child abuse and neglect, such as programs for children to prevent teen pregnancy or child sexual abuse. Preventive and family support programs may target a community, in an effort to make the area more family friendly and to encourage civic advocacy regarding the quality and availability of city services and schools. They may also involve improving linkages between service systems, to better identify families at risk of child abuse and neglect and offer services to ameliorate the problems, before a referral to child protective services becomes necessary.

Participation in prevention and family support programs is usually voluntary. These programs are intended for either the entire community or certain groups identified as "at risk," such as teenage parents and their children. Programs for parents who have been ordered by the court to improve family functioning to retain or resume custody of their children have mandatory participation and are usually more intense and focused on specific, serious problems and behaviors of parents. (These programs are discussed in Chapters 6, 7, 8, and 9.)

Although preventive and family support services vary widely in approach, population served, level of intensity, community auspices, professional disciplines involved, and specific program components, they share a focus on preventing child maltreatment and improving overall quality of life and developmental outcomes of children. They also share certain attributes and theoretical foundations.

Attributes of Preventive Services

Martin Bloom (1996) defined *prevention* as "coordinated actions seeking to prevent predictable problems, to protect existing states of health and healthy functioning, and to promote desired potentialities in individuals and groups in their physical and sociocultural settings over time" (p. 2). Preventive services are designed to ensure conditions in families and communities that reduce overall risks of social distress and offer opportunity for normal maturation of children and effective social functioning of all family members. The primary aim is to prevent situations from becoming unfavorable or hazardous to the well-being of children.

Preventive services are *oriented to the future.* In child protection, their purpose is to prevent abuse and neglect rather than to combat or cope with the effects of maltreatment after it has occurred, as is true of protective or therapeutic services. Because they are services offered in advance of harm to the child, they contain an essential component of teaching and learning in relation to recognized and accepted norms of family life. They utilize educational techniques not only in delivering services to families but also in teaching the community about the possible injurious influences in family life that can be prevented.

Preventive services are *grounded in the ecological perspective.* Bloom (1996) defined this perspective as the understanding "that each element in a given situation is ultimately related to every other element, often in an interactive way . . . [O]ne chooses what to do based on an analysis of all potentially relevant and interactive ingredients, the entire array of components in the ecology of the problem" (p. 5). The causes and correlates of child abuse and neglect are best understood with an ecological perspective, identifying parental, child, and community factors that, in combination, may lead to child maltreatment. (See Chapter 6.) Correspondingly, services to prevent maltreatment must also address some or all of the range of possible factors involved in abuse and neglect, including parental characteristics, child characteristics, support systems, community resources and supports or their absence, and the sociocultural values and conditions that surround the family.

Preventive services often use a helping philosophy emphasizing *empowerment.* This refers to a process of personal development in which individuals become increasingly aware of their strengths and abilities, build competency and self-esteem, and take steps to make positive changes in their family relationships and other immediate environments. Programs with an empowerment perspective are based on the fundamental idea that all persons have strengths but may need a supportive environment to realize them. These programs differ markedly from deficit models of helping, in which the deficiencies of clients are first identified and then a treatment, therapy, or educational program is supplied to address the defined area of weakness in the client's functioning (Bronfenbrenner, 1987; Cochran, 1993; Early & GlenMaye, 2000; Rose, 2000).

Prevention programs attempt not only to prevent negative outcomes, such as child abuse and neglect, but also to enhance participants' quality of life by taking a *developmental approach* to service delivery. The effort is not only to reduce the risk of child maltreatment but also to improve the overall quality of family life. Prevention and family support programs may offer or refer family members to developmentally enriched preschool programs, recreational and tutorial programs for school-age children and adolescents, and adult education and other personal development programs for adults. Through program activities, participants are offered opportunities to identify talents and possibilities within themselves and to find ways to use them that improve the quality of their lives.

Levels of Preventive Service

The field of public health, concerned with the prevention of epidemics and contagious diseases, has conceptualized three levels of prevention: primary, secondary, and tertiary. These levels have provided a framework for organizing the many disparate service initiatives to prevent child maltreatment, as described by Thomas and colleagues (2003, pp. 7–9).

❖ *Primary prevention* activities are directed at the general population and attempt to prevent abuse and neglect from occurring. They include public service announcements, universally available educational programs for parents, and nonstigmatizing, widely available, family support programs.

❖ *Secondary prevention* activities are directed at families who have "risk factors" for child abuse and neglect, such as teenage parents, parental mental health problems, or disabilities of children or adults. Approaches may include special respite programs for families caring for children with disabilities, home visiting programs for families with a new baby, family resource centers in low-income neighborhoods, and special family support and education programs for teen parents.

❖ *Tertiary prevention* activities are directed at families in which abuse or neglect has already occurred, with the goal of preventing its recurrence. Services include intensive family preservation services (see Chapter 7) and mental health services for parents and children.

Although these categories are useful for organizing conceptually all the different programs and initiatives that have a preventive focus, in reality, many programs cut across these categories and are not organized to focus on only one population group or treatment approach. Those involved in designing and providing preventive services may see their programs as part of a continuum of community services with the overall goals of preventing maltreatment and strengthening families.

Attachment Theory

Attachment theory provides a foundation for understanding the importance of relationships in attaining healthy developmental outcomes. A central tenet of attachment theory is that a strong attachment, reinforced by affectional bonds, is central to the personality development of infants and affects their ability to maintain healthy family relationships throughout life. It is also important in developing cognitive ability in children and may even determine the shape and functioning of the brain. Attachment starts with the loving relationship that infants first develop with their primary caregiver, usually the mother, and then grows over time to include other family members and a wider circle of relatives and friends. (The discussion that follows is based largely on an article by Patricia Van Horn, in the journal *The Source,* 1999.)

John Bowlby (1980), the leading figure in the development of attachment theory, has suggested that the need for infants to attach themselves to a parenting figure is deeply rooted in the biological drive for species survival. An infant ensures the protection of adults by developing a set of attachment behaviors that are linked to a reciprocal set of caregiving behaviors by an adult. The attachment system, in which the developing infant and the primary caregiver need and want to remain close to each other, is a fundamental part of our genetic heritage.

Attachment theory directs our attention to the caregiver as well as to the infant. The infant's need to attach is matched by the responsiveness of the primary adult. Together, through building a repertoire of reciprocal interactions, they create a strong psychological bond. The kinds of caregiving behaviors that the adult brings to the relationship are fundamental to the quality of the attachment that develops.

Attachment behaviors change as a child develops. A baby who is hungry or in need of attention will show signs of wanting to bring the caregiver close by crying, reaching out, or clinging. Toddlers may follow the caregiver and have a pattern of leaving the caregiver briefly to explore the world, then returning and reestablishing a sense of security. Older children have cognitive understandings of separations and rely less on the physical presence of the caregiver than on mental representations that provide needed security.

The need for attachment continues throughout life, as people develop intimate relationships. These bonds are built on the early experiences a child has with attachment to the caregiver. Ainsworth (1989, cited in Van Horn, 1999) identified the following qualities of a strong affectional bond, which apply to relationships between adults as well as between a child and an adult:

❖ It is persistent, not transitory.
❖ It involves a particular person, who is not interchangeable with another.
❖ It involves a relationship that is emotionally significant.
❖ The individual wishes to maintain contact with the person to whom he or she is attached.
❖ The individual feels sadness or distress if separated from the person to whom he or she is attached.
❖ The individual seeks comfort and security in the relationship.

Ainsworth (1978, cited in Van Horn, 1999) has identified different patterns of attachment between young children and their primary caregiver: securely attached, avoidant, and resistant. *Securely attached* babies actively seek out contact with their mothers. Babies showing *avoidant behavior,* in contrast, try to avoid the mother by such behaviors as refusing eye contact and ignoring her after she returns from a separation. They may prefer to be comforted by a stranger rather than their mother. *Resistant babies* alternate between seeking contact and pushing the mother away. They may prefer a stranger for comfort, but may also appear angry with both the stranger and the mother. Main and Solomon (1990, cited in Van Horn, 1999) have added another category: babies who show *disorganized/disoriented behavior.* These babies may act frightened of the caregiver or confused by her. Studies have linked disorganized/disoriented behavior in infants to mother's abuse of alcohol and to intimate partner violence (Lyons-Ruth, Connell, Zoll, & Stahl, 1987; Steiner et al., 1994; both cited in Van Horn, 1999).

These different styles of attachment may reflect different ideas the child has developed about himself or herself and about the trustworthiness and comfort available in the world. Developmental theorists call these ideas "internal working models" (George, 1996). For example, a securely attached baby may see himself or herself as worthy of being loved and also have a sense of self-efficacy, that he or she can make things happen in the world. Conversely, an avoidant child, who has received inconsistent or insensitive caregiving, may see himself or herself as unworthy and the world as unpredictable. The baby may believe that he or she is powerless to make the world respond to his or her needs.

Securely attached children as they grow older demonstrate self-confidence, competence, and a growing independence from caregivers. Children with attachment disorders may be more aggressive (particularly boys) or more dependent and passive (particularly girls). Serious attachment disorders involve emotional withdrawal from relationships or indiscriminate behavior in which superficial attachments may be sought with a number of different adults.

It is important to remember that the building of affectional bonds is an interactive process between two people. The mother does not have total responsibility for the quality of the attachment between her and her infant. Infants have varying temperaments; those with temperaments categorized as "slow to warm up" or "difficult" may present challenges to the adult caregiver trying to create a strong affectional bond (Greenberg, 1999). An ecological perspective directs attention not only to the mother's caregiving behaviors but also to the child's temperament and, in addition, to the quality of the environment in which the attachment process is taking place. Supportive family members, sufficient material resources, and lack of stress are very important environmental qualities in promoting secure attachments.

Attachment theory has obvious and significant implications for child welfare and family services. It directs our attention to prevention and early intervention strategies, because attachment begins in infancy and has long-lasting developmental repercussions. The home visiting and family support programs described in this chapter have, as part of their theoretical base, a focus on assessing attachment between mothers and their infants and young children, and offering environmental supports to strengthen it. Day care policy and programs also must take account of the importance of strong affectional bonds between children and a primary caregiver.

Family preservation services, as will be seen in Chapter 7, are premised on the understanding that children need secure and permanent attachments, with the implication that services should be directed at maintaining the family where possible, if the child is safe with the family. Family continuity, as a child welfare goal, suggests that placement decisions be made to protect as much as possible the attachments children have to siblings, extended family, or substitute caregivers, and discourages placement choices that will disrupt relationships already formed (Haight, Kagle, & Black, 2003). As described in Chapters 8, 9 and 10, the very disturbed behavior of some older children in foster and adoptive homes is related to their earlier experiences of attachment.

Difficulties in attachment may be amenable to therapeutic interventions. Many of the treatment interventions described in Chapters 4 and 9 to help parents and children cope are directed at resolving, strengthening, and protecting their attachments to one another, and to helping the avoidant child begin to trust the world and risk trying once again to develop attachments with adults (McLaren, 2003).

Social Learning Theory

Social learning theory attempts to explain how people think and learn, and what factors determine their behavior. According to this theory, a fundamental learning mechanism is operant conditioning, through which we learn the consequences that follow behavior. We tend to repeat behavior that results in positive consequences and stop behavior that tends to produce negative results. Other people can affect our behavior through positive or negative reinforcement. Another mechanism for learning is through imitation and modeling the behavior of others. Children seem to have strong imitative skills and learn to behave like those around them.

Albert Bandura (1976), the main architect of social learning theory, emphasized that learning does not occur in a vacuum; rather, it is the result of complex interactions among the individual's attitudes, skills, expectations, and knowledge, and the environment that may encourage or discourage different types of behavior. Social learning theory emphasizes that learning is an active process; as we learn new information, we actively engage in evaluating it, organizing it in terms of other information we have, and applying it to different situations. It addresses not only the acquisition of intellectual knowledge and physical skills but also the development of ideas about our own competence and self-worth, about what we can expect from others, and about how much we can influence our environment.

Many problems of children and adults are the consequences, according to this theory, of failure to learn or distortions in learning. Interventions may use respondent conditioning to change behavior, offering positive or negative consequences for different behavioral choices. They may also use imitation or modeling, by offering the learner opportunities to learn by example. Through a complex process, individuals may learn to incorporate many intangible qualities of another person, including their approach to life, values, and goals, into their own behavioral repertoires and their understanding of themselves and the world.

The following list identifies key elements of social learning theory that are relevant to the design of prevention and family support programs, and examples of how each element might be applied. (This material is partly based on information from the Resource Center for Adolescent Pregnancy Prevention, no date.)

❖ People have expectations about the consequences of their behavior. Application: Provide information on the likely consequences of different courses of action.

❖ People learn by observing others. Application: Identify positive role models; discuss the experiences others have had.

❖ People can change their behavior by learning new skills and gaining knowledge. Application: Provide opportunities to gain new skills.

❖ People can become more self-confident through persuasion, encouragement, and succeeding at making changes one small step at a time. Application: Point out strengths; help people set limited, sequential goals.

❖ The environment influences people's behavior, and in turn, people influence the environment in which they live. Application: Help people develop strategies for changing their environments; advocate for clients.

❖ People are likely to increase behavior that gets rewarded and decrease behavior that is punished or discouraged. Application: Provide incentives, rewards, praise, and encouragement; decrease negative responses.

Social learning theory is widely used in social work practice, and interventions based on social learning theory have demonstrated their success through numerous evaluations (Thyer, 1994; Bugental et al., 2002). Its fundamental tenets link easily with such prevention concepts as empowerment, early intervention, and orientation to the future. "By viewing client problems as arising from past and/or present environmental learning experiences and as a function of various physical, social, and psychological resources, an inherently nonpathological, respectful, and optimistic perspective arises from which to promote positive changes" (Thyer, 1994, p. 146). Social learning theory is also congruent with cultural competence, because it emphasizes individual assessments and does not make global assumptions (stereotypes) about people based on race or skin color (Thyer, 1994).

Parenting education classes use this theory extensively to help parents change their own behavior and also to change the behavior of their children and the way that family members interact with one another. The preventive programs for children and adolescents described in this chapter are based wholly or mainly on tenets of this theory.

Social learning theory is also used extensively in programs to help families and children recover from the effects of abuse and neglect. Intensive family preservation services (Chapter 7) and many of the child interventions used in treatment foster care, group home care, and residential treatment programs (Chapter 9) rely heavily on social learning theory and other closely related theories (cognitive-behavioral, behavior modification) in structuring their programs.

Risk and Protective Factors in Child Abuse and Neglect

Many factors are associated with the abuse and neglect of children. Similarly, factors have been identified that appear to help to protect children from abuse and neglect (Heyman & Slep, 2001). Programs designed to prevent child maltreatment benefit from the research that has identified these factors because they can give the program design focus and clarity. Programs may be designed to reduce the risk factors faced by a particular family or to strengthen the protective factors, or both. Box 3.1 lists some of the risk and protective factors for abuse and neglect, as identified by the Children's Bureau (2006). Note that these factors are not necessarily "causes" of maltreatment, but rather, are associated conditions that frequently coexist with abuse and neglect. Note further that many children may have several risk factors in their lives and still not be abused or neglected. The risk factors are conditions associated with increased risk but do not determine that it will occur. Risk and protective factors are best viewed within an ecological framework, which identifies areas for intervention at various system levels, including the larger social and community context, the family, and the child. The relationship of the risk factors listed below to abuse and neglect is described in more detail in Chapter 6.

Box 3.1

Risk and Protective Factors for Child Abuse and Neglect

Common Risk Factors	**Common Protective Factors**
Social/Environmental	*Social/Environmental*
Low SES	Mid to high SES (socioeconomic status)
Stressful life events	Access to health care and social services
Lack of access to medical care, child care, social services	Consistent parental employment
Parental unemployment; homelessness	Adequate housing
Social isolation/lack of social support	Family religious faith participation
Exposure to racism/discrimination	Good schools
Poor schools	Supportive adults outside of family who serve as role models/mentors to child
Exposure to environmental toxins	
Dangerous/violent neighborhood	
Community violence	
Parental/Family	*Parental/Family*
Personality Factors	Secure attachment; positive parent–child relationship
External locus of control	Supportive family environment
Poor impulse control	Household rules/structure; parental monitoring of child
Depression/anxiety	Extended family support and involvement
Low tolerance for frustration	Stable relationship with parents
Feelings of insecurity	Parents have a model of competence and good coping skills
Lack of trust	
Insecure attachment with own parents	
Childhood history of abuse	
High parental conflict/domestic violence	

(*continued*)

Box 3.1 (continued)

Family structure—single parent with lack of support, high # of children in household Social isolation, lack of support Parental psychopathology Substance abuse Separation/divorce, esp. high conflict divorce Age High general stress level Poor parent–child interaction, negative attitudes and attributions about child's behavior Inaccurate knowledge and expectations about child development	Family expectations of prosocial behavior High parental education
Child Premature birth, birth anomalies, low birth weight, exposure to toxins in utero Temperament: difficult or slow to warm up Physical/cognitive/emotional disability, chronic or serious illness Childhood trauma Antisocial peer group Age Child aggression, behavior problems, attention deficits	*Child* Good health, history of adequate development Above-average intelligence Hobbies and interests Good peer relationships Personality factors 　Easy temperament 　Positive disposition 　Active coping style 　Positive self-esteem 　Good social skills 　Internal locus of control 　Balance between help seeking and autonomy

Based on: Children's Bureau. (no date). Common risk and protective factors. Washington, DC: Child Welfare Information Gateway: Available: www.childwelfare.gov/preventing/overview/commonfactors.cfm.

An Ecological Model: Prevention of Maltreatment of Children with Disabilities

The ecological perspective provides a useful framework for linking information about the causes and correlates of child maltreatment with strategies for prevention. The following example uses an ecological framework for organizing information about one group of at-risk children, those with developmental disabilities.

Many of the factors in maltreatment are the same for all children, with or without disabilities, so the example also provides a general overview of an ecological approach to prevention. The example in Figure 3.1 shows that effective prevention of child maltreatment requires interventions at many levels of a child's environment and that factors interact and work in combination to increase risk. Attachment theory and social learning theory help explain how various factors in the child's environment work to increase risk, which leads logically to various prevention strategies. Some of the material for this ecological analysis comes from the National Clearinghouse for Child Abuse and Neglect (2001).

Figure 3.1 *An Ecological Model for Preventing Maltreatment of Children with Disabilities*

Society

Risk Factors: Attitudes, beliefs, and myths about children with disabilities

❖ Societal "devaluation" of children with disabilities.

❖ Segregation of children with disabilities reinforcing perceptions of difference, which, in turn, influence attitudes about the acceptability of violence.

❖ Interaction: Child may internalize negative societal attitudes about him or her and feel less worthy of being treated respectfully.

Prevention Strategies

❖ Public awareness campaigns on the extent of the problem.

❖ Coordination and cross-training of different professionals to increase awareness and identification of maltreatment.

❖ Reduce segregation of children with disabilities.

Family

Risk Factors

❖ Parental attitudes, such as viewing the child as "different," being embarrassed by the child, feeling anger at the child for not being the "normal" child they wanted.

❖ Disruptions in early bonding and attachment process.

❖ Increased stress due to special caretaking demands.

❖ Interaction: Child may seem unresponsive or unaffectionate, making bonding difficult.

❖ Interaction: Child may have needs for caretaking beyond the material or emotional capacity of the parents to meet, making child neglect or abuse more likely.

Prevention Strategies

❖ Family support services to increase parental knowledge of child, strengthen parenting skills, improve coping skills, reduce isolation, and improve access to resources.

❖ Linkage with school case management services through the Individualized Family Service Plan.

❖ Parent-to-parent group support.

Child

Risk Factors

Note: Some factors refer to people's response to the disability, not to inherent factors in the child him- or herself. Although some feel that any reference to child characteristics is "victim blaming," it is important to be aware of characteristics that make children more vulnerable, in conjunction with a constellation of other factors.

❖ Child may not know when behavior is wrong or inappropriate.

❖ Child may have physical limitations that prevent him or her from communicating or defending self.

❖ Children with emotional and behavioral disorders are most at risk for abuse and neglect, followed by children with speech/language impairments, mental retardation, and health impairments.

Prevention Strategies

❖ Prevention programs appropriate for children with different types of disabilities.

Institutional or Nonfamilial Maltreatment

Risk Factors

❖ Extreme power and control inequities, detachment from the children, isolation of children, clustering of children risking bullying by other children, an abusive subculture in the institution.

Prevention Strategies

❖ Improved agency policies and procedures: careful screening of job applicants, training in positive behavior management techniques, effective staff/client ratios, reasonable expectations of staff, strong supervision and support, explicit commitment to child protection.

❖ Families should get to know and be involved with nonfamilial caretakers. Discuss abuse awareness with the child.

Source: National Clearinghouse for Child Abuse and Neglect (2001, February), *In Focus: The risk and prevention of maltreatment of children with disabilities* (The Administration for Children and Families).

FAMILY SUPPORT SERVICES

Family support services is a term that covers a wide range of programs aimed at preventing abuse and neglect and strengthening family functioning. These programs can be helpful to all families, as they offer expert consultation on child health, child management, and family relationships, as well as social support and information on resources. However, they may be particularly useful to families with identified risk factors for child abuse and neglect: teenage parents; families affected by substance abuse or domestic violence; and families who face special challenges in family life due to single parenthood, physical or mental limitations of family members, poverty, social isolation, language barriers, or other impediments to family wellness.

Family support programs operate in many different kinds of communities and settings. Some are free-standing; others are under the auspices of hospitals, day care centers, faith communities, social service agencies, or universities. Services may take place through home visiting, at a center, or both in combination. Home visiting, if it is a part of the service, usually begins prenatally and continues through the child's infancy. Center programs tend to fit well with the needs of families with preschoolers, particularly if the program offers a preschool experience for children concurrently with the parental group sessions.

Typical program components include life skills training and parent education, developmentally appropriate experiences for children, parent–child and group activities, crisis intervention, and information and referral (Family Resource Coalition, no date). These programs attempt to create an atmosphere that parents and children find comfortable for exploring new ways of relating to each other, to professionals, and to other families.

In 1993, the federal government took a major step forward in addressing the need for family support services with the passage of the Family Preservation and Support Services Act. The Act defined family support services as

> primarily community based preventive activities designed to alleviate stress and promote parental competencies and behaviors that will increase the ability of families to successfully nurture their children; enable families to use other resources and opportunities available in the community; and create supportive networks to enhance child-rearing abilities of parents and help compensate for the increased social isolation and vulnerability of families. *(Highlights, 1994, p. 1)*

In this legislation, family *support* services and family *preservation* services are differentiated; family support services are preventive services available on a voluntary basis to a wide range of families, whereas family preservation services are remedial, intended for families who have already abused or neglected their children and need more intensive services to preserve their families and prevent foster care. Family preservation services are the subject of Chapter 7 in this text.

Home Visiting: Hawaii's Healthy Start Program

The case example at the beginning of this chapter is from Hawaii's Healthy Start Program, a service to promote child health and development in newborns of families at risk for abuse or neglect. Begun in 1985 as a demonstration project, it has inspired national and international adaptations and is currently being replicated in many sites by Healthy Families America.

Families are first identified at the hospital when the mother gives birth. They are screened for risk factors, such as a history of unstable housing, substance abuse, depression, parent's abuse as a child, late or no prenatal care, less than high school education, poverty, and unemployment. Because the program has resources for a limited number of families, only families with several risk factors are accepted. About 15 percent of reviewed families are considered as at risk; over 90 percent of those choose to participate in the program.

The trained paraprofessional home visitors are members of the community. They are close to the families served in social and cultural background and can approach the families in the helpful, nonthreatening way of a concerned neighbor or extended family member. Workers carry caseloads of twenty-five families and initially visit families weekly.

At the beginning, the workers and families often must cope with crises in housing, employment, or substance abuse. During this early period, workers also try to get the families established in using the medical system for preventive health care, encouraging them to keep regularly scheduled well-baby and immunization appointments, rather than waiting for medical emergencies.

Over time, as the family's situation stabilizes, the family begins to set goals and define its own level of participation. After a trusting relationship has been established with the worker, the focus may turn to parent–child relationships, child development, parenting skills, family planning, and relationships between adult partners. A child development specialist is available to visit the family concerning developmental issues of children. A male worker may visit the father to discuss the male role in the family. Gradually, the home visitor may decrease the visits to once a month. Group activities are also available to families and participation is encouraged. Families may remain in the program until the youngest child is 5 years old and ready to enter school.

A rigorous outcome evaluation of the project has raised questions about whether the Healthy Start Program has been successfully transformed from a focused, carefully implemented demonstration project to a statewide, ongoing service program (Duggan et al., 2004). Overall, the evaluation found no difference in likelihood of child abuse or neglect between Healthy Start families and families in a comparison group, who were not in Healthy Start but may have been receiving other family services in the community. The evaluation also found that the program model had drifted from its original focus on preventing child abuse and neglect to a more diffuse goal of "family empowerment" using strength-based approaches. The program also experienced more attrition of participants than did the early demonstration model, meaning that many families did not get a very large "dose" of service. This evaluation has raised questions about the next steps in the evolution of programs to prevent abuse and neglect (see below, Assessment of Family Support Programs).

Family Support Programs for Teen Parents

Family support programs for teen parents are needed because of the documented deficits in development that often occur in the teen parents and in their children (Butler, 1992). Early intervention is key, because the longer the teen parent takes to learn adequate parenting skills and to create a supportive environment, the greater the risk to her child. Family support programs for teen parents are similar to other types of family support programs, but according to the Family Resource Coalition (no date), they may have special emphases reflective of the parent's adolescent stage of development:

❖ emphasis on strong teen–staff relationships that are accepting yet firm and that foster high levels of trust;

❖ awareness of and sensitivity to the cultural milieu in which teens live, including understanding of kinship and extended family systems and of community norms;

❖ focus on teens' visions of the future, while working incrementally to attain skills needed for current goals and an improved sense of control;

❖ provision of long-term support, starting during pregnancy;

❖ coordination of services with health, education, and economic resources; and

❖ opportunities for peers to share and validate their experience. (p. 4)

One example of a family support program for teenagers is the New Futures School, an alternative school in the Albuquerque public school system. It provides educational, health, counseling, parenting education, and child care services to pregnant and parenting teens. The clientele include Latino, Caucasian, African American, and Native American adolescents. The goals of the program are to assist parents in completing their education, making informed decisions, having healthy pregnancies and healthy families, and being responsible parents (which may sometimes mean releasing the child for adoption). Through a comprehensive array of services, the program provides an environment that links teen parents' needs for an education and for the social experiences of adolescence with the developmental tasks they need to master to become competent parents and productive adults (Family Resource Coalition, no date).

Special Services for Pregnant and Parenting Teens

Sexual Abuse. An additional program focus concerns the relationship of sexual abuse to teen pregnancy. It is usually assumed that teen pregnancies are the result of voluntary sexual encounters between the teen mother and her teenage boyfriend. However, evidence is mounting that for some pregnant teenagers, particularly younger ones, the pregnancy may be the result of sexual abuse. The perpetrator is usually a family member or known to the family. Legal, health, and social work professionals who work with teen parents must be aware of the possibility that the pregnancy may have been the result of forced intercourse, make referrals to child protective services as appropriate, and offer services for survivors of sexual abuse as well as family support services (Mayden, 1997; Moore & Driscoll, 1997). (See Chapter 6.)

The Decision to Parent or Choose Adoption. The number of infants relinquished for adoption has sharply declined in the past 30 years. Currently, only about 5 percent of children of teenage mothers are released, in contrast to 19 percent in the early 1970s (Lewin, 1992). Changes in society's acceptance of single mothers and increased employment opportunities for women make the decision to be a single parent more feasible than in earlier times.

Research shows that teenagers who choose to relinquish their child for adoption tend to have the most to lose by teenage parenthood. They are likely to be in school, to have parents who went to college, and to have aspirations for college or other personal achievement goals. In contrast, characteristics associated with deciding to keep the baby include living in poverty and dropping out of high school (Bachrach, 1986).

The ability of the mother to weigh alternatives wisely and think through the consequences may also affect her decision to place or parent. In the past, some agencies and caseworkers have been reluctant to broach the subject of adoption with pregnant teenagers, under the principle of client self-determination or because they were unprepared to counsel teenagers on the difficult issues of grief and loss inherent in a plan of relinquishment. The Infant Adoption Awareness Training Program was passed by Congress in 2000. The purpose of the program is to develop a training program for health care professionals that is designed to increase their knowledge of adoption and their capacity to counsel adoption, along with other options with persons who have unintended or unwanted pregnancies (Children's Bureau, no date). Caseworkers can help pregnant teenagers weigh the burdens and benefits of keeping or placing the child, and imagine the future for themselves and the child given different decisions about adoption (Cervera, 1993). It is important to give teenagers "psychic space" to weigh alternatives and consider possibilities, and to keep the focus on reality issues. Some programs have had success with involving teenagers who have already made different decisions about keeping or placing, to facilitate clarification and discussion on these difficult issues. (See Chapter 10.)

Family Support Programs in Economically Deprived Communities

Family support services depend for their success on acceptance by the local community. Ironically, the low-income neighborhoods in which family support programs are most needed are also the places where they will take the longest to become established. A unique feature of this program model is that relatively large expenditures of time must be allocated to start-up tasks that build credibility. Experience has shown that it may take a year or more for a family support program to become a trusted, integrated component of the community.

Residents in poor communities often have attitudinal and other barriers to participation. They may have learned to distrust new programs because they have seen so many come and go over the years, after raising everyone's expectations for improvements that never materialized. In many low-income areas, the only parenting services known to residents are those that abusive and neglectful parents are mandated to attend, so family programs have become stigmatized as punishment for "bad" parents. Another problem is that people who have experienced multiple failures in school, work, and personal relationships may feel that they cannot be helped. Parents may believe that parenting "comes naturally" and is not a skill that can be taught (Downs, 1997). Many have had no positive experiences with social service systems and have no expectations that such encounters can be helpful.

Recruitment. For all of these reasons, recruitment of families requires careful strategizing and expenditure of program resources. Flyers, posters, and radio ads tend to attract mainly people who already know that family support services could be beneficial. For other potential participants, additional approaches are necessary, such as door-to-door canvassing, recruitment in welfare and health clinic waiting rooms, and the endorsement of community leaders, such as pastors, teachers, and housing project leadership councils. Offering small incentives, such as snacks or food coupons, to newcomers gives tangible evidence that the program cares about participants. Community baby showers have been used as recruiting devices; for these, area merchants and charitable organizations donate baby supplies. Child care and transportation are necessary components of some programs. Family support programs located in a host setting, such as a community center, health clinic, or school, often have more success than stand-alone centers because they have easier access to potential participants (Downs & Walker, 1996).

Assertive Outreach. Family support programs attempt to improve family and individual functioning but also to prevent child maltreatment. Unfortunately, families most at risk may be the least likely to participate initially. It is a mistake to believe that if families who know about the program will not come, then nothing more can be done unless the situation warrants a report to Child Protective Services. There is room to maneuver between totally voluntary participation and forced participation through the child protection system. *Assertive outreach* is the term given to focused, persistent, yet respectful recruitment efforts targeted to needy but reluctant families. In general, if the program offers families a tangible benefit and does not label them *dysfunctional,* they eventually can be recruited. As the case example at the beginning of this chapter shows, the family visitor had to make many visits to the family's home before she was finally admitted into the house. However, eventually she was able to win the family's trust (Downs & Nahan, 1990).

Advocacy and Cultural Competency. Family support programs in poor communities need to offer ongoing advocacy on behalf of the families in the program. Family support is not enough in communities that lack basic public services, have ineffective schools, and are dangerous. Advocacy must occur both in helping individual families access services and in helping groups of residents work for change in their neighborhoods. These efforts give credibility to the programs and address the reality that the risk factors for many of the residents lie outside the family.

Cultural competency needs to occur at all levels of the program. Successful family support programs are comprised mainly of staff of the same ethnic or racial group as the families served. The foods, music, holidays, celebrations, and beliefs about parenting and family life of participants' cultures are infused into all areas of the program. Languages other than English may be used.

Assessment of Family Support Programs

Family support programs have proliferated in the last two decades, outpacing the development of research and evaluation studies that could guide and shape them. Family support programs present challenges to rigorous evaluation designs. The development of instruments suitable for measuring changes in parenting has lagged. Rigid designs requiring pre- and posttests and comparison groups are difficult to implement without disrupting the voluntary, empowering qualities of the programs and are financially beyond the reach of most programs. Sometimes, funding imperatives require that evaluation take place before the programs have had enough time to become fully established.

Despite these difficulties, several recent reviews of research have pointed to modest but measurable effects of family support programs (Weiss & Halpern, 1990; Powell, 1994; MacLeod & Nelson, 2000; Harder, 2005; Daro, 2006.) Parents have been shown to increase their knowledge of child development and their skills in managing their children's behavior. Studies of comprehensive programs have shown effects on parents' general coping ability and personal development, such as returning to school or taking other steps toward economic self-sufficiency. Infants have shown improvements in developmental tests. Home visiting programs have demonstrated fewer low birthweight babies, fewer reported cases of child abuse and neglect, and higher rates of immunizations (Olds et al., 1998).

Because of the wide range of program designs, generalizing about overall program effects is difficult. There is evidence that some family support programs can have a positive impact on the quality of family life and reduce the likelihood of child maltreatment (McGuigan, Katzev, & Pratt, 2003). However, evidence is increasing that, to meet the goal of child abuse and neglect prevention, family support programs need to strengthen those aspects of their services that are known to be effective in meeting this goal. Significantly, research shows that intervention in domestic violence and substance abuse can effectively reduce child maltreatment. Yet many staff of family support programs are not trained to intervene confidently in these areas (Chaffin, 2004). At this time, family support programs should be considered "works in progress" that need to incorporate the findings of research into their program design and continue to work to increase effectiveness. They do not represent a fully developed service model that can be expected to reduce child abuse and neglect consistently or predictably. They may, however, have other important benefits to families, such as reducing isolation, increasing access to health and social services, and improving family interaction patterns.

Social Work Roles in Family Support

The role of professional social work in maltreatment prevention and family support programs is not clearly defined. Social workers are the dominant profession in the therapeutic approaches to individuals, families, and groups that are described below. However, many of these services are not available to or used by families most at risk of maltreatment, and generally speaking they have not been conceptualized primarily as programs to prevent child maltreatment. Nonetheless, they are well established in most communities and provide a strong line of defense in preventing the kinds of family dysfunction that may lead to child maltreatment.

Family support programs have a very different focus and history from traditional individual, family, and group work approaches in social work, although they share some of the same knowledge and theory base. They grew largely out of grassroots initiatives to offer help to families in underserved inner-city communities, and staff have come from a variety of disciplines, including health care, education, and early childhood development. Many of the front-line staff are paraprofessionals. As these programs become better established, social workers are increasingly involved as administrators, program planners, evaluators, group work facilitators, community organizers, consulting therapists, information and referral specialists, and direct service providers. The programs are inherently multidisciplinary, so successful social workers in these settings have good teamwork and collaboration skills; interpersonal practice skills of assessment, treatment planning, and engagement, with individuals and groups; and community organizing and advocacy skills.

Other Approaches to Strengthening Families

Besides family support programs, a range of social services is available to support family life.

Therapeutic Services. Therapeutic services stem from the identification of a serious problem, the development of an assessment, and the engagement of an individual or group in a course of social treatment whose goal is to stimulate change from maladaptive functioning to more adaptive behavior. People may seek these therapeutic services on their own initiative or be strongly encouraged to seek help; in any case, in varying ways and degrees they acknowledge a problem and choose to engage themselves in the treatment process. Typical examples are the casework treatment of a seriously emotionally disturbed boy or girl, the group work treatment of a number of children with similar handicapping behavior problems, the treatment of a parent who is mentally ill in an outpatient facility or hospital setting, and therapy based on the interaction of family members as a vital part of both the cause and the treatment of family problems. Therapeutic services are essential for the deeply troubled family or the seriously upset young person. These services are specialized and relatively well developed among the agencies that offer family and child services; however, such services are too frequently not available in communities where children and families most need them.

Casework with Individual Parents. A principal method in family and child services is working with individual parents. A commonly used approach is one that is strength-based and solution-focused. In this approach, the social worker and parent together usually arrive at an assessment early in the intervention process, emphasizing the issues the parent wishes to address and identifying strengths the parent brings to the plan for resolving them. Through helping the parent identify the problem that is causing stress in the family, understand some of its roots, and recognize the feelings and behaviors the problem produces, the social worker hopes to enable the parent (and indirectly other family members) to act more effectively. Social workers may lend strong emotional support to parents. They may offer interpretations of the parents' feelings and behaviors to help them gain insight into the behaviors that affect all family members.

Individual and Group Work with Children. Many children can best be helped by participating directly in the modification of their troubling behavior, in which case a social worker may give therapy to the individual child. Social workers blend theories and techniques in various ways to help children reach certain developmental goals, learn about themselves and the world around them, utilize opportunities, meet an unexpected crisis, or resolve a conflict that impairs their social functioning. Both social-cognitive theory and ego psychology are used as the basis for planning interventions.

Group work is an increasingly common approach used in working with children. Groups may take place at schools or social service agencies and have been used successfully with children as young as 4 or 5. Groups are commonly organized around an experience children share, such as having a substance-affected family member, living in a divorced family, suffering abuse or neglect, or having adjustment difficulties at school. Many groups for children have both an educational and a therapeutic purpose, encouraging children to learn new ways of coping and also to explore feelings in a safe environment.

Family Therapy. In its various forms, family therapy is based on the view that family life is a system of relationships between people. Family therapy may provide several advantages: attention to each member as well as the family as a whole; an opportunity for the reenactment of crucial themes within a family and a broader and more balanced diagnostic view of the strengths and weaknesses in the family; a reduction of the pressure on a single family member, particularly a child, who may have been singled out by other family members as their special problem; and an increase in the probability that improvement in a child's behavior and direction of growth will be sustained by changes and adaptations of family interaction patterns (Hartman & Laird, 1983).

PREVENTION PROGRAMS FOR CHILDREN AND ADOLESCENTS

In contrast to family support programs, which are targeted to both parents and children, some prevention efforts are focused solely or mainly on children.

Sexual Abuse Prevention Programs

Sexual abuse prevention programs have become a very common strategy to reduce the risk of sexual abuse to children, both in this country and abroad. Most of these programs are offered through the schools. Finkelhor and Dzuiba-Leatherman (1995, in Rispens, Aleman, & Goudena, 1997) estimate that about two-thirds of American school children will participate at some time in a school-based sexual abuse prevention program. The intent of these programs is to empower children to an extent that will enable them to exercise more control over what happens to them in an often unfriendly world.

A number of programs are available for educators. One common curriculum, developed and widely used in Atlanta, Georgia, is Good-Touch/Bad-Touch. This curriculum is designed for children from preschool through the sixth grade and focuses on knowledge and skills to help children protect themselves from abuse. Included is information on what abuse is, body safety rules, and strategies the child can use if threatened or harmed. The intent is not to provide sex education, but to prevent violence. Specific objectives are

❖ To give children language and information about abuse that is positive, nonthreatening, and practical;
❖ To teach children their body is their own;
❖ To teach children they can say "NO" to abuse;
❖ To help children identify people who can help if there is a problem with abuse/sexual abuse, bullying, or other situations that make them feel uncomfortable or give them an "uh-oh feeling." (Good-Touch/Bad-Touch, no date)

Sexual abuse prevention programs have been criticized for inadvertently giving children the understanding that they bear most of the responsibility for protecting themselves from adult behaviors that adults themselves do not understand sufficiently and find abhorrent. Another criticism is that teaching "good touches," "bad touches," "private zones," and skepticism of strangers is a simplistic approach. Most sexual abuse of children goes on in the child's own home and involves someone he or she has been led to trust. Critics question how much empowerment a young child can maintain in such situations (Costin, 1985; Reppucci & Haugaard, 1989).

Defenders have argued that sex offenders often gravitate toward children who seem vulnerable, and that they may be less likely to victimize a child who has participated in such a program. Such children would tend to be suspicious of adults who wanted special "alone time" with them or offered "special relationships" that needed to be kept secret from others. Children who have been exposed to a sexual abuse program, it is thought, might be less likely targets for sexual offenders in the first place, even if they were not able to thwart an attack once attempted.

During the past two decades, the evidence from evaluations has consistently shown that these programs are effective in teaching self-protection concepts and skills, even for children younger than 5 years, and that although retention decreases over time children's retention is at a satisfactory level (Rispens et al., 1997). Currently, research is addressing more complicated questions including whether children are able to transfer skills learned to a real-life situation, the extent to which the programs reduce sexual abuse, and the presence of undesirable side effects, such as increasing fearfulness in children (Davis & Gidycz, 2000; Adair, 2006). A recent retrospective study, in which college women completed survey questionnaires on their experiences with sex abuse prevention programs and with sexual abuse, found that "young women who had not participated in a school prevention program in childhood were about twice as likely to have experienced child sexual abuse as those who had participated in a program" (Gibson & Leitenberg, 2000). Future research is needed to clarify further the benefits and possible risks of these programs (Weisz & Black, in press).

Teenage Pregnancy Prevention Programs

In contrast to earlier decades, when teenage pregnancy was seen as a manifestation of maternal pathology, today, services related to teenage pregnancy usually take an ecological approach to understanding parenthood. Teenage pregnancy is seen as a complex phenomenon with multiple causes such as social and economic conditions; cultural attitudes about early parenthood, family, school, and peer influences; and developmental and psychological issues related to individual teenagers.

Public concern about the costs and consequences of teenage pregnancy has led to increased interest in developing effective programs to prevent teenagers from becoming parents. The welfare reform legislation of 1996 contains funds for grants to states to develop pregnancy prevention programs. See the earlier section, Early Childbearing and the Family.

During the past twenty-five years, extensive research on teenage pregnancy has identified promising practices that have been shown to reduce sexual activity or pregnancy among teenagers (Ooms & Herendeen, 1990; Kirby, 2001). Kirby (2001), in his review of research on promising practices, categorizes pregnancy prevention programs as falling into one of three types:

❖ those that focus on knowledge and skills about sex and sexual behavior, including abstinence programs, sex education programs, and clinics that offer access to condoms and other contraceptives
❖ those that focus on a broader range of risk factors, such as detachment from school, work, and other social institutions, lack of positive relationships with adults, and disadvantaged families and communities. These programs include service learning and other youth development programs
❖ those that address both reproductive health and youth development

Sex Education and Clinic Programs. Sex education programs often use social learning theory as the foundation of the curriculum, with a focus on gaining knowledge about the advantages of abstinence, the consequences of sexual intercourse including pregnancy, the dangers of sexually transmitted diseases and HIV/AIDS and how they are spread, and biological concepts of reproduction and contraception. The programs give students an opportunity to practice communication, negotiation and refusal skills, and other behavioral aspects of sexual health. They also incorporate discussions on social pressure, cultural attitudes about teen sexuality, and media messages about sexuality. Some programs, connected to clinics, provide access to health services including condoms and other contraceptives.

Many curricula and program models exist for sex education programs in schools, health clinics, and other settings. *Reducing the Risk: Building Skills to Prevent Pregnancy, HIV and STD* is a widely used and well-established curriculum. It contains sixteen lessons for middle school students. Based on social learning and cognitive-behavioral theories, it emphasizes knowledge and skill objectives regarding sexual choices and consequences (Kirby, Barth, Leland, & Fetro, 1991). A new curriculum, *Be Proud! Be Responsible!*, is designed for small groups of inner-city youth, in school or community settings. In addition to the approaches discussed earlier, this curriculum also addresses specific cultural issues for inner-city youth. Its curriculum includes information on how sexually transmitted diseases and HIV/AIDS have affected inner-city communities, and the importance of protecting the community as a motivation for changing behavior. Recognizing the confusion and shame that surround much adolescent sexuality, the curriculum emphasizes the theme of making proud and responsible sexual choices (Select Media, no date). Kirby (2001) found that successful programs deliver a consistent message about abstinence from sexual activity and, if abstinence is not the choice, using condoms or other contraceptives.

In reviewing the research on sex education programs, Kirby (2001) found that some well-developed curricula can have measurable, positive outcomes, such as delaying the onset of intercourse, increasing condom or other contraceptive use, and preventing teen pregnancy. Programs offering access to contraceptives have increased the use of contraceptives and thereby decreased the occasions of unprotected sex. Critics of sex education programs, and especially of school-based clinics, believe that their presence encourages youth to engage in sexual activity that they would not do if the services were unavailable. However, for both the sex education programs and those that include a clinic component offering condoms and other contraceptives, Kirby (2001) found no evidence from published research that they hasten the onset of sex or increase sexual activity among participants.

Youth Development Programs. Studies have shown linkages among dropping out of school, delinquency, substance abuse, and teen pregnancy, indicating that unprotected sexual activity is part of a cluster of high-risk behaviors. Youth development programs try to reduce risky behavior through exposure to careers, community service, remedial education, and job counseling. Service learning programs include voluntary service by teens in the community (tutoring, working in nursing homes or day care centers, fixing up parks); they usually have a component of discussion and reflection concurrently with the service activity, which may also include writing in journals. Kirby (2001) found that these programs "may have the strongest evidence of any intervention that they reduce actual teen pregnancy rates while the youth are participating in the program" (p. 14). It is not clear why they are so successful, but possibilities include

> participants develop relationships with program facilitators, they gain a sense of autonomy and feel more competent in their relationships with peers and adults, and they feel empowered by the knowledge that they can make a difference in the lives of others. All such factors, in turn, may help increase teenagers' motivation to avoid pregnancy. In addition, participating in supervised activities—especially after school—may simply reduce the opportunities teens have to engage in risky behavior, including unprotected sex. (*p. 14*)

Other youth development programs, such as the Job Corps, with more of a vocational focus, did not achieve these same pregnancy prevention outcomes.

Some programs address both sex education and youth development simultaneously. One very comprehensive (and very expensive) such program is the Children's Aid Society—Carrera Program. This long-term program offers participants family life and sex education, tutoring, assistance with college entrance exams and college applications, work-related activities, help with establishing bank accounts, self-expression through the arts and sports, and comprehensive health care including mental health services. It has found positive impact on sexual and contraceptive behavior on girls that lasts as long as three years. However, the program did not reduce sexual risk taking among boys (Kirby, 2001).

Current research on outcomes of pregnancy prevention programs shows encouraging results. Several different kinds of approaches are achieving positive outcomes. Kirby (2001) cautions, however, that it is important for program planners to replicate faithfully the program components of models that have been shown to be effective, to attain similar successful outcomes.

COMMUNITY APPROACHES

The programs described in this section illustrate some of the many ways that community factors influence the treatment children receive at home. Some of these programs are not conceptualized as "prevention" but as "developmental" programs to strengthen family functioning. Although the programs described here vary widely in the community elements involved, program design, populations served, and goals, they are alike in demonstrating that strengthening communities and strengthening the linkages between service systems are important components of efforts to reduce harm to children and strengthen families. They illustrate the ecological principle that family interaction patterns and individual functioning are affected by the environments in which families live.

Multiservice Centers for Chinese Immigrant Families

Although not focused primarily on preventing child maltreatment, multipurpose centers located in immigrant communities are included here because they exemplify the developmental, family strengthening approach that is a characteristic of family support programs. For many recently arrived immigrant families, they may be the only formal social services that are available or perceived as acceptable. They are a potential resource for the identification of problem situations and resolving them within a context familiar to the children and their parents, thus avoiding potentially confusing and threatening encounters with child protective services.

Multiservice centers for new immigrants build on the American settlement house tradition. Settlement houses were founded in the late nineteenth century to address an emerging problem: the dislocation and lack of support felt by families who had recently immigrated to U.S. cities from their rural homes in the United States or Europe. These families lacked the extended family and neighborly supports that had been available in their previous communities. They also faced special stressors of immigration: family breakup, exploitation by landlords and employers, unsafe living conditions, language barriers, and lack of political power, which meant that local politicians often ignored their neighborhoods.

A major function of the settlement houses was to work toward better living conditions for urban slum dwellers through political activism. Settlement house workers and local residents were effective in securing better street lighting, garbage pickup, and police protection. Settlement houses also helped families to adapt to their new life situation and to create a sense of community through mutual support. English language classes, political and discussion groups, sewing and child care classes, employment referrals, and recreational and arts programs drawing on the cultural traditions of participants were among the services commonly offered.

The settlement house model has contributed substantially to the development of prevention and family support programs. Although they did not use the term, founders of settlement houses such as Jane Addams took an "ecological approach" to services. Settlement houses were among the first social service programs to recognize that the neighborhood influenced the way families functioned and to develop interventions at the neighborhood as well as the family and individual levels. Settlement houses were also a model for organizing and delivering services to all members of a community, not targeting services only to those previously identified as needing special help. Further, they showed how professionals could work with local residents so that they would be empowered to take action on their own behalf (Addams, 1909; Wald, 1915; Husock, 1992).

An updated version of the settlement house model is the multiservice centers for recently arrived Chinese immigrants. They exist in three major U.S. cities: Los Angeles, New York, and Chicago. Developed over the past two decades, they provide a practice model for culturally competent and integrated service delivery. Asian Americans are a fast-growing minority group in the United States, the majority of whom are from China. About 70 percent of the Chinese in this country are foreign-born, first-generation immigrants. Many have settled in "Chinatown," which are among the most prominent ethnic enclaves in American cities (Chow, 1999).

Chow (1999) has described the service approach of these centers. It is developmental and preventive, and is designed to meet "the normative needs of the population rather than the few who are having problems" (p. 72). The centers are part of the community, where people can drop in and relax. The prevention focus is seen in the range of services offered. According to Chow (1999),

> [Most] recent immigrants arrived as whole families. Therefore, the entire family, not just the individual, is in need of services. It is not unusual, for example, to see parents attending English lessons and job training, their younger child attending the day care center, their teenage child going to the after school program, and their elderly parents drinking tea and playing chess next door in a senior citizens' center. Involving the entire family also helps in the early discovery of potential problems, thereby strengthening the center's primary prevention focus. (*p. 74*)

The after-school programs for youth "teach Chinese culture, so that ethnic identity and solidarity can be developed and maintained. These programs are successful in involving at-risk youths in healthy activities in a safe environment" (p. 72).

Cultural competence is another important aspect of these centers. According to Chow (1999), "frontline staff and workers are bilingual. . . . From the front entrance where the receptionists sit, to the intake workers, to the professionals, the centers are full of the sights and sounds familiar to service users. Art work, posters, brochures, displays, as well as background music, all fit into the cultural context" (p. 77). The Chinese cultural ideals of harmony and cooperation are reflected in the management structure of the centers. The focus is on teamwork and boundary spanning roles (p. 75).

Empowerment strategies help residents learn to be effective advocates for the needs of their community. Chow (1999) pointed out that for many recent Chinese immigrants, political activism is a new experience; part of the acculturation process is to learn the responsibilities and rights of citizenship. The centers offer help with voter registration, census counts, citizenship classes, and fund-raising events for local politicians (p. 75).

Interagency Cooperation to Prevent Child Maltreatment

The link between childhood disability and increased risk for child maltreatment is well known. One study has reported that children with disabilities are four times as likely to be abused or neglected as other children (Sullivan & Knutson, 1998); other research has shown that abuse and neglect can cause children to have disabilities (National Center on Child Abuse and Neglect, 1993). Yet, despite the evidence that the child welfare system and the health, mental health, and educational systems were often serving the same children with disabilities, until recently government programs for these children were entirely separate from services for abused and neglected children. To address this problem, in 2003, Congress passed the Keeping Children Safe Act; key provisions encourage increased cooperation among the child welfare, educational, mental health, and community-based service systems. These are:

❖ Requirements that hospitals notify Child Protective Services (CPS) of all children born affected by illegal substance abuse, and requiring CPS to develop a "plan of safe care" for these infants.

❖ Requirements that children under age 3 who have a substantiated case of abuse and neglect be referred to early intervention services funded under Part C of the

> Individuals with Disabilities Education Act (IDEA). IDEA funds intervention ser-
> vices systems for infants and toddlers with disabilities and their families. Eligible
> families may receive services such as speech, language, and physical therapy, fam-
> ily counseling, home visits, medical care, nursing, and nutrition assistance.

This last provision has potential to improve the lives of many young children with disabilities who
are suffering abuse and neglect. However, a major problem with mandatory referrals to IDEA is
that these programs serve only a small proportion of eligible children. For the 2003 Keeping Children Safe Act to reach its potential for serving young children, funding of IDEA, Part C will need
to be increased considerably. In addition, child advocates, parents, attorneys, and others concerned about the rights of children will need to be trained on the provisions of this Act and how it
can be implemented locally (Musheno, 2006; Davidson, no date)

Community Awareness Campaigns

Public health social marketing campaigns to prevent drinking and driving, smoking, and HIV/AIDS,
have been a model for child maltreatment initiatives directed at the entire community. For example, a
current campaign to prevent shaken baby syndrome has produced bumper stickers and billboards
admonishing, "Never Never Shake a Baby!" Several of the prevention web sites listed at the end of
this chapter have information for organizing public information initiatives in local communities.

Most sexual abuse prevention programs focus on teaching children how to avoid sexual abuse
(see Sexual Abuse Prevention Programs section). An innovative campaign in Vermont, called
STOP IT NOW!, addresses child sexual abuse as a public health issue. It uses social marketing and
public education to emphasize the responsibility of adults for prevention. A help line for adults
with questions about or experience of sexual abuse and for social agencies seeking information
about sexual abuse is available. Linkages with the legal system allow self-disclosed offenders to
seek treatment within the framework of the criminal code on court processing of alleged perpetrators (Pollard, 2006; Richard, 2003).

The program was evaluated in 1997 by surveying sex offender treatment programs and state attorneys' offices to assess self-reported abuse by adults and adolescents. During a two-year period,
fifty persons self-reported sexual abuse through the influence of the campaign, including thirty-
nine adolescents who entered treatment as a result of a parent soliciting help. The evaluation
found that community factors were critical to the program's success. Vermont has sufficient quan-
tity of sex offender treatment programs to guarantee a place for anyone who enters the legal system, has accessible media markets, and has a coalition of victim and abuser treatment
organizations that supported the initiative. The Centers for Disease Control recommends more
evaluations of the efficacy of public information campaigns to prevent child abuse, and suggests
that "a collaborative effort between public health officials, sex offender treatment providers, and
the criminal justice system in the model of STOP IT NOW! may benefit the well being of children" (Centers for Disease Control, 2001).

Fatherhood Programs

The high level of interest in services to fathers reflects research showing that children whose fathers are positively involved with them tend to have higher levels of functioning and are more

likely to receive child financial support (Child Trends, no date; Salovitz, 2002). These findings increase concern about the trend toward fatherless families. Additionally, an increasing number of fathers are raising children alone (U.S. Census Bureau, 2004). The problem of the "disappearing father" must be addressed at a number of levels, including improving preventive and supportive services to fathers, facilitating paternity establishment procedures, assisting low-income and low-skill fathers to find employment, and improving child support enforcement procedures (Pearson, 2003).

Social services, often explicitly or implicitly directed mainly at women and children, are challenged to find ways of reconnecting fathers to their families (Miller, 1997). The Fatherhood Project of New York City has identified that articulating clear expectations for fatherhood is a first step toward changing the practices of social agencies that have discouraged father participation and toward reengaging fathers with their families. This project publicizes that a father who behaves responsibly toward his family does the following: He waits to make a baby until he can support the child emotionally and financially; he establishes paternity; he shares parenting with the mother; and he shares with the mother ongoing financial responsibility for the child (Levine & Pitt, 1995, p. 5). Family support programs can promote father involvement by including both parents in activities, providing opportunities for fathers to network with each other, and being sensitive to the shame fathers may feel if unemployed, emphasizing their role as emotional nurturers as well as financial providers (Saleh, Buzi, Weinman, & Smith, 2006).

Establishing Paternity. Important benefits accrue to children for whom paternity has been established. These benefits include financial support and eligibility for benefits such as Social Security and health insurance. Although young, unmarried fathers may have little income to contribute to their newborn children, their ability to contribute increases over time. Psychologically, paternity establishment gives children a stronger sense of their identity and the security that comes from having been "claimed" by both parents. Early establishment of paternity can strengthen the bond the father has with the child and encourage a pattern of responsible parenting. Despite the benefits of establishing paternity, many children are without this protection. Disincentives to establishing paternity include fear of becoming involved with the "system" and bureaucratic hurdles to accomplishing the paperwork involved.

Growing evidence suggests that the best time to establish paternity is at birth. This capitalizes on the "glow of the moment"; most fathers are present at the birth of their child and find it a moving experience. Some states have had good results when they simplified their paternity establishment procedures and enabled hospital staff to distribute paternity papers and encourage new parents to complete them (Pearson & Thoennes, 1996; Turner, 2001).

Child Support. For many fathers, failure to pay child support is related to their low earnings level or unemployment. A recent demonstration project, the Parents' Fair Share, involving seven sites and two thousand participants, showed that comprehensive job placement and skill-building services increased only modestly the extent of child support payments made by these low-earning, low-skill fathers. The National Association of Child Advocates recommends that until programs for noncustodial fathers demonstrate more substantial benefits to children's well-being they should not replace more traditional means of providing public support for children. More experimentation with innovative approaches to strengthening families through interventions with noncustodial, low-income fathers is needed (Feeley, 2000).

TRENDS AND ISSUES

Controversy over Corporal Punishment

Prevention programs aimed at parents offer instruction on parenting practices that will increase the likelihood of good developmental outcomes and reduce the risk of child maltreatment. There is substantial agreement among parents, educators, other professionals, and researchers on many of these practices, such as the importance of communication and mutual respect, and the concept of "authoritative parenting," which combines parental warmth with the willingness to set limits on children's behavior (Maccoby & Martin, 1983; Steinberg, Elman, & Mounts, 1989). These and similar concepts guide and inform much of the curriculum of parent education programs. Research has shown that they increase the odds of creating good developmental outcomes in children.

However, there are areas of disagreement on optimal or acceptable parenting practices. One major disagreement concerns the acceptability of corporal punishment. Murray Straus (2000), a nationally known researcher on family violence, defines corporal punishment as: "the use of physical force with the intention of causing a child to experience pain, but not injury, for the purpose of correction or control of the child's behavior. This includes spanking on the buttocks and slapping a child's hand for touching a forbidden or dangerous object" (p. 1110). He points out that discussion of the acceptability of corporal punishment (CP) is curiously missing from discussions of maltreatment prevention. For example, *Child Abuse & Neglect,* a major scholarly journal on maltreatment, in a special issue called "A National Call to Action: Working Toward Elimination of Child Maltreatment" (1999), did not include discussion of elimination of CP in any of its nine articles. National surveys find that CP is widespread; a 1995 Gallup survey found that 94 percent of parents reported using CP and 35 percent hit infants, making its omission from the public debate quite troubling (Straus & Stewart, 1999). Straus cites a number of highly respected research studies that have linked CP both with negative developmental outcomes and with increased risk of child maltreatment.

In seeking for answers to the question of why the elimination of CP is not on the prevention agenda, despite its link to child maltreatment, Straus (2000) dismisses two common arguments for tolerating CP. To the argument that most parents who use CP do not abuse their children, he retorts that the same can be said of poverty, as most poor parents do not maltreat their children, yet everyone thinks that eliminating poverty would go a long way in reducing child maltreatment. Another common argument is that we cannot take away CP as a parental tool without first giving parents alternatives for managing children's behavior. Straus's response is that in other areas of interpersonal violence, such as spousal abuse, we are clear as a society that the behavior should stop regardless of whether the abuser knows alternative ways of handling conflict and disagreement.

Straus (2000) argues that the main reason that CP has not been targeted in prevention efforts is that CP raises deeply contradictory feelings. Many people believe that it is best to avoid CP, while at the same time believing that it is justified in some instances, or that it should be available as a "last resort." This position is held by many child protection agencies, which do not consider physical punishment of children as cause for substantiated abuse if they are done in the context of "reasonable discipline." (See Chapter 6.) Straus sees this position as inconsistent: "It is just as contradictory as being against slapping a spouse for misbehavior, while also believing that a slap may sometimes be necessary, and is harmless if done in moderation by a loving partner" (p. 1113).

Straus (2000) urges an all-out public media campaign against CP, because of its pervasiveness in American society and its proven link to poor developmental outcomes and child maltreatment. As part of this campaign, he suggests that it be called "hitting" and "physically attacking." He suggests that words in more common use, such as *spanking, whooping,* and *licking,* should be avoided because they suggest that "hitting children may be an approved disciplinary strategy" (p. 1113).

Child Maltreatment Prevention and the Schools

For at least three decades, there has been recognition that closer linkages between schools and child welfare agencies would improve services to children and families (Barth, 1985). Human service programs have been conducting innovative school-based and school-linked services for many years. As Landsman (2001), pointed out: "As a universal point of access for children, youth, and families, schools are increasingly being recognized as potential sites for innovation in attempts to tackle some of the vexing challenges facing youth, families, and communities today" (p. 1).

Schools are involved in both maltreatment prevention and family support efforts. There are a number of examples of school-linked prevention efforts. The schools have been a primary source of reports of child maltreatment to child protection agencies (see Chapter 6) and educators are mandatory reporters in every state. Prevention efforts aimed at children are often conducted in schools, such as the sexual abuse prevention and teen pregnancy prevention programs discussed earlier in this chapter. After-school programs frequently include elements aimed at prevention of delinquency, substance abuse, and other unhealthy behaviors.

Increasingly, family support and family development programs are linked to the schools. These programs are characterized by the strong partnerships they form with the school, including sharing of resources and expertise, and mutual responsibility for being accountable for outcomes (Blank & Melaville, 1999; Blank & Berg, 2006.)

Although various initiatives linking schools, maltreatment prevention, and family support show promise and are increasing in number, the potential for collaboration between child welfare and school service systems has not yet been realized. A major challenge is to find productive ways of collaboration for two of the major public service systems for children and families, the schools and the child welfare system (Dupper & Evans, 1996; Horton & Cruise, 2001).

Chapter Summary

Services to prevent maltreatment and support families are based on the principle that all families need help from time to time to fulfill their societal function of promoting the well-being and development of all family members. Some families face special stresses from a combination of factors: parental problems, such as teen parenthood or substance abuse; special conditions of children, such as developmental disabilities or low birth weight; and insufficient supports and resources in the extended family and community. Families of color, gay and lesbian families, and immigrant families may face special stresses because of societal oppression and discrimination.

The United States has lagged behind other Western countries in establishing preventive and supportive services to parents, so many families do not get help until the home situation has become dangerous to children and a referral to child protective services becomes necessary.

However, since the early 1990s, there has been increased interest in establishing supportive programs for families.

Preventive and family support services are oriented to the future, use an ecological perspective, emphasize empowerment, and take a developmental approach. Attachment theory and social learning theory provide a conceptual foundation for many preventive approaches.

Family support programs have the dual function of preventing maltreatment and improving family life. Services may be offered through home visits, centers, or both, and are offered to parents and (usually) preschool children. Services may include parenting education on child management and child health, developmental services for parents, preschool programs for infants, referral and linkage to other services, assessment, and advocacy. Traditional social work services, including casework, group work, and service to children are not usually considered to be family support services but are also very helpful in preventing child maltreatment and supporting families.

Another type of prevention program focuses directly on children, attempting to empower them to develop healthy, safe habits. Sexual abuse prevention programs attempt to teach children to avoid sexual abuse. Teen pregnancy prevention programs offer education on sexual issues and try to help teens make healthy choices and implement them in daily life. Some youth development programs, though not focusing directly on pregnancy prevention, are nonetheless very successful in preventing pregnancy.

Community approaches to prevention reflect the understanding that the environment affects maltreatment of children and family well-being. Many different types of prevention programs exist: Examples given in this chapter are multiservice centers for new immigrant families; a program to link child welfare services with services to children with disabilites; public health information campaigns; and programs to encourage responsible, involved fatherhood.

A controversial issue in the field of maltreatment prevention is the acceptability of corporal punishment in child management. From the point of view of community organization in linking human service systems, it is important to try to strengthen linkages between schools and the child welfare system, and to make use of the opportunities this collaboration provides for prevention and family support.

FOR STUDY AND DISCUSSION
STUDY AND DISCUSSION QUESTIONS

1. Individually or as a class, select a population at risk for child maltreatment (e.g., children of teen parents, children of substance abusing parents), and conduct an ecological assessment such as that presented in Figure 3.1, listing risk factors and possible prevention strategies at the community, family, and child levels.

2. For an ethnic or racial group with which you are familiar, consider the group's definition of family, its childrearing patterns, and the family roles. How would you design a culturally competent family support program for this group?

3. What are the arrangements for establishing paternity in your state? Which agencies or courts are responsible? Are parents routinely counseled on paternity establishment at the hospital? Do procedures and practices work to encourage or discourage voluntary avowal of paternity?

4. Visit a sexual abuse prevention program or a teen pregnancy prevention program, and report to the class your impressions. What were the themes covered? Did the program seem to use a social learning theory approach? How were the participants responding?

5. Visit a family support program. Learn the auspices under which it operates, funding sources, program goals, types of families served, range of services offered, and eligibility requirements, if any. Assess the benefits you see to the program and ways it could improve. Find out the results of any evaluations of the program. If possible, interview staff and participating families.

Internet Sites

Child Welfare Information Gateway. Child Welfare Information Gateway provides access to information and resources to help protect children and strengthen families. A service of the Children's Bureau, Administration for Children and Families, U.S. Department of Health and Human Services.
www.childwelfare.gov

The National Campaign to Prevent Teen Pregnancy. The National Campaign to Prevent Teen Pregnancy, founded in February 1996, is a nonprofit, nonpartisan initiative supported almost entirely by private donations. Its mission is to improve the well-being of children, youth, and families by reducing teen pregnancy. The goal of the National Campaign to Prevent Teen Pregnancy is to reduce the rate of teen pregnancy by one-third between 2006 and 2015.
www.teenpregnancy.org

National Fatherhood Initiative. National Fatherhood Initiative's mission is to improve the well-being of children by increasing the proportion of children growing up with involved, responsible, and committed fathers.
www.fatherhood.org

National Indian Child Welfare Association. Since its founding, the National Indian Child Welfare Association (NICWA) has served hundreds of American Indian tribes throughout the country by helping to strengthen and enhance their capacity to deliver quality child welfare services.
www.nicwa.org

Prevent Child Abuse America. Since 1972, Prevent Child Abuse America has led the way in building awareness, providing education, and inspiring hope to everyone involved in the effort to prevent the abuse and neglect of our nation's children. Working with their chapters, they provide leadership to promote and implement prevention efforts at both the national and local levels.
www.preventchildabuse.org

References

Adair, J. (2006). The efficacy of sexual violence prevention programs: implications for schools. *Journal of School Violence, 5*(2), 89–97.

Addams, J. (1909). *The spirit of youth and the city streets.* New York: Macmillan.

Ainsworth, M. (1989). Attachments beyond infancy. *American Psychologist, 44,* 709–716 (cited in Van Horn, 1999).

Allen, M., & Pittman, K. (1986). *Welfare and teen pregnancy: What do we know? What do we do?* Washington, DC: Children's Defense Fund, Adolescent Pregnancy Prevention Clearinghouse.

Amato, P. R. (1993). Children's adjustment to divorce: Theories, hypotheses, and empirical support. *Journal of Marriage and the Family, 55*(1), 23–28.

Aponte, R. (1993). Hispanic families in poverty: Diversity, context, and interpretation. *Families in Society, 74*(9), 527–537.

Bachrach, C. A. (1986). Adoption plans, adopted children and adoptive mothers. *Journal of Marriage and the Family, 48,* 243–253.

Bandura, A. (1976). *Social learning theory.* Englewood Cliffs, NJ: Prentice-Hall.

Barkan, S. (1996, December). *Teen parent provisions in the new law.* Washington, DC: Center for Law and Social Policy. Available: www.handsnet.org/handsnet2/welfarereform/ Articles/ art.849902466. html.

Barnes, S. L. (2001). Stressors and strengths: A practical examination of nuclear, single-parent, and augmented African American families. *Families in Society, 82*(5), 449–460.

Barth, R. (1985). Collaboration between child welfare and school social work services. *Social Work in Education, 8*(1), 32–47.

Bean, R. A., Perry, B. J., & Bedell, T. M. (2001). Developing culturally competent marriage and family therapists: Guidelines for working with Hispanic families. *Journal of Marital and Family Therapy, 27*(1), 43–54.

Bending, R. L. (1997). Training child welfare workers to meet the requirements of the Indian Child Welfare Act. *Journal of Multicultural Social Work, 5*(3–4), 151–164.

Billingsley, A. (1992). *Climbing Jacob's ladder: The enduring legacy of African-American families.* New York: Simon & Schuster.

Billingsley, A. (2002). *Mighty like a river: The black church and social reform.* New York: Oxford University Press.

Black, L. (1996). Families of African origin: An overview. In M. McGoldrick, J. Giordano, & J. Pearce (Eds.), *Ethnicity and family therapy* (2nd ed.) (pp. 57–65). New York: Guilford Press.

Blank, M., & Berg, A. (2006). *All together now: Sharing responsibility for the whole child.* Washington, DC: Association for Supervision and Curriculum Development.

Blank, M., & Melaville, A. (1999). Creating family-supportive schools: Taking the first steps. *Family Support, 18*(3), 37–40.

Bloom, M. (1996). *Primary prevention practices.* Thousand Oaks, CA: Sage.

Boonstra, Heather (2002). Teen pregnancy: Trends and lessons learned. *The Guttmacher Report on Public Policy, 5*(1), 1–5.

Bowlby, J. (1980). *Attachment and loss, vol. 3: Loss.* New York: Basic Books.

Boyd-Franklin, N. (2006). *Black families in therapy* (2nd ed.). New York: Guilford.

Bronfenbrenner, U. (1987). Foreword. In S. L. Kagan, D. R. Powell, B. Weissbourd, & E. F. Zigler (Eds.), *America's family support programs: Perspectives and prospects.* New Haven, CT: Yale University Press.

Bruner, C., & Carter, J. L. (1991, November). *Family support and education: A holistic approach to school readiness. Network Briefs.* Denver and Washington, DC: National Conference of State Legislatures.

Bugental, D. B., Ellerson, P. C., Lin, E. K., Rainey, B., Kokotovic, A., & O'Hara, N. (2002). A cognitive approach to child abuse prevention. *Journal of Family Psychology, 16,* 243–258.

Butler, A. C. (1992, March). The changing economic consequences of teenage childbearing. *Social Service Review,* 1–31.

Centers for Disease Control. (2001, February 9). Evaluation of a child sexual abuse prevention program. *MMWR Weekly,* Available: www .stopitnow.com.

Cervera, N. J. (1993). Decision making for pregnant adolescents: Applying reasoned action theory to research and treatment. *Families in Society: The Journal of Contemporary Human Services, 74*(6), 355–365.

Chaffin, M. (2004). Invited commentary: Is it time to rethink Health Start/Healthy Families? *Child Abuse & Neglect, 28*(6), 589–595.

Child Trends. (no date). What do fathers contribute to children's well-being? *Child Trends Research Brief.* Available: www.childtrends.org.

Children's Bureau. (no date). *Infant adoption awareness training program.* Available: www.acf.dhhs.gov/programs/cb.htm.

Children's Bureau. (2006). *Child neglect: Guide for prevention, assessment, and intervention.* Washington, DC: Child Welfare Information Gateway.

Choi, N. G. (2001). Social work practice with the Asian American elderly. *Journal of Gerontological Social Work, 36*(1–2), 1–3.

Chow, J. (1999). Multiservice centers in Chinese American immigrant communities: Practice, principles, and challenges. *Social Work, 44*(1), 70–81.

Cochran, M. (1993). Parent empowerment: Developing a conceptual framework. *Family Science Review, 5*(1–2), 81–92.

Coohey, C. (2001). The relationship between familism and child maltreatment in Latino and Anglo families. *Child Maltreatment, 6,* 130–142.

Costigan, C., & Dokis, D. P. (2006). The relations between parent-child acculturation differences and adjustment within immigrant Chinese families. *Child Development, 77,* 1252–1267.

Costin, L. (1985). Protective behaviors. *Social Work in Education, 7*(4), 210–211.

Cross, T. L. (1986). Drawing on cultural tradition in Indian child welfare practice. *Social Casework, 67,* 283–289.

Cross, T. L. (1996, Spring). Developing a knowledge base to support cultural competence. *The Prevention Report, 2*–5.

Daro, D. (2006, September 27). Testimony before the Subcommittee on Education Reform: Hearing on "Perspectives on Early Childhood Home Visitation Programs." Available: www.house.gov/ed_workforce/hearings/109th/edr/inhomeed092706/daro.htm.

Daro, D., & Donnelly, A. (2002). Charting the waves of prevention: Two steps forward, one step back. *Child Abuse & Neglect, 26,* 731–742.

Davidson, H. (no date.) Significant new changes to the federal Child Abuse Pevention and Treatment Act: Practical implications for child and family advocates. American Bar Association Center on Children and the Law. Available: http://aia.berkeley.edu/media/pdf/davidson_capta_sen.doc.

Davis, M., & Gidycz, C. (2000). Child sexual abuse prevention programs: A meta-analysis. *Clinical child psychology, 29*(2), 257–265.

Downs, S. W. (1997). Parenting pioneers and parenting teams: Strengthening extended family ties in family support programs. *Family Preservation Journal, 2*(1), 33–46.

Downs, S. W., & Nahan, N. (1990, Fall). Mixing clients and other neighborhood families: Neighborhood family support centers offer services plus peer support. *Public Welfare, 48*(4), 26–33.

Downs, S. W., & Walker, D. (1996, June–July). Family support while you wait: The waiting room approach. *Zero to Three, 16*(6), 25–32.

DuBray, W., & Sanders, A. (1999). Interactions between American Indian ethnicity and health care. *Journal of Health and Social Policy, 10*(4), 67–84.

Duggan, A., Fuddy, L., Burrell, L., Higman, S. M., Windham, A., Sia, C. (2004). Randomized trial of a statewide home visiting program: Impact in preventing child abuse and neglect. *Child Abuse & Neglect, 28*(6), 597–622.

Dupper, D. R., & Evans, S. (1996). From bandaids and putting out fires to prevention. *Social Work in Education, 18*(3), 186–192.

Early, T. J., & GlenMaye, L. F. (2000). Valuing families: Social work practice with families from a strengths perspective. *Social Work, 45*(2), 118–130.

Emery, R. E. (1999). *Marriage, divorce, and children's adjustment* (2nd ed.). Thousand Oaks, CA: Sage.

Family Resource Coalition. (no date). *Family support programs and teen parents.* Available: www.ericeece.org.

Feeley, T. (2000, February). Low-income noncustodial fathers: A child advocate's guide to helping them contribute to the support of their children. *Issue Brief.* National Association of Child Advocates.

Finkelhor, D., & Dzuiba-Leatherman, J. (1995). Victimization prevention programs: A national survey of children's exposure and reactions. *Child Abuse & Neglect, 19,* 129–139.

Fix, M., & Passel, J. (2001). *U.S. immigrants at the beginning of the 21st century.* Washington, DC: The Urban Institute.

Freeman, E. M. (1990). The black family's life cycle: Operationalizing a strengths perspective. In S. M. L. Logan, E. M. Freeman, & R. G. McRoy (Eds.), *Social work practice with black families* (pp. 55–72). White Plains, NY: Longman.

Furstenberg, F. F., & Harris, K. M. (1990, April). *The disappearing father? Divorce and the waning significance of biological parenthood.* Paper presented at the Albany Conference on Demographic Perspectives on the American Family: Patterns and Prospects.

Garcia-Preto, N. (1996). Latino families: An overview. In M. McGoldrick, J. Giordano, & J. Pearce (Eds.), *Ethnicity and family therapy* (2nd ed.) (pp. 141–154). New York: Guilford Press.

Gartrell, N., Banks, A., Reed, N., Hamilton, J., Rodas, C., & Deck, A. (2000). The national lesbian family study. *American Journal of Orthopsychiatry, 70*(4), 542–548.

George, C. (1996). A representational perspective of child abuse and prevention: Internal working models of attachment and caregiving. *Child Abuse & Neglect, 20*(5), 411–424.

Gibson, L., & Leitenberg, H. (2000). Child sexual abuse prevention programs: Do they decrease the occurrence of child sexual abuse? *Child Abuse & Neglect, 24*(9), 1115–1125.

Good-Touch/Bad-Touch. (no date). *About good-touch/bad-touch.* Available: www.goodtouch-badtouch.com.

Greenberg, M. (1999). Attachment and psychopathology in childhood. In J. Cassidy & P. R. Shaver (Eds.), *Handbook of attachment: Theory, research, and clinical applications* (pp. 469–490). New York: Guilford Press.

Haight, W. I., Kagle, D. J., & Black, J. E. (2003). Understanding and supporting parent-child relationships during foster care visits: Attachment theory and research. *Social Work, 48*(1), 195–207.

Haight, W. L. (1998). "Gathering the spirit" at First Baptist Church: Spirituality as a protective factor in the lives of African-American children. *Social Work, 43*(3), 213–221.

Halgunseth, L., Ispa, J. M., & Rudy, D. D. (2006). Parental control in Latino families: An integrated review of the literature. *Child Development, 77*, 1282–1297.

Harder, J. (2005). Prevention of child abuse and neglect: An evaluation of a home visitation Parent aide program using recidivism data. *Research on Social Work Practice, 15*(4), 246–256.

Hartman, A., & Laird, J. (1983). *Family centered social work practice.* New York: Free Press.

Hetherington, E. M. (1999). *Coping with divorce, single parenting, and remarriage: A risk and resiliency perspective.* Mahwah, NJ: Lawrence Erlbaum.

Heyman, R. E., & Slep, A. M. S. (2001). Risk factors for family violence: Introduction to the special series. *Aggression and Violent Behavior, 6*, 115–119.

Highlights from the family preservation and support services program instruction. (1994, January). Washington, DC: U.S. Department of Health and Human Services.

Hill, R. B. (1997, Spring). Supporting African-American families: Dispelling myths, building on strengths. *Children's Voice, 2*(3), 4–7.

Hines, P. M., & Boyd-Franklin, N. (1996). African-American families. In M. McGoldrick, J. Giordano, & J. Pearce (Eds.), *Ethnicity and family therapy* (2nd ed.) (pp. 66–84). New York: Guilford Press.

Horton, C. B., & Cruise, T. K. (2001). *Child abuse and neglect: The school's response.* New York: Guilford Press.

Hunter, A. G. (1997). Counting on grandmothers: Black mothers' and fathers' reliance on grandmothers for parenting support. *Journal of Family Issues, 18*(3), 251–269.

Hurdle, D. E. (2002). Native Hawaiian traditional healing: Culturally based interventions for social work practice. *Social Work, 47*(2), 183–192.

Husock, H. (1992, Fall). Bring back the settlement house. *The Public Interest, 109*, 53–72.

Indian education: A national tragedy: A national challenge. (1969). Washington, DC: Committee on Labor and Public Welfare, Special Subcommittee on Indian Education; U.S. Senate, 91st Cong., 1st Sess.

Johnson, B. B. (1981). The Indian Child Welfare Act of 1978: Implications for practice. *Child Welfare, 60*(7), 435–446.

Jones, D. J., Forehand, R., Brody, G., Armistead, L. (2002). Psychosocial adjustment of African American children in single-mother families: A test of three risk models. *Journal of Marriage & Family, 64*, 1, 105–115.

Jung, M. (1996). Family-centered practice with single parent families. *Families in Society, 77*(9), 583–590.

Kirby, D. (2001). *Emerging answers: Research findings on programs to reduce teen pregnancy (Summary).* Washington, DC: National Campaign to Prevent Teen Pregnancy.

Kirby, D., Barth, R., Leland, N., & Fetro, J. (1991). Reducing the risk: Impact of a new curriculum on sexual risk-taking. *Family Planning Perspectives, 23*(6), 253–263.

Korbin, J. E. (2002). Culture and child maltreatment: Cultural competence and beyond. *Child Abuse & Neglect, 26*, 637–644.

Landau, J. (1982). Therapy with families in cultural transition. In M. McGoldrick, J. Pearce, & J. Giordano (Eds.), *Ethnicity and family therapy.* New York: Guilford Press.

Landsman, M. (2001). Schools in partnership with families and communities. *The Prevention Report,* 2001(1).

Levine, J. A., & Pitt, E. W. (1995). *New expectations: Community strategies for responsible fatherhood.* New York: Families and Work Institute.

Levy, E. F. (1992). Strengthening the coping resources of lesbian families. *Families in Society: The Journal of Contemporary Human Services,* 23–31.

Lewin, T. (1992, February 27). Sharp decline found in number of children up for adoption. *New York Times,* p. 10.

Light, H. K., & Martin, R. E. (1986). American Indian families. *Journal of American Indian Education, 26*(1), 1–5.

Lott-Whitehead, L., & Tully, C. T. (1993). The family lives of lesbian mothers. *Smith College Studies in Social Work, 63*(3), 265–280.

Lyons-Ruth, K., Connell, D., Zoll, D., & Stahl, J. (1987). Infants at social risk: Relations among infant maltreatment, maternal behavior, and infant attachment behavior. *Developmental Psychology, 23,* 223–232 (cited in Van Horn, 1999).

Maccoby, E., & Martin, J. (1983). Socialization in the context of the family: Parent–child interaction. In E. M. Hetherington (Ed.), *Handbook of child psychology, vol. 4: Socialization, personality, and social development* (4th ed.).

MacLeod, J., & Nelson, G. (2000). Programs for the promotion of family wellness and the prevention of child maltreatment: A meta-analytic review. *Child Abuse & Neglect, 24*(9), 1127–1149.

Main, M., & Solomon, J. (1990). Procedures for identifying infants as disorganized/disoriented during the Ainsworth Strange Situation. In M. T. Greenberg, D. Cicchetti, & E. M. Cummings (Eds.), *Attachment in the preschool years* (pp. 121–160). Chicago: University of Chicago Press (cited in Van Horn, 1999).

Mayden, B. (1997). Child sexual abuse: Teen pregnancy's silent partner. In *Adolescent sexuality, pregnancy, and parenting: Selected readings* (pp. 57–60). Washington, DC: Child Welfare League of America.

Mayden, B., & Brooks, T. R. (1996). *Welfare reform and teen parents.* Washington, DC: Child Welfare League of America.

Maynard, R. A. (Ed.). (1996). *Kids having kids: A Robin Hood Foundation special report on the costs of adolescent childbearing.* New York: Robin Hood Foundation.

McGuigan, W. M., Katzev, A. R., & Pratt, C. C. (2003). Multi-level determinants of retention in a home-visiting child abuse prevention program. *Child Abuse & Neglect, 27,* 363–380.

McLanahan, S., & Sandefur, G. (1994). *Growing up with a single parent: What hurts, what helps.* Cambridge, MA: Harvard University Press.

McLaren, M. (2003). Empathic care: An attachment based parenting model for infants and children of substance using women. *The Source, Newsletter of the National Abandoned Infants Assistance Resource Center, 12*(2), 1–5, 28.

Miller, D. B. (1997). Adolescent fathers: What we know and what we need to know. *Child and Adolescent Social Work Journal, 14*(1), 55–69.

Moore, K. A., & Driscoll, A. (1997). Partners, predators, peers, protectors: Males and teen pregnancy. In *Not just for girls: The roles of boys and men in teen pregnancy* (pp. 5–10). Washington, DC: National Campaign to Prevent Teen Pregnancy.

Morgan, K. (2000). Mother—not mother. *The Family Therapy Networker, 24*(1), 54–59.

Mosley-Howard, G. S., & Evans, C. B. (2000). Relationships and contemporary experiences of the African American family: An ethnographic study. *Journal of Black Studies, 30*(3), 428–452.

Musheno, K. (2006). Children with disabilities and the Child Abuse Prevention and Treatment Act. *Impact: Feature issue on children with disabilities in the child welfare system, 19*(1). Available: http://ici.umn.edu/products/impact/191/default.html.

National Association of Social Workers. (2001). *NASW standards for cultural competence in social work practice.* Washington, DC: National Association of Social Workers.

National Center on Child Abuse and Neglect. (1993). *A report on the maltreatment of children with disabilities.* Washington, DC: National Clearinghouse on Child Abuse and Neglect Information.

National Clearinghouse for Child Abuse and Neglect. (2001, February). *In focus: The risk and prevention of maltreatment of children with disabilities.* Available: www.calib.com/nccanch/prevmnth/actions/risk.cfm.

Nobles, W. G. (1988). American family life: An instrument of culture. In H. P. McAdoo (Ed.), *Black Families* (2nd ed.) (pp. 44–53). Beverly Hills, CA: Sage.

O'Connell, A. (1993). Voices from the heart: The developmental impact of a mother's lesbianism on her adolescent children. *Smith College Studies in Social Work, 63*(3), 281–299.

O'Dell, K. (2001, July). Reducing out-of-wedlock childbearing through pregnancy prevention. *Welfare Information Network Issue Notes, 5*(10). Available: www.welfareinfo.org/reducingwedlockissuenote.htm.

O'Dell, S. (2000). Psychotherapy with gay and lesbian families. *Clinical Social Work Journal 28*(2), 171–182.

O'Hare, W. (2001). *The child population: First data from the 2000 Census.* The Annie E. Casey Foundation and the Population Reference Bureau.

Olds, D., Perritt, L. M., Robinson, L., Henderson, C., Ekemode, J., Kitzman, H., Cole, B., & Powers, J. (1998). Reducing risks for antisocial behavior with a program of prenatal and early childhood home visitation. *Journal of Community Psychology, 26*(1), 65–83.

Ooms, T., & Herendeen, L. (1990). Teenage pregnancy programs: What have we learned? *Background briefing report and meeting highlights: Family Impact Seminar.* Washington, DC: American Association for Marriage and the Family.

Ortiz, V. (1995). The diversity of Latino families. In R. E. Zambrana (Ed.), *Understanding Latino families* (pp. 18–39). Thousand Oaks: Sage.

Padilla, Y. C. (1997). Immigrant policy: Issues for social work practice. *Social Work, 42*(6), 595–606.

Patterson, C. J. (1992). Children of lesbian and gay parents. *Child Development, 63,* 1025–1042.

Pearson, J. (2003). *OCSE responsible fatherhood programs: Client characteristics and program outcomes.* Washington, DC: Children's Bureau, Administration for Children, Youth, and Families.

Pearson, J., & Thoennes, N. (1996, Summer). Acknowledging paternity in hospital settings. *Public Welfare, 54,* 44–51.

Pollard, P. (2006, May). Marketing sexual abuse prevention. *Behavioral healthcare online.* Available: http://behavioral.net/issues/2006/05/008/.

Powell, D. R. (1994). Evaluating family support programs: Are we making progress? In S. L. Kagan & B. Weissbourd (Eds.), *Putting families first: America's family support movement and the challenge of change* (pp. 441–470). San Francisco: Jossey-Bass.

Reardon-Anderson, J., Capps, R., & Fix, M. (2002). *The health and well-being of children in immigrant families.* The Urban Institute. Available: www.urban.org/urf.cfm?ID=310584.

Reppucci, N., & Haugaard, J. (1989). Prevention of child sexual abuse: Myth and reality. *American Psychologist, 44*(10), 1266–1275.

Resource Center for Adolescent Pregnancy Prevention. (no date). Social learning theory's major concepts. ETR Associates. Available: www.etr.org.

Richard, D. (2003). Stop it now! Helpline answers the call. *Contemporary Sexuality, 37*(12), 3–6.

Rispens, J., Aleman, A., & Goudena, P. (1997). Prevention of child sexual abuse victimization: A meta-analysis of school programs. *Child Abuse & Neglect, 21*(10), 975–987.

Rose, S. M. (2000). Reflections on empowerment-based practice. *Social Work, 45*(5), 403–412.

Saleh, M., Buzi, R., Weinman, M., & Smith, P. (2006). The nature of connections: Young fathers and their children. *Family Therapy, 33*(1), 17–27.

Salovitz, B. (2002, February). Reintroducing dad into the family equation. In *Making a difference that matters.* Duluth, GA: Child Welfare Institute.

Schiele, J. H. (1996). Afrocentricity: An emerging paradigm in social work practice. *Social Work, 41*(3), 284–294.

Schmitz, C. L. (1995). Reframing the dialogue on female-headed single parent families. *AFFILIA, 10*(4), 426–441.

Schorr, L. (1991). *Successful programs and the bureaucratic dilemma: Current deliberations.* New York: National Center for Children in Poverty.

Select Media. (no date). *Be proud! Be responsible!* Available: www.selectmedia.org.

Solomon, B. B. (1985). Assessment, service, and black families. In S. S. Gray, A. Hartman, &

E. S. Saalberg (Eds.), *Empowering the black family* (pp. 9–20). Ann Arbor: University of Michigan, National Child Welfare Training Center.

Steinberg, L., Elman, J., & Mounts, N. (1989). Authoritative parenting, psychosocial maturity, and academic success among adolescents. *Child Development, 60,* 1424–1436.

Steiner, H., Zeanah, C., Stuber, M., Ash, P., & Angell, R. (1994). The hidden faces of trauma: An update on child psychiatric traumatology. *Scientific Proceedings of the Annual Meeting of the American Academy of Child and Adolescent Psychiatry, 31* (cited in Van Horn, 1999).

Straus, M. (2000). Corporal punishment and primary prevention of physical abuse. *Child Abuse & Neglect, 24*(9), 1109–1114.

Straus, M., & Stewart, J. (1999). Corporal punishment by American parents: National data on prevalence, chronicity, severity, and duration, in relation to child and family characteristics. *Clinical Child and Family Psychology Review, 2,* 55–70.

Sullivan, P. M., & Knutson, J. F. (1998). The association between child maltreatment and disabilities in a hospital-based epidemiological study. *Child Abuse and Neglect, 22,* 271–288

Sutton, C. T., & Broken Nose, M. A. (1996). American Indian families: An overview. In M. McGoldrick, J. Giordano, & J. Pearce (Eds.), *Ethnicity and family therapy* (2nd ed.) (pp. 57–65). New York: Guilford Press.

Tafoya, N., & Del Vecchio, A. (1996). Back to the future: An examination of the Native American holocaust experience. In M. McGoldrick, J. Giordano, & J. Pearce (Eds.), *Ethnicity and family therapy* (2nd ed.) (pp. 45–54). New York: Guilford Press.

Thomas, D., Leicht, C., Hughes, C., Madigan, A., Dowell, K. (2003). *Emerging practices in the prevention of child abuse and neglect.* Washington, DC: Children's Bureau Office on Child Abuse and Neglect.

Thompson, R. A., & Amato, P. R. (Eds.). (1999). *The postdivorce family: Children, parenting, and society.* Thousand Oaks, CA: Sage.

Thyer, B. (1994). Social learning theory: Empirical applications to culturally diverse practice. In R. Greene (Ed.), *Human behavior theory: A diversity framework.* Hawthorne, NY: Aldine de Gruyter.

Turner, M. D. (2001). Child support enforcement and in-hospital paternity establishment in seven cities. *Child and Youth Services Review, 23*(4/5), 543–561.

Updegraff, K., McHale, S. M., Whiteman, S. D., Thayer, S. M., & Crouter, A. C. (2006). The nature and correlates of Mexican American adolescents' time with parents and peers. *Child Development, 77,* 1470–1486.

U.S. Census Bureau. (April, 2004). *Facts for features: Father's Day, June 20.* Available: *www.census.gov/Press-Release/www/releases/archives/facts_for_features_special_editions/001792.html.*

U.S. Department of Justice. (2003). *2001 statistical yearbook of the Immigration and Naturalization Service.* Washington, DC: U.S. Government Printing Office.

Van Horn, P. (1999). Understanding attachment disorders in infants and young children. *The Source, 9*(3), 1ff. National Abandoned Infants Resource Center.

Vega, W. A. (1990). Hispanic families in the 1980s: A decade of research. *Journal of Marriage and the Family, 52*(1), 1015–1024.

Visher, E. B., & Visher, J. S. (1990). Dynamics of successful stepfamilies. *Journal of Divorce & Remarriage, 14*(1), 3–12.

Wainright, J. L., & Patterson, C. J. (2006). Delinquency, victimization, and substance use among adolescents with female same-sex parents. *Journal of Family Psychology, 20*(3), 526–530.

Wainright, J. L., Russell, S. T., & Patterson, C. J. (2004). Psychosocial adjustment, school outcomes, and romantic relationships of adolescents with same-sex parents. *Child Development, 75*(6), 1886–1898.

Wald, L. D. (1915). *The house on Henry Street.* New York: Henry Holt.

Wallerstein, J. (2005). Growing up in the divorced family. *Clinical Social Work Journal, 33*(4), 401–418.

Wallerstein, J. S., & Blakeslee, S. (1996). *Second chances: Men, women, and children a decade after divorce.* Boston: Houghton Mifflin.

Weaver, H. (1998). Indigenous people in a multicultural society: Unique issues for human services. *Social Work, 43*(3), 203–211.

Weisberg, C. (2001). The school of the 21st century. *The Prevention Report, 2001*(1), 4.

Weiss, H. (1990). *Innovative models to guide family support and education policy in the 1990s: An analysis of four pioneering state programs.* Cambridge, MA: Harvard Family Research Project, Harvard Graduate School of Education.

Weisz, A., & Black, B. (in press). *Relationships should not hurt: Programs that reach out to youth to reduce dating violence and sexual assault.* New York: Columbia University Press.

Weiss, H., & Halpern, R. (1990). *Community-based family support and education programs: Something old or something new?* New York: National Center for Children in Poverty, Columbia University.

Zambrana, R. E., Silva-Palacios, V., & Powell, D. (1992). Parenting concerns, family support systems, and life problems in Mexican-origin women: A comparison by nativity. *Journal of Community Psychology, 20*(4), 276–288.

CHAPTER 4

Child Welfare Principles and Practices

If you can teach me how to cling to that which is real to me while showing me a way into a larger society, then not only will I drop my defenses and my hostilities; but I will sing your praises and help you to make the desert bear fruit.

—*Ralph Ellison, The Invisible Man (1948)*

Child welfare practice is one of the most challenging and difficult areas of social work practice. Every child welfare case is unique. This case is presented to demonstrate the progression of a family through the child welfare system. Comparatively speaking, it is a "simple" case. It is presented so that readers have one set of facts to use in a discussion of how child welfare practice can utilize consistent social work approaches irrespective of the particular child welfare service or program. In other words, while the particular tasks are different in the child welfare services array, that is, prevention, family preservation services, foster care services (including court-ordered kinship care), adoption and postadoption services, subsidized guardianship, planned permanent foster care services, and aging out services, there are fundamental principles and approaches that form the framework for providing any of these services. If the caseworker can master these fundamental principles and approaches, then a difficult job becomes less so.

There is no perfect way to do child welfare work. What the mastery of these fundamentals will provide is an evidence-based methodology for approaching and engaging the parent and child in resolving any of the situations you might confront as a child welfare caseworker. Given the limitations of this text, you are encouraged to pursue the resources listed in the For Additional Study and Reference sections at the end of this chapter for more comprehensive explanation of the fundamentals discussed.

The **Jones Family** includes
>   Ethel, the grandmother, age 65
>   Jennie, the mother, was killed approximately 1 year ago,
>   Danny, age 15
>   Mark, age 8
>   Moses, age 4 and
>   Jackie, 17 months.

The children's fathers, none of whom live with the children, are
>   Dan Bobcat, Danny's father, who died approximately nine years ago,
>   John Quick, Mark's father,
>   Mack Phillips, Moses' father, and
>   Jack Smith, Jackie's father.

The Jones' Family came to the attention of Children's Protective Services (CPS) for the first time approximately two years ago. Danny, Mark, and Moses had lived with their mother and grandmother since birth. Ms. Jones' mother, Ethel Jones, reported to CPS that Ms. Jones had taken Danny, Mark, and Moses from her (Ethel Jones') home because she refused to let Jennie Jones return to the home until she agreed to get some help for her substance abuse problem and ended her relationship with Jack Smith. Jack Smith had beaten Jennie frequently. Further, he had hit Danny once when Danny came to his mother's defense during a fight. Mrs. Jones was quite concerned about her grandsons' safety because Ms. Jones was using crack and Danny had told her that they were living with Jack Smith. CPS investigated the report and found no evidence of abuse or neglect of the children or of Jack Smith living in the home.

Danny ran away from his mother's home and returned to his grandmother's home about six months after his grandmother's referral to CPS. He refused to return to his mother's home. He told his grandmother that Jack Smith and his mom were always fighting. Mrs. Jones did not report this to CPS because she didn't think that they would do anything and, if she did, her daughter might take Danny from her.

A second CPS referral was made by a hospital social worker when Jackie was born with cocaine in her system. CPS substantiated this referral. Based on Ms. Jones' agreement to cooperate with substance abuse treatment services, CPS recommended in-home services. The caseworker documented, in the case file:

❖ She met with Ms. Jones in her home once a month at a scheduled time.
❖ The substance abuse treatment center provided a report each month that stated Ms. Jones had met all aspects of her treatment plan.
❖ She did not observe any neglect or abuse of Moses and Jackie during her monthly visits. The house was clean and there was food in the cabinets and refrigerator.
❖ Ms. Jones took Jackie for the required medical appointments.
❖ Ms. Jones participated in parent–teacher conferences about Mark's behavior problems in school at least once a month.
❖ Danny lived with his grandmother, Ethel Jones.
❖ Ms. Jones stated that Jack Smith was not living in the home.

After about six months of in-home services, CPS petitioned for removal of all the children because Ms. Jones was hospitalized after being severely beaten by Jack Smith. The petition was granted and the children were placed with their grandmother, Ethel Jones. Two months after placement, Jennie Jones died. Jack Smith was charged with murder and convicted. He is serving life in prison without parole.

Ethel Jones retired approximately 15 years ago after working 30 years in an automobile factory. Her husband, James, who worked at the same factory, died from a heart attack approximately 20 years ago. She has income from her husband's pension, her pension, and Social Security. In addition, she receives foster care payments and medical coverage for the children. She owns the home where she has lived for 45 years. She is very involved in her church and block club. She has one sister, Erma, who lives with her daughter, Patricia, four houses down the block. Erma and Patricia assist her with the children when needed.

Prior to the placement, Mrs. Jones had not seen Mark and Moses since their mother took them from her home two years earlier. She had never seen Jackie. Jennie Jones was angry with her for calling CPS and would not allow her any contact with the children. She had not had any contact with Jennie in over 15 months except to tell her that Danny was with her and he refused to return to Jennie's house. Jennie said "fine" and that ended the conversation.

The court ordered the agency to evaluate the children's fathers as possible caregivers. Dan Bobcat, the father of Danny, acknowledged paternity when Danny was born. He was killed in an automobile accident approximately nine years ago. His mother, Annie Bobcat, had maintained contact with her grandson until she died from pneumonia approximately two years ago. Mrs. Jones reports that there are no other family members on the Bobcat side. Annie Bobcat was an only child of parents who were only children. Both paternal great-grandparents are deceased. Dan is the child of a rape. The rapist was never identified. John Quick, the father of

Mark, has never seen Mark and expressed no interest in caring for or seeing him. Mack Phillips, the father of Moses, stated that he was unable to plan for Moses because he was unemployed and "living around," although he said he would like to "keep in touch with him." Jack Smith, the father of Jackie, is in jail, convicted of murder of Jennie Jones. He is serving a life sentence without parole. His mother, a drug addict and prostitute, abandoned him in the hospital at birth. None of her family wanted anything to do with him because he was biracial. His father was never identified. Jack Smith grew up in foster care.

The children have lived with their maternal grandmother for approximately 10 months. Here's what we know about the children and their experiences to date.

❖ **Danny** is 15 years old. There were no complications with the birth and he has developed within normative expectations. His mother became pregnant with him at 15 years of age. She and Danny's father had been friends since first grade and began dating in ninth grade. Jennie continued with high school during her pregnancy and graduated on time. Ethel Jones was the primary caregiver for Danny while his mother completed high school. In addition, she provided care for him while his mother attended the local college for three years. Annie Bobcat cared for Danny when Ethel Jones could not.

   Mrs. Jones reported that Danny was a quiet child from birth. He did not cry much as a baby, but she thought that might have been because she had him on a regular schedule for feeding, sleeping, and being changed from the "first day he came home." Jennie and Dan took on some of these responsibilities during the evenings and on weekends during high school and college. Jennie and Dan were planning to marry after Dan completed college. However, he was killed in an automobile accident on his way home for winter break. Jennie took Dan's death extremely hard. She began experimenting with drugs shortly after his funeral. Danny cried and would ask when his Daddy was coming back. Mrs. Jones and Mrs. Bobcat tried to console him "as best we could."

   Danny is in the tenth grade. He is an A/B student. In addition, he excels in basketball, football, and track. His teachers report that he is self-motivated, inquisitive, insightful, and helpful to students who are having difficulties with the subject matter or with behavioral expectations. He is well respected by all students.

   Danny had not seen nor spoken with his mother since he left her house about a year before her hospitalization. When he heard of his mother's hospitalization, he told his grandmother that he should have stayed with her to protect her. Mrs. Jones said she told him that he should not feel bad because it "was not his place to protect his mother. A mother is supposed to protect her children." He went to the hospital to see his mother every day until she died. He didn't want to talk about her when he got home so she "just let it be." A favorite teacher later told her that when Dan became very quiet and withdrawn, she asked him what was going on and he told her the story of his visits to the hospital and his feelings of guilt. She just let him talk and cry and tried to support him. When she asked if he wanted to talk with a social worker, he said "No. Nobody can help me with this. It will just take time." She reported that he seemed to change back to "his old ways" about a couple of months after his mother died.

❖ **Mark** is 8 years old. There were no complications with the birth and he developed within normative expectations for the first five years. His mother became pregnant with him while attending a party at college. She did not maintain any relationship with Mark's father. He initially denied that he was the father. After the paternity test concluded that he was the father, he paid child support; but never saw the child nor acknowledged him. He says that Mark was conceived while he was in a drunken state and he has no recollection of having sex with Jennie Jones. He is now a lawyer who is happily married with two children. He wants to relinquish his parental rights to Mark "as soon as possible and get this nightmare out of my life."

Mark met or exceeded all developmental milestones during his first five years. When he began kindergarten, he was already reading, knew his numbers, and could print his name, address, and telephone number. He was quite helpful with the other children who did not know the alphabet, numbers, or colors. His teacher described him as well-liked by everyone.

Mark began first grade in a different school because of his mother's move. During the two years that he lived with his mother, brother, and sister, his school performance and behavior changed significantly. He had difficulty paying attention in the classroom, frequently did not complete assignments, and often fought with other children. On many days, he seemed "in another world." The school social worker saw Mark once a week but little progress was made.

When Mark was placed with Mrs. Jones, there were about three months left in the school year. This placement required a change of schools for him. Mrs. Jones told the Principal and Mark's teacher the full story of Jennie's situation on the first day of school so they would understand his behavior and help him to cope. She also talked with both when Jennie died. Despite his poor performance, he was passed on to third grade. The current teacher reports that Mark is very bright, but has problems focusing sometimes. She thinks these problems are related to his mother's injury and death. She meets with Mark individually at least once a week to tutor him in his academic work. The school social worker meets with Mark on a weekly basis after school to "just talk." He seems to be getting more focused in classes. He is quite good at soccer and is picked early to play on teams at lunchtime. This has helped him develop some "friendships." He seems to smile more and volunteer answers more often. Four months into his third grade year, his academic performance is at grade level; but the teacher thinks it is below his intellectual capacity. She says, "Once he can resolve some of the emotional issues, he should skyrocket ahead of most of his peers."

His grandmother reported that she thinks that Jack Smith lived with her daughter and the children on and off for the entire two years. She doesn't know if Jennie or the children were abused by Jack before the most recent incident. Mark is slowly beginning to talk about the incident. He was home when Jack Smith beat his mother and actually saw Jack throw her against the kitchen counter. About four months ago, he told his grandmother that when the incident happened, he was supposed to be hiding under the bed with Moses and Jackie because that is what his mother told him to do when Jack "got crazy." He was scared because the fight was so loud that he crawled to the phone in the hall and called the police. He cried a little when he told the story and she comforted him but didn't press for more since he "went through so much with police, lawyers, and social workers during the trial." Mrs. Jones reported that she will continue to support Mark in telling the story "in his own time."

His grandmother describes him as a "very independent" child who seems a lot moodier than he was when he lived with her before. He still learns fast, likes to figure things out for himself, and is always watching adults. The first thing he does when he gets home from school is go to Moses and Jackie. While he had to have them in his sight until they went to bed when he first came to live with her, he now checks on them and plays with them for a little while and then goes to play or does his homework alone.

❖ **Moses** is 4 years old. His grandmother reports that his birth was normal and first-year developmental milestones were achieved as expected. Jennie had dated Moses' father for approximately two years before becoming pregnant. They talked of marriage, but he began using drugs and Jennie said "she didn't want to go there."

Ethel Jones was the primary caregiver for Moses until he left her home at 1 year. We don't know anything about Moses' development between ages 1 and 3.

During the first two weeks of placement with her, Mrs. Jones concluded that Moses may be "slow," meaning intellectually challenged. He talked very little and used only one or two words. He had occasional "accidents," meaning he urinated and defecated on himself, and "cries without making noise." He clung to Mark. The caseworker gave her a checklist to write down her observations for a month. The caseworker then scheduled an evaluation. It was determined that Moses was "intellectually delayed, most likely due to environmental deprivation." He was enrolled in an early intervention program to improve his intellectual and social skills. After a year in the program, he is functioning approximately six months below expectations in all domains.

❖ **Jackie** was seven months old on the day she moved to her grandmother's home. Mrs. Jones says she is a "fretful child." When initially placed, she cried a lot even after she has been fed or changed, was scared of loud noises, maybe slept for an hour or so, and then woke screaming. It took about "five months" for her to "settle down." She didn't crawl until she was about 12 months. She walked with support at 14 months. She started saying words at about 16 months. She doesn't talk much. Jackie was already enrolled in a program for children with disabilities when she was placed with Mrs. Jones. She continues in that program.

It is expected that she always will be intellectually challenged. At the present time, the severity of the long-term intellectual deficits cannot be determined. It is expected that she will have developmental delays in motor skills and be small for her age throughout her life.

Mrs. Jones stated that she never stopped loving her daughter or her grandchildren. Jennie was born after 10 years of trying and both she and her husband considered her a "gift from God." Jennie was a compliant child and an exceptional student, even after Danny's birth. She received a full scholarship to college and wanted to be a nurse. Mrs. Jones was disappointed that Jennie got pregnant in high school. However, she understood that "these things happen." She had known Dan Bobcat his entire life. He was a responsible young man who provided financial and emotional support for Danny and Jennie until his death. Mrs. Jones supported their decision to marry after each finished college.

After Dan Bobcat was killed, Jennie became very depressed, began to use drugs, and dropped out of college. She would be away from home for days at a time. Each time she returned home, Mrs. Jones would try to get her to go for treatment "for Danny." She stayed clean for about five years, then started using again about three years ago when she became involved with Jack Smith. Mrs. Jones feared for both Jennie and the children when Jennie became involved with Jack Smith. About two years ago, she told Jennie to "break it off with him or else get out of my house." She deeply regrets making that statement. Jennie left and they had no further contact. After Jennie was beaten, she prayed daily that Jennie would recover and "move back home." Once she understood that even if Jennie came out of the coma, she would not be able to function, she prayed that "God would take her and give me the strength to take care of my grandchildren." Two months after the children were placed with her, Jennie died.

Jack Smith is serving life in prison without parole. He refused to agree to voluntarily relinquish his parental rights. The caseworker filed a petition for termination of his parental rights on the basis that he is incarcerated for life and will have no opportunity for parole, thus no ability to assume care of Jackie. John Quick and Mack Phillips, the fathers of Mark and Moses had agreed to voluntarily relinquish their parental rights when the children were placed with Mrs. Jones; but the court refused because "these fathers should not be allowed to avoid child support payments." This petition also included a request to terminate the parental rights of John Quick and Mack Phillips on the basis that the children have been in the grandmother's care for over eight months and neither father has visited his child nor shown any interest in parenting his child. Further, it would be in Mark and Moses best interests to remain in placement with their grandmother and their siblings, Danny and Jennie. The petition also included termination of parental rights of Jennie Jones and Dan Bobcat, since both are deceased. The agency's permanency plan for the children is adoption. At the court hearing held six months after the children were placed, the court terminated parental rights of all parents and ordered the agency to proceed with adoption planning for all the children.

Danny, who has a legal right to express his permanency desires, says he wants to live with his grandmother and his brothers and sister. He doesn't want to be adopted by anyone. He is scared sometimes when he thinks that his grandmother might get sick and not be able to take care of them. He knows his aunt and cousin would "take them in if anything happens to Granny," but he isn't sure that they could handle Mark, Moses, and Jackie. He doesn't want them to split up ever again. He would like to attend the state university because they have better academics and he could easily get an athletic scholarship that would pay for everything according to his high school coach, but he's planning to attend college in town. By staying in town, he will continue to live with his grandmother and be available to help her take care of Mark, Moses, and Jackie. This college does not have full athletic scholarships. He's concerned about financing college without an athletic scholarship.

Mrs. Jones has agreed to "take care of the children until they are grown." She knows for certain that she does not want Jackie to have any contact with her father. Mark's father has never had any contact with him and she thinks it would be better for Mark if she could say "he's dead" because Mark doesn't understand why he doesn't want to see him. In the ten months that the children have been with her, Moses' father stopped by once about seven months ago. He was high on drugs at the time. She did not let him see Moses. She told him to come back when he wasn't "strung out." He hasn't been back. Mrs. Jones is not sure that she wants to legally adopt the children. She feels that adoption is unnecessary because they are already family. She said that she would not let her grandchildren be adopted by anyone else.

> The caseworker shared Danny's and Mrs. Jones' feelings about adoption with her supervisor. The supervisor told her that this plan was not acceptable and she should meet with Mrs. Jones to her to encourage her to adopt the children and, if she still says "No," to inform her that the caseworker must begin to look for another family to adopt Mark, Moses, and Jackie because they are so young.

INTRODUCTION

In Chapter 1, we presented the Pyramid of Child and Family Service. Kadushin (1970) takes a broad view of "child welfare" and submits that all of the services in the pyramid constitute child welfare services. However, the narrower view is that child welfare is limited to the range of services provided to prevent child abuse or neglect and services provided after child abuse or neglect has occurred to ensure child safety and permanency. In the narrower conceptualization, child welfare services typically include the following: child abuse and neglect prevention, child protection investigation, family preservation, intensive family preservation services, informal and formal relative/kinship placement services, nonrelated foster home placement services, residential care or residential treatment placement services, adoption services, postadoption services, independent living services, and legal guardianship services. These services are discussed in-depth in Chapters 7, 8, 9, and 10.

Child welfare practice requires a broad knowledge base and a broad skill base. The referenced chapters discuss specific knowledge and skill requirements for the particular service. In this chapter, we focus on the commonalities of casework process and child welfare tasks irrespective of the particular service provided. While no two child welfare cases are the same, every child welfare case presents the caseworker with the challenge of where to begin and what to do.

Nature and Use of Authority

So where does the caseworker begin? First, the provision of child welfare services involves governmental intrusion into the family to ensure the safety of children.

To make effective use of this governmental authority, all persons who provide child welfare services must understand its nature and source, and convey it clearly and objectively to the persons being investigated. The parents, in turn, must be able to accept to some degree the authority to improve their child care and family functioning. A major difficulty for child welfare is that it operates with conflicting values: On the one hand, we are protecting children, but we also believe in the integrity and autonomy of the family. This conflict sometimes leaves caseworkers caught in a double bind, and at best requires a careful weighing of factors before a decision is reached (Forsythe, 1987).

Sociolegal and Psychological Authority. Authority is a complex phenomenon. It is the power to influence or command thought, opinion, or behavior. The key concepts—*power, influence,* and *behavior*—appear in definitions of authority, sometimes used in such a way as to result in a sociolegal emphasis, and in other instances, to focus more on the psychological aspects of authority.

Sociolegal authority stems from the authority of an office or designated position; the possession of this formal power is a legitimate one, a matter of right attached to the person who occupies a specified and socially endorsed position in the institutional structure of a society. Psychological authority, the power to bring about change through influencing behavior, is subject to another person's perception of authority and readiness to be influenced, directed, or controlled.

To be effective in protecting children from neglect and abuse, the caseworker must rely on and use both the sociolegal and the psychological aspects of authority. The child welfare caseworker is given sociolegal authority by the law that authorizes the agency to act in ways that will protect children from neglect and abuse. A caseworker's position and role in a publicly mandated child protective agency embodies a legitimate and formal assignment of authority. This legal aspect of authority in child welfare is expressed most centrally in the caseworker's duty to investigate complaints about the care of children, and if substandard care or maltreatment is found, to continue to visit the home until the level of care is improved or until the children are cared for adequately in another setting. Legal authority, then, brings what DeSchweinitz and DeSchweinitz refer to as the power "to be there" (1964, p. 288).

Although legal authority is a necessary element in child welfare services, it is not sufficient by itself. The power of someone else to be there can lead to an oppressive sense of restriction on parents that may only exacerbate their feelings of inadequacy, resulting in resistance to change. Whether the agency representative who exercises the authority to be there can then motivate neglecting or abusing parents to face their need to change—the first step toward improved child care—will depend in large measure on the extent to which the psychological aspect of his or her authority (that is, knowledge and skill in ways of helping people) is developed and used.

Psychological authority does not imply some intangible quality that a child welfare caseworker may happen to possess; it can be learned through study and experience. It encompasses an understanding of the law and administrative policies that relate to child protection, as well as a community's standards in such areas as family life, health, and housing; the capacity to ascertain and evaluate relevant facts; a grasp of the nature of the child welfare caseworker's authority and an ability to use it constructively; sound judgment about the capacities of a particular parent; and an ability to develop, interpret, and implement a variety of treatment plans (DeSchweinitz & DeSchweinitz, 1964).

Use of Authority in Practice.   Authority need not be a necessary but negative part of child welfare services; it can be used as a factor to enable parents to fulfill their responsibility to their children more satisfactorily. The caseworker who presents authority skillfully can use it to create a climate of communication that may motivate resistant parents toward change.

Certain difficulties commonly occur, however, and the caseworker cannot expect parents to be motivated simply because he or she comes to them representing an agency with authority. This very action may tap a variety of negative feelings on the part of parents who probably already have had harsh and demeaning experiences with persons in an authoritative relationship. Parents who involuntarily become clients respond to the agency's offer of help in varying ways, such as superficial compliance, hostility, passive resistance, and belligerent defiance. Some parents are deeply distrustful of authority, while others may welcome it as a means of escaping their burdens and responsibilities.

Whatever the parents' initial response, the caseworker attempts to accept the basis for their feelings with empathy but proceeds to objectively identify the areas of child care that are of concern to the community and tells the parents the first concrete tasks they can perform in using the service; for example, taking a child to a medical clinic, getting him or her off to school each day, serving food regularly, following through on a search for employment, or applying for public assistance.

One of the principal tasks of the social worker is to develop alternatives or choices of action for the parents to consider, and to create opportunities for them to use their own initiative to improve their situation. The caseworker must convey that their freedom is restricted in only one direction—they are not free to neglect or abuse their children. Furthermore, the community endorses the right of the parents to receive help in improving their level of child care before declaring them neglectful, and the caseworker stands ready to try to help them without resorting to legal action; but the community will not cease to be concerned until the level of child care is improved, and the caseworker "will not disappear or be denied" (Moss, 1963, p. 388)

The caseworker cannot expect marked improvement immediately. Expectations, presented consistently, must be reasonable in light of the parents' problems, their capacities, and their resources. Encouragement and endorsement of minimal achievements toward improved family functioning are necessary.

In extending child welfare services, one of the most difficult matters facing the agency and its staff is the maintenance of proper balance in the use of authority. The families and their situations are difficult, often exasperating, and defeating. The children are vulnerable and dependent on others for improvement in their care. Citizens in the neighborhood and community are affronted by the family and expect the social agency to act and effect improvement in the situation promptly. Under such pressure, administrative actions that dangerously erode the right to direct one's own life may come to be regarded as inevitable. It is important that administrative and legal procedures be in place to safeguard the rights of the families, or these rights may be ignored as the caseworker and the community respond to the problems parents present to their children and to the community.

Engagement. Engagement is the process of establishing a helping relationship. The engagement process in child welfare is initially difficult and, as with any relationship, is forever changing. Imagine yourself in the parent's situation—a stranger comes to the door and says, "I am here to investigate a call to Child Protective Services reporting that you are neglecting or abusing your child." The initial process of engaging the parent and child under these circumstances requires the caseworker to:

- ❖ openly and respectfully acknowledge the hostility, anger, and defensiveness;
- ❖ explain exactly and specifically the duties and processes he or she is required to complete;
- ❖ explain the potential actions that could be taken;
- ❖ explain that the parent has a right not to volunteer any information and the consequences of making that choice;
- ❖ and be non-judgmental in the process. (Altman, 2005; Compton, Galaway, & Cournoyer, 2005; Schene, 2005; Mather & Lager, 2000)

Effective engaging behaviors by the caseworker contribute to the sharing of the power and authority inherent in child welfare. This sharing of power and authority is important in developing and supporting the parent's acceptance for the need for change and accepting responsibility to make those changes with the help of the caseworker and others. While engagement ultimately is a two-way process, initially, the work of engaging rests on the caseworker, who must create an environment of genuineness, honesty, and respectful acknowledgment of the client's nonengaging behaviors, irrespective of the point on the child welfare continuum when the caseworker assumes service responsibility for the family.

Informed Consent. Recently, issues of informed consent have arisen in relation to child welfare services. In the context of child welfare, informed consent should follow Ethical Standard 1.03 (d) of the National Association of Social Workers (NASW) Code of Ethics. It states:

> (d) In instances when clients are receiving services involuntarily, social workers should provide information about the nature and extent of services and about the extent of clients' right to refuse services. (*NASW, 2006*)

In addition, in child welfare services, the agency needs to consider not only the interest of the client but also the interests of the community, raising an ethical dilemma regarding limitations on confidentiality and its relationship to informed consent. Social workers need to be aware of the limits of confidentiality in child protective services practice and to inform their clients that information gathered and shared during the course of social service intervention may be used in court and may be shared with others. See Chapter 12 for a further discussion of ethical issues in child welfare practice.

Application of Concept of Authority to the Jones' Case. In the Jones' case, child protective services (CPS) commenced its first investigation based on a complaint from the grandmother, alleging that Ms. Jones was using drugs and living with a man that beat her frequently. CPS's investigation revealed no evidence of abuse or neglect of the children or violence toward Ms. Jones. Therefore, the case was closed. Clearly, CPS had a right to intervene because there was a potential risk or harm to the children because of the alleged substance abuse and domestic violence. However, because CPS found no evidence of substance abuse, domestic violence, or neglect or abuse of the children, there was no alternative but to close the case. That is, CPS "had no further right to be there."

In the second referral to CPS, the evidence was clear that Jackie had been born with cocaine in her system. The presence of cocaine in the system at birth is evidence of abuse under the state's child protection law. Thus, CPS investigated and found credible evidence that Jackie was born with cocaine in her system. Given the caseworker's assessment of Ms. Jones' desire to provide for her children and no previous or current abuse or neglect of them as corroborated by Ms. Moore and Mrs. Jones, she felt comfortable providing in-home services. In-home services were provided until Ms. Jones was severely beaten by Mr. Smith. Although there was no evidence that the children had been harmed by Ms. Jones or Mr. Smith, with Ms. Jones in a coma and unable to care for her children there was evidence that their environment posed a risk of harm to them; that is, domestic violence and the absence of an adult caregiver. Thus, CPS requested a court order to place the children with an alternate caregiver.

As time went on and more information was collected and assessed, the caseworker determined that none of the birth parents were available or desirable to provide for the long-term care of the children. With this evidence, she proceeded to request that the court terminate the parental rights of all birth parents based on the state's statute identifying conditions under which the court could terminate parental rights.

FUNDAMENTAL PRINCIPLES OF CHILD WELFARE PRACTICE

The fundamental policy provisions and principles of the United States' child welfare system were established in the Child Abuse Prevention and Treatment Act of 1974 (CAPTA) and the Adoption Assistance and Child Welfare Act of 1980 (AACWA), as amended by the Adoption and Safe

Families Act of 1997 (ASFA) and the rules promulgated to implement and monitor the provisions of these statutes. In Chapter 1 we discussed the interrelationship of federal and state policies. Suffice it to mention again here that the states typically adopt the federal policy provisions in their individual statutes because they must do so if they choose to access federal funding for the provision of child welfare services. Thus, while each state's laws and policies may be different, they are developed within the federal policy framework because states want to access the federal funds.

Child Safety, Well-Being, and Permanency

While there are several provisions of these statutes that are specific to implementation of specific services, the fundamental principles are

- ❖ child safety is paramount;
- ❖ services are to be child focused and family centered;
- ❖ services should be provided within the child's home if the child can safely remain in the home;
- ❖ services should be provided to enhance the child's well-being and improve the ability of the child's parent(s) to successfully meet the needs of the child;
- ❖ services should be culturally sensitive and culturally responsive; and
- ❖ services should be time limited and focused on safety, well-being, and permanency for the child.

Each of these provisions is discussed and applied specifically in Chapters 6 to 10. The importance of identifying these principles here is to emphasize the interrelationship between policy and practice in child welfare. Policies guide practice. For example, knowing that child safety is paramount helps the caseworker focus on these questions:

- ❖ Is the child safe in this home?
- ❖ If not, are there any services that can be provided that will ensure his or her safety in the home?
- ❖ If not, what alternative placement will ensure the child's safety?

Answering these questions guides the caseworker in selecting the appropriate initial service array for the child and family. At each contact, given that safety is paramount, these three questions are asked along with additional questions related to service planning for well-being and toward permanency. For example, a caseworker who provides foster care services to a child who has been in foster care for over a year additionally asks:

- ❖ What services have been provided to alleviate the conditions that resulted in the child's removal?
- ❖ What have been the results?
- ❖ What precludes the child safely returning to the parent's home now?
- ❖ Is it reasonable to expect that the child can safely return home within the next six months?
- ❖ Should an alternative permanency plan be implemented? If so what?

Child-Focused, Family Centered Practice

What do we mean by "child-focused, family centered practice"? As discussed in Chapters 1 and 2, the history of child welfare is rooted in rescuing children from harmful environments and placing them in stable, loving families. That "rescue" approach gave way to "family preservation" in the 1970s and 1980s. Some commentators and child advocates argued that the family preservation approach went too far and did not consider the child's interests, safety, and well-being sufficiently. Thus, in the mid-1990s the ASFA clarified that child welfare is first and foremost concerned with the safety and well-being of the child. Therefore, the child is the focus. However, children are not independent beings who are capable of caring for themselves. They primarily depend on their parents and others in their families to provide them with basic necessities, nurturance, and developmental support. Therefore, to achieve safety, well-being, and permanency for children, our practice is centered on working with individuals in those families and the family as a whole—hence, family centered.

THE CASEWORK PROCESS

All child welfare practice involves the following processes:

- ❖ intake;
- ❖ investigation;
- ❖ assessment;
- ❖ identifying interventions designed to achieve desired outcomes;
- ❖ developing the case plan;
- ❖ implementing the case plan;
- ❖ evaluating and modifying interventions and the case plan, as necessary, to reach a desired outcome/goal; and
- ❖ goal-attainment, evaluation, and case closure.

Casework is the "how-to" of child welfare practice, That is, casework is the primary means used by child welfare caseworkers to gather information, develop and modify service plans, and provide interventions. Both group work and community organization practices have been used and continue to be expanded in the child welfare systems, but casework has been and continues to be the dominant methodology in the field. Before using group work or community organization practice methods with a specific client, it is necessary to determine the situation and identify interventions that are acceptable to the client that will move the client toward accomplishing his or her desired goal and that of the community (i.e., child safety and child well-being). To accomplish this entails using casework processes or methods, that is, focusing on understanding the individual in the context of his or her environment. Composites and evaluations of the results of group work and community organization interventions with these individual clients provides evidence-based group work and community organization approaches that are effective in meeting the needs of the community of adults and children who face child abuse and neglect issues.

What Is Casework?

Perlman (1957) said, "The most difficult knowledge to transfer from teacher to learner is that of how to do." With that in mind, we will discuss the basic structure of casework, as developed by Richmond (1922) and modified by Perlman (1957), Hollis (1964), Towle, and others. You will forever be engaged in refining your casework knowledge and skills! At this point, we hope to provide the basic framework for beginning your quest in mastering casework knowledge and skills, to show how casework remains most important in the child welfare system, and to show how it survives the "child welfare fads of the day." It is important to revisit the historical development of casework practice to understand that it, like most social work, is an iterative process that is refined out of the actual "doing." The development of casework process is a good model for what child welfare practice entails—continuous information gathering, assessment, evaluation, and modification of interventions based on the new information. It is a process, not a product!

Problem-Solving. Casework practice is rooted in problem-solving. Problem-solving is a goal-directed process that involves:

❖ obtaining information about the situation that brings the person to your attention,
❖ assessing that information,
❖ reaching a conclusion on the nature of the problem,
❖ determining what actions can be taken to alleviate the problem,
❖ developing a plan to achieve the desired goals,
❖ implementing an intervention or series of interventions designed to correct the problem,
❖ assessing the effectiveness of those interventions, and
❖ modifying the plan as necessary, based on the effectiveness assessment. (Richmond, 1922; Perlman, 1957; Hollis, 1964; Perlman, 1969; Compton, Galaway & Cournoyer, 2005)

Richmond's (1922) conceptualization of casework practice has been modified over the years as we have learned more about human beings and interaction and as social work practice has moved away from a psychoanalytical orientation. Early criticism of Richmond's casework model was that it was "problem-centered" not "people-centered." In modifying her own thinking about casework, Richman wrote "I place the study of process first. . . . The process common to all case treatment deserves our special attention" (Richmond, 1922).

Towle clarified this conceptualization:

> Modern casework strives to be client centred rather than procedure centred. . . . Thus in casework today we consider that the outcome of our activity in every instance is contingent on three factors—the client's motivation, that is, his needs and wants; his capacity, physical, mental, emotional and environmental; and the opportunity for help afforded him. We face the fact that we cannot motivate him, or provide capacity, but we can provide an opportunity which either uses and strengthens motivation or breaks it down, one which also either uses and reinforces capacity or ignores or undermines it. Social casework therefore is client centred in the sense of according the individual the right to self-determination within social limits. (*Perlman, 1969 p. 157*)

Towle goes on to say:

> Social work at all operating levels is continuously concerned with defining and solving problems. In working with a client in casework there is always a problem in order that it may be

solved and an early determination reached as to whether or not it lends itself to solution. The nature of the problem is not the decisive factor—but instead the nature of the person and the meaning of the problem to him. The meaning of the problem to him throws light on his nature. *Our aim continuously is that of engaging the client's participation in both defining and solving problems.* (Perlman, 1969, p. 158, Emphasis added)

Perlman conceptualized the casework event as "A *person* with a *problem* comes to a *place* where a *professional representative* helps him by a given *process*" (Perlman, 1957, p.4). Further, she clarified the intended purposes of the casework process and its inherent challenges.

Perhaps the chief complexity of casework lies in the fact that its concern is always twofold: to promote the solution of the client's problems in social living and by this process to promote his capacity for growth. One eye of the caseworker must be kept on the object and the other on the subject, and it is small wonder that in this task of double perception the caseworker's vision at moments becomes blurred or strained. Yet we must hold to what we know to be true—that the conditions for the human being's social development are the use of his own powers in coping with the people and situations he encounters and the presence of pliant opportunity in his social environment. Thus, social casework attempts simultaneously to provide these two kinds of conditions: the resources and influences by which its client's social needs may be met and the modes which promote its client's personal and social effectiveness. (p. 84)

At first glance, the early conceptualizations of casework as problem and problem-solving focused and the current child welfare system's stressing "strengths-based" approaches may appear to be in conflict. The strengths-based approaches are rooted in resilience theories; that is, most individuals, despite the adversities in which they find themselves, have inner resources that can be harnessed to help them overcome adversity. The strengths-based approaches acknowledge that the person has a problem; that is, something with which they or society are not finding acceptable. Careful examination of the problem-solving casework model conceptualized by Richmond (1922), Towle (1935), and Perlman (1969), shows that the client's strengths are identified as essential in solving the problem, or the condition that led the client to seek professional help. Clearly, the transition from early casework to current casework in child welfare is a transition from language that is rooted in client pathology to language that is rooted in client strengths. *"A strengths perspective informs the assessment, underpins the strategies, and communicates to families a sense of respect and hopefulness that is crucial for successful family engagement and planning"* (Pennell and Anderson, 2005, p. 225). We will explore in more depth strengths-based approaches in Chapters 7 to 11.

Further analysis of these early conceptualizations finds the roots of four other concepts critical to the casework process in child welfare today: ecological assessment; client self-determination; culturally sensitive and culturally responsive practice; and task-centered, solution-focused casework practice.

Ecological Assessment. Ecological assessment is based in the person-in-environment framework of social work practice. In this framework, the caseworker and the client must understand the interconnectedness of the client and his or her environment to effectively assess the problem, design a solution, and ensure goal achievement and sustainability. Two tools were pioneered in child welfare in the 1970s by Ann Hartman to help gather information about families in their environments—the genogram and the ecomap—to help the caseworker make a comprehensive ecological assessment and engage the family and its natural network in solving the situation.

The ecomap, a drawing of the family and its interactions with other individuals and organizations outside the family, is an effective tool in helping the child welfare worker and the family capture, appreciate, and organize the complexities of the family's life and identify other people, agencies, and organizations that might help them.

Another useful tool in ecological assessment is the genogram. A genogram is like a family tree. In the context of child welfare, it is useful in identifying and locating potential relatives for support and placement, uncovering genetic illnesses or patterns of health, and providing a sense of family connectedness for the child (e.g., "these are my people"). In addition to these basic purposes, the development of a genogram with the client can help to identify unresolved emotional issues, patterns of behavior within the family, occupations, places of birth and death, family expectations, communication structures, and the like. As you complete your assessment of the family and its individual members, this data helps you to understand and better serve them. It is important to include both the paternal and maternal family lines. The reader should consult Hartman and Laird's (1983) *Family-Centered Social Work Practice* or Compton, Galaway, and Cournoyer's (2005) *Social Work Processes* for an explanation of how to complete the ecomap and the genogram.

Completing these tools is not the assessment. Rather, utilizing these tools provides a good way to organize basic information about the family that will be needed in the assessment. The assessment occurs after you have collected information from multiple perspectives. Assessment is the process of determining what you know, how you know it, and what difference this knowledge makes to addressing the client's situation. Assessment answers the "So what?" question. We will discuss assessment in more detail later in this chapter, as well as in Chapters 6 to 11.

Client Self-Determination Client self-determination is a basic social work value. Clients are provided the opportunity to make informed decisions about how they choose to handle a specific situation or what will happen to them. Ethical Standard 1.02 of the NASW Code of Ethics states:

> Social workers respect and promote the right of clients to self-determination and assist clients in their efforts to identify and clarify their goals. Social workers may limit clients' right to self-determination when, in the social workers' professional judgment, clients' actions or potential actions pose a serious, foreseeable, and imminent risk to themselves or others. (*NASW, 2006*)

In the child welfare system, client self-determination is subject to the broader societal value of child protection. Thus, a parent who neglects or abuses his or her child has some aspects of his or her self-determination limited by agency or court involvement and requirements. However, the child welfare system involvement does not eliminate client self-determination; rather, it constrains it only in the area of child safety. For Jennie Jones, this meant that once CPS determined that her children were at risk because Jackie was born with illegal drugs in her system, and she was ordered to participate in a drug treatment program and demonstrate that she was not continuing to use drugs, she would be provided with a choice of providers, locations, and times for meeting the requirement. She knew what was expected of her, she was given provider choices, and then it was up to her to decide to participate.

Culturally Sensitive, Culturally Competent Practice.

> *"Culture" refers to integrated patterns of human behavior that include the language, thoughts, communications, actions, customs, beliefs, values, and institutions of racial, ethnic, religious or social groups. — National Standards for Culturally and Linguistically Appropriate Services in Health Care: Final Report 2001, U.S. Department of Health and Human Services, Office of Minority Health; March 2001.*

Cultural competence has been defined as "a set of congruent behaviors, attitudes, policies, and structures which come together in a system, agency, or among professionals and enables that system, agency, or those professionals to work effectively in the context of cultural differences" (Cross, 1988, p. 1). This definition emphasizes that cultural competency needs to be ingrained into the administrative structure and procedures of an organization, and also needs to be a part of each social worker's personal set of beliefs and skills. The definition makes the point that cultural competency is not simply "the right thing to do," but is essential to effective provision of services.

The National Association of Social Workers formulated Standards for Cultural Competence in Social Work Practice in 2001 with the intent of helping individuals and agencies to develop high levels of cultural competence so that they can respond more appropriately to diverse clients and communities. The Standards identify guidelines for cultural competence in aspects of professional social work practice and administration, including social work values, ethics, self-awareness, professional knowledge base, social work skills, and service delivery. Five of the ten Standards are reproduced below.

1. *Ethics and Values.* Social workers shall function in accordance with the values, ethics, and standards of the profession, recognizing how personal and professional values may conflict with or accommodate the needs of diverse clients.
2. *Self-Awareness.* Social workers shall develop an understanding of their own personal and cultural values and beliefs as a first step in appreciating the importance of multicultural identities in the lives of people.
3. *Cross-Cultural Knowledge.* Social workers shall have and continue to develop specialized knowledge and understanding about the history, traditions, values, family systems, and artistic expressions of major client groups served.
4. *Cross-Cultural Skills.* Social workers shall use appropriate methodological approaches, skills, and techniques that reflect the workers' understanding of the role of culture in the helping process.
5. *Service Delivery.* Social workers shall be knowledgeable about and skillful in the use of services available in the community and broader society and be able to make appropriate referrals for their diverse clients. (NASW, 2001)

Specific discussions and examples of cultural competency in child and family welfare practice are infused in other chapters—kinship care and family group conferencing (Chapter 8); same race and interethnic adoption (Chapter 10); differential effects of major public programs such as income security, child protective services, foster care, and juvenile justice on children and families of different ethnic groups (Chapters 5, 7, 8, 9, and 11).

Improving cultural and linguistic competence to improve the delivery of child welfare services within the context of the broader cultural value and expectation of child safety continues to be a challenge. Numerous studies have shown associations between poverty and minority status and casework decisions in child welfare resulting in an overrepresentation of poor and minority children in the child welfare systems. Perceived discrimination, mistrust, and ineffective communication have long been identified as barriers to effective and timely case resolution (U.S. Department of Health and Human Services, 2006; Hill 2006; Rockymore, 2006; McRoy, 2005; Derezotes, Poertner, & Testa, 2004; U.S. Department of Health and Human Services, 2001; Chibnall, Dutch, Jones-Harden, & Brown, 2003; Walczyn, Hislop, & George, 2000; Roberts, 2002; Hill, 1972).

Task-Centered, Solution-Focused Casework Practice. Task-centered, solution-focused casework practice "is a technology for alleviating specific target problems perceived by clients, that is, particular problems clients recognize, understand, acknowledge, and want to attend to" (Epstein, 1992, p. 115). This conceptualization is important in child welfare services because the child welfare system is increasingly focused on time-limited interventions designed to achieve solutions to the problems that brought the family to the child welfare system. It encourages immediate, focused engagement of the client on resolving the problems as identified by the client and the caseworker with each assuming responsibility for problem resolution in a brief period. The task-centered, solution-focused model is ideal within this structure. It has four basic steps.

Step 1   Identify problems to be addressed.
Step 2   Prioritize the problems, set goals, assign caseworker and client tasks, set a timeframe in which tasks will be completed, and develop a written agreement/contract between the caseworker and client.
Step 3   Implement contract/agreement negotiated in Step 2.
Step 4   Attain goals, evaluate, and terminate services. (Compton, Galaway, & Cournoyer, 2005; Miller, Hubble, and Duncan, 1996; Epstein, 1992)

The value and importance of casework services in child welfare has been documented recently in the results of the Child and Family Services Reviews (CFSR) of the child welfare systems conducted by the Children's Bureau in all states and Puerto Rico. In summary, the reviews documented that when child welfare agencies focused on the safety and well-being of the child, case planning, and goal achievement during casework visits with the child, parents, and the child's caregivers, they were better able to determine risk to children, identify services needed, engage children and parents in planning for themselves, and determine the need for pursuing a permanency option other than reunification earlier in the case (U.S. Department of Health and Human Services, Children's Bureau, 2005). A report of the National Conference of State Legislatures, relying in large part on the data discovered during the CFSRs, states:

> Every state has a public agency that is charged with the delivery of services in response to reports of child abuse and neglect. These child welfare agencies also play a role in prevention and early intervention, and they are required to ensure a child's safety when the child is abused or neglected or when a caregiver is unable or unwilling to protect his or her child. . . . Child welfare agencies conduct these activities by assigning caseworkers to families that come to the attention of the child welfare system. Caseworkers work closely with families, conducting regular visits with intact families and with children in foster care and facilitating visitation between family members when children are placed outside the home. . . . These

casework visits are a critical component of child welfare system procedures for ensuring the safety of children and the well-being of families. . . . Those findings suggest a need for a more comprehensive approach to enhancing caseworker visits. (*2006, pp. 3–4*)

Because of these findings, the Child and Family Services Improvement Act of 2006 recognized the importance of caseworkers. That Act:

❖ provides funding to states for "providing training, professional development, and support to ensure a well-qualified child welfare workforce." (P.L. 109-288, Section 6 (a))

❖ amends the State Plan Requirement of the Social Security Act that requires all states to provide no later than October 1, 2007, a description of the state's standards for "the content and frequency of caseworker visits for children in foster care." It is expected that children will be visited no less than once a month and that the "caseworker visits are well-planned and focused on issues pertinent to case planning and service delivery to ensure the safety, permanency, and well-being of the children." (P.L. 109-288, Section 7 (a))

❖ expects states to achieve a 90 percent monthly caseworker visitation level by 2011.

Thus, for the foreseeable future, casework will remain the methodology of choice for serving children and families in the child welfare system.

Group work approaches have been used in child welfare services primarily for education and support group services to parents and children. Recently, the use of team decision-making models, using basic group work processes, have been incorporated into the child welfare services to assist the caseworker in information gathering, assessment, service planning, and service plan implementation (Pennell & Anderson, 2005; Annie E. Casey Foundation, 2006; U.S. Department of Human Services, Children's Bureau, 2005; McGowan, 2005; Kemp et al., 2005; Chahine & Higgins, 2005).

Macro-practice approaches are also being used to promote community engagement in helping individual families address child abuse and neglect as well as changing communities, in general, so that they are more responsive to the well-being of all its members (Annie E. Casey Foundation, 2006; U.S. Department of Human Services, Children's Bureau, 2005; Kretzmann & McKnight, 1993).

BASIC TASKS IN CHILD WELFARE PRACTICE

Having a basic understanding of casework, let's apply it to child welfare practice. Five basic tasks common to all child welfare practice are information gathering, assessment, case documentation, service planning and service delivery, and crisis intervention and stabilization.

Child welfare intervention begins with someone, sometimes even the parent, contacting the state's child welfare agency or the police and reporting that in their opinion a particular child has been or is at risk of abuse or neglect. With this referral, the caseworker begins to collect information. The primary tasks of intake are to gather enough information to determine if there are sufficient facts to meet the agency's services criteria and to determine what must be done immediately to ensure the child's safety. These determinations can be made by seeking information during your interviews and document reviews that will answer questions such as those in Box 4.1.

Box 4.1

Basic Child Welfare Questions at Intake

1. What specifically happened to the child, when did it happen, and who caused it to happen?
2. What were the parents' actions in relation to the incident?
3. What makes this incident neglect/abuse or not neglect/abuse?
4. If this incident is not neglect/abuse, are there any other actions I should take before closing the case?
5. If this incident is neglect/abuse, what must happen for the child to be safe in the parents' home?
6. What resources are available to help maintain the child safely in the parents' home?
7. If the child must be removed from the home, what is the exact reason?
8. If the child must be removed from the home, is there a relative or family friend with whom the child can be safely placed?
9. What are the child's specific needs in an out-of-home placement?
10. What agencies can provide the services necessary to meet the mutual and individual needs of parents and each child?

Information Gathering

Information is gathered through interviews with the child, parents, persons involved with the child and/or family—professionals and nonprofessionals—and review of written documents pertaining to the child and/or family. Child welfare and juvenile justice investigations need to be conducted in ways that preserve the information collected or "the evidence" and limit the attack on the caseworker's methods in collecting that information or evidence.

Because of the nature of child welfare services, nonvoluntary and government intrusive, it is advisable to approach the situation from the beginning, using a forensic interviewing and case documentation process, even though the vast majority of situations referred for child abuse and neglect are never processed through the court system (U.S. Department of Health and Human Services, 2006).

It is suggested that all investigations follow a forensic interviewing and documentation approach because this approach provides for an unbiased, multiperspective reporting of the incident from which the caseworker can make an informed conclusion as to the truthfulness of the neglect or abuse allegations and to determine the most appropriate intervention.

The interview process for court purposes is different from the interview for treatment purposes. In essence, the goal of interviews for court purposes, that is, forensic interviews, is to obtain descriptions of the events that occurred from people who experienced them from their experiential perspective as victim, perpetrator, observer, and professional interventionist. In these interviews, the caseworker is attempting to determine what happened, when it happened, how it happened, and who was involved in the act (victim, perpetrator, and protectors/interveners).

Having gathered this information from a variety of perspectives, the caseworker then identifies the variances in the accounts and seeks to resolve those variances through additional interviews and review of written materials.

The fundamental elements of forensic interviewing are

❖ creating a nonthreatening environment by stating clearly your reason for wanting to talk with him or her, how the information that he or she provides will be used, and ensuring that his or her comfort needs are met.
❖ interviewing children outside the presence of parents or caretakers to the extent that it can be done without further trauma to the child.
❖ determining the developmental and language and linguistic levels of all persons interviewed.
❖ using simple, open-ended questions that encourage the person being interviewed to describe in his or her own words the who, what, when, how, and where of the incident(s) under review.
❖ asking clarifying questions for the purpose of ensuring that you understand what the interviewee has said or described, not to offer your assessment, judgment, or conclusion of what he or she said.

Interviews and document reviews occur throughout the case's history. An example of an abbreviated first interview with Jennie Jones is in Box 4.2. This abbreviated interview addresses the substance of the report. The caseworker should also gather demographic information on the parents and all children, identify natural supporters and obtain their addresses and telephone numbers, explain the child protective services process, and make an initial determination of immediate actions necessary to ensure the child's safety.

After this interview, Ms. Brown scheduled meetings with Janice Moore and Ethel Jones. Jack Smith refused to be interviewed. During these visits, using forensic interviewing techniques, she discussed the reason for protective services involvement, asked about each person's relationship with Ms. Jones, and talked with Mark and Moses about the situation in their mother's home. She talked with Danny about his reasons for leaving his mother's home and living with his grandmother. In these interviews, Mark confirmed that his mother and Jack would fight, "but not as much as they use to." He said they fought about once or twice a month. He said that Jack never hit them, but yelled a lot. He also said that Jack and his mother would "smoke" a pipe together a couple of times a week. Sometimes his mother didn't want to, but Jack made her. Mark said that he would like to stay with his Mom, but wanted Jack to leave. He wasn't really scared of Jack but thought they would see his grandmother if Jack wasn't around. He missed his grandmother and Danny. Moses could not be engaged in a verbal discussion. She did not observe any marks or bruises on either Mark or Moses.

Danny said he could not stay with his mother and watch Jack beat on her. He thought his mother wanted to be with Jack more than she wanted to have him with her. He was okay with that. He hasn't had any contact with her since he left home. He was waiting for her to make the first move. He worried about his brothers, but knew his Mom would not hurt them; however, he wasn't sure about Jack. His grandmother told him that "eventually she will get herself together."

Mrs. Jones said she knew something like this would happen. This was why she told Jennie that she could not come back to her home until she left Jack Smith and committed to stop using drugs. She said she would be willing to take Mark, Moses, and Jackie if the agency decided that they needed to be taken from Jennie.

She understood why Jennie did not want to call her. While she wanted to go to the hospital to see Jennie and the new baby, she did not think it would be useful because Jennie was quite

Box 4.2

Initial Interview with Jennie Jones

In the Jones' case, the agency received a report of suspected child abuse and neglect from the Women's Hospital stating that Jennie Jones had given birth to Jackie Jones. Jackie was born with cocaine in her system. Prior to the interview with the mother, the caseworker reviewed the medical report and interviewed the medical personnel to confirm that the results of the test were accurate and to identify the specific reasons to explain how a child could be born with cocaine in her blood. With this knowledge, the caseworker then interviewed the mother.

Caseworker:	Hello, Ms. Jones. I am Jane Brown. I am from the Children's Protective Services. We received a report from the hospital that your daughter, Jackie, was born with cocaine in her blood. It is my responsibility to investigate this report and determine what action, if any, we must take to ensure that Jackie is safe. I have talked with the doctors and reviewed the medical reports. Please tell me how this happened.
Ms. Jones:	I don't know.
Ms. Brown:	Did you use cocaine at any time during the pregnancy?
Ms. Jones:	Yes. (reluctantly)
Ms. Brown:	When was the last time you used cocaine?
Ms. Jones:	I think it was the day before Jackie was born.
Ms Brown:	In our state, if a child is born with drugs in the blood, it is automatically opened as a children's protective services case.
Ms. Jones:	You aren't going to take my kids away from me are you?
Ms. Brown:	We don't always have to remove children from the parent. We must determine what you are willing to do to make sure Jackie is not harmed further. You said "children." How many children do you have?
Ms. Jones:	I have three others besides Jackie. Two live with me and one lives with my mother.
Ms. Brown:	What are the children's names and ages?
Ms. Jones:	Danny is 14; Mark is 7; and Moses is 3.
Ms. Brown:	Why is Danny living with your mother?
Ms. Jones:	He didn't like living with me and Jackie's father.
Ms. Brown:	What specifically did he say he didn't like?
Ms. Jones:	Sometimes, Jack gets drunk or high and we get into fights.
Ms. Brown:	Oh. What did Danny do when you "got into fights"?
Ms. Jones:	He would jump on Jack and try to get him away from me.
Ms. Brown:	Did Jack ever hit Danny?
Ms. Jones:	Once.
Ms. Brown:	Has Jack ever hit Mark or Moses?
Ms. Jones:	No.
Ms. Brown:	How often do you and Jack fight?
Ms. Jones:	We don't that much anymore. Maybe once a month.
Ms. Brown:	Does he use cocaine also?
Ms. Jones:	Yes.
Ms. Brown:	Given this discussion, I am concerned about the safety of Jackie, Mark, and Moses. I need to talk with Mark and his teacher. Also, I must talk with Danny, your mother, and Jackie's father. Who's taking care of Mark and Moses while you are in the hospital?
Ms. Jones:	Mark and Moses are staying with a friend of mine, Janice Moore. She lives at 4800 Young Street. Please don't take my kids. I will do anything I have to do to keep them with me. My Mom lives at 156 Brush.

Box 4.2 (Continued)

	Anything. . . . (with tears)
Ms. Brown:	I am pleased to hear you say that. Why isn't your mother taking care of Mark and Moses now?
Ms. Jones:	She and I had a falling out over my drug use and moving in with Jackie's father. We haven't talked in a while.
Ms. Brown:	I see. Well, I can't say what I will recommend until after I talk with everyone and talk with you again. I will try to contact everyone today and come back to see you tomorrow. Then we can talk further about what needs to be done. You must understand that at this point the primary focus will be on making sure all the children are safe. You, your family, and your friends will be actively involved in helping me decide what needs to be done to accomplish that. Do you think you could call Ms. Moore and your mother and let them know that I will be calling them to schedule a meeting to talk with them about this?
Ms. Jones:	I don't think I can call my Mom. She will be so disappointed with me. I suppose I will have to talk with her sometime, but I just can't do it now. I will call Janice and tell her you will be calling.
Ms. Brown:	Okay. I understand. I will call later to arrange a time to come tomorrow.

"strong willed." Jennie would have to make the first move to reconciliation for it to work. She was not personally aware how the children were being treated in the home. Occasionally, Janice Moore would call her to let her know how Jennie and the children were doing and to find out about Danny. She was sure that Janice was sharing this information with Jennie. She was sure that Jennie would not hurt any of the children; but she wasn't sure about Jack. She knew him to be a violent person and he had hit Danny once. She said Danny told her that his mother told Jack at that time, "Don't you ever hit any of my children again."

Janice Moore has been Jennie's friend since high school. She frequently takes care of Mark and Moses. She has had many conversations with Jennie about Jack's abuse and told her she needed to leave him before something bad happens. She thinks Jennie would stop using drugs if Jack was not around "pushing her to use them." She says Mrs. Jones truly loves Jennie and the grandchildren. She thinks that having no contact with Jennie hurts her more than she admits. Janice thinks that it would be a problem if the children were placed with Mrs. Jones because Jennie wants to save face and show her mother that she can change Jack. She confirmed that Jennie and Mark told her that the fighting between Jack and Jennie is less frequent now and the noticeable bruises seem less frequent also, maybe once a month. She will do anything she can to help Jennie keep her children. She is sure that Jennie will do whatever is necessary to keep her children, including having Jack move out. However, knowing Jack, she is not convinced that he will stay away.

Assessment

Assessment is the process of taking the information you have gathered from multiple sources, evaluating it, and coming to a conclusion about the actions you and the parent(s), individually and collectively, need to take to ensure the child's safety and well-being. Specifically, you need to reach conclusions to these questions based on the information you have gathered.

1. What happened to the child?
2. How did it happen?

3. Who made it happen or did not take action to prevent it from happening when it was reasonable to do so?
4. Who is available to help the family?
5. What do I need to do to ensure that the child is safe?

It is important to remember that assessment is a process. You will gather additional information as the services unfold and you will use this information to modify the initial assessment. (Cohen, Hornsby, & Priester, 2005; Schene, 2005; Dubowitz and DePanfilis, 2000; Hartman & Laird, 1983).

The Jones Referral Assessment. After all interviews and written reports are gathered and reviewed in the Jones case, the caseworker determined that Jackie was born with cocaine in her blood. The only means by which this could occur was perinatal transmission from the mother. Under state law, court intervention was required. Furthermore, she determined that removal of the children was not necessary to ensure their safety because there had been no previous abuse or neglect of the children, she did not observe any current or unexplained healed bruises on Mark or Moses, the mother committed to "doing whatever was necessary" to keep the children safely at home, including having Jack Smith ordered out of the home, and she had the support of her friend Janice Moore in caring for the children. The caseworker filed the required petition. The court found that Jackie had been born with cocaine in her blood and made Mark, Moses, and Jackie court wards in their mother's home. The court ordered the mother to submit weekly drug screening results to the agency, participate in an appropriate substance abuse treatment program, and participate in a domestic violence education program. Further, it found Jack Smith to be the legal father of Jackie, ordered him out of the home, and ordered him to submit weekly drug screening results to the agency, participate in an appropriate substance abuse treatment program, and participate in a domestic violence education program. He was given weekly one-hour visitation with Jackie at the agency.

In providing ongoing services to the family after the court had adjudicated the case and entered specific dispositional orders, the caseworker conducted similar fact-finding interviews and received written documentation to determine the mother's compliance with the orders.

If the orders had not been complied with, the caseworker sought to determine the specific reasons for noncompliance, using the fact-finding processes of forensic interviews with all involved parties. Jennie Jones met all expectations of the service plan. After one month, Jack Smith stopped submitting drug test results and did not attend the substance abuse treatment program nor the domestic violence program. He continued to visit Jackie at the agency regularly for about eight weeks and then stopped coming for visits. The caseworker could not locate him. These facts were then used to adjust the service plan to ensure the children's safety and well-being and were reported to the court for its consideration in modifying the current orders. The reader should consult the For Additional Study section for references that will provide more specifics on how to conduct forensic interviews with adults and children and how to complete assessments in child welfare.

Service Planning and Service Delivery

All child welfare services require the development of a case services plan and delivery of services identified in that plan. This case services plan is the formal summary of the information gathered, the assessment of that information, and the specific actions or what will be done based on that assessment. Service plans are like roadmaps guiding you to the final place on your journey. Effective service planning requires

❖ completing child safety assessments at each contact;

❖ clarifying the nature and severity of the neglect or abuse;

❖ identifying the underlying behaviors and conditions of the neglect or abuse;

❖ specifying the changes required to ensure the child's safety and well-being;

❖ identifying parental strengths, challenges, and needs;

❖ developing approaches to achieve desired changes given parent's strengths, challenges, and needs in partnership with the parent(s);

❖ identifying child's strengths, challenges, and needs;

❖ developing approaches to achieve desired changes given the child's strengths, challenges, and needs in partnership with the child as age appropriate;

❖ identifying the people in the parent's and child's natural support networks and communities that can be engaged in helping them and for you to ensure that the child and family are able to achieve safety and permanency;

❖ engaging the parent and the child in defining and accomplishing the tasks necessary to achieve the child's safety, well-being, and permanency; and

❖ continuously assessing and modifying approaches as the plan is implemented, change occurs, and new information is known.

While we discuss service planning with parents and service planning with children separately in the following sections, actual child welfare service planning requires concurrent assessments and interventions with the parent, child, other caregivers, natural supporters, and service providers. In addition, subsequent chapters will address specific parental or child behaviors or conditions common in child welfare practice and the promising or evidence-based interventions to address them.

Service Planning with Parents. Parental interventions require focused child welfare practice because it is the parental condition or behavior that led to or contributed to the child welfare system involvement. The ultimate first goal is that the child will be safe in the parent's care. If that goal is not possible, then the goal is to secure an alternative permanent family for the child. Achieving either goal requires focused attention on changing the parental conditions or behaviors that led to or contributed to the unacceptable level of child care. There is no infallible way to intervene with an individual or family that will guarantee changes. What is clear is that the more we engage the parents in partnership to solve the behaviors or conditions, the more likely we will achieve success in a shorter period. What is equally clear is that the child welfare system is doing an extremely poor job of engaging parents (U.S. Department of Health and Human Services, Children's Bureau, 2005; Altman, 2005). We talked about the difficulty in engaging involuntary or mandated clients previously. But without engagement, the services cannot go forward with any expectation of success. There is limited research on what works in engaging involuntary or mandated clients. The limited research available supports the caseworker who is creating an environment of honesty, genuineness, and respect. Altman (2005), in a study of caseworkers, parents, foster parents, and supervisors, found the following elements necessary for effective engagement.

❖ Establishing mutually acceptable and specific goals in partnership;

❖ Maintaining belief that change can occur;

❖ Acknowledging and understanding of the situation that brought child welfare system into the family;

❖ Parental motivation to change;

❖ Identifying and acknowledging cultural differences;

❖ Truthful, honest, and respectful communications by the caseworker; and

❖ Persistent, diligent, and timely efforts to help families.

Service Planning with Children. Children in the child welfare system require individual focus to ensure that the lasting effects of neglect and abuse are minimized. The further up the pyramid of services one goes, the greater the potential for the abuse or neglect to have lasting effects on the child. However, every child is different and the impact of neglect or abuse is correlated with age at the time of the neglect or abuse, prior relationship between child and neglector or abuser, intensity and duration of the neglect or abuse, and presence of supportive persons in the child's life. (Garbarino, 2005) Furthermore, the child continues to grow, develop, and change in all domains as child welfare services are provided. Every child has strengths, needs, and challenges. The services and supports provided by child welfare are used to meet the needs, maximize the strengths, and minimize or eliminate the challenges. They must be adjusted to encourage and support development of the individual child to his or her maximum potential in all domains. In addition to emotional and physical safety, the child's educational, physical health, and mental health needs must be fully addressed in any child welfare service plan.

Children in the child welfare system should be engaged in the development of their service plan, consistent with their age and developmental capacities.

Engagement principles of truthfulness, honesty, respectfulness, persistence, diligence, timeliness, and partnership in decision making are just as important, if not more important, when serving the child client. Children are watching what you do as well as what you say!

Parent–Child–Agency Agreements. Three specific tools are helpful in service planning: Parent–Agency Agreements, Child–Agency Agreements, and engaging and mobilizing the parent's and child's natural support systems. Agreements state who is responsible for doing what, by when, so that the child is safe at home, can be safely returned home, or achieve an alternate permanency goal, and is provided the care and support needed to achieve satisfaction and success in all domains to his or her full potential. Further, Agreements state the consequences for failure to carry out the terms of the Agreement. The consequences should be verbalized and written nonjudgmentally and factually.

Agreements are completed in partnership—the child, parent, and anyone else identified as important to assisting in developing and implementing the service plan, along with the caseworker, acknowledge the realities of the situation and together develop the terms of the Agreement. Agreements are negotiated and not imposed; although there may be limitations imposed on options, given the nature of child welfare services. Agreements should include incremental steps toward the larger outcome so that hope is maintained and reinforced by accomplishment and success. All parties to the Agreement accept responsibility to do what he or she agrees to do and is held accountable. Therefore, the Agreement should be written clearly and specifically at a linguistic level that is understandable to the parent or child signing the Agreement. They should be discussed until it is clear that there is a common understanding of what each person understands the Agreement terms to mean. Agreements should be updated whenever the service plan is updated. Agreements should be reviewed frequently, by telephone or in person, to

❖ keep everyone focused on accomplishing his or her tasks.
❖ provide positive feedback on actions taken thus far to make sure desired outcome is achieved by the due date.
❖ identify any barriers and discuss how to eliminate them or modify the provision(s) in the Agreement to acknowledge the realities.
❖ determine if other events have occurred that impact the ability of any party to fulfill his or her tasks under the Agreement.

Engaging and Mobilizing Natural Support Systems.　Engaging and mobilizing the parent's and child's natural support systems recognizes that these are the people the child and parent turn to in their daily living and not a caseworker or agency. For the most part, they will always be available to the parent and child. In general, their primary interest is in the well-being of the parent and child. They can be effective partners in helping to remove or alleviate the conditions that led to child welfare system involvement and supporting the parent and child after the child welfare system is no longer around.

It is the parent's or child's responsibility to identify the people he or she views as supportive and who he or she wants to include in helping with the service planning—remember client self-determination and confidentiality! However, it is important that the caseworker fully assesses and reassesses whether these people provide positive or negative support and influence and whether they are beneficial or harmful to accomplishing the child welfare outcomes. Even if some of the natural supporters identified by the parent or the child do not initially appear to support the parent or child in ways the caseworker deems positive and supportive, the caseworker should consider engaging them in the service planning if the assessment is that the person will not be harmful to the child or parent. The caseworker should discuss any concerns, including any person identified by the parent or the child, openly and honestly with the parent or child and then with the identified support person. The same principles of engagement apply: truthfulness, honesty, and respect.

Implementing, Monitoring, and Updating Service Plans.　Implementing the service plan involves providing direct services, facilitating acquisition of needed services from others, and managing for results and outcomes. In some child welfare systems, the caseworker is the case manager and does little provision of direct services. In others, the caseworker provides the full range of services needed by the child and family. Both systems require the caseworker to know what services offer the best opportunity for the client to succeed, what services are available in the community to meet the clients' needs and how to access those services, and how services should be sequenced to achieve maximum impact. If services are provided by others, the caseworker remains ultimately responsible for ensuring that the services provided support the client in accomplishing his or her responsibilities under the case service plan.

Monitoring the service plan involves discussing the services provided with the parent, child, and service provider; eliciting each person's perception of the benefit and relevance of the services to the case goals; modifying the services in partnership with the parent, child, and service provider; recording and assessing the services provided in relation to the impact of those services on the case objectives; and assisting the parent, child, or service provider with engagement and compliance concerns.

Updating the service plan involves summarizing and assessing what has occurred since the last service plan was developed and making changes in the services and service plan based on the changed conditions of the people involved, that is, results of the previous services and the changed behaviors and capacities of the parent(s), child(ren), and natural supports as a result of these services. Just as engagement and partnership with the parent, child, and support persons—professional and natural—was important in the development of the initial service plan; their participation in updated service plans is equally important.

Case Record Documentation

Properly documented case records are critical in the child welfare system's increasingly rapid march toward permanency for children. One of the unfortunate realities of the system is that staff turnover remains a major barrier to effective services for children and families. When workers leave and relevant information is not documented in the case file, the new worker looses much needed case intervention time in obtaining information that was known to the previous worker. In addition, it is annoying to parents and children to repeat "their story" over and over again!

What Should Be Recorded?   Each agency has its own case record documentation requirements. Much of the case record documentation is incidental to the reason the child and family are under the jurisdiction of the court, for example, eligibility determinations, computer system input forms, supervisory case review forms, etc. Other information, while helpful to ensuring the child's well-being and development, might be incidental to the court process unless it is connected to a reason the court took jurisdiction, for example, education reports, medical reports, etc. Often, the case plan and the court orders appear to have no connection. A case record for a child that is under court jurisdiction and subject to the ASFA requirements for expedited permanency for children in out-of-home care should have a specific section in the original case plan that states the reasons the court took jurisdiction, the orders it entered, and the agreements between the parent, child, and agency stating the specific actions each will take and the projected time by which the actions will be taken to fulfill the orders of the court.

Updated case plans would be completed based on contemporaneous documentation that is specific to dates and actions related to the previous case plan and focus on the progress of the parent, child, and agency in complying with previous court orders that were crafted to alleviate the conditions that brought the child and family to the attention of the court as well as modifications to orders based on subsequent findings of the court. Thus, a contact case documentation structure, consistent with ASFA requirements, would include:

❖ date of contact;
❖ location of contact;
❖ statement of the purpose of contact;
❖ identity and role of persons participating in the contact;
❖ description of what happened—the facts;
❖ caseworker's assessment of information gathered in the contact;
❖ actions to be taken, by whom, and by when as a result of the contact; and
❖ worker's signature and date entered in the case record.

This information should be recorded as soon as possible after the contact. It should be factual and unbiased. While you are required to make an assessment, this assessment should be based on the information you have gathered and not your personal opinions. The information would be summarized in the initial and updated case service plans. Some agencies provide copies of these contact notes to parents, children, and other service providers as reminders of what each agreed to do as a result of the contact. Case recording is discussed in more detail in Chapter 5.

Crisis Intervention and Stabilization Services

Most child welfare situations are the outgrowth of long-standing behaviors and conditions within the family, individual, and/or his or her environment that suddenly develop into a crisis. The crisis can be a call to child protective services by a neighbor, relative, friend, or mandated reporter. Or the crisis can be a call from a substitute caregiver asking that the child be removed from his or her home. Or the crisis can be a call from the school stating that the child is being suspended because of fighting. Anytime a crisis occurs, the caseworker is required to immediately assess the child's safety and assist the caregiver and child in resolving the crisis. The involvement of the caseworker in crisis intervention and stabilization depends on the nature of the crisis, the safety assessment of the child, and the capacity of the caregiver and the child to resolve the crisis.

For example, the crisis in the Jones case was Jennie Jones' hospitalization as a result of being severely beaten by Jack Smith. Until that point, in-home services were being provided and all indications were that Ms. Jones was complying with the court-ordered treatment plan. With Ms. Jones in the hospital and Jack Smith in police custody, the children needed a responsible adult to care for them. Consistent with Federal policy, the agency sought first to place the children with relatives and other siblings. This was accomplished by placing them with their maternal grandmother and brother, Danny. This resolved the immediate crisis and provided safety and stability for the children.

TRENDS AND ISSUES

The child welfare system is constantly under attack from outside sources—media, advocacy groups, federal agencies, state agencies, children who have exited the system, parents and families who have been involved with the system, lawyers representing children and parents involved in the system, and caseworkers and others within the child welfare system. Everyone expects the system to perform better!

The problem is that the system and all those who interact with it, observe it, and criticize it have expectations that appear to be beyond the capacity of the system. Specifically, they appear to want the child welfare system to be an ideal system in which no child is ever neglected or abused by his or her parent(s) or substitute caregiver and in which all children and families who come in contact with the system are provided timely services and supports necessary to ensure that the child and family, as individuals and as a unit, remain safe and able to achieve success in all domains of life. These ideals are appropriate. Unfortunately, the resources to accomplish these ideals have never been made available. It appears that, for the foreseeable future, our child welfare system will remain underfunded, under resourced, and under attack.

The federal CFSR process, a "results-oriented comprehensive monitoring system designed to promote continuous improvement in the outcomes experienced by children and families who come into contact with public child welfare agencies," found no state met all the expectations in its first round of reviews, which began in 2000 (U.S. Department of Health and Human Services,

Children's Bureau, 2005). However, the findings of these reviews informed child welfare practice and federal and state legislatures, awoke the advocacy community, and reinforced the importance of the caseworker–parent–child relationship in the child welfare system. In 2006, federal legislation was passed to provide additional funding to the states to support caseworker and supervisor training and development and to promote no less than monthly contacts between caseworker, child, and parents. In addition, the CFSRs have provided opportunities for sharing promising practices in child welfare across states. They have raised awareness of the complexities of child welfare services and reiterated the importance of collaboration and coordination across systems. They have provided clarity of purpose and focus for the system: child safety, child permanency, and child well-being within the family of origin or a family by adoption. There is hope that the CFSR process will not be just another federal monitoring of the states with no consequence! Furthermore, it is clear that the consequence desired by the federal government is improvement in services to children and families and not sanctions on the states.

The movement toward broader community involvement in child welfare services also continues to gain support. The child welfare system recognized the need to engage the full community in child welfare in the early 1970s. It still continues to be a challenge to effect this involvement. While reports of child abuse and neglect by different groups in the community have increased steadily over this period, the process of engaging these different groups in actually helping and supporting families who are at risk of abuse or neglect or in which the agency has found abuse and neglect to exist remains elusive. The Family to Family Initiative of the Annie E. Casey Foundation (2006) offers promise for identifying practices that facilitate and encourage broader community engagement, although the 2002 evaluation of its Initiative identified this area as still challenging to the child welfare system. Another evaluation will be completed in 2008. We are hopeful that some of the strategies show better results.

A renewed focus on engaging the family, its supporters, and the caseworker in teaming for decision making, case planning, and service implementation offers promise for more timely outcomes. Unfortunately, there are too few published reports on the success and replicability of these efforts broadly in the child welfare system.

CHAPTER SUMMARY

This chapter focused on basic principles of the child welfare system, irrespective of the specific programmatic area; that is, prevention, family preservation, child protection, foster care, adoption, and delinquency. The purpose is to demonstrate that irrespective of program, there are knowledge, skills, and processes common to all. While the child welfare system is extremely complex, a caseworker who has a basic orientation to the child welfare process can succeed.

The fundamental principles of child welfare services are that child safety is paramount and services should be child focused and family centered to promote child well-being and permanency. The basic methodology for child welfare services is casework practice and process, although group methodologies such as team decision making or family group conferencing or family group decision making are being used more often in recent years. Casework practice is problem-solving oriented with ecological assessment and task-centered, time-limited interventions as its cornerstones. In addition, it acknowledges, supports, and encourages client self-determination, cultural sensitivity and cultural responsiveness, and a strengths-based philosophy.

The basic tasks of child welfare include information gathering, assessment, case planning, case file documentation, service delivery and case management, and crisis intervention and stabilization.

The complexity of the child welfare system arises because there are individual, family, community, and societal interests, conditions, behaviors, values, and biases that must be addressed and resolved in each instance of child abuse and neglect. This requires that the caseworker has broad range and depth of knowledge in many areas—some of which change daily (e.g., resources available within the community).

FOR STUDY AND DISCUSSION
STUDY AND DISCUSSION QUESTIONS

1. Ask a child welfare worker to answer these questions: Describe the most rewarding experience you have had as a child welfare worker. Describe the most troubling experience you have had as a child welfare worker. What impact did these experiences have on your view of working in child welfare?

2. Prepare a list of questions to ask children in an initial investigatory interview. How would the questions change in relation to the child's age and developmental level?

3. Reflect on your personal values, biases, and experiences with respect to child abuse and neglect. How might these impact your performance as a child welfare caseworker?

4. Identify some of the issues in community engagement in child abuse and neglect issues in general and in specific case situations.

5. Develop a service plan for the Jones children if the grandmother says she will not proceed with a legal adoption.

Internet Sites

Children's Bureau. The Children's Bureau is one of six bureaus within the Administration on Children, Youth and Families, U.S. Department of Health and Human Services. It seeks to provide for the safety, permanency, and well-being of children through leadership, support for necessary services, and productive partnerships with states, tribes, and communities.
www.acf.hhs.gov/programs/cb/index.htm

Child Welfare Information Gateway. Established by the U.S. Children's Bureau to provide access, information, and resources on all areas of child welfare to help protect children and strengthen families. Excellent source to connect with other credible web sites on any child welfare issue.
www.childwelfare.gov

References

Altman, J. C. (2005). Engagement in children, youth, and family services: Current research and promising approaches. In G. P. Mallon & P. M. Hess. (Eds.), *Child welfare for the 21st century: A handbook of practices, policies and programs*. New York: Columbia University Press.

Altman, J. C. (2004). Engagement in neighborhood-based child welfare services. Garden City, NY: Adelphi University School of Social Work.

Annie E. Casey Foundation (2006). The Family to Family Initiative. Retrieved from www.aecf.org/Majorinitiatives on November 10, 2006.

Behrman, R. (Ed.) (2004). *The future of children.* Los Altos, CA: The David and Lucile Packard Foundation.

Bronheim, S., Goode, T., & Jones, W. (2006, Spring). *Policy Brief: Cultural and linguistic competence in family supports.* Washington, DC: Georgetown University, National Center for Cultural Competence.

Chahine, Z., & Higgins, S. (2005). Engaging families and communities: The use of family team conferences to promote safety, permanency, and well-being in child welfare services. In G. P. Mallon & P. M. Hess (Eds.), *Child welfare for the 21st century: A handbook of practices, policies and programs.* New York: Columbia University Press.

Chibnall, S., Dutch, N. M., Jones-Harden, E., Brown, N. (December 2003). *Children of color in the child welfare system: Perspectives from the child welfare community.* Washington, DC: U.S. Department of Health and Human Services, Children's Bureau.

Child and Family Services Improvement Act of 2006, P.L. 109-288.

Cohen, E., Hornsby, D. T., & Priester, S. (2005). Assessment of children, youth, and families in the child welfare system. In G. P. Mallon & P. M. Hess (Eds.), *Child welfare for the 21st century: A handbook of practices, policies and programs.* New York: Columbia University Press.

Compton, B. R., Galaway, B., & Cournoyer, B. R. (2005). *Social work processes.* Belmont, CA: Thomson Learning.

Cross, T. L. (1988). Services to minority populations: Cultural competence continuum. *Focal Point, 3*(1), 1–4.

Derezotes, D., Poertner, J., & Testa, M. (2004). *Race matters in child welfare: Overrepresentation of African American children in the system.* Washington, DC: Child Welfare League of America.

DeSchweinitz, E., & DeSchweinitz, K. (1964). The place of authority in the protective function of the public child welfare agency. *Child Welfare, 43*(6), 286–291.

Dubowitz, H., DePanfilis, D. (Eds.). (2000). *Handbook for child protection practice.* Thousand Oaks, CA: Sage Publications, Inc.

Ellison, R. (1952). *The invisible man.* New York: Random House.

Epstein L. (1992). *Brief treatment and a new look at the task-centered approach.* New York: Macmillan Publishing Company.

Forsythe, P. (1987). Redefining child protective services. *Protecting Children, 4*(3), 12–16.

Garbarino, J. (2005, October). *It depends.* Presentation for Michigan Governor's Task Force on Children's Justice Annual Summit.

Garrett, A. (1942). *Interviewing: Its principles and methods.* New York: Family Service Association of America.

Hartman, A., & Laird, J. (1983). *Family-centered social work practice.* New York: The Free Press: A Division of Macmillan.

Hess, P. M. (2005). Visits: Critical to the well-being and permanency of children and youth in care. In G. P. Mallon & P. M. Hess (Eds.), *Child welfare for the 21st century: A handbook of practices, policies and programs.* New York: Columbia University Press.

Hill, R. (1972). *The strengths of black families.* New York: Emerson Hall.

Hill, R. (2006). *Syntheses of the research on disproportionality in child welfare: An update.* Baltimore, MD: Casey-CSSP Alliance for Racial Equity.

Hollis, F. (1964). *Casework: A Psychosocial therapy.* New York: Random House.

Kadushin, A. (1970). *Child welfare services: A sourcebook.* New York: The Macmillan Company.

Kemp, S. P., Allen-Eckard, K., Ackroyd, A., Becker, M. F., & Burke, T. K. (2005). Community family support meetings: Connecting families, public child welfare, and community resources. In G. P. Mallon & P. M. Hess (Eds.), *Child welfare for the 21st century: A handbook of practices, policies and programs.* New York: Columbia University Press.

Kretzmann, J. P., & McNight, J. L. (1993). *Building communities from the inside out: A path toward finding and mobilizing a community's assets.* Evanston, IL: Northwestern University.

Mallon, G. P., & Hess, P. M. (Eds.). (2005). *Child welfare for the 21st century: A handbook of practices, policies and programs.* New York: Columbia University Press.

Mather, J. H., & Lager, P. B. (2000). *Child welfare: A unifying model of practice.* Belmont, CA: Thomson Learning.

McGowan, B. G. (2005). Historical evolution of child welfare services. In G. P. Mallon & P. M. Hess (Eds.), *Child welfare for the 21st century: A handbook of practices, policies and programs.* New York: Columbia University Press.

McRoy, R. G. (2005). Overrepresentation of children and youth of color in foster care. In G. P. Mallon & P. M. Hess (Eds.), *Child welfare for the 21st century: A handbook of practices, policies and programs.* New York: Columbia University Press.

Miller, S. D., Hubble, M. A., & Duncan, B. L., (Eds.). (1996). *Handbook of solution-focused brief therapy.* San Francisco: Jossey-Bass Publishers.

Moss, S. Z. (1963). Authority—An enabling factor in casework with neglectful parents. *Child Welfare*, *43*(8), 385–391.

National Association of Social Workers. (2000). *NASW code of ethics.* Washington, DC: NASW Press. Retrieved from www.naswdc.org/pubs/code/code.asp August 14, 2007.

National Association of Social Workers. (2001). *NASW standards for cultural competence in social work practice.* Washington, DC: National Association of Social Workers.

National Conference of State Legislatures. (2006, September). *Child welfare caseworker visits with children and parents.* Denver, CO: Author.

Netting, F. E., Kettner, P. M., & McMurtry, S. L. (1998). *Social work macro practice.* New York: Longman.

Pennell, J., & Anderson, G. (Eds.). (2005*). Widening the circle: The practice and evaluation of family group conferencing with children, youths, and their families.* Washington, DC: NASW Press.

Perlman, H. H. (1957). *Social casework: A problem-solving process.* Chicago: The University of Chicago Press.

Perlman, H. H. (Ed.). (1969). *Helping: Charlotte Towle on social work and social casework.* Chicago: The University of Chicago Press.

Richmond, M. (1922). *What is social casework?: An introductory description.* New York: Russell Sage Foundation.

Roberts, D. (2002). *Shattered bonds: The color of child welfare.* New York: Basic Books.

Rockymore, M. (2006, April). *The role of the caseworkers in identifying, developing and supporting strengths in African American families involved in child protection services.* St. Paul, MN: Minnesota Department of Human Services.

Schene, P. (2005, May). *Comprehensive family assessment guidelines for child welfare.* New York: National Resource Center for Family Centered Practice and Permanency Planning.

Tower-Crosson, C. (2007). *Exploring child welfare: A practice perspective.* Boston: Pearson Education.

University of North Carolina, School of Social Work. (1988). *The evaluation of family to family.* Chapel Hill, NC: Author.

U.S. Department of Health and Human Services. (2001). *National standards for culturally and linguistically appropriate services in health care: Final report 2001.* Washington, DC: Author.

U.S. Department of Health and Human Services. (2006). *Children's Bureau fact sheets.* Washington, DC: Author.

U.S. Department of Health and Human Services, Children's Bureau. (2005). *CFSR 50 state report: 2005 Report to congress.* Washington, DC: Author.

Walezyn, F., Hislop, K. B., & George, R. M. (2000). *An update from the multistate data archive: Foster care dynamics 1983–1998.* Chicago, IL: University of Chicago, Chapin Hall Center for Children.

Weil, M., Karls, J. M., & Associates. (1985). *Case management in human service practice: A systematic approach to mobilizing resources for clients.* San Francisco: Jossey-Bass Publishers.

CHAPTER 5

Law and Procedure

Court Intervention with Children, Youth, and Families

Juvenile court history has again demonstrated that unbridled discretion, however benevolently motivated, is frequently a poor substitute for principle and procedure.

—Justice Abe Fortas, In re Gault, 1967, p. 18

INTRODUCTION

Perhaps no social institution was founded with higher hopes for its contribution to justice for children than the juvenile court. In the past five decades, however, it has been a center of controversy. Its philosophy, procedures, and achievements have undergone scrutiny, challenge, and demands for radical change. At the heart of the controversy are differences over the proper purpose, focus, and procedures of the juvenile court.

The division of authority between courts and social agencies, particularly state child welfare agencies and the private child welfare agencies providing services under purchase-of-services arrangements with the public agencies, is a constant source of tension for the caseworker. In the period of the juvenile court's history when its rules and procedures were informal, caseworkers were consulted for their expertise in "what's best for the child." Their opinions were given, generally with little questioning of the evidentiary bases for them, and the court acted with significant deference to those recommendations. As the juvenile court system became more structured to conform to legal requirements for admissibility of evidence, standards of proof, rights to attorney representation, and other procedural protections for children and their parents, the caseworker's approach has had to adapt.

A constant source of conflict for caseworkers is that they are required to gather and act on both social evidence and legal evidence. Some situations of children and families do not yield clear legal evidence. Because the questions at issue in such cases are often not simple, caseworkers may rely on many sources of information, some of which is nonadmissible hearsay evidence or other information acquired informally. In such cases, they look for repeated patterns of parent and child behavior and environmental influences. They may offer "voluntary" services to the family with the hope of resolving the concern. Frequently, these offers of "voluntary" services are rooted in their knowledge that they have insufficient evidence to proceed to court intervention. This practice is receiving greater scrutiny and commentary within the social work and legal communities. Many argue that when the state intrusion and the treatment plan do not rest on a documented basis that could pass judicial scrutiny, caseworkers must carefully evaluate the reliability of any social evidence that in any way affects the rights of children and families and their ability to direct their own lives.

The challenge to caseworkers is to understand the nature of evidence and the court process, to become skillful in finding and organizing facts, and to integrate this knowledge and skill into their social work values and approaches to helping. In this chapter, we focus on the basics of the courts in the handling of abuse, neglect, and delinquency matters. Our intent is to orient the student to the structure and processes of the legal systems and their roles in them.

THE JUVENILE COURT MOVEMENT

Juvenile courts were created by a legal and social work cooperative venture. In a spirit of mission, late nineteenth- and early twentieth-century social reformers enjoined the "child welfare" purpose to that of "youth correction." Historical factors in large measure account for the highly complex commingling of the child welfare system and the juvenile justice system that exists today: "The most significant fact about the history of juvenile justice is that it evolved simultaneously with the child welfare system. Most of its defects and its virtues derive from that fact" (Flicker, 1977, p. 27).

Philosophy and Purpose

From its inception, the juvenile court had high aims, combined with heavy responsibilities. Its purpose was conceived of as protection and rehabilitation of the child in place of indictment and punishment. It was based on a philosophy of "individualized justice," which directs the application of law to social ends by individualization, that is, by "dealing with each case as in great measure unique and yet . . . on a basis of principle derived from experience . . . developed by reason" (Pound, 1950, p. 36). The intent was a humanitarian one, based on the conviction that the individual child and his or her needs rather than an offense and its legal penalty should be the focus of consideration.

The concern of the juvenile court founders was directed toward the youthful lawbreaker and children whose circumstances were likely to lead them into delinquency, rather than those who were grossly neglected or in need of other protections.

Judge Julian Mack, one of the early leaders in the juvenile court movement, described procedures prior to the passage of juvenile court legislation:

> Our common criminal law did not differentiate between the adult and the minor who had reached the age of criminal responsibility, seven at common law and in some of our states, ten in others, with a chance of escape up to twelve, if lacking in mental and moral maturity. The majesty and dignity of the state demanded vindication for infractions from both alike. . . . The child was arrested, put into prison, indicted by the grand jury, tried by a petit jury, under all the forms and technicalities of our criminal law, with the aim of ascertaining whether it had done the specific act—nothing else—and if it had, then of visiting the punishment of the state upon it. *(Mack, 1909–1910, p. 106)*

An early description of the aims and the humanitarian concerns of the new court will serve to draw the contrast between the old and the new philosophy:

> Emphasis is laid, not on the act done by the child, but on the social fact and circumstances that are really the inducing causes of the child's appearance in court. The particular offense that was the immediate and proximate cause of the proceedings is considered only as one of the many other factors surrounding the child. The purpose of the proceeding here is not punishment but correction of conditions, care and protection of the child and prevention of a recurrence through the constructive work of the court. Conservation of the child, as a valuable asset of the community, is the dominant note. *(Flexner & Baldwin, 1914, pp. 6–7)*

To implement such a philosophy, the juvenile court was of necessity a court of equity, one intended to temper the strict application of the law to the individual needs of the child. Its justice represented a departure from the concept of justice personified by the traditional symbol: a statue of a woman holding a balanced scale. In one scale, the crime is measured, and in the other, the punishment. When the two sides of the scale balance evenly, it was held, justice prevails. This symbol of justice wears a blindfold so that the wealth or poverty of the accused or other individual characteristics or station in life cannot influence her. She is blind to individual differences, all objective and evenhanded. There were historical reasons for this symbol. It marked a revolt against the tyranny and the inequities of earlier centuries when law was made and interpreted differently for nobles and peasants, rich and poor. It marked a claim of the ordinary person for equal treatment before the law.

But in the philosophy of the juvenile court, the blindfold was, in effect, stripped from the symbol of justice. The characteristics of the child became crucial to the judge, who was under obligation to examine the child and a particular situation with all its differences and to turn away from a scrutiny of the offense and its legal penalty. Julia Lathrop, one of the juvenile court's early founders, said that the outstanding contribution of the juvenile court was that "it made the child visible" (Lundberg, 1947, p. 119).

Founding

The first juvenile court in the United States was created in Illinois on April 2, 1899. The attainment of this significant and far-reaching piece of legislation came through cooperation among a group of discerning and energetic social workers in Chicago, lawyers for the Chicago Bar Association, and civic leaders from various organizations, particularly the Chicago Woman's Club.

The leading female reformer among those who assumed responsibility for securing the juvenile court was a social worker, Julia Lathrop. An early resident of Hull House, she had been challenged by the spirit and potentiality of youths and distressed at the careless and neglectful treatment of many of them.

In 1898, at the annual meeting of the Illinois State Conference of Charities, Julia Lathrop showed leadership in planning an entire conference program on the topic "The Children of the State." Different organizations were found to be considering legislative proposals for benefits to children. The various groups merged their efforts and appointed a committee to secure the cooperation of the Chicago Bar Association to bring about a draft of a juvenile court act. While there were many revisions, the bill that emerged was approved as a Bar Association bill and introduced into the state legislature (Lathrop, 1925, pp. 290–297). The task of proposing and testifying on behalf of the juvenile court bill was assigned to the lawyers, while the woman's club took responsibility for securing support for the bill (Rosenheim, 1962, pp. 18–19).

This initial piece of legislation, which served as a model for legislation in other states, was broadly titled "An Act to Regulate the Treatment and Control of Dependent, Neglected, and Delinquent Children." Thereafter, children who violated laws or ordinances were classified as delinquents instead of criminals. The new act was considered a magnificent accomplishment, attained against the weight and opposition of tradition. Jane Addams believed that the new court brought such change that

> there was almost a change in mores when the Juvenile Court was established. The child was brought before the judge with no one to prosecute him and no one to defend him—the judge and all concerned were merely trying to find out what could be done on his behalf.
> *(Addams, 1935, p. 137)*

Roscoe Pound said that the juvenile court represented "the greatest advance in judicial history since the Magna Carta" (National Probation and Parole Association, 1957, p. 127). The movement had strong appeal to individual citizens and to groups working on behalf of children. This exciting concept of justice for children and the new legal machinery for helping them was achieved during a period of support for social reforms generally and special interest in the needs of children, a factor that helped to speed the creation of juvenile courts in other states.

By 1945, all states plus the District of Columbia, Hawaii, Alaska, and Puerto Rico had enacted juvenile court legislation, and Congress had authorized similar procedures for use in the federal courts (Nutt, 1949, p. 270).

The Early Question of Constitutionality

Some opposition to the initial passage of the acts came from members of the bar who believed that the court procedures, although intended to protect children, actually took away their constitutional rights. Nevertheless, by finding that juvenile proceedings were not adversarial, the courts firmly established the constitutionality of the juvenile court statutes, substantially reinforcing and extending the doctrine of *parens patriae* to include juvenile delinquents. In all the leading test cases, the *parens patriae* tenet was called up and used to justify the state's authority in the new acts, even though this old doctrine had not been a direct antecedent of the juvenile court (Flexner & Oppenheimer, 1922; Lou, 1927). The first major test of the constitutionality of juvenile court procedures was that of the Pennsylvania Act of 1903. An excerpt from the decision is illustrative of the philosophy that prevailed.

> To save a child from becoming a criminal, or from continuing in a career of crime, to end in maturer years in public punishment and disgrace, the legislature surely may provide for the salvation of such a child, if its parents or guardian be unable or unwilling to do so, by bringing it into one of the courts of the state without any process at all, for the purpose of subjecting it to the state's guardianship and protection. . . . There is no probability, in the proper administration of the law, of the child's liberty being unduly invaded. Every statute which is designed to give protection, care, and training to children, as a needed substitute for parental authority and performance of parental duty, is but a recognition of the duty of the state, as the legitimate guardian and protector of children where other guardianship fails. No constitutional right is violated. (*Commonwealth v. Fisher, 1905*)

When the new juvenile court statutes were challenged on constitutional grounds, the state supreme courts successively upheld them on the basis that the juvenile court was not a criminal court and no child was brought before the juvenile court under arrest and on trial for a crime; hence, constitutional guarantees accorded defendants in criminal cases did not apply to juvenile procedures. The weight of decision was an overwhelming endorsement of the new laws.

Practically, this meant that the child was brought under the power of the juvenile court without the legal safeguards claimed as a constitutional right by an adult accused of law violations. These safeguards are embodied in such procedures as open hearings, right to counsel, proof beyond a reasonable doubt, limitations on the use of hearsay evidence, protection against self-incrimination, and right to bail. This practice of failing to provide the minor with these constitutionally guaranteed protections eventually led to extensive criticism of the juvenile court, on the basis that the rights of the child should be no less highly regarded and no less strictly observed than those of an adult in any court. Over time, this philosophy was extended to child abuse and neglect cases.

Supreme Court Decisions: New Procedural Directions

The *Kent* and *Gault* decisions of the United States Supreme Court began the constitutional review of the juvenile court processes that had been the subject of heavy criticisms. Youth and their parents frequently were not informed of their right to counsel. The absence of suitable facilities had led to the use of jails for children who had been arrested but not adjudicated. The social investigation, designed as a basis for helping the judge make an informed decision, often was sparse or superficial, thus negating its purpose. Clear proof of charges was often lacking, even though the result was undesirable labeling of the child or loss of liberty through commitment to training schools. Frequently, there had been no transcripts of court proceedings, or incomplete ones, which made an appeal to a higher court difficult (Ellrod & Melaney, 1950; Rubin, 1952; Beemsterboer, 1960; Elson, 1962; Handler, 1965). Too often there had been failure on the part of the state to provide true rehabilitative facilities following the removal of a child from parental custody, what Ketcham (1962) termed substitution of "governmental for parental neglect."

Supreme Court Justice Abe Fortas cogently pinpointed two of the major problems before the juvenile court, the lack of constitutional guarantees and the lack of rehabilitative treatment resources.

> There is much evidence that some juvenile courts . . . lack the personnel, facilities and techniques to perform adequately as representatives of the state in a parens patriae capacity, at least with respect to children charged with law violation. There is evidence, in fact, that there may be grounds for concern that the child receives the worst of both worlds: that he gets neither the protections accorded to adults nor the solicitous care and regenerative treatment postulated for children. *(Kent v. United States, 1966)*

The issue in the *Kent* case was the juvenile's constitutional rights during a transfer, or waiver, from the juvenile court to the adult criminal court. A District of Columbia law provided that a person 16 years of age could be waived to the adult court for trial after a full investigation by the juvenile judge on any offense that would be a felony if committed by an adult. Kent was charged with robbery, rape, and breaking and entering. He was waived. He challenged the waiver on the grounds that he was not afforded a hearing, no reasons for the waiver were provided to him, and his lawyer was denied access to his records. The U.S. Supreme Court stated that under the Due Process Clause of the Fourteenth Amendment, a juvenile was entitled to a hearing, full access to records and reports used by the court in arriving at its decision, and a statement of the reason for the juvenile court's decision (*Kent v. United States*, 1966).

The second major U.S. Supreme Court decision in relation to procedural protections for juveniles was *In re Gault*. The issue in this case was the due process and equal protection requirements in juvenile court proceedings.

Gault was a 15-year-old charged with making a lewd telephone call to a neighbor. He was on probation at the time of the call. He was arrested without notification to his parents, detained, not provided a lawyer, and never given a formal hearing. The Arizona court found him delinquent and committed him to the state training school until 18 years of age. He challenged the decision. The U.S. Supreme Court reversed the decision of the Arizona Supreme Court and established the due process rights of juveniles.

Justice Fortas made two statements in this decision that challenged the basic foundation of the juvenile court system and signaled the scope of constitutional protections for juveniles.

> Neither the Fourteenth Amendment nor the Bill of Rights is for adults alone. *(In re Gault, 1967, p.13)*
>
> Juvenile court history has again demonstrated that unbridled discretion, however benevolently motivated, is frequently a poor substitute for principle and procedure. *(Ibid., p. 18)*

While the Court made it clear that juvenile court proceedings on an adjudication of delinquency need not conform to all the requirements of a criminal trial, it held that such action must measure up to the essentials of due process and fair treatment guaranteed by the Fourteenth Amendment to the Constitution. Specifically, (1) the child and his or her parents must be given written notice of a scheduled hearing sufficiently in advance to provide opportunity to prepare for the hearing, and this notice must set forth the alleged misconduct "with particularity"; (2) the child and his or her parents must be notified of the child's right to be represented by counsel retained by them, or if they are unable to afford this, counsel will be appointed to represent the child; (3) the constitutional privilege against self-incrimination (the right to remain silent instead of admitting or confessing) is applicable in the case of juveniles as well as adults; and (4) the child or young person has a right to confront and cross-examine witnesses who appear against him or her (*In re Gault,* 1967).

Three other U.S. Supreme Court decisions are important in shaping the adjudication phase of a delinquency procedure. *In re Winship* (1970) established the principle of proof beyond a reasonable doubt as a requirement for a finding of delinquency (although not necessarily for finding a child "in need of supervision"). While *Winship* affirmed a required level of proof for minors, two other decisions, *McKeiver v. Pennsylvania* (1971) and *Schall v. Martin* (1984), were in the direction of limiting the legal rights of a minor. *McKeiver* held that the due process clause of the Fourteenth Amendment does not require jury trials for youths charged with delinquent acts that could result in incarceration, leading to the criticism that *McKeiver* "continues the tradition of conceptual oscillation when juvenile court procedure is at issue," resulting in "the extension of some rights and the denial of others" (Schultz & Cohen, 1976, p. 28). The *Schall* court decided that pretrial detention to protect an accused juvenile and society from the "serious risk" of pretrial crime is compatible with the "fundamental fairness" demanded by the due process clause. The interest of the state in promoting juvenile welfare is a *parens patriae* interest, and is what "makes a juvenile proceeding fundamentally different from an adult criminal trial" (*Schall v. Martin,* 1984, pp. 253, 263). Liberty can therefore be circumscribed by the power of *parens patriae.*

The doctrine of *parens patriae* found further expression in the first Supreme Court decision that established a standard in the dispositional stage of juvenile proceedings. *Thompson v. Oklahoma* (1988) overturned the death penalty for a boy who was 15 at the time he participated in the brutal murder of his former brother-in-law. The Court's majority held that to execute a person who was under 16 at the time of committing a crime was cruel and unusual punishment and therefore unconstitutional. The court distinguished juveniles from adults in terms of a basic assumption of society about children as a class: "We assume that they do not yet act as adults do, and thus we act in their interest. . . . It would be ironic if these assumptions that we so readily make about children as a class—about their inherent difference from adults in their capacity as agents, as choosers, as shapers of their own lives—were suddenly unavailable in determining whether it is cruel and unusual to treat children the same as adults for purposes of inflicting capital punishment" (*Thompson v. Oklahoma,* 1988, p. 2693, n. 23).

The minimum age for the death penalty was established at 18 years in the *Roper v Simmons* decision issued in 2005.

These precedent-setting cases affirm that in instances of alleged delinquency, juveniles are granted legal rights that are differentiated from those of adults, and at the same time are afforded due process protections (see Box 5.1).

Box 5.1

Due Process in Juvenile Courts

These are the due process rights for parties in juvenile court matters.

❖ *Right to notice and opportunity to be heard.* This means they have a right to know in advance what the charges are, who is making them, what evidence there is to support the charges, the date and time for the court hearing, and the right to bring evidence in support of their side of the story.

❖ *Right to representation.* This means that parents charged with abuse or neglect and youth charged with delinquent offenses have a right to an attorney. If they cannot afford one, then they have a right to have one appointed at public expense. Children in neglect and abuse matters may or may not have a right to attorney representation, depending on the state statute. They do have the right to have someone speak on their behalf—often a guardian *ad litem.*

❖ *Right to remain silent or privilege against self-incrimination.* This means that parents and youth charged with delinquent offenses can choose not to speak on their own behalf and the court cannot interpret that as an admission of or presumption of guilt.

❖ *Right to confront and cross-examine witnesses.* This means that parents charged with abuse or neglect and youth charged with delinquent offenses have a right to challenge verbally and with documents the testimony and statements of any witness.

THE FAMILY COURT MOVEMENT

The first family court was established in Cincinnati, Ohio, in 1914, just fifteen years after the founding of the juvenile court. Family courts, in general, have jurisdiction over a broad range of legal issues involving children and families. Specific jurisdictional issues include divorce; child support, custody, and visitation; paternity establishment; child abuse and neglect, including termination of parental rights; juvenile delinquency; guardianship; emancipation; and emergency medical and mental health treatment authorization. The underlying rationale is that family legal issues are not isolated. A family experiencing child abuse and neglect may already have custody and visitation orders that could conflict with orders arising out of the child abuse and neglect matter. Divorcing parents frequently charge each other with abuse or neglect. The family courts, having the comprehensive jurisdiction to adjudicate all matters arising out of the same situation, spare the parties the multiplicity of court appearances with their potential for conflicting results. One jurist knows all the facts and is responsible for the resolution of all the legal issues (Szymanski, 1995).

Currently, twenty-five states have family courts. These are in various stages of development. In the past 10 years of surge in the development of family courts, it is clear that development of the systems to support the concept is expensive and time-consuming (Jones, 2006; American Bar Association, 2007). To date, there has not been a comprehensive outcome evaluation of this new system. In jurisdictions where evaluations have occurred, case resolution post-family court implementation is faster; however, there is little evaluative information as to the quality of the resolutions. Furthermore, it has been difficult to isolate whether the change is in the structure itself or other factors caused this result (National Council of Juvenile Justice, 2002; Schepard & Bozzomo, 2003).

Ross (1998) identified four components necessary to classify a court as a "family court":

❖ comprehensive jurisdiction, that is, the ability to adjudicate a range of legal issues so that there is an integrated approach to the resolution of problems within the same family;

❖ efficient administration designed to support the concept of "one family, one team," that is, the provision of continuity in decision-makers so that individual solutions are crafted based in knowledge of the family and its total situation;

❖ broad training for all court personnel, that is, establishing mechanisms so that judges, lawyers, social workers, and other support personnel are trained in the social, medical, psychological issues that arise in connection with the legal issues;

❖ comprehensive services, that is, having a broad array of services available to the family that can be accessed as soon as the family assessment is completed. (pp. 15–28)

As the family court movement progresses, there is a need for critical evaluation of outcomes. In theory, the decisions should be more timely with little, if any, conflicts in orders, and services should be available when needed and in the "dosage" required for the individual family situation. Mark Hardin (1998) commented:

> If, in the end, it appears doubtful that the resources and organization needed to achieve excellence in child protection cases will be in place when a unified family court is established, then advocates will have to ask themselves whether the proposed unified family court will be an improvement for abused and neglected children or, if not, an improvement for children overall. Where the resources are not in place, advocates in some locations may ultimately choose to work for improvement through specialized juvenile courts. . . . In either event, child protection advocates should be aware of the significance of court reform to achieving change beneficial to abused children. (*p. 199*)

THE CRIMINAL COURT MOVEMENT

In the 1980s, the juvenile justice system was challenged with the "just desserts" or "adult crime–adult time" punishment approach. Under this approach, if juveniles were to commit certain statutorily enumerated offenses, generally the most serious offenses, they could be tried and sentenced in the adult criminal court system. It is the current policy approach for serious and/or chronic juvenile offenders.

This approach rests on the assumption that the juvenile court system has not been effective in deterring juvenile crime or correcting juvenile offenders' behaviors. Clearly, the data supported that conclusion; that is, there was a group of serious, chronic juvenile offenders who continued to commit increasingly more serious offenses while under the supervision of the juvenile courts and the juvenile justice treatment systems. Since the mid-1980s, all states have modified their juvenile codes to provide that juveniles could or would be adjudicated by the criminal courts and incarcerated in adult prisons if the crimes were serious enough. The crimes vary by state. In general, they include offenses found in Box 5.2.

Box 5.2

Offenses for Which a Juvenile May Be Tried as an Adult

Although states vary, in general youths aged 14 to 17 may be tried as adults for the following types of offenses:

- ❖ burning a dwelling
- ❖ assault with intent to commit murder
- ❖ assault with intent to commit great bodily harm less than murder
- ❖ assault with intent to rob—unarmed
- ❖ assault with intent to rob—armed
- ❖ attempted murder
- ❖ first-degree murder
- ❖ second-degree murder
- ❖ kidnapping
- ❖ criminal sexual conduct
- ❖ assault with intent to commit criminal sexual conduct
- ❖ armed robbery
- ❖ unarmed robbery
- ❖ possession, manufacture, or delivery of a controlled substance

Howell (1997) noted: "Once again, punishing the offense rather than the offender is the object of the current crime policy" (p. 23). Chapter 11 discusses in detail the prosecution and treatment of the serious, chronic juvenile offender in both the juvenile justice and criminal justice systems.

THE STRUCTURE OF THE LEGAL SYSTEM

The legal system is complex. Law is the body of rules set and enforced by the government. Its function is to provide order and stability to society. Laws are changed when the society, as a whole, determines that the changes are required to advance the goal of order and stability in an ever-changing society. Laws are established in federal and state constitutions, by statutes or ordinances passed by the legislative branch of federal, state, and local governments, by regulatory agencies in administrative rules and regulations, and by federal and state court case decisions.

The ultimate law of the land is the U.S. Constitution. No federal or state statute and no administrative rule or regulation that violates a provision of the U.S. Constitution will prevail when challenged on constitutional grounds and the federal courts find that the statute, rule, or regulation is in violation of the U.S. Constitution.

Assuming that a specific statute, ordinance, administrative rule, or case decision is constitutional, when there is a conflict, the general rule is that

- ❖ federal law supercedes state law and administrative rules if the federal law provides a greater benefit;
- ❖ state law supercedes administrative rules and local ordinances; and
- ❖ administrative rules supercede agency policies.

Case decisions, that is, case law or decisional law, serve to clarify the intent and meaning of federal and state constitutions, statutes, and administrative rules as applied in a specific fact situation or to clarify legal principles if there is no existing statute. Once a higher court of appropriate jurisdiction has ruled on the matter, that ruling serves as the interpretation of the law that all lower courts within the jurisdiction covered by the deciding court must follow.

Trial and Appellate Courts

The court system is comprised of the federal and state courts. Different courts have different jurisdictions, that is, types of legal matters over which they have authority to hear and decide. A trial court is a court in which decisions are based on receipt, examination, and evaluation of witness testimony and evidence. Either a jury or judge makes decisions. An appellate court is a court in which decisions are based on receipt and review of the written record of the trial court. Parties can submit written and oral arguments that identify the alleged errors made at the trial court level. Appellate courts can overturn (*reverse*) or support (*uphold*) the decision of the lower court based on the record as submitted, or can return the case to the trial court with specific instructions or orders (*remand*).

Different states have different statutes and court rules governing appeals. In general, there are appeals of right and appeals by application and leave granted. An appeal of right is taken when a specific statute provides that the decision of a lower court can be appealed to and must be heard by the appellate court. If a specific statutory provision granting an appeal of right is not present, the appeal is taken "by leave granted," that is, petition to the appellate court with the court having discretion as to whether to hear the case. Very few abuse, neglect, and juvenile delinquency matters ever proceed beyond the trial court stage.

Jurisdiction

The **jurisdiction** of a court (that is, its legal authority to hear and decide a particular matter) is determined by state statutes. The judge's authority in decision making is limited to those situations authorized by the statute. In juvenile matters, the primary factors enumerated in the statutes are the subject matter, the maximum age of the children for original jurisdiction, the geographic boundaries of the court, and the matters in which the court has exclusive and/or shared or concurrent jurisdictions.

The **age** of the young person in question is a primary factor that enters into a decision as to whether a juvenile court has jurisdiction. For delinquency matters, in most states the maximum age for original jurisdiction is 17 years; in some states the maximum age is as young as 15 years. Most states allow the juvenile court to continue jurisdiction over juvenile offenders, once they are adjudicated, beyond the maximum age of original jurisdiction. For abuse and neglect matters, in most states the juvenile court now has original jurisdiction up to 18 years, and, if jurisdiction were assumed prior to 18 years, it could continue jurisdiction beyond 18 years when provided by statute. For status offenses and adoption matters, in most states the jurisdictional age limit is 18 years.

The **subject matter** jurisdiction of the juvenile courts, in general, includes four general areas: abuse, neglect, abandonment, and dependency; delinquency; wayward minor, status offender, and minor in need of supervision; and adoption. With the family court movement, the decisional capacities in many states have been expanded to include paternity establishment; child custody, support, and visitation; guardianship; and emancipation. The specific facts of the case determine the appropriate jurisdictional basis. It is not atypical for dependency, neglect, abuse, and delinquency to overlap in the same case: "Parental neglect can precipitate delinquent conduct and the delinquent child may have been subjected to hostility and child abuse in the home. The neglected child may also be a delinquent who has not yet been caught" (Brieland & Lemmon, 1985, p. 139).

Jurisdictional elements are state-specific. Refer to the specific statutes and court rules for the state in which you are practicing.

Evidence

Evidence includes the full range of information, written and verbal, provided to the court in support of the allegations or statements made. Rules of evidence direct the type of information and the method for presenting that information to the court. These rules are promulgated to ensure the fair administration of justice. You should review the rules for the state in which you will be practicing, specifically, the rules related to hearsay, business records, and expert witness testimony. You should document cases and prepare for hearings or trials with these evidentiary rules in mind.

Standards of Proof

A **standard of proof** is the degree of evidence required for the party who has the burden of proof to present to the court in order to sustain its burden, that is, to prove what the party asserts. The standard of proof varies depending on the stage of the hearing process—adjudicatory or dispositional—and the type of case being heard.

The three standards of proof are preponderance of the evidence, clear and convincing evidence, and beyond a reasonable doubt.

Preponderance of the Evidence. This refers to the greater weight of the evidence or evidence that is more credible and convincing. In delinquency matters, this is the standard used in most states for dispositional phase. In neglect or status offense matters, which are not treated as delinquency cases, this is the standard used by most states for adjudicatory phase.

Clear and Convincing Evidence. This proof is beyond preponderance but less than beyond a reasonable doubt. Some say that this means proof beyond a well-founded doubt. This is the standard used in the adjudicatory phase for cases involving Indian Child Welfare Act cases and in termination of parental rights for all children except Indian children. In some states, this standard is used in delinquency matters when the recommended disposition is placement in a secure facility.

Beyond a Reasonable Doubt. This proof must satisfy a moral certainty, be entirely convincing; the facts proven must establish guilt. In delinquency matters, this is the standard used in adjudicatory hearings. It is also the standard used in termination of parental rights of children covered by the Indian Child Welfare Act.

Indian Child Welfare Act: An Example of Federal Law Superseding State Law

The Indian Child Welfare Act, P.L. 95-608, was passed in 1978. Its intent was to curb an excessive rate of placement of Indian children in non-Indian foster and adoptive homes. The legislation came about after years of agitation by Indian groups and other advocates of civil liberties who maintained that out-of-home placements contributed to disruption of tribal culture and to identity confusion on the part of Indian children and encroached on the sovereignty of tribes.

The federal legislation was a significant social policy development, unique in acknowledging and protecting cultural values and self-determination of a minority group within the larger American society. In passing the legislation, Congress stated that the policy of the nation was to promote the stability and security of Indian tribes and families by establishing minimum federal standards for the removal of Indian children from their families. The placement of such children in foster homes hereafter would reflect Indian preferences for placement in priority order: extended family; homes licensed by a nontribal entity; or institutions approved by an Indian tribe.

Tribal courts have exclusive jurisdiction over child custody proceedings involving most Indian children regardless of whether they reside on the reservation. This means that the state court has the responsibility to notify the tribal court that it has a custody matter involving an Indian child before it, and if the tribal court elects to take the case, the state court must transfer the case to the tribal court. Custody proceedings include all foster care or adoptive placements of Indian children resulting from abuse or neglect; termination of parental rights; or status offenses of running away, truancy, and curfew violation. The legislation provided for federal funding to assist tribes in developing and operating child and family service programs.

The U.S. Supreme Court has heard one case involving interpretation of the Indian Child Welfare Act, *Mississippi Band of Choctaw Indians v. Holyfield* (1989). That case involved twins born to an Indian mother who was a member of the Choctaw tribe and who lived on the reservation. The children were born off the reservation, and the mother and father released their parental rights to allow the Holyfields to adopt them. The Holyfields proceeded with the adoption, and the tribe brought a motion to vacate the adoption on the basis that the children were Indian children and the parents did not have the right to release them for adoption by non-Indian persons without tribal permission. The Court stated:

> We agree with the Supreme Court of Utah that the law of domicile Congress used in the ICWA cannot be one that permits individual reservation-domiciled tribal member to defeat the tribe's exclusive jurisdiction by the simple expedient of giving birth and placing the child for adoption off the reservation. Since, for the purposes of ICWA, the twin babies were domiciled on the reservation when adoption proceedings were begun, the Choctaw tribal court possessed exclusive jurisdiction pursuant to 25 U.S.C. Section 1911(a). *(Ibid., 1989, pp. 1610–1611)*

The Court expressed its concern about the fact that the children had lived with the Holyfields for three years while the case proceeded through the appellate process.

> We have been asked to make the decision as to who should make the custody determination concerning these children—not what the outcome of that determination should be. The law places that decision in the hands of the Choctaw tribal court. Had the mandate of the ICWA (Indian Child Welfare Act) been followed in 1986, of course, such potential anguish might have been avoided, and in any case the law cannot be applied so as automatically to reward those who obtained custody, whether lawfully or otherwise, and maintain it during any ensuing (and protracted) litigation. . . . It is not ours to say whether the trauma that might result from removing these children from their adoptive family should outweigh the interest of the Tribe—and perhaps the children themselves—in having them raised as part of the Choctaw community. Rather, we must defer to the experience, wisdom, and compassion of the Choctaw tribal courts to fashion an appropriate remedy. (*p. 1611*)

The legislation and this decision should leave no doubt that matters involving Native American children that come to the attention of the state child welfare system should be immediately referred to the appropriate tribal authority. State systems have authority to act to protect these children from immediate harm while awaiting response from the tribal authority.

LEGAL MATTERS FOR THE CHILD WELFARE SYSTEM

There are many legal matters that involve children, including child abuse, neglect, abandonment, or dependency; juvenile delinquency; status offenses; adoption; guardianship; paternity establishment; support and visitation; child custody, support, and visitation; and emancipation. It is not atypical for a caseworker in child welfare or juvenile delinquency to have a single case with a multitude of legal complexities involving the various issues identified.

Abuse, Neglect, Abandonment, or Dependency

The state's reporting law describes procedures for professionals and other citizens to use in reporting suspected instances of child abuse and neglect to the local child welfare agency and/or the local police department. After the report is received and investigated, the agency or police department decides whether to file a petition with the juvenile court. The factors that go into this decision vary. (See Chapter 6.) Important to note is that the child protection agency can find evidence of abuse, neglect, abandonment, or dependency and not bring the matter to the attention of the court.

The juvenile codes of the states typically provide for jurisdiction when it is alleged that the child

❖ lacks proper guardianship because his or her parents are minors, the parents' whereabouts are unknown, the parents are dead, or the parents are unable to provide acceptable care because of some established mental or physical incapacity;

❖ has been physically, mentally, or emotionally abused by a parent or guardian; or

❖ whose basic needs for food, shelter, clothing, medical care, and education have not been met by the parent or guardian. (See Chapter 6.)

Once the court takes jurisdiction (adjudicates) because of abuse, neglect, or dependency, it has a number of dispositional alternatives, including leaving the child in the home; referring the child to a child welfare agency for placement in foster care, including foster homes (relative and nonrelative), group homes, or residential treatment facilities; and, in extreme situations, immediate termination of parental rights.

Caseworkers have a particularly important role in juvenile court cases involving abuse and neglect because their agencies usually have the following key responsibilities:

❖ determining whether and when to file a petition alleging abuse or neglect;

❖ recommending that the child remain at home or be placed out of the home;

❖ in the case of a recommendation for out-of-home placement, showing that the agency made "reasonable efforts" to keep the family together;

❖ recommending a specific out-of-home placement, including placement with relatives, after investigating all possibilities;

   ❖   establishing a treatment plan with the parent and monitoring progress;

   ❖   reporting to the court on the parent's progress and recommending reunification or termination of parental rights;

   ❖   monitoring and supporting reunification, if that is the plan;

   ❖   preparing evidence to support a judicial decision for termination of parental rights, if it seems unlikely that the child can ever go home and can be adopted; and

   ❖   testifying in court.

It is not an exaggeration to say that the extent to which the juvenile court successfully protects children while supporting continuity of family relationships for children depends to a large extent on the competence of the caseworker and his or her knowledge of the case and of court procedures (Downs & Taylor, 1980). Continuous, meticulous documentation of all contacts with family members is essential if the caseworker wishes to influence the decisions that courts make concerning children.

The following quotation, while over twenty-five years old, has no less relevance today than when made.

> *A primary, essential, unavoidable rule is document, document, document. Admittedly, the tedium of the practice is at times overwhelming, and if the parent improves and the children return home, it may not have been necessary. However, proper recording of the worker's activities is directly related to success in court. Depending on legal practices in your state, your case record may be submitted as an evidentiary exhibit. Any issue with possible controversy is secured by case recording and supporting correspondence.* (A child welfare supervisor—Downs & Taylor, 1980)

Juvenile Delinquency

Delinquency jurisdiction arises when a juvenile, as defined by the state or federal statute, is alleged to have violated any federal or state law, or municipal ordinance. States vary somewhat by excluding certain minor offenses such as vagrancy or loitering, by treating traffic offenses differently depending on whether they are heard in traffic court or juvenile court, and in how they define and handle status offenses, that is, those acts that are illegal because of the youth's age or status. However, the primary criterion in defining delinquency is whether the act would be a crime if committed by an adult.

Although delinquency matters account for almost two percent of the juvenile court dockets nationwide, they receive the headlines and are perceived to be of significantly higher volume (Office of Juvenile Justice and Delinquency Prevention, 2006).

Nearly all states have some provision to permit a juvenile or, where appropriate, a family court to waive jurisdiction in the case of major offenses. This means that the juvenile or family court has the right to transfer a case to the criminal court for adjudication, following procedures delineated in the statutes or court rules that are consistent with those required by *Kent v. United States* (1966). In some states, the case may start in adult court, and it is up to the juvenile to prove that he or she is amenable to treatment in the juvenile system; in still others, the prosecutors have absolute discretion to file cases in adult court, without any hearing at all in juvenile court. (See Box 6.2 for the types of offenses that may be processed in criminal courts.)

Once the court adjudicates, the dispositional alternatives are similar to those it has in abuse and neglect matters. The youth can remain in the home; be placed in foster care, including foster homes, group homes, and residential treatment facilities; or be placed in a secure facility. The dispositional choice is based on the type of offense committed as well as social factors. Chapter 11 provides a detailed discussion of the juvenile delinquency services system.

The caseworker or probation officer is charged with monitoring the treatment and rehabilitation process and making periodic reports to the court.

Status Offenses

Many states provide separate jurisdictional sections for status offenders, wayward minors, or minors in need of supervision within their juvenile codes. For most, jurisdiction arises when it is alleged that the youth is beyond the control of his or her parents or other guardians and displays patterns of conduct deemed incorrigible, uncontrollable, or likely to develop into more serious and dangerous behavior. These situations are often referred to as "status offenses" because the conduct that brings the youth before the court is held to be illegal only because of the youth's age and would not be regarded as illegal if he or she were not a minor. Examples of status offenses include truancy, running away, curfew violations, sexual promiscuity, undesirable companions, and disobedience to parents. Youth who commit status offenses may be referred to as persons (or minors or children) in need of supervision, with the corresponding acronym PINS, MINS, or CHINS. Maintaining status offenses within the jurisdiction of the juvenile court remains highly controversial. Some authorities challenge the wisdom and justice of authorizing the juvenile court to assume jurisdiction over youth who behave in ways encompassed under such general terms as *incorrigibility* and *in need of supervision.* Given the scope, vagueness, and equivocal language of the statutes in many states, almost any child could be brought within the jurisdiction of the juvenile court (Simonsen, 1991).

Concern is expressed that a too-ready transfer of responsibility to bureaucratic discretion is seriously weakening the traditional responsibility of the family for control of children's misbehavior. Within an increasingly adversarial context, some believe the juvenile justice system is being forced to deal with delinquents and status offenders in the same way, that is, to treat status offenses as delinquent acts (Simonsen, 1991). (See Chapter 11.)

Once the court adjudicates, it has a number of dispositional alternatives, including leaving the youth in the home or placement in foster care, such as foster homes (relative and nonrelative), group homes, or residential treatment facilities. (See Chapter 11.)

Adoption

Adoption is the full transfer of parental rights and responsibilities to persons other than the biological parents, after termination of parental rights or voluntary relinquishment of parental rights. The legal process of adoption, relatively speaking, is simple. A petition is filed, along with the appropriate verifications—original birth certificates, child-specific information as required by statute, an adoptive family home study—and the court may or may not hold a hearing. The court orders the placement with or without supervision, depending on the state's statutory requirements. (See Chapter 10.)

Guardianship

Custody, guardianship, and *in loco parentis* are frequently confused. *Custody* generally relates to physical/legal placement with a parent; *guardianship* generally refers to physical/legal placement with someone other than the parent, because parents are by law the natural guardians of their children; and *in loco parentis* generally refers to a designated individual having authority to engage in certain parental acts on behalf of a child through statutory authority or a specific court order—for example, foster parents.

There are important differences between the rights and responsibilities of parents and those of a court-appointed guardian. Guardianship through court appointment is subject to the continuing supervision of the court. Guardianship, unlike parenthood, does not involve the duty to support and educate the child, who is generally called a "ward," except from the economic resources of the child, that is, his or her estate. It does not carry the right to the ward's earnings and services. The parent of a child has the right to control incidental assets of the child such as income from gifts and typical childhood employment. Control over other assets of the child such as insurance settlements, lawsuit awards, distributions from wills and trusts, or income from professional employment during minority generally requires a specific appointment of the parent or someone else as guardian of the estate. This triggers court oversight of the management of the estate. Children under court-appointed guardianship have statutory rights to inherit from their parents should the parents die without a will (intestate succession); they do not have any statutory rights to inherit from their guardians. If the guardians want the ward to inherit from them, they must specifically identify them and what they wish them to have in the guardians' wills. Parents have the right to choose where their child shall live as long as the care given does not fall below the minimal standards demanded by the community. In contrast, a guardian of the person may or may not have the authority to independently change the ward's residence. Parents cannot independently transfer their rights of legal guardianship. Whether the transfer of guardianship is voluntary or involuntary, the state court having jurisdiction over guardianship matters must be involved, and that court remains involved, so long as the guardianship is in effect.

There are two basic types of guardianship: guardian of the person and guardian of the estate. The **guardian of the person** becomes responsible for the care and control of the child. Depending on the state law, the guardian can decide the kind of medical care, including permission for major medical, psychiatric, and surgical treatment; or decisions about education, employment, permission for marriage, and permission for entry into the armed forces; and the right to represent the child in legal actions. In certain instances, the guardian of person may have been invested by court action with the power to consent to the adoption of the minor when the parent–child relationship has been fully terminated by judicial decree. Guardians of the person do not have the right to receive and manage property that their wards may acquire unless specifically authorized to do so through a separate appointment as the guardian of the estate.

Guardian of the estate creates a means by which a minor can deal in the business world. Guardians of the estate have power to govern the estate and act for their wards in matters involving property. The guardian of the estate can mortgage, sell, or otherwise transfer property and make the resources available for the ward's needs during his or her minority. Guardians of estate are persons of presumed integrity and are subject to the continuing supervision of the court. In general, they must submit periodic accountings of the ward's assets and their transactions to the court. Unless the guardian of estate is also named guardian of person, the guardian does not have the right to interfere in personal affairs of the minor but must confine his or her activities to the management of the estate.

While state laws vary, parents in most states can provide for **standby guardians** and **testamentary guardians.** These options are particularly useful in effecting permanency plans in child welfare cases in which the parent has a terminal illness, such as HIV/AIDS. A standby guardian is a person named by the parent to assume guardianship of the child should the parent become disabled and/or unable to care for the child. A testamentary guardian is a person named by the parent in his or her last will and testament to assume guardianship of the person of the child on the parent's death. Both are voluntary, independent acts of parents. Both require court approval before the guardians assume their responsibilities. Only a legal parent can name a testamentary guardian, and the testamentary guardian does not automatically assume guardianship responsibilities if another legal parent survives the one designating the testamentary guardian.

Guardianship often has been insufficiently understood as a resource for children who are abused, neglected, or abandoned. Guardianship is a practice and a policy issue in child welfare practice. The use of guardianship arrangements instead of foster care for the substitute care of children has been acknowledged as a viable resource for children in the child welfare system by national standard-setting agencies. The Children's Bureau position, stated in 1961, remains unchallenged in principle to this date.

> All children are entitled to an individual guardian "by birth or adoption or a judicially appointed guardian." This guardian is responsible for safeguarding the child's interests, making important decisions in her or his life, and maintaining a personal relationship with the child. (*p. 3*)

The practice of guardianship placement in lieu of foster care or adoptive placement can, depending on the specifics of the state's guardianship statutes, raise significant due process issues for the children, the legal parents, and the guardians. It is not uncommon to see legal guardians charged with neglect or abuse of their wards. Nor is it uncommon to have legal guardians rescind their guardianships when the child becomes "unruly." In voluntary guardianship arrangements, the parent usually retains authority to return and demand physical custody of the child at any time. In involuntary guardianships, the parent's rights may be terminated if he or she fails to complete the agreed-on plan in the specified time. Often, courts do not provide supportive services to parents whose children are under guardianship arrangements, whereas those services are provided to parents whose children are under abuse or neglect jurisdictional arrangements. All of these concerns raise the fundamental issue of protection and permanency for the child. To minimize these concerns and ensure the best use of legal guardianship in child welfare cases, social workers should assess each case situation with these principles as guides.

❖ Children are individuals with the right to develop their fullest capacities in a stable, supportive adult–child relationship.

❖ Parents have the first right and responsibility to give care, protection, stability, and support to their children.

❖ When parental efforts fall short of society's minimum standards, the state has the authority and responsibility to provide substitute care and protection, using the jurisdictional basis that will provide the best due process, equal protections, and permanency for child and parent.

❖ The judicial review and oversight responsibility for legal guardianship should be no less than that imposed for abuse, neglect, or dependency, that is, children under legal guardianship arrangements should be entitled to frequent judicial review of their status as wards and the quality of care provided by substitute caregivers.

❖ The choice of legal guardianship should not be made because the process is easier for the child welfare worker, but because it is in the best interests of the child.

Irrespective of whether the transfer of guardianship is voluntarily or involuntarily sought, the state court that has jurisdiction over guardianship matters must be involved. Further, that court remains involved so long as the guardianship is in effect. (See Chapters 8 and 9 for additional discussion of the role of permanent guardianship in child welfare cases.)

Paternity Establishment, Support, and Visitation

If a child is born to unmarried parents, the paternity of the child must be established for the father to legally assume the privileges, benefits, and responsibilities of parenthood. State statutes govern the process for paternity establishment. In general, there are two procedures:

❖ acknowledgment voluntarily signed by the mother and father
❖ adjudication of parentage through a court process should either the mother or father object to a voluntary acknowledgment

Once paternity has been established, by whichever method, the parents' individual and collective abilities to support the child and the visitation rights, if the parents live apart, may be voluntarily agreed to or determined by the court.

The caseworker should proceed with paternity establishment early in the processing of a child welfare case, because it is critical to case planning. From a legal perspective, the legal father and his family become potential care providers if identified early in the case processing, and furthermore, proceeding to permanency through termination of parental rights requires identification of the father and termination of his rights. (See Chapter 8, 9.)

The Federal Parent Locator Service, a national database, is available to child protection agencies to assist in locating parents and securing child support payment (Jones, 2006).

Child Custody, Support, and Visitation

Most controversy over custody, support, and visitation arises with a divorce action. Divorce statutes in all states make provision for awards of custody of children of the marriage. When there are issues of child abuse and neglect or delinquency in the family, child custody, support, and visitation present additional considerations. Specifically, unless the case is in a "family court" jurisdiction, at least two judges and two different courts will likely handle it. These judges and courts may or may not coordinate decision making, which may or may not result in conflicting orders with respect to the children's custody, support, and parental visitation.

Some jurisdictions no longer use the adversarial term *custody* and favor instead "allocating parental responsibilities" or "parenting plans following divorce." Many different options are available regarding custody, support, and visitation. While custody with the mother had been the norm until the early 1980s, joint custody became the preference of many courts during the 1990s. This generally results from a court order or a court-approved agreement between parents that provides for joint decision making concerning a child's education, medical treatment, religious training, and care. In some joint arrangements, physical custody is also shared. Rarely does a court, in deciding child custody in a divorce matter, order custody of a child to a third party when the parent(s) are alive. When a child's best interests require it, most states provide for custody to be granted to someone other than one of the parents. Generally, in such situations, relatives or friends are given preference over social agencies.

The most frequent social work roles in custody actions that arise from divorce are mediation with parents to arrive at the best plan for the child or, failing that, carrying out a family evaluation and recommending a particular custody or shared parenting time plan to the judge. Caseworkers handling child welfare matters may, from time to time, be confronted with conflicting court orders. The divorce order may grant custody to the father, whereas the child abuse/neglect order grants custody to the mother. In general, each state handles these conflicts by court rule. The caseworkers should know the rules and advise the juvenile court that a prior custody order exists.

Emancipation

Emancipation is the legal process by which a person younger than the age of majority, which is usually 18 years, is given the status and privileges afforded someone who is over the age of majority. State statutes specify the conditions under which emancipation can occur. Typically, they provide that persons who marry or join the military are emancipated by operation of law, that is, automatically on execution of the marriage or joining the military. Otherwise, a petition is required that must state the reasons for the emancipation and the young person's means of support.

COURT PROCEDURES

Processing the Abuse/Neglect or Delinquency Case in Juvenile or Family Court

An orderly process involving four steps is generally followed when a child or juvenile comes to the attention of the court: intake, investigation, adjudication, and disposition.

Initiating the Case. Courts do not act as casefinders. Generally, a court concerns itself with children only when a complaint or petition is filed by law enforcement (delinquency matters), the designated child protection agency (neglect, abuse, and dependency matters), the parent or person acting *in loco parentis* (status offenses, and minors in need of supervision), or in some states the child through an adult acting for him or her (adoption, guardianship, emancipation, and termination of parental rights).

Depending on the state statute and court procedures, the police or child protective services agency files either a complaint or a petition. In filing the complaint or petition, the complainant or petitioner must allege sufficient facts to show that the case comes within the jurisdiction of the court. For example,

> John Brown, born October 1, 1990, was treated at the Children's Hospital for a broken arm. The parent's statement as to how the arm was broken was inconsistent with medical evidence. The hospital filed a complaint with the child protection agency. In addition to the hospital's report, the investigating worker interviewed the parent's mother, who stated that she saw the parent "yank the child by the arm." The worker submits that this is evidence of abuse within the juvenile code. Further, the child and his mother reside in Little Town within the jurisdiction of this Court.

or, in a delinquency matter,

> Susan Sharp is a 14-year-old residing in Midville. On July 3, 1998, she took a sweater from the Big Department Store located in Midville without paying. This act was recorded on security cameras. This act constitutes a violation of the Criminal Code Section 101.

The court clerk or another designated official determines if the complaint or petition meets the requirements for filing. If it does, a date is set for a hearing. The timing of the hearing date is provided in statute or court rules. The child's parents or guardians must be notified of the petition, the time of the hearing, and their right to be represented by counsel.

Preliminary Inquiry or Hearing. Before the court can adjudicate the matter, it must first ensure that it has jurisdiction—that is, the court must establish its authority to hear and decide the case. The court does so by ascertaining certain facts, such as the age of the child, where he or she lives, where the alleged acts took place, and who committed the acts. If these established facts fit the kinds of situations over which the court has been given authority by statute, then it may proceed with the case. The court also makes a preliminary assessment of the evidence supporting the allegations and, consistent with state law or court rules, determines whether the child should remain with the parent or be removed pending the adjudication or whether the case should be diverted, dismissed, or authorized for adjudication.

Adjudication. The adjudication is the fact-finding or trial phase of the processing of the case. Here the court weighs the facts, properly presented under the rules of evidence by both sides, and decides whether the child, under the law, is delinquent, neglected, or dependent; or is in need of supervision; or requires an award of custody or guardianship. In reaching a decision in a neglect, abuse, or dependency allegation, the judge is expected to determine whether a preponderance of the evidence presented supported the allegations. If it did, then there is basis for taking wardship. If it did not, then the case should be dismissed. In reaching a decision in a delinquency allegation, the judge is expected to determine whether the evidence presented proved beyond a reasonable doubt that this juvenile committed the alleged offense.

Disposition. All court orders entered after the adjudication are dispositional. The disposition is, in essence, the decision as to how the child shall be treated—that is, what is to be ordered or arranged for him or her following the adjudication or case reviews. Judges have a great deal of discretion in the dispositional phase, in contrast to the adjudicatory phase in which they are bound by statutes and court rules. After a finding or plea that an act occurred within the statutory definition of abuse, neglect, delinquency, or status offense (adjudication), the judge must decide what to do to alleviate or remedy the condition(s).

If, at the conclusion of the adjudicatory hearing, the judge decides that there is sufficient evidence for the court to take wardship of the child, he or she may order a family and child assessment or social investigation to assist in the establishment of an appropriate disposition and treatment plan. The Adoption and Safe Families Act of 1997 requires courts to assume greater oversight in monitoring the case plan and services to the child and family to ensure permanency as soon as possible. Thus, the social investigation and case plan become more important to the legal process as well as the social work intervention. (See Chapters 7 and 8 for a more detailed discussion of the Adoption and Safe Families Act of 1997.)

The social investigation may be carried out by the probation staff or by a social agency as a service to the court. Typically, probation staff handles delinquency matters and social agencies handle all other matters. In some states, where the social agency also supervises delinquency wards, those agencies are expected to present the social investigation on youth already under their supervision who commit new offenses. In any case, it is important that the court have all the facts necessary to act properly in the best interests of the child and, if a delinquency matter, the promotion of public safety as well. The investigation presents facts and evaluations that help the judge determine what treatment plan is appropriate and what orders, if any, the court needs to make to ensure that the treatment plan is carried out in a timely manner.

Prior to the mid-1990s, judges had almost total discretion in dispositional alternatives. With increasing attacks on family preservation, children in foster care limbo, and community placement for juvenile delinquents, many states through statutory changes have limited the discretion of the judge. If a juvenile commits a certain offense, the disposition is prescribed in statute. If the abuse is so severe or is continuing and chronic, the disposition is prescribed in statute. The most common dispositions remain as follows:

❖ *Warn and dismiss.* No further action is needed and therefore the case is closed, as in instances of a single, minor delinquent act or status offense when it is believed that the family is able to prevent further misconduct on the part of the child.

❖ *Probation.* The child is found to be delinquent or guilty of a status offense and is placed on probation and permitted to remain in the community under the official supervision of the court.

❖ *Temporary wardship with in-home supervision.* The child is found to be neglected or abused and is allowed to remain at home under the protective supervision of a social agency.

❖ *Temporary wardship with out-of-home placement.* The child, whether delinquent, guilty of a status offense, neglected, abandoned, or abused, may be placed out of the home for protection, care, and treatment. Placements may be in foster homes, group homes, relatives' homes, an independent living situation if the youth is of appropriate age and maturity, institutions, or privately operated/state training schools or secure facilities.

❖ *Permanent wardship.* Increasingly, state statutes are providing for immediate termination of parental rights in serious abuse cases or when prior children have been removed and parental rights terminated. Further, all statutes provide specific conditions under which parental rights to a child who has been a temporary ward may be terminated.

❖ *Termination of court wardship.* This disposition is used when the child has exceeded the age limit for jurisdiction; the conditions that led to neglect or abuse wardship no longer exist, the child is adopted, or the juvenile has been rehabilitated and no longer poses a threat to public safety.

In delinquency matters, the juvenile court appears to be abandoning its historical tradition of basing its dispositional decisions on the individual characteristics of the juvenile and his or her need for rehabilitation, and moving toward a system of making dispositional decisions based on punishment, accountability, and public safety or offense-based dispositions (Office of Juvenile Justice and Delinquency Prevention, 1998, p. 32). The goals appear to be retribution and deterrence (Howell, 1997).

This change in the juvenile court processing of juvenile offenders is its acknowledgment of the increasing presence of serious, chronic juvenile offenders, the increasing use of drugs and alcohol by juvenile offenders within the system, and the need to hold juveniles accountable for their actions earlier in their delinquency careers to deter more effectively the tendency to continue and escalate their delinquent behaviors. The National Council of Juvenile and Family Court Judges endorsed a number of recommendations relating to the problem of serious juvenile crime in 1984, the first of which was this: "*Serious juvenile offenders should be held accountable by the courts. Dispositions of such offenders should be proportionate to the injury done and the culpability of* the juvenile and to the prior record of adjudication, if any". The Council added that "the principal purpose of the juvenile justice court system is to protect the public," and qualified this position only by the statement, "Although rehabilitation is a primary goal of the court, it is not the sole objective and not always appropriate" (Heck, Pindur, & Wells, 1985, p. 29).

This position has been tempered by the concept of balanced and restorative justice, which has taken hold in most jurisdictions. This approach advocates concurrent attention to public safety, individual accountability to victims and the community, and helping offenders develop skills to live law abiding and productive lives (Office of Juvenile Justice and Delinquency Prevention, 2006, p. 98).

Review Hearings. Dispositional decisions are reviewed by the court at specific intervals established by statute or court rule or at any time on motion by the supervising agency, the prosecutor, the youth, or other person acting on his or her behalf. At review hearings, the situation is reassessed and a determination is made on whether to order a new disposition. For example, the judge might decide to send a child home from foster care if the conditions that led to the child's removal had been alleviated to a degree that the child could be safe at home. In a delinquency matter, the judge could decide to move the youth from a secure to a nonsecure facility based on reports of the youth's progress in rehabilitation and the risk to public safety.

The review hearing is a monitoring mechanism to ensure that there is progress toward a permanent solution for the child. The review hearing can be used as a device to resolve controversies between the agency and parent when the agency has custody, such as a dispute over visitation or case planning. It can be used to clarify expectations of all parties and set a time certain for final disposition.

The Adoption and Safe Families Act of 1997 strengthened the responsibilities of the courts in conducting review hearings. The first round of the Child and Family Services Reviews (CFSR), completed in 2005, found that the timeliness expectations of permanency planning hearings and review hearings were not met. The Children's Bureau determined that the courts were not engaged in the CFSR planning or program improvement planning (PIP) process to the extent necessary. Thus, in June 2005, it issued a directive to the states to demonstrate actual involvement of the courts in these processes and adapted the Children's Bureau technical assistance and on-site processes to ensure court and state child welfare agency coordination in planning and performance improvements (U.S. Department of Health and Human Services, Children's Bureau, 2005; Fiermonte & Salyers, 2005).

Termination of Parental Rights. Termination of parental rights is the second most extreme action the legal system can take in abuse and neglect cases. The first, of course, is the initial intrusion into the family's autonomy with the removal of the child from the parent. In general, termination of parental rights is based on the following:

❖ Children need permanency and stability in their lives.
❖ The child before the court has been in out-of-home care for a statutorily specified period.
❖ The conditions that led to the removal have not been corrected.
❖ There is no reason to believe that they will be corrected in the foreseeable future.

Specific grounds for termination of parental rights are described in the statutes of each state. Pike et al. (1977) identified four overarching reasons for termination of parental rights that are present in some form in every state statute to this date: abandonment, desertion, parental condition, and parental conduct.

❖ *Abandonment and Desertion.* State statutes enumerate the failure of parents to identify the child, visit, establish paternity, contribute to the child's support, or maintain contact with the child's custodian for a prescribed period of time as grounds for termination of parental rights.

❖ *Parental Condition.* State statutes enumerate conditions such as mental illness, emotional illness, mental deficiency, narcotic or dangerous drug addiction, and alcohol addiction which have lasted or are expected to last for a certain period of time as grounds for termination of parental rights.

❖ *Parental Conduct.* State statutes enumerate conduct such as the chronic and continuing physical neglect of the child, serious physical abuse of the child or a sibling of the child, sexual abuse of the child or a sibling of the child and failure of parent to correct the conditions or conduct which lead to the child's removal as grounds for termination of parental rights. (pp. 5.1–5.8)

The social work issues related to a decision to seek termination of parental rights are discussed in greater detail in Chapter 9. The legal requirements are established in each state's statutes. A hearing to terminate parental rights is usually a formal proceeding such as the adjudicatory hearing, even though it is a dispositional action. When contested, it can be lengthy and involve many elaborate, technical, legal procedures.

The burden of proof is clear and convincing evidence, a higher standard than preponderance of evidence but somewhat less stringent than the beyond a reasonable doubt standard. Another indicator of the seriousness of this state action is the attention to ensuring that any adult with possible parental rights to the child is notified and has the opportunity to present evidence in court. This is particularly salient in the case of unmarried fathers, whose rights were at one time disregarded. (See Chapter 1 for a discussion of U.S. Supreme Court decisions on the standard of proof and on the rights of unmarried fathers.)

How a Juvenile Offender Comes before the Criminal Court

The states vary as to the procedure used to effect these transfers—judicial waiver, prosecutor discretion, or legislative exclusion. In the judicial waiver situation, the case originates in the juvenile court, and prior to holding an adjudicatory hearing, the juvenile court, consistent with state statutory guidelines, determines that the nature of the offense, the age of the juvenile, and the juvenile's past history are such that the juvenile is unlikely to benefit from juvenile court intervention. Then the case is waived to criminal court.

In the prosecutorial discretion situation, the prosecutor—the official who brings the charge on behalf of the people of the state—has full authority to decide, consistent with the state statutory requirements, whether he or she will prosecute the juvenile in the juvenile court or in the criminal court.

If he or she originates the action in juvenile court, the juvenile judge has authority to waive the case. However, if he or she chooses to originate the action in criminal court, the criminal court does not have authority to return the case to the juvenile court in most states. In the legislative exclusion situation, certain crimes that are committed by juveniles of certain ages are automatically within the exclusive jurisdiction of the criminal courts, meaning only the criminal court can hear the case.

While the names of the phases differ, the substantive processes are similar and the rights granted to the juvenile are the same.

Processing a Juvenile Offender in Criminal Court

Again, the courts do not seek out cases. Cases are brought to them. In criminal offenses, the police usually receive a complaint from a victim or are called to the scene of a crime by an individual in the community. They investigate and apprehend or arrest the suspected offender. After investigation, they can choose not to file charges to divert the juvenile for other services. If they choose to go forward, the police submit their information to the prosecutor, who determines the specific crime to charge, based on the evidence submitted by the police, and files a complaint with the court.

Once it is determined that a juvenile offense is to be prosecuted in the criminal courts, the prosecutor must file a complaint. The matter is then scheduled for preliminary examination or probable cause hearing. When probable cause is found, it is scheduled for arraignment or bail hearing if these matters are not scheduled as part of the preliminary examination or probable cause hearing, and a date is set for trial. If the juvenile is found guilty at trial or pleads guilty, a sentencing hearing is scheduled.

The Complaint.   This complaint is similar to the complaint or petition filed in juvenile court in that it contains specifics about the offense, the law it violates, and the name, age, and address of the person who is alleged to have committed the offense. The prosecutor is given discretion to charge a crime less than the one supported by the evidence.

The Preliminary Examination or Probable Cause Hearing.   This procedure is a review of the evidence against the juvenile by the judge and results in a determination as to whether the evidence is sufficient to believe that this juvenile committed the charged offense, should be charged with a lesser offense, or should be diverted.

The Arraignment or Bail Hearing.   If the person has been arrested, he or she must be arraigned on the charges, that is, given an opportunity to appear in court and hear the charges and the evidence, enter a plea (guilty or not guilty), and have bail set (an amount of money to be posted with the court to guarantee appearance at the trial). Many states do not permit bail to be set if a serious crime such as murder or rape is charged. There is no proscription as to the maximum amount of bail that can be set. Thus, many courts set high bails for juvenile offenders as a way of keeping them in custody until the trial. If the juvenile cannot post bail, he or she is held in jail. There is some debate as to whether a juvenile charged as an adult must be confined separately from adults.

The Trial.   The trial in criminal court is similar in form and process to the adjudication in juvenile court. The juvenile has a right to have the facts determined by a judge or jury. During the trial, the evidence is presented in accordance with the state's rules of evidence. If the evidence does not prove beyond a reasonable doubt that the juvenile committed the crimes charged, he or she must be found not guilty and released. If the evidence proves beyond a reasonable doubt that the juvenile committed the crimes charged, he or she must be found guilty and the matter set for sentencing.

The Sentencing.   The sentencing is the phase in which the punishment is rendered. In some states, sentencing guidelines require the judge to issue certain sentences for certain offenses. In other states, it is totally within the judge's discretion to determine the sentence. Most sentencing decisions are based on the crime, the juvenile's participation in the crime, the juvenile's past history, and any unique factors made known to the court in the sentencing report or by the juvenile.

Traditional sentences include

- ❖ probation
- ❖ suspended sentence

- ❖ fine
- ❖ community service
- ❖ restitution
- ❖ jail and probation
- ❖ periodic imprisonment (to permit the juvenile to continue employment while serving sentence)
- ❖ confinement in jail or prison
- ❖ death (Jacobs, 1995; 1997; Saltzman & Proch, 2000; Kramer, 1994, 2002)

THE ROLE OF THE CASEWORKER IN THE COURT PROCESS

Caseworkers that function as child welfare workers or juvenile probation workers provide social investigations, dispositional recommendations, and casework services for both the parents and the child until the court dismisses the case. In carrying out these responsibilities, the caseworker must gather and document information to

- ❖ support the allegations in the petition,
- ❖ advise the court on the actions taken to comply with previous court orders,
- ❖ support the caseworkers recommendations for dispositional actions, and
- ❖ present this information orally and/or in writing to the court when the case requires court intervention.

Although many child abuse and neglect interventions occur without court involvement—that is, the parent acknowledges that the event occurred and agrees to voluntary interventions to ensure the child's safety—the practices suggested in this section ensure that the rights of all parties are protected and the facts are determined so as to promote appropriate interventions.

This section provides a brief summary of the critical elements in forensic interviewing, case documentation, court report writing, and oral testimony. The reader is directed to the references section of this chapter for materials providing comprehensive coverage of these areas.

Critical Elements in Forensic Interviewing

It is suggested that all investigations follow a forensic interviewing and documentation approach because this approach provides for an unbiased, multiperspective reporting of the incident from which the caseworker can make an informed conclusion as to the truthfulness of the allegations and the most appropriate intervention.

Information is gathered through interviews with the child or juvenile, persons involved with the child and/or family, and a review of written documents pertaining to the child and/or family. Child welfare and juvenile justice investigations need to be conducted in ways that preserve the evidence and limit the attack on the social worker's methodologies in collecting that evidence. The interview process for court purposes is different from the interview for treatment purposes. In essence, the goal of interviews for court purposes—that is, forensic interviews—is to obtain descriptions of the events that occurred from people who experienced them from their experiential perspective as victim, perpetrator, observer, or professional interventionist. In these interviews, the caseworker is attempting to determine what happened, when it happened, how it happened, and who was involved in the act (victim, perpetrator, and protectors/interveners). Having gathered this information from a variety of perspectives, the caseworker then identifies the variances in the accounts and seeks to resolve these variances through additional interviews and review of written materials.

In Chapter 4, we discussed the critical elements of forensic interviewing. While we encourage the use of forensic interviewing principles in all child welfare cases, they are especially important in cases that proceed to court for adjudication and disposition.

Case Record Documentation

Case records, properly documented, are critical in the child welfare system's increasingly rapid march toward permanency for children. One of the unfortunate realities of the system is that staff turnover remains a major barrier to effective services for children and families. When workers leave and relevant information is not documented in the case file, the new worker loses much needed case intervention time in obtaining information that was known to the previous worker.

Each agency has its own case record documentation requirements. Much of the case record documentation is incidental to the reason the child and family are under the jurisdiction of the court, for example, eligibility determinations, computer system input forms, and supervisory case review forms. Other information, while helpful to ensuring the child's well-being and development, might be incidental to the court process unless it is connected to a reason the court took jurisdiction, for example, education reports and medical reports. Many times, the case plan and the court orders appear to have no connection with each other. A case record for a child that is under court jurisdiction and subject to the Adoption and Safe Families Act (ASFA) requirements for expedited permanency for children in out-of-home care should have a specific section in the original case plan stating the reasons the court took jurisdiction, the orders it entered, and the agreements between the parent, child, and agency stating the specific actions each will take and the projected time by which the actions will be taken to fulfill the orders of the court. Updated case plans would be completed based on contemporaneous documentation that is specific to dates and actions related to the previous case plan, which is related to the progress of the parent, child, and agency in complying with previous court orders crafted to alleviate the conditions that brought the child and family to the attention of the court, as well as modifications to orders based on subsequent findings of the court. Thus, a very simplified case documentation structure for the legal aspects of the case plan, consistent with ASFA requirements, would include

❖ date of contact,
❖ type of contact,
❖ statement of the purpose of contact,
❖ identity of persons participating,
❖ location of contact,
❖ description of what happened,
❖ summary of actions to be taken and by whom as a result of the contact, and
❖ worker's signature and date of entry.

Example: Case Documentation

On January 31, 2002, the court took jurisdiction of Rosie Jones and ordered, in part, that the mother get substance abuse treatment services from the Women's Substance Abuse Treatment Program, obtain weekly drug screens and submit the results to Child and Family Services, visit the child at the grandmother's home at least once a week, and attend weekly parenting education classes for parents with young children at the Parenting for Children Center.

The worker's documentation of a contact with the child's mother is shown in Box 5.3. As you can see, this contact documentation is factual and not filled with the worker's conclusions. This type of contact documentation, combined with others as well as the receipt and review of various reports from the involved agencies, provides the blueprint for the updated service plans and court reports. It minimizes lost information in the event of worker turnover, while helping to effect permanency for children by keeping the focus on what must be done to achieve that permanency through the court system. It ensures that case records do not subject the agency and its social workers to attacks from lawyers who allege that the caseworker is biased or prejudiced against the mother, fails to assist the mother in obtaining needed services, is inexperienced or incompetent, and that the agency, through a stream of workers, provides inconsistent instructions or directions regarding the court's expectations.

Example: Court Report

Courts vary as to expectations about what is included in written court reports and when they are to be submitted to the court and parties. In addition, requirements will vary depending on the role the caseworker has in the court process. A caseworker who is providing child welfare services would be expected to focus his or her report on the status of the child and the parents with respect to the specific orders of the court. This report should provide the facts and be well documented by reports or testimony from those providing the direct service to the child and parent, as shown in Box 5.4.

A caseworker who is providing mental health treatment would be expected to report on the nature of the mental illness or condition being treated, its impact on the parent's ability to perform parenting responsibilities in a manner sufficient to ensure child safety, the parent's degree of participation in treatment, the prognosis, and the expected length of time required for treatment before the parent is able to resume parenting responsibilities. Because of space limitations, an example of a mental health treatment report is not included here.

Testifying

In the court process itself, caseworkers are frequently called on to give testimony in addition to written progress reports, either as a fact witness or as an expert witness. A fact witness is one who gives information as to what he or she saw, heard, said, or did in relation to a specific issue before the court. An expert witness is one who is asked to give opinions or provide specialized knowledge on facts presented by others or themselves because they have specialized education, training, and experience. A caseworker, depending on the circumstances, can function in both capacities (Dickson, 1995).

Box 5.3

Rosie Jones Case Documentation

On March 4, 2002, I met with Mrs. Jones at the Child and Family Services offices to discuss the status of her participation in the substance abuse treatment program, weekly drug screens, weekly visitation with her child at the grandmother's home, and enrollment in the parenting education program as ordered by the court.

Mrs. Jones stated that she has been going in for weekly drug screens at the Drug Screening Center since the week after the court hearing. She signed a paper so they could send the results directly to me. She stated that she had not gone to the substance abuse treatment program. She did not give any reason for not going. She said she would go next week.

She said that she has been going to visit her child "just about every day." They read and play together while she is there. She said she frequently picks Rosie up from Head Start and walks her to her (Mrs. Jones's) mother's house.

I told Mrs. Jones that the agency has her on a waiting list for parenting classes. She would not be able to start the parenting classes until July 8. We reviewed the list of available locations and times for those classes. She picked Monday morning from 9 A.M. to 11:30 A.M. at the Jefferson Library on Jefferson and Dickerson. She told me that the library is down the street from the house where she is currently staying. She stated that she is living with her cousin, and the cousin says she can stay there until she finishes her treatment and her (Mrs. Jones's) mother lets her move back to her house. The address is 1201 Dickerson, MyTown 00014. Her phone number is (123) 456-7890.

Follow-Ups:

1. Mrs. Jones will go to the Women's Substance Abuse Treatment Program, enroll in the program, and fulfill the participation requirements. She will call me if she has any problems with this.
2. She will continue to get the drug screens weekly.
3. She will continue to visit Rosie as often as possible.
4. I will notify the Parenting for Children Center of the time and location she chose for the parenting education classes.
5. I will notify the court of her new address.

Signature: Charles W. Worker 03/04/02

Although the thought of testifying may be terrifying to the beginning child welfare worker and a source of ongoing anxiety for the experienced child welfare worker, testifying becomes easier with advance preparation and documentation of evidence. Preparation requires knowing the law involved, knowing the facts of the case, and understanding how those facts and the law relate to one another. Documentation requires distinguishing fact from opinion. Fact, as supported by documents or witnesses, is evidence. Opinions that are based on the application of theoretical knowledge to the facts of the case are important, but opinions that are not based in fact or knowledge provide attorneys with the opportunity to totally discredit the caseworker's testimony. If the caseworker approaches testifying prepared with factual documentation and applicable theoretical

Box 5.4

Rosie Jones Court Report

ANY JURISDICTION FAMILY COURT
CHILD ABUSE AND NEGLECT DOCKET

Hearing Date: May 05, 2002

Case Name: Rosie Jones

Court File No: 2002-1050

Parent's Name: Anna Jones, mother
Father unknown

Progress Report for Review Hearing

On January 31, 2002, the court ordered Rosie Jones placed with the maternal grandmother, enrolled in Head Start, and provided a complete physical examination and required medical treatment. The mother was ordered to receive services from the Women's Substance Abuse Treatment Program, submit the results of weekly drug screens to Child and Family Services, visit the child at the grandmother's home at least once a week, and attend weekly parenting education classes for Parents with Young Children at the Parenting for Children Center.

Rosie was placed with the maternal grandmother, Sarah Jones, on February 1, 2002, and remains with her. This worker has visited Rosie in the home four times since the placement. She has her own room, several age-appropriate toys and books, and new clothing. She is an active child who loves to talk as long as her grandmother is in the room. Her grandmother calms her by hugging her and lifting her up to sit on her lap. Rosie does not attempt to break away from these hugs.

She was enrolled in Head Start on February 14, 2002, and remains enrolled. She shows intellectual and social development at or above age level. A copy of the Head Start report dated April 30, 2002, is attached.

She received a complete physical examination from Dr. Sarah Cooper on February 8, 2002. She received the necessary immunizations for Head Start enrollment on this date. On February 20, 2002, the grandmother received a call telling her that, based on the results of the blood work, additional screening for sickle cell trait or anemia was necessary. The grandmother scheduled a follow-up appointment with the recommended specialist for June 1, 2002. This was the earliest possible date for the appointment. A copy of Dr. Cooper's medical report is attached.

Mrs. Jones sought services from the Women's Substance Abuse Treatment Program (WSATP) on February 17, 2002. She was told to return on February 18, 2002, because she arrived too late in the day to be processed. She did not return to the agency until March 18, 2002. Mrs. Jones told this worker that she couldn't get a ride before then. She had not contacted the worker for assistance with a ride. She was enrolled in the program on March 18, 2002. The program required daily attendance for four hours in either the morning or the afternoon. Bus tickets were provided for each day of attendance. Between March 18 and April 30, Mrs. Jones attended 6 days according to WSATP. Given the infrequency of her attendance, WSATP has insufficient information to provide an assessment or recommendation regarding her ability to care for her child. A copy of the WSATP report dated May 1, 2002, is attached. Mrs. Jones had reported to the worker that she had attended most of the sessions. When asked to explain the difference in her statement of attendance and that of the agency, she said she didn't like the people in the group and just stopped going after the first week. When asked

(*continued*)

Box 5.4 (continued)

if she discussed this with WSATP staff, she said, "No." When asked if she understood that the court order required her to attend this program, she said, "Yes." When asked what she intended to do to comply with the court order, she said she did not know.

Mrs. Jones obtained weekly drug screens from the Drug Screening Center starting February 5, 2002. The center submitted written statements of the results directly to the agency each week. Mrs. Jones tested positive for cocaine in 35 percent of the screens. Copies of the weekly reports from Drug Screening Center are attached.

This worker sent the referral to the Parenting for Children Center on February 5, 2002, as required by its contract with Child and Family Services. Mrs. Jones is on a waiting list for parenting education services. The Parenting for Children Center will start a new class series in July.

Mrs. Jones visits Rosie just about every day according to Sarah Jones, the child's grandmother. She came to visit "high" on three occasions and Sarah Jones asked her to leave. The mother became loud and threatening, to which Sarah Jones said she just "stood my ground" and eventually Anna left. Generally, during the visits, Rosie and her mother read books, play with her toys, and prepare and eat a sandwich or dinner. The child is excited to see her mother. The grandmother says she is concerned that Anna will not acknowledge that she cannot handle her drug problem without help. The grandmother says she will help her in any way she can; but will not let her move back into the home until she stays in a treatment program.

Recommendation

Based on the progress to date, this worker recommends that Rosie be continued in placement with her maternal grandmother and continue to receive Head Start services. We recommend that the court continue the order for Mrs. Jones to participate in substance abuse treatment at WSATP. That agency has the best reputation for working with women who have children in foster care.

It appears that Mrs. Jones was attempting to blame her drug abuse on everyone else and not assume responsibility for her actions. When confronted by group members and staff, she just did not return to the group. Mrs. Jones needs to understand that the court expects her to take responsibility for her drug use and abuse and that her parental rights could be terminated in the next nine months if she fails to obtain the required substance abuse treatment services.

She has complied with the order for weekly drug screens and has, within the relapse expectations, maintained "clean" drug screens. She has complied with the visitation order and shows a genuine interest in her child's development. She has been unable to participate in the parent education program through no fault of her own. She is expected to enroll in the program in July and complete it in September.

knowledge coupled with a clear head, then the techniques used by attorneys in the examination and cross-examination processes should be immaterial.

The basic principles for giving testimony are as follows.

❖ Keep your temper. If you lose your temper, you discredit yourself and your testimony.

❖ Answer a question in the shortest possible way. The more you talk, the more likely you will provide the attorney an opportunity to find a small discrepancy in your testimony and use it to discredit you. Do not withhold information; but once you have responded to the question, be quiet.

❖ Always be willing to admit ignorance, or that your memory has failed you or that you are not sure. If you don't know the answer, say, "I don't know." To respond when you do not know opens you up to giving conflicting testimony.

❖ Never show partiality, or vindictiveness, to either party to the litigation. You have no personal interest in this matter. You represent the state. You are charged with providing facts and opinions based on those facts. If you waiver from the charge, you are subject to rigorous examination designed to show that you are not presenting facts but biased statements.

❖ Never show reluctance to concede a point in the opposition's favor. If the other side is right, it is better for you to recognize it and move on. To do otherwise exposes you to challenge as biased.

❖ Use short, simple language so that your point is immediately comprehensible. Avoid social work jargon. If you must use a specific social work term, explain what it means in plain English.

❖ Ask for a question to be repeated or rephrased if you do not understand it.

❖ Prepare ahead of time; but do not memorize your testimony. If you memorize testimony you may forget some parts of it under the pressure of testifying or could lose all memory of the facts. Your preparation should include knowing the pertinent facts and the applicable law so that you can correlate the two while testifying.

❖ Expect to feel nervous. You never know how you will be examined or cross-examined. Thus, you will always feel tense until the process is completed.

❖ State the facts as you know them based on an unbiased, well-documented inquiry. Do not start with conclusions. The more you rely on facts that you have documented, the less likely you will be to get confused by an attorney's questions. Further, if the attorney engages you in a hypothetical ("what if . . .") discussion, you are able to differentiate the facts in the hypothetical from the facts in your actual case.

❖ If you are asked for an opinion or recommendation, first give the facts on which you base your opinion, then state your opinion or recommendation.

❖ Remain cool, calm, and collected. If you have prepared your case well and available evidence is not brought out by the attorneys or jurists, it is their fault not yours (Saltzman & Proch, 1990; Stein, 1991; Dickson, 1995; Stern, 1997; Jones, 2006).

Working with Other Professionals

Caseworkers are required to work with attorneys or guardians *ad litem* for the children and the parents as well as a myriad of service providers to effect case resolution. Most attorneys and guardians *ad litem* are appointed by the courts to represent either the child or the parents. Many have more cases than they have time to adequately represent. Therefore, many times they, like the caseworker, are operating in "crisis mode." This, in addition to their perceived higher power position in the court process, can be intimidating to caseworkers. The caseworker who is prepared and knowledgeable of his or her case as well as the pertinent law and procedures can confidently overcome this power imbalance and develop strong collaborative or cooperative working relationships with attorneys based on shared commitments to the goal of safety and permanency for the child. Attorneys can be engaged to assist the caseworker in explaining the court orders to the parents and the child, explaining the consequences of not complying with the court's orders, and encouraging their active cooperation. Furthermore, they can be engaged to advocate for the parent or child with agencies from whom services are needed to meet court orders (Jones, 2006).

In addition to attorneys, caseworkers must work with a myriad of agencies whose stated mission is to provide the services needed by the parents or child. The court expects the caseworker to support the parents' and child's efforts to comply with court orders. In fact, the "ability of the caseworker to access quality services on a timely basis distinguishes caseworkers in the eyes of judges" (Jones, 2006, p. 71). Frequently, the agencies from which the caseworker must obtain services have too much demand for the services available or, in some cases, the services are not designed to address the complexity of life circumstances of those involved in the child abuse and neglect or delinquency service systems. Whenever there is an apparent or real mismatch between service needs and service availability, there is opportunity for discord between the parties. The caseworker can attempt to mitigate this discord by proceeding with respect, acknowledging the agency's constraints, and discussing alternatives for how the needs might be met. Once the client is being served by an agency, the caseworker should maintain frequent contact, share updated information, understand what the agency is doing and what has been accomplished, determine how he or she might assist with client compliance or client support, and achieve consensus on case direction.

TRENDS AND ISSUES

There are several old and several new trends and issues that bear watching in the next few years: family court development and results; increase in the number of legal orphans in the child welfare system; the use of mediation or alternative dispute resolution; the number of abused and neglected children who are subsequently adjudicated delinquent; the impact of illegal immigration on child welfare and delinquency systems; and the active engagement of the court system in the Child and Family Services Review (CFSR) process. The development of family courts continues to be worth watching. While 50 percent of the states have adopted statutes and court rules that encourage the development of unified family courts, this system change is taking far longer than desired and the effectiveness has not been documented to date.

As predicted, the number of children whose parental rights have been terminated has increased dramatically since the passage of the Adoption and Safe Families Act of 1997. One of the fundamental issues is that on average, 10,000 more children have parental rights terminated each year than the number placed for adoption. This creates the "legal orphan" backlog, that is, children for whom parental rights have been terminated, but for whom no adoption is effected. At the end of Fiscal Year 2005, there were 114,000 children for whom parental rights had been terminated who were waiting for adoption. In addition, there were approximately 35,000 children for whom parental rights had been terminated who had goals of emancipation, long-term foster care, living with relatives, or guardianship (U.S. Department of Health and Human Services, Children's Bureau, AFCARS Reports).

Mediation or alternative dispute resolutions are becoming more commonplace in the juvenile system. In general, cases are referred to mediation after the court has taken jurisdiction. The primary purpose is to have the parties come to an agreement on the plan for resolving the issues that necessitated court involvement. As with family group conferencing or team decision making, it gives the family members a voice in decision making and provides greater opportunity for their adherence to the case plan. Many states have piloted mediation in child abuse and neglect matters. See the Reference section for further information.

The issues that surround illegal immigration are beginning to impact the child welfare system and the juvenile/family courts. Specifically, cases in which the parents are being deported and their children or some of their children are U.S. citizens whom the parents do not wish to take from the United States as well as cases of abuse, neglect, or delinquency in which the parent is found to be an illegal immigrant and is reported.

Both the Children's Bureau and the Pew Commission Report on Children in Foster Care found that court engagement and improvements in legal representation for children and parents were critical to positive outcomes for children and their families. Approaches to improve the training of jurists, lawyers, and other court personnel, systems reforms for better tracking of cases, and systematic inclusion of a broader court representation in the CFSR planning and PIP processes are being implemented.

CHAPTER SUMMARY

This chapter focused on the historical development of the juvenile court system, its transition from a benevolent system with full discretion given to the jurists to a system subject to rules providing for the protection of the parties in abuse, neglect, and delinquency matters. The movement toward family courts is growing throughout the United States. These courts have broader jurisdictions over the multiplicity of matters that arise when children are abused, neglected, or commit delinquent acts. It is hypothesized that family courts will provide administrative efficiency and ensure a consistent treatment of the various independent legal issues. In addition, the adult criminal courts have been given more jurisdictional authority over juveniles.

The standard processing of a case through the juvenile court system has been reviewed, for both child abuse and neglect and delinquency cases. In addition, the processing of juveniles in adult criminal courts has been discussed. The role of the child welfare worker in the court system has changed as the juvenile court has become more "procedural." The caseworker remains responsible for marshalling factual information to assist the court in determining the best plan for the child/juvenile and his or her parents; however, that information is now subject to more stringent examination by attorneys for the child and the parent. Child welfare and delinquency workers must understand the roles and responsibilities of their position and those of all the persons involved. This chapter provided a brief summary of these roles and responsibilities.

FOR STUDY AND DISCUSSION
STUDY AND DISCUSSION QUESTIONS

1. Explain and evaluate the aims and guiding philosophy of the early founders of the juvenile court. Discuss ways in which the implementation of the juvenile court deviates from those aims and guiding philosophy.

2. Give arguments to support either the traditional rehabilitative model of the juvenile court or a model based on constitutional guarantees of due process and legal justice.

3. Obtain a copy of the juvenile court act in your state. Review it in these terms:
   a. What is the expressed intent of the act? How well does this intent reflect a modern juvenile court philosophy?
   b. Compare the act's definitions of classes of children who come under the jurisdiction with those discussed in this chapter.
   c. What does the statute provide with respect to the child's and parent's constitutional rights? Are there different provisions based on the type of case, that is, neglect or delinquency?

4. Read your state's statute and interview agency and court personnel to find out what the provisions are in your state for termination of parental rights. How well does the statute protect the parent's rights and also provide for the child's need for permanency?

5. What is your assessment of the potential for family courts to provide for better administration of justice as compared with the juvenile court?

6. Distinguish the court process in your state from the standard process discussed in this chapter.

7. Why is paternity establishment so important in child welfare practice? How would you proceed to determine whether paternity had been established in one of your cases?

8. Identify a specific case that you will be testifying on in the next month. State the type of hearing for which testimony will be given. What information does the court need to accomplish the purposes of the hearing as stated in the statute? What information do you have? What are your sources for the information? What information are you lacking? How can you obtain the information you currently lack?

9. Should juveniles be prosecuted as adults for serious offenses? What factors should be considered in determining whether to treat them as adults or juveniles?

10. Review your state's statute for criminal prosecution of juveniles, and its impact.
   a. Compare the offenses for which a juvenile could be tried as an adult in your state with those listed in this chapter.
   b. Obtain data from your local juvenile and criminal courts for two years before and two years after the legislative change, on the number of juveniles adjudicated or convicted of each offense.
   c. Review media files' coverage of juvenile offenders during the same period.
   d. How is the public safety better protected after the legislative change?

11. If you were designing the ideal court system for handling matters involving children and youth, what would it look like?

Internet Sites

The following sites provide copies of statutes, case decisions, analyses, and commentary on legal issues affecting children in the juvenile and family court systems.

American Bar Association Center on Children and the Law.
www.abanet.org/child/home.html

National Archives and Records Administration, Code of Federal Regulations.
www.access.gpo.gov/nara/cfr/cfr-table-search.html

National Clearinghouse on Child Abuse and Neglect Information
www.calib.com/nccanch

National Council of Juvenile and Family Court Judges.
www.ncjfcj.unr.edu

THOMAS, Library of Congress.
http://thomas.loc.gov

United States of America, All federal governmental agencies.
www.firstgov.gov

References

Addams, J. (1935). *My friend, Julia Lathrop.* New York: Macmillian.

American Bar Association, ABA Unified Family Court Coordinating Council. (2007). Available: www.aba.net.org/unifiedamcrt/about/html

Anderson, G., & Whalen, P. (2004). *Permanency planning mediation pilot program: evaluation final report.* Michigan State Courts Administrative Office.

Babb, B. A. (1998, Summer). Where we stand: An analysis of America's family law adjudicatory systems and the mandate to establish unified family courts. *Family Law Quarterly, 32,* 31–57.

Babb, B. A. (2003). Symposium editor's note. *Family Law Quarterly, 37*(3), 327–328.

Beemsterboer, M. J. (1960). Benevolence in the star chamber. *Journal of Criminal Law, Criminology, and Political Science, 50,* 464–475.

Brieland, D., & Lemmon, J. A. (1985). *Social work and the law* (4th ed.). St. Paul, MN: West.

Carmen, R. V., & Trulson, C. R. (2006). *Juvenile justice: The system, process and law.* Belmont, CA: Wadsworth/Thompson Learning.

Children's Bureau. (1961). Legislative guide for the termination of parental responsibilities and the adoption of children. (Publication No. 136). Washington, DC: U.S. Government Printing Office.

Commonwealth v. Fischer, 213 Pa. 48 (1905).

Courtney, M. E., & Blakey, J. (2003, October). Examination of the impact of increased court review on permanency outcomes for abused and neglected children. *Family Court Review, 41*(4), 471–479.

Davidson, H. A., & Gerlach, K. (1984). Child custody disputes: The child's perspective. In R. M. Horowitz & H. A. Davidson (Eds.), *Legal rights of children.* Colorado Springs: Shepard's/McGraw-Hill.

Dickson, D. T. (1995). *Law in the health and human services: A guide for social workers, psychologists, psychiatrists, and related professionals.* New York: Free Press.

Downs, S. W., & Taylor, C. (1980). *Permanent planning in foster care: Resources for training.*

(DHHS Publication No. [OHDS] 81-30290). Washington, DC: U.S. Government Printing Office.

Ellrod, F. E., Jr., & Melaney, D. H. (1950, Winter). Juvenile justice: Treatment or travesty. *University of Pittsburgh Law Review, 11,* 277–287.

Elson, A. (1962). Juvenile courts and due process. In M. K. Rosenheim (Ed.), *Justice for the child* (pp. 95–117). New York: Free Press.

Fiermonte, C., & Salyers, N. S. (2005, June). *Fostering Results: Improving outcomes together: court and child welfare collaboration.* Champaign, IL: Children and Family Research Center, School of Social Work, University of Illinois at Urbana-Champaign.

Flexner, B., & Baldwin, R. N. (1914). *Juvenile courts and probation.* New York: Century.

Flexner, B., & Oppenheimer, R. (1922). *The legal aspect of the juvenile court.* (Children's Bureau Publication No. 99). Washington, DC: Children's Bureau.

Flicker, B. D. (1977). *Standards for juvenile justice: A summary and analysis* (Institute of Judicial Administration and American Bar Association, Juvenile Justice Standards Project). Cambridge, MA: Ballinger.

Gatowski, S., Dobbin, S., Litchfield, M., & Oetjen, J. (2005). *Mediation in child protection cases: An evaluation of the Washington, D.C. Family Court Child Protection Mediation Program.* Reno, NV: National Council of Juvenile and Family Court Judges.

Glover, L. (2001). Michigan court improvement program annual program report. Lansing: Michigan Supreme Court.

Greacen, J. M., & Barnes, J. H. (2003, Spring). Unified family courts: Recent developments in twelve states. *Judges' Journal, 42*(2) 10–14, 43–44.

Green, B. A., & Dohrn, B. (1996). Forward: Children and the ethical practice of law. (Proceedings of the Conference on Ethical Issues in the Legal Representation of Children). *Fordham Law Review, 64*(4), 1281–1323.

Handler, J. F. (1965). The juvenile court and the adversary system: Problems of function and form. *Wisconsin Law Review, 7,* 7–51.

Hardin, M. (1998, Summer). Child protection cases in a unified family court. *Family Law Quarterly, 32,* 147–203. Chicago: American Bar Association.

Heck, R. O., Pindur, W., & Wells, D. K. (1985). The juvenile serious offender/drug involved program: A means to implement recommendations of the National Council of Juvenile and Family Court Judges. *Juvenile and Family Court Journal, 36,* 27–37.

Howell, J. C. (1997). *Juvenile justice and youth policy.* Thousand Oaks, CA: Sage.

In re Gault, 387 U.S. 1 (1967).

In re Winship, 397 U.S. 358 (1970).

Indian Child Welfare Act, P.L. 95-608. (1978).

Jacobs, T. A. (1995, supp. 1997). *Children and the law: Rights and obligations.* St. Paul, MN: West.

Jones, W. G. (2006). *Working with the courts in child protection.* Washington, DC: U.S. Department of Health and Human Services, Children's Bureau.

Kelley, B. T., Thornberry, T. P., & Smith, C. A. (1997). *In the wake of childhood maltreatment.* Washington, DC: Office of Juvenile Justice and Delinquency Prevention.

Kent v. United States, 383 U.S. 541 (1966).

Ketcham, O. W. (1962). The unfilled promise of the American juvenile court. In M. K. Rosenheim (Ed.), *Justice for the child* (pp. 95–117). New York: Free Press.

Kramer, D. T. (1994, supp. 2002). *Legal rights of children* (2nd ed.). Colorado Springs: Shepard's/ McGraw-Hill.

Landsman, M., & Thompson, K. (2000). *The Iowa mediation for permanency project.* Davenport: Family Resources, Inc.

Lathrop, J. C. (1925). The background of the juvenile court in Illinois. *The child, the clinic, and the court.* New York: New Republic.

Lou, H. H. (1927). *Juvenile courts in the United States.* Chapel Hill: University of North Carolina Press.

Lundberg, E. O. (1947). *Unto the least of these: Social services for children.* New York: Appelton-Century-Crofts.

Lutheran Social Services of New England. (2000). *Lutheran Social Services of New England cooperative permanency mediation program.* Worcester, MA: Lutheran Social Services of New England.

Mack, J. W. (1909–1910). The juvenile court. *Harvard Law Review, 23.*

McKeiver v. Pennsylvania, 403 U.S. 538 (1971).

Mississippi Band of Choctaw Indians v. Holyfield, 490 U.S. 51 (1989).

National Council of Family Law Judges. (1998). *Court appointed special advocates.* Reno, NV: National Council of Family Law Judges.

National Council of Juvenile Justice (2002, January). *Ohio family court feasibility study.* Pittsburg, PA: Author.

National Probation and Parole Association. (1957). *Guide for juvenile court judges.* New York: National Probation & Parole Association.

Nutt, A. S. (1949). Juvenile and domestic relations court. In *1949 social work yearbook* (pp. 270–276). New York: Russell Sage Foundation.

Oetjen, J. (2003). *Improving parents' representation in dependency cases: A Washington State pilot program evaluation.* Reno, NV: National Council of Juvenile and Family Court Judges.

Office of Juvenile Justice and Delinquency Preventation. (1998). *Juveniles in adult courts.* Washington, DC: Office of Juvenile Justice and Delinquency Prevention.

Office of Juvenile Justice and Delinquency Prevention. (2000). *Statistics.* Available: www.ojjdp. nc/rs.org/statistics.

Office of Juvenile Justice and Delinquency Preventation. (2006). Juvenile offenders and Victims: 2006 national report. Washington, DC: Author.

Pike, V., Downs, S. W., Emlen, A., Downs, G., & Case, D. (1977). *Permanent planning for children in foster care.* (No. OHDS 77-30124). Washington, DC: U.S. Department of Health, Education and Welfare.

Pound, R. (1950). The juvenile in the service state. In *1949 yearbook.* New York: National Probation and Parole Association.

Pruett, E., & Savage, C. (2004). Statewide initiatives to encourage alternative dispute resolution and enhance collaborative approaches to resolving family issues. *Family Court Review, 42*(2), 232–245.

Roper v. Simmons, 543 U.S. 551 (2005).

Rosenheim, J. K. (Ed.). (1962). *Justice for the child.* New York: Free Press.

Ross, C. J. (1998, Summer). The failure of fragmentation: The promise of a system of unified family courts. *Family Law Quarterly, 32,* 3–30. Chicago: American Bar Association.

Rubin, S. (1952, November–December). Protecting the child in the juvenile court. *Journal of Criminal Law, Criminology and Political Science, 43,* 425–440.

Saltzman, A., & Proch, K. (1990). *Law in social work practice.* Chicago: Nelson-Hall.

Saltzman, A., & Proch, K. (2000). *Law in social work practice* (2nd ed.). Chicago: Nelson-Hall.

Schall v. Martin, 467 S.Ct. 253 (1984).

Schepard, A., & Bozzomo, J. W. (2003). Efficiency, therapeutic justice, mediation, and evaluation: Reflections on a survey of unified family courts. *Family Law Quarterly, 37*(3), 327–328.

Schultz, L. L., & Cohen, F. (1976). Isolation in juvenile court jurisprudence. In M. K. Rosenheim (Ed.), *Pursuing justice for the child.* Chicago: University of Chicago Press.

Simonsen, C. (1991). Status offenders: An attempt to clarify the system. *Juvenile Justice in America.* New York: Macmillan.

Stein, T. J. (1991). *Child welfare and the law.* White Plains, NY: Longman.

Stern, P. (1997). *Preparing and presenting expert testimony in child abuse litigation: A guide for expert witnesses and attorneys.* Thousand Oaks, CA: Sage.

Szymanski, L. A. (1995). *Family courts in the United States.* Washington, DC: Office of Juvenile Justice and Delinquency Prevention.

Thompson v. Oklahoma, 487 U.S. 815 (1988).

Trosch, L., Sanders, L., & Kugelmass, S. (2002). Child abuse, neglect, and dependency mediation pilot project. *Juvenile and Family Court Journal, 1,* 67–77.

U.S. Department of Health and Human Services, Children's Bureau. (2005, June). *ACYF-CB-IM 05-05: Court involvement in child and family service review.* Avalilable: http:www .acf.hhs.gov.

U.S. Department of Health and Human Services, Children's Bureau. AFCARS Reports. Available at http:www.acf.hhs.gov

Protecting Children from Neglect and Abuse

The little world in which children have their existence, whosoever brings them up, there is nothing so finely perceived and so finely felt, as injustice.

—*Charles Dickens*

To raise up and to restore that which is in ruin
To repair that which is damaged
To rejoin that which is severed
To replenish that which is lacking
To strengthen that which is weakened
To set right that which is wrong
To make flourish that which is insecure and undeveloped.

—*Huisa M. Karenga, Selections from the Huisa: Sacred Wisdom of Ancient Egypt*

CHAPTER OUTLINE

CASE EXAMPLE:
A Protective Services Investigation

No case can stand as a typical example of a protective services investigation because of the great range of family situations that are reported. The alleged maltreatment may be categorized as neglect, physical abuse, sexual abuse, emotional maltreatment, other concerns about poor child care, or a combination of problems. The case presented here shows the protective services investigator "in action," as she attempts to understand the extent of a family's problems and the risk they represent to the children.

Jennifer Rogers, a protective services worker in a large midwestern city, received a call on a Friday morning from a concerned citizen who saw a mother crossing a busy street with her five children. The reporter stated that although the mother was carrying the youngest child and holding the hand of another, one of the smaller children was lagging behind. The mother screamed at the child to "hurry up" but then just kept walking. The child, whom the reporter thought was about 3 years, was almost hit by a car while the mother walked on ahead. Oncoming traffic had to stop while the child got across the street. The mother seemed unconcerned with the commotion and got into a car with the children. The reporter took down the license plate number and called Child Protective Services (CPS).

Jennifer, after speaking with her supervisor, decided to wait until the following week to investigate the case, as she had two other cases in which the children seemed at imminent risk of harm. She needed to speak with their caregivers that same day and perhaps take other action. Although the newly reported situation was clearly a risky one, there was no indication of injury or other maltreatment. Jennifer did, however, contact the police for a license check on the car.

The following Wednesday, Jennifer received information on the name of the person who owned the car. It was Gloria Miles, a name Jennifer recognized immediately. Gloria was well known to CPS. She had five children, ages 7, 5, 3, 2, and 10 months. In a previous report to CPS last winter, Gloria had been seen in a public rest room with her children who were crying because they didn't have mittens and their hands were cold. Gloria was holding their hands under hot water trying to warm them up and yelling at them to be quiet.

The woman who reported the situation had offered to help, but Gloria told her to mind her own business and left with the children. She left her purse in the restroom and thus her name became known. Gloria had also been previously reported by a neighbor, who had called to say she had gone to Gloria's door one night about 10 P.M. and there was no adult there. The 7-year-old answered the door. The neighbor said that Gloria didn't show up until the next morning. When CPS investigated that incident, they were told that an aunt had been sleeping in the house, which the aunt, when contacted, confirmed.

Gloria had been diagnosed in the past with schizophrenia and is supposed to be taking medication regularly. She has never liked taking this medication, feeling that it does "weird things" to her mind. When she does take it, she is able to provide for the children adequately. She keeps the children clothed, although they are often underdressed for the weather, and she keeps the house clean, although she has little furniture. The neighborhood is poor, with high unemployment. Although Gloria has a car, it often breaks down. She frequently uses the bus system, which is difficult to use with all the children. The children have been interviewed and examined; no injuries have been noted. They appear to mind Gloria and also to love her. She appears to be affectionate with them. She very much resents any outside interference in her life and frequently yells and screams at caseworkers to leave her alone and "get out of my life." Support services have been provided to help Gloria with her child care duties, but she is so unpleasant to the support providers that they do not remain. The children occasionally go to live with Gloria's sister when Gloria is "not feeling well," but the sister is not able to sustain care for the children for long periods due to her own family obligations. Gloria is poor, lives on food stamps, and has recently been placed on an employment program to earn her public assistance. Although she has not yet found employment, she is required to spend twenty hours a week at the income assistance/employment agency.

The CPS worker is very concerned about the children's welfare because of Gloria's continued marginal caregiving ability, now compounded by the work requirement. However, she knows that if Gloria has a work requirement, she also should be getting child care assistance. In thinking through options for this family, she is aware that a child care provider could help to provide a safety net for the children. Jennifer feels that the children are at continual risk. She decides to try to persuade Gloria to accept support services again, at least so that the children's condition can be monitored somewhat. However, she is aware that Gloria may refuse outside help, as she has in the past. A plan to engage the psychiatrist who is prescribing her medication might be in order. Perhaps a "case staffing" could be set up in an effort to work toward more consistency in Gloria's medication intake. Jennifer also decides to try Family Group Conferencing, in which family members and others who know the family convene to try to make a safety plan for the children. Jennifer decides to "substantiate" the case on the basis that the children are at continual risk of harm, which is a basis for substantiation in her state. She does not believe that the children are at imminent risk of serious harm and is aware that there is some extended family involvement, so she will try to keep the children in the home and provide supportive services to the mother. She also knows that, given Gloria's temperament and mental illness, family preservation services may not be able to help Gloria create a home that would provide for their ongoing nurture and safety.

T his case shows how complex the world of children's protective services can be. The worker needs to continually balance concerns for the safety of the children with preservation of family bonds. Although there are clear-cut cases of abuse and neglect, CPS cases are often characterized by ambiguity and uncertainty about the dangers to children and the appropriate level of involvement of the agency. The CPS worker is also aware that there are limits to the services that can actually be offered to this client and the client's ability to use them effectively. This chapter will explore what constitutes abuse and neglect, the role of protective services, and the need for multisystem involvement in child maltreatment.

In child welfare and perhaps all social services, there is no situation that raises such concern and outrage as does the neglect, abuse, or exploitation of children by parents or others responsible for their care. Fueled by media coverage of sensational instances of abuse and by considerable research and other scholarly attention, the last thirty years have witnessed a dramatic new concern for these child victims.

INCIDENCE

The primary source of information on the incidence of child maltreatment comes from the National Child Abuse and Neglect Data System (NCANDS), maintained by the U.S. Department of Health and Human Services. It combines official reports of absue and neglect made to child protective agencies in each state and the District of Columbia. It is important to remember that the data include only cases reported to local CPS agencies. In 2004, the most recent year in which data are available, states received about three million reports of child abuse and neglect. Of these, only about one in four reports was confirmed after investigation as involving abuse or neglect, for a total of about 872,000 children. The victimization rate in 2004 was about twelve abused or neglected children per thousand children in the population of the United States, a rate that has declined from a high of 15.3 in 1993.

Child neglect is the most common type of maltreatment and surpasses by far the incidence of child abuse. In 2004, children suffered the following types of maltreatment:

Neglect	62%
Physical Abuse	18%
Sexual Abuse	10%
Emotional Maltreatment	7%
Medical Neglect	2%

About 15 percent of victims suffered other types of maltreatment, such as abandonment, congenital drug addiction, and "threats to harm the child." Many states count victims in more than one category if more than one type of maltreatment has occurred, so the total of the percentages is more than 100 percent (U.S. Department of Health and Human Services, 2006).

The NCANDS data show that younger children are somewhat more likely to be maltreated than older children. Boys and girls suffer equal rates of maltreatment, except in sexual abuse, which is more likely to be inflicted on girls. About half of all victims are white, a quarter are African American, and 17 percent are Hispanic. Most of the perpetrators are parents, although about 17 percent are relatives. Perhaps the most disturbing finding of the NCANDS data is that children who have been previously maltreated are much more likely to suffer maltreatment again than are children without such history (U.S. Department of Health and Human Services, 2006).

Other studies have also reported estimates of child abuse and neglect in the United States, usually much larger than the NCANDS data show. The most complete survey to date is the National Study of the Incidence and Severity of Child Abuse and Neglect, which collected data periodically from 1979 to 1994. Taking into account not only cases reported to CPS but also cases known to other human service agencies such as hospitals and schools, the study estimated that over one and a half million children suffered maltreatment in 1993 (Sedlak & Broadhurst, 1996).

Surveys have been conducted of parents of victims of maltreatment, asking them questions concerning their participation in child abuse or neglect. Like the National Incidence Studies data, these surveys show higher rates of maltreatment than those reported to public agencies (Straus & Gelles, 1986; Finkelhor, Hotaling, Lewis, & Smith, 1990). In a 1995 Gallup poll, the self-reported behavior of parents led researchers to conclude that about three million children suffered physical abuse from their parents, a rate that is sixteen times higher than that reported to public agencies. The same poll found that 23 percent of adults reported having been sexually abused as children by an adult or an older child, counting both contact and noncontact abuse (Gallup, Moor, & Schussel, 1997).

Behind each statistic is a child, a child whose immediate safety, comfort, welfare, and future development are jeopardized or whose very life may be at stake. Parents also exist behind these numbers, parents who may have their child removed from their care or at least have their autonomy as parents eroded. For society, the costs are similarly high. Balancing society's desire to maintain and support the integrity of the family while protecting the welfare of its children is a complicated proposition that requires clarification of national values. The relative value society places on child safety or family sanctity and preservation changes from time to time and influences how resources will be allocated.

AIMS AND SPECIAL ATTRIBUTES OF CHILD PROTECTIVE SERVICES

Child protective services are intended to reduce the risks to children's safety or well-being, prevent further risk of neglect or abuse, and restore adequate parental functioning whenever possible. If it does not appear that children will be adequately protected, steps are taken to remove children from their homes and establish them in alternative living situations in which they will receive more adequate care.

Protective services today reflect the conviction that many parents whose level of child care is unacceptable can be reached on behalf of their children and can be helped to improve their parental functioning. The focus of child protective services is on both the investigation of reported maltreatment that initiates agency responsibility and on stabilizing and improving the children's homes by helping parents to perform more responsibly in relation to their children's care. Protective services also are concerned with social planning to organize and coordinate collaborative efforts among community agencies involved in the child protection system.

Child protective services are characterized by certain distinctive features: (1) the way in which service is initiated; (2) the increased agency responsibility that accompanies work with parents of children at risk; (3) the kind of agency sanction or community authorization; and (4) the balance required in the use of authority in relation to the rights of parents, the child, and society.

1. ***Child protective services are authoritative.*** The protective agency initiates the service by approaching the parents about a complaint from some source in the community such as

police officers, school personnel, public health nurses, neighbors, or relatives. Because the protective service is frequently involuntary, the situation that justifies an agency's "intruding" into family life must strongly suggest that parents are not providing the basic care or protection a child needs for healthy growth and development.

2. *Child protective services carry significant social agency responsibility, because they are directed toward families in which children are at risk.* Children are highly vulnerable when their homes lack minimal levels of care or protection. Children cannot make effective claims by themselves for the enforcement of their rights. If appropriate and quick initiation of services does not follow a complaint from the community, lasting harm may result for a child who is being maltreated.

Caseworkers in the protective agency must act promptly; their decisions about the nature or seriousness of the complaint and objective assessment as well as subsequent actions, must be based on accurate fact-finding. Moreover, the social agency cannot withdraw from the situation if it finds the parents uncooperative or resistant to taking help, as it may in situations in which individuals have voluntarily sought help. Once protective services have been initiated, the agency can responsibly withdraw only when the level of child care in the home has improved to acceptable levels or when satisfactory alternative care has been arranged elsewhere, as in a relative's home or in foster care.

The protective agency, then, has a high degree of responsibility to the child at risk; to the child's parents, who are frequently experiencing great stress; and to the community, which charges the agency to act for it in the provision of child protection.

3. *Child protective services involve agency sanction from the community.* A child protection agency has been delegated responsibility by federal and state laws to receive reports about instances of unacceptable child care, to investigate them, and if necessary, to initiate services for the family even though the parents have not requested help. Other social agencies expect and look to the child protection agency to act. The provision of child protective services is mandated by federal law as a fundamental public agency responsibility.

4. *Child protective services require a crucial balance in the use of the agency's authority.* Child maltreatment is both a social and a legal problem. The fact that the agency approaches a family about its problems without a request from the family itself denotes some invasion of privacy, however well motivated the services may be. Furthermore, an integral part of the protective agency's methods is to reserve the right to invoke the authority of the court by filing a petition alleging parental neglect or abuse if the parents do not improve their level of care. This "threat," implied or acknowledged, is recognized by the family and may be perceived as either subtle or overt coercion—pressure to cooperate or conform to other ways of child care. Today, protective services workers must operate within narrow time frames in treating families or petitioning for termination of parental rights. This sense of urgency may communicate to parents a message that their own concerns and problems are not important and that the agency expects them to fail.

The protective agency has the difficult task of maintaining a just and effective balance in its use of authority in relation to the child at risk, whose rights and protection depend on other persons; to parents, whose right to rear their children without outside intervention is being questioned; and to society, which has delegated a responsibility for the protection of children from neglect or abuse. These four attributes of child protective services will assume fuller meaning as we consider the specific social services that are extended to the family and the issues involved in doing so. But first, it is important to look at the origins and subsequent growth of the protective services idea.

HISTORICAL DEVELOPMENT OF PROTECTIVE SERVICES

Early Attitudes toward the Treatment of Children

Accepted ideas on ways to rear children have undergone many changes through the centuries (Myers, 2006). We tend to lose sight of how recently the general public has strongly objected to indifferent parental care or to aggressive actions toward children by other members of society.

For hundreds of years, history has recorded mistreatment of children. The Bible contains examples of cruelty to children, including Herod's order to slay "all the children that were in Bethlehem, and in all the coasts thereof, from two years old and under" (Matthew 2:16). Infanticide by different means was carried out in a number of societies to assure the survival of only strong, healthy infants who could become able to serve the state in combat, and to rid the society of "undesirable" offspring—females, out-of-wedlock children, or any infant who did not seem to be a promising child. Parents who were poor sometimes abandoned children, exposing them to weather and hunger, to escape the burdens of rearing them; richer parents often did the same to avoid dividing property into too many small parts.

During colonial times and even later, parents often enforced absolute obedience of children to the demands of adults in an attempt to "break their will" and free them from the evil disposition with which they supposedly had been born. Drugs, particularly laudanum (a form of opium), were given by parents and servants "almost indiscriminately" to infants to stop their crying (Sunley, 1963). Flogging and caning were used extensively and brutally by schoolmasters. Child labor was accepted and endorsed: "In colonial life, the labor of children was a social fact and a social necessity, not a social problem" (Cohen, 2000, p. 18).

Beginnings of Care for Neglected Children

After the Revolutionary War, various states passed legislation that recognized the needs of neglected children to the extent of authorizing the binding out, or commitment to almshouses, of children who were found begging on the street or whose parents were beggars. In 1790, the first public orphanage was established in South Carolina, which cared for and educated not only orphaned children but also those whose parents could not afford to care for them (Abbott, 1938).

Homer Folks cited the year 1825 as the beginning of more general recognition and application of the principle that public authorities have a right and duty to intervene in cases of parental cruelty or gross neglect of children and "to remove the children by force if necessary, and place them under surroundings more favorable for their development" (Folks, 1911, pp. 168–169). Before the end of the nineteenth century, special laws were passed in nearly all states to provide for the protection of children from neglect or ill treatment by authorizing the courts to remove them from parents or guardians and commit them to some proper place of care.

Societies for the Prevention of Cruelty to Children

The new laws provided a legal basis for acting on behalf of maltreated children if they became objects of attention by a child-saving agency or a children's institution, or if the police chose to bring the situation to the attention of the court. However, there were no clear lines of responsibility among agencies or officials for *finding* neglected or abused children unless families were already requiring support from public or voluntary relief funds. As a consequence, societies for the prevention of cruelty to children (SPCCs) were established.

Examining the circumstances under which the first SPCC came into existence provides an aid to understanding the purpose and focus of the early societies. In 1873, Etta Wheeler, a church worker visiting tenement homes in New York City, heard the story of 9-year-old Mary Ellen, who for two years had been cruelly whipped and frequently left alone, locked in an inner room during long days. The thin partitions between the tenement apartments let other occupants hear the child's cries and other evidence of the cruel treatment inflicted on her by the man and woman with whom lived. They had obtained the child from an institution at 2 years of age, but institution personnel had made no inquiry about her well-being during the intervening seven years. Concerned neighbors had not known to whom to complain or how to get help for the child. The tenement visitor went to great lengths to investigate the report and establish evidence of the abuse and neglect. Then, when she sought advice as to how to obtain protection for the child, no one seemed to know of any legal means to "rescue" the child. Up to that time, the legal removal of children from cruel or neglectful parents was rare if not impossible.

Finally, Henry Bergh, who had founded the New York Society for the Prevention of Cruelty to Animals, arranged to file a petition to have the child removed from her custodians and placed with persons who would treat her more kindly. The abusing foster mother was sentenced to prison and Mary Ellen eventually gained loving parents. In 1875, the New York Society for the Prevention of Cruelty to Children was established.

The Mary Ellen case was not the sole cause of the emerging child protection movement. Large social movements rarely, if ever, are traceable to accidental causal beginnings. The emergence of the SPCCs is best explained by a coming together and fusing of various forces. Public awareness had been awakened by various stories about the lack of public response to the plight of children. Gaining in influence was the women's movement of the 1870s and its overarching influence on various thrusts toward social justice, one of which was the ideal of a protected childhood and cultural rejection of child abuse and punitive corporal punishment.

The formation of the New York SPCC triggered a rapid growth of other child cruelty societies. By 1898, more than 200 SPCCs had come into existence in the United States. Their primary function was to investigate cases of alleged maltreatment, present facts to the courts, and assist in the prosecution of adults responsible for the maltreatment (Costin, 1992).

Who Should Do Protective Work?

After the "discovery" of child abuse in 1874, child abuse seemed to disappear from public consciousness, only to be "rediscovered" in the 1960s. After the turn of the century, child welfare practice was marked by confusion and uncertainty as to which agencies should undertake the protective work. There was little public interest in creating a public agency with a mandate to intrude into the privacy of family life to protect children. The private agencies, for their part, continued to move away from child protection work. The use of authority, necessary in protective work, made social workers uncomfortable.

The Rediscovery of Child Abuse: The Battered Child Syndrome

The rediscovery of child abuse began in the 1960s, when Kempe and colleagues identified "battered child syndrome" (Kempe et al., 1962). Advances in the technology of radiology made it possible for physicians to identify patterns of injuries, observable by X-rays, that were likely to have been inflicted rather than accidental. In the deluge of interest and publicity that followed this discovery, public interest in addressing child maltreatment was renewed. The interest quickly took the form of establishing official procedures in which those who knew of instances of child abuse could report them to authorities.

The Child Abuse Prevention and Treatment Act

In 1974, the federal Child Abuse Prevention and Treatment Act (CAPTA) was passed. The Act established a National Center on Child Abuse and Neglect, which was to be a clearinghouse for the development and transmittal of information on research in child protection. The Act also provided for grants to the states if they passed reporting laws, requiring certain groups of people, called "mandated reporters," to report alleged child maltreatment to the state child protective services agencies (Schene, 1998). See the section, Reporting Child Maltreatment, for more information on this law.

Shifting Priorities: Child Safety and Family Preservation

This history of children's protective services shows that society has changed from time to time in the mandate given to agencies to intrude into family life for the protection of children. Legislation in this country has reflected this uncertainty, swinging from an emphasis on child safety to an emphasis on family preservation and back to an emphasis on child safety. CAPTA was primarily concerned with child safety, and changes to it in 1996 reinforced this emphasis. In 1990, the Indian Child Protection and Family Violence Protection Act extended mandatory reporting to reservations (Earle, 2000).

However, other legislation reflects a priority of preserving families. The 1980 Adoption Assistance and Child Welfare Act encouraged agencies to serve children in their own homes. Before removing a child from home, agencies were required to show the courts that they had made "reasonable efforts" to preserve the family by offering services to the parents. The Family Preservation and Support Act of 1993 increased the funding for family preservation efforts and for preventive services before maltreatment occurred. In 1997, the pendulum seemed to swing again, with the passage of the Adoption and Safe Families Act. While it expanded family preservation and support services, it clearly shifted the national priority to child safety. The Act clarified that child safety should not be jeopardized to meet the reasonable efforts requirement of earlier legislation. It also established clear and shortened time frames for deciding to terminate parental rights so the child could be placed in a permanent, adoptive home. It is too soon to tell whether this Act will improve safety to children, or whether we will find that child safety depends, ultimately, less on streamlined bureaucratic and judicial procedures, and more on improving the social and economic conditions in which children are raised. It is paradoxical that federal legislation, while mandating procedures to protect children, has consistently failed to provide the supports to families they need to keep their children safe. Legislation to protect children is necessary, but so are resources to help families raise their children in safety.

THE DEFINITIONAL DILEMMA

There is no consensual definition of either child abuse or neglect. There is wide agreement that the type of extreme case most frequently reported by the media constitutes maltreatment, but such cases are relatively rare. The great majority of cases fall into more ambiguous categories in which complex sets of factors must be taken into account. The difficulty and the importance of developing clear definitions can be understood if viewed as society's attempt to establish minimum standards for the care of children. The development of research-based knowledge, treatment, and prevention of child abuse and neglect depends on a foundation of agreement on what constitutes child maltreatment. Legislative and judicial mandates must share in this foundation.

CAPTA, reauthorized in 1996, gave a national definition of child maltreatment. Child abuse and neglect is, at a minimum:

❖ Any recent act or failure to act on the part of a parent or caretaker which results in death, serious physical or emotional harm, sexual abuse or exploitation; or

❖ An act or failure to act which presents an imminent risk of serious harm. (Child Abuse Prevention and Treatment Act, 1974, 1996)

This definition clarifies that only parents or other caregivers can be charged with abuse or neglect. Harmful behavior to children committed by other adults is considered assault and is usually handled by the criminal justice system. Note that the definition includes "emotional harm" as well as physical and sexual abuse and neglect. Also, it includes "endangerment" as a category of child maltreatment, through the use of the term *imminent risk of serious harm*. This means that child protective services could make a finding of abuse or neglect even though the child had not yet been observably injured, if the parent's threat to harm or extreme neglect seemed to represent a serious risk to the child. In the following section, we discuss these and other definitional issues in child maltreatment.

The CAPTA legislation left many specific details of defining abuse and neglect to the states, and states vary considerably in their definitions. For example, some states include educational neglect (caregiver's failure to ensure the child's school attendance) while others do not. Every state includes nonaccidental physical injury and sexual abuse in its definition of child abuse, but the definitions vary in how specific they are. States differ on whether newborns who show signs of prenatal substance exposure must be reported. Some states, but not all, require reporting of suspected maltreatment in out-of-home placements such as foster care. Other states handle these situations differently (U.S. Department of Health and Human Services, 1999a; Children's Bureau, 2006).

Dimensions of Child Maltreatment

Harm comes to children from many sources and in many forms. The difficulty in defining child maltreatment is deciding what elements must be present in a situation for it to be officially considered parental maltreatment of a child, and not just one of the myriad hazards of childhood. One definitional problem is whether the motivation of the parent to harm the child is necessary for abuse to be said to have occurred. It is not always easy to differentiate between intentional and accidental behavior. Often, child abuse reflects a mixture of intentional and chance elements, such as, for example, when harm to the child results from parental discipline. Another definitional controversy is whether to include endangerment in the definition of maltreatment, when the situation seems very risky but no actual harm has occurred. Related to this issue is the question of *cumulative harm*. This term refers to the cumulative effects of repeated moderate abuse or prolonged neglect, which are damaging in their cumulative effect, but do not cause a discrete injury. Examples of cumulative harm include ongoing verbal abuse or neglect to get medical care. These behaviors may not have an immediate effect on the child's development, but are damaging in the long run (Hutchinson, 1990; English, 1998; English, Bangdiwala, & Runyan, 2005).

Whether a broad or a narrow definition of child maltreatment is selected has implications for the policy and practice of child protective services. Proponents of a narrow definition would prefer to see only cases of observable harm, such as broken bones or burns, handled by child protective services. This policy would simplify the operation of protective services and provide clarity for all concerned—parents, those reporting maltreatment, and other professionals—on the scope and role of protective services in the community. Proponents of a broad definition, on the other hand, are concerned that many children suffering endangerment or cumulative harm would be left entirely unprotected and unnoticed if a narrow definition were adopted. They argue that the definition should include situations in which the child is at serious risk of suffering harm or negative developmental outcomes in the future.

Cultural Attitudes

In the culturally diverse society of the United States, differences among cultures in childrearing practices and perceptions of acceptable parental behavior complicate the problem of providing clear definitions of child abuse and neglect (Giovannoni & Becerra, 1979; Garbarino & Ebata, 1983; Ahn & Gilbert, 1992). Korbin (1994; 2002; 2003) points out the dilemma posed by cultural factors in determining whether a situation constitutes abuse or neglect: An extreme ethnocentric position, which disregards all cultural differences and imposes a single standard for child care on everyone, risks including situations that appear to constitute maltreatment but do not. On the other hand, an extreme position of cultural relativity runs the risk of ignoring situations that may in fact be harmful to children, even if accepted by the children's culture.

Korbin (1994) offers the example of "coin rubbing" among Southeast Asians to illustrate this dilemma. The practice of *cao gao,* believed to cure illness, involves pressing metal coins "forcefully on the child's body, leaving a symmetrical pattern of bruises" (p. 187). These bruises are, indeed, nonaccidentally inflicted and may leave a pattern of marks that appear more serious than the bruises resulting from being hit with a belt. An ethnocentric position would require that the case be reported for child abuse, even though the bruises were inflicted in a medical context. In fact, these cases are rarely reported because it is recognized as a cultural practice with good intentions. It should be noted however, that sometimes children involved in this procedure become very sick, not because of the procedure itself but because they did not receive standard medical care. In such a situation, some people might take the position that the child was discriminated against on the basis of ethnicity/race, because he or she did not receive the same level of protection as other children in American society.

Sometimes, a cultural practice that is acceptable within the community is taken to an extreme and then becomes a form of maltreatment. For example, a frequent cause for a child neglect report among the Navaho Indians is that children have been left alone or unattended. Parents justify this behavior by pointing out that Navaho culture endorses sibling caregiving of younger children and entrusts children with a high level of responsibility. However, a survey of Navaho parents found that most mothers disapproved of leaving young children alone or with siblings who were not much older overnight or other long periods. Many of the neglect cases were for children as young as 5 years. These situations could not be justified as culturally acceptable, but were in fact a departure from the cultural norms exacerbated by problems of poverty and alcohol (Korbin, 1994; 2003). Sibling caregiving as it was meant to be practiced within this culture should not be condemned, Korbin points out, but should be kept within acceptable limits.

Similarly Korbin suggests that culturally acceptable forms of physical discipline cannot always be considered abuse. Within the culture, physical discipline may be considered appropriate and necessary if it does not harm the child. Child protective services workers tend to see only the cases in which children are left with bruises, welts, and other wounds, yet most physical discipline within the culture leaves the children without such marks. (For another point of view, see the discussion of corporal punishment in the Trends and Issues section of Chapter 3.)

In an acknowledgment of diversity in beliefs on acceptable childrearing practices, the majority of states include provisions in their reporting laws stating that parental religious beliefs should be considered prior to a determination of abuse or neglect (U.S. Department of Health and Human Services, 1999b, p. 12).

REPORTING CHILD MALTREATMENT

Every state and the District of Columbia require reporting of suspected abuse and neglect by professionals who see children in the course of their work, including physicians and other medical personnel, mental health professionals, caseworkers, teachers, other school officials, child care workers, and law enforcement personnel. Some states require all citizens, both professionals and nonprofessionals, to report suspected cases, and all states permit any citizen to report when they suspect abuse and neglect (National Association of Social Workers, 2000). Those required by statute to report suspected maltreatment are the state's "mandated reporters."

The past twenty years have witnessed radically improved performance in the reporting of suspected child maltreatment. The reporting process is strengthened by publicity campaigns, 24-hour hotlines, and administrative linkages between agencies likely to report, such as schools, welfare, and visiting nurses, and the legally mandated child protection agency in the community. Knowledge of the law is improving among those who are mandated to report, and they have increased their reports to state authorities. The rate of reported child maltreatment was ten cases per thousand children in 1976, while by 2004, the rate was forty-three children per thousand (U.S. Department of Health and Human Services, 2006). As a result of improvements in reporting, many children have been saved from serious injury or death (Besharov & Laumann, 1996).

Most reports of alleged maltreatment come from professionals, who are the "mandated reporters." Family members, the victims themselves, and neighbors and friends also make reports. Figure 6.1 shows the sources of reports for 2004.

Problems with the Reporting Law

Despite improvements in reporting, two major problems remain: the large number of cases that go unreported and the large number of unfounded reports. The plight of many vulnerable children continues to go unreported. Although legally mandated to do so, many professionals still do not report cases in which they suspect child maltreatment. Reasons for this reluctance to report include lack of clarity on which situations require reporting, concern about confidentiality and the effect of reporting on the therapeutic relationship, concern about lawsuits or reprisals from clients, reluctance to become involved, and a belief that reporting will not help the situation (Deisz, Doueck, George, & Levine, 1996; Warner-Rogers, Hansen, & Spieth, 1996).

A second problem is the large number of reports that, on investigation, are found to be without enough basis to warrant further action. These "unfounded" or "unsubstantiated" reports currently constitute 60 percent of all reports made to child protection agencies (U.S. Department of Health and Human Services, 2006). Figure 6.2 shows the disposition of child maltreatment reports for

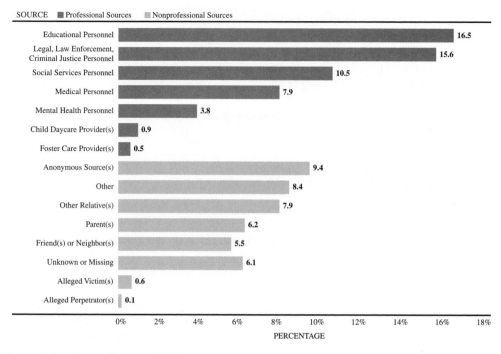

Figure 6.1 *Report Sources, 2004*

Source: U.S. Department of Health and Human Services (2006). *Child maltreatment 2004.* Washington, DC: U.S. Government Printing Office.

2004. Very few of these unfounded reports are made by malicious people trying to cause trouble. Many are made by "nonmandated reporters," such as neighbors and relatives (U.S. Department of Health and Human Services, 2006), who may not know the definitions of child maltreatment used by the local child protection agency. However, there is a significant number of reports made by persons involved in child custody disputes.

Another reason for the large number of unfounded reports concerns agency policy on which kinds of situations to substantiate. As indicated earlier, states vary in the inclusiveness of their definitions of abuse and neglect, and local and county agencies also vary in what kinds of situations they believe warrant a thorough investigation or a decision to substantiate (English, 1998, p. 41).

Unfounded reports are of concern because of the possible conflict between a family's right to privacy and the state's interest in protecting children who may be abused or maltreated. A protective service investigation is intrusive. Workers must inquire into intimate details of family life. The children usually must be questioned in addition to friends, school personnel, day care workers, clergy, and others who know the family. The fact of the investigation is stigmatizing, even if the report is later unfounded. Justice Hugo Black pointed out that the parent "is charged with conduct— failure to care properly for her children—which may be viewed as reprehensible and morally wrong by a majority of society" (*Carter v. Kaufman,* 1970, p. 959). Critics question a system that infringes on the family's right to privacy without giving much assurance that the lives of children will be improved as a result of this infringement (Lindsay, 1994; Besharov & Laumann, 1996).

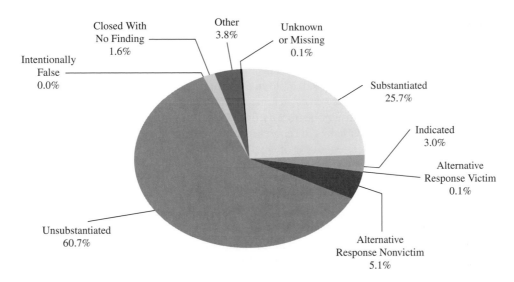

Figure 6.2 *Investigation Dispositions, 2004*

Source: U.S. Department of Health and Human Services (2006). *Child maltreatment 2004.* Washington, DC: U.S. Government Printing Office.

Another troublesome aspect of the large number of unfounded reports is that the agency resources are necessarily deployed to investigate reports, while children already identified as abused are insufficiently served by the agency. The large increase in reports of child maltreatment has not been accompanied by sufficient increases in appropriations for child protection agencies, so staff must spend time investigating new cases rather than treating families already known to them.

Waldfogel (1998) offered strategies to address the dilemma of both underreporting (thus missing some serious cases) and overreporting (thus tying up caseworkers unnecessarily, which also results in missing serious cases). She urged that definitions provide more clarity about such contentious issues as severity, endangerment versus actual occurrence, type of maltreatment, type of caregiver, and burden of proof. Waldfogel also suggested more training for mandated reporters and better communication between mandated reporters and the agency investigators. This could create a "feedback loop," giving investigators more information about a family and educating reporters on what kinds of situations are likely to receive attention from the agency (p. 116).

Some states are attempting to reduce the number of unfounded reports by dividing the most serious cases from the less serious ones, and treating less serious cases with support services rather than with a full-fledged investigation. Figure 6.2 shows that 5.1 percent of 2004 cases—those designated as "Alternative Response Nonvictim"—were offered services right from the start, rather than a maltreatment investigation.

Filing a Report

Mandated reporters must report suspected child abuse and neglect, and may face civil and criminal penalties if they fail to do so. They have immunity from legal action by parents for reporting.

They are also protected by confidentiality provisions in the reporting laws; the identity of the reporter is supposed to remain unknown to the parents.

Those who report child abuse and neglect are not expected to have conducted an investigation to ascertain whether child maltreatment occurred. They are asked to report instances in which they have "reasonable cause to suspect" child maltreatment. Then child protective services will conduct the investigation. As indicated earlier, many professionals are confused about what types of situations are considered abuse or neglect by their local child protective agency. However, the general rule for mandated reporters is to report all cases in which they have "reasonable cause to suspect" child abuse or neglect, regardless of whether they believe that the child protective agency will act on the referral. By doing so, they are protecting themselves from any possible legal penalties as well as working to protect children.

The procedures for filing a report are quite simple in most states and are described in the state's reporting law. Generally, the reporter may make an oral report, such as a telephone call, to be followed by a written report within twenty-four hours. Reporters are encouraged to give as much information as possible, such as relevant names, addresses, and phone numbers, and specific information regarding the maltreatment, such as physical evidence and the statements of children or perpetrators. In some states, child protective services is required or encouraged to let the reporter know the results of the investigation.

AN ECOLOGICAL VIEW OF CHILD MALTREATMENT

Conditions leading to the neglect or abuse of children cannot be identified in simple, discrete terms. Multiple causes and conditions interact, reinforce each other, and generate new influences that lead to family malfunctioning. No single factor causes child maltreatment; rather, the interaction among environmental, parental, and child characteristics creates situations in which child maltreatment is likely to occur (Belsky, 1993; English, 1998; Heyman & Slep, 2001; Children's Bureau, 2006). In this section, we discuss factors that research suggests is correlated with abuse and neglect, using the framework presented in Chapter 3, Box 3.1: Risk and Protective Factors for Child Abuse and Neglect.

Social/Environmental Risk Factors

Community Deficits.   Environmental conditions that contribute to child neglect and abuse often can be identified within a community's system of social services. There can be lack of early case-finding techniques, resulting in a pattern of providing social services only after a child is observed to be in an already dangerous situation, or when the care he or she is receiving finally reaches such a low level that it defies what a neighborhood or community can tolerate. A deficiency in "case accountability" is another factor, reflected in such practices as (1) giving inadequate or incomplete services, (2) failing to follow through on referrals for another service, (3) setting up barriers of communication or bureaucratic procedures that cut off some people from asking for or receiving help, (4) showing concern only about fragments of family life that present symptoms troublesome to the community, and (5) failing to develop an agency function that is an active part of a community-wide program of services. Preventive services may be unavailable to avert the onset of family problems. The situation in Miami, Florida, reported in 2002, in which a young child who was supposed to be under the oversight of the Department of Social Services, but instead could not be found, is an extreme example (and fortunately a rare one) of problems with case accountability.

Serious social problems abound in our communities today, and all of these, directly or indirectly, tend to increase the incidence of child neglect and abuse. Some of the most pressing social problems are a large-scale incidence of mental illness and substance abuse; escalating health costs and unequal medical services; poverty in the midst of affluence; lack of jobs for youth and heads of families; deplorable housing for large numbers of the population; high rates of delinquency; inadequate and irrelevant education for much of the nation's youth, with a lack of preparation for jobs, higher education, parenthood, and other aspects of adult responsibility; and a pervading sense that individuals lack the power of self-direction and are subject to the restrictive rules of bureaucracies or intangible outside forces that limit daily experiences for them and their children.

Societal Attitudes. We live in a culture that is saturated with images of violence. The media glamorize violence in movies, books, television, and music, and reinforce the widely held view that violence is a culturally approved way of resolving disputes. Toys and computer games for children glamorize "the thrill" of violent encounters. Child abuse must be viewed within the context of a society that accepts and too often condones violence in the domestic sphere and in the community. Physical force is still considered by many, including many school districts, to be an acceptable means to govern children's behavior.

Poverty. The relationship of poverty to child maltreatment has been recognized at least since the nineteenth century. Research consistently shows a correlation between socioeconomic status and child maltreatment rate. In one national study, the poorest children were three times as likely to suffer maltreatment than were children in families with incomes between $15,000 and $29,000, and more than twenty-five times as likely to be maltreated than were children in the most affluent categories (Sedlak & Broadhurst, 1996). Of course, child abuse and neglect occur at all income levels. To some extent, the differences in rates between income groups may reflect differences in recognition of maltreatment rather than differences in occurrence. Although most states mandate that a petition alleging neglect be for reasons other than poverty, this distinction does not always get made in practice. Families of higher socioeconomic status may be able to conceal child maltreatment because of access to greater resources and less scrutiny by social services. It is also important to remember that most poor families do not abuse or neglect their children, and raise their children successfully in the face of great obstacles. Nevertheless, the magnitude and consistency of the difference in maltreatment rates among income groups makes clear that children in poor families are at greater risk of maltreatment.

Many factors work to increase the risk to poor children. Poor families frequently live in poor neighborhoods with few services. They face the ongoing stress of living in chronically poor conditions, and their children's safety is but one concern among many. Poor people may be less well informed about developmentally sound ways of disciplining their children than are middle-class families. The integral connection between poverty and all types of maltreatment (with the possible exception of sexual abuse) will become clearer in the sections describing each category of abuse and neglect.

When welfare reform was enacted in 1996, with its strict work requirements for families, there was concern that the increased burden on poor families might result in greater risk of child maltreatment. In a review of recent research, Slack (2002) concluded that it is "too early to tell" whether welfare reform will affect the child maltreatment rate, but recommended increasing the safety nets and conducting longitudinal research on how children fare under welfare reform.

RACE

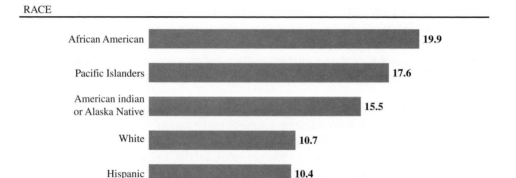

Figure 6.3 *Race and Ethnicity of Victims, 2004*

Source: U.S. Department of Health and Human Services (2006). *Child maltreatment 2004*. Washington, DC: U.S. Government Printing Office.

Race and Ethnicity. Some racial and ethnic groups are more likely to be reported for child maltreatment than others. As Figure 6.3 shows, African American children and Pacific Islander children have particularly high rates (twenty and eighteen per thousand children in the population, respectively). White children are more likely than other races to be reported for sexual abuse (U.S. Department of Health and Human Services, 2000a). However, the relationship of race to maltreatment is a complicated one. Misunderstandings about cultural beliefs and practices, such as those discussed earlier in this chapter, play a part in whether a situation gets reported. African American children are more likely to be reported, particularly if they are poor, because they are more likely to come to the attention of mandated reporters. It is difficult to separate out the distinct effects of race, poverty, and substance abuse, all closely linked to child maltreatment. Berrick, Needell, Barth, and Jonson-Reid (1998), after a major review of research, have concluded, in line with other researchers (Sedlak & Broadhurst, 1996; Ards, Chung, & Myers, 1998), that ethnicity by itself does not increase risk of maltreatment for children. It seems reasonable to conclude that race is often linked to a constellation of factors, including poverty and substance abuse that, together, represent increased risk to children.

Parental Characteristics. Abusive and neglectful caregivers often have inappropriate expectations of their children. They may lack parenting skills and knowledge of child development, and are likely to have unreasonably high expectations of their children to care for themselves, to care for younger siblings, and to comply with parental demands. When these expectations are not met, the parent may assume the child is being willful or defiant and lash out physically. For example, a parent may believe that a 3-month-old infant who keeps on crying after being told to stop, just "won't mind" and needs a spanking.

Some parents have a very limited repertoire of techniques for guiding their children's behavior. They know how to spank a child but not how to use time-outs, explanations, negotiation, diversion, and positive reinforcement. Lack of knowledge of parenting skills, combined with lack of empathy and belief in authoritarian control can precipitate child maltreatment.

Maltreating parents may express more negative and neglectful feelings about their children than do other parents. Their interactions with their children are often limited, negative, controlling, and lacking in emotional nurturance. They may make many requests of their children but at the same time are unlikely to respond to requests from them.

Having been mistreated as a child puts a parent at greater risk of abusing and neglecting a child. Widom (1989), after reviewing research, estimated that about one-third of those who were abused as children will neglect or abuse their own offspring, and that two-thirds will not. Thus, the "cycle of violence" from one generation to the next does exist, but it is not inevitable.

The ability to form attachments is thought to depend on the quality of care the parent received as a small child, so failure to bond tends to get transmitted intergenerationally. Steele (1987) observed that parents who suffered massive emotional deprivation and physical abuse in early life often manifest a marked lack of empathy for their children. They seem unaware of and insensitive to their children's affective needs and moods, and are unable to respond appropriately. This deficit is observable in hospital maternity wards in the first interactions of the parent and child. The parent may seem cold, uninterested, and unwilling to attend to the newborn infant's needs. She may avoid eye or body contact with the child. Particularly when under stress, unempathic parents find the satisfaction of their own needs to be so compelling that they disregard those of the child (Erickson & Egeland, 1996; Goldman, Salus, Wolcott, & Kennedy, 2003).

Substance Abuse. Drug abuse has increased tremendously in recent years, with devastating effects on the lives of adults and children. Substances such as alcohol, marijuana, cocaine, crack, PCP, heroin, and methamphetamine are widely available. In 1997, a study of state child welfare agencies estimated that 67 percent of parents in the child welfare system required substance abuse treatment services (Child Welfare League of America, 2001). Parents who abuse substances, especially if they are addicted, are often unable to provide consistent, nurturing care that promotes their child's development. Feeding the addiction takes needed resources from the family, so that children may lack sufficient food and clothing and decent housing. Use of psychoactive drugs also increases the risk of abuse. Chemical substances lower inhibitions; an angry parent when drunk may become a physically abusive parent. Some parents recruit their children into selling drugs, prostitution, or other extremely damaging activities in order to obtain money to buy drugs or alcohol (Zuckerman, 1994; Breshears, Yeh, & Young, 2004).

Often, addiction is related to a constellation of other problems that also affect the parent's ability to provide an adequate level of care for his or her children. Many women who are addicted experienced sexual or physical abuse as children. For them, use of drugs and alcohol may be an effort to dull the painful memories associated with these events. Domestic violence, depression, and substance abuse are interrelated conditions, which together compound the risks to children's healthy development (Zuckerman, 1994; Malow et al., 2006; Nicholas & Rasmussen, 2006).

Although child welfare professionals have been aware for many years of a link between child maltreatment and drug and alcohol abuse, only recently have efforts been made to link the child protective and substance abuse service systems. In the past decade, professionals in both service systems have become more aware of the importance of an integrated approach, incorporating substance abuse treatment and help with parenting (Azzi-Lessing & Olsen, 1996).

One way that communities have attempted to assist those with substance abuse issues is through family treatment courts. These courts bring together legal services, social welfare services, and substance abuse services in the same courtroom with a permanently assigned judge to the case. Case managers whose task it is to link clients with services and monitor their use assist the judge. This close linkage of the judicial, social service, and substance abuse treatment arenas can help to keep everyone aware of progress and in compliance with time frames set out by, the Adoption and Safe Families Act (ASFA) (American Humane Association, 2002a).

Domestic Violence. Physical assault on children is much more common in households in which women are battered. Even if the children are not themselves abused, they may suffer neglect or psychological maltreatment associated with the abuse of a parent by another adult (Osofsky, 1999; Levandosky & Graham-Bermann, 2001). According to Barnett, Miller-Perrin, and Perrin (1997):

> Families where marital violence is occurring are generally experiencing high levels of stress. Children in such families are subject to self-blame, feelings of helplessness, neglect, abuse, and injury. Most likely, mothers in these families are psychologically unavailable for their children and are inconsistent in their parenting style. Fathers in violent families appear more irritable than other fathers and less likely to be involved in parenting. The children are traumatized by the threat of observing violence or becoming the object of physical assault. (*p. 146*)

Even very young children may be affected by violence in the home. Osofsky (1999) reported finding infants and toddlers showing "excessive irritability, immature behavior, sleep disturbances, emotional distress, fears of being alone, and regression in toileting and language. Additionally, some researchers have claimed that children may well suffer from Post Traumatic Stress Disorder (PTSD) and impaired development of trust and autonomy" (p. 36).

Despite the clear link between children's development and domestic violence, professionals working in protective services and domestic violence services have often viewed themselves as having different mandates. Child protective services (CPS) are highly regulated while domestic violence services generally operate with much less government oversight. Domestic violence workers generally are not named in state statutes as mandated reporters for child abuse and neglect and may view child protective services as indifferent to the needs of battered women or as punitively blaming them for their own abuse. CPS workers may view domestic violence as a failure of the mother to protect herself and her children.

Federal legislation has addressed domestic violence, in particular, the Violence Against Women Act (VAWA) of 1994. States have started to enact legislation to require a connection between domestic violence services and CPS. Some states use child endangerment standards to prosecute batterers who attack their partners in the presence of the children. Approximately sixteen states now include children who witness acts of domestic violence in the category of children in need of protection. As with substance abuse, domestic violence treatment dynamics often conflict with decision-making time frames set out by ASFA. Co-training and cross-training of child welfare and domestic violence workers are recommended (Nuszkowski et al., 2007).

Animal Abuse. Emerging research suggests that a link may exist between animal abuse and child abuse and other domestic violence. The American Humane Association's program, "The Link," looks at these possible connections. One study found that higher rates of animal abuse were found in homes where physical abuse of children was substantiated (DeViney, Dickert, & Lockwood, 1983, cited in Ascione & Arkow, 1999). Garbarino (1999, cited in Ascione & Arkow, 1999) argued that professionals need to cultivate a "generic empathy for the victimized." Child protection investigators should be aware of the possibility for animal abuse, while animal abuse officers should conduct a brief assessment of the children in households where pets are abused.

Louisiana has mandated cross-reporting for animal humane officers and people who are investigating allegations of child abuse. California has legislation stating that county child and adult protective services workers may report animal abuse. Clearly, this is an area for further research and legislative intervention. (Migliaro, Ryan, 2004)

Child Characteristics. Younger children, premature infants, children with developmental delays or physical or mental disabilities and disordered behavior, and children with irritable temperaments are at higher risk for abuse and neglect. Girls are at higher risk for sexual abuse. Infants with fragile bodies are more likely than other children to die of maltreatment (Berrick et al., 1998; English, 1998). Sadly, children already victimized are much more likely to experience recurrence of maltreatment than are children without a prior history of victimization (U.S. Department of Health and Human Services, 2001b).

TYPES OF CHILD MALTREATMENT

Most state statutes and child protection agencies recognize the following types of child maltreatment: child neglect, child abuse, psychological maltreatment, and child sexual abuse. Often, more than one type of maltreatment is involved in a particular case.

Child Neglect

The term "child neglect" refers to parental failure to meet a child's basic needs and provide an adequate level of care. It is the predominant form of child maltreatment in the United States. Child protective services agencies found that over 550,000 children were neglected in 2004 (U.S. Department of Health and Human Services, 2006). The consequences of child neglect can be very serious. It is the leading cause of child fatalities, and many may cause serious long-term damage to children (Garbarino & Collins, 1999; Hildyard & Wolfe, 2002; English et al., 2005b).

Given the prevalence of child neglect and its long-term, serious consequences, it is surprising that neglect has not received the same level of attention as have other forms of maltreatment. One reason for the "neglect of neglect" is that often it does not cause observable harm. Much of the damage from neglect accrues overtime. It is the cumulative effect of malnutrition, lack of medical care, inattention to education, and emotional deprivation that has serious long-term consequences to the developing child (Erickson & Egeland, 1996). A second reason that child neglect has not received the attention its severity merits is that it is closely linked to poverty. Solving the problem of child neglect would require large public expenditures to address the social and economic conditions associated with substandard child care. A third reason for the comparative lack of attention to neglect is that the medical and mental health professions have treatment modalities that are better suited to abuse than neglect. Physicians and emergency room staff are equipped to deal with the observable injuries suffered by abuse victims. Mental health professionals have focused disproportionately on child sexual abuse (Chaffin, 2006). However, child protective service workers have always been heavily involved in identifying and alleviating child neglect, and there are recent indications that policy, research, and treatment professionals are beginning to join them in this concern.

Definition of Neglect. Neglect is generally defined as "deprivation of adequate food, clothing, shelter or medical care" (U.S. Department of Health and Human Services, 1999a.) This definition is not entirely helpful, because it leaves both "deprivation" and "adequate" open to subjective interpretation, and because it does not cover all forms of neglect. It has proved difficult historically to reach a national consensus on the definition of neglect. States define it differently, as do professionals in various disciplines (Zuravin, 2001). DePanfilis (2006, p. 2) identified unresolved issues in defining neglect; the following minimum requirements in caring for a child are adapted from her work

❖ whether the caregiver's action or inaction is intentional (for example, a physically disabled parent may not intend to neglect his or her toddler who is dangerously close to the stairs);

❖ impact of the neglect on the health, safety, and well-being of the child;

❖ whether the failure to protect a child from abuse by another person in the home constitutes neglect;

❖ whether the lack of ability to provide for the child because of poverty should be considered neglect; and

❖ whether risk of harm should be included in the definition; for example, if a child is improperly clothed for cold weather but has not yet suffered frostbite.

Furthermore, the age and developmental level of the child is a consideration in deciding whether neglect has occurred. For example, leaving a preschooler unattended for an hour is quite different from leaving a 12-year-old. In addition, the concept of "continued risk" poses problems in defining neglect. Many professionals now believe that the damage from neglect comes more from emotional or physical deprivation over a long period than from a single or temporary situation. Yet it is difficult to define "continued risk" in a way that everyone consistently understands and applies to concrete situations.

Neglect may be classified according to severity, with implications for what level of intervention the child protection agency may deem appropriate. *Mild neglect*, such as failing to use a car seat, may not warrant a child protection investigation, but rather a referral to a preventive service. *Moderate neglect* covers situations in which previous referrals to preventive services have not solved the problem, and the child faces some harm from parental inaction, such as inadequate clothing or nutrition. In these situations, the child protection agency may stay involved, in partnership with a family support program. *Severe neglect* describes situations in which the child has suffered harm for a long time, or the harm has been severe; for example, a child who has been deprived over a long period of medication needed for a chronic condition, resulting in frequent hospital admissions. In these situations, the child protection agency will be very much involved, as will the legal system (DePanfilis, 2006).

Types of Neglect

Neglect may be classified by type. Common categories include: physical neglect, medical neglect, inadequate supervision, educational and environmental neglect, and newborns addicted or exposed to drugs and alcohol. Each of these is discussed below. Another type of neglect—emotional neglect—is discussed in Psychological Maltreatment.

Physical Neglect.   Involves failure to provide for children's basic needs for food, clothing, safety, and shelter. An infant may be undernourished for a long period, resulting in a condition known as "failure to thrive" (Wallace, 1996; Zanel, 1997). Inadequate clothing and hygiene and reckless disregard for the child's safety such as driving while intoxicated are other instances of physical neglect. There is controversy on whether homelessness should be considered neglect.

Usually, consideration is given to the reason for homelessness; neglect would certainly be said to occur if the family were homeless because the parent used the family's finances for drugs. *Expulsion* refers to situations in which a child, usually an adolescent, is told to leave home with no adequate provision made for his or her care, or is not permitted to return home (U.S. Department of Health and Human Services, 2002). *Shuttling* refers to a pattern of leaving children repeatedly with a variety of caregivers, possibly due to the parent's unwillingness to provide a stable home for the child. *Abandonment* refers to the desertion of a child without leaving provision for his or her care, and usually not picking him or her up within two days.

Medical Neglect.   Occurs when a parent denies or delays seeking needed health care for a child. States may have legislation that permits parents to take into account their religious beliefs in using health care. These situations may be controversial and get resolved through litigation.

Inadequate Supervision.   Refers to situations in which children are without a caregiver or the caregiver is inattentive or unsuitable, and therefore the children are in danger of harming themselves or possibly others. Children's need for supervision varies with age, and cultural factors may also influence the level of unsupervised time that is considered acceptable, so it is not possible to set specific guidelines on what constitutes inadequate supervision. However, children who are exposed to safety hazards such as poison, stairs, and drug paraphernalia; to second-hand smoke; to guns and other weapons; or to unsanitary conditions in the home, such as rotting food, feces, and lack of sanitary facilities, are receiving inadequate supervision, even if their exposure to hazards has not yet resulted in observable harm to them.

An important consideration is the problem of single, poor, working parents, who struggle to maintain the family income while ensuring adequate child care. For families in this situation, the appropriate response is active and effective advocacy to help the family get the child care it needs; a child protective services investigation of inadequate supervision of the child seems unlikely in itself to address the problem, and may make the situation worse, unless that is the only way to get the family the child care help it needs (Jones, 1987; Nam, Meezan, & Danziger, 2006).

Educational Neglect.   Refers to a child's habitual absence from school, when the parent has been informed of the problem and does not take steps to remedy it. The term also covers situations in which parents refuse to permit their children with special needs to receive the services they need.

Newborns Addicted or Exposed to Drugs.   Although it has been known for many years that pregnant women sometimes behave in ways that may harm a growing fetus, only recently have some of the behaviors been categorized as fetal neglect and come to the attention of child welfare agencies. Neglecting to get prenatal care and not acting on sound medical advice are ways that pregnant women might show insufficient care for the developing fetus. Reasons for maternal medical neglect include mental illness, particularly depression, mental retardation, and addiction to chemical substances (Kent, Laidlaw, & Brockington, 1997). Psychoactive substances used by pregnant women can affect the fetus's developing brain and cause learning disabilities and behavior problems such as those encompassed by the term fetal alcohol syndrome. The problem is widespread and serious. It is estimated that between 400,000 and 800,000 children are exposed prenatally to drugs or alcohol each year, and research has shown that children prenatally exposed to cocaine are much more likely than nonexposed children to suffer later abuse and neglect. In response to this problem, the federal government enacted the Keeping Children and Families Safe Act of 2003, which requires that newborns who test positive for drugs be referred to child protection agencies. As of 2005, twenty-four states also had such statutory provisions.

The controversy over the appropriate level of intervention in cases of fetal neglect illustrates the dynamic interplay of rights and responsibilities of child, parent, and society, as described in

Chapter 1, in the arena of child protection. Scientific advances have made it possible to diagnose problems in the fetus and to treat the fetus directly, raising policy questions concerning the competing rights of the fetus and the mother. Judges and other policymakers are tempted to create laws that use restrictions or punishments to force pregnant women to adhere to medical advice as a way of protecting the fetus and ensuring its healthy development. Some women's advocates oppose such restrictions, on the grounds that they constitute an impermissible infringement on the rights of women. Some states, such as Wisconsin, do allow custody of a pregnant woman with evidence of ongoing substance abuse and inability to control it.

Some state reporting laws require that newborns who test positive for drugs be referred to child protection agencies, although usually more evidence of ongoing drug use is required to trigger removal of the child from the home (Stein, 1998). States opting for statutes that require the reporting of parents who use drugs during pregnancy should include safeguards against race and class bias. A county in Florida that has mandated reporting for mothers known to have used alcohol or illicit drugs during pregnancy, found that African American women were reported at approximately ten times the rate of white women. Poor women were also more likely to be reported. The rates of substance abuse among all groups were quite similar, suggesting that race and class bias influenced the decision to report (Chasnoff, Harvey, Landress, & Barrett, 1990).

It is necessary to look at the reporting of fetal abuse in relation to the aid such action will make available to the parents. If the purpose of such a report is to lay the groundwork for removing the child from the mother's custody immediately after the child's birth, mothers may become wary of using medical services for fear of this outcome. However, if the purpose of the report is to help the mother access services that would otherwise be unavailable, the report will further the effort to have a caring and capable parent for the arriving baby. "In examining the legal and social policy implications of fetal abuse, the question that must be asked is whether society's goal is control of the woman or protection of the baby. Ultimately, the child's interests will best be served by supporting the mother and providing the resources to meet her diverse needs" (Madden, 1993, p. 139).

Signs of Neglect. The condition of neglected children reflects the lack of attention they have received to even their most basic needs. Common signs of possible child neglect include chronic hunger; inappropriate dress, such as a lack of warm clothing in cold weather; poor hygiene, as shown by unclean clothing and hair and possibly lice or other skin conditions; and unattended medical needs. Neglected children may display such behaviors as stealing and hoarding food; falling asleep at odd times or listlessness; frequent unexplained absences from school; self-destructive activity, including abuse of alcohol and drugs; and frequent reports that no caregiver is at home (American Humane Association, 1997, Child Welfare Information Gateway, 2006.)

Neglectful families are likely to be poor, to be headed by a single parent, and to have many children. They are often socially isolated. The parents may appear to lack empathy, have difficulty relating to others, and have ineffective communication skills. They tend not to demonstrate nurturing behaviors to their children, and their interactions with the children lack warmth. Their lives often seem chaotic, with many conflictual relationships (Berrick, 1997). Neglectful parents tend to have a low opinion of their own competency and abilities, and lack a sense of well-being (Gaudin & Dubowitz, 1997).

Child Abuse

Each year in this country substantial numbers of children are physically injured by their caregivers in circumstances that cannot be explained as accidents. Moreover, their injuries usually result from recurring acts of violence rather than from a single expression of anger or loss of control by the adults who care for them. The severity of such injuries ranges from a mild form of abuse, which may not come to the attention of a doctor or other persons outside the home, to an extreme deviancy in child care, resulting in extensive physical damage to the child or even death. After physical neglect, physical abuse is the most common type of child maltreatment. Boys and girls are about equally likely to be physically abused. Boys are more likely to be abused in the early grade school years, girls at the onset of puberty (U.S. Department of Health and Human Services, 2002; 2006).

Physical abuse includes such parental actions as hitting with a hand, stick, or other object and punching, kicking, shaking, throwing, burning, stabbing, or choking the child. The primary symptom of child abuse is the evidence on the child of suspicious injuries that the parents cannot explain satisfactorily. Children often get bumped or bruised in the course of play and their daily activities, so not all injuries lead to a suspicion of child abuse. Physical indicators include unexplained bruises, welts, bite marks, bald spots, burns (especially cigarette-shaped burns or immersion burns in the shape of a glove or stocking), fractures, and lacerations. Some marks leave the shape of the object that was used to hit the child, such as belt buckles or hot irons (American Humane Association, 2003a).

Abused children may also display behaviors that are suggestive of physical abuse. For example, they may be very aggressive or very withdrawn; they may complain of soreness, move uncomfortably, or wear inappropriate clothing to cover their body; they may be afraid to go home or continually run away.

Besharov (1990a) has identified a number of factors that lead to the suspicion that an injury was caused by abuse rather than by an accident. The location of the injury is important: Accidents cause injury to chins, foreheads, hands, shins, and knees, but injuries to other parts of the body, such as thighs, genitals, buttocks, and torso are often caused by physical assault. Corner or joint fractures are usually not caused by accidents but by violent shaking or twisting. Another indicator is the presence of old as well as new injuries. Although physical abuse can occur in a single episode, it is often a pattern of behavior that goes on over time. Children with injuries such as those described here should be reported to the child protection authorities. An accurate determination of the exact cause of the injury can then be made through medical diagnosis and social services investigation.

Physical Abuse and Reasonable Discipline. Society sanctions corporal punishment of children. Even though many people believe that any physical punishment of children is wrong and contributes to their emotional maladjustment, all states recognize the rights of parents to use physical force to discipline their children. The difficulty, for those concerned with reporting child abuse, is to differentiate between reasonable discipline and child abuse. Besharov (1990a) has provided guidelines for making this distinction. Discipline would be considered unreasonable if its *"reasonably foreseeable consequence was or could have been the child's serious injury.* This includes any punishment that results in a broken bone, eye damage, severe welts, bleeding, or any other injury that requires medical treatment" [italics added for emphasis] (p. 67). He points out that physical punishment of infants is always of concern because infants are not developmentally able to understand the reason for the physical assault on them and because their soft tissues make any physical violence dangerous. A forceful attack on the head of a child of any age is also dangerous and unreasonable punishment. In assessing cases of physical punishment, a number of factors should be considered, including "the child's age and physical and mental condition, the child's misconduct on the particular occasion and in the past, the parents' purpose, the kind and frequency of punishment inflicted, the degree of harm done to the child, and the type and location of the injuries" (p. 68). (See the Trends and Issues section, Chapter 3.)

Parent and Family Characteristics. Families of abused children tend to be larger than average. The caregivers tend to be young, with higher rates of abuse reported for parents under 27 years than for other age groups (Connelly & Straus, 1992; Wolfner & Gelles, 1993). Poverty is strongly linked to child abuse, as families with low income and parents who are unemployed or lack a high school diploma are at greater risk of child abuse (Wolfner & Gelles, 1993).

Mothers' boyfriends are thought to increase the risk for abuse. Margolin's study (1992) supports this view. She pointed out that boyfriends have characteristics often associated with higher risk of abuse: being nongenetic caregivers, being male, and being located in a single-parent family. She suggests that the lack of an accepted, legitimate social role may put boyfriends on the defensive and make them more likely to react to perceived threats to their authority. Particularly if they are not supporting the family or fulfilling a parental role in other ways, they may be challenged by the children when they try to exercise authority and may then react with violence. Further, a mother's boyfriend may be in conflict with the children because both are competing for the mother's time, and the children may feel that the boyfriend is displacing their own father's role in the family.

Abusive parents are more likely than other parents to have suffered abuse themselves as children. They have learned negative behavioral models of parenting that they duplicate when they themselves become parents. Substance abuse or a psychiatric diagnosis of hostile or explosive personality are linked to higher rates of physical child abuse. Abusive parents tend to see their children in a more negative light than do nonabusive parents. They are apt to have inconsistent childrearing practices, characterized by sporadic, harsh coercion. Family members tend to communicate through arguments and other negative, hostile interactions (Kolko, 1996).

Shaken Baby Syndrome. Shaken baby syndrome occurs when a baby is violently shaken, which "repeatedly pitches the brain in different directions." Frequently, there are no physically evident signs of injury to the child's body, but the injury, on examination, is found in the child's head or behind the eyes. Injuries that can occur include "brain swelling and damage, subdural hemorrhage, mental retardation or developmental delays, blindness, hearing loss, paralysis, and speech and learning difficulties and death" (American Humane Association, 2002b). Shaken baby syndrome can be part of a pattern of abuse or the result of the caregiver's frustration with a young child. Sometimes caregivers simply play too roughly with infants, unaware of the infants' undeveloped neck muscles and fragile brain tissue.

Munchausen Syndrome by Proxy. Munchausen syndrome by proxy (MBP) is a rare and bizarre form of child maltreatment. The name is derived from Munchausen syndrome, a condition in which a person, usually an adult, harms him or herself to induce symptoms of serious illness, followed by extensive and persistent involvement with the medical system. MBP refers to the situation in which a parent induces such symptoms in his or her child. MBP has been defined as an illness that meets the following conditions:

1. Illness fabricated (faked or induced) by the parent or someone *in loco parentis*;
2. The child is presented to doctors, usually persistently, and the perpetrator (initially) denies causing the child's illness;
3. The illness goes when the child is separated from the perpetrator; and
4. The perpetrator is considered to be acting out of a need to assume the sick role by proxy or as another form of attention-seeking behavior. (Meadow, 2002)

The incidence of MBP is less well established than other forms of maltreatment, partly because of difficulties with definition and categorization. Is it physical abuse or, as some claim, psychological abuse accompanied by physical abuse? Another problem is the difficulty of making the diagnosis and ruling out other organic causes of the child's symptoms of illness, and the likelihood that it has been concealed for years by parents who move children from doctor to doctor. However, increasing recognition of the problem suggests that it is more common than was previously thought.

A review of research on MBP identified fifty-nine articles on the syndrome, describing 122 cases from twenty-two countries (Feldman & Brown, 2002). In these cases, the mother was most often the perpetrator, and the majority of children were between the ages of 4 and 12. Over half (54 percent) of the children were male. The parents' methods of inducing the symptoms of illness in the child included "fabricating or inducing bleeding, administering harmful substances, falsely reporting seizures, and falsifying or inducing fever or failure to thrive" (p. 519).

The causes of MBP are not well understood, but seem to include both individual psychopathology and dysfunctional family interactions. To some extent, modern medicine provides a compatible environment for those with the syndrome to operate, with its invasive procedures, diagnostic testing, and medication trials, and with a lack of history taking, getting to know the family, and "expressions of empathy" (p. 519).

Psychological Maltreatment

The study and identification of psychological maltreatment, also referred to as emotional abuse and neglect or mental injury, has been hampered by the lack of a sound definition of the problem. In general, psychological maltreatment refers to a repeated pattern of behavior that conveys to a child that he or she is unwanted, worthless, valued only to the extent that he or she can meet others' needs, or is threatened with physical or psychological attack. Hart, Brassard, and Karlson (1996) developed an operational definition comprising six categories of behavior:

- ❖ *Spurning,* including belittling, degrading, shaming, ridiculing; singling out one child to do most of the household chores or to criticize and punish; and publicly humiliating
- ❖ *Terrorizing,* including threatening to hurt, kill, or abandon a child; placing a child in recognizably dangerous situations; and threatening or perpetuating violence against a child's loved ones or objects
- ❖ *Isolating,* including confining the child or placing unreasonable limitations on the child's freedom of movement or on social interactions with peers and adults in the community
- ❖ *Exploiting/corrupting,* including modeling, permitting, or encouraging such antisocial behavior as prostitution, performance in pornography, criminal activity, or substance abuse; encouraging developmentally inappropriate behavior such as parentification or infantilization of the child; extreme overinvolvement or intrusiveness; and restricting cognitive development
- ❖ *Denying emotional responsiveness,* such as being detached and uninvolved, interacting only when absolutely necessary, and failing to express love and affection to the child
- ❖ *Mental health, medical, and educational neglect,* such as ignoring or refusing to provide for the child's needs in these areas (p. 74)

Psychological maltreatment is related to other forms of maltreatment; it is the psychological dimension of abuse, neglect, and sexual abuse. Terrorizing may be embedded in physical abuse; denying emotional responsiveness may be the psychological aspect of physical neglect. However, psychological maltreatment may also exist by itself, without other forms of maltreatment (Burnett, 1993; Moore & Pepler, 2006).

It seems very likely that psychological maltreatment is underreported to child protection agencies. Although most states require reporting such maltreatment, the definitions given in state statutes are often vague or ambiguous. Psychological maltreatment is often difficult to prove, and generally must be tied to some observable harm to the child, such as "severe anxiety, depression, withdrawal, or untoward aggressive behavior, or as evinced by discernible impairment of the child's ability to function within a normal range of performance" (U.S. Department of Health and Human Services, 1999a, p. 10).

Psychological maltreatment can have long-lasting effects on children and can be more damaging in the long run than physical abuse (Glaser, 2002). Children subjected to this form of maltreatment may have "hidden scars" that are manifested in poor self-esteem, cruelty to others or to animals, fire-setting, emotional withdrawal, abuse of drugs and alcohol, suicide, and, as adults, instability in the realms of love and work (American Humane Association, 2006).

Children evidencing these behaviors have not necessarily been psychologically maltreated, so by themselves these signs of dysfunction are insufficient evidence that a child is suffering maltreatment. As a general guide for identifying a situation as psychological maltreatment, Besharov (1990a) suggests a two-tiered approach. For extreme acts of mistreatment, such as close confinement or torture, the parental behavior is sufficient evidence to ascertain that mistreatment has occurred. For less extreme forms, such as not allowing the child social and emotional growth or failure to provide a loving home, some relationship should be established between the parental behavior and the child's problems. Particularly important in a finding of psychological maltreatment would be the parent's refusal to accept help for the child's emotional problems.

Sexual Abuse of Children

After many years of child sexual abuse being hidden, ignored, and covered up, this topic is widely discussed today, although it is still not well understood. An expanding body of literature, including survivor's stories of abuse and recovery and professional clinical and research reports, have helped shed light on this disturbing phenomenon. Over the past twenty years or so, child protective services, courts, and police have improved procedures for identifying and intervening in situations that involve child sexual abuse.

According to the American Humane Association, the definition of child molestation is an "act of a person, adult or child, which forces, coerces, or threatens a child to have any form of sexual contact or to engage in any type of sexual activity at the perpetrator's direction" (2003a, p. 1). The term "sexual abuse" encompasses a wide range of behaviors, categorized by the American Humane Association as follows:

Touching sexual offenses include:
fondling,
making a child touch an adult's sexual organs, and
penetrating a child's vagina or anus no matter how slightly with a penis or object that doesn't have a valid medical purpose.

Non-touching sexual offenses include:
  engaging in indecent exposure or exhibitionism,
  exposing children to pornographic material,
  deliberately exposing a child to the act of sexual intercourse, and
  · masturbating in front of a child.
Sexual exploitation can include:
  engaging a child or soliciting a child for the purposes of prostitution, and
  using a child to film, photograph, or model pornography. (2003a, pp. 1–2)

An unresolved definitional issue is when experimentation among children who are peers, or close to being peers, changes from exploration to abuse. A 17-year-old having intercourse with a 15-year-old may not be desirable, but may appear consensual with no ill effects that can be documented. Clearly, this is a different situation from one in which a 35-year-old is having sex with a 15-year-old.

Every year, many children are sexually abused. Girls are more likely to be victims of sexual abuse than are boys and tend to be older when victimized; the median age of victimization for girls is 11 years: for boys, the median age is 8 years. In the past twenty-five years, studies have revealed that sexual abuse is much more common than people thought. Reports of sexual abuse have increased greatly since mandatory reporting began in the mid-1970s. This trend probably reflects increased willingness of the public to identify and report sexual abuse, not an increase in incidence (Berliner & Elliott, 1996). Unlike other more obvious forms of maltreatment, child sexual abuse can remain hidden unless the victim chooses to disclose it. In the past, victims very often chose to remain silent because they feared retribution from their attackers, because they were ashamed and blamed themselves for the abuse, or because they felt, often correctly, that they would not be believed. With increased understanding of the dynamics of sexual abuse, victims are more likely than in previous years to tell someone about the abuse, although it is still underreported.

Parent and Family Characteristics.   Some family characteristics place children at greater risk for abuse. Although most stepfathers do not abuse their stepchildren, the presence of stepfathers in the home does somewhat increase the risk of sexual abuse for girls. Children in single-parent families and those in which the mother is disabled, dead, mentally ill, or out of the home for extensive periods are at somewhat higher risk than are other children, particularly if there are no other caring female adults for the child to confide in. Other parental characteristics associated with increased risk for children include reliance on punitive discipline, extreme marital conflict, social isolation, disorganized family life, substance abuse, and depression. Children from such families may be emotionally deprived and more susceptible to the ploys of child molesters who offer attention and affection (Finkelhor, 1993; Fleming, Mullen, & Bammer, 1997). Children with disabilities are more likely to be sexually abused than are other children (National Center on Child Abuse and Neglect, 1993). However, these characteristics are too general to be useful in identifying specific cases of sexual abuse. They are perhaps most helpful to caseworkers in selecting groups of children for prevention programs.

Sexual abuse that comes to the attention of child protective services is usually perpetrated by a family member, neighbor, or friend. The police handle cases of stranger rape and abuse. Patterns of sexual abuse vary widely. Multiple abuse episodes are common (Berliner & Eliott, 1996). In Faller's (1988a) clinical sample of 148 Michigan cases, on average, a given perpetrator victimized a child twenty-three times. Sexual contact was the most prevalent type of abuse, with noncontact abuse accounting for only 15 percent of the sexual acts. In more than half the cases, some form of force was used by the perpetrator to gain compliance. In cases in which force was not used or threatened, the children had a history of deprivation and abuse, and viewed sexual abuse as a way of receiving nurturance. Victims reported the abuse about three months after it began, on average. About half the perpetrators made some kind of admission or confession to the abuse (Faller, 1988a).

The vast majority of perpetrators are male, although women also commit sexual abuse. Perpetrators are characterized by a failure to control their sexual impulses toward children. They are likely to have suffered sexual abuse themselves as children (Sebold, 1987). As adults they often have ambivalent or hostile relationships with members of the opposite sex and have limited ability to develop intimate relationships or show affection. They also demonstrate excessive self-centeredness, strong dependency needs, and poor judgment (Bresee, Stearns, Bess, & Packer, 1986). Alcohol and drugs, which act as disinhibitors and also weaken guilt pangs, are frequently used by perpetrators.

Mothers of sexual abuse victims frequently have been abused themselves as children, or they were nonvictimized members of incestuous families (Faller, 1988a).

CASE EXAMPLE

The following protective services investigation concerns incestuous attacks by a father on his two young teenage daughters. It illustrates some of the dynamics of incest.

The Smith family was referred to the agency by the police department. When Jill Smith was picked up for shoplifting earlier in the day, she informed the police that she shoplifted in order to get someone's attention. Her father had been making sexual advances toward her, and she was frightened. Jill indicated that the same thing had happened to her older sister, Nicki. [Nicki, Mr. Smith's daughter by a previous marriage, lives with her mother but saw Mr. Smith on visits.]

When Mr. Smith was questioned by the police, he admitted that he made sexual advances toward both Nicki and Jill. The incident with Nicki occurred about two years ago when she was visiting the family for the summer. She was 13. Mr. Smith had removed her panties, touched her breasts and genital area, and penetrated her vagina with his finger. The incident with Jill occurred about a year later. Mr. Smith kissed her, putting his tongue in her mouth, and he attempted to reach inside her blouse and touch her breasts. He did not try to undress her or convince her to do so.

Nicki returned to her mother's home immediately after her father made sexual advances toward her. She has not visited at her father's home since then.

According to Jill, her father had not made any other sexual advances toward her since that incident. However, he had begun to ask her to sit near him and to put his hands on her thighs even though she asked him not to do it. She described it as "creepy" and was afraid that he would try to become more intimate with her.

After questioning Jill and Mr. Smith, the police referred the case to the state attorney's office. The police also informed Mrs. Smith that she should not leave Jill alone with Mr. Smith under any circumstances.

[The CPS worker interviewed the family and learned that] the family consisted of Mr. Smith (age 39), a sales representative, Mrs. Smith (age 34), director of a day care center, and their daughter, Jill. Jill, age 13, is an eighth grader who is making satisfactory academic progress. The Smiths have been married for fourteen years. This is Mrs. Smith's first marriage and Mr. Smith's second.

Mr. Smith moved out of the home immediately after the police filed the report with the agency. He stated that he would continue to live away from home until the agency allowed him to return. He has scheduled an appointment with a psychiatrist at the local mental health center. He denies being sexually attracted to either Nicki or Jill, and he cannot offer any explanation for his sexual advances toward them. "It was just something that happened." He would like to resolve his problems and return to his wife and daughter.

Mrs. Smith cannot understand why her husband made sexual advances toward Nicki and Jill, and why neither girl had told her what had happened. She thought that she had a close relationship with them and that they trusted her. She is ambivalent about her husband; she did not feel that she could accept him as her husband again, but she hated the thought of living without him. She believes perhaps he did it when he was drunk and unable to control himself. Mrs. Smith expressed anger and concern over Jill's shoplifting. She thinks Jill told the police about her father not because she was afraid he would assault her but in order to elicit sympathy and get out of a sticky situation.

Jill reiterated the sequence and details of her father's sexual advances toward her to the child protection worker. She denies she told the police about his advances as a way of distracting attention from the shoplifting. She is adamant that she shoplifted purposely in order to have the opportunity to talk with someone. When asked why she did not simply call the police to report her concerns, she stated that she did not know that a report could be made by telephone. She hopes her mother will divorce her father. She said she hates him for what he did to her, for forcing Nicki to leave the family and therefore depriving her of a sister, and for the embarrassment his frequent intoxication caused her. (Proch, 1982, pp. 49–51)

Identifying Child Sexual Abuse.   Child protective service workers may have great difficulty substantiating allegations of sexual abuse, unless the child or a witness discloses the abuse. Physical indicators include torn or stained underclothing, pain or injury in the genital area, difficulty walking or sitting, venereal disease, and frequent urinary or yeast infections (American Humane Association, 1997). Physical evidence exists in only a small percentage of cases (Rosenberg & Gary, 1988).

Sexually abused children may exhibit such behaviors as depression, excessive seductiveness, sudden massive weight loss or gain, substance abuse, suicide attempts, hysteria, sudden school difficulties, avoidance of physical contact, devaluation of self, and inappropriate sex play or premature understanding of sex (Browne & Finkelhor, 1986; Hibbard & Hartman, 1992; Chandy, Blum, & Resnick, 1996; Harrison, Fulkerson, & Beebe, 1997; American Humane Association, 2003a). Other symptoms can include enuresis, encopresis, fire-setting, and cruelty to animals. By themselves, without physical evidence, these behaviors may not be enough for child protective agencies to substantiate sexual abuse (Oberlander, 1995).

Corroborating witnesses are a good source of evidence, but they rarely exist because sexual abuse usually takes place in secrecy. Perpetrators are likely to deny that they have engaged in sexual abuse, fearing rejection, shame, and criminal prosecution.

Children do not often make false allegations or misunderstand innocent behavior. However, interviewing sexual abuse victims requires specialized knowledge and techniques. Children making true allegations can usually give detailed information about the context in which the incidents occurred, and describe the sexual victimization and their own emotional state (Faller, 1988b; Oberlander, 1995; Goodman, 2006; Lyon & Saywitz, 2006).

Legal Intervention. Legal entities that may intervene in sexual abuse cases include child protective services, law enforcement, the juvenile court, prosecuting attorneys, and the criminal courts. These agencies often are not well coordinated. Children who are sexual abuse victims may suffer additional trauma by having to describe the circumstances of their abuse to many investigators. If the case is criminally prosecuted, children face public court appearances, confrontation with their abuser, and cross-examination. The process may be even more painful if the accused is a family member rather than a stranger, because the child and others in the family may have mixed feelings about criminally prosecuting a close relative of the child. The child wants the abuse to stop but may not understand the need for legal interventions to stop it (Berliner & Barbieri, 1984). Decisions on whether to prosecute a sex abuse case through the criminal justice system depend on the plan that is developed to protect the child.

Social Work Intervention. The first goal of intervention is to stop the sexual abuse. Victims need protection not only from further abuse but also from retribution from family members for disclosing the sexual abuse. Intervention possibilities include permanently removing the child from the home, criminal prosecution of the perpetrator, permanent exclusion of the perpetrator from the family unit, and reunification. Careful assessment of each parent is needed to guide case planning decisions. Nonoffending parents who are financially independent, or are able to become so, and who are loving and protective to their children can be fruitfully involved in a family rehabilitation plan. For perpetrators, key factors are their general level of functioning as providers and family members, the extent to which they acknowledge and feel guilty about the abuse they have inflicted on a child, and the duration, intensity, and frequency of the abuse (Faller, 1988c).

Individual and group treatment of sexual abuse victims can be effective in ameliorating the effects of abuse. Therapy is usually supportive and psychoeducational; topics include feelings about the abuse and the offender, education on sex abuse prevention, preparation for court appearances, and development of a support system. Treatment for victims with sexual behavior problems usually follows standard interventions for other types of child behavior problems, with a close focus on changing specific behaviors. Family therapy is often needed because the families function poorly; issues specific to the sexual abuse include helping parents work through their initial negative reactions to the disclosure and to the court procedures, and addressing the psychological distress of siblings, if incest was involved (Berliner & Elliott, 1996).

Cases of child sexual abuse raise particularly difficult issues for professionals in the human services. Many people are bewildered or repelled to learn that adults could have sexual feelings toward children. Discounting or disbelieving the child or rage at the perpetrator are understandable but unhelpful reactions, as are blaming the victim or the mother (Faller, 1988a). Another reason that sexual abuse cases are difficult to manage is that they require the specialized knowledge of several disciplines. As with other forms of abuse, the medical, legal, mental health, and child welfare fields each contribute needed knowledge to the resolution of sexual abuse cases. Multidisciplinary teams are an effective way for the community to respond to sexual abuse cases.

Through a team approach, the resources of the community can be effectively coordinated to arrange a case plan that is most likely to assist the victim's recovery (Faller, 1988a).

Survivors of Sexual Abuse. Children suffer in many ways from sexual abuse. The behaviors listed in the section Identifying Child Sexual Abuse show the powerful effects that these traumatic events can have on children's emotional and social functioning. Sexual behavior is common, manifested by excessive masturbation, sexual play with dolls, sexual statements, or behavior interpreted by others as seductive. These behaviors are the result, not the cause, of the abuse, and they do not imply acceptance of the sexual role by the victim (Faller, 1988a; Ryan, 1996). Many victims, particularly boys, become sexually aggressive, thus perpetuating the abusive cycle by victimizing other children (Burton, Nesmith, & Badten, 1997).

The effects of child sexual abuse can last into adulthood. Adults who were abused as children, in comparison to adults with no history of child sexual abuse, are more likely to have sexual disturbance or dysfunction, to have a diagnosable anxiety disorder, to show evidence of depression, to have difficulty expressing anger, and to have suicidal ideas and behavior. They are also susceptible to revictimization; they may be victims of battering, sexual assault, or rape. Adults who have multiple personality disorder or borderline personality disorder may have child sexual abuse or physical abuse in their background. They are at risk for sexual dysfunction and of becoming sex abuse perpetrators (Beitchman et al., 1992).

Persons who have suffered overwhelming trauma may develop posttraumatic stress disorder (PTSD), which is manifested by recurring memories of the traumatic events through flashbacks, nightmares, and intrusive thoughts. Studies show that between one-third and two-thirds of sexual abuse survivors have PTSD, particularly if the abuse was severe and of long duration (Berliner & Elliott, 1996).

Some survivors cope with the overwhelming pain of memories of sexual abuse through dissociation, including disengagement, depersonalization, psychic numbing, and amnesia. Clinicians and survivors report the phenomenon of an adult recalling traumatic abuse that occurred in childhood, after a period of not remembering these events. A controversy has arisen over whether these events did in fact ever happen, or if the adult is fantasizing (Loftus, 1993). Research in this area is still preliminary, but one recent study has found that many adult survivors of abuse report that they had periods in their lives when they could not remember their abuse, suggesting that it is possible for people to repress memories of traumatic events (Melchert & Parker, 1997). More research is needed to understand the relationship between memory and childhood trauma (Lyon & Saywitz, 2006; Goodman, 2006).

The effects of child sexual abuse on adult behavior vary; some survivors report very few symptoms, while others experience overwhelming difficulties. The severity of the adult survivor's problems are related to characteristics of the abuse he or she experienced. Serious, long-term adjustment problems are more likely to be reported by adult survivors who suffered abuse that was of long duration; was accompanied by violence, force, or threat of force; involved penetration; or was committed by a parent or stepparent rather than another member of the family or a nonrelative. Disclosure may increase the trauma to the child if it leads to the breakup of the family or to blaming the victim. Families that are supportive and have higher general functioning can help the victim's recovery. The ability of the mother to be warm, supportive, and caring makes a big difference in the long-term adjustment of her child to the abuse (Beitchman et al., 1992; Berliner & Elliott, 1996; Mapp, 2006).

Ritualism and Child Sexual Abuse. Social workers helping families and children involved in sexual abuse may encounter, at some time in their practice, stories of bizarre, perverse, and sadistic sexual events. Descriptions of these events come from children and from adults recalling past abuse. Events including these kinds of elements have been termed *ritualistic abuse,* defined as "abuse that occurs in the context linked to some symbols or group activities that have a religious, magical, or supernatural connotation, and where the invocation of these symbols or activities, repeated over time, is used to frighten and intimidate the children" (Finkelhor, Williams, & Burns, 1988).

Reliable estimates of the prevalence of ritualistic abuse do not exist, but the National Center for Child Abuse and Neglect surveyed professionals regarding their contact with such cases. The study found that 31 percent of mental health professionals and 23 percent of prosecutors, law enforcement agencies, and child protection agencies who responded to the survey had encountered at least one case of ritualistic or religion-based abuse. The respondents overwhelmingly believed both the ritualistic abuse and the religion-related allegations (Goodman, Bottoms, & Shaver, 1994).

Reports of ritualistic sexual abuse usually involve multiple perpetrators and multiple victims, with males and females about equally likely to be victims (Kelley, 1996).

Therapists are aware of the extremely serious effects ritualistic abuse has on children. Affected children experience greater psychopathology than do other sexually abused children, with increased symptomatology and persistent fears related to their victimization (Jones, 1991; Kelley, 1996).

A central issue for therapists and law enforcement officials is the credibility of those who allege to have been abused. To date, most of the evidence for ritualistic practices comes from children and adults who claim they were abused as children. Very little evidence has come from police to corroborate these stories. Investigations of crime scenes have not found corpses or other physical evidence of violent murders (Lanning, 1991). More research is needed on this important topic before questions on the extent and effects of this phenomenon are understood.

CONSEQUENCES OF CHILD MALTREATMENT

Children experience disruptions to normal development as a result of maltreatment, leading to physical, psychological, cognitive, and social impairments that last well into adulthood (Malow et al., 2006; Gorske et al., 2006; Whisman, 2006; Veltman & Browne, 2001; Thrane et al., 2006; Leitenberg, Gibson & Novy, 2004). The extent of these effects varies depending on the age of the child when maltreatment occurred, the severity and duration of the maltreatment, the type of maltreatment suffered, and the individual makeup of the child. The family's response to the maltreatment also matters greatly; children whose parents are able to become more protective and nurturing are likely to suffer less long-term damage (Nicholas & Rasmussen, 2006). Effects on children of various types of maltreatment were discussed previously in the individual sections on types of maltreatment. Here, we discuss two aspects that cut across categories: the tragedy of child fatalities and the phenomenon known as "the resilient child."

Child Fatalities

Keeping children from being killed by their caregivers is an essential and basic task of any child protection system. Each child homicide by a parent or caregiver represents a failure of the system. To develop better community systems that can identify and monitor potentially lethal family situations, all fifty states plus the District of Columbia have established Child Fatality Review Teams. These teams are made up of representatives from health services, law enforcement, child protective services, the medical examiner's office, and the prosecutor. These multidisciplinary groups review the circumstances leading to the death, including the extent to which social and health agencies were involved with the family. The purpose of the reviews is to prevent future child death or serious injury through improved case identification, more effective response and intervention, and better coordination among the involved agencies. Many teams now focus on all injury and child deaths, not just child maltreatment fatalities (Daro & Mitchel, 1989; McCurdy & Daro, 1994; Durfee, Durfee & West, 2002; Hochstadt, 2006).

Each day, about two children per 100,000 in the United States die from abuse or neglect. In 2004, an estimated 1,490 children died from maltreatment. The incidence of child fatalities due to maltreatment is probably underreported because some deaths that are officially listed as accidental death, homicide, or sudden infant death syndrome (SIDS) would be attributed more accurately to mistreatment (McCurdy & Daro, 1994). Fatalities reported in 2004 were more often due to neglect (36 percent) than to physical abuse (28 percent), while 30 percent were due to a combination of both. Most child maltreatment fatalities occur to children under age 4, a fact that highlights the extreme vulnerability of young children. Fatalities can occur in many types of family and caregiver arrangements. As Figure 6.4 shows, 31 percent of child fatalities were perpetrated by the mother acting alone, and 14 percent by fathers alone. Overall, over three-quarters (79 percent) of fatalities were caused by one or more parents. Other caregivers, such as day care providers, foster parents, or residential facility staff were responsible for about 11 percent of fatalities (U.S. Department of Health and Human Services, 2006).

Of particular importance to child welfare agencies is information on the incidence of child fatalities among children who are already known to the agency. An important goal of child protection work

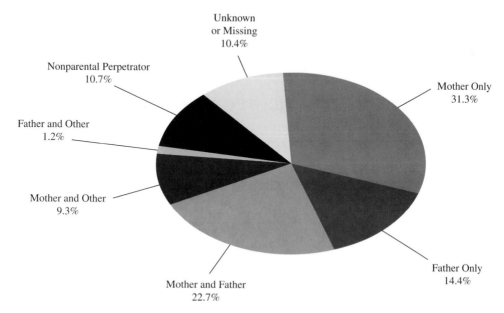

Figure 6.4 *Perpetrator Relationships of Fatalities, 2004*

Source: U.S. Department of Health and Human Services (2006). *Child Maltreatment 2004.* Washington, DC: U.S. Government Printing Office.

is that its intervention should result in keeping children alive. In the 2004 data, children whose families had received "family preservation services in the past 5 years accounted for 12.4 percent of child fatalities. Nearly 2 percent (1.7 percent) of the child fatalities had been in foster care and were reunited with their families in the past 5 years" (U.S. Department of Health and Human Services, 2006). In reviewing these numbers, it is important to keep in mind that the families served by the child protection system are among the most troubled in the country. Although the preventable death of any child is unacceptable, it is to be expected that the death rate of children already in the child welfare system would be somewhat higher than in the nation as a whole. It is also important to consider the painful reality that the cost of never losing a child to infanticide would be an unacceptable level of intrusiveness into the lives of very many families, and a massive build-up of the child protection system. With our current level of knowledge, it is not possible to predict with accuracy which situations are very likely to become lethal, but it is possible to continually work to improve the ability of the system to predict, identify, and respond to situations that are extremely dangerous to children.

The Resilient Child

Some children seem to transcend seriously neglectful or abusive childhoods to become successful adults. It would be useful to know how this happens, as such knowledge could guide improvements in treatment interventions. Both environmental and personal factors seem to account for resiliency. Personal qualities of resilient children include good intellectual ability, a positive attitude toward others, physical attractiveness, enthusiasm, and an internal locus of control. External protective factors that may make a difference are the presence of caring adults outside the abusive family who take a strong interest in the child, and parents who, despite being abusive, are able to offer some family stability, expectations of academic performance, and a home atmosphere in which the abuse is sporadic rather than a constant, pervasive element. In addition, such factors as access to good health care, education, social services, and other benefits of well-functioning communities seem to promote resiliency in children (Starr & Wolfe, 1991; Fraser, 1997; Smith & Carlson, 1997).

THE PRACTICE OF CHILD PROTECTION

Public child welfare agencies have a number of functions related to the protection of children. They are best known for their work in investigating allegations of abuse and neglect within families. However, public agencies also have other programs that provide protection for children. In every state but Alaska, the protective services agency conducts investigations of abuse and neglect in licensed child care facilities, such as day care, group care, foster family care, and residential care. In many states, the public agency is also responsible for investigating maltreatment allegations against nonfamily members such as strangers, clergy, school employees, coaches, and baby-sitters. However, many states have assigned responsibility for investigating nonfamilial maltreatment to law enforcement agencies (National Clearinghouse on Child Abuse and Neglect Information, 2002).

Core Services of Child Protective Services

Child protective services (CPS) in a democracy must provide safeguards for the rights of the child, the parents, and society; the development of clear standards and rules, as a basis for agency intervention; and the proper observance of legal provisions that will help to ensure that decision making is reasonable and based on relevant criteria.

CPS agencies provide full geographic coverage throughout each state. These agencies vary in size and complexity, but they all should offer a basic set of services to protect children. Guidelines created by the National Association of Public Child Welfare Administrators (1988) emphasize that the purpose of CPS agencies is to assure the child's safety, but "all decisions and activities should be directed toward enhancing the family's functioning and potential for growth. The agency's policies, procedures, and practices should reflect its focus on 'family based' child welfare" (p. 27). Figure 6.5 shows the steps followed by cases through the child welfare system, beginning with a report of abuse or neglect.

All CPS agencies provide a basic set of core services, as follows.

Intake.   The intake service receives reports of abuse and neglect. When a member of the community makes a report to CPS, it is the function of intake to take the report and screen it for suitability for investigation (Wells, Stein, Fluke, & Downing, 1989). Agencies may screen out reports if the situation is not within the legally mandated mission of the agency, such as reports of delinquency, family eviction, or mental health problems.

Investigation.   The investigation involves the timely gathering of information, through contact with the child, the parents, and individuals who can provide collaborating information. CPS staff should be trained to conduct an investigation in an objective, thorough, but unobtrusive manner that is sensitive to the difficulties an investigation imposes on the family. The investigation should be done within specified time limits. In some states, CPS work cooperatively with the police to conduct investigation of selected cases (Cross, Finkelhor, & Ormrod, 2005).

Disposition Determination.   The disposition determination involves timely decisions about the status of the abuse or neglect report and the need for further CPS action. In making the disposition, the agency should put the case in one of three categories:

1. ***Unsubstantiated (not confirmed).*** No or insufficient credible evidence of abuse or neglect has been identified.
2. ***Substantiated (or confirmed).*** Credible evidence has been identified that abuse or neglect has occurred.
3. ***Critical sources of information not accessible.*** For example, family moved, unable to locate; this category records the fact that the agency was unable to take action on the report.

The terms *unsubstantiated* and *not confirmed* are often misunderstood. They mean that the agency was unable to find credible evidence of maltreatment according to its definitions. However, it is quite possible that the family has some deficits in childrearing that are not serious enough to be labeled abuse or neglect but need attention. In this case, the families should be referred to agencies from which they can receive help on a voluntary basis.

Crisis Intervention.   Crisis intervention services should be available from CPS as needed during the time that CPS is engaged with the family, including the intake phase. These services should provide for immediate protection of the child and help families remain together during short-term emergencies. Crisis nurseries, domestic violence shelters, emergency housing, short-term placement with relatives, removal of the perpetrator, and twenty-four-hour emergency homemakers should be available to help stabilize families during a crisis (Gentry, 1994).

Case Planning and Coordination.   Case planning and coordination services are also the responsibility of CPS. For substantiated cases, the agency workers should design an individualized, goal-oriented case plan that clearly sets out what the agency expects parents to do to

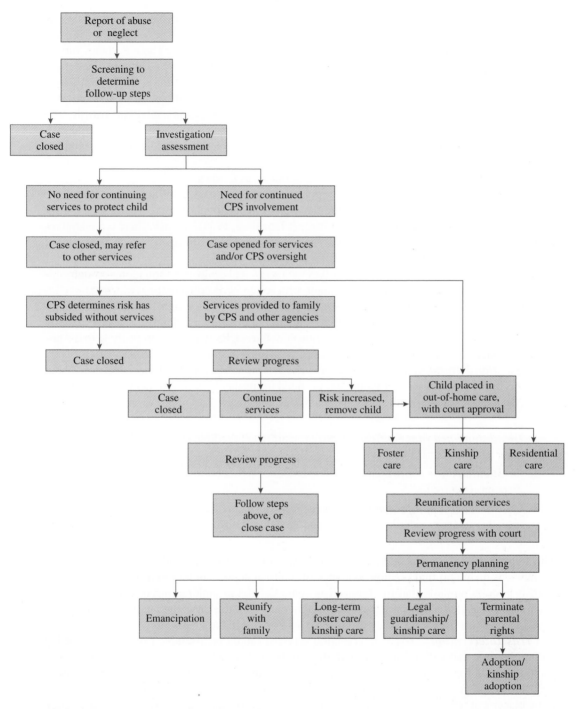

Figure 6.5 *Overview of Steps Followed by Cases through the Child Protective Services (CPS) and Child Welfare Systems*

Source: P. Schene (1998), Past, present, and future roles of child protective services, *The Future of Children: Protecting Children from Abuse and Neglect, 8*(1). Reprinted with the permission of the David and Lucile Packard Foundation.

maintain children in the home. ASFA requires that parents be actively involved in developing the case plan and be aware of the time frames within which they must work.

Discharge.   Discharge services are appropriate when the CPS agency determines that one of the following conditions exist: (1) The child is no longer at sufficient risk to warrant CPS involvement; or (2) the family is voluntarily receiving services from another agency to strengthen family functioning, and CPS involvement is not needed because the child is no longer at risk.

Central Registries.   A central registry is a centralized data system of child abuse and neglect reports maintained by states in compliance with their child maltreatment reporting laws. These registries are used to aid CPS agencies in their investigations and to maintain statistical information. In addition to CPS agencies, other individuals and organizations such as police officers, court personnel, and physicians may have access. Increasingly, registries are being used as screening devices for child care workers and foster parents. Central registries have come under criticism because the information is not always accurate or updated, and because of concerns about confidentiality for both the reported families and the reporter.

Shortcomings in CPS.   Although this is the model for most CPS agencies, it must be acknowledged that CPS is not always able to carry out these functions well. CPS suffers from high community expectations combined with insufficient resources. Staffing problems exist, including rapid turnover and low morale. Working with resistant, problem parents, with unsatisfactory care of children the pressing concern, is a heavy responsibility, that requires a range of knowledge and acquired competencies. Increased staff-development programs, lower workloads, improved relationships with the juvenile court, and skilled, available supervision are needed if CPS workers are to meet society's expectations of them.

Other considerations also interfere with the ability of CPS to meet the sometimes unrealistic expectations of society. It must be remembered that the job is complex and most of the decisions are not clear-cut. Very few of the family situations are of the sort that make headlines; most are in the gray area of marginally adequate child care. In addition, there is tremendous variation across jurisdictions in the staffing and organization of CPS. The values of court personnel and the workload of individual courts also significantly affect both service provision and length of involvement of children's protective services with the case.

These problems make it difficult to gain a consensus on what reforms are needed and what the appropriate focus of CPS should be. A further problem is that there are limits on the knowledge we have about how to intervene effectively in some families. Finally, a major difficulty for CPS is that it operates with conflicting values: On the one hand we are protecting children, but we also believe in the integrity and autonomy of the family. This conflict sometimes leaves CPS workers caught in a double bind and at best requires a careful weighing of factors before a decision is reached (Forsythe, 1987; Wells, 2006.)

Decision Making in Child Protective Services

Casework in child welfare involves a complex set of skills. The worker, operating within a framework of public policy and agency mandates and procedures, must fulfill the obligation of completing a thorough, unbiased investigation for the purpose of protecting the child. The investigative process often is hampered by the natural resistance of parents and by the lack of evidence from eye witnesses. At the same time that the worker is undertaking this difficult task, he or she must also try to form an alliance with the family for the purposes of deciding on a future course of action with the goal of improving the child's and the family's situation. These caseworker roles and responsibilities are intertwined, making it difficult to separate out skills needed for the investigative phase from those needed for the treatment phase. In this text, an integrated approach to casework in child welfare is presented in Chapter 4, which describes how caseworkers investigate and intervene, using sound casework principles within a public policy context. Chapter 5 links child protection to the legal system, with information on forensic interviewing. In this chapter we present material specific to child protection agencies that relates to the decision-making process. Readers are encouraged to use this material in conjunction with the information presented in Chapters 4 and 5.

A number of factors influence the protective service worker's decision to substantiate a report of abuse and neglect (Jones, 1993).

Direct Evidence. Direct evidence of maltreatment includes physical evidence on the child and in the home; parental admission of maltreatment; the child's statements about the maltreatment; and the reports of witnesses. This evidence is valuable but is not always available. Sexual abuse in particular is often hidden; witnesses are not present, and parents have a powerful motivation to deny that the abuse occurred. Children may not be believed or may not be able to tell the story clearly. The nature and severity of the injury is often used as an indicator of abuse by investigators (American Humane Association, 1996). Medical research has provided useful information on differentiating between intentional injuries and accidents. However, workers may rely too heavily on the severity of the injury in substantiating abuse, and overlook more subtle evidence of chronic maltreatment (Jones, 1993).

Parental Response. The parent's response is often a key factor in the worker's decision to substantiate, particularly when direct evidence is not available. Workers assess the appropriateness of the parent's response to the situation and whether they can provide consistent and credible explanations of the child's injury. Workers are more likely to substantiate abuse if parents are uncooperative with the investigation. Assessing cooperation can be quite subjective; some families are uncooperative because of the way they perceive they are being treated by the agency; other families may be deemed uncooperative because of their appearance, because of their inability to verbalize feelings, or because of the worker's class or cultural biases. On the other hand, some parental responses are "red flags" of serious problems. In cases of obvious maltreatment, workers assess the extent to which the parents take responsibility for the maltreatment, express remorse, and acknowledge that the treatment the child received is harmful. (DeRoma et al., 2006).

Child's Vulnerability. Workers are more likely to substantiate if the child is very young, has a serious mental or physical illness, exhibits unusual behavior problems, or is developmentally delayed. Other considerations are the interactions between the parent and child and the child's reaction to the parent, such as flinching or avoiding contact (Dale, Green, & Fellows, 2005).

Assessing Risk and Safety

Risk assessment can be defined as the "systematic collection of information to determine the degree to which a child is likely to be abused or neglected at some future point in time" (Doueck, English, DePanfilis, & Moote, 1993, p. 442). Risk assessment, like an investigation of a report of abuse or neglect, involves collecting information on the family. However, risk assessment is oriented toward the future; it attempts to establish the likelihood, or an educated prediction based on a careful examination of the data, that the child will be maltreated at another time. Risk assessment should be a process that continues throughout the course of CPS involvement, from time of initial screening of a report to discharge (National Association of Public Child Welfare Administrators, 1988; Fitch, 2006; Schene, 2005.) CPS agencies use risk assessment to prioritize cases for investigation and services, and to help determine the level of service that a family will receive. For example, a family rated as "high risk" would receive immediate and intense interventions, compared with a family rated as "low risk."

Items on risk assessment instruments are those that research and practice experience have shown to predict later maltreatment of a child, regardless of whether maltreatment has already occurred. The following is a list of risk factors compiled by the National Association of Public Child Welfare Administrators (1988).

❖ impact of parental behavior: CPS intervenes if behavior is serious and harmful, even if harm to the child is not easily observed, such as psychological maltreatment or sexual abuse
❖ severity of abuse or neglect
❖ age and physical and mental ability of the child
❖ frequency and recency of alleged abuse or neglect
❖ credibility of the reporter
❖ location and access of child to perpetrator
❖ parental willingness to protect child and cooperate
❖ parental ability to protect

Risk assessment instruments hold promise of standardizing data collection and helping to make decisions more consistent within an agency, because all workers will collect the same areas of information on families and share, to some extent, a common understanding on how to assess the information collected (Schene, 1996). Risk assessment instruments are still under development and have received little validation so far when used under field conditions (Doueck, Bronson, & Levine, 1992). Proponents of risk assessment instruments emphasize that they are intended as an aid to worker judgment. They are not yet accurate enough to replace the experienced judgment of seasoned caseworkers and should not be relied on as the sole basis for case decisions (Doueck et al., 1993; Schene, 1996; Hughes & Rycus, 2007). See Chapter 4 for information on assessment in casework services.

Protecting Children at Home or in Foster Care

A crucial phase of child protective work is the determination that children can be properly protected within their own home, or that they should be in foster care. The Adoption Assistance and Child Welfare Act of 1980 required agencies to make "reasonable efforts" to preserve families before placing children in foster care and encouraged the decision to leave the child in his or her own home. Social workers today generally hold that it is better to serve children in their own homes, whenever possible, and to extend social work effort to the strengthening of their family situations.

Nevertheless, not all children can remain at home, and some must be removed for their own safety and well-being. The Adoption and Safe Families Act of 1997 has specified situations in which "reasonable efforts" to prevent foster care are no longer required. These are

❖ parent subjecting the child to "aggravated circumstances" (e.g., abandonment, torture, chronic abuse, and sexual abuse);
❖ parent was convicted of (or involved in) murder or involuntary manslaughter of another child of the parent;

❖ parent was convicted of a felony assault resulting in serious bodily injury to the child or another child or the parent; or

❖ the parental rights of the parent to a sibling have been involuntarily terminated in the past. (U.S. Department of Health and Human Services, 2000b, p. 9)

In these situations, the agency may choose to place a child immediately in foster care.

Families that show only moderate child neglect are more hopeful in terms of preserving and strengthening the home as a place for the care of children. Parents in these families often have greater adequacy in their social functioning. They can be expected to respond in greater numbers to a constructive use of agency authority and social work services. In addition, if a greater investment of the nation's resources is made to alleviate some of the serious social problems that impinge on these families, the outlook should be improved very considerably for strengthening not only these homes but also the level of child care so that foster placements need not occur (National Coalition for Child Protection Reform, 2006).

ASPECTS OF COMMUNITY SUPPORT AND INFLUENCE

The way in which a protective agency discharges its responsibilities is influenced not only by the quality of its staff and its organization and structure, but also by factors within a community. Public attitudes and level of community support affect the responses of government, the professions, and voluntary associations to protect children from abuse and neglect.

Multidisciplinary Teams

An increasingly prevalent model for organizing community professionals in protective services is the multidisciplinary team. Teams consist of professionals from different fields, including social work, psychology, nursing, and law enforcement. Experience with the team approach shows that it is working in many areas across the country to provide consultation to child protective services agencies. Most teams have been involved in case planning, and some have also provided crisis service, case management, direct services to the family and child, public education, community organization and program planning, and advocacy. The team can work out of a hospital or be affiliated with a private or public child welfare agency (Bross et al., 1988; Winterfield & Sakagawa, 2003; Smith, Witte, & Fricker-Elhai, 2006).

The use of a multidisciplinary team in relation to a particular case provides flexibility in the kinds of arrangements that can be made when a family crisis occurs. It helps to prevent a service from becoming wholly committed to traditional methods or narrow professional identifications because the variations in background, training, and special interests of the team members can be used to foster a climate that will stimulate innovation and response to newly perceived needs of families. It provides an opportunity for mutual support among staff members, which can lessen their need to receive some appreciation from a family or see some sign of progress prematurely. It can spread responsibility for crucial decision making—for example, for deciding when an infant can safely be left in the care of a parent who has injured him or her.

Multidisciplinary Interview Centers. If there are allegations of sexual abuse or severe physical abuse that may involve criminal charges of a perpetrator, it is recommended that children be interviewed in multidisciplinary interview centers (Crimes against Children Research Center, 2006). These settings provide a comfortable atmosphere for children, support staff who can answer parents' and children's questions about the investigative and legal processes, and the opportunity for prosecutors and police to observe the interview behind one-way glass or by TV monitor. This procedure will eliminate the need for children to undergo multiple interviews on the painful circumstances of their abuse. The centers usually have the facilities for videotaping interviews, although videotapes may not be acceptable as evidence in court (Vandevort, 2006).

Advocacy Organizations

Tremendous public and media attention has been given to the plight of abused and neglected children since the reporting laws were passed in the early 1970s. Public concern for these children has found expression in a number of national advocacy groups. The Children's Trust Fund provides state revenue to fund programs to prevent child abuse and neglect, bypassing the traditional legislative appropriation process. Kansas was the first state to establish such a trust in 1980; currently, most states have established trusts. Revenues for the trust program are raised in various ways in the different states, including surcharges placed on marriage licenses, birth certificates, or divorce decrees, or voluntary checkoff plans using state tax refunds. The common feature of these methods is that they are separate from the ordinary state tax and revenue-collecting processes, and the money is earmarked especially for child abuse and neglect prevention.

The American Humane Association: Children's Division is a private, nonprofit organization located in Denver, Colorado. Founded in 1877 to protect children from abuse and neglect, its mission continues to be the protection of children and the prevention of child maltreatment. Its chief functions are to provide information on child maltreatment and to be an advocate for children and families in relation to effective service delivery systems in all communities.

The National Committee to Prevent Child Abuse is a volunteer-based organization dedicated to involving all concerned citizens in actions to prevent child abuse. Donna J. Stone, a Chicago philanthropist, founded the committee in 1972 out of concern for the number of infant deaths that appeared to be caused by inflicted injury. The committee's mission is to prevent child abuse through prevention programs, public awareness, education and training, research, and advocacy.

A backlash to child maltreatment investigations has developed in the formation of a citizen's organization called Victims of Child Abuse Laws (VOCAL), founded by people who stated that they were wrongly accused of abuse. It has lobbied state legislatures to drastically decrease the scope of child protective service investigations. The public also became aware of the possibilities of false accusations and false denials from caregivers, perpetrators, and sometimes children, particularly in the context of child custody disputes. However, these countertrends do not appear to have lessened public interest in reducing child abuse.

The Child Welfare League of America (CWLA) is an association of more than 1,100 public and nonprofit agencies involved in the prevention and treatment of child abuse and neglect. CWLA establishes standards of excellence for child welfare practice and works to pass child welfare legislation. The staff publish child welfare materials, are available for consultation with public and private child welfare organizations, and convene conferences, seminars, and training sessions.

Trends and Issues

Child Protective Services in a Comprehensive System

Child protective services fits into a comprehensive system of child welfare. Many are concerned that child protective services has absorbed a large proportion of resources available to child welfare, leaving gaps in services. Kamerman and Kahn (1990), in a survey of state child welfare agencies, found that public child welfare agencies focus on investigating allegations of abuse and neglect and on treating those families for whom maltreatment is substantiated. Families with less severe problems are not able to find help. Resources are also limited for needed foster care and adoption services for children whose families cannot maintain a minimally sufficient level of care.

A number of proposals exist for reconfiguring the child welfare system so that child protective services becomes part of a larger whole rather than the force driving the entire system. The U.S. Advisory Board on Child Abuse and Neglect has called for a national child protection strategy that integrates the contributions of social service, mental health, and educational and legal professionals into a service delivery system offered at the neighborhood level (U.S. Advisory Board, 1993).

Jane Waldfogel (1998) suggests that a "differential response" is needed in the child protection system. In her proposed plan, levels and types of service would be available for different family and child needs. She recommends that informal helpers such as relatives and neighbors be more involved in preventing and intervening in child maltreatment. She points out that child protective services are not well integrated into the service system of the community.

Schene (2001) also recommends a two-tiered system, in which the most serious reports go to an "investigative track" while the less serious but still risky situations go on as "assessment track." The assessment track would include cases that are not substantiated. The alleged perpetrator's name would not go on the state child abuse and neglect registry. The important planning consideration for these families would be their level of need for services. This approach would allow ongoing assessment along with the provision of ameliorative services. A difficulty with the plan is that families would participate on a voluntary basis, which might cause some potentially very harmful situations to fall away from agency scrutiny.

Ultimately, the solution to enhanced child safety goes beyond the reorganization of child protective services. Clearly needed also is a renewed societal commitment to creating an environment in which children and their families can survive and flourish—a guaranteed, minimal level of income for all families that would provide adequate food, shelter, and medical care. Such a program would greatly reduce the stress on poor families and the child maltreatment associated with it. Sufficient long-term, effective programs for substance abusers would go a long way in reducing substance abuse–related child maltreatment, particularly neglect. School systems that are adequately staffed, with creative, energized personnel, can help to reduce children's problematic behaviors, which trigger some cases of maltreatment. A ban on the use of corporal punishment in schools would encourage parents and others in authority to learn other ways of managing children's behavior. A public backlash against the violence promoted by the entertainment industry would also encourage everyone to develop nonviolent strategies to resolve problems.

Chapter Summary

Media reports of abused and neglected children disturb us and make us aware of the appalling conditions in which many children live. Child protective services represents the organized response of each community to the circumstances of mistreated children and their families. Every year, about

3 million children come to the attention of child protective services, although only a percentage of the situations reported are "substantiated" or "confirmed" for abuse and neglect. Child abuse and neglect are often hidden from the scrutiny of neighbors and professionals, and these cases are not reported, so the actual extent of child maltreatment is unknown. However, various surveys indicate that the number of cases reported to child protective services is only a small proportion of the total.

Types of maltreatment are neglect (including physical neglect, abandonment, lack of supervision, and medical neglect), which comprise more than half of all cases of mistreatment; abuse; sexual abuse; psychological maltreatment; and educational neglect. Many times, more than one type of maltreatment is involved.

Violence toward children has been pervasive in American history. During the nineteenth century, concerned citizens formed societies for the prevention of cruelty to children, to investigate instances of child abuse and report them to the police. These societies (SPCCs) are the precursors of today's child protective services agencies. In the 1960s, the "discovery" of the battered child syndrome led to the passage of the Child Abuse Prevention and Treatment Act in 1974 and ushered in a new era of child protection.

Today, all states have reporting laws that require professionals to report all cases of suspected child abuse or neglect to CPS. However, the implementation of these laws is hampered by the lack of clear definitions of types of child abuse and neglect. Factors to be considered in definitions are the severity of the harm, the cumulative harm to the child over time, endangerment of the child even if the child has not yet suffered observable harm, intentional harm versus accidental harm, and cultural issues.

There are problems with overreporting and underreporting child maltreatment. Fewer than half of all reports are substantiated, which leaves many parents feeling that they have suffered an invasion of privacy and the stigma of having been the focus of a child abuse investigation. On the other hand, many cases of maltreatment are not reported because the potential reporters believe that reporting will not help the family and may make matters worse.

The causes of child maltreatment are complex and overlapping, and are best understood from an ecological perspective. No one factor causes abuse or neglect, but rather a combination of circumstances. Risk factors include social conditions such as deprived, dangerous neighborhoods with few supports or social services and widespread societal tolerance for interpersonal violence. Poverty is highly associated with all forms of maltreatment and is the single most important risk factor for children. Race and ethnicity do not appear to be related to maltreatment, although people of color are more likely to be reported to CPS. Many family and parental characteristics and conditions are associated with abuse and neglect, including single parenthood, mental illness, substance abuse, domestic violence, social isolation, and a history of having been mistreated as children (although many children who are maltreated do not grow up to mistreat other children). Maltreating parents tend to lack empathy, express negative attitudes and hostility to their children, lack the ability to form attachments, and use the children to meet their own needs.

Children suffer in many ways from maltreatment, including death, permanent injury, and impaired physical, cognitive, social, and emotional development.

All child protective service agencies offer a set of core services, including intake, investigation, and case planning. While investigating families, the workers must also assess the current and future risk to the child, and take steps to remove the offender or child from the home when necessary. The preference is to maintain the child in his or her own home, if possible, by providing services to help the family. CPS workers have the legal authority to intervene in the lives of families and must develop strategies for using that authority to help parents achieve a minimally sufficient level of care.

A major issue today is the appropriate scope and authority of child protective services. One view is that CPS should be involved only for serious cases of child maltreatment and that less serious situations should be referred to other social service agencies. It is thought that this would protect families from needless intrusive investigations and free up resources for the most serious situations. Others believe that CPS should be expanded, because many abused and neglected children are not receiving any services and may, in fact, be unknown to any social service agency. Many policymakers believe that CPS must become more connected to the community, through partnerships with schools, police, and neighborhood groups, to form a comprehensive system for protecting and serving children.

FOR STUDY AND DISCUSSION
STUDY AND DISCUSSION QUESTIONS

1. Discuss how the ecological approach is useful in understanding child maltreatment. What interventions using an ecological approach would be most effective for each of the different categories of child maltreatment?

2. Discuss how the historical development of children's protective services has resulted in the system we have today. What benefits do you see in today's child protection system? What are the disadvantages?

3. Discuss whether you think that some forms of child maltreatment are more serious than others and why.

4. Discuss the feasibility of having two levels of definitions of child abuse and neglect: narrow definitions of the various categories of maltreatment for legal purposes and broad definitions for the purpose of determining the need for services. Give examples of narrow and broad definitions for one of the categories of child maltreatment.

5. In view of the characteristics of neglected and abused children as you have come to see them, make suggestions for new treatment approaches in direct work with such children.

6. Draw together what you regard as significant aspects of agency organization and community support if effective protective services are to be provided. Then study the protective service agency in your community in relation to these aspects.

Internet Sites

American Bar Association Center for Children and the Law. The American Bar Association Center for Children and the Law aims to improve children's lives through advances in law, justice, knowledge, practice, and public policy. Its areas of expertise include child abuse and neglect, child welfare, and protective services system enhance-ment, foster care, family preservation, termination of parental rights, parental substance abuse, adolescent health, and domestic violence. **www.abanet.org/child/**

American Humane Association. American Humane Association has a long and established

history of protecting children from abuse and neglect. It supports the development and implementation of effective community, state, tribal, and national systems to protect children and strengthen families. Through consultation, training, research and evaluation, advocacy, and information dissemination, American Humane Association continues its legacy of child protection.
www.americanhumane.org

Child Welfare Information Gateway. Child Welfare Information Gateway provides access to information and resources to help protect children and strengthen families. A service of the Children's Bureau, Administration for Children and Families, U.S. Department of Health and Human Services.
www.childwelfare.gov

National Center on Substance Abuse and Child Welfare. The mission of the National Center on Substance Abuse and Child Welfare is to improve systems and practices for families with substance use disorders who are involved in the child welfare and family judicial systems by assisting local, state, and tribal agencies.
www.ncsacw.samhsa.gov

References

Abbott, G. (1938). *The child and the state, vols. I & II.* Chicago: University of Chicago Press.

Ahn, H. N., & Gilbert, N. (1992, September). Cultural diversity and sexual abuse prevention. *Social Service Review, 66,* 410–427.

American Humane Association. (1996). *Guidebook for the visual assessment of physical child abuse.* Englewood, CO: Author.

American Humane Association. (1997). *Guidelines to help protect abused and neglected children.* Englewood, CO: Author.

American Humane Association. (2002a). Family treatment court: Significant results in recovery and reunification. *Child Protection Leader.* Englewood, CO: Author.

American Humane Association. (2002b). Fact sheet: Shaken baby syndrome. Available: www.americanhumane.org.

American Humane Association. (2003a). *Fact sheet: child physical abuse.* Available: www.americanhumane.org.

American Humane Association. (2003b). *Fact sheet: child sexual abuse.* Available: www.americanhumane.org.

American Humane Association. (2006). *Fact sheet: emotional abuse.* Available: www.americanhumane.org.

Ards, S., Chung, C., & Myers, S. (1998). The effects of sample selection bias on racial differences in child abuse reporting. *Child Abuse & Neglect, 22*(2), 103–115.

Ascione, F. R., & Arkow, P. (1999). *Child abuse, domestic violence and animal abuse.* West Lafayette, IN: Purdue University Press.

Azzi-Lessing, L., & Olsen, L. J. (1996). Substance abuse affected families in the child welfare system: New challenges, new alliances. *Social Work, 41*(1), 15–23.

Barnett, O., Miller-Perrin, C., & Perrin, R. (1997). *Family violence across the lifespan.* Thousand Oaks, CA: Sage.

Beitchman, J. H., Zucker, K. J., Hood, J. E., DaCosta, G. R., Akman, D., & Cassavia, E. (1992). A review of the long-term effects of child sexual abuse. *Child Abuse & Neglect, 16,* 101–118.

Belsky, J. (1993). Etiology of child maltreatment: A developmental-ecological analysis. *Psychological Bulletin, 114,* 413–434.

Berliner, L., & Barbieri, M. K. (1984). The testimony of the child victim of sexual assault. *Journal of Social Issues, 40*(2), 125–137.

Berliner, L., & Elliott, D. M. (1996). Sexual abuse of children. In J. Briere, L. Berliner, J. A. Bulkley, C. Jenny, & T. Reid (Eds.), *The APSAC handbook on child maltreatment* (pp. 51–71). Thousand Oaks, CA: Sage.

Berrick, J. D. (1997). Child neglect: Definition, incidence, outcomes. In J. D. Berrick, R. P. Barth, & N. Gilbert (Eds.), *Child welfare research review, vol. 2* (pp. 1–12). New York: Columbia University Press.

Berrick, J. D., Needell, B., Barth, R. P., & Jonson-Reid, M. (1998). *The tender years: Toward developmentally sensitive child welfare services for very young children.* New York: Oxford University Press.

Besharov, D. (1990a). *Recognizing child abuse: A guide for the concerned.* New York: Free Press.

Besharov, D. (1990b). Gaining control over child abuse reports. *Public Welfare, 48,* 34–41.

Besharov, D. J., & Laumann, L. A. (1996). Child abuse reporting. *Society, 33*(4), 40–46.

Bresee, P., Stearns, G. B., Bess, B. H., & Packer, L. S. (1986). Allegations of child sexual abuse in child custody disputes: A therapeutic assessment model. *American Journal of Orthopsychiatry, 56*(4), 560–569.

Breshears, E. M., Yeh, S., & Young, N. K. (2004). *Understanding substance abuse and facilitating recovery: A guide for child welfare workers.* Rockville, MD: U.S. Department of Health and Human Services, Substance Abuse and Mental Health Services Administration.

Bross, D., Krugman, R., Lenherr, M., Rosenberg, D., & Schmitt, B. (Eds.). (1988). *The new child protection team handbook.* New York: Garland.

Browne, A., & Finkelhor, D. (1986). Impact of child sexual abuse: A review of the research. *Psychological Bulletin, 99,* 66–77.

Burnett, B. (1993). The psychological abuse of latency age children: A survey. *Child Abuse & Neglect, 17,* 441–454.

Burton, D. L., Nesmith, A. A., & Badten, L. (1997). Clinician's views on sexually aggressive children and their families: A theoretical exploration. *Child Abuse & Neglect, 21*(2), 157–170.

Carter v. Kaufman, 8 Ca.App.3d 783, 87 Ca. Rptr. 678 (1970), *cert. denied,* 402 U.S. 964 (1971). (J. Black dissenting in separate opinion at 402 U.S. 954, 959).

Chaffin, M. (2006). The changing focus of child maltreatment research and practice within psychology. *Journal of Social Issues, 62*(4), 663–684.

Chandy, J. M., Blum, R. W., & Resnick, M. (1996). History of sexual abuse and parental alcohol misuse: Risk, outcomes and protective factors in adolescents. *Child and Adolescent Social Work Journal, 13*(5), 411–432.

Chasnoff, I. J., Harvey, M. D., Landress, J., & Barrett, M. E. (1990). The prevalence of illicit-drug or alcohol use during pregnancy and discrepancies in mandatory reporting in Pinellas County, Florida. *The New England Journal of Medicine, 322*(17), 1202–1206.

Child Abuse Prevention and Treatment Act, Public Law 93-247, 42 U.S.C.A. 510g (1974, amended 1996).

Child Welfare Information Gateway. (2006). *Recognizing child abuse and neglect: Signs and symptoms.* Washington, DC: The Children's Bureau. Available: www.childwelfare.gov/pubs/factsheets/signs.cfm.

Child Welfare League of America. (2001). *Alcohol, other drugs and child welfare.* Washington, DC: Author.

Children's Bureau. (2006). *Prenatal drug use as child abuse: Summary of state laws.* Washington, DC: Child Welfare Information Gateway. Available: www.childwelfare.gov/systemwide/laws_policies/statutes/drugexposedall.pdf.

Cohen, N. A. (Ed.). (2000). *Child welfare: A multicultural focus.* Boston: Allyn & Bacon.

Connelly, C. D., & Straus, M. (1992). Mother's age and risk for physical abuse. *Child Abuse & Neglect, 16*(5), 709–718.

Costin, L. B. (1992). Cruelty to children: A dormant issue and its rediscovery, 1920–1960. *Social Service Review, 66*(2), 177–198.

Crimes against Children Research Center. (2006). *Executive summary: findings from the UNH multi-site evaluation of children's advocacy centers.* Durham, NH: University of New Hampshire.

Cross, T., Finkelhor, D., & Ormrod, R. (2005). Police involvement in child protective services investigations: Literature review and secondary data analysis. *Child Maltreatment, 10*(3), 224–244.

Dale, P., Green, R., & Fellows, R. (2005). *Child protection assessment following serious injuries to infants: Fine judgments.* Hoboken, NJ: John Wiley and Sons.

Daro, D., & Mitchel, L. (1989). *Child abuse fatalities continue to rise: The results of the 1988 annual fifty-state survey.* (Working Paper Number 808). Chicago: National Committee for the Prevention of Child Abuse, National Center on Child Abuse Prevention Research.

Deisz, R., Doueck, J. J., George, N., & Levine, M. (1996). Reasonable cause: A qualitative study of mandated reporting. *Child Abuse & Neglect, 20*(4), 275–287.

DePanfilis, D. (2006). Definition and scope of neglect. In *Child neglect: Guide for prevention, assessment, and intervention.* Washington, DC: Children's Bureau, U.S. Department of Health and Human Services.

DeRoma, V., Kessler, M., McDaniel, R., & Soto, C. (2006). Important risk factors in home-removal decisions: Social caseworker perceptions. *Child and Adolescent Social Work, 23*(3), 263–277.

DeViney, E., Dickert, J., & Lockwood, R. (1983). The care of pets within child abusing families. *International Journal for Study of Animal Problems, 4,* 321–329.

Doueck, H. J., Bronson, D. E., & Levine, M. (1992). Evaluating risk assessment implementation in child protection: Issues for consideration. *Child Abuse & Neglect, 16*(5), 637–646.

Doueck, H. J., English, D. J., DePanfilis, D., & Moote, G. T. (1993). Decision-making in child protective services: A comparison of selected risk-assessment systems. *Child Welfare, 72*(5), 441–452.

Durfee, M., Durfee, D., & West, P. M. (2002). Child fatality review: An international movement. *Child Abuse & Neglect, 26,* 219–236.

Earle, K. A. (2000). *Child abuse and neglect: An examination of American Indian data.* Seattle: Casey Family Programs and NICWA.

English, D. (1998). The extent and consequences of child maltreatment. *The Future of Children: Protecting Children from Abuse and Neglect, 8*(1), 39–53.

English, D. A., Bangdiwala, S. I., & Runyan, D. K. (2005). The dimensions of maltreatment: Introduction. *Child Abuse & Neglect, 29,* 441–460.

English, D. A., Thompson, R., Graham, J., & Briggs, E. (2005b). Toward a definition of neglect in young children. *Child Maltreatment, 10*(2), 190–206.

Erickson, M. F., & Egeland, B. (1996). Child neglect. In J. Briere, L. Berliner, J. A. Bulkley, C. Jenny, & T. Reid (Eds.), *The APSAC handbook on child maltreatment* (pp. 4–20). Thousand Oaks, CA: Sage.

Faller, K. C. (1988a). *Child sexual abuse: An interdisciplinary manual for diagnosis, case management, and treatment.* New York: Columbia University Press.

Faller, K. C. (1988b). Criteria for judging the credibility of Children's statements about their sexual abuse. *Child Welfare, 67*(5), 389–401.

Faller, K. C. (1988c). Decision-making in cases of intrafamilial child sexual abuse. *American Journal of Orthopsychiatry, 58*(1), 121–128.

Feldman, M. D., & Brown, R. (2002). Munchausen by proxy in an international context. *Child Abuse & Neglect 26,* 509–524.

Finkelhor, D. (1993). Epidemiological factors in the clinical identification of child sexual abuse. *Child Abuse & Neglect, 17,* 67–70.

Finkelhor, D., Hotaling, G., Lewis, I. A., & Smith, C. (1990). Sexual abuse in a national survey of adult men and women: Prevalence, characteristics, and risk factors. *Child Abuse & Neglect, 14*(1), 19–28.

Finkelhor, D., Williams, L. M., & Burns, N. (1988). *Nursery crimes: Sexual abuse in day care.* Newbury Park, CA: Sage.

Fitch, D. (2006). Examination of the child protective services decision-making context with implications for decision support system design. *Journal of Social Service Research, 32*(4), 117–134.

Fleming, J., Mullen, P., & Bammer, G. (1997). A study of potential risk factors for sexual abuse in childhood. *Child Abuse & Neglect, 21,* 49–58.

Folks, H. (1911). *The care of destitute, neglected, and delinquent children.* New York: Macmillan.

Forsythe, P. (1987). Redefining child protective services. *Protecting Children, 4*(3), 12–16.

Fraser, M. W. (Ed.). (1997). *Risk and resilience in childhood.* Washington, DC: NASW Press.

Gallup, G. H., Moor, D. W., & Schussel, R. (1997). *Disciplining children in America.* Princeton, NJ: The Gallup Organization.

Garbarino, J. (1999). *Lost boys: Why our sons turn violent and how we can save them.* New York: Free Press.

Garbarino, J., & Collins, C. C. (1999). Child neglect: The family with a hole in the middle. In H. Dubowitz (Ed.), *Neglected children:*

Research, practice, and policy (pp. 1–23). Thousand Oaks, CA: Sage.

Garbarino, J., & Ebata, A. (1983). The significance of ethnic and cultural differences in child maltreatment. *Journal of Marriage and the Family, 45,* 773–783.

Gaudin, J. M., & Dubowitz, H. (1997). Family functioning in neglectful families. In J. D. Berrick, R. P. Barth, & N. Gilbert (Eds.), *Child welfare research review, vol. 2* (pp. 28–62). New York: Columbia University Press.

Gentry, C. E. (1994). *Crisis intervention in child abuse and neglect.* Washington, DC: U.S. Department of Health and Human Services, National Center on Child Abuse and Neglect.

Giovannoni, J. M., & Becerra, R. M. (1979). *Defining child abuse.* New York: Free Press.

Glaser, D. (2002). Emotional abuse and neglect (psychological maltreatment): A conceptual framework. *Child Abuse & Neglect (26),* 697–714.

Goldman, J., Salus, M., Wolcott, D., & Kennedy, K. Y. (2003). What factors contribute to child abuse and neglect? In *A coordinated response to child abuse and neglect: A foundation for practice.* Washington, DC: The Child Welfare Information Gateway, Children's Bureau. Available: www.childwelfare.gov.

Goodman, G. S. (2006). Chidlren's eyewitness memory: A modern history and contemporary commentary. *Journal of Social Issues, 62*(4), 811–832.

Goodman, G. S., Bottoms, B. L., & Shaver, P. R. (1994). *Characteristics and sources of allegations of ritualistic child abuse* (Executive summary of the final report to the National Center on Child Abuse and Neglect [Grant No. 90CA1405]). Washington, DC: National Center for Child Abuse and Neglect.

Gorske, T., Larkby, C., Daley, D., Yenerall, E., & Morrow, L. (2006). Childhood abuse and psychiatric impairment in a sample of welfare to work women. *Children and Youth Services Review, 28*(12), 1528–1541.

Harrison, P. A., Fulkerson, J. A., & Beebe, T. J. (1997). Multiple substance use among adolescent physical and sexual abuse victims. *Child Abuse & Neglect, 21*(6), 529–539.

Hart, S. N., Brassard, M. R., & Karlson, H. C. (1996). Psychological maltreatment. In J.

Briere, L. Berliner, J. A. Bulkley, C. Jenny, & T. Reid (Eds.), *The APSAC handbook on child maltreatment* (pp. 72–89). Thousand Oaks, CA: Sage.

Heyman, R. E., & Slep, A. M. S. (2001). Risk factors for family violence: Introduction to the special series. *Aggression and Violent Behavior, 6,* 115–119.

Hibbard, R. A., & Hartman, G. L. (1992). Behavioral problems in alleged sexual abuse victims. *Child Abuse & Neglect, 16,* 755–762.

Hildyard, K. L., & Wolfe, D. A. (2002). Child neglect: Developmental issues and outcomes. *Child Abuse & Neglect, 26*(6–7), 679–695.

Hochstadt, N. J. (2006). Child death review teams: A vital component of child protection. *Child Welfare, LXXXV*(4), 653–670.

Horejsi, C. (1996). *Assessment and case planning in child protection and foster care services.* Englewood, CO: American Humane Association.

Hughes, R. C., & Rycus, J. S. (2007). Isssues in risk assessment in child protective services. *Journal of Public Child Welfare, 1*(1), 85–116.

Hutchinson, E. D. (1990). Child maltreatment: Can it be defined? *Social Service Review, 64*(1), 60–78.

Jones, L. (1993). Decision making in child welfare: A critical review of the literature. *Child and Adolescent Social Work Journal, 10*(3), 241–262.

Jones, M. A. (1987). *Parental lack of supervision: Nature and consequence of a major child neglect problem.* Washington, DC: Child Welfare League of America.

Jones, P. H. (1991). Ritualism and child sexual abuse. *Child Abuse & Neglect 15*(3), 163–170.

Kamerman, S. B., & Kahn, A. J. (1990, Winter). If CPS is driving child welfare—Where do we go from here? *Public Welfare, 48,* 9–13.

Kelley, S. J. (1996). Ritualistic abuse of children. In J. Briere, L. Berliner, J. A. Bulkley, C. Jenny, & T. Reid (Eds.), *The APSAC handbook on child maltreatment* (pp. 90–99). Thousand Oaks, CA: Sage.

Kempe, C. H., Silverman, F. N., Steele, B. T., Droegemueller, W., & Silver, H. K. (1962, July). The battered child syndrome. *Journal of the American Medical Association, 181.*

Kent, L., Laidlaw, J. D., & Brockington, I. F. (1997). Fetal abuse. *Child Abuse & Neglect, 21*(2), 181–186.

Kolko, D. J. (1996). Child physical abuse. In J. Briere, L. Berliner, J. A. Bulkley, C. Jenny, & T. Reid (Eds.), *The APSAC handbook on child maltreatment* (pp. 21–50). Thousand Oaks, CA: Sage.

Korbin, J. E. (1994). Sociocultural factors in child maltreatment. In G. B. Melton, & F. D. Barry (Eds.), *Protecting children from abuse and neglect: Foundations for a new national strategy* (pp. 182–223). New York: Guilford Press.

Korbin, J. (2002). Culture and child maltreatment: Cultural competence and beyond. *Child Abuse & Neglect, 26*, 637–644.

Korbin, J. (2003). Children, childhoods, and violence. *Annual Review of Anthropology, 32,* 431–446.

Lanning, K. V. (1991). Ritual abuse: A law enforcement view or perspective. *Child Abuse & Neglect, 15*(3), 171–173.

Leitenberg, H., Gibson, L., & Novy, P. (2004). Individual differences among undergraduate women in methods of coping with stressful events: The impact of cumulative childhood stressors and abuse. *Child Abuse & Neglect, 28*, 181–192.

Levandosky, A., & Graham-Bermann, S. (2001). Parenting in battered women: The effects of domestic violence on women and their children. *Journal of Family Violence, 16*(2), 171–193.

Lindsay, D. (1994). *The welfare of children.* New York: Oxford University Press.

Loftus, E. F. (1993). The reality of repressed memories. *American Psychologist, 48,* 518–537.

Lyon, T. D., & Saywitz, K. J. (2006). From post-mortem to preventive medicine: Next steps for research on child witnesses. *Journal of Social Issues, 62*(4), 833–861.

Madden, R. G. (1993). State actions to control fetal abuse: Ramifications for child welfare practice. *Child Welfare, 72*(2), 129–140.

Malow, R., DeEvieux, J., Martiniez, L., Peipman, F., Lucenko, B., & Kalichman, S. (2006). History of traumatic abuse and HIV risk behaviors in severely mentally ill substance abusing adults. *Journal of Family Violence, 21*(2), 127–135.

Mapp, S. C. (2006). The effects of sexual abuse as a child on the risk of mothers physically abusing their children: A path analysis using systems theory. *Child Abuse & Neglect, 30,* 1293–1310.

Margolin, L. (1992). Child abuse by mothers' boyfriends: Why the overrepresentation? *Child Abuse & Neglect 16,* 541–551.

McCurdy, K., & Daro, D. (1994). *Current trends in child abuse reporting and fatalities: The results of the 1993 annual fifty-state survey.* Chicago: National Committee to Prevent Child Abuse.

Meadow, R. (2002). Different interpretations of Munchausen syndrome by proxy. *Child Abuse & Neglect, 26,* 501–508.

Melchert, T. P., & Parker, L. (1997). Different forms of childhood abuse and memory. *Child Abuse & Neglect, 21*(2), 125–135.

Migliaro, M., & Ryan, G. (2004). The correlation between child abuse, animal abuse and domestic violence. *National Child Advocate, 5*(3,4), p 2–4.

Moore, T. E., & Pepler, D. J. (2006). Wounding words: Maternal verbal aggression and children's adjustment. *Journal of Family Violence, 21*(1), 89–93.

Myers, J. (2006). *Child protection in America: Past, present, and future.* New York: Oxford University Press.

Nam, Y., Meezan, W., & Danziger, S. (2006). Welfare recipients' involvement with child protective services after welfare reform. *Child Abuse and Neglect: The International Journal, 30*(11), 1181–1199.

National Association of Public Child Welfare Administrators. (1988). *Guidelines for a model system of protective services for abused and neglected children and their families.* Washington, DC: American Public Welfare Association.

National Association of Social Workers. (2000, July). *Social workers and child abuse reporting: A review of state mandatory reporting requirements.* Silver Springs, MD: NASW Press.

National Center on Child Abuse and Neglect. (1993). *A report on the maltreatment of children with disabilities.* Washington, DC: U.S. Department of Health and Human Services.

National Clearinghouse on Child Abuse and Neglect Information. (2002). *State statutes.* Available: www.calib.com/nccanch/statutes/civilstats.cfm.

National Coalition for Child Protection Reform. (2006). *Ten ways to do child welfare right: Successful alternatives to taking children from their parents.* Alexandria, VA: Author.

Nicholas, K., & Rasmussen, E. (2006). Childhood abusive and supportive experiences, inter-parental violence, and parental alcohol use: Prediction of young adult depressive symptoms and aggression. *Journal of Family Violence, 21*(1), 43–61.

Nuszkowski, M., Coben, J., Kelleher, K., Goldcamp, J., Hazen, A., & Connelly, C. (2007). Training, co-training, and cross-training of domestic violence and child welfare agencies. *Families in Society, 88*(1), 35–41.

Oberlander, L. B. (1995). Psycholegal issues in child sexual abuse evaluations: A survey of forensic mental health professionals. *Child Abuse & Neglect, 19*(4), 475–490.

Osofsky, J. (1999). The impact of violence on children. *The Future of Children: Domestic Violence and Children, 9*(3).

Proch, K. (1982). *Child welfare case notebook.* Urbana: University of Illinois at Urbana Champaign, School of Social Work.

Rosenberg, D. A., & Gary, N. (1988). Sexual abuse of children. In D. C. Bross et al. (Eds.), *The new child protection team handbook.* New York: Garland.

Ryan, K. (1996). The chronically traumatized child. *Child and Adolescent Social Work Journal, 13,* 287–310.

Schene, P. (1996). The risk assessment roundtables: A ten-year perspective. *Protecting Children, 12*(2), 4–8.

Schene, P. (1998). Past, present, and future roles of child protective services. *The Future of Children, 8*(1), 23–38.

Schene, P. (2001, Spring). Meeting each family's needs. *Best Practice, Next Practice,* 1–6.

Schene, P. (2005). *Comprehensive family assessment guidelines for child welfare.* Washington, DC : Administration for Children and Families, Childrens Bureau.

Sebold, J. (1987). Indicators of child sexual abuse in males. *Social Casework, 68*(2), 75–80.

Sedlak, A. J., & Broadhurst, D. D. (1996). *Third national incidence study of child abuse and neglect: Final report.* Washington, DC: U.S.

Department of Health and Human Services, National Center for Child Abuse and Neglect.

Slack, K. (2002). Assessing the influence of welfare reform on child welfare systems. *Focus, 22*(1), 98–105.

Smith, C., & Carlson, B. E. (1997, June). Stress, coping, and resilience in children and youth. *Social Service Review,* 231–256.

Smith, D. W., Witte, T. W., & Fricker-Elhai, A. E. (2006). Service outcomes in physical and sexual abuse cases: A comparison of child advocacy center-based and standard services. *Child Maltreatment, 11*(4), 354–360.

Starr, R. H., Jr., & Wolfe, D. A. (Eds.). (1991). *The effects of child abuse and neglect: Issues and research.* New York: Guilford Press.

Steele, B. (1987). Psychodynamic factors in child abuse. In R. E. Helfer & R. S. Kempe (Eds.), *The battered child* (4th ed.) (pp. 81–114). Chicago: University of Chicago Press.

Stein, T. (1998). *The social welfare of women and children with HIV and AIDS.* New York: Oxford University Press.

Straus, M., & Gelles, R. (1986, August). Societal change and change in family violence from 1975–1985 as revealed by two national surveys. *Journal of Marriage and the Family, 48,* 465–479.

Sunley, R. (1963). Early nineteenth-century American literature on child rearing. In M. Mead & M. Wolfenstein (Eds.), *Childhood in contemporary cultures.* Chicago: University of Chicago Press.

Thrane, L., Hoyt, D., Whitbeck, L., & Yoder, K. (2006). Impact of family abuse on running away, deviance, and street victimization among homeless rural and urban youth. *Child Abuse & Neglect: The international journal, 30*(10), 1117–1128.

U.S. Advisory Board on Child Abuse and Neglect. (1993). *The continuing child protection emergency: A challenge to the nation.* Washington, DC: U.S. Government Printing Office.

U.S. Department of Health and Human Services. (1999a). *Current trends in child maltreatment reporting laws.* Washington, DC: U.S. Government Printing Office.

U.S. Department of Health and Human Services. (1999b). Religious exemptions to criminal child abuse and neglect. *Child abuse and neglect state statutes elements, domestic violence.* (No. 41). Washington, DC: U.S. Government Printing Office.

U.S. Department of Health and Human Services. (2000a). *Child maltreatment 1999: Reports from the states to the National Child Abuse and Neglect Data System.* Washington, DC: U.S. Government Printing Office.

U.S. Department of Health and Human Services. (2000b). *Rethinking child welfare practice under the Adoption and Safe Families Act of 1997.* Washington, DC: U.S. Government Printing Office.

U.S. Department of Health and Human Services. (2001b). Child witness to domestic violence. *Child abuse and neglect state statutes elements, domestic violence* (No. 41). Washington, DC: U.S. Government Printing Office.

U.S. Department of Health and Human Services. (2002). *Child maltreatment 2000: Reports from the states to the National Child Abuse and Neglect Data System.* Washington, DC: U.S. Government Printing Office.

U.S. Department of Health and Human Services. (2006). *Child maltreatment 2004.* Washington, DC: U.S. Government Printing Office.

Vandevort, F. E. (2006). Videotaping investigative interviews of children in cases of child sexual abuse. *Journal of Criminal Law & Criminology, 96*(4), 1353–1416.

Veltman, M., & Browne, K. (2001). Three decades of child maltreatment research: Implications for the school years. *Trauma, Violence & Abuse, 2*(3), 215–239.

Waldfogel, J. (1998). *The future of child protection.* Cambridge, MA: Harvard University Press.

Wallace, H. (1996). *Family violence: Legal, medical and social perspectives.* Boston: Allyn & Bacon.

Warner-Rogers, J. E., Hansen, D. J., & Spieth, L. E. (1996). The influence of case and professional variables on identification and reporting of physical abuse: A study with medical students. *Child Abuse & Neglect, 20*(9), 851–866.

Wells, R. (2006). Managing child welfare agencies: What do we know about what works? *Children and Youth Services Review, 28,* 1181–1194.

Wells, S. J., Stein, T. J., Fluke, J., & Downing, J. (1989). Screening in child protective services. *Social Work, 34*(1), 45–48.

Whisman, M. (2006). Childhood trauma and marital outcomes in adulthood. *Personal Relationships, 13,* 375–386.

Widom, C. S. (1989). Child abuse, neglect, and adult behavior: Research design and findings on criminality, violence, and child abuse. *American Journal of Orthopsychiatry, 59*(3), 355–367.

Winterfield, A. P., & Sakagawa, T. (2003). *Investigation models for child abuse and neglect: Collaboration with law enforcement, final report.* Englewood, CO: American Humane Association.

Wolfner, G. D., & Gelles, R. J. (1993). A profile of violence toward children: A national study. *Child Abuse & Neglect, 17,* 197–212.

Zanel, J., Jr. (1997). Failure to thrive: A pediatrician's perspective. *Pediatrics in Review, 18*(11), 371–378.

Zuckerman, B. (1994). Effects on parents and children. In D. J. Besharov (Ed.), *When drug addicts have children* (pp. 49–63). Washington, DC: Child Welfare League of America and the American Enterprise Institute.

Zuravin, S. (2001). Issues pertinent to defining child neglect. In T. D. Morton & B. Salovitz (Eds.), *The CPS response to child neglect: An administrator's guide to theory, policy, program design and case practice* (pp. 37–59). Duluth, GA: National Resource Center on Child Maltreatment.

CHAPTER 7

Family Preservation Services

*Each family is so complex as to be known and understood only in part
even by its own members. Families struggle with contradictions as
massive as Everest, as fluid and changing as the Mississippi.... Yet
when practical the preference should be for family.*

—*Maya Angelou*

CHAPTER OUTLINE

CASE EXAMPLE:
Using Intensive Family-Based Services to Prevent Placement

The following case example is one of countless family preservation efforts—each complex and unique—that successfully holds a family together when the events of that family's existence threaten a profound dislocation.

Amy is a 23-year-old mother of three young children. Jimmy, who is the father of Jeremy, age 6, and Tiffany, age 4, drifts in and out of their lives. When he is sober he visits and sometimes brings toys or food. When he has been drinking he becomes sullen and verbally abusive. Amy has learned to keep him from bothering them. Amy's youngest child, Ashley, is medically fragile—Amy was using crack heavily during her pregnancy.

Amy doesn't remember who Ashley's father might be. Amy's life has been a blur of misfortune in the past few years. She has been evicted from apartments twice for nonpayment of rent. They spent weeks going from homeless shelter to homeless shelter until her cousin took them in. Both Amy's stepmother and Jimmy have threatened to have the children taken from her. She struggles to stay free of crack. As a result of substance abuse treatment after Ashley's birth, Amy has had periods of nonuse and a brief relapse. Her nerves are frayed from the children's constant fighting and whining and Ashley's irritable, fretful crying. Amy tries to keep the children quiet because they annoy her cousin, who threatens to kick her out. She needs a drink or a joint to tolerate the children when they get out of control. Amy is frightened because she has been hitting the children in futile discipline attempts. She left bruises on Jeremy's buttocks and left arm after hitting him with a belt to show him that he couldn't hit his sister. When she took Ashley to the emergency room because the infant seemed very congested, a nurse noticed Jeremy's bruises and was concerned about Ashley's nutrition, as she was below the twentieth percentile. The hospital called child protective services.

Fifteen to twenty years ago, the children might have been placed in foster care. After a careful assessment of risk, the CPS worker referred Amy to a program that offers intensive, comprehensive, family-based services designed to preserve the family unit, protect the children, and keep the children out of care.

Carolyn, the family-based services worker, carries a cell phone so that she is available to Amy and the children around the clock, if needed. Because her caseload is limited to two or three families at a time, she is available, during the next six weeks, to work with the family. She will work to keep the family together by identifying and supporting their strengths, bringing in resources, teaching them problem-solving skills, and providing hope. She will engage Amy by helping her to locate housing and furniture, working with her at household tasks, and being an understanding, caring, and consistent figure in her life. Carolyn will use a wide range of techniques and strategies, drawn from family therapy and social learning sources, to enable Amy to face and solve the problems that have led to the threat of child placement. She will also begin to put into place a safety net of ongoing community resources that will meet the children's developmental needs and Amy's needs during a long recovery process.

CONTROVERSY CONCERNING FAMILY PRESERVATION PHILOSOPHY AND SERVICES

Although social work has long been concerned with the family—the first direct practice journal was named *The Family*—at first the focus of child welfare was on the child. However, in the 1980s, the rapidly developing field of family therapy intersected with a strong government response to the problems of child welfare. Mandatory reporting of child maltreatment, combined with the substance abuse epidemic's devastating effect on families, had led to a great increase in the numbers of children identified as abused or neglected. However, services were inadequate or nonexistent to help their families improve the quality of their care (Sudia, 1981). It was clear to all that foster care was not the solution for every abused or neglected child, and that many families could be helped to retain their children at home if services were available to them. The 1980 Adoption Assistance and Child Welfare Act established mandates that "reasonable efforts" be made to keep families together. It gave federal support to state efforts to preserve the family before placing a child in foster care. The intent was to protect children from unnecessary separation from their parents and to encourage agencies to work with families in more than a cursory way.

The nation responded to the call to improve services to families and maintain children in their homes if possible. The U.S. Children's Bureau established a National Resource Center in Iowa to help agencies establish family preservation programs. Between 1981 and 1993, thirty states established statewide family-based programs, and twenty-seven state associations for family-based services were developed (Allen & Zalenski, 1993). The Family Preservation and Support Services Act of 1993 bolstered services that enhanced parental functioning; the child welfare field saw it as an opportunity to establish a continuum of coordinated, culturally relevant, family-focused services. An air of optimism stimulated the family and children's services system in the early 1990s. "That family preservation can be the catalyst for rehabilitating the entire service delivery system is the hope, already glimpsed and beginning to be realized, of its advocates" (Barthel, 1992, p. 75).

Soon, however, the concept of family preservation began to be called into question by professionals and media alike. Widely publicized failures to protect children from harm while they and their families were receiving family preservation services caused a growing backlash against family preservation (Hartman, 1993). Lindsey (1994), writing for a professional audience, observed, "the risk with inappropriate removal of a child is that it may tear apart a family unnecessarily. However, the risk of leaving a child in an endangered home is a child fatality. Neither is acceptable, but protecting the child's life must always be paramount" (p. 279).

In response, Maluccio, Pine, and Walsh (1994) acknowledged that family preservation is viewed as competing with child protection, and in particular cases, these may be incompatible goals. However, they stated, "At the philosophical and policy levels family preservation and child protection are complementary rather than competing values. In essence, the best way to protect children is to preserve as much of their families as possible" (p. 295). Others argued that the goal of services to support families should change focus from placement prevention to child development and be part of a wide system of support services (Wells & Tracy, 1996). McCroskey (2001) noted that child welfare decisions involve weighing a complex set of factors: "These decisions are based on judgment calls and may not turn out always to have been justified, but no child welfare worker or agency wants to leave children in danger, even when they believe there may be some possibility of bringing the family together again" (p. 5). Professionals have acknowledged that family preservation services were originally oversold and that the backlash is to some extent a reaction to unrealistically high expectations about what family preservation could accomplish. Dennis (1997) pointed out that, in an effort to persuade legislatures to fund services to families, unrealistic claims were made about the cost-effectiveness of family preservation services. They were not given enough funding to meet the goals expected of them; many were short term and ill suited to the profound, systemic problems that the families presented.

The passage of the Adoption and Safe Families Act in 1997 culminated the philosophical and political shift away from some of the original tenets of family preservation. The act emphasizes child safety in the home, which reflects the public concern that the family preservation philosophy went too far in maintaining children at home, risking their safety in some cases. However, the act continues funding for preventive services to strengthen families (see Chapter 3) and for family preservation when children can be safely maintained at home. It increases treatment options for families, particularly for the problems of substance abuse, domestic violence, and homelessness. Even though the initial optimism that family preservation programs could reduce the need for foster care has diminished, family preservation remains a vital part of the child welfare service continuum (Whittaker, 2002).

CHARACTERISTICS OF FAMILY PRESERVATION SERVICES

Principles of Family Preservation Services

Family-based services for the prevention of placement represent a philosophy that families are important, that they should be kept together, and that intensive, focused efforts will mobilize family strengths. As articulated by the National Resource Center on Family-Based Services, this philosophy is rooted in the belief that

❖ children need permanency in their family relationships to develop into healthy, productive individuals;
❖ families should be the primary caregivers of their own children; and
❖ social service programs should make every effort to support families in this function. (National Resource Center, 1994; Child Welfare League of American 2003)

Common elements of intensive, family-based placement prevention programs include the following aspects:

❖ commitment to maintaining children in their own homes
❖ focusing on the entire family system rather than on individuals
❖ accepting for service only those families at actual risk of having children placed
❖ beginning service as soon as the referral has been made—no waiting lists
❖ seeing and working with families in their own homes
❖ maintaining flexible hours seven days a week, with round-the-clock response to family needs
❖ providing intensive service over a limited period (from one to five months)
❖ keeping caseload size small—often two to three cases at a time—enabling the worker to deliver intensive services

❖ providing comprehensive services meeting a variety of therapeutic, concrete, and supportive needs

❖ teaching family members skills

❖ offering counseling or therapy within the home

❖ basing services on client need rather than agency categories

❖ having access to flexible funding to support the case plan

❖ offering ongoing, in-service training and support to staff

❖ following up and evaluating family progress and program success (Edna McConnell Clark Foundation, 1985; Nelson, Landsman, & Deutelbaum, 1990; Whittaker, Kinney, Tracy, & Booth, 1990; Whittaker, 2002).

Theoretical Base

The conceptual frameworks for family-based prevention services draw from and integrate a number of theoretical sources. The ecological systems metaphor examines the transactions and exchange of energy and resources between the family and its environment, and views the family holistically in terms of interrelationships of systems. When children experience problems, for example, those difficulties need to be viewed in the context of the child's family, the family's community, and the community's involvement in the larger society.

Theories of coping and adaptation in both maturational and situational life transitions (Germain & Gitterman, 1996) are also applied, with the understanding that coping with ongoing conditions is part of family functioning. According to Bain (1978; Olson, 1997), the family capacity to cope is a function of the magnitude of the stress and the richness, relevance, and coherence of the "social container" within which the stress is experienced. The concept of the social container includes both the family's social networks and its formal institutional relationships. Such a view of family dysfunction suggests several options for intervening to enhance family coping, to reduce stress, to facilitate the response of formal institutions, to strengthen the social network, or to enhance the effectiveness of family members.

Another theoretical source for many family-based prevention programs is crisis intervention theory (Parad, 1965; Caplan, 1974; Ell, 1996). Families seen in family preservation programs are usually experiencing one of two crises: (1) Child protective services has said that the family is not providing adequate child care and is planning to remove one or more children, or (2) problems between parents and children have grown so severe that a parent is refusing to allow the child to continue to live at home, or the child is running away (Kinney, Haapala, & Booth, 1991; Kinney & Dittmar, 1995). Crisis intervention theory postulates that people's familiar coping mechanisms break down during periods of high stress so that they become more open to change. With competent intervention, the opportunity is created for healthier adaptation following resolution of the crisis.

Many family-based service programs, especially Homebuilders, integrate social learning theory into their approach. See Chapter 3. A key to understanding behavior is recognizing the rewards or penalties that follow the behavior and the antecedents that stimulate or trigger the behavior (Patterson, 1975). The expectations and cognitions about behavior also provide reciprocal influence with the behavior itself (Bandura, 1977). The clarity and specificity of cognitive-behavioral approaches fit with the focused intervention of most programs.

Family-systems theory, which takes note of family structure, family roles, family life cycle, multigenerational family issues, and the nature of family transactions, also undergirds a family-based services approach. It helps the social worker to understand the circular nature of interactions and behaviors that may jeopardize the safety of the child in his or her own home. The use of family-systems theory enhances the assessment of how the family "works." Many therapeutic techniques—such as ecomaps and genograms, increasing the clarity of communication, understanding the structure of the family, working with boundary issues, helping families change maladaptive roles, and establishing positive family rituals—come directly from family therapy sources (Murray, 2006; Smith & Walton, 1999).

Although many models of social work practice start with problems or pathology, the *strengths perspective* (Saleeby, 2002) emphasizes the strengths in people. The role of the social worker is framed as one of identifying and building on strengths. Noble, Perkins, and Fatout (2000) use the analogy of the athletic coach, who trains athletes to develop their muscles, to describe the role of the child welfare worker who trains clients to develop their strengths. In applying the strengths perspective to family preservation, they stress the importance of hope in the ability of people to change for the better and to achieve success in areas of life such as housing arrangements, education, social support, leisure, relationships, health, personal care, and finances. The worker's optimism in the client's ability to achieve success must be balanced by good sense and realism. (See Chapter 4.)

Programs That Prevent Placement and Preserve Families

Currently, the federal government contributes to family preservation programs in all fifty states. While there is tremendous variety and diversity within the existing programs, they have in common a commitment to intensive, family-based services.

The Homebuilders Model

Homebuilders, an intensive in-home crisis intervention and education program for families, has pioneered concepts of family preservation since 1974. The families are referred by state workers when there is a child at imminent risk of placement. Workers serve only two families at a time, providing a wide range of services, including help with basic needs and counseling regarding family relationships. The Homebuilders philosophy includes several important assumptions: It is our job to instill hope, clients are our colleagues, and people are doing the best they can (Kinney, Haapala, & Booth, 1991; Kinney & Dittmar, 1995).

When a family is accepted into the program, a face-to-face meeting takes place within twenty-four hours. Homebuilders therapists are on call to the client families and have flexible schedules so that they can meet with clients as needed, even on weekends, nights, or holidays. While much of the work takes place in the home, therapists also go where the problems are, whether that is a school or a teen hangout. The goal of all services is to enable families to resolve their own problems. Program goals are limited: to prevent out-of-home placement and to teach families the skills necessary to remain living together.

The therapist is involved in doing concrete tasks such as cleaning the apartment or driving to the grocery store with the family members. The therapist also uses a variety of educational and therapeutic techniques as the situation warrants, including teaching behavior-management skills, assertive skills, problem-solving skills, cognitive skills, and communication skills.

The brevity of the Homebuilders model, four to eight weeks, fits with a crisis-intervention theoretical foundation. The services are intense during the time-limited period, serving to keep therapist and family focused on the specific goals established by the family.

In addition to initiating the family preservation approach in 1974, Homebuilders has made several significant related contributions to the field. From its inception, an evaluation component was built into the model. This focus on accountability provided impetus for widespread adoption of Homebuilder concepts. It also convinced state legislatures that the program was cost effective and would save money if placement were avoided. Many states have family preservation programs based on the Homebuilders model.

Other Models

A model of family preservation services with two workers has been used in a number of places, from Maryland to Adelaide, South Australia. Advantages of having a staff pair to work with a family include the ability of the team to keep each other on target, to provide extra energy for difficult or complex tasks, and to keep a positive focus on family progress. The following case illustrates the need for teamwork.

> A family preservation team intervened in a situation in which the parent had allowed garbage and trash to pile up to the ceiling in the home. The media had photographed the housing inspector staring at the huge mounds of refuse and ran the photograph on the front page of the local newspaper with the headline "The Dirtiest House in the State." The mother was so shamed that it took three days before the family preservation team could go into the house. They met with the mother on the front porch and made cleanup plans. It took a contractor with three dumpsters to empty the house of rubbish, and a large group of relatives and volunteers to scrub, clean, and paint. When the house had been restored to order and the mother engaged with mental health services in the community, the team members reflected on their success. They realized that it would have been much harder to counter the media criticism, ameliorate the depression and shame of the mother, and handle the overwhelming nature of the mess if they had been working singly, not as a team.

Typically, such an arrangement consists of a professional social worker and a paraprofessional or case aide. The pair is usually part of a larger team that meets regularly to provide support and celebrate success.

A variation on the use of brief, intensive family preservation services (IFPS) was found in an experimental program in which IFPS workers were assigned to families at the front end of a child protective services investigation, before rather than after a CPS determination has been made. The family preservation workers assessed families in terms of strengths, and the CPS workers assessed risks in a collaborative decision-making process. The IFPS workers helped families establish a network of services for a strengthened environment, including informal support such as extended family members, friends, neighbors, and clergy. Families in the experimental group had fewer cases opened than did those in the control group and were more satisfied with the agency's services. By front-loading services to the time of CPS intake, child safety may be enhanced (Walton, 1997; 2001).

Family Preservation and Domestic Violence

Research and practice wisdom affirm that children in homes where partner abuse occurs are at risk of being battered by the adult abuser (Edleson, 1999). (See Chapter 6.) A collaborative model between the domestic violence and child welfare service delivery systems in Michigan (Findlater & Kelly, 1999) has shown that through policy development, resource sharing, and training, children can stay safe while remaining with their battered mothers. Family preservation workers help battered women and their children in a variety of critical areas, including establishing an independent home, safety planning, parenting issues such as supporting the mother's authority, and developing a social support network. They coordinate case services with domestic violence staff, who provide expertise on resources for battered women and consultation on the dynamics of abusive situations.

Family Preservation and Children's Mental Health Needs

Another form of services targeted at the prevention of placement addresses the needs of children and youth at risk of being sent from the community into costly residential care, or young people returning to family and community from a more structured setting. The "wraparound" approach, developed in Alaska by the former coordinator of Children's Mental Health Services, has been replicated in over 100 sites nationwide (VanDenBerg, Grealish, & Schick, 1993; VanDenBerg, Bruns, & Burchard, 2003). A wraparound service is developed by a community-based child and family team, which may include parents ("customers"), child welfare, mental health, juvenile justice, education, law enforcement, health, vocational rehabilitation, clergy, developmental disabilities, family advocates, and other concerned staff and community representatives. An individualized resource coordinator identifies those people already in the child's life and configures a wraparound team. This team, operating on the premise "never give up," develops culturally competent individualized services in the life domain of the child and family. Life domains include basic human needs such as a place to live, family, social interaction, friends, psychological/emotional ties, safety, and so forth. Family strengths—"the good news about families"—are assessed, and problems are reframed. A family resistant to assistance might be commended for being a wise shopper for services, or an assaultive child might be reframed as someone who tries to stick up for himself. Creative approaches to meeting life domain needs might include hiring a college student who models acceptable behavior while keeping a youth from running away or doing destructive behaviors. Parent involvement is key to the wraparound approach. Wraparound services are funded through integration of funding streams for children's services and are cost effective in the prevention of expensive residential care or hospitalization.

Family Preservation for Substance-Affected Families

Models to coordinate substance abuse treatment with child welfare and maternal health services have been implemented in response to the epidemic of crack cocaine addiction (Gruber, Fleetwood, & Herring, 2001).

Parental addiction is seen as "a chronic relapsing disorder" (Besharov, 1994, p. ix) that requires that current child welfare programs must be radically reoriented. Recognition of the severity of substance abuse and addiction—especially to crack cocaine—has led to a number of collaborative approaches that often involve health, substance abuse treatment, child development, and child care and child welfare services. Many of these initiatives involve longer-term case management than the typical family preservation, short-term, crisis-intervention program. While working with the family they may help to substantiate that there is a problem, help parents consider the need for treatment, help parents access treatment, and help develop structures for the child's safety.

Time-limited, intensive family preservation services are not adequate for substance-affected families. Such cases need ongoing services, including transitional housing for recovering parents, family-focused treatment, family planning services, and child care options. Recovering addicts should be trained to anticipate their own drug-using episodes and seek protection for their children before the crisis hits (Jones, 1994). Kinship care can be viewed as a form of family preservation that provides safe and supportive environments for children of addicts (Johnson, 1994). Barth (1994) proposes that intensive family preservation programs for drug users should be augmented by ongoing case management, shared family care, early childhood services, developmentally focused services, and child care to improve developmental outcomes while protecting children.

The National Council of Juvenile and Family Court Judges developed a "reasonable efforts" protocol for substance abuse cases. In examining the social service agency response to a substance-abusing parent, some of the questions to be asked are as follows:

> Has there been adequate intra-agency coordination to ensure that concrete services have been made available in a timely manner?
>
> Have all relatives been contacted and their ability to care for the child been assessed?
>
> How has the social service agency helped the substance-abusing parent obtain treatment?
>
> Have referrals to treatment programs been appropriate . . . to programs experienced in treating women with the mother's particular addiction and problems with small children?
>
> Has the availability of the following service programs been examined:
>
>> family-centered drug treatment services
>> intensive family preservation services
>> emergency housing
>> in-home caretaker
>> out-of-home respite care
>> teaching and demonstrating homemakers
>> parenting-skills training
>> transportation, etc.

(*National Council of Juvenile and Family Court Judges, 1992, p. 19*)

> *I was so scared that I'd lose my kids. I guess I might have deserved it because I'd been messing up and staying high for days at a time. If my worker hadn't gotten me into treatment I could be dead today. She gave us all a second chance, and we want to make it work. (A parent)*

THE PRACTICE OF FAMILY-BASED SERVICES

The family-based services practitioner operates on values that form the bedrock of the family work. These values and beliefs enable the practitioner to enter a troubled family system effectively, engage family members, build hope, and begin the change process. One of the most important beliefs is that workers and clients are partners in change. Another belief is that a crisis is an opportunity for change. However, the most important belief is that the child's safety is paramount. (See Chapter 4.)

Family preservation programs generally focus on such practice components as engaging and building trust carefully; working in the clients' home whenever possible; providing concrete services; being available nights and weekends, with twenty-four-hour-on-call backup; deemphasizing diagnostic labeling; building on family strengths; setting specific client generated goals; and using client priorities (Kinney, Haapala, & Booth, 1991; Pecora et al., 1992). The following case example illustrates the unique aspects of family-based services practice.

CASE STUDY:
Protecting Children from Sexual Abuse and Domestic Violence in a Rural Setting

Reason for Referral.   Tammie had fled with her children, Kelly, age 3, and Bethany, age 1, to a domestic violence shelter in another county after being beaten by Pete, the father of her children. At the shelter she and the staff discovered that Kelly's statements seemed to indicate sexual abuse by Pete. Fearing a referral to child protective services, Tammie left the shelter precipitously, moved in with a new boyfriend, Tom (who lived with several other men), and hid the children at her great-aunt's house so their father couldn't find them. She told her relative that she would get the children as soon as she found housing, but at the present time there was no room for them at Tom's place.

The great-aunt knew about the possibility of sexual abuse and was concerned about getting help for the children, so she called the local child protective services. The CPS worker was aware that Tammie had a previous referral in the county where the domestic violence shelter was located, and that her earlier living conditions had exposed the children to sexual and physical abuse. Other concerns were that Tammie's ability to protect the children was uncertain and that there appeared to be substance abuse in the mother's current living situation. Tammie needed to learn how to protect her children and to fulfill her parenting responsibilities, and she needed assistance in establishing a home. The case was referred to the local family preservation program.

Family Members.   Tammie, age 20, had run away from home at age 16 and lived on the streets of the nearest small city using drugs and occasionally trading sex for food or shelter. She was taken in by Pete, who fathered at least one of her two children. Tammie had left high school before her sixteenth birthday. As a young teen she had been sexually abused by her father when her mother was in a mental hospital. She left home before her mother returned from the hospital. Before the birth of her first child she tried to reach out to her parents, only to find that they had moved away and left word that they did not want her to try to follow them. She is ambivalent about her parents, alternately missing them and hating them. Tammie is petite, attractive, and looks much younger than her years.

Kelly is 3 years old. She appears healthy and strong for her small size although she eats mostly junk food. She resists going to sleep, but generally sleeps well with only occasional nightmares. She has had recurring bladder infections and is behind on her immunizations.

Bethany is 1 year old. She is quite small in size, which may be related to her mother's petite stature. She appears slightly developmentally delayed in motor skills in that she attempts to crawl but has not tried to stand yet. She appears attached to her mother.

Engagement and Developing Trust.   Elise, the family preservation services worker, met Tammie at the child welfare office. Tammie was angry with her great-aunt for calling child protective services, dismayed that she was "in trouble," and angry that she couldn't just pick up her children and move on. Elise drove Tammie to see the children and listened on the way to her tearful explanation of why she had left the children. Their father, Pete, had taken Tammie in when she was on the streets at age 16. When Tammie became pregnant by Pete, she realized that she was terribly dependent on him because her parents had moved away without her and she had nowhere to go. Before Tammie gave birth to Kelly, Pete became increasingly physically abusive to her. She tried working at a fast food restaurant to earn enough money to be able to leave Pete, but she was afraid to leave Kelly at home with him. She became increasingly depressed, quit her job, and was completely isolated. When she came home from the hospital after having their second child, Bethany, Kelly complained to her of a "sore bottom." Tammie wondered if Kelly had been sexually abused, but was too afraid and depressed to confront Pete, and too ashamed to ask for help. When she was ready to leave Pete, she took the children with her to the shelter, planning to leave the children with her great-aunt as soon as possible.

She felt lucky that Tom was taking care of her, but knew that it wasn't a good place to bring the children. She didn't know whether Tom or his friends could be trusted and Tom didn't want kids around anyway. Besides, she was just too upset to take care of them at the moment.

Elise listened quietly to the outpouring of despair as they drove to the great-aunt's home. She noted that Tammie was shaking and offered her a jacket to help keep her warm. She waited while Tammie visited with the children and observed that the little ones ran to their mother, clinging to her and kissing her. After the visit she dealt with Tammie's tears by asking how she could help and by reminding Tammie that the purpose of family preservation services was to keep families together. Tammie identified her first goal—finding housing—and her greatest fear—that Pete would find her or the children.

Assessment of Strengths. Although Tammie had had a traumatic adolescence and appeared very young because she was physically petite, she showed maturity in her wish to be a good parent to her daughters and to locate housing. Tammie and the children appeared bonded to each other and showed appropriate emotion at their visit. Tammie is attractive, personable, and shows normal intelligence. She has made efforts to remove herself from a difficult situation, the first time when she tried to work so that she could leave Pete, and the second time when she actually left and found a safe place for the children. Tammie was excited that family preservation services would work with her to locate housing and establish a home for the children.

Goal Setting. Tammie, with Elise's help, established four goals for the time they would be working together:

1. secure affordable housing and furnishings for the family that could be maintained over time
2. protect the children from further physical or sexual abuse and herself from Pete's violence
3. improve parenting and child management skills
4. improve her self-esteem regarding relationships with men and her ability to select men who would not be a danger to her and the children

Action Steps to Reach Goals. Elise and Tammie worked together to locate a mobile home that could be rented reasonably. FPS flexible funding paid the security deposit and the first month's rent. Tammie applied for Temporary Assistance for Needy Families (TANF), food stamps, and WIC. Elise took Tammie to the distribution point for free commodities. They went grocery shopping together, and Tammie learned that nutritious snack foods such as apples and bananas are actually cheaper than potato chips and cheese curls. Elise referred Tammie to the county extension family nutrition program. They purchased a copy of "The Cheapskate's Gazette," a local bargain-hunter's newsletter, and scoured thrift shops in order to furnish the trailer and locate equipment such as a toddler car seat for Bethany. Tammie was also referred to the public assistance employment program with the goal of finding work that would fit her long-range goal of obtaining a GED or completing high school. Tammie and Elise talked about how to network with her new neighbors and barter goods or services such as child care or a ride to town. These action steps related to the goal of being able to live on assistance and maintain housing until she found adequate employment.

Legal action was begun for a restraining order to protect Tammie from Pete. According to the prosecuting attorney, there was insufficient evidence to initiate criminal charges of sexual abuse against him. However, medical exams, and the great-aunt's report that Kelly was displaying the sexual behavior of "humping" with her toys, indicated that sexual abuse had in all likelihood occurred. Elise provided Tammie with several books and a videotape about protecting children from sexual abuse and discussed protection plans with her. They discussed sleeping arrangements for the children, who could be trusted with the children, and how to manage sexual acting-out behaviors. They also worked on other safety issues, putting all cleaning substances and other poisonous or hazardous supplies in high or locked cupboards, and generally childproofing the inside and the yard of the mobile home.

In preparation for the return of the children from the great-aunt's house, Elise began teaching Tammie child-management skills, including environmental controls, time-out, active listening, positive reinforcement, and natural and logical consequences. The children were returned to their mother several days after the mobile home was ready. Tammie and the worker spent many hours together as Tammie tried her new parenting techniques. One resource available in the rural community was a Head Start program that provided transportation and had a parent support group. Kelly was enrolled in Head Start after having been reunited with her mother for two weeks. Elise took Tammie to the first parent support group at the Head Start Center. The county nutritional aide began visiting. Tammie went to the county health department for the well-baby clinic and family planning services.

Tammie thought carefully about her dependency on men and the reasons she had gravitated to a relationship that would turn abusive to her and the children. Elise gently helped her see that she had characteristics, such as intelligence and sensitivity, that were as important as the "sexiness" that Tammie thought was her prime attribute. As her capacity to parent increased, Tammie realized that she had strengths of her own which meant she was not dependent on a male for survival. Tammie's relationship with her boyfriend Tom continued, but she began to look at how she might survive if the relationship should end. She began to examine this relationship for clues that Tom, too, might be abusive to her or the children. She listened to tapes on how to overcome past dysfunctional family rules in order to have healthier adult relationships. Elise coached Tammie on assertiveness-training skills.

Termination. After five weeks the goals had been attained and the safety net of ongoing services was in place. The child protective services case would remain open. A public health nurse would make home visits, watch Bethany's development, and ensure that the children's immunizations continued. The nutrition aide would assist Tammie in meal planning and accessing commodities. Head Start and the parent support group would help her meet Kelly's developmental needs. The great-aunt would provide child care for brief periods if Tammie needed a break. Tammie could get transportation to town with a neighbor or her landlady. A restraining order against Pete would remain in effect, and Tammie's location remained a secret.

Elise had spent sixty-eight hours providing services to Tammie, including many hours of driving to services in the rural area. She had also spent slightly over $800 in flexible funds to cover initial costs of housing and furnishings, plus some lunches and reading materials. Elise reflected in retrospect, "All that time I spent driving paid off. When Tammie and the kids were in the car with me we talked and interacted productively. When they weren't with me I used my recorder for dictation. Working in a rural area has its problems, like isolation and poverty, but you know all the key players in the helping system so you can get things done quickly. Besides, I appreciate the fresh air and wide open spaces."

Case Commentary. Family preservation services adapts well to rural social work. The worker creates clinical interventions and brings them to the home, compensating for the lack or inaccessibility of services for a young mother isolated in a trailer in the hills with two small children. If Tammie had lived nearer to the battered women's shelter or had known earlier how to access that service system in the nearest city, she might have left an abusive relationship before her child was ever molested and would not have come to the attention of child protective services.

One might wish that a local sexual abuse survivors group or support group for women who had experienced battering had been available, so Tammie could continue to look at her dependent relationships with men. It is also clear that she has many unresolved family of origin issues. Perhaps she will be able or willing to address them as she matures; perhaps she will not. But Tammie is young and resilient. She has one family member in her support network who can help provide some stability. It is unfortunate that in this somewhat isolated county there is no children's play therapist available to work with Kelly regarding the trauma of sexual abuse, witnessing violence, and experiencing temporary separation from her mother. For the time being the family is together and has survived a crisis. Protective services involvement could be helpful in negotiating future developments with Pete or in financing other needed services. The short-term goals have been accomplished, and the family is stabilized. There are supportive services in place, as a step down from the intensive family-based services, which should help the family to stabilize further and begin working toward long-range goals. In the future as Tammie grows and pursues her goals there will be time for more changes.

This case illustrates the importance of providing concrete services to keep a family together and the use of multiple techniques to strengthen a parent's competence. The worker's reflections capture much of the essence and challenge of rural social work.

Culturally Competent Family Preservation Services

Family-based services for family preservation are congruent with the social work emphasis on cultural competence. Family preservation has been adapted successfully to serve families of diverse ethnic and racial backgrounds, including African American families (Gray & Nybell, 1990), Native American families (Cross, 1987; Mannes, 1993), Hispanic families (Sandau-Beckler, Salcido, & Ronnau, 1993), and lesbian families (Faria, 1994). Respecting clients' beliefs and culture, learning about the family's cultural context, sorting out differences between these beliefs and one's own values, advocating for clients, and dispelling stereotypes and myths are ways in which family preservation workers can operationalize social work knowledge, values, and skills about diversity.

Understanding the nuances of culture is a critical skill for family preservation workers engaging families across ethnic and cultural boundaries. Social workers need to ask about important traditions of the family of origin and country of origin. Culturally competent workers are sensitive to issues of shame in the family and the cultural prohibitions about discussing family business with an outsider (Sandau-Beckler, Salcido, & Ronnau, 1993).

Napoli and Gonzales-Santin (2001) discuss family preservation with Native American families living on a reservation. They place family preservation services within a Native American framework, which looks at the total ecology of the extended family network and understands wellness as a healthy connection to the land, the community, the spirit world, and the family. A team that includes representatives of the tribal community provides the family preservation services. To engage the family and increase trust, the team and family share personal stories while engaging in communal activities. Teams have successfully used a medicine wheel as an instrument to restore harmony and balance. They have also used cultural traditions such as the talking circle to frame engagement and intervention.

Like other models of social work practice, family preservation is most successful when adapted to the unique needs of a particular family. In a sense, each family has its own cultural stance and its own permutation of cultural origins. The family preservation worker is a cultural explorer, discovering traditions, meanings, values, and customs of the family in order to intervene most effectively.

OTHER APPROACHES THAT HELP HIGH-RISK FAMILIES

In addition to family preservation services, many other approaches also are used to protect the child and preserve the family. Children can be maintained in homes and family life can be sustained through a variety of programs, including family counseling, parent education, recreational groups, day treatment, drop-in or respite child care, homemaker services, parent aides, foster grandparents, employment and educational opportunities, and developmental early childhood education programs such as Head Start. These programs are used in a variety of combinations to work with families' diverse situations and family members' unique needs for nurture, stimulation, comfort, competence, contact, well-being, and protection. (See Chapter 3.)

Many of the treatment approaches described here can be used with families and children regardless of whether the child has been removed from the home. In some cases they are part of a family reunification plan. (See Chapter 9.) These services constitute "reasonable efforts" to keep families together and are often offered as long-term follow-up after the intensive phase of family preservation services (about two months) has been completed. (Staudt, 2001).

Treating Loneliness

This phrase grew out of the observation that "among neglectful parents are many who make their circumstances worse by self-imposed aloneness, and who must thus deal with dreadful loneliness" (Polansky, Chalmers, Battenmeier, & Williams, 1981, p. 210). Although the roots of isolation may lie in circumstances of the parent's childhood, it can to some extent be remedied by providing parents the opportunity to be with people.

Group treatment of parents being served by CPS has been used to deal with individual problems, marital problems, and child-management techniques. An often-overlooked function of these groups, apart from other benefits, is that they give parents an opportunity to interact with other adults.

An example of groupwork with abusive parents is a twelve-week program designed to build social support networks for low-income abusive mothers who received training in conversational skills, self-protection, and assertion. In the first session, women examined various types of friendships and were encouraged to identify features or patterns in their social networks. The term *friend* carried negative connotations—members reported being hurt and taken advantage of by persons they had considered friends. In the second session they identified danger signs of relationship problems, such as drug problems or lying. In the fourth session the right to feel safe was emphasized, with discussion of protective techniques. During the next few sessions participants focused on basic social skills such as initiating, maintaining, and ending conversations. In sessions eight through eleven, the women learned how to assert themselves and handle criticism. In the final session a shopping outing provided an opportunity for members to practice new social skills (Lovell, Reid, & Richey, 1992).

Treatment with individual parents can also incorporate the concept of strengthening social networks. Tracy, Whittaker, Pugh, Kapp, and Overstreet (1994) report that social network mapping used with family preservation clients yielded rich data about the importance of social support in helping families avert placement.

For example, the goals for one socially isolated abusive family were to teach basic child care skills and to capitalize on the support system that was in place. Family meetings were held to strengthen family relationships. The parents were encouraged to contact family or friends when they needed help (Tracy et al., 1994, p. 487).

Help with Reality Problems

For neglecting and abusing parents, actions usually speak louder than words. The disorganized daily living pattern of neglecting families means that family workers must relate to everyday problems and behaviors, and give direct help with pressing reality problems. These parents are not ready to deal with introspective questions.

Reality-oriented services are typically used when problems have been detected that are not quite serious enough to warrant removal of the children without an attempt to rectify the problem and meet the needs of the family and children. Each type of service can have multiple functions. In a "dirty house" case, a homemaker can mobilize the family to clean up the litter of dirty laundry, decaying food, animal feces, and dirt piles. The homemaker may also demonstrate housekeeping skills, teach basic techniques, model positive attitudes toward housecleaning, help the mother develop a cleaning routine, and break through the atmosphere of discouragement and depression surrounding the neglected home environment.

A parent aide can bring new input to an entropic situation of a young parent marooned with small children. She may provide transportation for shopping, set up recreational activities to stimulate and cheer a depressed mother, and counteract the isolation that heightened the risk of child maltreatment. Yet the success of a parent aide may depend more on intangible qualities of the relationship that develops between parent and aide than on activities. Kind and supportive comments by the aide may nurture the parent and provide role modeling of effective interaction, which can carry over into discipline of the children.

Head Start, which stimulates social and cognitive development to prepare preschoolers to succeed in school, also has additional benefits for other family members, even as it is nurturing the child. Aside from the obvious respite it provides to stressed parents, it also offers adult socialization and learning opportunities, as parents engage in parent groups and programs. (See Chapter 3.)

Housing is an extremely important element of family preservation. In the past, many children were at risk of placement due in part to homelessness or inadequate housing. The Family Unification Project is unique in that its central element is housing assistance. This program brings together child welfare agencies and housing agencies to make the needs of child welfare families and persons in domestic violence shelters a top priority (Doerre & Mihaly, 1996).

EVALUATION OF FAMILY PRESERVATION PROGRAMS

Family-based services present a number of problems to evaluation. Recently, Jacobs (2001) has enumerated some of the most troubling. The first, defining the mission of family-based services, must take into account the changes in mission that have taken place since they began in the 1980s. At the beginning, the goal was defined as preventing placement, but the mission has since been expanded to other goals, such as enhancing child development, improving family functioning, reducing child welfare expenditures, and enhancing collaborations across human service systems. The addition of new goals complicates the evaluation process. Second, the field lacks useful theories of change, making it difficult to show how or why a particular program produces desired results. Often, it is not clear whether change in family functioning that has been observed by researchers can be attributed to the interventions of the family preservation services. Third, there are numerous program models and definitions of the term *family preservation services,* making it difficult to compare evaluation results of different programs. Finally, there is a lack of good data due to poorly organized state management information systems, and a scarcity of instruments to measure progress in some outcome areas (DeVoe & Kantor, 2002). A review of the history of evaluation of family preservation highlights these difficulties.

As the prototypical family preservation program, Homebuilders set an expectation for program evaluation. It used "prevention of placement" and "cost-effectiveness" as desirable outcomes. Working with a population considered to be "at imminent risk of placement," Homebuilders defined success as the prevention of placement at twelve months from the initiation of service. Using this measure, Homebuilders' success rate was over 70 percent of families served. The per-child cost of Homebuilders compared favorably with the average cost of placement, suggesting that family preservation could result in huge savings by avoiding foster care, group care, or psychiatric hospitalization of children (Kinney, Haapala, & Booth, 1991). Other early family preservation programs used the Homebuilders evaluation model, measuring success by the percentage of children served who did not end up in foster care. Estimated savings in foster care expenses suggested that the programs were very cost effective (Bergquist, Szwejda, & Pope, 1993).

However, a damper on these optimistic estimates of cost savings and placement prevention came in 1992, from an extensive evaluation of Illinois' Family First program. This study found that the risk of placement of children served by family preservation was actually quite low; most of these children were not expected to go into foster care even without family preservation services. This evaluation also found that the Family First program had no effect on subsequent reports of maltreatment by participating families after the program intervention was finished (Schuerman, Rzepnicki, & Littell, 1992). The media used this information to reach the simplistic conclusion that family preservation services didn't work.

Schuerman's research raised the issue that the program was not limited to those for whom it was originally intended, families with children at "imminent risk" of placement. Instead, the services were offered to a larger and more diverse group of families in the child welfare system. The researchers suggested that family preservation services should take place in a reformed, more expansive child welfare service system, because the families receiving services had great needs and the services were not necessarily being wasted (Schuerman, Rzepnicki, Littell, & Budde, 1992; Denby & Curtis, 2003; Kirk & Griffith, 2004).

This research started a movement away from evaluations that looked only at placement rates. Courtney (1997) recommended that "service and support approaches should be developed for clearly defined subpopulations of families and children . . . one size simply doesn't fit all" (p. 73), and "a retreat from the unrealistic early objectives of the family preservation movement is reasonable" (p. 74). Recently, researchers have directed attention toward specific issues, including attempts to measure change in family functioning due to family preservation services intervention. Scannapieco (1993) found improved family functioning in 75 percent of families who had participated in a family preservation program.

Wells and Whittington (1993) studied family functioning among families with an emotionally disturbed child served by a mental health agency. They found that family functioning improved as a result of the services offered, and the children were able to remain in the home. However, the researchers questioned whether in some cases this was a desirable outcome. The families still had many difficulties, and it seemed possible that both they and the child would be better served if the child were admitted to residential treatment that could help him or her substantially.

Research has also addressed the question of what kinds of families can be helped by family preservation services (Littell, 2001). Bath and Haapala (1993) found outcomes less positive for neglectful than for abusive families. Neglectful families were affected by a greater range of environmental, social, and personal difficulties, and suffered the effects of poverty more than their abusive counterparts. Berry (1992) also found that neglectful families were less likely to be served successfully.

A key dimension of program evaluation in family preservation services is client satisfaction. Consistent with a family empowerment value orientation, most programs ascertain client perceptions of services given. Research has consistently shown that families are satisfied and even enthusiastic about this form of service delivery. In one typical study of family satisfaction, over 90 percent of families who responded to the family satisfaction surveys expressed high levels of satisfaction with the quality of the interaction with the worker and the willingness of the worker to listen to them and understand their situation. Over 80 percent reported positive behavioral change in family interactions as a result of the intervention in such areas as improved communication, appropriate discipline, and care of children (Berguist et al., 1993). An important result of the family preservation movement has been the endorsement by families, often labeled as "resistant," "multiproblem," and "hard to reach," of this form of service, with its focus on practical change in an empowerment and strengths-based framework. Not enough attention has been given to this quite remarkable discovery, considering the many years of "client blaming" and failure to engage clients that preceded the family preservation movement. For many families, this is their first positive experience with the social service system.

Recently, there have been calls for research to examine which models of family preservation are most effective and, particularly, to study the relationship of family preservation services to child cognitive, emotional, and social development outcomes (Heneghan, Horwitz, & Levanthal, 1996). Jacobs (2001) noted that "over the past five years or so, the number of evaluation reports . . . has tailed off quite dramatically, suggesting some loss of interest among funders and researchers alike in evaluating FPS" (p. 4). Jacobs suggested that a combination of "evaluation fatigue," a spate of bad publicity, and renewed interest in other areas of child welfare, particularly adoption, are responsible for the scarcity of new research.

KINSHIP CARE AS FAMILY PRESERVATION

A tradition of mutual assistance within kinship networks is common to many cultures. From the villages of Africa and the clans of Scotland, our ancestors brought to the New World an understanding that the extended family cared for children when parents were incapacitated or unavailable. Despite widespread concern following the World Trade Center attack of September 11, 2001, no children affected by the disaster were placed in the foster care system. Most children who lost a parent continued with a surviving parent. The few who lost both parents were quickly absorbed into kinship care arrangements (Rabin, 2001). This example, drawn from a great tragedy, aptly illustrates that kinship care is normative in American society when the nuclear family cannot fulfill its child caring function.

In the field of child welfare, kinship care has become an integral part of family preservation practice. Kinship care can take either of the following forms:

❖ informal kinship care that takes place outside the child welfare system, as, for example, when a child goes to live with an aunt
❖ formal kinship care, made through the child welfare system, including kinship foster care, kinship guardianship, and kinship adoption

One could consider that *all* kinship placements of whatever type are a form of family preservation, if "family" is defined as the entire extended family network.

The Child Welfare League of America has affirmed the importance of kinship care: "Care of children by kin is strongly tied to family preservation. Family strengths often include a kinship network that functions as a support system. . . . The involvement of kin may stabilize family situations, ensure the protection of children, and prevent the need to separate children from their families and place them in the formal child welfare system" (Child Welfare League, 1994, p. 1).

The Cultural Tradition of Kinship Care among American Indian Families

It was through the efforts of the original people of the United States that concepts of kinship care were first enacted into child welfare law. The Indian Child Welfare Act of 1978, reversing a century of policies that intentionally or unintentionally separated large numbers of Indian children from their families, affirmed the extended family structure of Indian families as the primary resource for Indian children who could not live with their parents. Before the era of dominance by non-Indian influences, childrearing was shared within the extended family network and the community (Cross, 1986). (See Chapter 3.) The Indian Child Welfare Act highlighted the importance of kinship networks in child placement for the entire child welfare system and was a precursor of the family preservation movement.

Since implementation of the Indian Child Welfare Act, Indian child welfare programs have developed placement standards that are culturally sensitive to tribal traditions and living standards. Indian children and youth unable to live at home are now more likely to be placed with relatives or other Indian families than before the Act was passed. Non-Indian child welfare professionals sometimes mistakenly view these placements as foster care settings and are concerned about permanency planning for the child. However, from the point of view of many tribal child welfare organizations, these placements are made within the context of permanency planning and are considered to be legitimate long-term placements. To them, kinship care *is* family preservation, because their definition of "family" extends to a wide network of relatives. It should be noted that Indian child welfare organizations, in addition to using kin placements, also have intensive family preservation and reunification programs to work with the nuclear family (Mannes, 1993).

The Cultural Tradition of Kinship Care among African American Families

Kinship care, long a strength of the African American community, came into prominence in the child welfare system as a possible solution to the family breakdowns caused by the substance abuse epidemic of the 1980s. Kinship care in the foster care system had earlier been called "relative placement" and was used infrequently. By 1990, kinship care had been reconceptualized as a form of family preservation and was a recognized part of the child welfare system. The increase in status and acceptability of this form of care reflected new awareness of the importance of kinship ties to children and also the reality that the formal child welfare system lacked resources for protecting this new influx of children.

Although every ethnic group has felt the effects of the epidemic of crack cocaine in this country, it has had particularly noxious effects on many African American communities. A disproportionate number of African American children live with grandparents. Many of these arrangements are informal, as differentiated from formal placements made by the child welfare system. In informal situations grandparents, aunts, and other relatives simply assimilate into the household the children of mothers incapacitated by substance abuse or other difficulties. In some instances, the mother and the extended family caregivers may share a common household. "Recognizing the adaptive and healing power of the African American kinship network, and indeed the importance of kinship to all people, enriches the child welfare worker's ability to help the family develop creative solutions to child welfare issues" (Mills, Usher, & McFadden, 1999, p. 13).

Family Group Decision Making

Indigenous people in many countries have become aware of the Indian Child Welfare Act and its implications. In New Zealand, the Act influenced a movement of the indigenous Maori people to reform the child welfare system so that it would be more responsive to Maori culture and processes for protecting children. In turn, the New Zealand family decision-making model has evoked wide interest in the United States. (Crampton, 2004). It has been adapted by other Pacific Island peoples and in Australia.

New Zealand's Children, Young Persons, and Their Families Act of 1989 acknowledged the right of the Maori people to make decisions for their own families and to retain the child within the extended family network (Worrall, 2001). A key innovation of the New Zealand model is to return much of the decision-making power in child protective services to the extended family and to develop processes for mutual collaboration between the child welfare system and the family. The family and the child welfare bureaucracy are conceptualized as equal partners in this process.

In New Zealand, the family decision-making model involves a conference of extended family members following an investigation of child abuse by a child protection worker. The parents are asked to agree to involve their extended family in planning. The kinship network is then invited to participate; the child welfare system facilitates the transportation of family members from all over the two islands that constitute this country. The meeting takes place in a comfortable setting and may last for several days. During the conference, professionals share information about factors that place the child at risk. They leave the family alone to develop a plan for protecting the child, but are available for consultation if requested. The plan involves deciding on whom the child will live with and what supportive roles other family members will play. The conference coordinator, who is a child welfare staff member, records decisions and accesses resources needed for implementation of the plan (Smith & Featherstone, 1991).

Adapting the family decision-making model to an American setting raises many issues (Zalenski, 1994; Merkel-Holguin, 1998). Legal constraints around confidentiality, court processes, and liability make it difficult to involve the extended family in planning (Hardin, 1994). Yet the model is being transplanted to a number of states and communities in the United States.

In practice in the United States, the child protection worker investigating a case determines that the case will be referred to a family group conference coordinator. In most states families are referred voluntarily, although in a few locations such meetings may be court ordered. Merkel-Holguin (1998) identified four distinct phases in the process:

Phase 1: referral to hold a family group decision-making (FGDM) meeting
Phase 2: preparation and planning
Phase 3: the family conference or meeting
Phase 4: follow-up

The coordinator prepares and plans for the meeting, a process that may take weeks. This involves working with the family; identifying concerned parties and members of the extended kinship network; clarifying their roles and inviting them to a family group meeting; establishing the location, time, and other logistics; and managing other unresolved issues. At the meeting, the coordinator welcomes and introduces participants in a culturally appropriate manner, establishes the purpose of the meeting, and helps participants reach agreement about roles, goals, and ground rules. Next, information is shared with the family, which may involve the child protection workers and other relevant professionals such as a doctor or teacher involved with the child. If the program strictly adheres to the New Zealand model, the coordinator and other professionals withdraw from the meeting in the next stage, to allow the family privacy for their deliberations. (Some programs have adjusted the model to their local norms and allow the coordinator to remain in the meeting.) As a result of this process, the kinship network responds to several issues, including the safety of the child and the care of the child if it considers that protection is needed (American Humane Association, 1996). There is generally some type of follow-up involved to provide support to the designated caregivers and to plan for permanence when needed. It should be noted that the coordinator and/or child protection worker retain the right to veto a family plan if he or she believes the child will not be protected. In reality, this veto is rarely used.

Working with family group decision making requires a new approach to family-centered practice. The social worker must expand his or her ideas about the family to recognize the strength and centrality of the extended kinship network, particularly in communities of color. Use of the strengths perspective is critical. The worker must understand the greater investment of kin in the well-being of the child and should also understand that, even when parts of the kinship system may seem to be compromised or dysfunctional, the healthier kinfolk may effectively assess and deal with the problem. One of the greatest challenges for the American child welfare system is incorporating the sharing of power or returning of power to the kinship network (American Humane Association, 1998). Generally speaking, most FGDM workers welcome the opportunity to work in partnership with kin families and find it to be congruent with their values.

A comprehensive evaluation of family group decision making in one Michigan county found that it was a valuable addition to the child welfare service continuum; that children placed through family group conferences were less likely to have additional contact with children's protective services; that they moved less between temporary homes; that they were less likely to be placed in an institutional setting; that in two-thirds of cases children remained with their extended family members in legal guardianship; and that families "taking care of their own" is family preservation (Crampton, 2001).

The following case illustrates the implementation of the model within the child protection system of the United States.

CASE STUDY:
Mental Health Consumers

Judy and Ronnie R. are parents of a 7-year-old son, Chad. Judy and Ronnie had met in a community drop-in center for consumers of mental health services. Judy, the adopted daughter of Tom and Sandy J., had complex special needs, including developmental and learning disabilities, occasional seizures, and motor difficulties. Ronnie, the son of Mary Ellen R., was diagnosed with a mental illness. Both received SSI for their disabilities. When Judy's pregnancy became evident, both families supported the marriage of the young couple and became actively involved as grandparents for Chad. From time to time Judy and Ronnie would leave their child with paternal or maternal grandparents when they felt unable to cope. Several times Tom and Sandy had gone to the R.'s apartment to pick up Chad and actively intervene in his behalf. Gradually Judy and Ronnie began to isolate themselves from the extended family and refuse to allow Chad to have his regular visits with the relatives.

A referral was made to child protective services by Chad's teacher and the school social worker. Chad had missed twenty days of school in the first semester and appeared dirty and hungry when he was in school. He had difficulty focusing on his work, slept in class, and cried frequently. The school social worker had attempted to engage the parents but was not allowed into their apartment. Ronnie was threatening and belligerent to the school social worker and refused to let Judy speak.

When the protective service worker visited the home, he found it to be dirty to the point of being a health hazard. He noted that Ronnie appeared to spend much of his time locked in the bedroom, and Judy was absorbed in the TV. In a visual assessment of Chad he noted several bruises. The medical evaluation of Chad's condition was that he was suffering from malnutrition, was neglected, and that bruises on his back and buttocks were in the shape of handprints. In discussions with Judy, the protective service worker discovered that the grandparents had been involved with Chad before Judy and Ronnie had shut them out. Both parents indicated that they would rather have the grandparents reinvolved with Chad than risk the possibility of placement outside the family. Ronnie and Judy agreed to have a family group decision-making conference. Chad was allowed to stay temporarily with the paternal grandmother, Mary Ellen, while the case was referred to a family group conference coordinator.

The coordinator received the names and telephone numbers of both paternal and maternal grandparents. She met with Tom and Sandy, and also with Mary Ellen, doing genograms with each family to identify members of the kinship network. Both sets of grandparents helped contact other family members. The conference coordinator talked with each potential participant to explain the FGDM process and purpose.

The conference was held within two weeks of the initial referral, at the small grassroots agency where the coordinator worked. A number of persons attended the conference, including both sets of grandparents, Judy's two sisters and their husbands, her godparents, and her cousin. Ronnie's father, stepmother, and brother also attended. Ronnie and Judy chose not to attend the meeting. The coordinator explained the purpose of the meeting: to plan for the care and protection of Chad. After people became comfortable, with introductions and light refreshments, the coordinator invited the protective service worker to speak. He discussed the medical report, the teacher's concerns, and the condition of the apartment when he had called. The coordinator then asked the family to decide whether they thought Chad needed care and protection by his extended family. The professionals left the room, explaining that the family could have their discussion in private, but that the coordinator would be available as a consultant if they needed her. Within fifteen minutes, she was called back into the room by Tom, the maternal grandfather. The grandparents took turns speaking. First Tom stated that their family was aware of Judy's limitations and that they had tried hard to support her, until they found themselves shut out by Ronnie. They believed that Chad needed to live away from his parents to receive proper care. Mary Ellen, the paternal grandmother, stated that their family had been increasingly concerned about Chad over the past several years and that she knew from having Chad with her the past several weeks that he had not been properly cared for by his parents. Ronnie's father stated that everyone realized that Chad had been neglected and abused and that it was time for the family to step in decisively.

The coordinator then outlined several options and asked the family to develop a plan for caring for Chad. Again, the coordinator let the family plan privately. After an interval of about three hours, during which the coordinator worked in her office on other matters and lunch was brought in to the family, she was summoned back to the family meeting. This time, Judy's sister and brother-in-law, Marjorie and Ed, served as spokespersons for the family. They stated that the families had looked at many complicated issues, including Judy and Ronnie's disabilities, and had decided that in all likelihood Chad might need a home within the extended family for all of his growing-up years. Thus they reasoned that, while the grandparents wanted to remain strongly involved, it might be best for Chad to live with younger family members. Marjorie and Ed, who lived near both sets of grandparents, felt that they could raise Chad to adulthood, if needed, and could keep him in contact with both maternal and paternal relatives. Ronnie's father and brother stated that they would make sure Ronnie would not further abuse Chad or make trouble for Marjorie and Ed. Mary Ellen would provide day care for Chad on school holidays, and Tom and Sandy would provide respite care as needed. Marjorie and Ed would apply for guardianship of Chad. All grandparents would contribute to Chad's support through the purchase of clothing, furniture, and provision of money for allowance and incidentals. The family would try to work with Judy and Ronnie on cleaning up their apartment and using mental health services. Until the situation stabilized, the parents would have to visit Chad at the grandparents' homes. The family would make sure they continued to have a part in Chad's life.

This understanding was written down in a "family compact," which was approved by the coordinator and the protective service worker.

Case Commentary.   Not all family group decision-making cases are as easily resolved as this one. Both maternal and paternal relatives were able to reach a position of agreement and trust with each other. Both sets of kin had attempted to support the family and protect the child earlier. However, until empowered by protective service intervention, they were unable to overcome the barriers posed by the parents' isolation. Thus empowered, they promised to take specific roles in supporting the placement of the child and assisting the parents. This case illustrates the strengths and potential of a kinship network to develop a realistic plan based on the needs and situation of the child and family. It appears that both of the parents have conditions that will continue to affect their parenting. It should be noted that this family system had tried diligently to support the child prior to protective service intervention, but they were shut out by the parents. The protective service worker and family group conference coordinator empowered the extended family, enabling them to continue and intensify their efforts with the child.

Several key elements that contributed to the success of this family group conference were the consent of the parents, the strengths of the extended family members, the ability of the coordinator to enlist the cooperation of all members through careful planning, and the family's focus on the long-term needs of Chad. The signed family compact clarified the roles of all, the financial arrangements, the legal arrangement to be made, and the conditions under which protective services might have to be reinvolved.

Policy and Program Issues in Kinship Care

Kinship care, as a program alternative for children in need of child welfare services, spans various categories of child welfare programs and traditional legal arrangements: family preservation, foster care, guardianship, and adoption. The linkage of formal child welfare services and kinship care is congruent with current thinking on the importance of culturally competent human service delivery systems and on the psychosocial need of children for continuity and ongoing attachments.

However, there are a number of unresolved issues and concerns regarding the use of kinship care in the child welfare system. Legal and financial structures designed to define family relationships, protect children, and support families were not intended to apply to kinship care and are not suited to easy linkage with it in many cases (Johnson, 1994). There are also questions about whether to assess kinship homes for safety and as environments for child development in a different way from the assessment of nonkinship placements (Billing, Ehrle, & Kortenkamp, 2002).

The issues are complex and somewhat overlapping. One issue on which there is general agreement concerns the need of kin providers for social support and access to resources for themselves and their young relatives (Dubowitz, 1990; Berrick, Barth, & Needell, 1994; Terling-Watt, 2001; Ehrle & Geen, 2002). Children in relative placement may have very conflicted histories and present daunting behavioral, educational, and medical challenges. In addition to the aftereffects of abuse and neglect, the children may have serious diseases such as HIV/AIDS (Linsk & Mason, 2004). Children with incarcerated parents are frequently in the care of relatives and are thought to have significant unresolved issues around separation and trauma (Hungerford, 1996; Slavin, 2000). Children with many different kinds of complex problems may need—in addition to the love, support, and sense of belonging they have in an extended family context—access to professional services of many types if they are to be helped and if the placement is to stay intact (Edelboch, Liu, & Martin, 2002).

Family caregivers also have needs. If employed, they may have concerns about continuing to work while undertaking new caretaking responsibilities. Older relatives, such as grandparents, may have health concerns for themselves or their spouse. Their lives may have grown to include interests and activities that conflict with child caring demands but which they are loath to put aside. They may need improved housing, respite care, support groups, and access to legal counseling.

Family dynamics in kinship arrangements may be complicated and volatile. For example, Warren (2001) noted that parent-absent adolescents may feel contempt for the parent who failed them, and they can turn their anger against themselves in depression or displace it onto grandparents who are raising them. Such situations require expert mental health services and family therapy (Minkler, Roe, & Price, 1992). One group of kin caregivers, adult siblings of children needing care, may have special issues of family dynamics and role conflicts. These arrangements often do not come to the attention of the child welfare system and very little is known about them.

Many child welfare and other organizations are increasing their efforts to help kinship caregivers. For example, the American Association of Retired Persons funds telephone "warm lines" for grandparents to use when feeling overburdened and at wit's end, grandparenting classes, and support groups (McFadden & Downs, 1995; Crumbley & Little, 1998; Jackson, Mathews, & Zuskin, 1999). However, overall, the service systems around the country to support kin placements are fragmented, lacking in many areas, and hard to access (Scannapieco & Hegar, 2002; Cuddleback & Orme, 2002).

Financial and Legal Issues.   A serious unresolved problem is providing financial support to kin caregivers, and the problem is exacerbated by the linkage between legal status and eligibility for various forms of public support. One source of financial assistance is TANF, formerly known as public welfare. However, the financial support available for "child only" cases is extremely low. If the grandparent applies for funds on his or her own behalf, the grandparent is subject to the same work requirements as any other applicant, which may not be feasible or helpful to the child (Takas, 1993; Anderson, 2006).

It is possible in some instances for kin providers to be licensed foster parents. These situations are often referred to as *formal kinship care* to distinguish them from *informal kinship care,* which takes place without changes of custody made through the child welfare system. In formal kinship care, the child is placed by the court in the legal custody of the child welfare agency; financial support for the care of the child is made through foster care payments if the kinship homes meet licensing or approval standards for foster parents; and the kinship caregivers are generally expected to comply with the foster parenting role, such as participating in training and cooperating with the agency in implementing a case plan. If they do not meet licensing/approval standards, then payments are made from TANF funds or special relative/kinship care funds.

Treating kin caregivers like foster parents allows them to receive foster care payments, much higher than TANF child only grants. However, many people, including many kin caregivers, have philosophical disagreement with classifying relatives as foster parents; they think that people should not get paid for taking care of their own. Agencies and caregivers alike may see conflicts between the foster parent role and that of relatives; foster parents are in some sense agents of the agency and answerable to it, whereas relatives may not feel that they are fundamentally accountable to the agency (Geen, 2004).

Problems with financial support, role conflict, and legal status also arise in permanency planning, if the preferred option for the child is a permanent living arrangement with relatives. Some kin caregivers are willing to make a home for a grandchild or other young relative on a permanent basis, but may be reluctant to legalize this arrangement through adoption (Thornton, 1991). Grandparents, in particular, may find it difficult to assume the parents' role and may be particularly reluctant to be part of a process in which their child's parental rights to his or her child are terminated so the grandparent can legally take that parent's place. Such an arrangement feels unnatural, is contrary to cultural expectations, and may mean a final relinquishment of hope that their adult child will recover from the problems that led to the placement of the children. For these caregivers, long-term foster care or guardianship might be a more workable permanency solution.

> *After all, he knows I'm his granny, I always was and I always will be. I'll always love him and I'll always take care of him. He knows we're permanent. We don't need no adoption to feel permanent.* (A grandmother)

If the grandparent is given guardianship and the case moves out of the system, the caregiver may lose the foster care pay rate as well as foster care support services. On the other hand, if the grandparent adopts the child, she will probably be eligible for an adoption subsidy. Proponents of kinship care suggest that subsidized guardianships may promote a new kind of permanency in formal kinship care (Child Welfare League of America, 1994). Others advocate for a new form of adoption—kinship adoption (Takas, 1993; Hegar & Scannapieco, 1999).

Assessment and Psychosocial Issues. An attitudinal barrier to the use of kinship care is expressed in the adage: "The apple doesn't fall far from the tree," indicating that the problems of the child's parents are related to their family of origin. A competent assessment of the relative's home is necessary to address safety and protection issues. A national body has developed the following list as factors to consider in kinship assessment (Child Welfare League of America, 1994, pp. 44–45).

- ❖ The quality of the relationship between the relative and the child
- ❖ The likelihood that the relative can/will protect the child from further maltreatment
- ❖ The safety of the kinship home and the ability of the relative to provide a nurturing environment (including presence of alcohol or drug involvement)
- ❖ The willingness of the relative to accept the child into the home
- ❖ The ability of the relative to meet the developmental needs of the child
- ❖ The nature and quality of the relationship between the birth parent and the relative, including the birth parent's preference about placement of the child with kin

Assessment of kin homes also requires that workers be aware of their own biases. Kin providers may be much older than the worker and of a different socioeconomic class and race (Dubowitz, 1990; Thornton, 1991; Berrick, Barth, & Needell, 1994). Workers may feel less comfortable working with kin caregivers and prefer working with established foster parents who are known to the agency, have more financial resources, and are better educated. In assessment, workers need to be aware of the possibility that their biases are affecting their perceptions.

A possible disadvantage of kinship care is that the maltreating parent could have too easy access to a child or the caregiver may have difficulty establishing boundaries with the parent. Although relatives may appear stable, they may also have some denial about the risk the parent represents to the child, or there may be undetected substance abuse or maltreatment patterns in the family system. It is reassuring that one research project found that children may be less at risk in relative care than in foster care (Zuravin & DePanfilis, 1997). However, there is also less monitoring of relative homes than of unrelated foster homes, raising the possibility of undetected maltreatment (Berrick, Barth, & Needell, 1994). One recent study reported that there was a higher rate of disruption among kin placements than with other types of permanent placements. Reasons for disrupted placements included health limitations of the caregiver, difficulties in the relationship with the children's parents, and difficulty in caring for special needs children (Terling-Watt, 2001). This finding highlights the importance of good assessment in making kin placements and of providing adequate levels of support after they are made.

In spite of these concerns, practice experience and research to date suggest that relatives are a viable resource for many children in the child welfare system who need safe, loving homes with people who think they are very special. The home of a relative can give a child a sense of belonging and promote the formation of cultural and personal identity. Kin caregivers may have more positive perceptions about children placed with them than do nonrelated family foster caregivers (Gebel, 1996; Berrick, Barth, & Needell, 1994). If the case plan supports it, the child can have easier access to parents for visiting and possible reunification. Children may be better able to address unresolved issues of loss and family trauma when placed in an extended family context (Crumbley & Little, 1997). More research is needed on effective strategies for strengthening kin placements and on the outcomes of children placed with relatives, including educational attainment, health status, and ongoing safety and protection.

TRENDS AND ISSUES

Assessment of Family Functioning

Outcome research conducted in Los Angeles County with two voluntary agencies examined changes in family functioning during home-based family preservation services, as well as changes in child behavior, home environment, traits of parents, and placement outcomes for children (McCroskey & Meezan, 1997). The experimental program differed from the typical family preservation program in that the services provided were for a three-month period (as opposed to the four- to six-week crisis intervention model); the program provided less intensive service to a broader range of families than those with imminent risk of placement; and the program had different standards of program success than the avoidance of placement or cost savings. In many respects, the program appears to address significant issues raised by earlier evaluation (see Evaluation of Family Preservation Programs), especially with its approach to assessing family functioning.

The two agencies involved used a specially developed family assessment form (Children's Bureau of Southern California, 1997) that addressed family functioning in the following areas: (1) environment (physical environment, family finances, and social supports), (2) caregiver (caregiver's history, personal characteristics, and child-rearing ability), (3) family interactions (caregiver to children, children to caregiver, and caregiver to caregiver), and (4) children (developmental status, behavioral concerns, and child summary). It should be noted that studies of family preservation have used various tools to assess family functioning. For example, the Child Well-Being Scales (Magura & Moses, 1986) have been used in studies of family preservation with drug-exposed infants, while the Family Risk Scale (Magura, Moses, & Jones, 1987) was used in research (Thieman & Dail, 1997) on predictors of out-of-home placement.

The Family Assessment Form used in Los Angeles is a practice-oriented assessment protocol that allows the worker to monitor the progress of families. It has been used with families in many different program settings in agencies all over the world (Children's Bureau of Southern California, 1997).

CHAPTER SUMMARY

Intensive family-based services, typically known as family preservation, have been demonstrated to be helpful to families struggling with multiple problems. These services are time limited and are provided primarily in the home and other environments within the family's ecosystem. Within an overall family-systems framework, a variety of approaches and techniques may be used, including but not limited to the following: cognitive-behavioral, crisis intervention, provision of concrete resources, parent education, mobilization of community supports, and operating from a strengths-based perspective. Flexible funds and the availability of the worker on around-the-clock basis if necessary help to stabilize families in crisis and provide a wide range of resources for change. The approach is congruent with social work's historic concern and values about families.

While proponents of the services believe that they often prevent out-of-home placement of children and ensure the safety of children who remain in the home, program evaluations call into question the targeting of services to families at risk of placement and the concept of placement prevention. There is some agreement on the usefulness of the services to families, but researchers and practitioners alike call for further research on developmental outcomes for children, the effect of services on levels of family functioning and child safety, and the types of families for whom the family preservation approach is most effective. The trend appears to be toward a wider application of family-based services and greater flexibility in the area of time limitation.

Another important form of family preservation is the use of kinship care. Program approaches borrowed from New Zealand to involve the extended kinship network in the protection of children from abuse and neglect through family group decision making show promise.

A significant concern for proponents of kinship care is the lack of congruent policy and supports for kinship caregivers. Federal support and policy development for kinship care has been inconsistent.

FOR STUDY AND DISCUSSION
STUDY AND DISCUSSION QUESTIONS

1. In your community, is there an intensive family-based services program that works for family preservation with families of children at imminent risk of placement? Visit the agency or invite a staff member to class to discuss assessment and safety issues. How does the agency operationalize the value "safety is our first concern"? How does it respond to attacks in the media? How is it evaluating the effectiveness of its program? What is the practitioner's role in evaluation?

2. Identify those agencies in your community providing support to relatives who are involved in kinship care. Are there support groups and/or advocacy groups? They may be framed as "grandparents raising grandchildren groups," forums for kinship caregivers, or parent-education classes for relative caregivers. Is there a "warm line" or information and referral service available to them? Talk to kinship caregivers and find out what they need.

3. Does your community have any community collaboratives for family support and family preservation? How do service delivery systems (mental health, child protective services, schools, and family preservation agencies) work together to identify needs, allocate resources, provide interdisciplinary team planning for wraparound services and coordinate the "step-down" services when a family moves from family preservation to community-based family support?

4. Talk with your child protection agency. Has your state or community piloted a project on family group decision making? Why or why not? If so, what involvement do the courts and child protection play in the process? What follow-up is available for assuring the children's safety and permanence?

5. Examine current media (newspapers, magazines, television, and talk shows) to identify issues being raised in your state and community about family preservation and safety of children. Do a simple content analysis to identify recurrent themes. Then research the evaluation of family preservation and write a letter to the editor or similar rejoinder to correct any media distortions.

6. Contact your local domestic violence, children's mental health, or HIV support agency. Inquire how it sees family preservation and what intensive, family-based services are being offered to its clientele.

7. Invite a family preservation social worker to speak to your class on the *specifics* of his or her job. How does he or she engage families? How does he or she provide hope? How do families respond to the worker's identifying strengths? What are the greatest challenges? What are the rewards?

Internet Sites

American Humane Association. This nationally recognized organization, known primarily for work in the area of child protection, provides references to publications specific to family group decision making.
www.americanhumane.org

The Child Welfare Information Gateway. The Child Welfare Information Gateway provides access to information and resources to help protect children and strengthen families. A service of the Children's Bureau, Administration for Children and Families, U.S. Department of Health and Human Services.
www.childwelfare.gov

Child Welfare League of America. This organization has a general child welfare site, with specific pages related to developments in family preservation and lists of topically related publications provided by CWLA.
www.cwla.org

National Family Preservation Network. The central coordinating point for a network of family preservation staff and programs.
www.nfpn.org

References

Allen, M., & Zalenski, J. (1993, Spring). Making a difference for families: Family-based services in the nineties. *The Prevention Report,* 1–3.

American Humane Association. (1996). The practice and promise of family group decision-making. *Protecting Children, 12*(3).

American Humane Association. (1998). *1997 National roundtable series on family group decision-making: Summary of proceedings, assessing the promise and implementing the practice.* Englewood, CO: Author.

Anderson, S. G. (2006). The impact of state TANF policy decisions on kinship care providers. *Child Welfare, 85*(4), 715–736.

Angelou, M. (1985). Introduction. In *Keeping families together: The case for family preservation.* Edna McConnell Clark Foundation.

Bain, A. (1978). The capacity of families to cope with transitions: A theoretical essay. *Human Relations, 31*(8), 675–688.

Bandura, A. (1977). *Social learning theory.* Englewood Cliffs, NJ: Prentice-Hall.

Barth, R. P. (1994). Long-term in-home services. In D. Besharov (Ed.), *When drug addicts have children* (pp. 175–194). Washington, DC: Child Welfare League of America, American Enterprise Institute.

Barthel, J. (1992). *For children's sake: The promise of family preservation.* Philadelphia: Winchell Company.

Bath, H., & Haapala, D. (1993). Intensive family preservation services with abused and neglected children: An examination of group differences. *Child Abuse & Neglect, 17,* 213–225.

Bergquist, C., Szwejda, D., & Pope, G. (1993, March). *Evaluation of Michigan's Family First program summary report.* Lansing, MI: University Associates.

Berrick, J., Barth, R., & Needell, B. (1994). A comparison of kinship foster homes and foster family homes: Implications for kinship foster care as family preservation. *Children and Youth Services Review, 16*(1–2), 33–63.

Berry, M. (1992). An evaluation of family preservation services: Fitting agency services to family needs. *Social Work, 37*(4), 314–321.

Besharov, D. (Ed.). (1994). *When drug addicts have children: Reorienting child welfare's response.* Washington, DC: Child Welfare League of America, American Enterprise Institute.

Billing, A., Ehrle, J., & Kortenkamp, K. (2002). Children cared for by relatives: What do we know about their well-being? In *New Federalism: National survey of America's families.* Washington, DC: The Urban Institute.

Caplan, G. (1974). *Principles of preventive psychiatry.* New York: Basic Books.

Child Welfare League of America. (1994). *Kinship care: A natural bridge.* Washington, DC: Child Welfare League of America.

Child Welfare League of America. (2003). *CWLA Standards of excellence for services to strengthen and preserve families with children.* Revised edition. Washington, DC: Child Welfare League of America.

Children's Bureau of Southern California. (1997). *Family assessment form: A practice-based approach to assessing family functioning.* Washington, DC: Child Welfare League of America Press.

Courtney, M. (1997). Reconsidering family preservation: A review of *Putting Families First. Children and Youth Services Review, 19*(1–2), 61–76.

Crampton, D. (2001). Making sense of foster fare: An evaluation of family group decision making in Kent County, Michigan. Dissertation, University of Michigan.

Crampton, D. S. (2004). Family involvement interventions in child protection: Learning from contextual integrated strategies. *Journal of Sociology and Social Welfare, 31*(1), 175–198.

Cross, T. (1986). Drawing on cultural tradition in Indian child welfare practice. *Social Casework,* May, 283–289.

Cross, T. (1987). *Cross-culture skills in Indian child welfare: A guide for the non-Indian.* Portland, OR: Northwest Indian Child Welfare Association.

Crumbley, J., & Little, R. (Eds.). (1997). *Relatives raising children: An overview of kinship care.* Washington, DC: Child Welfare League of America Press.

Cuddleback, G. S., & Orme, J. G. (2002). Training and services for kinship and nonkinship foster families. *Child Welfare, 81*(6), 879–909.

Denby, R. W., & Curtis, C. M. (2003). Why special populations are not the target of family preservation services: A case for program reform. *Journal of Sociology and Social Welfare, XXX* (2), 149–173.

Dennis, K. (1997). Advocate's narrative. In R. Golden (Ed.), *Disposable children* (pp. 169–172). Belmont, CA: Wadsworth.

DeVoe, E. R., & Kantor, G. K. (2002). Measurement issues in child maltreatment and family violence prevention programs. *Trauma, Violence, & Abuse, 3*(1), 15–39.

Doerre, Y., & Mihaly, L. (1996). *Home sweet home: Building collaborations to keep families together.* Washington, DC: Child Welfare League of America Press.

Dubowitz, H. (1990). *The physical and mental health and educational status of children placed with relatives: Final report.* Baltimore: University of Maryland.

Edelboch, M., Liu, Q., & Martin, L. (2002). Unsung heroes: Relative caregivers in child-only cases. *Policy and Practice of Public Human Services, 60*(1), 26–30.

Edleson, J. L. (1999). The overlap between child maltreatment and woman battering. *Violence Against Women, 5*(2), 134–154.

Edna McConnell Clark Foundation. (1985). *Keeping families together: The case for family preservation.* New York.

Ehrle, J., & Geen, R. (2002). Chlidren cared for by relatives: What services do they need? In *New Federalism: National survey of American's families.* Washington, DC: The Urban Institute.

Ell, K. (1996). Crisis theory and social work practice. In F. J. Turner (Ed.), *Social Work Treatment* (4th ed.), New York: Free Press.

Faria, G. (1994). Training for family preservation practice with lesbian families. *Families and Society, 75*(7), 416–422.

Findlater, J., & Kelly, S. (1999, May). Reframing child safety in Michigan: Building collaboration among domestic violence, family preservation, and child protection services. *Child Maltreatment* (pp. 167–174). Thousand Oaks, CA: Sage.

Gebel, T. (1996). Kinship care and nonrelative family foster care: A comparison of caregiver attributes and attitudes. *Child Welfare, 75*(1), 5–18.

Geen, R. The evolution of kinship care policy and practice. (2004). *Future of Children, 14*(1), 130–149.

Germain, C., & Gitterman, A. (1996). *The life model of social work practice* (2nd ed.) New York: Columbia University Press.

Giarretto, H. A. (1982). *Integrated treatment of child sexual abuse.* Palo Alto, CA: Science and Behavior Books.

Gray, S. S., & Nybell, L. (1990). Issues in African-American family preservation. *Child Welfare, 69*(6), 513–523.

Gruber, K., Fleetwood, T., & Herring, M. (2001). In-home continuing care services for substance-affected families: The Bridges Program. *Social Work, 46*(3), 267–277.

Hardin, M. (1994, May). Family group conferences in New Zealand. *ABA Journal and Child Welfare Law Reporter.*

Hartman, A. (1993). Family preservation under attack. *Social Work, 38,* 509–512.

Hartman, A., & Laird, J. (1983). *Family centered social work practice.* New York: Free Press.

Hegar, R., & Scannapieco, M. (1999). *Kinship foster care: Policy, practice, and research.* New York: Oxford University Press.

Heneghan, A., Horwitz, S., & Leventhal, J. (1996). Evaluating family preservation programs: A methodological review. *Pediatrics, 97*(4), 535–542.

Hungerford, G. (1996). Caregivers of children whose mothers are incarcerated: A study of the kinship placement system. *Children Today, 24*(1), 23–27.

Jackson, S., Matthews, J., & Zuskin, R. (1999). *Supporting the kinship triad: A training curriculum.* Washington, DC: Child Welfare League of America.

Jacobs, F. (2001). *What to make of family preservation services evaluations.* Chicago: Chapin Hall Center for Children at University of Chicago.

Johnson, I. (1994). Kinship care. In D. Besharov (Ed.), *When drug addicts have children,* (pp. 221–228). Washington, DC: Child Welfare League of America, American Enterprise Institute.

Jones, B. (1994). The clients and their problems. In D. Besharov (Ed.), *When drug addicts have children* (pp. 115–124). Washington, DC: Child Welfare League of America, American Enterprise Institute.

Kinney, J., & Dittmar, K. (1995). Homebuilders: Helping families help themselves. In I. M. Schwartz, & P. AuClaire (Eds.), *Homebased*

services for troubled children. Lincoln: University of Nebraska Press.

Kinney, J., Haapala, D., & Booth, C. (1991). *Keeping families together: The homebuilders model.* New York: Aldine de Gruyter.

Kirk, R. S., & Griffith, D. P. (2004). Intensive family preservation services: Demonstrating placement prevention using event history analysis. *Social Work Research, 28*(1), 5–16.

Lindsey, D. (1994). Family preservation and child protection: Striking a balance. *Children and Youth Services Review, 16*(5–6), 279–294.

Linsk, N. L., & Mason, S. (2004). Stresses on grandparents and other relatives caring for children affected by HIV/AIDS. *Health and Social Work, 29*(2), 127–136.

Littell, J. H. (2001). Client participation and outcomes of intensive family preservation services. *Social Work Research, 25*(2), 103–113.

Lovell, M., Reid, K., & Richey, C. (1992). Social support training for abusive mothers. *Social Work with Groups, 15*(2–3), 95–107.

Magura, S., & Moses, B. (1986). *Outcome measure for child welfare services: Theory and applications.* Washington, DC: Child Welfare League of America Press.

Magura, S., Moses, B., & Jones, M. (1987). *Assessing risk and measuring change in families.* Washington, DC: Child Welfare League of America Press.

Maluccio, A., Pine, B., & Walsh, R. (1994). Protecting children by preserving their families. *Children and Youth Services Review, 16*(5–6), 295–307.

Mannes, M. (1993). Seeking the balance between child protection and family preservation in Indian child welfare. *Child Welfare, 72*(2), 141–152.

McCroskey, J. (2001). *What is family preservation and why does it matter?* Chicago: Chapin Hall Center for Children.

McCroskey, J., & Meezan, W. (1997). *Family preservation & family functioning.* Washington, DC: Child Welfare League of America Press.

McFadden, E. J., & Downs, S. W. (1995). Family continuity: The new paradigm in permanence planning. *Community Alternatives: The International Journal of Family Care, 7*(1), 44.

Merkel-Holguin, L. (1998). Transferring the family group conferencing technology from New Zealand to the United States. Paper presented at the twelfth International Congress on Child Abuse and Neglect, Auckland, New Zealand.

Mills, C., Usher, D., & McFadden, E. J. (1999, Fall). Kinship in the African American community. *Michigan Sociological Review, 13,* 1–16.

Minkler, M., Roe, K., & Price, M. (1992). The physical and emotional health of grandmothers raising grandchildren in the crack cocaine epidemic. *The Gerontologist, 32*(6), 752–761.

Murray, C. E. (2006). Controversy, constraints, and context: Understanding family violence through family systems theory. *The Family Journal, 14*(3), 234–239.

Napoli, M., & Gonzales-Santin, E. (2001). Intensive home-based and wellness services to Native American families living on reservations: A model. *Families in Society, 82*(3), 315–324.

National Council of Juvenile and Family Court Judges. (1992). *Protocol for making reasonable efforts to preserve families in drug-related dependency cases.* Reno, NV: National Council of Juvenile and Family Court Judges.

National Resource Center on Family Based Services. (1994). Project proposal. Iowa City, IA.

Nelson, K., Landsman, M., & Deutelbaum, W. (1990). Three models of family-centered placement prevention services. *Child Welfare, 69*(1), 3–21.

Noble, D., Perkins, K., & Fatout, M. (2000). On being a strength coach: Child welfare and the strengths model. *Child and Adolescent Social Work Journal, 17*(2), 141–153.

Olson, D. (1997). Family stress and coping: A multisystem perspective. In S. Dreman, (Ed.), *The family on the threshold of the 21st century: Trends and implications.* Mahwah, NJ: Lawrence Eribaum Associates.

Parad, H. J. (Ed.). (1965). *Crisis intervention: Selected readings.* New York: Family Service Association of America.

Patterson, G. (1975). *Families.* Champaign, IL: Research Press.

Pecora, P., Whittaker, J., Maluccio, A., Barth, R., & Plotnick, R. (1992). *The child welfare challenge.* Hawthorne, NY: Aldine de Gruyter.

Polansky, N., Chalmers, M., Battenmeier, E., & Williams, D. (1981). *Damaged parents: An anatomy of child neglect.* Chicago: University of Chicago Press.

Rabin, R. (2001, November 18). What about the children? *Grand Rapids Press,* p. A13.

Saleeby, D. (2002). *The strengths perspective in social work practice* (3rd ed.). Boston: Allyn & Bacon.

Sandau-Beckler, P., Salcido, R., & Ronnau, J. (1993). Culturally competent family preservation services: An approach for first generation Hispanic families in an international border community. *The Family Journal, Counseling and Therapy for Couples and Families, 1*(4), 313–323.

Scannapieco, M. (1993). The importance of family functioning to prevention of placement: A study of family preservation services. *Child and Adolescent Social Work Journal, 10*(6), 509–520.

Scannapieco, M., & Hegar, R. L. (2002). Kinship care providers: Designing an array of supportive services. *Children & Adolescent Social Work Journal, 19*(4), 315–327.

Schuerman, J., Rzepnicki, T., & Littell, J. (1992). *Evaluation of the Illinois Family First placement prevention program: Progress report.* Chicago, IL: Chapin Hall.

Schuerman, J., Rzepnicki, T., Littell, J., & Budde, S. (1992). Implementation issues. *Children and Youth Services Review, 14,* 193–206.

Slavin, P. (2000). Children with parents behind bars. *Children's Voice, 9*(5), 4+.

Smith, C., & Walton, E. (1999). The genogram: A tool for assessment and intervention in child welfare. *Journal of Family Social Work, 3*(3), 3–20.

Smith, D., & Featherstone, T. (1991). Family group conferences—the process. In *Family Decision Making.* Lower Hutt, New Zealand: Practitioners Publishing.

Staudt, M. M. (2001). Use of services prior to and following intensive family preservation services. *Journal of Child & Family Studies, 10*(1), 101–114.

Sudia, C. (1981). What services do abusive and neglecting families need? In L. H. Pelton (Ed.), *The Social Context of Child Abuse and*

Neglect (pp. 268–290). New York: Human Services Press.

Takas, M. (1993, December–January). Kinship care: Developing a safe and effective framework for protective placement of children with relatives. *Zero to Three,* 12–17.

Terling-Watt, T. (2001). Permanency in kinship care: An exploration of disruption rates and factors associated with placement disruption. *Children & Youth Services Review, 23*(2), 111–126.

Thieman, A., & Dail, P. (1997). Predictors of out-of-home placement in a family preservation program: Are welfare recipients particularly vulnerable? *Policy Studies Journal, 25*(1), 124–139.

Thornton, J. (1991). Permanency planning for children in kinship foster homes. *Child Welfare, 70*(5), 593–601.

Tracy, E., Whittaker, J., Pugh, A., Kapp, S., & Overstreet, E. (1994). Support networks of primary caregivers receiving family preservation services: An exploratory study. *Families in Society, 75*(8), 481–489.

VanDenBerg, J., Bruns, E., & Burchard, J. (2003). History of the wraparound process. *Focal Point, 17*(2), 4–7.

VanDenBerg, J., Grealish, M., & Schick, C. (1993). *Wraparound guidelines.* Lansing, MI: Michigan Department of Social Services.

Walsh, R., Pine, B., & Maluccio, A. (1995). Essay, the meaning of family preservation: Shared mission, diverse methods. *Families in Society: The Journal of Contemporary Human Services,* 625–626.

Walton, E. (1997). Enhancing investigative decisions in child welfare: An exploratory use of intensive family preservation services. *Child Welfare, 76*(3), 447–461.

Walton, E. (2001). Combining abuse and neglect investigations with intensive family preservation services: An innovative approach to protecting children. *Research on Social Work Practice, 11*(6), 627–644.

Warren, D. H. (2001). Reaching for integrity: An Ericksonian life-cycle perspective on the experience of adolescents being raised by grandparents. *Child and Adolescent Social Work Journal, 18*(1), 21–35.

Wells, K., & Tracy, E. (1996). Reorienting intensive family preservation services in relation to public child welfare practice. *Child Welfare, 75*(6), 667–692.

Wells, K., & Whittington, D. (1993, March). Child and family functioning after intensive family preservation services. *Social Service Review,* 55–83.

Whittaker, J. K. (2002). The elegant simplicity of family preservation practice: Legacies and lessons. *Family Preservation Journal, 6,* 9–29.

Whittaker, J., Kinney, J., Tracy, E., & Booth, C. (1990). *Reaching high-risk families.* New York: Aldine de Gruyter.

Worrall, J. (2001). Kinship care of the abused child, the New Zealand experience. *Child Welfare, 80*(5), 495–511.

Zalenski, J. (1994). A new/old practice to care for children: New Zealand's family decision making model. *The Prevention Report* (pp. 11–14). Iowa City, IA: National Resource Center on Family Based Services.

Zuravin, S., & DePanfilis, D. (1997). Factors affecting foster care placement of children receiving child protective services. *Social Work Research, 21*(1), 34–42.

8

Foster Care: History, Laws, Policies, and Structure

What the best and wisest parent wants for his child, society should want for all its children.

—John Dewey

CHAPTER OUTLINE

G iven the complexity of foster care, we are devoting two chapters to it. In this chapter, we focus on the history of foster care; the laws and policies, federal and state roles, types of foster care, and professional issues of recruitment, training, monitoring, and supervision of staff; foster parents; and contracted providers of services. In the next chapter we focus on foster care practice with children and their parents, including concurrent planning, services to ensure the safety and well-being of children, addressing the specific needs of children with conditions or behaviors requiring specialized interventions, assisting youth for successful transitions from foster care, addressing parental conditions and behaviors that led to the foster care placement, case planning for timely permanency, and unique issues in serving children and families in relative care or kinship placements.

Foster care is the placement of children out of the custody of their parents or legal guardians after a court finding that they have been abused or neglected, are a person in need of supervision (status offender), or have committed delinquent acts. Foster care is a social system with many component parts and complex interrelationships between those parts. The foster child, parents,

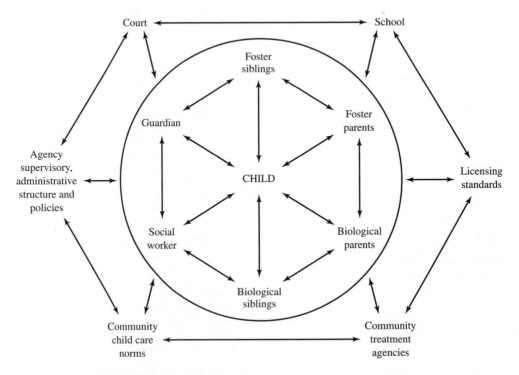

Figure 8.1 *Foster Care System*

siblings, paternal and maternal extended family members, foster parents, foster siblings, the agency caseworker, peers in placement, child care staff, social workers, therapists, the court-appointed guardian or attorney, support organizations, jurists, schools, community organizations — each party is an integral element of the whole system.

The social agency responsible for the child in care and the court authorizing the placement have continuing obligation to monitor the placement situation to see that proper care and treatment are given, and to consult with children, parents, and caregivers in a teamwork approach.

WHY CHILDREN ARE PLACED IN CARE

Problems relating to parental characteristics and social conditions that precede foster care are in most instances very serious, and are not easily corrected by preventive, therapeutic, or family preservation services. In some instances they are so hazardous that these services are not attempted. The primary reason that children come into foster care is found in family breakdown or incapacity, exacerbated by severe environmental pressures. The breakdown reflects a cluster of critical and visible individual and environmental problems, in addition to the neglect or abuse of children, such as mental or emotional problems of parents, substance abuse, domestic violence, and chronic poverty.

Contrary to popular belief, children entering care are not orphans; meaning, they have not lost their parents through death. Children in foster care usually have at least one living parent who may or may not visit and assume responsibility.

Family Characteristics

Children who enter foster care, particularly those who are likely to remain in care a long time, usually have parents who have a configuration of serious personal and environmental problems that have grown over time and the child does not have sufficient support from other adults. Nor has social services been able to help these families continue to care for their children in their own homes. Because almost all families whose children enter foster care have multiple problems and needs, it is difficult to identify a single principal reason for each placement. For example, a neglecting or abusing parent may also be mentally ill and trying to self-medicate with alcohol or other drugs. Some children come into care because of family homelessness or the incarceration of the mother. A series of studies and reports over the past several decades indicate that the major problems bringing children into care are not their emotional or behavioral disorders, but *problems relating to parental functioning* (Phillips, Shyne, Sherman, & Haring, 1971; Jenkins & Norman, 1972; Jones, Magura, & Shyne, 1976; Besharov, 1994; Zuravin & DePanfilis, 1997; Semidei, Radel, & Nolan, 2001).

Since the 1980s, a major reason that children have come into care is the substance abuse of their parents, linked to other debilitating conditions (Horn, 1994; Groze, Haines-Simeon, & Barth, 1994). Addicted mothers of children in foster care are likely to be unemployed, have unstable housing, have dysfunctional families of origin, and have violent and unhealthy relationships. They often do not receive prenatal care and have many untreated health problems (Chasnoff, 1990). Children are *not* placed in care simply because their parent abuses drugs, but because they are abused or neglected (Wightman, 1991) or they may be born drug exposed and the state's child abuse and neglect statutes define that condition as child abuse or neglect and require foster care placement (Child Welfare Information Gateway, 2006).

Parental drug use is related to another reason that children come into care: the presence of HIV/AIDS in the parent, the child, or both (Taylor-Brown & Garcia, 1995). About a quarter of children whose parents have HIV/AIDS are in the foster care system; the rest are in the care of their parents or relatives (Stein, 1998). Some of these children have HIV/AIDS themselves, transmitted to them prenatally; they may have developmental problems in addition to the illness and present a substantial caregiving challenge. Specialized foster homes have been recruited and trained to meet the complex needs of these children.

CHARACTERISTICS OF CHILDREN IN CARE

Age, Ethnicity, and Other Variables

Current data on foster care are available through the federal government's Adoption and Foster Care Analysis and Reporting System (AFCARS). Before AFCARS, the American Public Welfare System collected foster care program data from 1982 through 1990. However, not all states were able to provide all data requested, so the Voluntary Cooperative Information System (VCIS) data were considered "rough" national estimates. In 1986 the U.S. Congress provided for the establishment of a national mandatory data collection system for foster care and adoption of children from foster care, which became the current AFCARS system. Fifty-two jurisdictions (including the District of Columbia and Puerto Rico) participate in AFCARS.

On September 30, 2005, there were 513,000 children in foster care. This represented the sixth consecutive year of decline—from 552,000 at the end of 2000. In addition, the total number of children served in foster care (799,000) in 2005 represented a decline from the total number served (811,000) in 2000, although 813,000 children were served in 2001 and 2002. During this period, entries into foster care continued to exceed exits from foster care. Children waiting to be adopted declined from 131,000 in 2000 to 114,000 in 2005. Likewise, terminations of parental rights declined from 73,000 to 66,000. The number of children adopted from foster care was 51,000 in each year. (Children's Bureau, 2006)

The median age of the children in care on September 30, 2005 was 10.6 years. They had been in foster care for an average of 15.5 months with 37 percent in care for 24 months or more. Of these children, 52 percent were male and 48 percent were female. The group was 41 percent white–non-Hispanic, 32 percent black–non-Hispanic, 18 percent Hispanic, 3 percent two or more races, 2 percent American Indian or American Native, 1 percent Asian, and 2 percent unknown or unable to determine. They were placed in nonrelative foster homes (46%), relative foster homes (24%), institutions (10%), group homes (8%), pre-adoptive homes (4%), trial home visits (4%), supervised independent living (1%), and 2 percent were on runaway status. The case goal for these children were reunification with parents or legal guardians (51%), adoption (20%), placement with nonparent relatives (4%), long-term foster care or emancipation (13%), and guardianship (8%), and case goals had not been determined for 8% of the children (Children's Bureau, 2006).

Of the children who exited foster care during 2005, they had been in foster care for an average of 12 months. Of these children, 33 percent had been in foster care less than 6 months, 30 percent between 6 and 17 months, 20 percent for 18 to 35 months, and 17 percent for 3 years or more. Of the children exiting care, 45 percent were white, 28 percent were black, and 17 percent were Hispanic, 6 percent were multiracial or unknown, 2 percent were American Indian or American Native, and 1 percent were Asian. The majority of these children were reunified with parents (54%) or relatives (11%). The others exited to adoption (18%), emancipation (9%), guardianship (4%), runaway, or transferred to other agencies (4%). During 2005, there were 534 children who died while in foster care. These deaths were caused by medical conditions, accidents, and homicides (Children's Bureau, 2006).

BASIC CHARACTERISTICS OF FOSTER CARE

As a service to children and their families, foster care has certain distinguishing characteristics:

1. Foster care is arranged by a public, private nonprofit, or private for-profit social agency either under a court order or by parental request (voluntary placement).

2. Responsibility for children's daily care usually is transferred from the biological parents because of a serious situation—a complex set of interacting conditions or parental characteristics that makes the parents unable to care for their children properly and necessitates community assumption of responsibility.

3. Foster care is full-time care, twenty-four hours a day, outside the child's own home.

4. Foster care or out-of-home care may be given within a relative's home, a nonrelated family foster home, a treatment foster home, a small group home, a cottage setting, a larger residential care facility, or if the child is old enough, in his or her own residence with independent living program supervision.

5. In contrast with adoption, foster care is supposed to be a temporary arrangement, with the expectation that the child will return to the parents or extended family, be placed for adoption, or be discharged from care on reaching legal maturity.

Using social work methods, the social agency plays a major role in planning and carrying out the child's care. Typically, the parents retain many of their rights, even if the court has assumed temporary wardship of the child. Thus, the agency shares the broad responsibility for the child with the court, the parents, and the community, even while the foster parents, house parents, or child care staff provide the day-to-day services for the child.

Children and youths who enter care have usually had difficult experiences, including the maltreatment and/or parental problems that necessitate care, and this is compounded by the painful separation from parents, siblings, kinfolk, and familiar environments. They may have unresolved conflicts in relation to their parents or divided loyalties between original family and substitute caregivers. Because of their life experiences—physical neglect, abuse, emotional neglect, sexual abuse, abandonment, or exploitation—young persons in care often have many unmet developmental needs. Consequently, for the foster care experience to be nurturing and successful, it must involve far more than a change of setting.

Underlying Principles

Certain generalizations or principles underlie contemporary foster care practice. Some have remained relatively stable during this century, while others have evolved:

1. The parent–child relationship and adequate parenting are of utmost importance to the child. Society's first responsibility is to try to preserve the child's own home. If that is not possible, the kinship network or extended family should be supported to provide the

child continuity of relationships. The Adoption and Safe Families Act (ASFA) requires that relatives be given preference if out-of-home care is required.

2. If parental care cannot be restored to a level that will protect children and provide at least minimally adequate care, and the kinship network cannot maintain the child, then family foster care can provide nurture within a family setting until a permanent family situation can be achieved for the child.

3. Different settings within the foster care system—related and nonrelated family foster homes, specialized or treatment homes, group homes, and residential care—are an array of services from which the most appropriate placement service can be selected, based on the unique needs of the individual child and family.

4. In all settings, the entire family is the identified client. The initial service goal is usually family reunification, with improved family functioning and safety and permanency for the child.

5. The foster caregiver (foster parent, houseparent, or child care staff) is an integral part of the service team. The caregiver participates in forming a permanency plan, serves as a role model to the family, aids in facilitating family reunification, and ensures that the child's health, dental and medical; mental health; and educational needs are met.

6. When decisions crucial to the future of the child are made, special consideration must be given to ensure that the legal rights of the child are protected. This must be balanced with attention to constitutional rights of parents and the rights of children to be part of a family and maintain family connections.

HISTORICAL DEVELOPMENT

Indenture, Almshouses, and Institutions

In ancient times as throughout history orphaned children were usually cared for by their kinfolk through mechanisms embedded in clan or tribe and culture. Both Jewish and Christian religions made provisions for the care of children in family homes. Slingerland, in his treatise on foster care (1919), found no record of formal institutions for dependent children until about the end of the second century. These institutions have continued until very recently.

In England, the system of child placing for profit began under a system of indenture given national sanction in 1562. This system was imported into the American colonies, where it left a significant imprint on the development of child placing. By statute in many states, trustees of the poor were authorized to "bind out" to a master artisan a poor child, orphan, illegitimate child, or any other destitute child old enough to work. Such children would then become members of their master's household and be taught a craft or trade. In turn, the children were obliged to give their master obedience and labor, which was expected to pay for their keep and training by the time they reached maturity and the end of their indenture.

Indenture was seen as having two basic purposes: (1) to fix responsibility for the support and care of a dependent child on some person or family, and (2) to give training for work (it was a period of history when there was much work to be done for survival, and the growth of the country required most persons to acquire some skills or an occupation).

Homer Folks (1911) noted that the old-fashioned indenture or apprentice system passed largely into disuse and disrepute after 1874. The system had not been without merit and provided in varying degrees an experience of substitute family life for dependent children. However, changing industrial conditions in the nineteenth century tended to make the relationship of apprentice to master less intimate and kindly.

Not all poor children were indentured in the early years of this country. Sometimes "outdoor relief"—material supplied by the town to destitute parents in their own homes—preserved a child's own home. But punitive attitudes toward the poor made outdoor relief the least accepted form of care. When towns grew large enough to build almshouses, needy children were often sent to live in them. In 1842, Yates, then secretary of state of New York, surveyed the condition of paupers and strongly recommended the elimination of outdoor relief and that every county in the state maintain a poorhouse. The children of pauper inmates were to be educated and at a suitable age sent out for useful labor.

His plan was largely implemented in New York. However, thirty years after Yates's enthusiastic report on what the almshouse system would accomplish for children, an investigation of the poorhouses found them to be "most disgraceful memorials of the public charity" and "for the young . . . the worst possible nurseries" (*Report of Select Senate Committee*, 1857). Publicity about the poorhouse environment in which children were living led to the conviction that the placement of children there had been a serious mistake. As a result, various states began to remove children from the almshouse.

While the controversy was going on about outdoor relief, indenture, and almshouse care, some institutions for children apart from adults were being established. In the nineteenth century, public and private agencies set up institutions for special classes of children—the blind, deaf, mentally deficient, and delinquent—as well as orphanages for dependent children to protect them from neglect and abuse. While these institutions appeared to their founders as an improvement over the mixed almshouses (and many were), in some of the large congregate institutions there were problems of inadequate sanitation, poor medical care, inadequate diets, and epidemics of contagious disease from which many children died.

The trend toward orphanages grew, however, not only because of continuing dissatisfaction with the public almshouses but also because of the emerging practice of awarding assistance from the public treasury to voluntary agencies. Most of the orphan asylums were established under denominational auspices as various religious groups sought to provide for their own needy children and teach them their faith. Their programs combined religious duty with missionary zeal, lack of individualization of children, hard daily work for the children "to inure [them] to hardship and fatigue," and little chance for enduring relationships with particular adults. When children were received into care, the usual practice was to require parents to surrender their rights to their children. As they grew older and had been given some education, indenture was the means for moving them back into the community.

The vast majority of orphanages were operated by white people for white children. Many of the children were new immigrants whose families, migrating from Europe, had died or become separated during the migration process (Downs & Sherraden, 1983). By and large children of color were served by informal kinship placements, but in 1888 several African American women community leaders founded the St. Louis Colored Orphans Home. This agency evolved into the Annie Malone Children and Family Service Center, which still provides leadership in the African American service community today (Brissett-Chapman & Issacs-Shockley, 1997).

Orphan Trains and Free Foster Homes

Still another approach to the care of dependent children was the free foster home movement, best illustrated by the work of Charles Loring Brace, who in 1853 began the practice of taking needy or homeless children from the city in large parties to a rural locality, where they were placed in the homes of farmers and tradespeople. Brace was concerned about the increasing crime and poverty among the children of New York City and the plight of the many uncared-for, ignorant, and vagrant youth. In his book *The Dangerous Classes of New York*, he wrote that immigration "is pouring in its multitude of poor foreigners, who leave these young outcasts everywhere abandoned in our midst" (1872). The child "placing out" movement spearheaded by Brace took children from the cities by "orphan trains" to farm communities in the Midwest and South. Brace described his method as follows:

> We formed little companies of emigrants, and, after thoroughly cleaning and clothing them, put them under a competent agent, and, first selecting a village where there was a call . . . for such a party, we dispatched them to the place. The farming community having been duly notified, there was usually a dense crowd of people at the station, awaiting the arrival of the youthful travelers. The sight of the little company of the children of misfortune always touched the hearts of a population naturally generous. . . . The agent then addressed the assembly, stating the benevolent objects of the Society and something of the history of the children. The sight of their worn faces was a most pathetic enforcement of his arguments. People who were childless came forward. . . . Others, who had not intended to take any into their families, were induced to apply for them; and many who really wanted the children's labor, pressed forward to obtain it. *(pp. 231–232)*

Between 1853 and 1929, over 30,000 children were placed in family homes by way of the orphan trains (Thurston, 1930). Brace's movement attracted followers. It was bold; many children did get good homes, and it provided a stimulus generally to the placement of children out of almshouses and into families. But there were critics as well. Some of the child welfare leaders of religious faiths different from Brace's had little enthusiasm for his program, as most of the homes in which children were placed were Protestant. By contrast, most of the children came from immigrant families, largely Catholic. Objections that children had been removed from the religion of their parents added a stimulus to the growth of sectarian agencies and to legislating religious matching as one determinant in the choice of foster or adoptive homes. Brace's experiment also revealed the problem of lack of ongoing supervision of placements once made.

The White House Conference on Children

By the last quarter of the nineteenth century, foster homes and institutions prevailed as fairly well-developed forms of care for dependent children. A philosophy of child care centered on the question "What does the child really need?" began to emerge. A consensus developed, articulated at the White House Conference on Children in 1909, that all children need families and that family care was the preferred environment to meet the needs of developing children.

CHILD WELFARE REFORMS IN THE TWENTIETH AND TWENTY-FIRST CENTURIES

Child welfare policies and practices *appear* to be in constant "reform" mode. What has remained constant since the White House Conference on Children in 1909 is that all children need families and family care is the preferred environment for placement of children who are not safe with their parents or legal guardians. Additional constants dating from the 1970s include too little money to provide comprehensive services to children and parents in the foster care system; fragmentation in policies, procedures, service delivery philosophies, and methodologies across child welfare, mental health, education, substance abuse, housing, and public assistance departments or units within federal and state governments, the legislative and the judicial/legal systems; deprofessionalization of casework and supervisory staff; excessive caseloads; inadequate training, support, monitoring, and supervision of child welfare caseworkers; frequent turnover of casework staff; inadequate or incompetent legal representation for children and their parents; inadequate recruitment, training, and supervision of related and nonrelated foster parents; inadequate supply of competent relatives or foster parents to meet the demand for children requiring substitute caregivers; children remaining in foster care without adoption long after parental rights have been terminated; children experiencing multiple placements because chosen caregivers lack the desire, interest, skills, and/or supports to meet the child's needs; too few outcome-based evaluations of service interventions with children and parents; confusion about what works; and arbitrary decisions by ever changing political climates at the federal and state levels. Below we will review five federal "reforms" that have impacted child welfare policies and practices. As you read these summaries and the more detailed discussion of federal laws that follows, remember the discussion of the characteristics and number of children who were served in foster care in 2000 through 2005, and ask yourself —"How does this make a difference to the child in foster care?" Then you will begin to understand what "reform" really means.

Family Foster Care, a Response to Institutional Care

From the White House Conference in 1909 through the 1960s, the main goal of the foster care program was to provide a safe, nurturing environment for children who could not live at home because of parental maltreatment or inadequacy. Child welfare practice focused on helping the child adjust to the foster home and helping the foster family with the child's development. The serious limitations of this phase were the lack of incentives within the system to work toward family reunification and the lack of recognition that the family of origin was important to the child in care. Because the main emphasis was on the child's well-being, it usually appeared safer to leave the child in care indefinitely.

The Permanency Planning Movement

A major impetus for reform was the growing recognition that although foster care had been intended as a temporary substitute for the child's own home, many children remained in foster care for years, sometimes moving through many different foster homes (Maas & Engler, 1959). The work of Bowlby (1969) and others (Geiser, 1973; Littner, 1975) lent theoretical weight to the notion that separations and disruption of emotional attachments would lead to difficulties in forming healthy attachments and would be damaging to children.

In response to these concerns, and because the critical mass of children in care had risen to over 520,000 by 1977, the 1970s saw the advent of permanency planning. *Permanency planning* is the "systematic process of carrying out, within a limited period, a set of goal direct activities designed to help children and youths live in families that offer continuity of relationships with nurturing parents or caretakers, and the opportunity to offer lifetime relationships" (Maluccio & Fein, 1983, p. 197). Moving children out of care into adoption became a desired goal. Throughout the 1970s the legal, attitudinal, and procedural barriers to moving children into adoptive families were systematically addressed through a variety of demonstration programs and national dissemination efforts (Pike et al., 1977; Emlen, 1978; Fanshel & Shinn, 1978; Jones, 1978; Downs, 1981). In many states, statutes were revised to make clearer the grounds for termination of parental rights, and to mandate case review and case planning. Underlying this phase was the belief that "no child is unadoptable" (Churchill, Carlson, & Nybell, 1979).

Family Preservation

As professionals demonstrated that the backlog of children in indeterminate foster care could be reduced, they promoted the understanding that some children would not have needed care in the first place if services had been available to their families. In the early 1980s, this awareness sparked practice strategies and legal reform to prevent family breakup (Nelson, Landsman, & Deutelbaum, 1990). Two major pieces of federal legislation, the Indian Child Welfare Act of 1978 and the Adoption Assistance and Child Welfare Act of 1980, gave federal support to state efforts to make diligent and focused efforts to preserve the family before deciding to place a child in foster care (Ratterman, Dodson, & Hardin, 1987). By 1984 the number of children in foster care (both foster family and group care) declined to 275,000 as a result of vigorous permanence planning and family preservation services.

Family Continuity and Kinship/Relative Care

By 1991, however, the number of children in care had climbed once again, despite permanency planning, family preservation, and adoption reforms. The onset of the crack cocaine epidemic, the spread of HIV/AIDS to women and children, and economic stressors were contributing factors to the fragmentation of families. Although the number of children entering care increased, the number of foster families prepared to receive them was in sharp decline, creating a placement crisis (U.S. General Accounting Office, 1989). The term *lobby bodies* referred to a growing phenomenon, children filling up the waiting room of the child welfare office waiting for a placement.

For these and other reasons, the focus has turned to the possibilities of placing more children with relatives. Although "relative placement" had been a possibility for many years, it now has become a more explicit agency policy. Kinship care provides continuity of family relationships for the child, and its use also has helped alleviate the foster home shortage crisis (Allen, Lakin, McFadden, & Wasserman, 1992; McFadden & Downs, 1995). See Chapter 9 for a discussion of kinship care.

Figure 8.2 outlines the phases of child welfare reform in the twentieth century.

Current federal policy gives preference to relative placement over nonrelative placement when out-of-home placement is necessary. Section 505 of the Personal Responsibility and Work Opportunity Reconciliation Act (PRWORA) of 1996 amended Title IV-E (the federal funding law) by requiring, "States shall consider giving preference to an adult relative over a non-related caregiver when determining a placement for a child/youth, provided that the relative caregiver meets all relevant state child protection standards." (PRWORA, 1996.)

Safety, Well-Being, and Permanency

In response to growing concerns that family preservation practices were compromising the safety and well-being of children, The Adoption and Safe Families Act (ASFA) of 1997 was passed. ASFA clarified that the "safety of the child is paramount" in child welfare practice. It identified

Figure 8.2   *Child Welfare Reforms in the Twentieth Century*

Phase	Time	Reform	Focus	Cumulative Contribution to Field
One	1909–1970 White House Conference	Family Foster Care	Foster Family	Children belong in a family rather than an institution
Two	1970s	Permanency Planning	Adoptive Family	Children belong in a permanent family; no child is unadoptable
Three	1980s Adoption Assistance and Child Welfare Act	Family Preservation	Biological Parents	Children belong with their biological parents; reasonable efforts must be demonstrated to maintain family
Four	1990s	Family Continuity	Extended/ Augmented Family	Children belong in a family network that continues

Source: E. J. McFadden & S. W. Downs (1995, April), Family continuity: The new paradigm in permanence planning. *Community Alternatives, 7*(1).

parental behaviors toward the child or a sibling that did not necessitate consideration of "reasonable efforts to preserve the family," that is, family preservation services. It required the termination of parental rights for children who had been in foster care for fifteen of the last twenty-two months unless the situation met one of the few exemptions for not terminating parental rights (*Adoption and Safe Families Act of 1997, 1997*).

In addition, several statutes have been passed amending Title IV-E of the Social Security Act to ensure that children are age-appropriately engaged in permanency planning hearings, that foster care and adoption providers are screened for criminality and child abuse and neglect, and to encourage and facilitate placement of children transracially and across state boundaries (*The Child and Family Services Improvement Act of 2006, P.L. 109-288; The Multiethnic Placement Act of 1994 as Amended by the Interethnic Placement Provisions of 1996; The Deficit Reduction Act of 2005, P.L. 109-171; The Safe and Timely Interstate Placement of Foster Children Act of 2006, P.L. 109-239; The Adam Walsh Child Protection and Safety Act of 2006, P.L. 109-248*).

The Child and Family Services Review process has focused the system on outcomes that ensure child well-being, including preserving family ties with parents, relatives, and siblings; reducing the number of placements and maintaining stability in placements; meeting the educational, physical, and mental health needs of children in out-of-home care; preparing youth for emancipation from foster care and independent living; and ensuring that substitute caregivers are screened for criminality and child abuse and neglect (Children's Bureau, 2007)

All these statutes are discussed in more detail below and in Chapter 9.

Residential Care—Renewed Interest

Since the 1909 White House Conference, the place of residential care in the foster care system has been marginalized. Family-based care has been and continues to be the preferred alternative to own home care. However, the inability of the family-based system to competently provide for care that promotes the well-being, permanency, and stability of children, specifically those presenting behavioral or emotional challenges and older children who choose not to live in a family setting, has led to a renewed discussion of the role of residential care as a placement option for children. (Knapp, 2006; Children's Bureau, 2006; CWLA, 2005; McKenzie, 1998; Courtney & Maluccio, 1999; Wolins & Piliavin, 1964)

FEDERAL ROLE IN CHILD WELFARE

Federal, state, and local governments have shared responsibilities for defining, administering, and funding the foster care system. Essentially, the federal government's role is to provide funding to states to deliver child welfare services in accordance with federal policies designed to ensure the safety, well-being, and permanency of children and to monitor states' compliance with federal standards. The federal government does not require any state to comply with its policies and standards. However, any state that chooses to receive federal funds for its foster care services must comply. The states or local units of government, as determined by state laws, are responsible for the actual delivery of foster care services either directly or through purchase of service arrangements with organizations who meet the legal requirements established by the states. Further, states and local units of government are responsible for financing foster care services for children and families who do not meet the eligibility standards for federal funding and contribute matching funds for the federal funds.

Title IV-E of the Social Security Act, as amended by the Indian Child Welfare Act of 1978; the Multiethnic Placement Act of 1994, as Amended by the Interethnic Placement Provisions of 1996; and the Adoption and Safe Families Act of 1997 constitutes the basic federal policy and financing framework for foster care services. In 2006, four other federal statutes were passed that have provisions that reinforce ASFA's provisions for timely, safe, and permanent placements for children in the child welfare system through further amendments to Title IV-E. These were the Deficit Reduction Act of 2005, P.L. 109-171; the Safe and Timely Interstate Placement of Foster Children Act of 2006, P.L. 109-239; the Adam Walsh Child Protection and Safety Act of 2006, P.L. 109-248; and the Child and Family Services Improvement Act of 2006, P.L. 109-288. We will briefly discuss each of these. All are cited in the Reference section and are accessible on the Children's Bureau web site for the reader who wishes to review the complete statutes and the Children's Bureau interpretations and policy memoranda regarding the laws.

Title IV of the Social Security Act

Titles IV-B and IV-E of the Social Security Act are the primary sources of federal funds for state child welfare services, including protective services, family preservation, foster care, and adoption assistance. The federal government has been sharing the cost of foster care with the states since 1961. Prior to that time, foster care was a state responsibility. Federal foster care was part of the Aid to Families with Dependent Children (AFDC), Title IV-A appropriations and eligibility linked to AFDC from 1961 to 1980, when the Adoption Assistance and Child Welfare Act provided for authorizing foster care under Title IV-E. Over the years, various laws have been passed that amended Titles IV-B and IV-E. Here, we focus on the laws specific to Title IV-E

To receive federal funds, each state must submit a State Plan in accordance with established procedures, determine each child's eligibility for IV-E funding, and document expenditures made for the eligible children in four different categories: foster care maintenance payments, short and long-term training for staff and foster parents, administrative expenditures, and costs of required data collection system. The federal government matches the expenditures at different rates, ranging from 50 percent to 80 percent. As expected, these requirements are ripe for error and disputes and are time-consuming, without evident direct benefit to the child. No one disputes that the current structure is inflexible and, because of its noncapped entitlement, emphasizes removal from the home. However, to date, there has been no consensus on how to change this relationship. The federal government's latest or most recent budget is in excess of $6.8 billion per year in IV-E foster care and adoption assistance payments to states (U.S. Department of Health and Human Services, 2007; Radel, 2005; The Pew Commission on Children in Foster Care, 2004). All the Acts discussed in this section have amended or added provisions in Title IV-E, which the state then is required to meet to be eligible for funding.

The Indian Child Welfare Act of 1978

The Indian Child Welfare Act (ICWA) acknowledged the sovereignty of federally recognized Indian tribes to govern the care and custody of their children. ICWA grants Tribal courts exclusive jurisdiction to decide child welfare cases involving an Indian child who lives on a reservation, or is domiciled or resides on a reservation but temporarily lives elsewhere, or is a ward of the Tribal court. Its purpose is to protect the best interests of Indian children and to promote stability and security of Indian tribes and families by establishing federal standards for the removal of Indian children from their parents or Indian custodians. ICWA also sets the priority for the placement of such children in foster or adoptive homes that reflect the unique values of Indian culture. It provides financial assistance to Indian tribes for operation of child and family service programs.

"Indian child" is defined as any unmarried person under 18 who is a member of an Indian tribe or who is eligible for membership in an Indian tribe and is the biological child of a member of an Indian tribe [25 USC § 1903 (iv (4)].

States and tribes continue to negotiate the complexities of a quasi-sovereign nation within a sovereign nation. Currently, federal funding for child welfare services are provided through the states and not directly to the tribes, who have been lobbying since 1979 to have funding provided directly to them and place them in a "direct relationship" to the Children's Bureau. Legislation remains before the U.S. Congress to make these changes. The U.S. Government Accountability Office, in a 2005 report to Congress, stated:

> Twenty-five years after the passage of the Indian Child Welfare Act, we know very little about the effect of this law on moving American Indian children in foster care to permanent homes in a timely manner. The scarcity of data on outcomes for children subject to the law, along with variation in how individual states, courts, social workers, and tribes interpret and implement ICWA make it difficult to generalize how the law is being implemented or its effects on American Indian children. (GAO, April 2005, p. 58)

The Multiethnic Placement Act of 1994 as Amended by the Interethnic Placement Provisions of 1996

The Multiethnic Placement Act (MEPA) was passed to address the policy bias against transracial foster care and adoptive placements that have existed in the child welfare system since the 1970s.

The consensus in 1994 was that this bias resulted in minority children remaining in foster care for long periods when there were nonminority families available and willing to adopt them.

When passed in 1994, MEPA stated:

> An agency or entity that receives federal assistance and is involved in adoption or foster care placement may not
>
> (A) categorically deny to any person the opportunity to become an adoptive or foster parent, solely on the basis of the race, color, or national origin of the adoptive or foster parent or of the child involved; or
>
> (B) delay or deny the placement of a child for adoption or into foster care, or otherwise discriminate in making a placement decision, solely on the basis of the race, color, or national origin or the adoptive or foster parent, or the child, involved. (42 U.S.C. 5115a)

Practice basically continued as before until the "solely" language was removed by the Interethnic Placement (IEP) provisions of 1996. Current language is

> Neither the state nor any entity in the state that receives funds from the federal government and is involved in adoption or foster care placements may
>
> (A) deny to any person the opportunity to become an adoptive or a foster parent on the basis of race, color, or national origin of the person or of the child involved; or
>
> (B) delay or deny the placement of a child for adoption or into foster care on the basis of race, color, or national origin of the adoptive or foster parent, or the child involved. [42 USC § 1996 (h)]

MEPA and IEP do not apply to Indian children who are subject to the Indian Child Welfare Act of 1978. The goals of MEPA and IEP are to:

❖ decrease the length of time that children wait to be adopted;
❖ facilitate the recruitment and retention of foster and adoptive parents who can meet the distinctive needs of children awaiting placement; and
❖ eliminate discrimination on the basis of the race, color, or national origin of the child or the prospective parents.

The operative standard in foster care or adoptive placements has been and continues to be "the best interests of the individual child/youth." The Health and Human Services Guidance issued after the 1996 amendments stated, "Any decision to consider the use of race as a necessary element of a placement decision must be based on concerns arising out of the circumstances of the individual case" (Health and Human Services, 1997) Any consideration of race, color, or national origin in foster or adoptive placements must be *narrowly tailored* to advance the child's best interests and must be made as an *individualized determination* of each child's needs and in light of a specific prospective adoptive or foster care parent's capacity to care for that particular child.

MEPA/IEP requires states to develop plans that "provide for the diligent recruitment of potential foster and adoptive families that reflect the ethnic and racial diversity of children in the state for whom foster and adoptive homes are needed" [42 USC 622 (b) (9)]. A diligent recruitment plan should include the following:

- ❖ A description of the characteristics of waiting children.
- ❖ Specific strategies to reach all parts of community.
- ❖ Diverse methods of disseminating both general and child-specific information.
- ❖ Strategies for assuring that all prospective parents have timely access to the home study process, including location and hours of service that facilitate access by all members of the community.
- ❖ Strategies for training staff to work with diverse cultural, racial, and economic communities.
- ❖ Strategies for dealing with linguistic barriers.
- ❖ Nondiscriminatory fee structures.
- ❖ Procedures for a timely search for prospective parents for a waiting child, including the use of exchanges and other interagency efforts, provided that such procedures must ensure that placement of a child in an appropriate household is not delayed by the search for a same race or ethnic placement.

For the most part, the limited research on American children fostered or adopted transracially has relied on foster–adoptive parent statements of their impressions of their foster–adopted child's adjustment to the placement. However, if we look at the existing body of research, clinical summaries, and writings in which transracially adopted children speak out about their adoption experience and its impact on their development, we can identify areas for caseworkers and foster–adoptive parents to address prior to and during the foster–adoption process. Children and their parents report a need to have more information and support in handling issues involving race and racism. Children are reticent to raise concerns about racial incidents in school or the community with their parents. Children feel isolated or not fully accepted in families, schools, and communities where they are the only child or one of few children of their race or ethnicity. Children are constantly confronted with the fact that they are adopted and "don't really belong." Parents want to raise all their children in the same way.

Parents feel unaccepted by the communities to which their children are tied racially or ethnically. Parents feel that the agency should provide more information about the issues of transracial adoption before the adoption. Parents want to be connected with other parents who have adopted transracially (Trenka, Oparah, & Shin, 2006; Merz & Hightower, 2005; Weinberg, Waldman, van Dulmen, & Scarr, 2004; de Haymes & Simon, 2003; Lee, 2003: Steinberg & Hall, 2003; Patton, 2000; Eldridge, 1999; Crumbley, 1999).

It is critical for caseworkers to identify and acknowledge their personal biases and feelings about transracial adoption before engaging with children or potential adoptive parents to discuss the issue. Even though the laws have changed, caseworkers' personal biases and feelings continue to present unnecessary delays and denials of adoption of children by parents of different races. The caseworker has the professional duty and professional responsibility to put aside personal feelings and provide evidence-based information to the child and the potential adoptive parents. Finally, consideration must be given to whether the child is of an age to consent to his or her adoption under state laws, and the potential adoptive parent must decide if a transracial family is within his or her value system and capabilities.

The Adoption and Safe Families Act of 1997

The Adoption and Safe Families Act of 1997 (ASFA) was passed to clarify and change provisions of The Adoption Assistance and Child Welfare Act of 1980. Among other things, ASFA:

- ❖ clarified the reasonable efforts requirements—child safety is paramount;
- ❖ required case planning to focus on child safety, well-being, and permanency;
- ❖ established expedited timeframes for permanency hearings and termination of parental rights;
- ❖ provided for opportunity for child and his or her caregivers to be notified of and present for court hearings;
- ❖ mandated use of the Federal Parent Locator Services to locate absent parents;
- ❖ mandated criminal record checks for prospective foster and adoptive parents;
- ❖ clarified eligible populations for independent living services;
- ❖ required case documentation of efforts to place children for adoption;
- ❖ provided incentive payments to states to increase adoptions; and
- ❖ required a report to Congress on state policies and practices with respect to placement with relatives (kinship care).

With the passage of the Adoption and Safe Families Act of 1997, the American people, through their legislators, moved the issues of child safety, well-being, and permanency into the forefront of child welfare policy. Long intended as a "temporary" service for children and families, foster care—and the child welfare system—has become a way of life for too many children. Many children have not found permanency outcomes; in 2000, nearly a third of the 550,000 children in foster care had been in care for three years or more. About 130,000 children were identified as unlikely ever to return home and were awaiting a permanent plan. Minority children, who make up 55 percent of children in care, wait longer for permanent homes than do white children (AFCARS, 2002). To address the problem of too many children staying in foster care too long, the law expedites procedures and requires states to file termination of parental rights petitions for any child in foster care for fifteen of the most recent twenty-two months, unless the child is in the care of a relative or other possible compelling reasons, such as termination would not be in the child's best interests or the state has not provided the family of the child the services necessary for safe return of the child.

The issue of safety was also of concern to policymakers. Of the thousand or so children who die of abuse and neglect each year, nearly half are known to child protection agencies (Pizzigati, 1998). Public concern has mounted as citizens read in their daily newspapers about children at risk in their families or in the systems designed to protect them. ASFA addresses child safety by explicitly eliminating, in some dangerous situations, the requirement that child welfare agencies make "reasonable efforts" to preserve families before placing the child in care. To further protect children and promote quick permanency decisions, the law requires mandatory filing of termination of parental rights petitions in certain extremely dangerous situations: when there has been the murder of another child by the parent, abandonment of an infant, or felony assault resulting in serious bodily harm to a child. Criminal background checks for foster and adoptive parents are required. States must report annually to the federal government on their performance in protecting children.

Another aspect of the renewed focus on improving services to children themselves, apart from services to their families, is the requirement in the Act that agencies address the developmental needs of children. ASFA requires the Department of Health and Human Services to prepare an annual report on state child welfare agency attainment of child well-being standards in health, mental health, education, and continuity of placement (Maza, 2002). This focus reaffirms that foster care should be a service focused on children's needs and should be accountable for how children fare while under state care. However, compliance may force states into hard choices concerning resource allocation for child services as opposed to family preservation services.

ASFA addresses the issue of timely permanency by *permitting* states to engage in concurrent planning for reunification and placement for adoption with permanent legal guardians, and *requires* states to concurrently "identify, recruit, process, and approve a qualified family for adoption at the same time it petitions for termination of parental rights."

It permitted youth who accumulate assets of $5,000 or less to remain eligible for Title IV-E–funded independent living services.

The Foster Care Independence Act of 1999

The Foster Care Independence Act of 1999 replaced the Independent Living Initiative established in 1986 under Title IV-E. The Act:

❖ establishes the John H. Chafee Foster Care Independence Program, which
1. increases funding for independent living programs,
2. provides room and board payments for young adults under 21 years who are out of foster care,
3. provides that states can give Medicaid coverage to young adults aged 18 to 21 if they are in foster care on their eighteenth birthday,
4. bases the funding allocation on the total number of children in foster care irrespective of whether it is Title IV-E- or state-funded
5. requires participation of young people in the planning and assumption of responsibility for achieving independence,
6. increases funding for training staff and caregivers on adolescent issues, and
7. requires development of outcome measures and evaluation by the Department of Health and Human Services (HHS).
❖ increases the child's asset limit to $10,000 for Title IV-E eligibility.
❖ requires states to ensure that foster parents are trained to care for the children placed with them.

Children aging out of foster care with limited ability to support themselves or to pursue advanced education is a continuing challenge for all states. In Chapter 9, we will explore some promising practices developing out of the Chafee Independence Programs that might yield better outcomes.

The Deficit Reduction Act of 2005

In response to deficiencies found in the legal system during the first round of the Child and Family Services Reviews, the Deficit Reduction Act provides for training of judges, attorneys, and other legal personnel in child welfare cases, as well as cross-training with child welfare agency staff and contractors; collaboration with the courts; allows public access to court proceedings provided that the safety and well-being of the child, parents, and family is ensured; allows administrative costs for an otherwise Title IV-E eligible child when placed with an unlicensed/unapproved relative or facility; and provides adoption assistance eligibility for a child who was Aid to Families with Dependent Children (AFDC) eligible at the time of removal from a specified relative.

The Safe and Timely Interstate Placement of Foster Children Act of 2006

The Safe and Timely Interstate Placement of Foster Children Act, effective October 1, 2006, provides that states must have policies and procedures that will ensure that interstate home studies are completed within 60 days unless the delay is due to circumstances beyond the state's control; in that case, an additional 15 days is permitted. To eliminate barriers and delays in interstate foster care or adoptive placements, courts are to inquire about the availability of both in- and out-of-state placements when conducting permanency planning hearings and to provide mechanisms so that parents, children, caregivers, and witnesses do not have to travel to give testimony. Furthermore, it requires that the agency provide a copy of the child's health and education records to the caregiver at the time of placement and to the child at the time of emancipation from foster care.

The Adam Walsh Child Protection and Safety Act of 2006

The Adam Walsh Child Protection and Safety Act, effective October 1, 2006, provides that unless state legislation is required, the state must have procedures for conducting fingerprint-based checks of the National Crime Information Databases (NCID) for all prospective foster and adoptive parents and must check the child abuse and neglect registry in each state in which the prospective foster or adoptive parent or any adult member of the household resided in the previous 5 years.

The Child and Family Services Improvement Act of 2006

The Child and Family Services Improvement Act, recognizing the importance of the caseworker–child–parent relationship to positive outcomes for children and a strong correlation between caseworker visits and positive outcomes, requires that caseworkers make monthly visits to all children in foster care and encourages better training and support for casework staff. In addition, recognizing that between 60 and 75 percent of all foster care cases are reported to include substance abuse, it provides funding of regional partnerships to address methamphetamine or other substance abuse.

Child and Family Services Review Process

The Child and Family Services Review (CFSR) process is "a results-oriented comprehensive monitoring system designed to promote continuous improvement in the outcomes experienced by children and families who come into contact with public child welfare agencies" (Federal Register, 2006, p. 32969). This system was developed by the Children's Bureau to monitor the states. It is probably the most exciting and potentially beneficial "reform" to child welfare since federal and state governments entered into a partnership for serving children that required out-of-home placement. It is focused on safety, permanency, and well-being outcomes for the children and the systemic factors that support these outcomes. While sanctions are possible, the actual implementation has demonstrated a greater desire to improve the systems than to sanction the states. The Administration for Children and Families does not require the states to meet the national standards. Rather, it expects states to meet the progress agreed on in the approved Program Improvement Plans (PIPS).

The process is continuous one and involves the establishment of the seven outcomes and seven system factors, as well as expected national standards for each outcome and indicator; statewide assessment; on-site reviews by federal and state teams; completion of Summary of Findings; state development of PIPs; federal review and approval of the PIPs; and implementation and monitoring of the PIPs with quarterly federal monitoring. The complete process is repeated in each state every 5 years.

The outcomes are:

- ❖ Children are first and foremost protected from abuse and neglect.
- ❖ Children are safely maintained in their homes whenever possible and appropriate.
- ❖ Children have permanency and stability in their living situations.
- ❖ The continuity of family relationships and connections is preserved for children.
- ❖ Families have enhanced capacity to provide for their children's needs
- ❖ Children receive appropriate services to meet their educational needs.
- ❖ Children receive adequate services to meet their physical and mental health needs.

In addition to these outcomes, there are seven systemic factors required. States must have:

- ❖ a statewide information system,
- ❖ a case review system,
- ❖ a quality assurance system,
- ❖ staff training and development,
- ❖ an array of services to meet the needs of the child and family,
- ❖ a plan for responsiveness to the community, and
- ❖ foster and adoptive parent licensing, recruitment, and retention plans and services.

Based on the results and lessons learned from Round 1, the data methodology has been changed for some of the indicators for these outcomes and systemic factors in Round 2, begun in 2008. Instead of using single data measures, data composites will be used. Data composites will account for the states' strengths and weaknesses in a given area rather than relying on one measure. Furthermore, emphasis is placed on states assessing the "whys or reasons" for its performance in both the statewide assessment and the PIPs. The Administration for Children and Families begins round 2 of the CFSR process in 2008 (Milner, 2007; Federal Register, 2006).

All 50 states, the District of Columbia, and Puerto Rico were reviewed between 2001 and 2005. No state was found to be in substantial compliance with all measures. The CFSR's major findings are presented in Tables 8.1 and 8.2.

What can we learn from these results? First, it is clear that overall states performed better on systemic factors than they did on outcome factors. However, even on the systemic factors, less than half the states achieved substantial conformity in the adequacy of case review systems and service array—both critical components of service outcomes. Two indicators for the continuity of

Table 8.1 *Child and Family Services Reviews Findings from the First Round of 52 Reviews*

Findings on the Outcomes, Indicators, and National Standards
Number (%) of States Achieving Substantial Conformity with the 7 Outcome Measures, Number (%) Receiving a Rating of "Strength" on the 23 Indicators, and the Number (%) Meeting National Standards

Outcomes and Indicators	Number (%) Achieving Substantial Conformity	Number (%) Receiving a Rating of "Strength"	Number (%) Meeting National Standard*
Safety Outcome 1—Children are first and foremost, protected from abuse and neglect	6 (11.5)		
Item 1: Timeliness of investigations		21 (40.4)	
Item 2: Repeat maltreatment		17 (32.7)	17 (32.7)
Safety Outcome 2—Children are safely maintained in their homes when possible	6 (11.5)		
Item 3: Services to prevent removal		21 (40.4)	
Item 4: Risk of harm		17 (32.7)	
Permanency Outcome 1—Children have permanency and stability in their living situations	0		
Item 5: Foster care re-entry		26 (50.0)	26 (50.0)
Item 6: Stability of foster care placements		5 (9.6)	14 (26.9)
Item 7: Permanency goal for child		5 (9.6)	
Item 8: Reunification, guardianship, and placement with relatives (for 2002–2004). Independent living services (for 2001).		12 (23.1)	19 (36.5)
Item 9: Adoption		6 (11.5)	14 (26.9)
Item 10: Other planned living arrangement		17 (32.7)	
Permanency Outcome 2—The continuity of family relationships and connections is preserved	7 (13.5)		
Item 11: Proximity of placement		49 (94.2)	
Item 12: Placement with siblings		36 (69.2)	
Item 13: Visiting with parents and siblings in foster care		16 (30.8)	
Item 14: Preserving connections		21 (40.4)	
Item 15: Relative placement		21 (40.4)	
Item 16: Relationship of child in care with parents		21 (40.4)	
Well-Being Outcome 1—Families have enhanced capacity to provide for children's needs	0		
Item 17: Needs/services of child, parents, and foster parents		1 (1.9)	
Item 18: Child/family involvement in case planning		5 (9.6)	
Item 19: Worker visits with child		13 (25.0)	
Item 20: Worker visits with parents		7 (13.5)	
Well-Being Outcome 2—Children receive services to meet their educational needs	16 (30.8)		
Item 21: Educational needs of child		16 (30.8)	
Well-Being Outcome 3—Children receive services to meet their physical and mental health needs are met	1 (1.9)		
Item 22: Physical health of child		20 (38.5)	
Item 23: Mental health of child		4 (7.7)	

* Meeting the national standard for maltreatment in foster care was part of the assessment of substantial conformity with Safety Outcome 1. However, there was no specific item corresponding to maltreatment in foster care because the incidence is very low and it was determined that cases selected for the sample would rarely involve maltreatment in foster care.

Source: U.S. Department of Health and Human Services, Administration for Children, Youth and Families, Children's Bureau, (2006). *A report to Congress on the interjurisdictional placement of children. Appendix II.*

Table 8.2 *Findings on Systemic Factors for 52*

Systemic Factors	Number (%) Achieving Substantial Conformity	Number (%) Rated as "Strength"
I. Statewide Information System	45 (87)	
Item 24: System can identify the status, demographic characteristics, location, and goals of children in foster care		45 (87)
II. Case Review System	13 (25)	
Item 25: Process for developing a case plan and for joint case planning with parents		6 (12)
Item 26: Process for 6-month case reviews		42 (81)
Item 27: Process for 12-month permanency hearings		26 (50)
Item 28: Process for seeking TPR in accordance with ASFA		22 (42)
Item 29: Process for notifying caregivers of reviews and hearings and for opportunity for them to be heard		26 (50)
III. Quality Assurance System	35 (67)	
Item 30: Standards to ensure quality services and ensure children's safety and health		44 (85)
Item 31: Identifiable QA system that evaluates the quality of services and improvements		31 (60)
IV. Training	34 (65)	
Item 32: Provision of initial staff training		34 (65)
Item 33: Provision of ongoing staff training that addresses necessary skills and knowledge		27 (52)
Item 34: Provision of training for caregivers and adoptive parents that addresses necessary skills and knowledge		38 (73)
V. Service Array	23 (44)	
Item 35: Availability of services		25 (48)
Item 36: Accessibility of services in all jurisdictions		9 (17)
Item 37: Ability to individualize services to meet unique needs		30 (58)
VI. Agency Responsiveness to the Community	49 (94)	
Item 38: Engages in ongoing consultation with critical stakeholders in developing the CFSP		46 (88)
Item 39: Develops annual progress reports in consultation with stakeholders		40 (77)
Item 40: Coordinates services with other federal programs		45 (87)
VII. Foster and Adoptive Parent Licensing, Recruitment and Retention	43 (83)	
Item 41: Standards for foster family and child care institutions		51 (98)
Item 42: Standards are applied equally to all foster family and child care institutions		43 (83)
Item 43: Conducts necessary criminal background checks		50 (96)
Item 44: Diligent recruitment of foster and adoptive families that reflect children's racial and ethnic diversity		21 (40)
Item 45: Uses cross-jurisdictional resources to find placements		47 (90)

Source: U.S. Department of Health and Human Services, Administration for Children, Youth and Families, Children's Bureau (2006). *A report to Congress on the interjurisdictional placement of children. Appendix II.*

family relationships outcome were achieved—children are being placed geographically near their parents and they are being placed in greater numbers with their siblings. Otherwise, outcome conformity was dismal despite all the "reforms."

STATE ROLE IN CHILD WELFARE

Policy Framework

Each state establishes its own laws, policies, and procedures for the foster care program. If the state wants to receive federal funds to provide child welfare services to eligible children and their families, it must have laws, policies, and procedures that meet the minimum expectations established in the federal laws discussed previously. For example, ASFA states that a permanency hearing must be held 12 months after the child is placed in out-of-home care. Thus, for a state to comply, its laws for court or administrative hearings must provide that the permanency planning hearing be held no less than every 12 months. It may, if it chooses, require permanency hearings be held at shorter intervals; but it cannot specify that they be held less frequently.

Funding Framework

Each state must have a comprehensive child welfare system that provides for the protection and placement of all its children, not just those eligible for Title IV-E funding. Furthermore, Title IV-E funding must be "matched" with state funds at an amount established using the state's Medicaid participation rate. The State Plan system established for Title IV-E requires that the system provide the same protections and care options to all children, irrespective of the funding source. Thus, states participating in Title IV-E must fund services for Title IV-E ineligible children (U.S. Department of Health and Human Services, 23 January 2007).

States have total discretion in determining how it meets its match requirements and its obligations to fund non-Title IV-E services and placements. Most rely on some form of shared responsibility between the state and local units of government. Many seek financial support from individual donations and philanthropic organizations. The total non-federal expenditures for foster care is not known.

Service Delivery Framework

States define the scope of services provided and the manner in which services are delivered, consistent with federal standards. A state may choose to deliver services with state employees; local government employees; employees of private, nonprofits or private, for profit agencies; or individuals or some combination of those. Irrespective of who delivers the services, the state remains accountable to the federal government for the child welfare program.

Each state is required to develop certification, licensing, training, and monitoring systems to ensure that children are protected and services promote their safety, well-being, and permanency.

FOSTER CARE PLACEMENT OPTIONS

There are several options available for foster care placement. The choice of placement should rest on what meets the "best interests of the child." However, if this were the case, every placement decision would begin with an assessment of the child's needs and then identify the most appropriate placement that could meet those needs. The reality is that policy biases and resource availability dictate the actual placement of most children. Too frequently, children are placed with limited knowledge of their needs and desires. We will discuss this issue further in Chapter 9. In this chapter, we focus on identifying the different options and the characteristics of each.

Kinship/Relative Foster Care

Kinship or relative care—the term used in federal legislation and the CFSR process—is the preferred form of care for most children who must live away from their parents. Relative care that takes place within the foster care system, in which the relative caregivers are licensed or certified foster parents or the child is a court ward placed with the relative under the abuse/neglect provisions and the relative is not licensed or certified, is called formal kinship/relative care.

Policy and Program Issues in Kinship Care

Kinship care, as a program alternative for children in need of child welfare services, spans various categories of child welfare programs and traditional legal arrangements: family preservation, foster care, guardianship, and adoption. The linkage of formal child welfare services and kinship care is congruent with current thinking on the importance of culturally competent human service delivery systems and on the psychosocial need of children for continuity and ongoing attachments.

The issues are complex and somewhat overlapping. One issue on which there is general agreement concerns the need of kin providers for social support and access to resources for themselves and their young relatives (Dubowitz, 1990; Berrick, Barth, & Needell, 1994; Terling-Watt, 2001; Ehrle & Geen, 2002, The Pew Charitable Trusts, 2007). Children in relative placement may have very conflicted histories and present daunting behavioral, educational, and medical challenges. In addition to the aftereffects of abuse and neglect, the children may have serious diseases such as HIV/AIDS. Children with incarcerated parents are frequently in the care of relatives and are thought to have significant unresolved issues around separation and trauma (Hungerford, 1996; Slavin, 2000). Children with many different kinds of complex problems may need—in addition to the love, support, and sense of belonging they have in an extended family context—access to professional services of many types if they are to be helped and if the placement is to stay intact (Edelboch, Liu, & Martin, 2002; (The Pew Charitable Trusts, 2007).

Family caregivers also have needs. If employed, they may have concerns about continuing to work while undertaking new caretaking responsibilities. Older relatives, such as grandparents, may have health concerns for themselves or their spouse. Their lives may have grown to include interests and activities that conflict with child caring demands but which they are loath to put aside. They may need improved housing, respite care, support groups, and access to legal counseling (Generations United, 2006).

Family dynamics in kinship arrangements may be complicated and volatile. For example, Warren (2001) notes that parent-absent adolescents may feel contempt for the parent who failed them, and they can turn their anger against themselves in depression or displace it onto grandparents who are raising them. Such situations require expert mental health services and family therapy (Minkler, Roe, & Price, 1992). One group of kin caregivers, adult siblings of children needing care, may have special issues of family dynamics and role conflicts. These arrangements often do not come to the attention of the child welfare system and very little is known about them.

Many child welfare and other organizations are increasing their efforts to help kinship caregivers. For example, the American Association of Retired Persons funds telephone "warm lines" for grandparents to use when feeling overburdened and at wit's end, grandparenting classes, and, support groups, and is engaged in national advocacy for subsidized guardianship funding for relatives. (Generations United, 2006; McFadden & Downs, 1995; Crumbley & Little, 1997; Jackson, Mathews, & Zuskin, 1999). However, overall, the service systems around the country to support kin placements are fragmented, lacking in many areas, and hard to access.

Financial and Legal Issues. A serious unresolved problem is providing financial support to kin caregivers, and the problem is exacerbated by the linkage between legal status and eligibility for various forms of public support. One source of financial assistance is Temporary Assistance to Needy Families (TANF), formerly known as public welfare. However, the financial support available for "child only" cases is extremely low. If the grandparent applies for funds on his or her own behalf, the grandparent is subject to the same work requirements as any other applicant, which may not be feasible or helpful to the child (Takas, 1993).

It is possible in some instances as for kin providers to be licensed foster parents. These situations are often referred to as *formal kinship care* to distinguish them from *informal kinship care*, which takes place without changes of custody made through the child welfare system. In formal kinship care, the child is placed by the court in the legal custody of the child welfare agency; financial support for the care of the child is made through foster care payments if the kinship homes meet licensing or approval standards for foster parents; and the kinship caregivers are generally expected to comply with the foster parenting role, such as participating in training and cooperating with the agency in implementing a case plan. If they do not meet licensing/approval standards, then payments are made from TANF funds or special relative/kinship care funds (The Pew Charitable Trusts, 2007).

Treating kin caregivers as foster parents allows them to receive foster care payments, much higher than TANF child only grants. However, many people, including many kin caregivers, have philosophical disagreement with classifying relatives as foster parents; they think that people should not get paid for taking care of their own. Agencies and caregivers may see conflicts between the foster parent role and that of relatives; foster parents are in some sense agents of the agency and answerable to it, whereas relatives may not feel that they are fundamentally accountable to the agency.

Problems with financial support, role conflict, and legal status also arise in permanency planning, if the preferred option for the child is a permanent living arrangement with relatives. Some kin caregivers are willing to make a home for a grandchild or other young relative on a permanent basis, but may be reluctant to legalize this arrangement through adoption (Thornton, 1991). Grandparents, in particular, may find it difficult to assume the parents' role and may be particularly reluctant to be part of a process in which their child's parental rights to his or her child are terminated so the grandparent can legally take that parent's place. Such an arrangement feels unnatural, is contrary to cultural expectations, and may mean a final relinquishment of hope that their adult child will recover from the problems that led to the placement of the children. For these caregivers, long-term foster care or guardianship might be a more workable permanency solution.

> *After all, he knows I'm his granny, I always was and I always will be. I'll always love him and I'll always take care of him. He knows we're permanent. We don't need no adoption to feel permanent.* (A grandmother)

If the grandparent is given guardianship and the case moves out of the system, the caregiver may lose the foster care pay rate as well as foster care support services. On the other hand, if the grandparent adopts the child, she will probably be eligible for an adoption subsidy. Proponents of kinship care suggest that subsidized guardianships may promote a new kind of permanency in formal kinship care (Child Welfare League of America, 1994). Others advocate for a new form of adoption—kinship adoption (Takas, 1993; Hegar & Scannapieco, 1999).

Assessment and Psychosocial Issues. An attitudinal barrier to the use of kinship care is expressed in the adage: "The apple doesn't fall far from the tree," indicating that the problems of the child's parents are related to their family of origin. A competent assessment of the relative's home is necessary to address safety and protection issues. A national body has developed the following list as factors to consider in kinship assessment (Child Welfare League of America, 1994, pp. 44–45).

❖ The quality of the relationship between the relative and the child
❖ The likelihood that the relative can/will protect the child from further maltreatment
❖ The safety of the kinship home and the ability of the relative to provide a nurturing environment (including presence of alcohol or drug involvement)
❖ The willingness of the relative to accept the child into the home
❖ The ability of the relative to meet the developmental needs of the child
❖ The nature and quality of the relationship between the birth parent and the relative, including the birth parent's preference about placement of the child with kin

Assessment of kin homes also requires that workers be aware of their own biases. Kin providers may be much older than the worker and of a different socioeconomic class and race (Dubowitz, 1990; Thornton, 1991; Berrick, Barth, & Needell, 1994). Workers may feel less comfortable working with kin caregivers and prefer working with established foster parents who are known to the agency, have more financial resources, and are better educated. In assessment, workers need to be aware of the possibility that their biases are affecting their perceptions.

A possible disadvantage of kinship care is that the maltreating parent could have easy access to a child or the caregiver may have difficulty establishing boundaries with the parent. Although relatives may appear stable, they may also have some denial about the risk the parent represents to the child, or there may be undetected substance abuse or maltreatment patterns in the family system. It is reassuring that one research project found that children may be less at risk in relative care than in foster care (Zuravin & DePanfilis, 1997). However, there is also less monitoring of relative homes than of unrelated foster homes, raising the possibility of undetected maltreatment (Berrick, Barth, & Needell, 1994). One recent study reported that there was a higher rate of disruption among kin placements than with other types of permanent placements. Reasons for disrupted placements included health limitations of the caregiver, difficulties in the relationship with the children's parents, and difficulty in caring for special needs children (Terling-Watt, 2001). This finding highlights the importance of good assessment in making kin placements and of providing adequate levels of support after they are made.

Despite these concerns, practice experience and research to date suggest that relatives are a viable resource for many children in the child welfare system who need safe, loving homes with people who think they are very special. The home of a relative can give a child a sense of belonging and promote the formation of cultural and personal identity. Kin caregivers may have more positive perceptions about children placed with them than do nonrelated family foster caregivers (Gebel, 1996; Berrick, Barth, & Needell, 1994). If the case plan supports it, the child can have easier access to parents for visiting and possible reunification. Children may be better able to address unresolved issues of loss and family trauma when placed in an extended family context (Crumbley & Little, 1997). More research is needed on effective strategies for strengthening kin placements and on the outcomes of children placed with relatives, including educational attainment, health status, and ongoing safety and protection (The Pew Charitable Trusts, 2007).

Nonrelated Family Foster Care

Family foster care is care provided in the homes of persons who are certified or licensed according to standards established by the states. In general, the standards address the individual's ability to provide care for someone else's child, the types of conditions or behaviors they can handle or would be willing to learn how to handle, includes results of criminal record and child abuse and neglect registry checks for all persons in the household, includes references from people who know the parenting capabilities of the person, and the adequacy and safety of the physical environment, that is, the space available for the child to sleep and play. If a child who must be placed outside the parents' home cannot be placed with a suitable relative, nonrelated family foster care is generally sought.

Foster parents are expected to "parent" the child as they would their own. The supervising caseworker and foster parent negotiate the specific tasks to be performed by each; clarify roles of the child's birth parents, relatives, and foster parents; and work with the child, his or her parents, siblings, other relatives, teachers, counselors, lawyers, guardians, and other treatment professionals to ensure that the child's physical, emotional, and educational needs are being met and that he or she is physically and emotionally safe at all times.

What kinds of problems arise in family foster care, to which the foster parent and social worker must give attention? In undertaking the challenges of foster parenting, competent adults enter a new situation in which they risk failure. Fostering places increased demands to share relationship and possessions on the family, so problems of rivalry and jealousy come into play. Foster parents' own children may have difficulty coping with the loss implicit in the foster care situations (Twigg, 1995).

Foster parents may be unclear about their role or how to fill it appropriately. Foster mothers may see their roles more as "mothering" than providing care in a professional sense (Meidema & Nason-Clark, 1977). Foster parents may find themselves uncertain about actions to control behavior of the children, especially in light of agency discipline policies, which prohibit spanking and other child management techniques.

Being a foster parent is a demanding and intense experience that carries with it enormous pressure and expectations from the agency and the community. Despite the critical role foster parents play in the child welfare system, they are frequently neglected by agencies and social workers. One aspect of neglect is the low board rates paid to foster parents. Most states pay only enough to cover the actual costs of the child's care. In addition to monthly board payment, agencies cover the costs of medical and dental care (although it is hard for many foster parents to locate medical care providers who will accept Medicaid), clothing, and some incidental expenses. Most foster parents simply are not compensated for the services they provide (Downs, 1989).

A second aspect of the neglect of foster parents is their feeling that they do not receive the help they need from agencies. Very often, agencies do not provide sufficient training for foster parents or opportunities for mentoring or support from other foster parents. Little help is given to workers on how to improve worker–foster parent communications. This neglect is highly related to the large turnover of foster parents. In a recent study of why they leave fostering, foster parents cited lack of agency support, poor communication with caseworkers, lack of input into plans for the child, and difficulties with the child's behavior. Those foster parents who continued to foster tended to have more advanced training, services to meet their needs, and support from other foster parents (Rhodes, Orme, & Buehler, 2001).

Factors Predictive of Foster Parent Success. In a study of the maintenance of placements in the Casey Family Homes, Walsh and Walsh (1990) found four factors to be predictive of successful overall functioning of the foster family. These predictors related to the comfort of foster parents in their several roles, to their being motivated to take a foster child by a genuine liking for children, to the foster mother possessing strong emotional coherence, and to the ability of the family to tolerate unassimilated aspects of the child.

Foster Parent Recruitment. Foster parents are selected by means of a home study and licensing/approval process. Licensing standards are set by states. Recruitment that is specifically targeted to finding families for the kinds of children the agency places is a more productive strategy than are generalized campaigns to interest as many families as possible. Agencies recruit new foster parents using multiple sources including newspapers, radio, television announcements, faith communities, current foster parents, service groups, and others. Consultation with community leaders is vital to vigorous recruiting of foster parents from minority racial and ethnic groups. Agencies must also assess the cultural competence of their agency and staff in approaching minority communities (Lakin, Whitfield, & Anderson, 1997).

Foster parents give multiple reasons for wanting to give care: liking children, identifying with abused and neglected children or unhappy children, a wish to provide a community service, and so forth. Even though some reasons appear promising and others may appear suspect, it is more important to focus on parents' skills and strengths in working with children than on their stated motivations. Orientation meetings and preservice training provide opportunities for foster parents to self-select as they learn more about the responsibilities of their role and allow the agency to continue the screening process.

Types of Family Foster Homes

Shelter Homes. Family foster homes may provide temporary shelter for children during the period of initial assessment and determination by the court of a need for out-of-home care. Although children's agencies must have access to temporary shelter homes, assessment of children's need for placement can be made more reliably when they are still in their own homes rather than after they are abruptly separated from parents and placed in an unfamiliar temporary situation.

Long-Term Foster Homes. Long-term foster homes are sought for children who have no chance to return to their parents, who need permanent family living, and who do not wish to be adopted or who have been denied adoption because no adoptive home could be found for them. Some foster parents may feel unable to assume guardianship for or to adopt children in their care but are willing to give a particular child a stable environment and the assurance of a lasting relationship. The Casey Family Homes successfully provide well-resourced long-term care to young people with histories of multiple placements and other problems (Walsh & Walsh, 1990).

Specialized and Treatment Foster Care

Specialized family foster homes are used by some agencies for children who can profit from family living, although they may have emotional problems or developmental disabilities. Some homes specialize in adolescents and take a major role in preparing the youths for independent living. Remuneration is higher in specialized foster homes arrangements than in the usual family foster home arrangement.

Treatment Foster Care. The last decade has witnessed a tremendous increase in the use of treatment foster care and the development of new programs. The intensive service provided in the foster home distinguishes treatment foster care from regular foster care. Treatment foster care is "something of an adaptive hybrid combining elements of residential treatment programming and the foster family environment. . . . This model offers an alternative to both the family foster home and the institution for youngsters who are not appropriately or adequately served in either type of program" (Bryant & Snodgrass, 1990, p. 2). Treatment families have a high degree of training, with an emphasis on behavioral management theory and technique.

Shared Family Care

The newest form of out-of-home care is still at the stage of innovation and experimentation (Kufeldt & Allison, 1990). In this form of care, foster families house both children and their parents. Types of families who have used shared family care include those in which the parents are teens, parents have developmental delays, substance-abusing parents are in recovery, parents are homeless, and parents have unstable physical or mental health.

This form of care has the potential to help some parents learn parenting and home management skills while the child is protected and the family stays intact (Barth & Price, 1999). A major challenge to the development of this form of care is that many states have funding policies that do not permit foster payments for adults in care. Another challenge is recruiting and adequately supporting foster parents.

Residential Group Care

Most often when residential care is mentioned, the general public thinks of the large orphanages of the nineteenth and early twentieth centuries. Residential care, broadly defined, includes any congregate care facility that is owned or leased by an agency and licensed or certified by the designated state organization. In most cases, these facilities are staffed by rotating shifts of employees on a 24-hour basis. However, family-staffed residential care facilities with intensive staff support have shown promise in melding the policy bias that favors family care with the ability to meet the service needs of children who cannot function in typical family foster care. These facilities include group homes within residential communities, campus-based group homes or cottages, boarding schools, residential treatment facilities, emergency shelters, short-term diagnostic care, detention, and secure treatment facilities. These facilities provide a range of services to children with varying conditions or behaviors—counseling, education, health care, mental health services, daily living skills training, advocacy services, and general support for positive youth development (Child Welfare League of America, 2005).

Group care facilities include (1) residential group facilities for the care and protection of dependent and neglected children, including temporary shelters; (2) correctional institutions for delinquent and predelinquent young persons, including training schools, detention homes, and diagnostic reception centers; (3) treatment facilities for the emotionally disturbed, including psychiatric inpatient children's units, residential centers, and mental hospitals; (4) residential drug and alcohol programs; (5) facilities for developmentally disabled children and youth; and (6) private boarding schools.

Certain characteristics of the group residential care setting can be specifically useful in helping children and young persons. These characteristics, which are different from those of the family home, in principle permit a controlled living process and a consciously designed therapeutic environment that can be varied to meet the needs of a particular child or group of children.

In contrast to a family home setting, young people in residential care can be freed from an obligation to form close personal relationships. The troubled child can keep relationships with others diluted so that there is less need to persist in old ways of reacting. Thus, energy can be channeled into new learning processes. The group setting can allow greater variation in behavior than a family unit, and the impact of difficult behavior—"acting out"—may be less because it is diffused among a series of adults who work shifts, rather than being on duty twenty-four hours a day as are parents and foster parents.

The young person in group care has an opportunity for a variety of interpersonal relationships and patterns of behavior since he or she has access to more adult role models and other supportive relationships. The wider choice can permit the youth to remain relatively detached from relationships that in the past had been undesirably disturbing, but return to those relationships (parents, former foster parents, adoptive parents, mentors) that are rewarding, supportive, and productive. The peer group is an important resource and often a catalyst for constructive change. It offers an opportunity for interaction with others who share the same experience day by day.

A greater range of remedial and therapeutic programs and group activities can be brought together in a residential setting and made available for planning positive daily living experiences. The accessibility of the child to the staff facilitates diagnosis, observation, and treatment. Therapy for emotional problems, remedial programs for learning problems, and controls for behavioral problems can be integrated and related directly to the young person's daily life.

The consistent routine of group care may contribute to a child's sense of continuity, regularity, and stability. Many young persons requiring group care have come from very disorganized home environments and need structure to facilitate impulse control.

Staff members in group care, by accepting formal employment conditions, assume an obligation for professional functioning and can be readily accessible to regular in-service training and supervision. They work in a context of backup and support from other professionals, which helps to minimize their reactivity to the problems of young residents in the facility.

These attributes of group care, which can create a therapeutic environment, are not automatically self-fulfilling. If not used with professional skill, each attribute could become a barrier to treatment. Depersonalizing influences can also penalize children and youths who need individual personalized attention. In group living there is always an implicit lack of privacy. Opportunities to make choices may be lost. Some children are overstimulated by the variety of relationships and activities in group care. Without appropriate supervision and controls, acting-out behaviors by young people in care can jeopardize other group members. Although institutional staffs are increasingly aware of the need to involve children and youths in the mainstream of community life, often, the campus of the facility is geographically isolated from community influence. In the case of young people in trouble with the community, the isolation may be an advantage during the period in which new controls are being established but a disadvantage when it becomes time to reintegrate the youth back into the mainstream of community life. Within the past few years, greater attention has been paid to the need for working with a child's family if therapeutic change is to be maintained. Wraparound services are being used to reintegrate young people back into their families or into the community in other family settings such as family foster care or kinship care.

The range of specific approaches to a planned therapeutic residential environment includes individualized psychotherapy, trauma therapy, behavior modification, play therapy, milieu therapy, group work, and positive peer culture. In all such approaches, the attempt is to use the everyday living environment as a therapeutic tool.

Group work approaches have emphasized social and peer supports and sanctions as a means of establishing new patterns of behavior. Youths are given selected responsibilities for the day-to-day operation of the unit and for governing their own and each other's behavior. The youth group assigns, schedules, and monitors the necessary chores, activities, and privileges. The use of recreational challenges, such as wilderness trips, high-ropes courses, and camp situations also strengthens young persons' perceptions of responsibility to the peer group goals. Staff act as facilitators or guides with the group interactions, as well as maintaining standards of expected behavior.

Behavior modification remains a dominant treatment approach in many settings. This approach is based on the idea that behavior is learned and is largely controlled or reinforced by its consequences. The staff has the tasks of making both the desired behavior and the consequences explicit to residents and of managing the system of consequence—rewards and punishments—to support and reinforce expectations. Familiar techniques in this approach include token economies, in which young people work for points or tokens to attain varied levels of privilege.

Agency Group Homes

The agency-operated group home has been mostly used with adolescents. The group home is typically a large single dwelling or apartment, either owned or rented by an agency or other organization, and located in a residential part of the community. Child care staff members are usually viewed as counselors rather than as foster parents. Some agency group homes have a married couple—group home parents—and child care staff, giving young people the benefit of family-like contact plus the additional opportunity to relate to child care staff as young adult role models. Other professional personnel serve the group home regularly—social workers, a psychiatric consultant, a psychologist, and perhaps at times other resource persons such as recreational therapists, special education consultants, or nutritionists. While the parent agency or institution has administrative and supervisory responsibility, however, the group home reaches out to the community for many activities.

Meeting the expectations of multiple constituencies is a problem for group homes. The constituencies include schools, police, the children or youths' families, and neighbors. Group homes are an open system, so interaction is frequent. Community relations functions are extremely important in the management of a group home. Use of community volunteers and community advisory groups is helpful in promoting positive transactions and community understanding of the needs of the young people in care.

Unfortunately, existing research on residential care is too methodologically weak on the issues of the characteristics of children who are in residential facilities, the characteristics of children best served in residential care, and the outcomes of children served. Without empirical evidence to support policy and practice development in residential care, child welfare continues to promote family care and restrict residential care to those children who have "failed" in family care or for whom no family is found to care for them. As Stavsky stated in 1941,

> We have been swinging on a pendulum, with institutions at one end, and foster homes at the other. Today we should be ready to cease proselytizing for foster home care or defending institutional care, and begin to utilize child placing for what it is, an art, dealing with an individual and prescribing what he, as an individual, really needs. *(Wolins & Piliavin, 1964, p. 32)*

Whittaker commented that " the greatest tragedy would be to extend into the next century the polarizing debate that has engulfed group care throughout much of the last one hundred years. Group care, in any of its forms, is no panacea. Yet, it deserves thoughtful critical review to determine its proper place and function in an overall continuum of care and services" (Whittaker, 2000, p. 12). Sixty-four years after Stavsky's comments, the Child Welfare League of America, supported by many advocates, recommended that more resources be devoted to research and that child placing policies and practices be revised to move away from the linear placement process, that is, family care first and then residential care if it doesn't work, toward one that provides "appropriate interventions at various points in time." In essence, "give the child what he really needs; not what system biases mandates he be provided" (Child Welfare League of America, 2005, p. 3; Bullard & Johnson, 2005).

Independent Living Services

Increases in the number of adolescents in foster care triggered a new challenge to the child welfare system—the necessity of preparing large numbers of at-risk foster adolescents for independent living, or *interdependent living*, a phrase that underscores the emancipating youth's need to continue to relate to family and community (Maluccio, Krieger, & Pine, 1990). In the past, young people who remained in foster care until the age of majority have been discharged into the community with the expectation that they could assume care for themselves. For many young persons exiting care, the lack of planning had disastrous results, and they ended up in homeless shelters with no place to go, no financial resources, and no families to fall back on. Many youths leaving foster care ended up on public assistance (Allen, Bonner, & Greenan, 1988).

The Independent Living Initiative, established by Congress in 1988, provides funds for services to emancipating youth. The legislative intent was to enable youths to seek a high school diploma, participate in vocational training, enroll in a program for life skills, and use individual or group counseling. Agencies were charged with integrating services for youth and making individualized independent living case plans (Allen, Bonner, & Greenan, 1988). The Foster Care Independence Act of 1999 and the John H. Chaffee Foster Care Independence Program amended the 1988 Act to improve independent living and transitional living services for youth in foster care or exiting foster care (P.S. 196-169).

Currently, a wide range of programs exist, including special group homes that teach life skills, supervised apartment living, mentorship programs, group work for young people who are receiving in-home training from their foster parents, and specialized foster homes established to teach life skills and assist the emancipation process (Downs, 1990). A culturally specific African American rites-of-passage program teaches youth life care skills for the transition to adulthood using Afrocentric mentoring and ritual (Gavazzi, Alford, & McKenry, 1996).

> *He tells me, "You're going to move out on your own." No way, man, that's what I'll say. Not ready. Not ready. Not ready. (Young man in care, Martin & Palmer, 1997, p. 44)*

In addition to tangible independent living skills, young people emancipating from care often require assistance with the intangible aspects of emancipation, including reliving the original separation experience and confusion about their identity. Under the best of circumstances, emancipation can be a difficult process requiring a series of complex adaptations. The young person leaving placement often faces a double loss: leaving the foster home or group home and reexperiencing the original loss of the biological family (McFadden, Rice, Ryan, & Warren, 1989). The Chafee Program extended eligibility to all youth expected to remain in foster care to age 18 and those 18 to 21-year-olds who left foster care because they "aged out." It required youth participation in designing their independent living activities and accepting responsibility for achieving independence. Room and board payments could be made up to age 21. In addition, states could extend Medicaid benefits to eligible youth to 21 years (National Foster Care Awareness Project, 2000).

In addition to these services, most states have developed alternative living arrangements for older youth, generally 16 years and older, where they do not necessarily live with an adult caregiver twenty-four hours a day or where they have separate apartments or independent spaces with locking capacity within buildings with on-site adult supervisors/mentors. Some of these programs were developed in the early 1980s to provide for safe places for older adolescents who refused to remain in family or group care for various reasons and had no family home in which they could be placed. These alternatives began to be recognized as beneficial to a youth's transition to adulthood with the 1986 Independent Living Initiatives. They are expanding under the 1999 John Chafee Independent Living Program. They provide the youth with the opportunity to experience the requirements of self-sufficiency in daily living while still having the support and guidance of a caring adult, either a caseworker or "houseparent/mentor," who develops and improves personal capacities to handle the range of responsibilities that come with "independence."

PROFESSIONAL ISSUES IN FOSTER CARE

Volumes could be written on the professional issues in foster care, but space limitations preclude doing so in this text. There are some foundational issues that, if effectively resolved, would most likely concurrently eliminate many others.

Staff Education, Training, and Supervision

Despite efforts to engage more persons in the decision making for case planning or engaging the broader community in support of the child and parent, the caseworker is the director of outcomes. He or she sees the issues; hears the pain and concerns of the child, parents, and caregivers; feels the joys and frustrations; takes the actions necessary to engage others in moving the case plan forward; and prepares the reports and recommendations for the court and agency. He or she is the one who has too many cases and too little time. He or she is the one who needs to be knowledgeable in so much, but who has so little time to acquire the knowledge. He or she is the one who spends an inordinate amount of time trying to find information and resources and too little time working directly with children and their families. He or she is the one who is supposed to be the "broker of services," but who, in reality, is the "provider of services" because there are no other providers or the waiting lists for providers are so long and the child's or parent's need cannot wait. He or she is the one who seeks advice and direction from anyone around because his or her supervisor is in yet another meeting to discuss yet another "foster care policy and procedure change."

Worker Training. Foster care workers must be able to work across boundaries with many other disciplines. Training on legal issues related to permanency planning is necessary. Staff need to be grounded in legal terminology, understand legal processes related to permanency planning; know the legal basis of child welfare practice, including constitutional rights of parents; be able to document all aspects of casework; be able to present effective testimony and prepare for court hearings; and be able to work collaboratively with attorneys.

The skills of casework, while still valuable for foster care workers, must be supplemented with the ability to do groupwork, to develop resources within the community, to be an internal organizational change agent, and to advocate for families and children at the level of social policy. They must be generalists in their skills but specialists in their knowledge of issues affecting families and children.

Despite the range of persons staffing group homes and other residential facilities, child care staff spend the most time with the children. In addition to knowing what caseworkers should know, child care staff in residential facilities need extensive training on working with children who have many diverse conditions and behaviors in a group context. They are the arbiters of interpersonal disputes. They are the teachers of alternative behaviors. They are "there" for the child "in good times and in bad times." They control access to activities and, in many cases, determine when the child exits the facility. They help the child voice his or her thoughts and feelings. They advocate for the child's wants when the child cannot do so for himself or herself and model how to advocate. They are mom, dad, uncle, aunt, sister, brother, friend, mentor—the one caring adult that makes a difference for the child

Unfortunately, due to lack of training, too many child care workers forget that these are their roles. Too many bring harm to children or youth because they lack knowledge of effective intervention techniques for the multitude of issues presented by individual children in group environments.

Child Care Staff Training. Many agencies and organizations have developed career ladders for child care staff, with comprehensive curricula focused on the emotional, social, and behavioral needs of children and youth in care. In addition, the content of training may include topics on teaching families and children practical skills to cope effectively with their environments, and working to enhance natural support networks for families. Staff must have skills of relating to young people of different ethnic groups and also to gay and lesbian youth.

Foster care is the most complex of the child welfare services and, as yet, policymakers, administrators, practitioners, and educators have not been specific enough in defining the knowledge, skills, aptitudes, attitudes, and abilities needed by foster care caseworkers, therapists serving children in foster care, educators, and child care staff. This is a necessary prerequisite to developing and implementing comprehensive academic programs, recruitment and hiring practices, and on-the-job training and staff development programs that provide the necessary education, training, and development. Child welfare positions have been progressively deprofessionalized from the late 1970s and early 1980s when the Children's Bureau was providing funding for child welfare workers and supervisors to obtain masters' degrees in social work, and the challenges of the children, parents, caregivers, and the system have become more complex. Over the past six to seven years, some states have entered into agreements with colleges and universities to encourage employees to obtain masters' degrees in social work in programs that modify coursework content to the child welfare context or develop certificate programs specifically in child welfare. The Children's Bureau has awarded some grants to state–university partnerships to better define the educational, training, and supervision needs of child welfare caseworkers and supervisors. In addition, while most states now require social workers to be licensed or certified, child welfare caseworkers in many states are exempted from that requirement, even though they perform social work tasks.

Supervisors in child welfare have a similar fate to caseworkers. Their education and training does not prepare them to supervise caseworkers in such a complex milieu. Furthermore, the crisis nature of foster care and its bureaucratic administrative requirements challenge planned supervisor-casework conferences and supervisory review of all cases serviced by the supervisees. "Supervision on the fly" (SOF) is the norm in most foster care agencies, despite the best efforts to have planned supervision. SOF tends to be reactive and incomplete; for example responding to a caseworker's question without taking the time to discuss and get all the information. It tends to support the caseworker's desire for an "instant answer" rather than teaching him or her how to think and make decisions independently, because giving the answer is less time consuming than helping the caseworker to arrive at the answer.

The CFSR process documented the importance of the caseworker to child safety, well-being, and permanency outcomes and the necessity for the caseworker to visit the child and parent frequently and have focus to the visits. Additional federal resources have been made available to support casework efforts. Further supervisory support and monitoring is crucial to ongoing quality improvement in foster care services. We will provide a model for casework supervision in Chapter 9.

Education and training for therapists and educators infrequently address the unique circumstances of children and youth in foster care and the impact those circumstances have on the child's ability to engage in and benefit from "standard" therapy or educational programming. All service providers contracted to serve these children and families need to be provided specific information and training on the foster care system and its impact on children and families.

Conflicts in Providing Services to Children and Parents

Who is the client? (Some say "consumer" but a consumer has choices of where to spend his or her money, whereas a parent or child in the child welfare system doesn't have such choices.) Both the child and the parents are the caseworker's clients. Both require the best efforts of the caseworker to assist them in achieving their individual and family goals. But when a conflict arises, such as a parent who demands visits according to an existing court order and a child who refuses to visit the parent, what is the caseworker to do? ASFA offers some help in resolving this, but not all conflicts. The child is the primary client because the system focuses on the child's safety, well-being, and permanency. Caseworkers are there because the child has been harmed either by abuse or neglect. However, for caseworkers to achieve safety, well-being, and permanency for the child, they must work with the parents, the secondary client. Furthermore, parents have rights that must be respected. In the example given above, the caseworker has to ask the child why he or she does not want to visit with the parent, determine whether this reason relates to safety or well-being, and, if it does, secure court approval of a change in the terms and conditions of visitation, or negotiate an acceptable visitation arrangement with the parent and child that acknowledges and addresses the child's concern. See Chapter 12 for a discussion of professional ethics and resolution of ethical dilemmas.

Facilitating Effective Teamwork

There are many actors and actresses in the child welfare drama. The caseworker, as director, must work with them all and get them to work with each other to achieve the desired conclusion. Everyone—professional and nonprofessional—sees events through the lenses of his or her experiences, values, beliefs, biases, perceived and actual organizational expectations, and communication style. "Team" requires substituting the individual to the group. It requires knowing the rules of engagement, that is, what is to be done, by who, by when, and in accordance with what parameters. The caseworker facilitates common understanding of the rules and coordinates the team's communications.

Teamwork is necessary to achieve the purposes of out-of-home care. Caseworkers, primarily charged with implementing permanency plans, and the caregivers, who provide the day-to-day nurturing that promotes development and healing of earlier trauma, must coordinate their activities with collateral professionals who also provide service to children and their parents. These professionals include educators, health care providers, mental health professionals, and others who are part of the overall plan. The team is part of a larger helping system brought into play by the caseworker's brokering and coordinating functions. On a different level, there needs to be collaborative teamwork between the management of the child welfare agency, the courts, and the mental health and substance abuse treatment agencies (National Commission on Family Foster Care, 1991).

Today, there is particular interest in forming closer collaborations with the schools. Many have observed that the special education departments of public schools serve many of the same children as the child welfare system. Yet communication between these two systems is often nonexistent or adversarial. New approaches are needed to better coordinate these two service systems (Altshuler, 2003). Child welfare agencies are now accountable to the federal government for child development outcomes of the children they serve, which should encourage progress in these coordinating efforts. (See Chapters 1 and 9.)

The Children's Bureau has embraced the systems of care concept for child welfare (Pires, Lazear, & Cohan, 2006). Originally developed in the mental health system in the 1980s to serve children with emotional disorders, systems of care was defined as

> a comprehensive spectrum of mental health and other necessary services which are organized into a coordinated network to meet the multiple and changing needs of children and their families. *(Pires, 2002, p. 4)*

Systems of care practice in child welfare recognizes that the child welfare system must rely on multiple other systems to achieve those outcomes. While the development of the system of care initially rests with child welfare policymakers and administrators, their ongoing utility rests with the child welfare caseworkers' and supervisors' abilities to develop and maintain service teams across systems (Pires, 2006).

Resource Availability

Foster care requires a vast array of services for children and parents and placement options. As the CFSR results show, no state has the resources it needs to achieve the desired outcomes. Since the 1970s, the most frequently identified service needs of parents have not changed: mental health services for *Diagnostic Statistical Manual* (*DSM*) diagnoses, substance abuse treatment services (although the substances abused have changed over time), housing, parenting education, and economic support alternatives (literacy education, job training, public assistance benefits). Despite knowing this, the system has never developed the capacity to provide "just in time" linkages to these services. Waiting lists are the standard, even though the prime time to help a parent change is at the crisis of the child's removal. Too frequently, even after the parent has secured a place in a service or program, that service or program presents access issues—location, hours of operation conflicts, language barriers, too brief a service period to adequately address the parent's issues, inconsistent or conflicting expectations, and so on. The parent's failure "to adhere to the program requirements" results in termination of services and the "wait" cycle resumes.

Too many children spend too many hours in the lobbies of foster care agencies because the system lacks the capacity to identify an appropriate caregiver or, more often, it just doesn't have a relative or foster parent who wants the child. Intake systems to foster care are not child friendly. Some wish to be with their brothers and sisters but are placed in four different homes because there is no home available to take four children. At a time when the child needs the most nurturance and understanding support, he or she does not receive it.

Mention that a child is in foster care and most people automatically assume that the child is "deficient" in some way. Most foster children are "normal" kids! That is, they have not been classified as in need of special education services or early childhood intervention services (Children's Bureau, 2006, August) They are experiencing an abnormal situation that they expect adults to "make normal." They have adjustment problems, but wouldn't you if someone took you from what you knew and put you in a strange environment? The system offers them counseling when they would like to play on the basketball team—but there is no money for basketball. It offers them counseling when they would like to join the Girl Scouts—but the system can't pay for the uniforms and other activities. It offers them a foster family when they would rather go to a boarding school—but are told "families are best for you."

Some have severe emotional or behavioral problems and get "bounced" from foster home to foster home because the foster parents are not prepared for and supported in dealing with the child's problems. Some are not ready for a family, but that is what the system says they must have. Some wish to be able to read, but they don't stay in one school long enough and the next school doesn't teach reading the same way, so they have to start over. Some can't read because they can't see the book and they can't get glasses for a couple of months because the Medicaid coverage is "screwed up." What happened to "the best interests of the child"?

Foster Parent and Relative Caregiver Training and Monitoring

Foster parenting has evolved from just expecting the relative or foster parent to "do what comes natural." Given the needs of the children and their families, all substitute caregivers must receive training in how to identify, understand, interpret, and intervene effectively to ensure the child's safety and well-being, to promote normalization in the child's life, and to provide supportive interactions necessary for positive youth development. The caregiver must have an understanding of self and how that affects his or her interaction with the child, parents, caseworkers, and other service providers.

Foster parents' roles are becoming more professional, such as the roles of group home "parents" or "counselors" or residential care staff who may fill roles of milieu therapists. In general, all caregiver roles in out-of-home care have evolved from less specialized to more specialized, from lay to paraprofessional or professionalized, and from strictly child focused to work with child and family.

The value of systematic training for foster parents is well established. Foster parent training has been shown to reduce the incidence of failed placements, increase the number of desirable placements, and encourage foster parents to remain licensed. Foster parent training is now mandated in all states. Training formats bring together experienced foster parents as mentors and trainers of those who are just starting, and offer time for foster parents to share experiences and offer support to one another in an informal setting. Topics that may be covered in training include emotional development of children in care, working with biological parents, handling destructive behavior of children, fostering sexually abused children, and working as part of a team.

Protecting Children and Youth in Out-of-Home Care

When the community, through courts and agencies, intervenes in the life of a family, it has a moral and legal obligation to provide adequate care if the child is placed away from the family. The existence of maltreatment by caregivers and others in out-of-home settings is cause for serious concern and careful vigilance by foster care professionals. Long ignored, it has now been brought to national and professional attention mainly through class action lawsuits.

Agencies are now monitoring foster homes and institutions more closely. An unintended side effect of this increased scrutiny is that foster parents have felt that they were treated unfairly when allegations were brought against them and many have left fostering (Carbino, 1991). Agencies can reduce the chances of a child being maltreated in care through providing training, matching child with family, monitoring the child in the home, conducting a thorough initial home study, and decertifying a home known to be deficient. Some children are more at risk of maltreatment than others, including those with disabilities and severe emotional and behavioral problems, making it important to match children carefully with the specific capacities and strengths of foster parents.

Institutions for children are thought to place children at greater risk for abuse than foster care, although there is strong resistance to reporting abuse or believing that it can happen. Bloom (1992) recommended that institutions take the following steps when an allegation of abuse occurs: take allegations seriously, suspend the employee with pay during the initial investigation, reach out to the child's family, act to cut retribution by staff members or peers, and flood the child with support. He also urged treating the alleged perpetrator with respect and dignity during the investigation and finding ways of supporting the staff.

CFSR composites show that reported instances of child maltreatment in the nation is less than 1 percent for children in out-of-home care (Federal Register, 2006, p. 32980). Unfortunately, many instances of abuse of children in foster care go unreported either because the child does not disclose it until many years after the incident or the caseworker does not perceive children's comments about treatment in a foster home or facility as emotional abuse. There were 534 deaths of children in foster care in 2005. These included natural causes, suicides, and homicides. Unfortunately, the AFCARS data system does not distinguish the number by subcategory. (Children's Bureau, 2006, September)

Media or Advocacy Group Involvement

Foster care is a hot topic for media coverage. Most often, the coverage is of a child who dies or is seriously injured and the child welfare agency had been involved in the case and, in the opinion of the reporter, did not do what it should have done. Recently, there has been increased focus on telling the stories of young people who transition out of the system and are homeless, jobless, and have no one to help them. Sometimes the media reports the story of parents who are wrongly accused of abuse or neglect. There are also the stories of children who are medically compromised and parents who decide not to pursue further treatment and those in which parents seek "alternatives to traditional medicine." There are stories of children in foster care in need of dental or optometric care. There are stories asking for contributions to fund foster children participation in a broad range of recreational and leisure activities. Occasionally, there is a story of a child in foster care or exiting foster care who has achieved success in school or the community (University of Maryland, Casey Journalism Center on Children & Families, 2007). Advocacy groups take up similar issues. Sometimes they take their concerns to the media, sometimes to the agency, sometimes to the legislature or the Governor, and sometimes they engage in class action litigation, which is discussed below.

Media and advocacy groups can be instrumental in foster care change. However, their impact on actual foster care "reform" is questionable. Negative publicity frequently gets the attention of the top executive and legislative officials. If the reporting was especially revealing and negative, policies change, practices change, and laws change. In other cases, the change may be short-sighted and short-lived because another news story moves to the front page and the reporter does not come back to the earlier story. The foster care systems in several states have been the subject of series, that is, several stories over many days or weeks. These stories tend to generate more lasting changes.

Monitoring and Oversight

The objective of monitoring and oversight should be to identify where the system is not performing as expected in individual cases and as a whole and to make the necessary changes to get it to function. However, that has not been the case in foster care. Despite having multiple layers of monitoring and oversight, many of the challenges or failures of the system are identified over and over and nothing happens. In many states, the same case is reviewed by the caseworker's supervisor, an internal quality assurance team or peer review team, an administrative review board, a court-appointed special advocate, the guardian *ad litem* or the child's attorney, and the judge or other jurist. They all hear and read the same story for six months. That story is that the mother has a substance abuse problem and the agency has been unable to help her get into treatment because there are not enough drug abuse treatment services in the county where she lives and she can't go to the neighboring county that has vacancies because she is not in their geographic service area. They thank the caseworker for the report and ask her to "keep trying" and nothing happens. What is the benefit to the child and the parent to have the same problem identified six times and never corrected?

Child welfare "reform" starts with the individual child and parent receiving the services needed to ensure the child's safety, well-being, and permanency. Again, CFSR holds promise for being an effective monitoring and oversight process because in its second round, it is requiring states to explain the whys behind its performance data, and in its PIPs it must directly link the actions taken to correct the problem in performance to specific outcomes and commit to percentage improvements over current performance.

Trends and Issues

Privatization and Managed Care

There is serious interest in applying the concept of managed care, which has been used in health care, to child welfare. The principles of managed care—having diagnostic categories with related lengths of stay or paying a flat fee for certain types of care, no matter how long it might take to achieve the permanency goal—come from the medical model, which does not seem clearly related to the way the foster care system has operated in the past. Managed care has been applied for some children and youths receiving mental health treatment services under Medicaid funding.

The Child Welfare League of America has established the Managed Care Institute to identify and describe current and potential changes in the way child welfare agencies are delivering services consistent with managed care principles. Some thirty child welfare administrators say they are implementing or planning to implement initiatives that include managed care features (Hutchins, 1997).

Managed care is related to the privatization of child welfare services. Kansas was one of the first states to move in this direction, when, in 1996 and 1997, three major child welfare services—family preservation, foster care, and adoption—were transferred to contracted private providers in a modified form of managed care. This involves a capitated case rate for each family or child. This case rate is expected to meet all the crisis needs of the family and/or children for the duration of each of the services. While there was considerable agreement that the child welfare system had past problems and was in need of system change, not all reports on the new system have been positive. The Kansas chapter of the National Association of Social Workers enumerated concerns about the implementation of the new systems, and developed a set of recommendations, including:

- ❖ Develop community advisory boards.
- ❖ Adopt a set of best-practice standards to ensure child safety.
- ❖ Provide training for new case managers.
- ❖ Institute a grievance process.
- ❖ Create an ombudsman/advocate. (Kansas NASW, 1997)

Child welfare organizations are developing networks, partnerships, and mergers to successfully navigate the new managed care environment. Four key reasons for doing so are that they can provide more efficient and effective services, can have increased fiscal stability, and can increase their organizational control. Attention to leadership, economics, and qualitative improvements can develop strong organizations that can compete in the changing marketplace (Emenhiser, King, Joffe, & Penkert, 1998). As funding patterns are affected by managed care or become more flexible to move services toward the prevention end, foster care practice may see an increased emphasis on innovation such as shared family care, kinship care, family decision making for permanency planning, and other prospects that promote family continuity.

The Kansas managed care system was disbanded when the private agency charged with managing it went bankrupt. No other state has attempted widespread managed care for its foster care populations. Several have implemented managed care concepts in some of its services, for example, mental health treatment interventions.

All states are engaged in some aspects of privatization of both placements and services for children in out-of-home care. In general, these privatization efforts are seen as supplementing state systems, not supplanting them. Private nonprofits and private for profits are accepted contractors. Most must be licensed or certified under state laws to provide care for children. The states' maintain various degrees of monitoring responsibilities, and ultimately hold accountability. Frequently, privatization is used to develop and implement new programming in shorter periods than possible with state employees. There are no studies that document the superiority of public or private services.

Minority Overrepresentation

The issue of minority overrepresentation is an ongoing concern for the foster care policymakers and administrators. Black children are overrepresented in every state and Hispanic children of either race are overrepresented in some states. This has been a historical situation dating from the 1960s, when minorities were included in the publicly funded child welfare system. The predominate theories for disproportionate minority representation are:

❖ disproportionate need—minority children and families are poorer and lack resources.

❖ racial bias and child welfare decision making—minority children and families are treated differently by mandated reporters and caseworkers.

❖ interactions between family risk and child welfare practice—minority children and families have disproportionate needs and thus are referred to the child welfare system most often. Once referred, the racial bias and child welfare decision making leads to more placements of minority children. Once placed, they remain in care longer (GAO, 2007; Hill, 2006; Chibnall et al., 2003).

Frank discussions of race remain difficult in the United States. White people feel that they must defer to the thinking of minority individuals to explain why their group is overrepresented. Minority race people feel that they must put the issues of racial bias and institutional racism in every discussion. No one is bold enough to ask, "Why is it that blacks are overrepresented in every state and other minorities are only overrepresented in a small number of states?" Furthermore, if blacks are placed with relatives at higher percentages than whites, can we not expect that they will remain in foster care longer to have access to services and financial assistance that they would not otherwise have? Black people are resilient people! Black people are intelligent people! To frame a response to the issue of minority overrepresentation and to craft policies and interventions to reduce it, if that is what is found to be in the best interests of minority children and their families, the research methodologies must improve and, perhaps, current theories must be discarded so that the facts of individual case decisions can be searched out and sorted through without being directed to a finding to support a chosen theory.

Subsidized Guardianship

Subsidized guardianship is viewed as a permanency alternative for children who cannot be returned home and for whom adoption is not in their best interests or is not possible. In most cases, subsidized guardianship is viewed as a "common sense solution for children in long term relative foster care" (Generations United, 2006). Each state varies in its definition of legal guardianship. For ASFA permanency purposes, the federal definition of legal guardianship is

> A judicially created relationship between child and caretaker which is intended to be permanent and self-sustaining as evidenced by the transfer to the caretaker of the following parental rights with respect to the child: protection, education, care and control of the person, custody of the person, and decision-making. *(42 USC 675 (b) (7)*

Subsidized guardianship is when the guardian receives monthly payments from the government for the child's care, similar to foster care or adoption assistance payments. The rate of payments varies from state to state and is not necessarily equivalent to the foster care or adoption assistance payment rates (Godsoe, 2003). Ask yourself: What justifies a difference in the amount of the government's payment to the child's caregiver based on the caregiver's legal relationship to the child?

In 2003, subsidized guardianship was available in 31 states, with 9 of these states providing payments to relatives only (National Data Analysis System, retrieved April 15, 2007). As adoptive parents have found, postadoption services are limited and fragmented, and subsidized guardians are now beginning to experience some of the same issues. More outcome research is needed. The justification for it should not simply be that the number of children exiting foster care increases when subsidized guardianship is available. Rather, we should be equally concerned with their well-being and stability in those placements.

Paternal Relatives as Placement Options

Historically the child welfare system has not sought out paternal relatives. For many years, paternity establishment was not the norm for children entering foster care. If the mother didn't identify the child's father and his relatives or the father or his relatives did not come forward, the system did not pursue the issue until it was time to terminate parental rights. Now, ASFA and the CFSR require immediate identification of fathers and their relatives and engage them in the placement and planning process. Systems are in place to establish paternity for children for whom it has not been established.

Clearly this opens up opportunities for children and their families to remain with their "blood relations." However, it also opens up challenges for the child welfare system. Many times, paternal relatives have had no or limited, infrequent contact with the child. Therefore, they don't know the child and the child doesn't know them. However, just as with maternal relatives who frequently present the same issue, this can be overcome. The child doesn't know a nonrelated foster parent either. Furthermore, it is not uncommon for siblings in foster care to have the same mother but different fathers. Should the children be split for placement and permanency with their respective paternal relatives? How do we legalize the relationship between child and the paternal relatives of a sibling so that placement can be effected? What do we do when the paternal relative says, "I will take my son's child; but I won't take the others"? What do we do when the father of one child says, "I will take my son and his brothers and sisters too"? What do we do when the child says, "I don't know those people and I am not going to live with them"? Should maternal relatives be preferred over paternal relatives? Many questions should be answered through experience guided by the focus that it's all about the child's safety, well-being, and permanence.

Class Action Litigation

Class action litigation is increasingly being used to effect system reform. Children's Rights, a nonprofit organization based in New York, is the leading advocacy group using the class action strategy. Basically, a class action lawsuit is one in which it is argued that the class of foster children or some subset of it are not being provided the protections and services needed and granted by federal or state laws. They can be brought in federal or state courts. Children's Rights have brought class actions in approximately 14 states as of this writing. Settlement agreements, that is, negotiated agreements acceptable to both Children's Rights and the state, have been reached in most cases, and some cases have yet to be resolved. Marcia Lowry, the Executive Director, noted

> It's not that we ask for utopian things. We're just asking governments to do what the law requires of them, to protect children. But when it comes to governments taking action, the areas where there is pressure is where things get accomplished. And because these kids can't vote, it's up to us to produce that pressure on their behalf. Someone needs to give a voice to these kids. They don't have any power otherwise. *(Children's Rights, 2007)*

CHAPTER SUMMARY

Foster care is a service for children who cannot live with their parents because of parental incapacity. It is also a service to help parents resolve problems that led to placement so that they can resume care for their children. Foster care has a long and complicated history in the United States, evolving from nineteenth-century forms of care such as indenture, outdoor relief, almshouse care, orphanages and children's institutions, and free foster homes. During the twentieth century, foster care was established as the preferred form of care for most children, with institutions reserved for older children with serious problems. Foster care has changed from a program focused on stabilizing the child's placement to one emphasizing planning and movement of the child through the system and into a permanent home.

In the twenty-first century, a laser beam focus on the child's safety, well-being, and permanence *has the potential* to truly reform foster care practice and outcomes. Whether that potential is actually realized rests with how committed the federal government and states are to identifying, developing, and sustaining the service array to meet the needs of the children and their families and how committed they are to ensuring that all persons who have a role in the child's life have the knowledge, training, skills, attitudes, and beliefs necessary to make a difference in the life of the child and his or her family. Further, it rests on the commitment of all child welfare practitioners, those impacted by the system (caregivers, children, parents, relatives), educators, mental health professionals, substance abuse professionals, foundations, advocates, the media, and the community at large to do whatever is necessary to ensure that the child is safe, has access to services that promote well-being, and feels that he or she has someone who values him or her and wants what is for the best.

The characteristics of children entering care have not change significantly. Therefore, we should be able to better plan for their placement and service needs. The characteristics of parents also have not changed significantly. Therefore we should be able to better plan for their service needs.

Concurrently, we should refrain from intervening with all children or all parents with certain characteristics with the same services or methods. Every person presents in a complex interrelationship of individual, family, and community factors that impact how he or she engages in and is impacted by the system. Individual assessments are fundamental. Having an array of services to choose from makes the time spent on the individual assessment beneficial.

Foster care is a shared responsibility of the federal, state and local units of government. The federal government guides but does not mandate state policies through its Title IV funding system and Child and Family Services Review process.

There are several different types of out-of-home care for children, including kinship care, family foster care, treatment foster care, group homes, and residential treatment centers. Adolescents aging out of foster care receive independent living services to help them make the transition to adulthood.

Relative or nonrelative family care are the preferred placement options for children needing out-of-home care. Other forms of care are being critically evaluated for serving children who present emotional or behavioral challenges resulting in numerous family home placements before group care is considered. Conventional wisdom is that these children might be better served by group care first with step-down to trained family care with a provider who has participated in the child's group care.

The issues of staff and provider education, training, support, and supervision and resource availability are the two most persistent issues leading to poor outcomes for children and their families. Monitoring and oversight bureaucracy continues to grow but show little impact on positive outcomes for children. Minority overrepresentation, subsidized guardianship, engaging paternal relatives, and class action litigation are issues to watch in the next five years.

Foster care will always present challenges despite our best efforts. It is a system of human beings presenting many different issues, abilities, and disabilities. There is no singular, absolute, right answer to many situations, that is, there is no do X and it will result in Y every time. This is probably why the foster care system is in perpetual state of "reform." Yet most of the issues in the 1970s remain with us today. We must learn from our errors. We must become more data-driven while recognizing the constraints of data collection bias and errors. We must accept and support the roles the media and advocacy groups can play in holding the system accountable. We must rejoice in the successes of our children, their parents, and child welfare practitioners.

FOR STUDY AND DISCUSSION
STUDY AND DISCUSSION QUESTIONS

1. Identify both positive and negative vestiges of the historical development of foster care practice that may be seen in current agency practice.

2. Talk with a placement specialist from a child placing agency to determine which options (shared family care, kinship care, family foster care, treatment foster care, group homes, and residential care) are available in your community. What criteria are applied for selecting a particular care option for a child and family?

3. Meet with a protective services supervisor to determine under what circumstances children in your community would be removed from their families and put into care. What are the critical problems or clusters of problems causing foster care placement?

4. Attend a foster parent association meeting and survey foster parents on their perceptions of social worker teamwork. Talk with foster care social workers about what they believe constitutes characteristics of good foster parents. Compare points of convergence and discrepancies.

5. Determine the total expenditure for foster care placement and services for children and their families in your state in the last fiscal year. As you complete this task, ask yourself—Have I included all the expenditures? Are there some expenditures from other units of governments? Are there nongovernmental sources of financing these services? How will I ever know that I have found all expenditures?

6. Go to the Children's Bureau web site and review the CFSR report and PIP for your state. Identify one outcome in which your state was not in substantial conformity. Assess the impact of the PIP strategies. Identify other strategies.

7. Go to the Casey Family Programs, Race Matters Consortium web page. Review the latest discussion on minority overrepresentation in foster care. What is your opinion? What information would you need to feel comfortable discussing this issue with your classmates of different races?

8. Go to the University of Maryland, Casey Journalism Center on Children & Families' web site. Review the summary of articles on foster care printed across the United States in the past month. What are the issues of media attention? How did the agency officials respond to the media articles? What information was not covered that might have influenced public perception of the issue?

9. Imagine yourself assuming the top position for child welfare in your state. Identify your number one priority and develop an action strategy for implementation.

Internet Sites

Casey Journalism Center on Children & Families. is an academic unit of the University of Maryland's School of Journalism and is focused on providing support for journalists pursuing child and family issues. It maintains compilations of media publications on foster care throughout the United States. Casey Journalism Center on Children & Families
www.cjc.umd.edu

Child Welfare Information Gateway. Established by the U.S. Children's Bureau to provide access, information, and resources on all areas of child welfare to help protect children and strengthen families.
www.childwelfare.gov

Child Welfare League of America. This organization has a general child welfare site, with specific pages related to developments in foster care and lists of topically related titles by Child Welfare League of America Press.
www.cwln.org

Children's Bureau, Administration for Children and Families, Department of Health and

Human Services, Adoption and Foster Care Analysis and Reporting System (AFCARS). This government site provides data, laws, policies, and practices on foster care. **www.acf.hhs.gov/programs/cb**

Children's Defense Fund, Washington, DC. This site provides information on child care, current news as it relates to children, the black community, publications, and other related links. It also gives data on population and family characteristics, economic security, and federal program participation. **www.childrensdefense.org**

Children's Rights, Inc. is a New York-based advocacy organization for abused and neglected children that utilizes class action litigation as a source of change. **www.childrensrights.org**

International Federation of Social Workers. This organization has a central office in Switzerland, and links together social workers from around the globe. It is currently working with the United Nations on the Convention on Rights of the Child. **www.ifsw.org**

International Foster Care Organization. This organization meets biennially for educational conferences. A youth in care network is part of IFCO.

The organization links together child welfare agencies, nongovernmental organizations, foster parent groups, and child care groups from many countries. **www.internationalfostering.org**

National Data Analysis System. Integrates national child welfare data from many sources. Provides capability to complete statistical tables of data from all states on a many child welfare issues. **http://ndas.cwla.org**

National Foster Parent Association. Information on becoming a foster parent is available at this site. This site explains the purpose of the National Foster Parent Association and provides membership information. It offers a comprehensive site called KidSource, which addresses information on children, newborn through adolescence, as it relates to fostering. **www.kidsource.com/nfpa/index.html**

National Resource Center for Permanency Planning. Provides information services, training, and technical assistance to ensure that children have safe families to grow up in. This site focuses on the following issues: permanency planning, kinship foster care, concurrent planning, family group decision making, and HIV/AIDS. **www.hunter.cuny.edu/socwork**

References and Other Resources

Adoption and Foster Care Analysis and Reporting System (AFCARS). (2002, August 7). Available: www.acf.hhs.gov/programs/cb/publications/afcars/report7.htm

Adoption and Safe Families Act of 1997. Public Law 105–89.

Allen, M., Bonner, K., & Greenan, L. (1988). Federal legislative support for independent living. *Child Welfare, 67*(6), 515–527.

Allen, M., Lakin, D., McFadden, E. J., & Wasserman, K. (1992). *Family continuity: Practice competencies*. Ypsilanti, MI: National Foster Care Resource Center.

Altshuler, S. (2003). From barriers to successful collaboration: Public schools and child welfare working together. *Social Work, 48*(1), 52–64.

Altshuler, S. J., & Poertner, J. (2002, May–June). The Child Health and Illness Profile—adolescent edition: Assessing well-being in group homes or institutions. *Child Welfare, 81*(3), 495–514.

Barth, R. P. (2002). *Institutions vs. foster homes: The empirical basis for a century of action.* Chapel Hill, NC: University of North Carolina.

Barth, R. P. & Price, A. (1999, January-February). Shared Family care: Providing services to parents and children placed together in out-of-home care. *Child Welfare, 78*(1), 88–107.

Battistelli, E. (1998). *The health care of children in out-of-home care.* Washington, DC: Child Welfare League of America Press.

Besharov, D. (Ed.) (1994). *When drug addicts have children.* Washington, DC: Child Welfare League of America/American Enterprise Institute.

Berrick, J., Barth, R., & Needell, B. (1994). A comparison of kinship foster homes and foster family homes: Implications for kinship foster care as family preservation. *Children and Youth Services Review, 16* (1–2), 33–63.

Billing, A., Ehrle, J., & Kortenkamp, K. (2002). Children care for by relatives: What do we know about their well-being? In *New Federalism: National Survey of America's Families.* Washington, DC: The Urban Institute.

Billingsley, A. (1992). *Climbing Jacob's ladder: The enduring legacy of African-American families.* New York: Simon & Schuster.

Bloom, R. (1992). When staff members sexually abuse children in residential care. *Child Welfare, 71*(2), 131–145.

Bowlby, J. (1969). *Attachment and loss.* London: Hogarth Press.

Brace, C. L. (1872). *The dangerous classes of New York and twenty years' work among them.* New York: Wynkoop and Hallenbeck.

Brissett-Chopuon, S., & ISSACS-Shockley, M. (1997). *Children in social peril: A community vision for preserving family care of African-American children and youths.* Washington, DC: Child Welfare League of American Press.

Bryant, B. & Snodgress, R. (1990). Therapeutic foster care past and present. In P. Meadowcroft & B. Trout (Eds.), *Troubled youth in treatment homes: A handbook of therapeutic foster care.* Washington, DC: Child welfare league of America.

Bullard, L. B., & Johnson, K. (2005). *Residential services for children and youth in out-of-home care: A critical link in the continuum of care.* In G. P. Mallon & P. M. Hess (Eds). *Child welfare for the 21st century: A handbook of practices, policies and programs.* New York, Columbia University Press.

Burns, B. J., & Hoagwood, K. (2002). *Community treatment for youth: Evidence-based interventions for severe emotional and behavioral disorders.* New York: Oxford University Press.

Chasnoff, I. (1990). Maternal drug use. In *Crack and other addictions: Old realities and new challenges for child welfare* (pp. 110–120). Washington, DC: Child Welfare League of America.

Chibnall, S., Dutch, N. M., Jones-Harden, B., Brown, A., Gourdine, R., Boone, A., Snyder, S., (2003). *Children of color in the child welfare system: Perspectives from the child welfare community.* Washington, DC: U.S. Department of Health and Human Services, Administration for Children and Families.

Child Welfare Information Gateway, (2006). State statutes series. Washington, DC: Author.

Child Welfare League of America, (1994). *Kinship care: A natural bridge.* Washington, DC: Author.

Child Welfare League of America. (1995). *Standards of excellence for family foster care services* (rev. ed.). Washington, DC: Author.

Child Welfare League of America, (2005). *Position Statement on Residential Services.* Washington, DC: Child Welfare League of America. Availables: 222.cwla.org.

Children's Bureau. (1999). *Title IV-E independent living programs: A decade in review.* Administration for Children and Families. Washington, DC: U.S. Government Printing Office.

Children's Bureau (August 2006). *Trends in foster care and adoption—FY 2000–FY 2005.* Washington, DC: U.S. Department of Health and Human Services.

Children's Bureau (September 2006). AFCARS Report 13. Washington, DC: U.S.

Children's Bureau (2007). *The child and family service reviews.* Washington, DC: Author.

Children's Rights, Inc. (2007). Retrieved from www.childrensrights.org, April 15, 2007.

Churchill, S., Carlson, B., & Nybell, L. (Eds.). (1979). *No child is unadoptable.* Beverly Hills, CA: Sage.

Colon, F. (1978). Family ties and child placement. *Family Process, 17,* 289–312.

Courtney, M. E., & Maluccio, A. N. (1999). The rationalization of foster care in the twenty-first century. In P. A. Curtis, G. Dale, Jr., & J. C. Kendall (Eds). *The foster care crisis: Translating research into policy and practice.* Lincoln, NB: University of Nebraska Press.

Crumbley, J. (1999). *Transracial adoption and foster care: Practice issues for professionals.* Washington DC: CWLA Press.

Crumbley, J., & Little, R. (Eds.). (1997). *Relative's raising children: An overview of kinship care.* Washington, DC: Child Welfare League of America Press.

De Haymes, M.V., & Simon, S. (2003). Transracial adoption: Families identify issues and needed support services. *Child Welfare, 82*(2) 251–272.

Derezotes, D. M., & Poertner, J. (2004). Factors contributing to the overrepresentation of African American children in the child welfare system: What we know and don't know. In D.M. Derezotes, J. Poertner & M.F. Testa (Eds). *Race matters in child welfare: Examining the overrepresentation of African Americans in the child welfare system.* Washington, DC: CWLA Press.

Downs, S. W. (1981). *Foster care reform in the 70s: Final report of the permanency planning dissemination project.* Portland, OR: Regional Institute for Human Services.

Downs, S. W. (1990). Recruiting and retaining foster families of adolescents. In A. Maluccio, R. Krieger, & B. A. Pine (Eds), *Preparing adolescents for life after foster care: The central role of foster parents.* Washington, DC: Child Welfare League of America.

Downs, S. W. (1999). Foster parents of mentally retarded and physically handicapped children. In J. Hudson & B. Galaway (Eds), Specialist foster family care: A normalizing experience. *Special Issue of Child and Youth Services Review, 12*(1–2), New York: Haworth.

Downs, S. W., & Sherraden, M. (1983). The orphan asylum in the nineteenth century. *Social Service Review, 57* (2), 272–290.

Dubowitz, H. (1990). The physical and mental health and educational status of children placed with relatives: Final report. Baltimore: University of Maryland.

Edelboch, M., Liu, Q., & Martin, L. (2002). Unsung heroes: Relative caregivers in child-only cases. *Policy and Practice of Public Human Services, 60*(1), 26–30.

Ehrle, J., & Geen, R. (2002). Children cared for by relatives: What services do they need? In *New federalism: National survey of America's families.* Washington, DC: The Urban Institute.

Eldridge, S. (1999). *Twenty things adopted kids wish their adoptive parents knew.* New York: Dell Publishing.

Emenhiser, D., King, D. W., Joffe, S., & Penkert, K. (1998). Washington, DC: Child Welfare League of America Press.

Emlen, A. (1978). *Overcoming barriers to planning for children in care.* Portland, OR: Regional Research Institute for Human Services.

Fanshel, D., & Shinn, E. B. (1978). *Children in foster care: A longitudinal investigation.* New York: Columbia University Press.

Federal Register. (2006, June 7). *The data measures, data composites, and national standards to be used in the child and family services reviews.* Washington, DC: U.S. Government Printing Office.

Folks, H. (1911). *The care of destitute, neglected, and delinquent children.* New York: Macmillan.

Gavazzi, S., Alford, K., & McKenry, P. (1996). Culturally specific programs for foster care youth. *Family Relations, 45,* 166–174.

Gebel, T. (1996). Kinship care and nonrelative family foster care: A comparison of caregiver attributes and attitudes. *Child Welfare, 75*(1), 5–18.

Geiser, R. (1973). *The illusion of caring.* Boston, MA: Beacon Press.

Generations United (2006). *All children deserve a permanent home: Subsidized guardianships as a common sense solution for children in long-term relative foster care.* Washington, DC: Author.

Gillespie, J., Byrne, B., & Workman, L. (1995). An intensive reunification program for children in foster care. *Child and Adolescent Social Work Journal, 12*(3), 213–228.

Godsoe, C. (2003). Subsidized guardianship: A new permanency option. *Children's Legal Rights Journal,* 23(3), 11–20.

Golden, R. (1997). *Disposable children: America's child welfare system.* Belmont, CA: Wadsworth.

Government Accountability Office (GAO). (April, 2005). GAO-05-290 Indian Child Welfare Act. Washington, DC: U.S. Government Printing Office.

Groze, V., Haines-Simeon, M., & Barth, R. (1994). Barriers in permanency planning for medically fragile children: Drug affected children and HIV infected children. *Childand Adolescent Social Work Journal, 11*(1), 63–85.

Hegar, R., & Scannapieco, M. (1999). *Kinship foster care: Policy, practice, and research.* New York: Oxford University Press.

Hill, R. B. (2006). *A synthesis of research on disproportionality in child welfare: An update.* Washington, DC: Center for Study of Social Policy and Casey Family Programs. Available: http://www.cssp.org?major-initiatives/racialEquity.html.

Horn, W. (1994). Implications for policy making. In D. Besharov (Ed.), *When drug addicts have children* (pp. 165–174). Washington, DC: Child Welfare League and American Enterprise Institute.

Hudson, J., Nutter, R., & Galaway, B. (1994). Treatment foster family care: Development and current status. *Community Alternatives, 6*(2), 1–24.

Human Services Associates. (1998). *Finding our place: The inside story of foster care.* St. Paul, MN: Rummel Dubs & Hill.

Hungerford, G. (1996). Caregivers of children whose mothers are incarcerated: A study of the kinship placement system. *Children Today, 24*(1), 23–27).

Hutchins, H. (1997). Managing managed care for Families, *Children's Voice, 7*(1), 28–29.

Jackson, S., Matthews, J., & Zuskin, R. (1999). *Supporting the kinship triad: A training curriculum.* Washington, DC: Child Welfare League of America.

Jenkins, S., & Norman, E. (1972). *Filial deprivation in foster care.* New York: Columbia University.

Johnson, I. (1994). Kinship care. In D. Besharov (Ed.), *When drug addicts have children* (pp. 221–228). Washington, DC: Child Welfare League of America.

Jones, E. F. (2006). *Public policies and practices in child welfare systems that affect life options for children of color.* Washington, DC: Joint Center for Political and Economic Studies, Health Policy Institute.

Jones, M. (1978). Stopping foster care drift: A review of the legislation and special programs. *Child Welfare, 57*(9), 571–579.

Jones, M., Magura, S., & Shyne, A. (1976). *A second chance for families.* New York: Child Welfare League of America.

Jordan, C. (1994). Have external review systems improved the quality of care for children? Yes. In E. Gambrill & T. Stein (Eds.), *Controversial issues in child welfare* (pp. 136–140). Boston: Allyn & Bacon.

Knapp, M. (2006). The economics of group care practice: A Reappraisal. In L. C. Fulcher & F. Ainsworth (Eds.), *Group care practice with children and young people revisited.* London, UK: The Haworth Press, Inc.

Kufeldt, K., & Allison, J. (1990). Fostering children—Fostering families. Community Alternatives. *International Journal of Family Care, 2,* 1–18.

Lakin, D., Whitfield, L., & Anderson, G. (1997). Necessary components of effective foster care and adoption recruitment. (Working paper). Southfield, MI: National Resource Center on Special Needs Adoption.

Lee, R. M. (2003). The transracial adoption paradox: History, Research, and Counseling implications of cultural socialization. *The Counseling Psychologist, 31*(6), 711–744.

Littner, N. (1975). The importance of natural parents to the child in placement. *Child Welfare, 54*(3), 175–181.

Maluccio, A., & Fein, E. (1983, May–June). Permanency planning: A redefinition. *Child Welfare, 62*(3), 195–201.

Maluccio, A., Krieger, R., & Pine, B. (Eds.) (1990). *Preparing adolescents for life after foster care: The central role of foster parents.* Washington, DC: Child Welfare League of America.

Martin, F., & Palmer, T. (1997). Transitions to adulthood: A Child welfare youth perspective. *Community Alternatives, The International Journal of Family Core, 9*(2) 29–58.

Mass, S., & Engler, R. E. (1959). *Children in need of parents.* New York, NY: Columbia University.

Maza, P. L. (2002). The impact of ASFA on adoption. Presentation at National Conference on Child Abuse and Neglect.

McFadden, E. J., & Downs, S. W. (1995). Family continuity: The new paradigm in permanence planning. *Community Alternatives: The International Journal of Family Care, 7*(1), 44.

McFadden, E. J., Rice, D., Ryan, P., & Warren, B. (1989). Leaving home again: Emancipation from foster family care. In J. Hudson and B. Galaway (Eds.), *Specialist foster family care: A normalizing experience.* New York: Haworth.

McKenzie, R. B. (1998). *Rethinking orphanages for the 21st century.* Thousand Oaks, CA: Sage Publishing.

Meidema, B., & Nason-Clark, N. (1977). Foster care redesign: The dilemma contemporary foster parents face. *Community Alternatives, the International Journal of Family Care, 9*(2), 15–28.

Merz, H., & Hightower, M. (2005). *Knowing who you are: Helping youth in care develop their racial and ethnic identity.* Baltimore, MA: Casey Family Programs.

Milner, J. (2007, Spring). Child and family services review: The second round. In *Child welfare matters.* Portland, ME: National Child Welfare Resource Center for Organizational Improvement.

Minkler, M., Roe, K., & Price, M. (1992). The physical and emotional health of grandmothers raising grandchildren in the crack cocaine epidemic. *The Gerontologist, 32*(6), 752–761.

National Commission on Family Foster Care, (1991). *A blueprint for fostering infants children and youths in the 1990s.* Washington, DC: Child Welfare League of America.

National Data Analysis System. (2007). State use of subsidized guardianship, 2003. Retrieved from http://ndas.cwla.org. April 17, 2007.

National Foster Care Awareness Project. (2000). *Frequently asked questions about the Foster Care Independence Act.* Seattle, WA: Casey Family Programs.

Nelson, K., Landsman, M., & Deutelbaum, W. (1990). Three models of family-centered placement prevention services. *Child Welfare, 69*(1), 3–21.

Newton, R. R., Litrownik, A. J., & Landsverk, J. A. (2000). Children and youth in foster care: Disentangling the relationship between problem behaviors and number of placements. *Child Abuse and Neglect, 24*(10), 1363–1374.

Nowicki, S., & Duke, M. (1992). *Helping the child who doesn't fit in.* Atlanta, GA: Peachtree Publishers.

Patton, S. (2000). *Transracial adoption in contemporary America.* New York: New York University Press.

Personal Responsibility and Work Opportunity Reconciliation Act (PRWORA) of 1996. Public Law 104–193.

Pew Commission on Children in Foster Care. (2004). *Fostering the future: Safety, permanence and well-being for children in foster care.* Washington, DC: The Pew Commission on Children in Foster Care.

Phillips, M., Shayne, A., Sherman, E., & Haring, B. (1971). *Factors associated with placement decisions in child welfare.* New York: Child Welfare League of America.

Pike, V., Downs, S. W., Emlen, A., Downs, G., & Case, D. (1977). *Permanent planning for children in foster care* (No. OHDS 77-30124). Washington, DC: U.S. Department of Health, Education and Welfare.

Pires, S. A. (2002). *Building systems of care: A primer.* Washington, DC: National Technical Assistance Center for Children's Mental Health, Georgetown University.

Pires, S. A., Lazear, K. J., & Conlan, L. (2006). *Primer hands on — child welfare: A skill building curriculum.* Washington, DC: Human Services Collaborative.

Pizzigati, K. (1998). Safety and permanence: New federal law emphasizes both. *Children's Voice, 7*(3), 12–13.

Radel, L. (2005, August). *Federal foster care financing: How and why the current funding structure fails to meet the needs of the child welfare field.* Washington, DC: U.S. Department of Health and Human Services, Office of the Assistant Secretary for Planning and Evaluation.

Ratterman, D., Dodson, D., & Hardin, M. (1987). *Reasonable efforts to prevent foster care placement: A guide to implementation.* Washington, DC: American Bar Association.

Redding, R. E., Fried, C., & Britner, P. A. (2000). Predictors of placement outcomes in treatment foster care: Implications for foster parent selection and service delivery. *Journal of Child and Family Studies, 9*(4), 425–447.

Reddy, L., & Pfeiffer, S. (1997). Effectiveness of treatment foster care with children and adolescence: A review of outcome studies. *Journal of American Academy of Child and Adolescent Psychiatry, 36*(5), 581–588.

Rehnquist, J. (2002a). *Recruiting foster parents.* Department of Health and Human Services, Office of the Inspector General. Washington, DC: U.S. Government Printing Office.

Rehnquist, J. (2002b). *Retaining foster parents.* Department of Health and Human Services, Office of the Inspector General. Washington, DC: U.S. Government Printing Office.

Rhodes, K. W., Orme, J. G., & Buehler, C. (2001, March). A comparison of family foster parents who quit, consider quitting, and plan to continue fostering. *Social Service Review*, 84–114.

Robertson, R. (1997). Walking the talk: Organizational modeling and commitment to youth and staff development. *Child Welfare, 76*(5), 577–590.

Saunders, E., Nelson, K., & Landsman, M. (1993). Racial inequality and child neglect: Findings in a metropolitan area. *Child Welfare, 72*(4), 341–354.

Semidei, J., Radel, L. F., & Nolan, C. (2001, March–April). Substance abuse and child welfare: Clear linkages and promising responses. *Child Welfare, 80*(2), 109–128.

Shlonsky, A. R., & Berrick, J. D. (2001, March). Assessing and promoting quality in kin and nonkin foster care. *Social Service Review*, 60–83.

Simmons, D., & Trope, J. (1999). *P.L. 105-90 Adoption and Safe Families Act of 1997: Issues for tribes and states serving Indian children.* The National Indian Child Welfare Association, National Resource Center for Organizational Improvement. University of Southern Maine.

Slavin, P. (2000). Children with parents behind bars. *Children's Voice, 9*(5), 4.

Slingerland, W. (1919). *Child placing in families.* New York: Russell Sage Foundation.

Staff, I., & Fein, E. (1995). Stability and change: Initial findings in a study of treatment foster care placements. *Children and Youth Services Review, 17*(3), 379–389.

Stein, T. (1998). *The social welfare of women and children with HIV and AIDS.* New York: Oxford University Press.

Stein, T. J. (2000, November–December). The Adoption and Safe Families Act: Creating a false dichotomy between parents' and children's rights. *Families in Society, 81*(6).

Steinberg, G., & Hall, B. (2003). *What is transracial adoption?* Warren, NJ: EMK Press.

Takas, M. (1993, December-January). Kinship care: Developing a safe and effective framework for protective placement of children with relatives. *Zero to Three*, 12–17.

Taylor-Brown, S., & Garcia, A. (1995). Social workers and HIV-affected families: Is the profession prepared? *Social Work, 40*(1), 14–15.

Terling-Watt, T. (2001). Permanency in kinship care: An exploration of disruption rates and factors associated with placement disruption. *Children & Youth Services Review, 23*(2), 111–126.

Testa, M. F., & Rolock, N. (1999, January–February). Professional foster care: A future worth pursuing? *Child Welfare, 78*(1), 108–124.

The Pew Charitable Trusts. (2007). Time for reform; Support relatives in providing foster care and permanent families for children. Philadelphia, PA: Author. Available at: www.kidsarewaiting.org.

Thoennes, N. (1996). Foster care review: Reducing delay and expense in the juvenile court. Alexandria, VA: State Justice Institute.

Thornton, J. (1991). Permanency planning for children in kinship foster homes. *Child welfare, 70*(5), 593–601.

Thurston, H. S. (1930). *The dependent child.* New York: Columbia University Press.

Tourse, P., & Gunderson, L. (1988). Adopting and fostering children with AIDS: Policies in progress. *Children Today, 17*, 15–19.

Trenka, J. J., Oparah, J. C., & Shin, S. Y. (2006). *Outsiders within: Writing on transracial adoption.* Cambridge, MA: South End Press.

Twigg, R. (1995). Coping with loss: How foster parents' children cope with foster care. *Community*

Alternatives: The International Journal of Family Care, 7(1), 1–14.

U.S. Department of Health and Human Services, Administration for Children and Families. (2006). The data measures, data composites, and national standards to be used in the child and family services reviews. In *Federal Register* (pp. 32969–32987).

U.S. Department of Health and Human Services, Administration on Children, Youth, and Families. (23 January 2007). Foster care; non-profits; Title IV-E maintenance payments; interstate placements; home studies; foster and adoptive parents; background checks; title IV-E state plan amendments. (ACYF-CB-PI-07-02). Washington, DC: Author. Available: http://www.acf.hhs.gov/programs/cb.

U.S. General Accounting Office. (1989). *Foster parents: Recruiting and preservice training practices and evaluation.* Washington, D.C.: Author.

U.S. General Accounting Office. (1991). *Foster care: Children's experiences linked to various factors; better data needed.* (HRD-91-64). Washington, DC: Author.

University of Maryland, Casey Journalism Center on Children & Families, (2007, April). *News stories compiled.* Available: at www.cjc.und.edu

U.S. Department of Health and Human Services. (2000). *Rethinking child welfare practice under the Adoption and Safe Families Act of 1997: A Resource guide.* Washington, DC: U.S. Government Printing Office.

U.S. Department of Health and Human Services. (2007). *Budget in brief FY 2008.* Washington, DC: U.S. Government Printing Office. Available:http://hhs.gov/budget/docbudget.htm.

Walsh, J., & Walsh, R. (1990). *Quality care for tough kids.* Washington, DC: Child Welfare League of America.

Warren, D. H. (2001). Reaching for integrity: An Ericksonian life-cycle perspective on the experience of adolescents being raised by grandparents. *Child and Adolescent Social Work Journal, 18*(1), 21–35.

Weinberg, R. A., Waldman, I., van Dulmen, M.H.M., & Scarr, S. (2004). The Minnesota transracial adoption study: Parent reports of psychological adjustment at late adolescence. *Adoption Quarterly, 8*(2), 27–44.

Whittaker, J. K. (1987). Group care for children. In A. Minahan (Ed.). *Encyclopedia of social work* (18th ed.) (pp. 672–682). Silver Spring, MD: National Association of Social Workers.

Whittaker, J. K. (2000). The future of residential group care. *Child Welfare, 79*(1), 59–73.

Wightman, M. (1991). Criteria for placement decisions with cocaine-exposed infants. *Child Welfare, 70*(6), 653–663.

Wolins, M., & Piliavin, I. (1964). *Institutions or foster family: A century of debate.* New York: Child Welfare League of America.

Wood, L., Herring, A. E., & Hunt, R. (1989). *On their own: The needs of youth in transition.* Elizabeth, NJ: Association for the Advancement of the Mentally Handicapped.

Zambrana, R., & Dorrington, C. (1998). Economic and social vulnerability of Latino children and families by subgroup: Implications for child welfare. *Child Welfare, 77*(1), 5–27.

Zuravin, S., & DePanfilis, D. (1997). Factors affecting foster care placement of children receiving child protective services. *Social Work Research, 21*(1), 34–42.

Statutes, Administrative Rules, and Children's Bureau Interpretative Policies

Accreditation of Agencies and Approval of Persons Under the Intercountry Adoption Act of 2000 (IAA). 04/01/06 Edition. 22 CRF Chapter 1, Part 96.

Title IV of the Social Security Act, 42 U.S.C. Section 422 et. seq.

The following public laws amended sections of Title IV of the Social Security Act.

The Adam Walsh Child Protection and Safety Act of 2006, P.L. 109–248, amends 42 U.S.C. Sections 671(a) (20), 671(a) (20) (B).

The Adoption Assistance and Child Welfare Act of 1980, P. L. 96–272

The Adoption and Safe Families Act of 1997, P. L. 105-89 amending 42 U.S.C. Sections 601 et seq., 622b, 629 et seq., 653, 670-679, 671 at5, 675(5)(E), 677(a)(2)A, 675(1), 1320a-9.

The Child and Family Services Improvement Act of 2006, P.L. 109-288, amends 42 U.S.C. 620-628b,622(b), 629b(a)(8), 629b(b)(2), 629d, 629e(c), 629f(b), 629f(b)(3), 629g, 629g(a), 629g(b)(3), and 629(i).

The Deficit Reduction Act of 2005, P.L. 109-171, amending 42 U.S.C. Sections 429h©, 622(b), 629f(a), 629 h, 629H(a), 629h(b), 671, 672, 672a, 673(a)(2), and 674(a)(3).

The Indian Child Welfare Act of 1978, P.L. 95-608, 25 U.S.C. Sections 1901 – 1963. The John Chaffee Foster Care Independence Act of 1999, P.L. 106-169 amending 42 U.S.C. Sections 671a, 673b, 674(a)(4), 675, 677, and 139a(a)(10)(A)(ii).

The Keeping Children and Families Safe Act of 2003, P.L. 108-36, amending 42 U.S.C. Sections 670, 5101, 5104(b), 5104(c)(1), 5105, 5105(a), 5105(b), 5106(a), 5106a(a), 5106a(b), 5106a(c), 5106(b), 5105(c), 5106c(c), 5106d, 5111, 5113, 5114, 5116a, 5116b, 5116d, 5116e(a), 5116f, 5116g(3), 5116h, and 5116h(1).

The Multiethnic Placement Act of 1994 and Interethnic Placement Provisions of 1996, P.L. 103-382 as amended by P.L. 104-188, Section 1808 amending 42 U.S.C. Sections 622, 671(a)(18), 674(d), 1996 b, 1996(h), and 5115a.

The Personal Responsibility and Work Opportunity Reconciliation Act of 1996., P.L. 104–193.

The Safe and Timely Interstate Placement of Foster Children Act of 2006, P. L. 109-239

Children's Bureau Policies

Children's Bureau (2006, December). Child and Family Services Reviews Procedures Manua. Available at www.acf.hhs.gov/programs/cbcwmonitoring/tools_guide/index.htm

Children's Bureau, (2007). Child Welfare policy manual, section 4: MEPA/IEP. Available at www.acf.hhs.gov/programs/cb/laws_policies/laws/cwpm.

The following policy issuances of the children's Bureau are available at www. acf.hhs.gov/programs/cb/laws_policies/laws/cwpm

❖ ACYF-IM-CB-97-04: The Small Business Job Protection Act of 1996, Interethnic Adoption, and Multiethnic Placement Act.
❖ ACYF-CB-PI-07-04: Issued February 21, 2007. Title IV-E State Plan Amendment —The Tax Relief and Health Care Act of 2006 (Public Law (P.L.) 109-432)
❖ ACYF-CB-PI-07-03: February 22, 2007. Court Improvement Program Requirements of the Safe and Timely Interstate Placement of Foster Children Act of 2006)
❖ ACYF-CB-PI-07-02: Issued January 23, 2007. Title IV-E State Plan Amendments —New Legislation.
❖ ACYF-CB-IM 06-05: Issued: December 7, 2006. The Child and Family Services Improvement Act of 2006 (Public Law (P.L.) 109-288).
❖ ACYF-CB-IM 06-04: Issued: September 1, 2006. New Legislation—The Adam Walsh Child Protection and Safety Act of 2006 (Public Law (P.L.) 109-248.)

❖ ACYF-CB-IM 06-03: Issued: August 11, 2006. New Legislation—The Safe and Timely Interstate Placement of Foster Children Act of 2006 (Public Law (P.L.) 109-239).

❖ ACYF-CB-IM 06-02: Issued: June 9, 2006. New Legislation—The Deficit Reduction Act of 2005.

❖ ACYF-CB-IM 06-01: Issued: January 17, 2006. New Legislation—Public Law 109-113, the Fair Access Foster Care Act of 2005.

CHAPTER 9

Foster Care Practice and Issues

If you can't be touched, you can't be changed. If you can't be changed, you can't be alive.

— *James Baldwin*

It is the truly, truly remarkable person who will work in other people's pain.

—*Michael D. Clark*

CHAPTER OUTLINE

INTRODUCTION

The Adoption and Safe Families Act (ASFA) and the subsequent statutes discussed in Chapter 8, have two overarching goals. First, to move children who are in the child welfare system into permanent homes. Second, to change the experience of children who are entering the system today. The philosophy that guides ASFA is that the health and safety of children is the paramount concern that must guide all child welfare services and decisions (42 USC 671 (a) (15)).

ASFA seeks to ensure that the child welfare system respects the developmental needs of children, including the need for a permanent place to call home. To ensure that children move out of foster care and grow up in safe, permanent homes, the Act radically changes the time frames for making decisions regarding permanent placement. The law requires that states hold the child's first permanency hearing within twelve months (rather than eighteen months), and that states initiate or join termination of parental rights (TPR) proceedings for parents of children who have been in care for fifteen of the last twenty-two months (except in situations in which the child is placed safely with relatives and this placement is expected to be permanent, there is a compelling reason why TPR is not in the child's best interest, or the family has not received the services that were part of the case service plan). It reaffirms reunification as the preferred option for children whose families can provide them with a safe, nurturing environment and it promotes the timely adoption of children who cannot return safely to their own homes.

Standards for Decision Making

Child welfare decisions are made by caseworkers, supervisors, and jurists. These decisions occur when they apply agency guidelines, policies, or laws to the information gathered in a specific case. Important case decisions, including the decision to place, are being made by caseworkers with less specialized education and child welfare experience than in the past. Difficult tasks are often performed by persons who do not have the necessary skills and training. A majority of caseworkers in foster care lack professional graduate social work education. The situation is exacerbated by staff turnover.

The processing of information is influenced by contextual elements. Child welfare practitioners are forced to operate on a crisis-to-crisis basis, which limits the information collected and the time allowed for processing it. This can lead to decisions based on expediency. Another dimension of decision making is the range of persons involved in the process. Although the principal decision maker is usually the caseworker, this decision is rarely made unilaterally. There may be input from family members, other staff in the child welfare agency, and professionals within the community who have been working with the child and family. A casework decision to seek removal of a child from the family must be taken to the court and affirmed or denied through a legal process. (See Chapter 5.)

The decision about whether to place a child is influenced not only by the characteristics of the case and the decision-making context, but also by the criteria that have been established for such decisions. Standards for public agencies are promulgated through legislation, administrative rules, and policies. All states have statutes authorizing intervention to protect children. On a national level, ASFA of 1997 set these standards:

1. Child safety is the paramount consideration in decision making regarding service provision, placement, and permanency planning. Reasonable efforts to preserve and reunify the family should be made except
   ❖ where the parent has subjected the child to abandonment, torture, chronic abuse, sexual abuse or other exaggerated circumstances defined in state law;
   ❖ the parent has been convicted of murder or involuntary manslaughter or aided another person in these acts against another child of the parent;
   ❖ the parent has been convicted of felony assault to the child or another child; or
   ❖ the parent has had parental rights to another child involuntarily terminated.
2. Foster care is a temporary setting and not a place for children to grow up. A permanency hearing must be held within twelve months of placement into foster care. A petition for TPR must be filed for any child who has been in care fifteen of the last twenty-two months unless the child is safely placed with a relative, there is a compelling reason why TPR is not in the child's best interests, or the family has not, through no fault of their own, received the services that were part of the case plan.
3. Permanency planning efforts should begin as soon as the child enters care. Concurrent planning—that is, reasonable efforts to reunify and reasonable efforts to place for adoption/guardianship—can proceed at the same time.
4. The child welfare system must focus on results and accountability. Children are provided with quality services that protect their safety and health. Families are provided with quality services that increase their capacities to parent.
5. Innovative approaches are needed to achieve the goals of safety, permanency, and well-being, including helping states identify and address barriers to timely adoption placements addressing kinship care and identifying and addressing parental substance abuse. (U.S. Department of Health and Human Services, 2000)

Most states, in order to qualify for federal funds, have passed laws or administrative policies implementing these standards.

How has a service that affects so many children and that has such a long-established position in child welfare become so burdened with highly complex problems? To shed light on this question, this chapter focuses on foster care service delivery. Specifically, it explores casework practices that could take ASFA, the Multiethnic Placement Act as amended by the Interethnic Placement Provisions, the Indian Child Welfare Act, the John Chafee Foster Care Independence Act, Keeping Children and Families Safe Act, the Safe and Timely Interstate Placement of Foster Children Act, the Adam Walsh Child Protection and Safety Act, and the Child and Family Services Improvement Act, from well intentioned "child welfare reforms" on paper to a "child welfare reality" for the over 800,000 children impacted by the foster care system each year. Given the complexities of the foster care system and the limitations of space in this text, we will not comprehensively discuss every situation. However, we will discuss some of the major issues and suggest possible actions that could humanize the experience for everyone involved.

The core concepts of casework practice were discussed in Chapter 4. We will apply those concepts to the situations seen in the foster care program. For ease in reading throughout this chapter we use the term "child" to refer to all persons less than 18 years of age and "she" to include children of either gender unless there are specific gender differences or references to persons of certain genders, in which case, we use the appropriate gender term. In addition, we provide application exercises or opportunities for the reader to apply the identified concepts to case scenarios. Hopefully, these opportunities will stimulate and advance individual learning and group learning. We started with "concurrent planning" because it should be the framework for organizing interventions with children and parents from the first day.

CONCURRENT PLANNING

When the U.S. Congress passed the Adoption and Safe Families Act in 1997, several barriers to timely permanence for foster children were addressed. The law states that in certain serious situations, the courts do not need to require "reasonable efforts" toward family reunification, but can move forward without delay with termination of parental rights. In such cases, a permanency planning hearing must be held within thirty days. Additionally, in those cases in which "reasonable efforts" for family reunification are being implemented, the law permits the use of concurrent planning. This means that states may plan to place a child for adoption or with a legal guardian at the same time that family reunification is tried. The two plans are being implemented simultaneously, so that an alternative plan is already in place in the event that family reunification fails (Katz, 1999). Concurrent planning requires that agencies and workers prepare for different outcomes at the same time, instead of sequentially. While at times this may seem to present the practitioner with an ethical dilemma, the goal of reunification can be in the foreground of practice efforts, with the goal of adoption in the background as a fail-safe option if the primary goal is not achieved. The parent must be fully informed from the beginning that the agency is starting work on an adoption plan, but only as a backup plan if reunification becomes very unlikely. The case example below shows how the worker used concurrent planning in a way that was helpful to the parent.

CASE EXAMPLE:
Concurrent Planning

On an initial contact with Ms. Denton, the worker explored her family situation to see whether there was a potential relative placement. Ms. Denton stated that her mother was deceased and her father lived on the streets in another state. She did not know who was the father of Elena, and Ricky's father was serving time in prison for dealing controlled substances. Her only sibling was an unsuitable placement, she knew, as he had sexually abused her when they were children. She considered that the children were better off in the Williams foster home than with any of her friends.

At the court hearing, Ms. Denton acknowledged that her use of substances had caused her to leave the children home alone on more than one occasion and that her judgment had been impaired when she failed to return home on the dates alleged in the petition. The children were made temporary wards of the family court, and the judge instructed Ms. Denton that she must seek treatment for her substance use and be able to provide a home with proper supervision within legal time frames.

The case was transferred to Ms. Lee, the foster care worker. Immediately, Ms. Lee scheduled an appointment at the substance treatment center for an assessment of the effects of alcohol and other drugs on Ms. Denton's functioning and ability to parent. Ms. Denton was admitted for treatment but checked herself out the following morning and once again could not be found. The foster care worker did a "differential diagnosis" based on information collected from a variety of sources. The prognosis for recovery and family reunification was not good at that point, so Ms. Lee began to implement a concurrent plan. The plan was still for family reunification (if Ms. Denton addressed the issues that had caused the children to be placed), but an alternative plan was also developed, to be used if she defaulted on the plan.

Ms. Lee spoke with Mr. and Mrs. Williams on her second visit to the home to monitor the well-being of the children. The foster parents were experienced and well trained, so they were well aware of the deleterious effects of placement change on children. They committed to work intensively with Ms. Denton when she returned and to assist her in the reunification process. At the same time, they indicated they would be available as a resource for adoption if the children's mother did not follow through.

The next week, less than two weeks after the children had been placed in care, Ms. Denton reappeared and Ms. Lee provided the mother with a full disclosure of the situation. She emphasized the urgency of the time lines required by federal and state law and stressed that Ms. Denton had a limited time in which to show the court that she was ready to be reunited with her children. Ms. Denton wept when confronted with the reality that she might lose her children and vowed to work hard for their return. A signed agreement was developed that specified the time lines of court review, the steps that Ms. Denton would undertake, and the resources and assistance that would be provided by Ms. Lee and the agency. That day she returned to the substance treatment center.

Mr. and Mrs. Williams brought the children to visit their mother frequently. They had learned in their training the importance of maintaining the parent–child relationship. By sharing their observations of the children with the mother, they were able to show her how important she was to both Ricky and Elena. When Ms. Denton completed her inpatient stay, the Williamses brought her to their home for yet another visit. They also brought the children to the mother's apartment when the worker deemed the time for home visits had arrived.

Meanwhile, Ms. Lee was exploring the paternal claims to the children. Elena apparently had been the result of a "one night stand," and there was no knowledge of who the father might be. Corresponding with Ricky's father in prison, she ascertained that he was willing to relinquish parental rights in the event of an adoption. By attending to these details before the need to move to termination of parental rights and adoption, she was removing obstacles to timely permanency.

At the same time, the worker met with Ms. Denton's AA sponsor, who helped the newly recovering woman to attend frequent AA meetings to support sobriety. Ms. Lee also monitored other kinds of progress with the plan, including regular urine screens, enrollment in a parenting class, and the mother's use of appropriate discipline with the children. Mrs. Williams helped teach Ms. Denton to cook nutritious meals for the children when they visited.

After four months, the children were returned to their mother's care, and a family reunification worker supported Ms. Denton and the children with intensive family-based services (see Chapter 7). The family remained under foster care supervision for another six months. Occasionally, Ms. Denton would bring the children to visit with the Williams family when she needed a brief period of respite.

Had the reunification plan not succeeded, the children would have remained with the Williams family with whom they had made a good adjustment and were comfortable. When the case was dismissed from court jurisdiction, Ms. Denton confided to Ms. Lee that it was not until she was confronted with the reality that she might lose her children that she was able to move ahead to sobriety and learning to parent.

What Is Concurrent Planning?

In concurrent planning, the caseworker engages in active efforts to effect family reunification and simultaneously identifies an alternative permanency plan *with the knowledge of the parent, child, and foster parent/relative*. The concept of concurrent planning, though not the label, was first formulated in the late 1960s by Irmgard Heymann and colleagues in Chicago (Weinberg and Katz, 1998). Heymann and colleagues advocated an early, specific, honest discussion with the parent of the requirements for returning the child to his or her home and the consequences if those requirements were not met.

Child development professionals have long argued and proven that a child's positive growth and development rests on the child having a stable environment with continuity of caregivers who value the child and whom the child can rely on without question. The concurrent planning approach for children who have been removed from their parent(s) is an attempt to restore stability and caregiver permanency for these children as soon as possible.

The concurrent planning term and approach was adopted in 1983 and was further developed and demonstrated by Lutheran Social Services (LSS) of Washington State. LSS has shown over the past twenty years that concurrent planning can ensure safety and permanency for the child in a shorter period, while respecting the rights of parents (Cahn, 2003).

Concurrent Planning Practice

The nine core components of concurrent planning are

1. redefining success;
2. early differential assessment and prognostic case review;
3. full disclosure;

4. using crises and time limits as opportunities;
5. motivating parents to change;
6. frequent parent–child visitation;
7. establishing and working toward Plan A and Plan B simultaneously;
8. written agreements, scrupulous documentation, and timely case review; and
9. legal–social work collaboration. (National Resource Center Family Centered Practice and Permanency Planning, 2003)

Application exercise: *So what does the caseworker do?* As you read through the explanation of the core components, refer back to the Denton case and identify what the caseworker did. Remember that concurrent planning focuses on what needs to be done to achieve permanency. There are other aspects of child welfare case planning that will be discussed later in this chapter.

Redefining Success.   ASFA redefined success by instituting strict time limits for children to be returned to parents or placed with relatives, or for parental rights to be terminated and the child placed for adoption. The caseworker's job is to quickly direct the case to one of these resolutions. The policy preference is to pursue these options in the order listed, unless the parents' behavior toward the child or sibling is defined as "aggravated circumstances." Aggravated circumstances include abandonment, murder of a child, voluntary manslaughter of a child, the parent aided or abetted, attempted or conspired to commit such a murder of voluntary manslaughter, or a felony assault that resulted in serious bodily injury to their child or another child (42 USC 675 (5) (E)). Under these circumstances, states are not required to perform "reasonable efforts" to preserve or reunify the child and parents. State laws vary on this issue.

Early Differential Assessment and Prognostic Case Review.   To achieve timely resolution, the caseworker begins with culturally respectful parent and child assessments—including strengths, needs, and identifying core issues, problems, and challenges. Based on the initial assessment, the caseworker makes a *tentative conclusion* about the probability of the child returning home based on her assessment of the parents' capacities to benefit from reunification services. At the same time, based on the child's assessment, she identifies possible alternatives should return home not be achieved.

Full Disclosure.   To avoid any claims of duplicity or dishonesty, the caseworker engages in respectful, candid discussion with the parents about their rights and responsibilities, supports the agency will provide, importance of the time limits, and the specific consequences of not following through with the case plan. At each contact, open, honest discussions with all parties—parents, relatives, foster/adoptive families, attorneys, other service providers—about the status of the permanency plan and the next steps should be discussed and reevaluated. Statements should be used such as: "Our goal is to return your child to you as soon as you demonstrate that you are not using drugs and not engaging in behaviors that threaten your child's safety. We will help you find the services you need, but you are the only one who can make the changes. I am required to petition the court for termination of your parental rights if you do not demonstrate the necessary changes in twelve months. In some circumstances, we may determine that termination of your parental rights may not be in your child's best interests. If the court agrees, your rights may not be terminated. Also, while I am working with you to help you do what is necessary to have your children with you, I am also working on identifying an alternative permanent home for your child should you not be successful in doing what we have agreed needs to be done to get the children back." This type of direct conversation helps to set a nonjudgmental, respectful, and honest tone to go forward with concurrent planning.

Crises and Time Limits as Opportunities. Placement and clarity about time limits designated by law can create crises for parents. The caseworker uses time limits and the "crisis" of the placement as opportunities for the parents to make change. What did Mrs. Denton say made her change?

Motivating Parents to Change. The role of the worker is to engage parents in planning, to motivate them to change, and to support them in the process of change. The role of the parent is to make the changes necessary to ensure the child's safety, well-being, and permanency. The underlying conditions and behaviors that necessitate child placement are usually chronic and multiple. Therefore, we should not expect change will be easy for the parent. Relapse is not atypical, but it does not necessarily indicate failure. The caseworker has to show the parent how to "begin again," while understanding that the clock is ticking.

Frequent Parent–Child Visitation. Parents who visit regularly have the best chance of reunification with their children. In an ideal world, all siblings would be placed together and the parent and the child's substitute caregiver would develop a relationship that normalized visitations in the child's foster home. However, our world is far from ideal. The parents' hostilities and past behaviors, the caregivers' fears, the distances from parents' home and foster home, the need for caseworker-supervised visits, and insufficient placement resources to accommodate sibling groups are some of the reasons for office visits. The more structured the visitation plan, the more likely parents will participate. Involving foster parents and relatives in parent–child visits promotes more supportive relationships with the parents both during and after placement. In addition, it shows the child that her parent is respected.

Establishing and Working Toward Plan A and Plan B Simultaneously. Concurrent planning requires identifying, locating, and engaging fathers and maternal and paternal family as soon as removal from the parents is deemed necessary. Tell relatives and nonrelated foster parents that the plan is to return the child to the parents. Ask them if they would be willing to provide a permanent home for the child if reunification doesn't work out. If they are, begin acquiring the information necessary to effect permanent placement with them. Many states, recognizing that their primary sources of adoptive parents are relatives and nonrelative foster parents with whom the child is placed at the time of termination of parental rights, have combined their foster and adoptive home recruitment, family assessments, and required documentation to expedite adoptive placements after termination of parental rights. Partnerships between parents, caseworkers, and relatives/foster parents promote the child's emotional well-being and permanency planning—the child sees that the people who care about her get along and respect one another.

Written Agreements, Scrupulous Documentation, and Timely Case Review. What needs to be done? Who is responsible for doing it? When is it to be done? When will progress be reviewed? Writing down *specific goals*, *specific tasks*, and *specific time frames* helps motivate parents to follow through, provides clarity of responsibilities of parents and caseworker, and keeps the case on a sure trajectory to permanency for the child. A signed Parent–Agency Agreement, properly completed, is the approach used by most states. It is a useful "To Do" list for everyone.

A child welfare caseworker also must document services needed, services obtained or provided, services still needed, plans to obtain these services, and the implication for progress to permanency. As discussed in Chapter 4, the task-centered casework methodology is an effective model for child welfare services documentation. In essence, the Parent–Agency Agreement is the organizing framework for collecting and documenting information for agency and court reports. The Parent–Agency Agreement documents the promises. The agency and court reports document the behaviors, that is, what actually happened. Modifications to the permanency plan are based on the deviations of actual behavior from promised behaviors.

Important to the implementation of any plan is the ongoing review and modification based on new information, changed circumstances, or changed assessments. Early and ongoing case review to assess progress, to review continuing needs, and to modify and plan for the future is required by ASFA no less than every ninety days by the agency and court reviews no less than every six months. Many states have more frequent reviews.

Legal and Social Work Collaboration. Children enter foster care after a court has determined that the child's health or safety requires removal from the parents' home, or, in very limited circumstances, when the parent requests voluntary placement of the child. Foster care is intrusive in family matters held sacrosanct by the U.S. Constitution and specific state laws. Court engagement in the placement and ongoing decision-making processes protect the due process rights of children and parents. Consultation and support from legal staff assures legally sound case work and case planning. See Chapter 5 for a discussion of this collaboration.

WORKING WITH THE PLACEMENT PROCESS

When a child is referred to a social agency because placement outside her own home is likely to be necessary, the agency must undertake a series of tasks. The use of a systematic placement process helps to assure that the agency meets its responsibilities for

1. trying to reunify the child with her family;
2. selecting an appropriate form of care;
3. helping the child separate from parents and move into the new child care arrangement;
4. helping foster parents or child care staff carry out their responsibilities successfully; and
5. seeing that a permanent home is provided for the child, either with her parents or relatives, or in a new permanent home through adoption, guardianship, or other forms of planned long-term care providing a stable living environment.

Parental Involvement

Removing children from their homes to place them into the foster care system is a very serious step with far-reaching consequences. It cannot be stated too often that this step should be undertaken only when it becomes clear that even with outside help the children's parents cannot provide for their safety.

To make the child's placement less traumatic, the caseworker must reach out to the child's parents and try to understand them—their life experiences, the ambivalent feelings they may have about their child, and their strengths and weaknesses in parenting and how these affect the child. Parents should be involved in planning the placement to the greatest degree possible. Parents are to be viewed as partners (Maluccio & Sinanoglu, 1981; Pennell & Anderson, 2005) and as a valuable resource for the child in care (Blumenthal & Weinberg, 1983).

Parents are often the best source of information about the child's likes, dislikes, habits, and needs (McFadden, 1980; Ryan, McFadden, & Warren, 1981) and should communicate with the foster parents early in the placement process, preferably before the child goes to the foster home. The foster parent can answer the parent's questions about care and can benefit from detailed practical information about the child. Even if parents are in crisis, are angry about the removal of the child, or are highly negative about the child, the engagement process should be attempted by the foster care team at the earliest feasible time (Palmer, 1997).

When a child is in foster care, the court often orders parental visits and provision of child support. The caseworker makes realistic plans with the parents about their contributions to the child's support and arrangements to visit the child under circumstances that will reinforce their affection and commitment to the child. It is important that parents be helped to understand their continuing rights and responsibilities. They need to know the short time frame they have to make substantial, measurable progress, before federal mandates require a permanency planning hearing. It is essential that the social worker strive to help parents establish a realistically attainable plan to restore their home, or, if this is not possible, to release the child for adoption. Because many of the children who enter foster care do not have adoptive homes made available to them, even though they are legally free for adoption, it is all the more important that whatever is of value in the parent–child relationship be supported.

Considerable attention has been given to the effects on children of separation experiences. In contrast, insufficient attention has been given to understanding the experiences of parents when their children enter foster care. The separation of children from parents is a crisis for the parents and for the whole family system. A parent whose children were placed following an episode of serious abuse recollected the impact of the separation on her.

> I had already lost my husband. Now I was losing everything, my self-respect, my children, I was losing myself. I felt like a piece of shit. My father had told me that I'd get no help from the family because I had disgraced them. I knew that I'd lose my financial assistance [AFDC]. Something was dying in me. I wanted to kill myself. Thank God my Parents Anonymous sponsor came down to the hospital emergency room while my children were being examined and taken away. She told me I shouldn't kill myself because if I killed myself I wouldn't get my kids back. I think I probably would have done myself in if she hadn't been there to help me at a time when I lost everything. (*McFadden, 1984, p. 596*)

Parents should be prepared with anticipatory guidance for the painful feelings surrounding placement. In acknowledging the difficulty of the separation, the caseworker can help the parent identify the supportive people in the environment who can assist them in the sad and anxious hours following the separation. The caseworker's skill in restating visiting plans and the plans made to achieve reunification may provide a needed element of hope, which can sustain the parent's motivation. For the parent to provide a verbal or written message to the child about the reasons for the separation and the hopes for the placement period, can be helpful to both parent and child.

Selecting the Placement Type

Figure 9.1 gives an overview of the steps followed by cases through the foster care system. Children are placed with relatives, in a nonrelative home, or in a group home or institution. Their parents normally would be highly involved in reunification services, to help them correct the problems that brought their children into care.

Little empirical data exist to support decisions in selecting from a range of foster care facilities. Nevertheless, certain guidelines generally prevail in choosing among the different types of care for children.

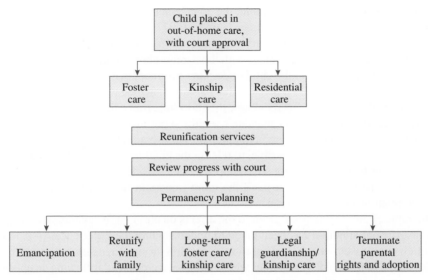

Figure 9.1 *Overview of Steps Followed by Cases through the Foster Care System*

Source: Adapted from P. Schene (1998). Past, present, and future roles of child protective services, *The Future of Children: Protecting Children from Abuse and Neglect, 8*(1), Adapted with the permission of the David and Lucile Packard Foundation.

Despite its difficulties, the foster home (relative or nonrelative) continues to be preferred for the majority of children if it appears that a child can participate in family life, attend community schools, and live in the community without danger to self or others. Especially for preschool-aged children, foster homes are considered almost mandatory except for those with very severe problems requiring specialized service. Kinship foster care is often preferred because it enables the child to remain in an extended family network and lessens the trauma of separation. Sibling groups should almost always be placed together, if possible, unless an older sibling abuses the younger one(s) and cannot be controlled. Children get comfort and stability from being placed with siblings (Rutter, 1985; Garbarino, DuBrow, Knostelny, & Pardo, 1992; Staff & Fein, 1992; Grigsby, 1994). For many children it may be very important to remain in their own school district so that their education is not disrupted and they can maintain their relationships with friends and teachers. For others, a complete change of environment might be more desirable and beneficial. About 24 percent of foster children are currently in kinship foster care, and 46 percent in nonrelative foster homes (Children's Bureau, 2006, September).

Treatment foster care is appropriate for children with emotional or behavioral problems that can be handled in a therapeutic family milieu. Specialized, highly trained foster homes take medically fragile children, such as those with HIV/AIDS, work closely with the hospital and medical team, and make it possible for these children to be in a home rather than a hospital (Hochstadt & Yost, 1991).

Group care is rarely used for young children and is generally considered to be appropriate for adolescents who are unable to tolerate the demands of family living. Many adolescents do well in general or treatment foster homes, and are desirous of having a positive experience with family life. For some adolescents, small or family-type group homes are a good solution. For others, group homes or cottages in which the child care staff are more role models than parent figures may be appropriate. In 2005, 8 percent of foster children were in group homes.

Children who cannot make use of family living are usually referred to institutions or residential treatment facilities; for example, troubled adolescents who are trying to free themselves of close family ties and for whom peer influences and group experiences may have greater value than family life. If youths have difficulty in forming relationships with substitute parenting figures because of past family experiences, they may fare better in a group setting. Some children have experienced successive replacements in poorly selected foster homes and can use the group home, residential treatment facility, or institution as a stable setting that provides continuity and physical, if not emotional, "roots" and a chance to seek out a few accepting or "safe" adult staff with whom to try to form ties.

Children and young persons who act out in aggressive ways dangerous to themselves or others or who display other behavior that the family or community will seldom tolerate are often served in a residential setting. Some children are cared for in residential facilities because their communities lack appropriate educational, medical, or psychiatric resources that they need. Usually, a family setting is preferred for the first placement, based on the belief that children should be in the "least restrictive environment" possible, and moved to residential facilities if they cannot make a satisfactory adjustment to family life. The trend is to move the child back into a community setting as soon as possible. In 2005, 10 percent of children in care were in institutional settings (Children's Bureau, 2006, September).

Older foster children are being supervised in their own residences and provided independent living services to help them make the transition from foster care to productive adulthood. These youth are placed in their own residences by default (no other placement is available) or by plan (they have attained sufficient maturity to live without twenty-four-hour supervision by an adult. In 2005, 1 percent of children were in supervised independent living services (Children's Bureau, 2006, September).

The hope is that the child will experience only one placement or, failing that, the absolute minimum of placements possible. The first placement can be a very significant one for the child's future, as it may become her permanent home if the parents cannot resume care of the child and concurrent planning efforts have resulted in a plan of adoption or guardianship by the foster parents. Even though the first placement may become a permanent one and should, therefore, be made with special care, unfortunately there is rarely the time available to do a thorough assessment of the child and foster family to ensure an appropriate match. The unfortunate reality is that choice of foster care placement is often determined by practical factors such as what is available, location of the home, and the constraints of agency contracts with other child placement agencies (Stein & Rzepnicki, 1984).

Child Assessment and Initial Placement Selection

One of the striking findings of the first round of CFSRs was that the child protective services system as a whole did not document a full assessment of children in the families. They lacked information on the child's educational attainments, medical conditions and services, behavioral conditions and services, and general behaviors unless extreme (Children's Bureau, 2005). Some states have child assessment centers or shelter facilities (family-based or group care) in which all children entering foster care are placed for assessment but many do not. States argue that the CFSR process does not support assessment centers because they are included in the "count" for the "placement stability" indicator. In the states that do not know much about the children, the foster care system generally makes placements based on the age and gender of the child and the ASFA philosophy; first-choice placement is with a suitable relative. If that is not possible, second-choice placement is in a nonrelated foster home. Too many of these placement decisions result in replacement for the child because there is no determination of the caregiver's ability to meet the needs of the specific child (Children's Bureau, 2005).

Often, neither parent is available to provide information to assist with the initial placement selection. How might a caseworker quickly determine what the child needs in placement with so little information? First, if the child can speak—ask her! Children know a lot more than caseworkers think. They may be a little reticent to share everything about themselves with a stranger, but you don't need to know everything at the initial placement. The caseworker must create a friendly, caring, and safe environment for the child. Explain what has happened and what will happen at the child's level of understanding. A statement–question format works well. For example, "Because we can't find your mom, we need to find another place for you to stay. Do you have any relatives or other adults that you would like me to ask if you can stay with them?" If the child gives you a name and location, investigate it. If the relative is unwilling or found unacceptable, explain why to the child. If she doesn't identify anyone, or the identified persons are unacceptable, a statement–question such as, "Since we can't find a relative or other adult you know for you to stay with, we need to find a foster home for you. Tell me what you would like me to look for in foster parents or foster homes when we sort through possible homes." Listen and take notes. Children want to see that you think what they say is important enough to write down for the case record.

Then ask, "Now tell me things about yourself that the foster parent should know." If the child doesn't say anything, follow up with questions that elicit responses for the child's strengths and challenges. For example:

Do you have any allergies?

What do you like to eat?

What don't you like to eat?

Do you like to have a lot of children around?

Do you have a certain bedtime?

When do you get up in the morning?

What do you like to do most of all?

Where do you go to school?

What grade are you in?

What subjects do you like most?

What subjects do you like least?

What grades do you get?

Do you get into fights at school or in the neighborhood?

What's the hardest thing for you today and what do you want me and the foster parent to do to help? (Compton, Galaway, & Cournoyer, 2005; Thompson & Rudolph, 2000; Trozzi & Massimini, 1999; Liberman, 1979)

Another accessible source is the child's teacher. You need to talk with her to let her know the child's situation so that she can be supportive when the child returns to school. Use this opportunity to ask about the child. Elicit her thoughts on the characteristics in a foster home that would best meet the child's needs. Every effort should be made to transport the child to her current school, unless that poses a danger to her, until it is determined that a change of schools will be required because the child will be in foster care for thirty days or more. Many states have adopted the philosophy of placing the child in her neighborhood of removal so she can remain in the same school (Casey Family Programs, 2006). These states report varying degrees of success.

For children who cannot talk, there are often older siblings who can tell you about the younger ones. In addition, the caseworker can talk and observe the child's reactions. If the child is one to five months ask: How does she respond to being held by you? When held by others in the office? When laid down? How does she respond to your voice? Does she follow sounds? Is she startled by loud noises? If she is eight months or older, ask: Does she react to her name? Does she follow simple commands like waving "bye-bye" or playing "peek-a-boo"? Most children should be using 3–20 words between 13 months and 18 months. Use a picture book to determine what words the child knows. Point to the picture and ask the child: "What's this?" A physical examination should be performed by an appropriate health care professional.

Because the caseworker wants to arrange a placement as soon as possible, the time taken to talk with and observe the child and attempts to talk with parents, relatives, teachers, or medical personnel before placement results in better opportunities to match the child's needs with the caregiver's abilities. This is critical when you think that these parents may become the child's permanent parents. A better matching provides more stability for the child. More stability for the child means fewer crises for the caseworker. Irrespective of how much the caseworker knows, too often, placement selection is dictated by resources available rather than the child's needs. The caseworker, as advocate, should provide information to her supervisor on the adequacy or inadequacy of foster home choices for individual children. Children should not continue to suffer because of a mismatch of resources needed and resources available.

Once the child has been safely placed, a more thorough child assessment process can begin. Some states use a standard process for all children and others use an individual behavior or condition-triggered process. This is discussed in Meeting the Needs of Children in Foster Care.

TEAM DECISION MAKING

The various models used for team decision making were discussed in Chapter 4. The use of teams to inform and facilitate decision making is as old as child welfare practice. The practice of team decision making has varied in form and substance over time. Early practice focused on convening multidisciplinary teams of caseworkers and other professionals to assess the family functioning and the nature and cause of harm to the child, and to formulate treatment plans and review progress. The most significant recent practice change is the inclusion of parents, children, and their natural helpers in team meetings and decisions (Pennell & Anderson, 2005; Weil et al., 1985). Using team decision making for children in foster care provides many benefits for them and for the child welfare system. Many perspectives provide a better understanding of the issues and possible resolutions, better understanding promotes better case interventions and better case interventions yield better results. Many helpers can lighten the load for the caseworker and offer the lifelong family supports that are needed by most families, irrespective of connection with the child welfare system. The issues of information sharing and engaging the children, parents, natural helpers, service providers, and others remain the greatest challenges to effective team decision making.

Information Sharing

One of the challenges to team decision making and service collaboration is the issue of client confidentiality and information sharing. In most situations, the parent's consent to the sharing of information about herself and her child—yes, the child is hers until the court terminates her rights—is all that is necessary to legally share the information. Competent casework practice in securing the parent's consent includes an explanation about the need to share information with others, the types of information to be shared, the parent's right to agree or disagree with the sharing of the information, the agency's authority to share specific information with specific individuals or agencies, and the court's authority to order the sharing of information if it finds that to be in the best interests of the child or the administration of justice. Consent to the release of information forms should be very specific as to what information is to be shared, with whom, and for what period.

Furthermore, the challenge is minimized or eliminated by federal and state laws on the sharing of information in foster care cases. For example, provisions of Title IV-E require the release of medical, educational, and service plan information to the child's caregiver and service providers. The Federal Educational Rights and Privacy Act (FERPA) and Individuals with Disabilities Education Act (IDEA) provide that education records may be obtained with parental consent, court order, or the child's consent if she is 18 years or older. Under IDEA, a "surrogate parent" may consent to the release of information. Many schools designate the relative/foster parent as the surrogate parent (Bussiere, English, & Teare, 1997).

Engaging the Children, Parents, Natural Helpers, and Service Providers

Frederick L. Collins stated, "There are two types of people— those who come into the room and say 'Here I am!' and those who come into the room and say, 'Ah, there you are.' The caseworker's best strategy for success is to be the one who says "Ah, there you are." (www.quotations page.com/quotes/Frederick_L._Collins)

Children. Children enjoy being the center of attention. In ecological graphics of foster care, that is always their position. However, what we hear from them is that no one listens to them (Jim Casey Youth Initiative, 2007; Represent, September 2006: Knipe & Warren, 1999).

The caseworker must listen and demonstrate that she understands the child's wishes, desires, or views. However, the caseworker must also be honest with the child. The child needs to know that while you will listen and hear what she says, there may be reasons that the wishes cannot be honored. The caseworker has to be able to clearly explain those reasons to the child and then engage the child in "alternative options" by brainstorming and planning. For example, "Your high school grade point average and your ACT scores are below the average for students accepted into the University of Michigan. While you may be admitted, I think you should apply to other colleges just in case you are not admitted to Michigan. What other colleges might you want to consider?"

Engaging and involving the child facilitates safety, well-being, and permanency. The child knows whether she is being hurt physically or emotionally. The child knows her feelings even though she may not know why she is feeling a certain way. The child knows what makes her feel hopeful and what makes her feel hopeless. The child knows what makes her happy and what makes her sad. She knows when she has someone who will "always be there" for her.

> **Application exercise:** Listen to Jeff. What does he want? How can you help him get what he wants? What do you predict will happen if he is returned to his mother? What do you and Jeff do to get his mother and grandmother to work together?

Jeff is an 11-year-old boy who entered foster care about 11 months ago because his mother was hospitalized after a drug overdose. His paternal grandmother said she would take him as soon as "the mother died or the agency terminated her rights." He has been in four foster homes in twelve months. He says, "They don't like me and I don't like them." The agency reported to the judge that he ran away from the foster homes. Jeff told the judge, "I don't run away, I walk to the agency and say I am not going back to the foster home." The agency's plan is to return him to his mother next month because she has made "significant progress" in drug treatment and the agency feels that the child will be safe with the mother. Jeff told his mother, his grandmother, and everyone monitoring his case —the caseworker, his Court Appointed Special Advocate (CASA) volunteer advocate, the judge, the agency supervisor, his teachers—that he does not want to go home with his mother because she will just "get on drugs again and I will be back with strangers."

Children should participate in every team meeting about them. They should be prepared in advance. They should know who is going to be in the meeting, what will be discussed, how long it will last, and what they can do and say during the meeting. They should have a signal to alert the worker that they are uncomfortable and want to leave. They should be permitted to sit or walk about during the meeting. Their participation and the duration of their presence should be based on their age and the nature of the issues being discussed. Clearly, they should be included in discussions about them. However, the child should be excluded from some of the details about the child's parents' accomplishments or failures out of respect for both the child and the parent.

Parents.   Respectful and honest communication with the parent on the first contact can set the tone for the caseworker–parent relationship. Understandably, parents are upset, worried about their child and how the child feels about the parent, angry with themselves, and angry with the system. If we put them in a room full of strangers before we have one-on-one conversations with them, we contribute to their defensiveness. The parent should be included in identifying who should be at the meeting, have prior knowledge of the purpose of the team meetings, know who will be there, what the people attending will already know about her (or think they know), how the meeting will be conducted, her right to speak or not speak without being judged as noncooperative or nonresponsive, and what she should do when she feels uncomfortable. Team decision making meetings that are held before the court has found abuse and neglect present some legal issues regarding the parents. Any statements made in such meetings can be reported to the courts. Attorneys and parent advocates are now beginning to raise the question of whether the agency facilitator should provide the parents with a warning that statements made during the meeting can be reported to the courts.

Natural Helpers.   Natural helpers are any persons whom the child and parent identify as important to them in their daily living. These are the people they look to when they are happy and want to share that happiness with someone, and they are the people they look to when they need support. These are the people who will be with them after the caseworker and agency are not. It is important for the children and parents to identify these people to the caseworker early in the process so that they can be additional supporters, along with the caseworker, for the children and parents. Further, they may be possible placement resources for the children. Natural helpers should be identified and invited to team meetings by the child or parent. The caseworker or facilitator should make sure that they feel included.

Service Providers.   Service providers include all persons who are being paid or will be paid to provide a service to the child or parent. The payment might be made by the child, parent, agency, other governmental agency, or private funding source. Their inclusion in the meeting is to receive their perspectives on the family's situation and to determine what service they provide or can provide and how provision of that service will enhance or impede the ability of the child or parent in improving individual and family functioning, which is necessary to ensure the child's safety, well-being, and permanency.

WORKING WITH PARENTS

Parents are the initial focus of service planning for permanency because what they did or did not do resulted in harm or threatened harm to the child. For the child to be safe, the parents' conditions or behaviors have to change so that they can provide a safe environment for the child. This is the reality. It sounds harsh on paper but it does not have to be presented harshly to the parents. Caseworkers cannot change them, they must change themselves. They need caseworkers to be direct, but kind. They need caseworkers who realize that they will not always succeed on the first try, but who don't give up encouraging them to reach deeper because their children are depending on them. They need caseworkers who care and who help create the critical conditions of desire, ability, reason, and need (Clark, 2007).

> **Application exercise:** Review the caseworker's approach with Mrs. Denton in the case presented earlier. Identify the instances in which the caseworker used an empathetic but direct approach to what happened, why it happened in her opinion, what needs to be done, by whom, and by when. What impact did this approach have on Mrs. Denton as the case progressed? The caseworker created an environment in which Mrs. Denton had the desire, the ability, the reason, and the need to change!

Addressing Parental Conditions and Behaviors

Most parents have co-occurring or multiple conditions or behaviors that lead to abuse or neglect of their children. The most prevalent conditions and behaviors include substance abuse, mental illness/mental health problems, domestic violence, and housing, economic, and parenting skills below the accepted community standard. The caseworker and parents wonder "What do we do first?" For example between 66 percent and 80 percent of foster care cases have parental substance abuse as one of the identified behaviors leading to placement. Most often, these cases include parental absence, homelessness, unemployment, mental illness, and poor parenting (Wheeler, 2007; Child Welfare Information Gateway, 2003). Until recently, practice was to secure substance abuse treatment first for any parent with that condition. Now, there is a shift in approach by the substance abuse treatment community. This shift resulted from recognition that substance use is interrelated with other events or conditions of the person. That is, substance use may be the parent's response to bipolar disorder, domestic violence, or homelessness. Unless the triggers are addressed, the substance use will not change and vice versa. Service interventions must be integrated if we expect to resolve these concerns sufficiently to ensure the safety of the child. However, the development of integrated programs lags far behind recognition of the need for them (Hardin, 2007; Barth, Gibbons, & Guo, 2006; Marsh, Ryan, Choi, & Testa, 2006; Kerwin, 2005; Suchman Mayes, Conti, Slade & Rounsaville, 2004; McAlpine, Marshall, & Doran, 2001). The caseworker is the person who tries to help the parent access the full continuum of services and integrate them to the degree possible in our specialized professional worlds with different values, intervention methodologies, eligibility criteria, and resource availability. The identification of the complete range of service needs and the parents' capacities in accessing those is the first step in the process. Chapter 7 discusses the different challenges faced by parents.

Family-Centered Practice for Family Reunification

Family reunification, usually the preferred goal for permanency planning, is the "planned process of reconnecting children in out-of-home care with their families by means of a variety of services and supports to the children, their families and their foster parents or other service providers" (Pine, Krieger, & Maluccio, 1993, p. 6). Despite many system problems, most children in foster care do return home. In 2005, 54 percent of children exiting foster care were reunified with a parent or primary caregiver. Another 11 percent were living with relatives (AFCARS, 2006).

> *My kids is my life. There is not much in this world for me but my kids, and I do love them. I do not want my kids taken away from me. I do not like to be separated from them.* (A parent—Marcenko & Striepe, 1997, p. 44)

It is a fundamental goal of the foster care system to work with the parents so that they can resume care of their children. Unfortunately, there is no guarantee that foster care will improve, not exacerbate, the family situation. Parents may become immobilized by the grief of losing their children, and the parent–child attachment may be compromised, particularly if visits are infrequent.

A number of factors make reunification more likely. Marcenko & Striepe (1997) found that parental qualities of strong love for one's children, help of spouse or partners, success at drug treatment, belief in oneself, and spirituality were linked to reunification. Workers helping parents regain their children work with these strengths to motivate and encourage the parent. Some parental qualities present high barriers to reunification, notably serious ongoing parental drug use and severe mental illness (Hohman & Butt, 2001).

Parental ambivalence can be a barrier to reunification (Hess & Folaron, 1991). Some parents are able to verbalize mixed feelings. Others have difficulty expressing their concerns to the worker and appear to sabotage the case plan with their behavior. When workers engage the parents and open up honest communication about the permanency plan, parental ambivalence can be addressed more effectively. Some parents can be helped to articulate their need or desire to relinquish parental rights. Others can be supported to move toward reunification.

In addition to parental characteristics and attitudes, agency factors are also important in whether a family is reunified. Casey Family Services applied family preservation–type services to reunify families with multiple and serious problems. The project demonstrated that reunification is achievable if the agency has the resources to offer intensive services (Fein & Staff, 1993). Unfortunately, not all agencies have the necessary resources to provide intensive family reunification services. Particularly with chemically dependent parents, reunification may be difficult to achieve without sufficient resources. Children who are in care because of parental substance abuse tend to stay in care longer than other children and are less likely to return home (Marsh, Ryan, Choi, Testa, 2006; National Black Child Development Institute, 1989; Besharov, 1990; Walker, Zangrillo, & Smith, 1991).

Many agency services for restoration of family life are of insufficient strength and direction to have a sustained impact. The more effective programs include the following elements: (1) a wide variety of helping options; (2) a primary and continuing social work staff team; (3) small caseloads; (4) crisis intervention services around the clock; (5) use of natural helping resources in the neighborhood and the community; (6) intensive counseling services; (7) provision of transportation, health services, respite care, and child care; and (8) availability and use of substance abuse treatment (Berry, 1988; Ten Broeck & Barth, 1986; Pecora et al., 2000; Besharov, 1994). Intensive family-based services—often the same services used to prevent placement—have been effectively used to reunify families in which placement has occurred (Walton et al., 1993; Gillespie, Byrne, & Workman, 1995).

Parent–Child Visiting

The overall purposes of visits are to maintain the parent–child relationship and to move toward the permanency goal of reunification. Many studies have emphasized the importance of regular, frequent visits to attain these two goals. Children who receive visits have improved emotional well-being and fewer behavioral problems (Cantos, Gries, & Slis, 1997). Fanshel and Shinn (1978), in a classic study, concluded that with few exceptions parental visiting is linked to discharge from foster care and that this holds across ethnic and religious groups and is persistent over time. They found visiting patterns of parents—whether they visit and how often they visit their children in foster care—to be the strongest correlate of discharge from foster care. Other studies have also affirmed continuing visits by parents as central to family reunification (Weinstein, 1960; Mech, 1985; Proch & Howard, 1986; Milner, 1987).

Caseworkers have major responsibility for organizing and facilitating visits. In good foster care practice, every visit between parent and child has a plan and a goal. The immediate goal of a particular visit might be to work on an aspect of parenting such as behavior management; to reassure the child; to celebrate the child's birthday and show the child he or she is important; to demonstrate a skill such as comforting a tremulous, substance-affected child; or to learn to take pleasure and enjoyment from contact with one another.

In order to facilitate visits, caseworkers may need to arrange transportation and a meeting place that is satisfactory to all involved. Visits can occur at the agency when strict supervision is needed, at the foster home if the parent needs to see how and where the child is living, in a relative's home if the kinfolk are involved, in the parent's home to prepare for reunification, or at a neutral site such as a restaurant or park.

Foster parents are an important part of the team in making visits successful. Trained foster parents can use the time of the visit to help teach skills to parents and to facilitate joint visits to the school, doctor, and so forth. Their accepting and caring attitude to parents may encourage parents to work for reunification. Foster parents can help children prepare for the visit through making cookies, making a picture, and assembling their mementoes to show their parents. If parents fail to keep the appointment, trained foster parents can help the child deal with the disappointment not by blaming the parents, but by providing reassurance and support to the children.

Caseworkers have a responsibility to observe visits to assess attachment, parenting skills, and parent–child interaction. They may also need to coach parents and be supportive of foster parents.

Engaging the Parent in the Child's Care during Foster Care

The parents should be encouraged to participate in a child's medical appointments, school conferences, sports and other after-school activities, and other important events in the child's life during the child's foster care placement. This provides opportunities for the caseworker or caregiver to model behaviors that will help the parent enhance her capacity to provide for her children's needs, a CFSR outcome. It reinforces the parent's continuing roles and responsibilities to the child.

It helps the child to "feel normal." It provides opportunity for continuity of care after the child is returned home.

Parent–Agency Service Agreement

Use of parent–agency service agreements (contracts) creates a sharply focused direction for practice (Stein, Gambrill, & Wiltse, 1974). It is an essential part of concurrent planning (Katz, 1999).

The contract typically relates to the allegations found on the petition leading to the court assuming jurisdiction over the child. If the court found that the parental home was filthy and unsafe, for example, and that the parents had neglected to feed or provide medical care to the child, then correcting those conditions would become key components of the contract. The contract spells out the permanency planning alternatives, the goal (usually return to the parents), what must be done to correct the elements of neglect found in the court petition, and who will do what to accomplish the goal. The contract might specify that the agency would provide homemaker services to assist the parent in cleaning up the filthy home, that the agency would refer the parent to nutrition classes, and that the parent would attend medical visits for the child.

The parent's responsibilities might include cleaning the home so that it would pass inspection by the health department, attending nutrition classes and demonstrating adequate food preparation skills, demonstrating an understanding of the child's medical needs, and participating in ongoing medical care. In contemporary practice, a frequent component of contracts is that the agency provide referral for substance abuse treatment and support group, and that the parent use treatment, attend the self-help group, and provide clean drug screens on a weekly basis. It is important to spell out in the contract what is an acceptable level of performance by the parent.

Recognize, for instance, that relapse is expected because recovery from alcohol and other drug addictions "is a lifetime process, one day at a time" (Young, 2007, Slide 16).

Alternatively, attending a parenting class does not necessarily mean that a parent will improve discipline techniques. The contract should show that attending parenting classes are related to the goal of using effective discipline without severe corporal punishment.

Case Review

Case review is a regular part of foster care programming. Its purpose is to ensure that time lines are being met in planning for permanency and that parent–child visits, efforts to help parents, and other necessary program components are occurring as planned. Case review exists at three levels: judicial, administrative, and citizen. Judicial reviews, mandated by federal law, occur at regular intervals at the juvenile or family court. They are the most authoritative and usually include testimony and a report from the social worker and testimony from the parents and other stakeholders. Administrative reviews are internal agency processes monitoring compliance with program goals and policy. Citizen reviews are conducted under the auspices of the court, an advocacy organization, or the agency, and are intended to provide oversight of the child welfare system by interested and knowledgeable citizens in the community (Jordan, 1994; Thoennes, 1996; National Association of Foster Care Reviewers, 1998). States vary in their use of each review method. Thoennes (1996) found that no single review model is decidedly superior in producing positive case outcomes and concluded that administrative and citizen reviews are advisable in systems that lack judicial resources to ensure regular, thoughtful review hearings.

CASE STUDY:
Family Reunification

Selena Q. had completed treatment for her addiction, attended a twelve-step support group, and was making steady progress in her recovery. Raymond, her estranged husband, was still using heavily and on the streets. Selena had returned to her earlier employment and located housing. She was responding to clear expectations spelled out in the parent–agency service agreement (contract). At first, she had felt angry with the foster care worker for telling her what she had to do to get the children back, but now she appreciated the help she had gotten in working toward her goals. She felt shaky and anxious about maintaining sobriety, but had a Narcotics Anonymous (NA) sponsor and a relapse prevention plan. She knew that she could not reconcile with Raymond unless he stopped using and was in recovery. She wanted the children back but felt that she could not cope with all of them at once.

Her two middle children, girls aged 5 and 7 years, had been placed with her aunt in a kinship foster care situation, but her son, aged 14 years, was in group care for treatment, as he had been a sexual abuse perpetrator to his 5-year-old sister. The baby was in a specialized foster home because he had special medical needs. Selena had maintained contact with all four children through visits, although she had spent the most time with the two children placed with her aunt.

The worker and the mother decided together it would be wise to phase the return of the children. First, Selena stayed on the weekends with her aunt to resume care of her two middle children. Then the children returned to her new home, with the aunt providing day care while Selena worked. The family reunification worker was available to her around the clock, seven days a week, and met with her every evening to help her reconnect with the two girls who had been returned. The girls showed some anger and defiance, telling their mother that they only had to listen to Aunt Fay, and they didn't have to listen to her. The worker showed Selena how to set limits and have family meetings.

They then had a meeting with the reunification team, which included the parent, her aunt, the foster care worker, the foster parent, the group care worker, and her son's therapist. They developed a plan in which the baby would be returned next, and her son would start to visit in the home, with close supervision by the mother and the family reunification worker.

Selena and her aunt spent time with the foster parent learning the special techniques involved in baby Jeffrey's care. She and the mother went together to the doctor, the rehab clinic, and the public health department. The plan was that Jeffrey would visit first for long weekends, with the foster parent "on call" for problems. When the baby returned home, Selena was able to reduce her work hours and still retain TANF eligibility. The first week that Jeffrey was at home, she called in her family reunification worker frequently, as she was feeling very stressed and found herself having cravings for her drugs. The worker and Selena's sponsor helped her get past the cravings, and the foster parent came in to provide respite so that Selena could get to more meetings of her twelve-step group. The sponsor, the reunification worker, and Selena developed a specific relapse prevention plan.

A serious concern was whether the return of Tyrone from group care would upset the precarious homeostasis and make Selena once again vulnerable to relapse. Selena was fearful that Tyrone might reoffend with the girls. She was also having flashbacks to her own sexual abuse as a child.

The family reunification worker helped Selena decide to get help for her survivor issues. She took Selena to a survivor's group and gave her some survivor workbooks. She helped Selena educate the girls about good touches and bad touches, the importance of "telling" and saying no. They decided that because Tyrone had completed the treatment program, it might be a good idea to bring him home while the family reunification worker was still involved.

The entire family, including Aunt Fay and the worker, went to a final treatment session at Tyrone's group facility. At this session, Tyrone got down on his knees in front of Jessica and apologized for his actions. He cried when he apologized to his mother for hurting one of the children. Aunt Fay promised to be the outside person who would monitor Tyrone's behavior to Jessica and Roshelle. Selena was helped to set very firm limits for Tyrone. Tyrone was to be enrolled in a new school and assigned an adult male mentor.

The first week Tyrone was back, Selena again went into crisis because Raymond, her estranged husband, showed up high, wanting money and demanding to take Tyrone with him for "some fun." The family reunification worker stepped in to support Selena in making Raymond leave and handling Tyrone's reactions to his father's visit.

Eight weeks after the first two children were returned home, the family was together, with the exception of Raymond, the father, who had not dealt with his addiction. Each of the older children had a support system, including school, Al-A-Tot or Al-A-Teen, neighborhood activities at a nearby church, and Tyrone's mentor. Their aunt was involved in their lives, and she was introducing them to other relatives who had distanced themselves earlier when Selena had been using.

Selena had good days and bad days. There were times when her cravings were hard to take. She used her twelve-step support group and her sponsor to deal with the urge to relapse. She attended the sexual abuse survivors group from time to time as painful feelings emerged. The family reunification worker got Selena on a waiting list for sexual abuse counseling at a local agency. Selena began to realize that part of her substance use had been to cover childhood pain. She also consulted an attorney about obtaining a divorce from Raymond. She was clear that she did not want to risk losing the children again. The family reunification worker ended her intensive services, although the family remained under supervision by the court and the foster care worker for another six months.

Case Commentary.   This case has been idealized to illustrate the strong points of contemporary foster care practice. The focus was family centered and involved the kinship network in planning and helping. Teamwork was essential, with active involvement by the foster parent, the group care facility, and community resources in implementation of the plan. The task of parenting was shared by the kinship caregiver, the parent, and the foster parent. The foster care worker and the family reunification worker used an empowerment focus, despite the strong element of social control underlying the child protection intervention. One limitation of the resolution of the case was that neither worker was able to

> reach Raymond, the children's father. They did, however, support and empower Selena in creating boundaries that would prevent his addiction from intruding into the reformed family in recovery. Special attention was paid to the realities of the recovery process, including development of a relapse prevention plan. The phased return of the children took into consideration the unique needs of the children and the mother's vulnerability to relapse. Although in some states there might be prohibitions against allowing Tyrone back into the home (certain statutes prohibit funding family reunification if there is a perpetrator in the home), he had completed a treatment program, and there was a plan for close supervision and monitoring of the sibling group.

Postreunification Services

Fifty-four percent of children exiting foster care in 2005 were returned to their parents. This continues a six-year trend of reunification as the most frequent outcome for children exiting the system (Children's Bureau, 2006, September). The caseworker's job is not finished when the child is reunited with the parents. Postreunification competes with initial removal as the most challenging time for the child, parents, and caseworkers. The equilibrium has been changed and everyone is adjusting. Postreunification requires the child and parents to learn new ways of living with one another after a significant separation. Visitation is one thing, living together twenty-four hours a day is another. Each person is happy but scared; each wants success but is haunted by fear of possible failure. What exactly should a postreunification services plan include to help with the readjustment and to ensure stability?

Application exercise: Review the Q family reunification example. Identify the postreunification services that were in place at reunification. How was each important to maintaining the reunification?

There are few studies of reunification to guide practice. Promising practices include continuing to build family strengths and capacity to meet the needs of the child; weekly caseworker–family contacts with planned decrease in frequency and duration over time as the family demonstrates capacity to resolve challenges; maintaining established linkages to therapeutic interventions and support services for the parents' substance abuse and mental health issues; ensuring availability of concrete services; securing needed educational, health, and mental health services for the child; and assisting the parents with recognizing and attending to the changing developmental needs of the child (Pine, Spath, & Gosteli, 2005; Wulczyn, 2004).

Re-entry into Foster Care

Re-entry into foster care occurs when the reunification plan was unsuccessful and the children are not safe in the family home. Families whose children re-enter foster care are characterized by lack of parenting skills, limited social support networks, and drug addiction. The pressure to move children quickly out of foster care to meet federal mandates may result in agency decisions to return children to unsafe homes, and thereby create a revolving door for some, with the attendant problems of upheaval and lack of stability.

The re-entry rate to foster care was 9.9 percent in 2003, the latest data available (U.S. Department of Health and Human Services, 2005). Re-entry into foster care is one of the measures for CFSR Permanency Outcome 1—Children Have Permanency and Stability in Their Living Situations. The measure for the second round reads: "Of all children discharged from foster care to reunification in FY 2003, what percent reentered foster care in less than 12 months?" Based on baseline data from all 50 states and the District of Columbia, the range for re-entry was 1.6 percent to 29.5 percent (Federal Register, 2006).

Why do children re-enter foster care? Other than a recurrence of abuse or neglect, there is no complete answer to the question. Clearly, parental drug addiction and mental illness are factors. However, many parents with these conditions have successful reunifications. A comprehensive evaluation of the cases that re-enter foster care is needed to determine the correlation between multiple parent and child characteristics; postreunification services provided including type, duration, and intensity; natural supports; and reunification stability. This type of evaluation could inform practice and reduce trauma to the child.

When children re-enter foster care, the caseworker should first seek to place the child with the former caregiver if that caregiver provided good care and is interested in providing a permanent home for the child. The chance of reunification decreases at each re-entry. While the caseworker does not want to immediately dismiss the possibility of reunification at each re-entry, prognostics dictate active pursuit of alternative permanency plans earlier than in previous entries.

Termination of Parental Rights

Some families do not respond to services provided or have difficulties so pervasive that children cannot remain with them in safety. In these situations, federal and state law require that children not languish in an impermanent and temporary setting. Generally speaking, after a child has been in care twelve months without family reunification being accomplished, a permanency hearing is held. For a child to be legally free for adoption, parental rights must be terminated or relinquished voluntarily. If the child is in foster care for fifteen of the last twenty-two months, then termination of parental rights must be initiated.

For foster care workers, planning for termination of parental rights can be very challenging. It typically involves teamwork with attorneys, knowledge of legal procedures, gathering evidence in a format that is admissible in court, contacting witnesses, and locating absent parents who have a legal interest in the child. (See Chapter 5.)

Workers may have feelings of failure, sadness, and anger that they have not been able to help parents fulfill the terms of the parent–agency agreement for permanency planning. Some workers dread the adversarial court proceedings when they must testify against parents.

OTHER PERMANENCY OPTIONS

For children who cannot return home, options for permanence include long-term foster care, guardianship, kinship care, independence/emancipation, and adoption. Proponents of long-term foster care argue that when a child or youth has strong connections to the original family, adoption will not serve the young person's interests. Ensuring continuity of family relationships for these children may entail staying in the foster home where emotional ties have been formed and where the foster parents will facilitate ongoing connection to the original family, when possible (Bryant, 1994).

The use of guardianship, particularly in kinship care, is also an option for permanence that maintains the child's bonds to family or to long-term caregivers (Child Welfare League of America, 2004). However, there are many forms of guardianship and some do not offer the level of permanence and protection that the family and the child need. (See Chapter 5.)

The preferred permanency option, once return to the original family has been ruled out and parental rights have been terminated, is adoption. Adoption offers an arrangement that is the legal equivalent of biological parenthood. Adoptions can be made in the context of family continuity, such as when long-term foster parents adopt a child, or when the child retains contact with parents or extended family members. (See Chapter 10.)

Long-Term Relative Care

Discussion of relative placement requires clarification of the different ways a child could be placed in relative care and the terminology associated with those placements. Formal placement is when the child is placed with the relative under the supervision of a child welfare agency after the court has determined that the child has been abused or neglected. The relative who cares for the child in formal care can be a licensed foster parent and can receive the same compensation and support services as a nonrelated foster parent. In most states, formal kinship/relative care is subject to the same requirements as nonrelated foster care. Children in the child welfare system who are placed with relatives are in foster care and the relative is a foster parent. This type of relative placement is the focus of our discussion in this chapter.

Informal placement or voluntary relative care is when the child is placed in the home of a relative by the parent without any abuse/neglect court involvement. In this case, the relative takes on primary care for the child outside the supervision of a child welfare system. A distinction has further been made between two types of informal care—"private" and "voluntary."

1. Private kinship care is when an arrangement is made between the parents and the relative without the involvement of the child welfare system.
2. Voluntary kinship placements exist when there is initial involvement with a child welfare agency, but the child is placed in the care of a relative without ongoing involvement of the child welfare system (Geen, 2004).

In legal guardianship kinship/relative placements, the relative or fictive kin is appointed by the court to take on specific legal rights, responsibilities, and decision-making powers of a parent (i.e., enroll child in school, make medical decisions) for the child. Legal guardianship can be ordered with or without the consent of the parent. This type of care arrangement is becoming an increasingly popular option for kinship families (Testa, 2004). Guardianship, unlike adoption, does not sever the legal relationships between parent and child. Relatives, even those who adopt, historically have had difficulties accepting the "legal" decisions that the child's birth parents no longer had any right to visit the child or parent the child after termination of parental rights and adoption. They continued their and the child's relationships with the child's parents as if the legal termination had not occurred. However, if this posed a safety threat to the child or themselves, they used the court order as leverage to change parental behaviors. Furthermore, they had difficulty with the adoption practice philosophy that their relationship with the child was changing from "grandmother" to "mother" or "aunt" to "mother." They continued to be "Granny" or "Auntie" or whatever other name the child called them before the adoption. New federal and state policies seem to make obtaining legal guardianship a more viable option for kinship caregivers (Testa, 2004).

An early experiment with relative care as the preferred placement for children in out-of-home care was in the federally funded Temporary Foster Care Project in Detroit, Michigan in 1976. Children could be placed with relatives under a legal guardianship arrangement with financial support equal to the foster care payment of which the child was eligible or as a temporary court ward with the relative licensed as a foster parent. Over 30 percent of children entering care in the first six months of the project were placed with relatives. Previously, less than 10 percent were placed with relatives at entry. This percentage continued to increase over the two-year span of the project (Moore, 1977).

Relative care placements received major supported in the *Miller v. Youakim* decision by the U.S. Supreme Court in 1979. That decision held that states were required to pay foster care board rates for Title IV eligible children placed with relatives who met the state's foster care licensing requirements. The preference for relative placements was made federal policy in the Indian Child Welfare Act of 1978 and, indirectly, in the Adoption Assistance and Child Welfare Act of 1980; it was reemphasized in the Personal Responsibility and Work Opportunity Act of 1996 and Adoption and Safe Families Act of 1997, as well as the Child and Family Services Review process. As of this writing, approximately 26 states and Puerto Rico have laws that give preference to relative placements for children requiring out-of-home care. All states have policies that give preference to relative placements (Child Welfare Information Gateway, 2006; Blair & Taylor, 2006; Geen, 2004). States define relative differently. In addition, states vary in the emphasis they place on licensing or certifying relatives so that Title IV-E payments can be made.

At the end of 2005, of the 513,000 children in out-of-home care, 124,153 were placed with relatives, or, approximately 24 percent. This percentage has been rather constant in the past five years. (Children's Bureau, 2006, September). The data is questionable, however, because states vary in how they define and code relative care. In some states, all relatives who are licensed or certified as foster parents are included in the foster home count and nonlicensed or noncertified relatives are included in the relative count. In some states, they are all coded as relative care.

Is Kinship Care Good for Kids? Research shows that children in kinship care experience greater stability, report more positive perceptions of their placements, have fewer behavioral problems, and are less likely to experience abuse and neglect after being removed from their homes (Conway & Hutson, 2007). Other studies have found that relative caregivers tend to be older, in poor health, have lower incomes, lower educational levels, receive less supervision and fewer services than nonrelative foster parents, and children placed with relatives are less likely to be reunited with parents and less likely to be adopted (Geen, 2004).

Blair and Taylor (2006) commented

> The ultimate impact of ASFA and TANF has been to increase the likelihood that kin will be the foster care placement of choice while also ensuring that caregivers will have to make do with the much smaller income assistance payments provided under the child-only provisions of TANF, along with significantly less services, training, and support provided to traditional foster care parents (Geen, 2004). All of this is happening despite evidence that kinship caregivers are typically very needy and the mounting evidence that shows that child-only caregivers are often more needy than the typical kinship caregiver. (*p. 6*)

Most kin/relatives who agree to become foster parents have various motivations. These include a sense of loyalty or obligation, the need to rescue the child from the child welfare system, anger at the parent who abuses or neglects the child, and desire to be paid to care for the child. Irrespective of motivation, the critical question is: What is the quality of their relationship with the birth parents and how will this experience influence their relationship with the child?

While relative caregivers offer many benefits to children, there is also the possibility that they can harm the child by demeaning the parents. Remember, the relative knows more about the parents and child than the agency will ever know. The relative can sabotage reunification with the parents. The relatives and parents can collude to have the child remain with the relatives to continue the increased benefits afforded the placement if the relative is a licensed foster parent or to continue TANF supports if the parents have received maximum years of benefits. While relatives adopt 25 percent of all the children adopted and provide permanent placements for 11 percent of the children exiting foster care to outcomes other than adoption, there is concern that relative placements are a contributing factor to the slowing reductions in the national foster care population totals because relatives choose not to adopt or obtain subsidized guardianship for fear the child will lose eligibility for services or benefits she would be eligible for if in foster care. The caseworker serving children in relative placements is required to provide those children with the same level of services as a child in nonrelative placement. However, the realities of caseload size preclude serving all children equally and most often it is the children in relative care who do not receive services.

Legal or Subsidized Guardianship

ASFA defines the term legal guardianship as "a judicially created relationship between child and caretaker which is intended to be permanent and self-sustaining as evidenced by the transfer to the caretaker of the following parental rights with respect to the child: protection, education, care and control of the person, custody of the person, and decisionmaking" (42 USC 675).

Subsidized guardianship is becoming increasingly popular to facilitate relatives and nonrelated long-term foster parents in obtaining guardianship of children in the child welfare system. It acknowledges the increasing number of related and nonrelated foster parents who agree to provide care until the child's emancipation, but who choose not to adopt. In most states, the child welfare case is closed when permanent guardianship is granted and the guardian receives ongoing governmental payments for the child's support. The payment amounts vary from state to state. Many subsidized guardianship payments are less than the foster care payments that the child would be eligible to receive under Title IV-E.

In an effort to reduce the number of children on the child welfare rolls, states provide legal services to assist related and nonrelated persons in completing the necessary paperwork and agency support systems so that kin can talk with others who have obtained guardianship. As of this writing, thirty-six states and the District of Columbia have subsidized guardianship programs. Ostensibly, these subsidized guardianships are in the child's interests and not just another way to show a decrease in the total number of children in out-of-home care and to reduce overall costs of administering the child welfare system by not having caseworkers providing services and ensuring the child's safety and well-being on an ongoing basis. Clearly, these subsidized guardianships reduce child welfare caseload counts. However, we have insufficient data to make any further analyses at this time as to whether they ensure safety, child well-being, and permanency (Child Welfare Information Gateway, 2006; Geen, 2004; Testa & Miller, 2005; Testa, 2004).

These placements are supposed to be "permanent." However, parental rights have not been terminated in many cases in which subsidized guardianship is being promoted by child welfare policy. In fact, policy discussion now is to use subsidized guardianship with relatives in lieu of termination of parental rights so that the family bond is not broken. Analysis of state guardianship statutes concluded that "most are easily revoked and provide inadequate legal protections for the guardian or custodian as well as inadequate permanence for the child. The forms of guardianship available in most states are too legally vulnerable to provide the permanency that are required" (Duquette, 2005, p. 371). Where the subsidized guardianship occurs after parental rights are terminated, the parents' challenge to the guardianship is not an issue.

> **Application exercise.** You are the newly assigned caseworker for John. Your supervisor tells you to pursue permanent subsidized guardianship with John and the Williams family because the agency is trying to reduce the number of children in foster care.
>
> John is a 14-year-old who has been in foster care placement with the Williams Family since he was 7 years old. His parents' parental rights were terminated when he was 9 years old. At first, the Williams family expressed interest in adopting John, but in the process of gathering all the documentation needed for the adoption, it was discovered that Mr. Williams owed child support. The state law precludes approval of adoptions by persons with outstanding child support payment obligations. John began lying and stealing from the Williams and in the neighborhood. The Williams family then said they would not adopt John, but that he could stay with them while the agency tried to find another adoptive family. John had visits with five families over three years, but none chose to adopt him. John told the caseworker he no longer wanted to be adopted. The previous caseworker documented that John said he wants to stay with the Williams family until he leaves foster care. The Williams family told that caseworker "he will always be one of the family, but we want the agency to keep providing John and us with services."

A policy debate is simmering as this book goes to print. What should be the policy for children who are expected to remain in foster care until they "age out"? Should parental rights be terminated if there is no expectation of reunification or permanent placement with relatives? The policy debate is rooted in the increased number of children in foster care for whom parental rights have been terminated—adoption is appropriate and desired by many of the children, but for whom the system can find no adoptive home. (Children's Bureau, 2007; Maza, 2005) Adoption is the preferred permanency option for children after termination of parental rights. See Chapter 10 for a discussion of adoption policies, issues, and practices.

Another Planned Permanent Living Arrangement

ASFA eliminated planned long-term foster care as a permanency goal and replaced it with "another planned permanent living arrangement." Is this semantics or a major shift in policy? What is the difference in practice? We lack the data to respond conclusively. The intent of the planned long-term foster care goal centered in the word "planned." Too many children were just drifting in foster care, even though most were in stable foster home placements, with no real plan for permanence. Planned long-term foster care required active engagement of the child and her caregivers in making an affirmative decision that the child–caregiver relationship would last and the child was expected to remain in the foster home until she exited foster care. Long-term foster care agreements were signed and filed. But policymakers thought this was just compliance with formalities.

In ASFA, the policymakers wanted to remove the opportunity to default to long-term foster care and add the component of creating a lifelong relationship between the child, caregivers, and others. Thus, in "another planned permanent living arrangement," "planned" remained but "permanent" replaced "long-term" and "living arrangement" replaced "foster care." What is the difference? There is continued emphasis on "planned." That is, affirmative action is required to establish this goal. Clearly "long-term" could be a shorter period than "permanent." "Foster care" includes all "living arrangements" outside the home of the parents or legal guardians that are under the auspices of the child welfare system. But "living arrangements" don't necessarily refer to just physical spaces for ASFA. It incorporates "relationships." The intent is that the system is actively working to connect the young person with caring, supportive adults who will remain connected as she transitions from foster care and throughout adulthood. This is different from the long-term foster care concept of a committed person until transition. For now, the following question remains for evaluators and researchers: Is this semantics or a major shift in policy?

Children need lifelong connections. Many of the children who are aging out of foster care have those connections in the parents, relatives, nonrelative foster parents, child care workers, and caseworkers. We rarely read about those young people. We often read about those who leave foster care and become homeless, who commit crimes and are incarcerated, who have no place to go for holidays, who are unemployed, and who feel alone in the world. Clearly, we did not serve this latter group as well as we should have.

Emancipation

Emancipation, or aging out, is the reality for about 25,000 young people each year. This group is about 10 percent of all children exiting foster care (Children's Bureau, 2006, September). Issues in serving this population are discussed below.

MEETING THE NEEDS OF CHILDREN IN FOSTER CARE

The experiences and behaviors that the child brings to foster care need to be **acknowledged, accepted, allowed,** and **adapted** *over time*. For the child, the best approach is the willingness of the caseworker and caregiver to understand the child's frustration, help her identify what she wants to happen, and then show her ways to successfully achieve those results.

The management of one's behavior is closely related to self-determination. Children generally understand that behaviors have consequences. The child welfare system experience complicates behavior and coping strategies. Children in the child welfare system are expected to adapt to the caregiver. Each caregiver has different expectations, rules, and consequences for the same behavior. For some, this constant need to adapt to the expectations of others does not make sense because they "are not here to stay." Thus, wanting to speed up the "moving on," the child uses behaviors she has used in the past to get that result. This is a standard defense mechanism—be in control and don't let others hurt me.

Children who feel a lack of control, recognition, and/or appreciation, find ways to sabotage their relationships with others *and themselves* in their determination to gain control. Based on past socialization and learned-behavior experiences, children in the child welfare system develop a system of coping with their lack of control of what happens to them by developing relationship patterns that keep them emotionally distant and isolated, even when they appear to be engaged. Many use aggressive or acting out behavioral responses to maintain distance, to prove that they are not wanted, and to have some control. This includes obnoxious and defiant behaviors, running away, stealing, intentional damage to other's possessions, or intentional violation of the rules. These behaviors need to be unlearned over time. The child needs to be shown that these behaviors are not necessary for her to "belong" and have some autonomy in the foster home. Some behavioral responses are because the "child doesn't know any better" or "hasn't been taught how to handle certain situations or emotions." Some behavioral responses of children in the child welfare system are directly related to the child welfare experiences.

Some of the behaviors might have been reasonable responses to the situations the child experienced. They were needed to survive some untenable challenges. The caseworker and caregiver need to teach and show her other ways of responding to situations that might help her achieve her desired result. The caseworker and caregiver needs to provide support as she practices new ways of responding. The caseworker and caregiver can help older children and youth by offering choices and sharing control in the process. This builds her healthy self-concept and ability to form healthy attachments and relationships. Older children must be allowed to make choices on the things that affect them whenever possible as a way of regaining control. Teach older children decision-making skills and allow them to own the responsibility—including the good feelings and the disappointments—of the decisions they make.

The caseworker and caregiver need to learn to distinguish what behaviors can be expected and changed over time with love, redirection, and support, and those behaviors that require therapeutic interventions.

Relationships Count: Attachment and Separation

Children who leave their own homes and enter foster care have experienced varying kinds and degrees of deprivation in parental care. Social workers have given considerable attention to assessing the likely long-term effects of poor parental care, particularly poor mothers, and to finding ways to help children with the distress they feel at separating from their parents, even neglectful or rejecting ones.

Assessing the child's attachment to parenting figures increases the worker's understanding of important relationships in the child's life. Attachment commonly refers to a close emotional bond that endures over time, beginning in infancy with the reciprocal relationship the child forms with the mother. As the child grows, he or she becomes attached to other family members as well. (See Chapter 3.) Children who have disordered, ambivalent, or anxious attachments may show some of the following behaviors: lack of comfort seeking when frightened, hurt, or ill; lack of warm and affectionate interactions or indiscriminate affection with unfamiliar adults; lack of compliance with caregiver request or, conversely, overcompliance; failure to check back with the caregiver in unfamiliar surroundings; and failure to reestablish interaction after separation (Levy & Orlans, 1998). Attachment problems create great difficulty in foster and adoptive homes, and later in life. Preserving the attachment to parents, siblings, and kinfolk is an important goal of contemporary child welfare practice (Bowlby, 1969; Goldstein, Freud, & Solnit, 1973; Fahlberg, 1991; Hegar, 1993; Grigsby, 1994).

Although each child's reaction to separation from parents is unique, certain painful feelings are common to the placement process. Children may be torn between conflicting feelings of love and anger toward their parents. No matter how appalling their homes might appear to others, the homes are familiar to children and they have developed ways of coping. In the situation of being separated from the parents for the purpose of placement, children almost inevitably feel powerless. Feelings of abandonment, rejection, helplessness, worthlessness, and fear are to be expected. They may feel shame or guilt about their "terrible" behavior that caused their parents to give them up or give up on them. These feelings can affect their self-concept and sense of reality and distort their interpretation of old and new environments (Freud, 1955; Littner, 1975).

The experience of repeated separations, as often happens in foster care, can elicit ever-increasing anger and related dysfunction. Attachment disorders underlie many of the clinical diagnoses that have been used traditionally to label extremely troubled foster children, such as conduct disorder (Delaney, 1991; Kools, 1997).

Children may also suffer from posttraumatic stress disorder (PTSD), characterized by intrusive imagery, somatic difficulties, sleep disturbance, hypervigilance, and inability to concentrate. A sound diagnosis is needed to identify PTSD.

Fahlberg (1991) summarized the factors that influence the child's reaction to separation:

❖ the child's age and stage of development
❖ the child's attachment to the parent
❖ the parent's bonding to the child
❖ the child's perceptions of the reasons for separation
❖ the child's preparation for the move
❖ the "parting message" the child receives
❖ the "welcoming message" the child receives
❖ the postseparation environment
❖ the child's temperament
❖ the environment from which he is being moved (p. 14)

These variables underscore the need for teamwork by worker, foster parents, and biological parents in the placement process and the treatment of the child.

Caseworkers and caregivers set the tone and philosophy for working with children by acknowledging that foster care placement is a painful process, creating a safe place for the child to talk about her feelings, engaging the child in the process of maintaining connections with the people and places she misses, listening to what she says, and responding honestly and truthfully using words she can understand. The caseworker explains the child's circumstances and concerns within the constraints of confidentiality promises made to the child, parents, caregivers, teachers, and other support persons to engage them in supporting the child as well.

Safety

The first issue is to make sure the child is physically and emotionally safe in the chosen placement. This involves caseworker inquiries about not only the adult caregivers, but adults who frequent the home. It involves inquiries about the other children in the home. How does each relate to the child and how does the child relate to each of them. Often, caseworkers forget that the child is the one who knows how she feels and if she is being hurt—the conversation is usually with the adults. In addition, the child is often not provided confidential space in which to talk with the caseworker. Put yourself in the child's place. What would you say if your abuser is standing there and will be there when the caseworker has left?

It is difficult to know sometimes that a child is being neglected or abused in a foster care placement. The child does not automatically speak up because this is supposed to be a safe place. In her mind, the agency took her from mom and put her here, so this must be okay. The caseworker doesn't always want to believe that a person who volunteers to care for someone else's child would hurt them. Children are harmed by substitute caregivers! Some reports made by youth exiting foster care suggest that there is more harm than the actual reported "maltreatment in foster care."

Most agencies have protocols specifying how the caseworker is to assess safety and respond to findings or concerns. This is a suggested casework practice protocol for meeting the safety needs of children in foster care.

❖ Create a separate space for the caseworker–child visits that affords privacy.
❖ Tell the child every time you see her that one of your jobs is to make sure she is safe and no one, child or adult, is hurting her.
❖ Observe the child for bruises and marks.
❖ Ask the child to explain how she got the bruises and marks.
❖ Ask the child if anyone ever does anything to her that she doesn't like.
❖ Ask the child about the other children in the home. If the child raises any concerns, ask if she has talked with the caregiver about them. If she has, ask what the caregiver did and if that made the situation better.
❖ Ask the child what she likes and dislikes about this home.
❖ Talk with the caregiver about any child-on-child abuse. Determine if the caregiver can ensure the safety of the child. If not, determine if the child needs to be removed immediately or can wait for a planned move. Assess the safety of other children in the home.
❖ Take the child with you when you leave if there is any concern about caregiver-on-child abuse. Make sure all foster children are removed before you leave.

The manner and style of the discussion is dependent on the caseworker–child relationship and the child's linguistic skills.

The caseworker has the continuous obligation to assess safety issues during parent–child visits.

Child Well-Being

In addition to safety, ASFA seeks to ensure that the child's educational, physical health, and mental health needs are met while in out-of-home placement. Meeting these needs supports the child's overall well-being. Well-being is not well defined, it is the most recent addition to the child welfare paradigm: safety, well-being, and permanency. It is just beginning to receive the focus afforded safety and permanency. Most of the research findings on the well-being of children in foster care are based on small samples of children in foster care pre-ASFA. ASFA added "well-being" to the child welfare system. The Urban Institute completed the first national overview of the well-being of children in foster care based on data from the 1997 and 1999 National Survey of America's Families (NSAF). The sample size was 819 children living in relative (69 percent) and nonrelative (31 percent) foster care. It found that about 28 percent of these children had a physical, learning, or mental health condition that limits their activities, whereas only 8 percent of the children in parent care and 14 percent of children in high-risk parent care have such severe problems. Compounding these findings was that 17 percent are living with foster parents and relatives who report poor mental health symptoms and 26 percent report high levels of aggravation (Kortenkamp & Ehrle, 2002). In CFSR-1, only sixteen states achieved substantial conformity on providing services to meet the child's educational needs, and only one state achieved substantial conformity on providing services to meet the physical and mental health needs of children in foster care (Children's Bureau, 2006a). The caseworker cannot be expected to be all-knowing about every condition the child presents. However, the caseworker needs to be knowledgeable about the general norms of child well-being in education, physical health, and mental health, and should seek professional assessments and interventions when indicated.

Education

Contrary to popular belief, most foster children do not receive special education services (McNaught, 2004). Is this a positive or a negative? Is this the result of foster children being assessed to determine need for special education services and having been found not to need them, or is it the result of foster children not being assessed? Existing educational attainment and educational needs data on children in foster care do not give the answers. CFSR requirements now make this an AFCARS data element, which means more reliable data should be forthcoming.

The NSAF found that 32 percent of the 12- to 17-year-old children in child welfare had been suspended or expelled from school and 17 percent skipped school in the past twelve months. Further, 28 percent were not involved in extracurricular activities, 3 percent were in special education, and 39 percent had low levels of school engagement (Kortenkamp and Ehrle, 2002). In CFSR-1, sixteen states achieved substantial conformity on the "children receive services to meet their educational needs" (Children's Bureau, 2006).

Educational attainment is an important marker for a productive life. Lack of educational attainment in the early grades leads to dropping out in high school, unemployment in adulthood, and increased criminal behavior and incarceration. Most agencies have protocols specifying how the caseworker is to assess educational needs and respond to findings or concerns. Below is suggested casework practice for meeting the educational needs of children in foster care.

❖ Keep the child enrolled in the same school unless placement in another school would be in the child's best interests or are the wishes of an older child.
❖ Educate the school personnel about the impact of foster care on children.
❖ Make sure the child has appropriate clothing or school uniforms and supplies as soon as possible after enrollment.
❖ Request the teacher to expect the child to perform and succeed and notify you if she believes the child is underperforming at any time.
❖ Review the child's school performance with the child, parents, caregivers, and teachers at each marking period. Determine what, if any, additional supports are needed for the child to perform at her maximum potential. The school has testing available to determine child's cognitive capacities and limitations. If there is any question, ask the schools to test the child. If the child is performing below capacity, determine why and then implement interventions to alleviate the specific cause or causes for the low performance.
❖ Talk with the child about school issues at each visit.
❖ Obtain special education services for children who are eligible for them.
❖ Conference with appropriate school personnel whenever a child is disciplined. Determine what supports are necessary to alleviate the underlying causes.
❖ Make sure the child is encouraged and supported in participation in extracurricular activities such as sports, clubs, etc.
❖ Attend extracurricular events with the child's approval, but identify yourself as a friend—not the caseworker.
❖ Keep the following information in the child's case file in summary form:
   1. standardized tests given: name, date, results, and actions taken based on results and outcomes
   2. grades achieved, including school, district, class, and grade

3. academic performance concerns, actions taken to correct, and results

4. behavioral performance concerns, actions taken to correct, and results

5. extracurricular activities and awards

6. teacher conferences and other contacts; summarize concerns discussed, decisions, actions, and results

7. copies of report cards

8. copies of Individualized Education Plan

❖ Include specific information about educational attainment, issues, corrective strategies, and outcomes in each quarterly review.

❖ Advocate, advocate, advocate. . . .
(Elz, Auslander, Stiffman & McMillen, 2005; Zetlin, Weinberg, & Kimm, 2005; McNaught, 2004)

Physical Health

David has been in severe pain for three months. He was accidentally hit in the mouth with a basketball. The dentist says he needs a root canal, but Medicaid will not pay for it. The alternative is to pull the tooth. David does not want the tooth pulled because it is a front tooth. His aunt has taken him to three dentists. All of them tell her the same thing. David has missed school an average of two days a week because of the pain. He is in jeopardy of failing this semester. Children in foster care have emergency and routine health care needs. The child welfare system needs to be responsive to both. David's story identifies one of the major issues in health care for children in foster care—Medicaid eligibility and payment rates. This appears to be a chronic concern nationally, specifically for dental services and optometric services. Children with dental problems or sight problems have difficulties performing in school, the community, and with the family and peer relations. Child welfare agencies committed to meeting the health care needs of children in foster care develop structured arrangements with a broad range of health care providers to meet the needs of children before the need arises. Medicaid payments are maximized and other funding sources are identified for nonreimbursable services.

NASF found that in the twelve months prior to the survey, 27 percent of children birth to five years, 21 percent of children six to eleven years, 40 percent of children twelve to seventeen years did not receive well-child care, 37 percent did not have a dental visit, and 10 percent were in poor or fair health (Kortenkamp & Ehrle, 2002). No state achieved substantial conformity on meeting the child's physical health needs, but 20 states did receive a rating of "strength" in CFSR-1 (Children's Bureau, 2006a).

Most agencies have protocols specifying how the caseworker is to identify and meet the child's physical health needs and respond to findings or concerns. This is suggested casework practice for meeting the physical health needs of children in foster care.

❖ Obtain an initial screening and comprehensive health assessment immediately upon placement from the child's doctor of record, if possible.

❖ Continue to obtain health care services from the provider of record when the child entered care.

❖ Engage the parents and the caregiver in partnership to manage the child's ongoing health care needs.

❖ Talk with the child about any chronic conditions during monthly contacts.

❖ Make sure the child has access to health care services and treatment identified through the screening and health assessment. Maintain lists of specialty clinics or health care providers who accept Medicaid or who will treat the child without payment. Know other funding sources that can be used for nonreimbursable services.

❖ Ask for copies of patient education information materials addressing the child's chronic health conditions.

❖ Ask the physician for a routine health care schedule for the child's age, gender, and health status.

❖ Monitor to ensure that the child receives routine health care.

❖ Manage health information and review it periodically, noting changes in diagnosis and prognosis for later discussion with the parents, caregiver, and health care provider.

❖ Coordinate care, if necessary, to support parents and caregivers while teaching them how to coordinate care.

❖ Be informed: Read patient education information provided on the web sites of the American Academy of Pediatrics, American Dental Association, the U.S. Department of Health and Human Services, Maternal and Child Health Bureau and National Institutes of Health, and the American Medical Association's Adolescent Health page. An excellent reference is Green and Palfrey's, *Bright Futures: Guidelines for Health Supervision of Infants, Children, and Adolescents,* available from the Health Resources Services Administration Clearinghouse.

❖ Keep the following information in the child's case file in summary form:

1. dates seen for health care, by whom, procedures, and results;

2. chronic conditions, date diagnosed, by whom, treatment plan, and treating physician or clinic; and

3. results of routine physical examinations.

❖ Include specific information about health care received, concerns, treatment modifications, and outcomes in each quarterly review.

❖ Advocate, advocate, advocate. . . .

Mental Health

Children enter foster care traumatized. An increasing number enter foster care with mental health diagnoses Some are former clients of the children's mental health system who have been discharged to parents who are ill-prepared to care for them. Without a doubt, these children will require ongoing mental health treatment by a mental health professional. Most of these children have ongoing services from a mental health professional or should be referred to the most current providers, unless the child objects, to maintain continuity in intervention methodologies.

The vast majority of children in foster care are children who are traumatized by the child welfare experience itself. This experience affects children differently. Some are so traumatized that mental health treatment services are necessary. Others benefit from kind, supportive discussions with the caseworker or caregiver who understands what they have experienced and are experiencing, and are willing to listen and help them normalize their situation. Sometimes in the course of these discussions, the need for more intensive intervention is identified and the child is referred to a mental health professional.

NASF found that 27 percent of the children in foster care had high levels of behavioral and emotional problems with 32 percent receiving no mental health services and 25 percent of all children in foster care receiving mental health services in the preceding twelve months (Kortenkamp and Ehrle, 2002).

Most agencies have protocols specifying how the caseworker is to identify and refer children with emotional or behavioral challenges. This is suggested casework practice for meeting the mental health needs of children in foster care.

❖ If the child enters care with a mental health diagnosis:

1. Tell her that you are not a therapist, but need to talk with her about her condition. Talk with her, if possible, about the diagnosis, previous and current therapeutic approaches, medications and their effects, how she feels about coming into foster care, what she needs in a caregiver, and a placement to help her feel safe and secure.

2. Immediately contact the mental health professional serving any child who enters care with a mental health diagnosis. Confirm continuity of treatment care arrangements, and elicit information about the diagnosis and its implications for placement decision making. Ask for specific approaches to interacting with the child to minimize trauma.

3. Engage the parent (if appropriate) and caregiver in managing the child's treatment.

4. Maintain ongoing contact with the mental health professional and the caregiver to ensure that the caregiver and support environments are supporting the child's mental health treatment.

5. Keep the following information in the child's case file in summary form:
   ❖ dates seen for mental health services, by whom, and results;
   ❖ diagnosis, by whom, treatment plan, and name of mental health professional; and
   ❖ results of interventions.

6. Include specific information about mental health care received, concerns, treatment modifications, and outcomes in each quarterly review.

7. Advocate, advocate, advocate. . . .

❖ For children entering foster care without a mental health diagnosis:

1. Provide casework services focused on minimizing the child's trauma from the neglect or abuse and placement in foster care.

2. Engage the parents and caregivers in observing the child using a specific parent observation and documentation format on an ongoing basis.

3. Obtain specific information from the parents about the child's past history of behavioral and emotional functioning.

4. Obtain teacher reports if the child is school aged.

5. Complete or refer for a mental health screen after the initial trauma issues have been addressed and the child is beginning to show signs of adjusting to the placement and when behaviors raise concerns. Refer for mental health services if indicated.

6. Provide ongoing casework services with counseling on behavioral or emotional issues as they arise.

7. Be informed: The National Institute of Mental Health–Child and Adolescent Treatment and Preventive Intervention Research Branch, and the Academy of Child and Adolescent Psychiatry web sites are excellent resources for information on child and adolescent mental health.

8. Advocate, advocate, advocate. . . .

Permanency

The CFSR outcomes of permanency and stability in living arrangements, preserving continuity of family relationships and connections, and enhancing the families' capacities to provide for children's needs, are all important to the child's permanency. These have all been discussed in previous sections. In this section, permanency is approached from the child's eyes and heart. The child needs permanency of place and permanency of person to achieve well-being—to feel whole. All that the caseworker does should be focused on the end goal of helping the child feel whole. The caseworker helps the child feel whole by:

❖ developing a nurturing and supportive professional relationship with her that is filled with praise for what she does well and positive redirection for what she does not do well.

❖ providing opportunities for the child to maintain continuity of relationships despite disruptions in placements. Encourage and facilitate frequent visits, telephone calls, and e-mails with parents, siblings not placed with each other, friends, relatives, and other caring adults.

❖ giving the child a voice in developing and achieving goals for her personal development.

❖ keeping the child informed of the permanency plan, progress, and setbacks so she doesn't feel "stuck."

❖ ensuring that the child is in a safe, caring living environment with caregivers who are concerned most about meeting the child's needs rather than the child meeting the caregivers' needs.

CHILDREN REQUIRING THERAPEUTIC INTERVENTIONS

Children with certain characteristics require additional services to meet their safety, permanency, and well-being needs. These children include children with emotional disturbances, children with behavior/conduct disorders, children with developmental disabilities, children with chronic medical conditions, sibling groups, older children and adolescents, children re-entering the foster care system, children in the system as legal orphans, and gay and lesbian youth. Some of these conditions require interventions by mental health professionals or highly educated and trained child welfare caseworkers, health care professionals, and/or educators, and some require increased frequency and focus of child welfare caseworker–child contacts.

The federal government is emphasizing "evidence-based" practices in child welfare services, that is, "practices whose effectiveness with specific populations or conditions has been demonstrated through rigorous scientific research and whose application is well defined and replicable" (Dore, p. 157). Unfortunately, there are very few evidence-based practices in child welfare because of the lack of "rigorous scientific research" (Children's Bureau, 2006b).

As mentioned in the child well-being sections, the caseworker, while not an expert in these conditions, must become an expert in the condition of the children she serves. Diagnoses, treatment interventions, and prognoses are constantly changing.

Therapeutic and socioeducational groups for children and young persons can help address the child's perceptions of the separation and assist in the child's adaptation to care (Palmer, 1990). One of the advantages of groupwork with children and youth in care is that they discover the similarity and normalcy of their feelings (Rice & McFadden, 1988). Another is that the faulty attributions and self-blame about the reasons for placement can be identified and resolved.

Individual treatment such as play therapy or counseling may also be helpful to the child making a transition into care. In working with the individual child to master past traumatic events, techniques such as bibliotherapy, puppet play, drawing, dollhouse play, or work with clay can help the child express hidden pain and reenact confusing or frightening events until some mastery is gained.

Mental health services are needed for an estimated 50 to 80 percent of children using the services of the foster care system. These services should be integrated into the service delivery system of child welfare agencies, should focus on prevention as well as dysfunction, and should be tailored to the various reasons for placement (Schneiderman et al., 1998).

Many children coming into care have critical health care needs. The approach to providing health care to children in out-of-home care varies from community to community. Because children entering care suffer from a variety of conditions, including the effects of lack of preventive medical care and the sequelae of various forms of maltreatment, it seems imperative to develop comprehensive medical services targeted at their unique needs and situation. The mandate of ASFA to focus on the developmental outcomes of foster children is calling renewed attention to educational, health, and mental health services for children in foster care.

CHILDREN REQUIRING INTENSIVE CASEWORK SERVICES

Some situations require casework visits more than once a month, the current expectation for foster care. These situations include sibling groups, older children and adolescents, children re-entering foster care, children in the system as legal orphans, and gay and lesbian youth. Depending on the specifics, these children could require weekly visits with telephone contacts between visits until their situation is stabilized. While this is difficult to manage in most child welfare environments, doing so may reduce the incidence of crises and redefine child welfare practice.

Sibling Groups

Whether siblings are placed together is more dependent on the availability of placement resources than on an assessment of the individual and group needs of the siblings. The importance of siblings to one another has been documented in numerous studies. To the extent possible, they should be placed together or in close proximity to facilitate frequent visitation and common schools, when age appropriate. If they are not placed together or close enough to see each other daily, the caseworker should make sure they have each other's telephone numbers, make sure the relative or foster parents understand the need for frequent contact and support it, and arrange for no less than weekly visits. When a specific sibling is a risk to the others, visitation should still occur, but should be supervised by an adult. If there is any expectation that the siblings will be reunited with the parents, the siblings need to be taught ways of safely interacting with one another.

Older Children and Adolescents

Forty-eight percent of the children entering care in 2005 were 8 years or older (meeting the federal definition of "older"). Recognizing the "aging" trend in the foster care population, the Keeping Children and Families Safe Act of 2003, P.L. 108-36, authorized additional funding to recruit and train foster and adoptive parents for older children and adolescents.

These children are most at risk for behavioral and emotional problems, school failure, and placement instability. More frequent casework visits and collateral contacts with caregivers, teachers, and therapists are indicated. The caseworker's responsibilities as broker and coordinator are also increased as more service providers are engaged to meet the child's needs.

Children Re-Entering Foster Care

We discussed the issue of re-entry in the section on Family Reunification. While less than 10 percent of children who are reunited with parents re-enter foster care, this event is extremely traumatizing for those who do re-enter. After addressing the initial trauma of re-entry and trying to minimize it by placing the child with the previous foster parents, the caseworker needs more frequent contact with the child to fully assess the impact re-entry is having. This increased contact time affords the caseworker the opportunity to discover how the child's wishes about reunification change over time and to work with the child and parents for permanency.

Children in the System as Legal Orphans

Maza coined the term "legal orphans" to identify those children who remain in foster care for extensive periods after parental rights are terminated. Some of these children have adoption as the goal, others do not. In any case, they are the "state's children"; that is, they have no individual person who has parental duties and obligations (Maza, 2000). Sixty-three percent of the 114,000 children waiting to be adopted as of September 30, 2005, had been in continuous foster care for 18 months or more. Of that number, 42 percent had been in foster care for 3 years or more. Of all the waiting children, 47 percent were 9 years or older and 74 percent were placed with relatives or nonrelated foster parents (Children's Bureau, 2006, September).

After the initial post-ASFA surge in termination of parental rights, terminations declined by 7,000 cases from 2000 to 2005. During the same period, the number of children waiting to be adopted declined by 26,000. These changes cannot be explained. After Maza coined the term in 2000, policymakers began to reexamine their original assumptions about the system's capacity to place all children for whom adoption was appropriate and desired with adoptive families. Significant efforts are currently being expended to recruit and train foster and adoptive parents for these children who tend to be over 8 years. There was a reexamination of the benefit in terminating parental rights if the child is in relative care that is expected to be permanent. There was a reexamination of whether adoption should be the permanency plan for some children and plans were changed. These actions might partially explain the decline. See Chapter 10 for more on this issue.

In the 1970s and 1980s, the child welfare system was focused on the large number of children "adrift in foster care" as temporary court wards. Now, there is a large number of children "adrift in foster care" as permanent court wards or state wards. The data shows, however, that these children might not be as "adrift" as the statement implies—74 percent are with relatives or nonrelative foster parents. What is the placement instability for children after termination of parental rights?

The foster care caseworker who thought her work with and for the child would be completed with termination of parental rights and transfer of the child to the adoption caseworker or affecting an adoption and terminating foster care involvement is left to provide services to the child until emancipation.

In these circumstances, the child who is expecting and wants to be adopted experiences rejection and loss with each potential family explored. The caseworker has to help the child understand the realities that she might not get adopted. The child needs to be helped to understand that not being adopted does not mean that she is not wanted—it means the agency hasn't done the right things to find the right family for her. She needs to be helped to understand that she is not "stuck." She needs to know that she has people who care about her that offer her some of the benefits of a "forever home" without legal adoption. She needs to hear from them their reasons for not adopting her and their commitment to her. She needs to know that if she chooses to reestablish a relationship with her parents and other birth relatives, she can do so, unless there is a specific reason that doing this would be harmful to her safety or well-being. She has many things to accomplish that do not depend on being adopted or not being adopted. The caseworker facilitates it all while grieving herself.

Gay and Lesbian Youth

Gay and lesbian youth in out-of-home care are underserved (Child Welfare League of America, 1991). A significant factor among agencies that retards help to gay and lesbian youths is an inability to distinguish them from other youths. These young people have been socialized to fear admitting their sexual orientation and often have internalized societal homophobia. They need skilled help and understanding from caregivers who can accept them, and a safe environment in which they can talk about their concerns, meet peers and adults who can become role models, and learn skills that will enable them to live as a gay or lesbian adult in a straight society (NASW, 1993). For many of these young people, a gay or lesbian foster home can be the placement of choice. Unfortunately, agency staff may hold homophobic attitudes based on myth and stereotype, and may lack training on how to help gay and lesbian teens (Quinn, 2002). For more information on gay and lesbian families, see Chapter 3.

Issues of gender and sexual orientation in the child welfare system have focused mostly on the issue of whether adults who are gay, lesbian, bisexual or transgendered (LGBT) should be foster or adoptive parents. Until very recently, there was very little acknowledgement of the needs of children who were LGBT in out-of-home care (Mallon, 1999). "The lack of leadership and professional guidance related to these key developmental issues has left a vacuum that is often filled by harmful and discriminatory practices based on personal biases related to adolescent sexuality and gender identity rather than informed, evidence-based policies and guidelines" (Wilber, Ryan, & Marksamer, 2006, p. ix).

The Child Welfare League of America issued guidelines in 2006 for serving LGBT youth. The standards identified "creating an organizational culture in which the inherent worth and dignity of every person is respected and every person is treated fairly" as the most critical factor in improving services to LGBT youth (Wilber, Ryan, & Marksamer, 2006, p. 9). While the organizations discuss how they will create this environment, the caseworker serving LGBT youth must create the environment for youth. First, the caseworker must develop a relationship with the youth in which the youth feels safe enough to talk about her sexual orientation. Too many LGBT youth never disclose their sexual orientation or gender identity to the caseworker and never receive supports for positive identity internalization. These youth need the same things that any other youth needs. They have an additional complicating factor—sexual orientation or gender identity that must be acknowledged, accepted, and interpreted in the context of U.S. society. Many LGBT youth feel confused, misunderstood, and afraid to talk about these issues. This places them at risk of emotional problems. With stable and supportive relationships, they can develop a strong sense of well-being (Ragg, Patrick, & Ziefert, 2006). Caseworkers and caregivers must be educated to the issues and must place personal biases aside and create an environment in which the youth can seek help (Ragg, Patrick, & Ziefert, 2006). Relationship development and building trust takes time. Disclosing an issue as personal as being LGBT that subjects one to lifelong discrimination is not done without a relationship and trust. Once the youth discloses to the caseworker, the caseworker must respect the youth's right to determine subsequent referrals.

PREPARING YOUTH FOR INDEPENDENT LIVING AND AGING OUT

Foster care is a temporary setting and not a place for youth to grow up. However, many children do grow up in foster care and age out without the benefit of family reunification or adoption. Recent research findings highlight the disturbing picture for youth who age out of the foster care system. They face increased risk for homelessness, poverty, incarceration, a diagnosable mental illness, substance abuse, chemical dependency, and victimization (Wald & Martinez, 2003). While this presents a grim picture, a renewed focus has been placed on helping these youth begin their adulthood. The Foster Care Independence Act of 1999, which established the John Chafee Foster Care Independence Program (Chafee), replaced and expanded the Independent Living Initiative Program (ILP) of 1986 (The Foster Care Independence Act, 1999).

Many of the provisions of the Act resulted from an evaluation of the programs and services implemented under the 1986 program. The evaluation was based on a review and analysis of the ILP final reports submitted by all 50 states and the District of Columbia for 1987 to 1996. Significant data limitations, including different reporting formats; different definitions; different timeframes; lack of information on the intensity, duration, and scope of services; and postdischarge outcome data. Nonetheless, it found that 37 percent of eligible youth did not receive any services. Most states engaged youth in the program design and ongoing evaluation. A broad range of services were provided and expanded over time. Services included educational and vocational supports, career planning, employment services, housing and home management, budgeting, health care, mental health, personal care, teen parenting classes, substance abuse education, decision-making classes, communication skills development classes, and conflict-resolution skills classes. Most states had difficulty tracking youth after exiting foster care.

Acknowledging data limitations, the evaluation recommended: structured reporting forms; consistent definitions; guidelines for data collection; longitudinal studies by external evaluators; increased federal funding so all eligible youth could be served; supported independent living as a continuous process by lowering the age for eligibility; expanded eligibility to youth 18 to 21 years; promoted greater coordination within child welfare agencies of permanency planning, adoption, and independent living units; expanded supervised independent living programs so youth "learn by doing"; increased services to youth with additional needs—teen parents, those with disabilities, those with substance abuse issues, and those with juvenile justice backgrounds; increased youth involvement in program planning, oversight, and evaluation; and increased collaboration with other agencies to provide a broader range of services and to teach youth to access services (U.S. Department of Health and Human Services, 1999).

Current policymaker discussions appear to disassociate meeting the well-being of children in foster care and permanency planning from preparation for independent living. Current media coverage of youth aging out portrays policymakers and practitioners as surprised that these youth have "aged out" without skills to "make it on their own" (Casey Journalism Center on Children and Families, 2007). Reflect back to the section on Meeting the Needs of Children in Foster Care. Preparing a child to exit out of foster care does not start when the youth is "aging out." The child welfare system should begin when they enter care, irrespective of age at entry. The fundamental prerequisites for self-sufficient, independent, or as some argue "interdependent," functioning in young adulthood and later life include educational and vocational supports, career planning, employment services, housing and home management, budgeting, health care, mental health, personal care, teen parenting classes, substance abuse education, decision-making classes, communication skills development classes, and conflict-resolution skills classes. The same range of services were offered to youth under the 1986 Act.

The child should be in a continuous learning and development cycle consistent with her age and cognitive capacity in all domains. Planning for the well-being of a child must include realistic discussions, in a developmentally appropriate way, of what she expects her life to be like after foster care—where she sees herself living, whether she wants to maintain a relationship with the current caregiver or previous caregivers, and what she wants that relationship to look like; and for the older youth, how she expects to support herself after foster care funding ends and when she, or the caseworker and she, will talk with her caregivers about their commitment to her after foster care ceases. Together everyone should establish a plan for academic improvement, vocational training, and training in daily living skills that will help her develop the knowledge, skills, and resources to succeed.

If a child is in any foster care placement for any period, to acknowledge that the child has no adult to whom she can call for support after foster care should raise alarms about how well the system is attending to the child's well-being while in foster care. Abrupt "emancipation" from foster care without sufficient preparation, education, or adult supports to assist her to survive and thrive as an adult should not happen if the system succeeds and the youth does her part while in foster care.

This does not mean that the young adult will not need support after exiting foster care at age 18. The Chafee Independent Living Program provides eligibility to youth exiting foster care to the age of 21 years. States can provide room and board (up to 30% of their allocation), Medicaid coverage, and services for youth who left foster care because they reached 18 years. All children who are expected to remain in foster care until their eighteenth birthday are eligible to receive independent living services under Chafee prior to that age. Even though the federal government began providing funding for independent living programs in 1986, the child welfare system is still challenged with providing the array of services that maximizes each youth's capacity to provide for her needs at exit. But, will a youth be any more self-sufficient at age 21 than she is at age 18?

SUPERVISION IN FOSTER CARE

A Martian asks, How do you keep your children safe?

A Human responds, Well, we hire a group of 24 year olds, we give them a month of training, we send them to look at incredibly complex and deeply disturbing, distressed families for a few hours a month, we tell them to make life or death decisions, and if they are wrong, remind them that something terrible will happen in the family and that they will be publicly crucified. That's how we do it. (National Child Welfare Resource Center on Family Centered Practice, "Frontline Worker from Mars," 2004)

The supervisor is responsible and accountable for the work performance of all her subordinates—caseworkers and support team. The supervisor must ensure that the agency's core child welfare work is done efficiently and effectively. The core child welfare work is described above. Efficient means producing with minimum waste or expense and effective means producing a desired or intended result. Caseworkers must be competent and committed and it's the supervisor's task to guide them in achieving both characteristics.

What Do We Mean by Competent and Committed?

A competent person knows what is required for successful accomplishment of the job task and has the knowledge and skills required to perform the task.

> **Application exercise.**   Joan was recently hired as a foster care worker. She has no experience, but she took one class on child welfare policy and practice in college. Is she competent to perform the tasks of a foster care worker?
>
> Paul has been employed as a foster care worker by the Best Agency for five years. He has been rated superior in the completion of case service plans by four different supervisors. He has achieved successful implementation of case service plans in 85 percent of his cases. Is he competent to perform the tasks of a foster care worker?

A committed person is motivated, that is, she demonstrates interest and enthusiasm, and is confident, that is, she demonstrates a sense of security and self-assuredness in performing the tasks required.

> **Application exercise.**   Phil has been employed by the agency for twenty years. He achieves satisfactory performance ratings. He develops and writes case service plans that meet the agency's requirements for content but his written work requires several corrections by the supervisor. Is Phil committed? Is Phil competent?
>
> Betty has been employed as a protective services worker for two years. She investigates complaints thoroughly, collecting more information than any other worker. Some of the information is relevant to the protective services decision and some is not. She is slow to complete the paperwork required for her findings because she needs to check into one more thing. Is Betty committed? Is Betty competent?

Competence and commitment are not absolutes; rather, they exist on a continuum for most individuals and are related to specific job tasks or job situations. Again, the supervisor's task is to guide each caseworker to achieve her maximum level of competence and commitment in the specific job tasks.

Techniques for Nurturing and Growing Staff

There are various supervisory styles. Each person develops a style with which they are comfortable and that achieves the agency's goals. The limitations of this text preclude a discussion of possible styles. Rather, we address some of the common elements. Each style uses some directive and supportive behaviors. Directive behavior includes telling staff what to do, when and how, structuring the work, controlling the work performance, and supervising work accomplishment. Supportive behavior includes listening to subordinates; providing support, encouragement, and praise; facilitating interaction; and involving subordinates in decision making.

The behavior used should be related to what the subordinate needs to accomplish the agency's work. All caseworkers want and need structure and support. Some require more planned, consistent support than others.

In general, supervisors must provide structure and support to achieve effective and efficient accomplishment of the agency's work. Structure focuses on worker task accomplishment. It defines the work to be done, the expectations of performance (content and process), and monitors performance. Support focuses on the affective dimensions. It shows trust, respect, and concern for the worker.

Structure includes

- ❖ defining what is expected, when, and how well it must be completed;
- ❖ providing regular, specific feedback on what the subordinate is doing well and what needs improving;
- ❖ informing the subordinates how what they are doing fits the overall mission and purpose of the agency;
- ❖ clarifying their level of authority—what decisions they can make on their own and what decisions need to involve others; and
- ❖ providing opportunities for each to develop skills and grow.

Support includes

- ❖ creating an environment of approval and openness;
- ❖ developing personal relationships—acknowledging unique nesses;
- ❖ providing fair treatment; and
- ❖ enforcing rules equitably. (Kadushin, 1981)

To move the individual and staff to the highest level of performance requires determining the causes of successes and difficulties. Both individual and organizational factors contribute to success and difficulty. Too often supervisors identify the individual factors (knowledge, skill, attitude) and fail to identify the organizational factors (policies, procedures, supports) in developing work performance improvement plans.

Planned Meetings

One of the greatest challenges in child welfare supervision is having planned meetings with staff. Child welfare supervision is most often "supervision on the fly" (SOF). The person needing help dashes in the supervisor's office or catches her walking down the hall, asks a question, gets an answer or direction, and dashes off. Crises for both the supervisor and the subordinate routinely interfere with planned supervisory conferences. Somehow, they never get reset for that day or that week. Thus, the SOF cycle continues. Recognizing that some crises are unavoidable, the supervisor should make every effort to have a planned meeting with each subordinate each week. A standard meeting agenda with caseworkers focuses supervisor and subordinate discussion on these core child welfare tasks:

- ❖ children in crisis
- ❖ court hearings—recommendations and results
- ❖ outstanding work and plans to complete
- ❖ supports needed

Support staff agenda items should be specific to the support functions each performs. For example, an agenda item for a transporter for parent–child visitations could be "children transported for visit but parent did not show up." The "outstanding work and plans to complete" and "supports needed" are common to all subordinates.

Serious performance deficits or issues necessitate formal conferences. These conferences should be well planned. The following steps are useful to a productive outcome for supervisor and subordinate.

- ❖ Gather specific data or information about the issue or concern.
- ❖ Plan the meeting for a specific date, time, and place.
- ❖ Define exactly what will be covered.
- ❖ Identify special problems of a subordinate that should be considered as you plan and conduct the conference; for example, motivational level, length of time on job, previous coaching on same topic.
- ❖ State the objective—demonstrated competence in performing X task.
- ❖ Set the proper climate for productive, positive discussion.
- ❖ Observe the employee performing the task or review written documents completed by the subordinate with her during the conference to determine if she knows the correct way to perform the task.
- ❖ Provide feedback on observation or written documents. Always begin with positive points, then areas needing improvement, and then areas needing corrective action.
- ❖ Demonstrate correct procedure. Show the worker how to perform the task correctly.
- ❖ Have the subordinate show you that she understood your explanation by actually performing the task.
- ❖ Provide feedback based on observation and continue the demonstrate–observe–review cycle until the subordinate demonstrates correctly.
- ❖ Develop follow-up plans specific to how monitoring will occur. Make sure the subordinate actively participates in the development and monitoring of the plan.

TRENDS AND ISSUES

Role of Youth in Foster Care

The Chafee Program has reemphasized the need to give youth a voice in foster care policies and practices. The establishment of Youth Boards, an approach advocated by the Jim Casey Initiative, is an excellent way of engaging youth. However, one of the remaining challenges for the system is to develop and support other ways to engage a more diverse group of youth in the process. The philosophy of youth engagement should extend to younger children as well. Children in foster care face many risks and challenges. Engaging them in resolving those risks and challenges in developmentally appropriate ways increases their capacity for self-sufficiency and improves overall well-being.

Children Who Are AWOL

On a given day, about 10,000 youth who are supposed to be in foster care placements are not in those placements (Children's Bureau, 2006, September). These children are "away without official leave," or AWOL. Some are AWOL because they have been abducted from placement by parents, but most are AWOL because they chose to leave placement. Are they safe? Many states have implemented procedures that strengthen the engagement of the police in "apprehending" these youth. Once apprehended, many are placed in detention facilities. These youth are in the revolving door. The child welfare system has not demonstrated capacity to develop services and programs to engage them.

CHAPTER SUMMARY

Foster care is a system that too frequently is presented negatively. For many children and parents it is more than a necessity. It is the system that restores their capacities and helps them change as individuals and families. It is a system that gives them opportunities to grow and learn better ways of dealing with their pain. For some, it remains the negative that is most often publicized. For all, it remains a system with too few resources, too much "grouping," too little "individualizing," and too little evidence-based practices. The caseworker makes the difference. The caseworker who understands the impact she has on the life of the child and her parents assertively works to meet the needs of the child for safety, well-being, and permanency. She enlists the active involvement of the parents, relatives, nonrelative caregivers, friends, support persons, other professionals, her peers, and her supervisor to overcome the inherent barriers to effective and efficient service delivery. The caseworker cannot possibly commit to memory all the information and resources needed to serve children and families. She must know where to look or who to talk with when she needs information. The caseworker is always an advocate for the child, while understanding that the family is the basic unit for meeting the child's needs. The caseworker must work with them to strengthen their capacities to meet the child's needs.

This chapter has offered many recommendations for how to apply the casework principles discussed in Chapter 4 to the situations presented by children in out-of-home care and their parents. Evidence-based practice for foster care is limited. Therefore, it is impossible to say definitively, "If you do X, you will get Y." While the parents and children present similar issues, each serves an individual function in an environment that affects how what the caseworker does will impact the outcome. These children and their parents are persons who have been failed by prevention services, protective services, family preservation services, and adoption services. Despite that, over 50 percent of the children are discharged from foster care to their parents, with only 10 percent re-entering foster care within twelve months of discharge. That's a 90 percent success rate for reunification!

While the foster care system has many challenges and systemic issues that have remained unresolved since the 1970s, there is incremental progress in the right direction—ensuring safety, well-being, and permanency for children. The CFSR process offers hope that systemic issues will be identified and services and programs implemented to resolve them.

For children who age out of foster care, renewed emphasis is being placed on establishing and maintaining positive relationships with birth families and others that will remain a part of the youth's life for years after she exits foster care. Further, there is renewed emphasis on helping to build capacity for independent functioning starting earlier in the youth's foster care experience.

Children with emotional disturbances, conduct or behavior disorders, developmental disabilities, and chronic medical conditions challenge the foster care system's capacity to build systems of care that include collaborations with mental health, education, and physical health systems.

Supervision is critical to effective and efficient child welfare practice.

FOR STUDY AND DISCUSSION
STUDY AND DISCUSSION QUESTIONS

1. Talk with a placement specialist from a child placing agency to determine which options (shared family care, kinship care, family foster care, treatment foster care, group homes, and residential care) are available in your community. What criteria are applied for selecting a particular care option for a child and family?

2. Invite a former foster child or a panel of young adults who have been in care to discuss their experiences with you in class.

3. Read more extensively on the needs and experiences of parents whose children are in care and talk with a parent in this situation in person.

4. The following scenarios represent three distinct supervisory issues. Identify the issues and structure your approach for efficiently and effectively resolving the issues.

Ann has worked in child welfare for five years. Prior to last month, she was an excellent worker who completed all her work timely, correctly, and was willing to help other caseworkers. In the last month, you returned several updated service plans and court reports to her because they were either incomplete or contained inconsistencies. Two staff members told you that she told them she didn't have time to "do their work" when they asked her opinion about what she would do in specific case situations they were experiencing. Another staff member told you that she thinks Ann's mother is dying and maybe everybody should "cut her some slack."

John has worked in child welfare for twenty years. Kids, birth parents, and foster parents rave about him. He has very few crises on his caseload. When there is one, he is quick to work out an appropriate resolution. He just doesn't do the paperwork. This has been his pattern for over fifteen years. His previous supervisor disciplined him for failure to meet paperwork requirements at least three times in the past two years. Each time he was disciplined, he would complete the work at the last minute. He was recently moved to your staff. Over half his caseload has overdue work. Concurrently, administration has issued a directive that service plans and eligibility determinations must be current for all cases within the next thirty days.

Maria has worked in child welfare for two years. She has struggled from the beginning to meet casework requirements. She has a positive attitude, tries hard, and seems to want to perform better. She has had three supervisors in two years. Her performance ratings indicated that she was a marginal performer who worked hard, but didn't seem to get all the work completed timely and accurately. No specific professional development plan or discipline had been implemented. She joined your staff (agency reorganization due to staff reductions) last week. Yesterday, a child on her caseload died. The child was placed in a foster home. Marie had not seen the child in two months. The news media, agency administration, and the judge want answers now.

5. Secure the AWOL policy and procedures for your service area. Identify areas that might be strengthened by utilizing a child safety and well-being framework.

Internet Sites

Children's Bureau. The Children's Bureau is one of six bureaus within the Administration on Children, Youth and Families, Administration for Children and Families, of the Department of Health and Human Services. It seeks to provide for the safety, permanency, and well-being of children through leadership, support for necessary services, and productive partnerships with states, tribes, and communities.
www.acf.hhs.gov/programs/cb/index.htm

Child Welfare Information Gateway. Established by the U.S. Children's Bureau to provide access, information, and resources on all areas of child welfare to help protect children and strengthen families. Excellent source to connect with other credible web sites on any child welfare issue.
www.childwelfare.gov

Child Welfare League of America. This organization has a general child welfare site, with specific pages related to developments in foster care and lists of topically related titles by the Child Welfare League of America Press.
www.cwla.org

Children's Defense Fund. This site provides information on child care, current news as it relates to children, the black community, publications, and other related links.
www.childrensdefense.org

First Gov. This web site accesses all agencies and departments of the federal government. It provides access to all the national clearinghouses and resource centers on mental health, substance abuse, and the child welfare national resource centers.
http://firstgov.gov

National Center on Substance Abuse and Child Welfare. The organization is funded by the Substance Abuse and Mental Health Services Administration's Center for Substance Abuse Treatment and the Administration on Children, Youth, and Families, Children's Bureau. Its charge is to develop and implement a comprehensive program of information gathering and dissemination, to provide technical assistance, and to develop knowledge that promotes effective practice, organization, and system changes at the local, state, and national levels specific to substance abuse and child welfare.
www.ncsacw.samhsa.gov

National Foster Parent Association (NFPA). Information on becoming a foster parent is available at this site. The web site explains the purpose of the NFPA and provides membership information. It offers a comprehensive site called KidSource, which provides information on children as it relates to fostering.
www.kidsource.com/nfpa/index.html

The National Resource Center for Family-Centered Practice and Permanency Planning. This center focuses on increasing the capacity and resources of state, tribal, and other publicly supported child welfare agencies to promote family-centered practices that contribute to the safety, permanency, and well-being of children, while meeting the needs of their families.
www.hunter.cuny.edu/socwork/nrcfcpp/index.html

References

Ainsworth, M. D. (1962). The effects of maternal deprivation: A review of findings and controversy in the context of research strategy. In *Deprivation of maternal care: A reassessment of its effects.* Geneva: World Health Organization, Public Health Papers (no. 14).

Allen, M., Bonner, K., & Greenan, L. (1988). Federal legislative support for independent living. *Child Welfare, 67*(6), 515–527.

Allen, M., Lakin, D., McFadden, E. J., & Wasserman, K. (1992). *Family continuity: Practice competencies.* Ypsilanti, MI: National Foster Care Resource Center.

Altman, J. C. (2004). *Engagement in neighborhood-based child welfare services.* Garden City, NY: Adelphi University School of Social Work.

Altman, J. C. (2005). Engagement in children, youth, and family services: Current research and promising approaches. In G. P. Mallon & P. M. Hess (Eds.), *Child welfare for the 21st century: A handbook of practices, policies and programs.* New York: Columbia University Press.

Altshuler, S. (2003). From barriers to successful collaboration: Public schools and child welfare working together. *Social Work, 48*(1), 52–64.

Altshuler, S. J., & Gleeson, J. P. (1999, January–February). Completing the evaluation triangle for the next century: Measuring child "well-being" in family foster care. *Child Welfare, 78*(1), 125–147.

Altshuler, S. J., & Poertner, J. (2002, May–June). The Child Health and Illness Profile—adolescent edition: Assessing well-being in group homes or institutions. *Child Welfare, 81*(3), 495–514.

American Psychiatric Association. (2000). *Quick Reference to the Diagnostic Criteria from DSM-IV-TR.* Arlington, VA: American Psychiatric Publishing.

Bank, S., & Kahn, M. (1982). *The sibling bond.* New York: Basic Book..

Barth, R. P., Gibbons, C., & Guo, S. (2006). Substance abuse treatment and the recurrence of maltreatment among caregivers with children living at home: A propensity score analysis. *Journal of Substance Abuse Treatment, 30*(2), 93–104.

Berry, M. (1988). A review of parent training programs in child welfare. *Social Service Review, 62*(2), 302–322.

Besharov, D. (1990, July–August). Crack children in foster care: Re-examining the balance between children's rights and parents rights. *Children Today,* 21–25.

Besharov, D. (Ed.). (1994). *When drug addicts have children.* Washington, DC: Child Welfare League of America/American Enterprise Institute.

Billingsley, A. (1992). *Climbing Jacob's ladder: The enduring legacy of African-American families.* New York: Simon & Schuster.

Blair, K. D., & Taylor, D. B. (2006). Examining the lives and needs of child-only recipient kinship caregivers: Heroes stepping up to help children. *Journal of Family Social Work, 10*(1), 1–23.

Blumenthal, K., & Weinberg, A. (1983). *Establishing parental involvement in foster care agencies.* New York: Child Welfare League of America Press.

Bowlby, J. (1969). *Attachment and loss.* London: Hogarth Press.

Brace, C. L. (1872). *The dangerous classes of New York and twenty years' work among them.* New York: Wynkoop and Hallenbeck.

Breshears E., Yeh, S., & Young, N. K. (2005). *Understanding substance abuse and facilitating recovery: A guide for child welfare workers.* Rockville, MD: National Center on Substance Abuse and Child Welfare, Center for Substance Abuse Treatment.

Brissett-Chapman, S., & Issacs-Shockley, M. (1997). *Children in social peril: A community vision for preserving family care of African American children and youths.* Washington, DC: Child Welfare League of America Press.

Bromley, B., & Blacker, J. (1991). Parental reasons for out-of-home placement of children with severe handicaps. *Mental Retardation, 29*(5), 275–280.

Bronheim, S., Goode, T., & Jones, W. (2006, Spring). *Policy Brief: Cultural and linguistic competence in family supports.* Washington, DC: Georgetown University, National Center for Cultural Competence.

Bryant, B. (1994). Panacea watch: Permanency planning. *The Review, 8*(3), 2–3.

Bryant, B., & Snodgrass, R. (1990). Therapeutic foster care past and present. In P. Meadowcroft, & B. Trout (Eds.). *Troubled youth in treatment homes: A handbook of therapeutic foster care.* Washington, DC: Child Welfare League of America.

Bussiere, A., English, A., & Teare, C. (1997). *Sharing information: A guide to federal laws on confidentiality and disclosure of information for child welfare agencies.* Washington, DC: American Bar Association.

Cahn, K. (2003). *Lutheran community services evaluation report.* Seattle, WA: University of Washington School of Social Work. Available:

http://depts.washington.edu/nwicf/EvalServ/ LCS Final Report.pdf.

Cantos, A., Gries, L., & Slis, V. (1997). Behavioral correlates of parental visiting during family foster care. *Child Welfare, 76*(2), 309–329.

Carbino, R. (1991). Child abuse and neglect reports in foster care: The issue of foster families and "false" allegations. *Child and Youth Services, 15*(2), 233–247.

Cautley, P. W. (1980). *New foster parents.* New York: Human Sciences.

Casey Family Programs. (2006). Family to family initiative. Available at www.caseyfamilyprograms.org.

Casey Journalism Center on Children and Families. (2007). CJC Summary. Available at www.casey.amd.edu

Chahine, Z., & Higgins, S. (2005). Engaging families and communities: The use of family team conferences to promote safety, permanency, and well-being in child welfare services. In G. P. Mallon & P. M. Hess (Eds.), *Child welfare for the 21st century: A handbook of practices, policies and programs.* New York: Columbia University Press.

Charles, G., & Matheson, J. (1990). Children in foster care: Issues of separation and attachment. *Community Alternatives, International Journal of Family Care, 2*(2), 37–49.

Chasnoff, I. (1990). Maternal drug use. In *Crack and other addictions: Old realities and new challenges for child welfare* (pp. 110–120). Washington, DC: Child Welfare League of America.

Chernoff, R., Coombs-Orme, T., Risley-Curtis, C., & Heisler, A. (1994). Assessing the health status of children entering foster care. *Pediatrics, 93,* 594–601.

Chibnall, S., Dutch, N. M., Jones-Harden, E., Brown, N., et. al (2003, December). *Children of color in the child welfare system: Perspectives from the child welfare community.* Washington, DC: U.S. Department of Health and Human Services, Children's Bureau.

Child and Family Services Improvement Act of 2006, P.L. 109-288. National Clearinghouse on Child Abuse and Neglect Information. (2005, April). *Concurrent Planning: What the Evidence Shows.* Washington DC: Author.

Child Welfare Information Gateway (2003). Substance abuse and child maltreatment. Bulletin for Professionals. Washington, DC: Author.

Child Welfare Information Gateway. (2005, April). *Concurrent planning: What the evidence shows.* Washington, DC: U.S. Department of Health and Human Services.

Child Welfare Information Gateway. (2006). *State statutes series.* Washington, DC: U.S. Department of Health and Human Services.

Child Welfare League of America. (1991). *Serving gay and lesbian youth: The role of child welfare agencies.* Washington, DC: Author.

Child Welfare League of America. (1994). *Kinship care: A natural bridge.* Washington, DC: Author.

Child Welfare Research Center. (2003). *Promising practices in concurrent planning.* Berkeley, CA: Center for Social Services Research University of California at Berkeley Schools of Social Welfare. Available: http://cssr.berkeley .edu/childwelfare.

Children's Bureau. (2005). *Findings from the 50 states.* Washington, DC: U.S. Department of Health and Human Services, Administration for Children and Families.

Children's Bureau. (2006a). *Placement instability.* Washington, DC: Author. Available: http//www.acf.hhs.gov/programs/cb.

Children's Bureau. (2006b). *Promising practices in child welfare services.* Washington, DC: Author. Available: http//www.acf.hhs.gov/programs/cb.

Children's Bureau. (2006, September). The AF-CARS report: Preliminary estimates as of September 2006 (13). Available: www.acf. hhs.gov/programs/cb/stats—research/afcars/ tar/report13.htm [2007 January 2]

Children's Bureau. (2007). Children's Bureau Express. Available: http://www.acf.hhs.gov/cb.

Churchill, S., Carlson, B., & Nybell, L. (Eds.). (1979). *No child is unadoptable.* Beverly Hills, CA: Sage.

Clark, M. D. (2007, April). The research on motivation and human behavior change: The critical conditions of desire, ability, reason, and need. Presented at: Substance Abuse: Paving the Road to Recovery and Reunification Conference, Lansing, MI.

Cohen, E., Hornsby, D. T., & Priester, S. (2005). Assessment of children, youth, and families in the child welfare system. In G. P. Mallon & P. M. Hess (Eds.), *Child welfare for the 21st century: A handbook of practices, policies and programs.* New York: Columbia University Press.

Colon, F. (1978). Family ties and child placement. *Family Process, 17,* 289–312.

Compton, B. R., Galaway, B., & Cournoyer, B. R. (2005). *Social work processes.* Belmont, CA: Thomson Learning.

Conway, T., & Hutson, R. Q. (2007). *Is Kinship Care Good for Kids?* Washington, DC: Center for Law and Social Policy. Available: www.clasp.org

Cordero, A., & Epstein, I. (2005). Refining the practice of family reunification: "Mining" successful foster care case records of substance abusing families. In G. P. Mallon & P. M. Hess (Eds), *Child welfare for the 21st century: A handbook of practices, policies and programs.* New York: Columbia University Press.

Crisp, C. (2006). The gay affirmative practice scale (GAP): A new measure for assessing cultural competence with gay and lesbian clients. *Social Work, 51*(2), 115–126.

Cross, T. L. (1988). Services to minority populations: Cultural competence continuum. *Focal Point, 3*(1), 1–4.

Delaney, R. (1991). *Fostering changes: Treating attachment-disordered foster children.* Fort Collins, CO: Walter J. Corbett Publishing.

Dore, M. M. (2005). Child and adolescent mental health. In G. P. Mallon & P. M. Hess (Eds.), *Child welfare for the 21st century: A handbook of practices, policies, and programs.* New York: Columbia University Press.

Dubner, A. E., & Motta, R. W. (1999). Sexually and physically abused foster care children and posttraumatic stress disorder. *Journal of Consulting and Clinical Psychology, 67,* 367–373.

Duquette, D. N. (2005). Establishing legal permanence for the child. In M. Ventrell & D. N. Duquette (Eds.), *Child welfare law and practice: Representing children, parents, and state agencies in abuse, neglect, and dependency cases.* Denver, CO: Bradford Publishing Company.

Elze, D. E., Auslander, W., Stiffman, A., & McMillen, C. (2005). Educational needs of youth in foster care. In G. P. Mallon & P. M. Hess (Eds.), *Child welfare for the 21st century:*

A handbook of practices, policies and programs. New York: Columbia University Press.

Emlen, A. (1978). *Overcoming barriers to planning for children in foster care.* Portland, OR: Regional Research Institute for Human Services.

Epstein, L. (1992). *Brief treatment and a new look at the task-centered approach.* New York: Macmillan Publishing Company.

Fahlberg, V. (1991). *A child's journey through placement.* Indianapolis: Perspectives Press.

Fanshel, D. (1975). Parental failure and consequences for children: The drug-abusing mother whose children are in foster care. *American Journal of Public Health, 65*(6), 604–612.

Fanshel, D., & Shinn, E. B. (1978). *Children in foster care: A longitudinal investigation.* New York: Columbia University School Press.

Federal Register, 2006, June 7.

Fein, E., & Staff, I. (1993). Goal-setting with biological families. In B. Pine, R. Warsh, & A. Maluccio (Eds.), *Together again: Family reunification in foster care* (pp. 67–92). Washington, DC: Child Welfare League of America.

Fenton, J. (2006, January). *Concurrent planning.* ACF Regional Office Teleconference.

Festinger, T. B. (1994). *Returning to care: Discharge and reentry in foster care.* Washington, DC: Child Welfare League of America.

Fimmen, M. D., & Mietus, K. J. (1988). *An empirical analysis of the impact of joint training upon child welfare practitioners.* (DHHS Award No. 05CT1022/01). Macomb, IL: Western Illinois University.

Folaron, G. (1993). Preparing children for reunification. In B. Pine, R. Krieger, & A. Maluccio (Eds.), *Together again: Family reunification in foster care* (pp. 41–154). Washington, DC: Child Welfare League of America.

Folaron, G., & Hess, P. (1993). Placement considerations for children of mixed African-American and Caucasian parentage. *Child Welfare, 72*(2), 113–125.

Folks, H. (1911). *The care of destitute, neglected, and delinquent children.* New York: Macmillan.

Folman, R. D. (1998). I was tooken: How children experience removal from their parents preliminary to placement into foster care. *Adoption Quarterly, 2*(2), 7–35.

Foster Family-Based Treatment Association. (2001). *Annotations of research in treatment foster care.* Teaneck, NJ: Author.

Freud, C. (1955). Meaning of separation for parents and children as seen in child placement. *Public Welfare, 13*(1), 13–17, 25.

Garbarino, J., DuBrow, N., Knostelny, K. & Pardo, C. (1992). *Children in danger: Coping with the consequences of community violence.* San Francisco: Jossey Bass.

Garnier, P. C., & Poertner, J. (2000, September–October). Using administrative data to assess child safety in out-of-home care. *Child Welfare, 79*(5), 597–613.

Garrett, A. (1942). *Interviewing: Its principles and methods.* New York: Family Service Association of America.

Gavazzi, S., Alford, K., & McKenry, P. (1996). Culturally specific programs for foster care youth. *Family Relations, 45,* 166–174.

Geen, R. (2004). The evolution of kinship care policy and practice. *The Future of Children: Children, Families, and Foster Care, 14*(1), 131–147.

Geiser, R. (1973). *The illusion of caring.* Boston: Beacon Press.

Generations United. (2006). *All children deserve a permanent home: Subsidized guardianships as a common sense solution for children in long-term relative foster care.* Washington, DC: Author.

Gillespie, J., Byrne, B., & Workman, L. (1995). An intensive reunification program for children in foster care. *Child and Adolescent Social Work Journal, 12*(3), 213–228.

Gilligan, R. (1997). Beyond permanence? The importance of resilience in child placement practice and planning. *Adoption and Fostering, 21*(1), 12–20.

Golden, R. (1997). *Disposable children: America's child welfare system.* Belmont, CA: Wadsworth.

Goldstein, J., Freud, A., & Solnit, A. (1973). *Beyond the best interests of the child.* New York: Free Press.

Government Accountability Office (2007, July). African-American children in foster care: Additional HHS assistance needed to help states reduce the proportion in care. GAO-07-816. Washington, DC: U.S. Government Printing Office.

Green, M., & Palfrey, J. S. (Eds.). (2000). *Bright futures: Guidelines for health supervision of infants, children, and adolescents* (2nd ed.). Arlington, VA: National Center for Education in Maternal and Child Health.

Grigsby, K. (1994). Maintaining attachment relationships among children in foster care. *Families in Society, 75*(5), 269–276.

Groze, V., Haines-Simeon, M., & Barth, R. (1994). Barriers in permanency planning for medically fragile children: Drug affected children and HIV infected children. *Child and Adolescent Social Work Journal, 11*(1), 63–85.

Gurdin, P., & Anderson, G. R. (1987). Quality care for ill children: AIDS-specialized foster family homes. *Child Welfare, 66*(4), 291–302.

Hamblen, J. (1999). *Fact sheet: PTSD in children and adolescents.* National Center for PTSD. Available: www.ncptsd.org/facts/specific/fs_children.html.

Harden, B. J. (2004). Safety and stability for foster children: A developmental perspective. *The Future of Children, 14*(1), 31–48.

Hardin, C. (2007). Bridging the gap between the court, child welfare, and treatment systems. Presented at Paving the Road to Recovery and Reunification: Courts, Child Welfare, and Treatment Partners. April 3, 2007. Lansing, MI.

Hartman, A., & Laird, J. (1983*). Family-centered social work practice.* New York: The Free Press.

Hegar, R. (1993). Assessing attachment, permanence, and kinship in choosing permanent homes. *Child Welfare, 72*(4), 367–378.

Hess, P. M. (2005). Visits: Critical to the well-being and permanency of children and youth in care. In G. P. Mallon & P. M. Hess (Eds.), *Child welfare for the 21st century: A handbook of practices, policies and programs.* New York: Columbia University Press.

Hess, P., & Folaron, G. (1991). Ambivalences: A challenge to permanency for children. *Child Welfare, 70*(4), 403–424.

Hill, R. (2006). *Syntheses of the research on disproportionality in child welfare: An update.* Baltimore, MD: Casey-CSSP Alliance for Racial Equity.

Hill, R. (1972). *The strengths of black families.* New York: Emerson Hall.

Hochstadt, N., & Yost, D. (Eds.). (1991). *The medically complex child: The transition to home care.* New York: Harwood Academic Publishers.

Hohman, M. M., & Butt, R. L. (2001, January–February). How soon is too soon? Addiction recovery and family reunification. *Child Welfare, 80*(1), 53–70.

Horn, W. (1994). Implications for policy-making. In D. Besharov (Ed.), *When drug addicts have children* (pp. 165–174). Washington, DC: Child Welfare League and American Enterprise Institute.

Hudson, J., Nutter, R., & Galaway, B. (1994). Treatment foster family care: Development and current status. *Community Alternatives, 6*(2), 1–24.

Human Services Associates. (1998). *Finding our place: The inside story of foster care.* St. Paul, MN: Rummel Dubs & Hill.

Hutchins, H. (1997). Managing managed care for families. *Children's Voice, 7*(1), 28–29.

Jackson, H., & Westmoreland, G. (1992). Therapeutic issues for black children in foster care. In L. Vargas & J. Koss-Chioino (Eds.), *Working with culture: Psychotherapeutic interventions with ethnic minority children and adolescents* (pp. 43–62). San Francisco: Jossey Bass.

Jenkins, S., & Norman, E. (1972). *Filial deprivation in foster care.* New York: Columbia University.

Jim Casey Youth Initiative. (2007). *Vision statement on youth engagement.* Available: www.jimcaseyyouth.org.

Johnson, P., Yoken, C., & Voss, R. (1990). *Foster care placement, the child's perspective.* Discussion paper No. 036. Chicago: University of Chicago, Chapin Hall Center.

Jones, M. L. (1978). Stopping foster care drift: A review of legislation and special programs. *Child Welfare, 57*(9), 571–580.

Jones, M., Magura, S., & Shyne, A. (1976). *A second chance for families.* New York: Child Welfare League of America.

Jordan, C. (1994). Have external review systems improved the quality of care for children? Yes. In E. Gambrill & T. Stein (Eds.), *Controversial*

issues in child welfare* (pp. 136–140). Boston: Allyn & Bacon.

Kadushin, A. (1981). *Supervision in social work,* 2nd Ed. New York: Columbia University Press.

Kansas chapter. National Association of social workers. (1997). Kansas talk back: Early responses to the privatization of child welfare services. www. naswdc.org/PRAC/Kansas.htm.

Katz, L. (1999, January–February). Concurrent planning: Benefits and pitfalls. *Child Welfare, 78*(1), 108–124.

Kemp, S. P., Allen-Eckard, K., Ackroyd, A., Becker, M. F., & Burke, T. K. (2005). Community family support meetings: Connecting families, public child welfare, and community resources. In G. P. Mallon & P. M. Hess (Eds.), *Child welfare for the 21st century: A handbook of practices, policies and programs.* New York: Columbia University Press.

Kerwin, M. E. (2005). Collaboration between child welfare and substance abuse fields: Combined treatment programs for mothers. *Journal of Pediatric Psychology, 30*(7), 581–597.

Klee, L., Soman, L., & Halfon, N. (1992, March–April). Implementing critical health services for children in foster care. *Child Welfare, 71*(2), 99–110.

Knipe, J., & Warren, J. (1999). *Foster youth share their ideas for change.* Washington, DC: Child Welfare League of America.

Knutson, J. (1995). Pyschological characteristics of maltreated children: Putative risk factors and consequences. *Annual Review of Psychology, 46,* 401–431.

Kools, S. (1997). Adolescent identity development in foster care. *Family Relations, 46,* 263–271.

Kortenkamp, K., & Ehrle, J. (2002, January). The well-being of children involved with the child welfare system: A national overview. *In New Federalism National Survey of America's Families, Series B, No. B-43.* Washington, DC: The Urban Institute.

Lee, D., & Nissivoccia, D. (1989). *Walk a mile in my shoes: A book about biological parents for foster parents and social workers.* Washington, DC: Child Welfare League of America.

Leeds, S. (1992). *Medical and developmental profiles of 148 children born HIV-positive and placed in foster families.* New York: Leake and Watts Services.

Levy, T., & Orlans, M. (1998). *Attachment, trauma and healing.* Washington, DC: Child Welfare League of America Press.

Liberman, F. (1979). *Social work with children.* New York: Human Sciences Press.

Littner, N. (1975). The importance of the natural parents to the child in placement. *Child Welfare, 54*(3), 175–181.

Maas, S., & Engler, R. E. (1959). *Children in need of parents.* New York: Columbia University.

MacFarlane, C. D. (2006). My strength: A look outside the box at the strengths perspective. *Social Work, 51*(2), 175–176.

Mallon, G. (1977). Basic premises, guiding principles and competent practices for a positive youth development approach to working with gay, lesbian and bi-sexual youths in out-of-home care. *Child Welfare, 76*(5), 591–610.

Mallon, G. P. (1999). Gay and lesbian adolescents and their families. *Journal of Gay and Lesbian Social Sciences, 10*(2), 69–88.

Mallon, G. P., & Hess, P. M. (Eds.). (2005). *Child welfare for the 21st century: A handbook of practices, policies and programs.* New York: Columbia University Press.

Maluccio, A., & Fein, E. (1983, May–June). Permanency planning: A redefinition. *Child Welfare, 62*(3), 195–201.

Maluccio, A., Krieger, R., & Pine, B. (Eds.). (1990). *Preparing adolescents for life after foster care: The central role of foster parents.* Washington, DC: Child Welfare League of America.

Maluccio, A., & Sinanoglu, P. (Eds.). (1981). *The challenge of partnership: Working with parents of children in foster care.* New York: Child Welfare League of America.

Marcenko, M., & Striepe, M. (1997). A look at family reunification through the eyes of mothers. *Community Alternatives: The International Journal of Family Care, 9*(1), 33–47.

Marquardt, S. M. (2000). *Implementing non-adversarial direct consent adoptions in Michigan.* Lansing, MI: Michigan Family Independence Agency.

Marsenich, L. (2002, March). Evidence-based practices in mental health services for foster youth. Sacramento, CA: California Institute for Mental Health. Available: www.cimh.org/downloads/Fostercaremanual.pdf.

Marsh, J. C., Ryan, J. P., Chol, S., & Testa, M. F. (2006). Integrated services for families with multiple problems: Obstacles to family reunifications. *Children and Youth Services Review, 28*(9), 1074–1087.

Martin, F., & Palmer, T. (1997). Transitions to adulthood: A child welfare youth perspective. *Community Alternatives, the International Journal of Family Care, 9*(2), 29–58.

Mather, J. H., & Lager, P. B. (2000). *Child welfare: A unifying model of practice.* Belmont, CA: Thomson Learning.

Maza, P. L. (2000, September–October). Using administrative data to reward agency performance: The case of the federal adoption incentive program. *Child Welfare, 79*(5), 444–456.

Maza, P. L. (2005, October). Adoption data update. Presented at: National Association of State Adoption Program Managers Annual Meeting. Washington, DC: Children's Bureau.

McAlpine, C., Marshall, C. C., & Doran, N. H. (2001). Combining child welfare and substance abuse services: A blended model of intervention. *Child Welfare, 80*(2), 129–149.

McFadden, E. J. (1980). *Working with natural families.* Ypsilanti, MI: Eastern Michigan University.

McFadden, E. J. (1984). Practice in foster care. In A. Hartman & J. Laird (Eds.), *Handbook of child welfare.* New York: Free Press.

McFadden, E. J. (1996). Family-centered practice with foster parent families. *Families in Society, 77*(9) 545–557.

McFadden, E. J., Rice, D., Ryan, P., & Warren, B. (1989). Leaving home again: Emancipation from foster family care. In J. Hudson & B. Galaway (Eds.), *Specialist foster family care: A normalizing experience.* New York: Haworth.

McGowan, B. G. (2005). Historical evolution of child welfare services. In G. P. Mallon & P. M. Hess (Eds.), *Child welfare for the 21st century: A handbook of practices, policies and programs.* New York: Columbia University Press.

McNaught, K. M. (2004). *Learning curves: Education advocacy for children in foster care.* Washington, DC: American Bar Association.

McRoy, R. G. (2005). Overrepresentation of children and youth of color in foster care. In G. P. Mallon & P. M. Hess (Eds.), *Child welfare for the 21st century: A handbook of practices, policies and programs.* New York: Columbia University Press.

Meadowcroft, P., & Grealish, E. M. (1990). Training and supporting treatment parents. In P. Meadowcroft & B. Trout (Eds.), *Troubled youth in treatment homes: A handbook of therapeutic foster care.* Washington, DC: Child Welfare League of America.

Mech, E. (1985). Parental visiting and child placement, *Child Welfare, 64*(1), 67–72.

Meidema, B., & Nason-Clark, N. (1977). Foster care redesign: The dilemma contemporary foster parents face. *Community Alternatives, the International Journal of Family Care, 9*(2), 15–28.

Miller, S. D., Hubble, M. A., & Duncan, B. L. (Eds.). (1996). *Handbook of solution-focused brief therapy.* San Francisco: Jossey-Bass Publishers

Milner, J. (1987). An ecological perspective on duration of foster care. *Child Welfare, 66*(2), 113–123.

Moore, E. (1977). *Wayne County Temporary Foster Care Project: Report #1.* Detroit, MI: Michigan Department of Social Services–Wayne County.

Munroe, F. (1997). Pathways to permanent placement for young children in high-risk situations. In E. Wattenberg (Ed.), *Redrawing the family circle: Concurrent planning—Pathway to permanency for young children in high-risk situations.* St. Paul, MN: University of Minnesota School of Social Work, Center for Advanced Studies in Child Welfare.

Murphy, S., & Helm, M. (1988). Group preparation of adolescents for family placement. In J. Trisiliotis (Ed.), *Groupwork in adoption and foster care.* London: B. T. Batsford, Ltd.

National Association of Foster Care Reviewers. (1994). Court improvement project: The citizen review role. *The Review, 8*(3), 1–2.

National Association of Foster Care Reviewers. (1998). *Safe passage to permanency: Using third-party review to improve outcomes for children in foster care.* Atlanta, GA: Author.

National Association of Social Workers. (1993, April). *NASW News.*

National Association of Social Workers. (2001). *NASW standards for cultural competence in social work practice.* Washington DC: National Association of Social Workers.

National Black Child Development Institute. (1989). *Who will care when parents can't: A study of black children in foster care.* Washington, DC: National Black Child Development Institute.

National Center for Substance Abuse and Child Welfare. (2003). Understanding substance use disorders, treatment and family recovery: A guide for child welfare professionals [curriculum]. Available: www.ncsacw.samhsa.gov/tutorials.

National Child Welfare Resource Center on Family Centered Practice. (2004, Winter). *Frontline Worker from Mars.* Des Moines, IA: Author.

National Clearinghouse on Child Abuse and Neglect Information. (2005, April). *Concurrent planning: What the evidence shows.* Washington, DC: Author.

National Commission on Family Foster Care. (1991). *A blueprint for fostering infants, children and youths in the 1990s.* Washington, DC: Child Welfare League of America Press.

National Conference of State Legislatures. (2006, September). *Child welfare caseworker visits with children and parents.* Denver CO: Author

National Foster Care Awareness Project. (2000, February). *Frequently asked questions I about the Foster Care Independence Act.* Seattle: Casey Family Programs.

National Foster Care Awareness Project. (2000, December). *Frequently asked questions II about the Foster Care Independence Act of 1999 and the John H. Chafee Foster Care Independence Program.* Washington, DC: Author.

National Resource Center Family Centered Practice and Permanency Planning. (2003, February). *Concurrent planning.* New York: Author.

National Resource Center for Foster Care and Permanency Planning. (2002). Concurrent Planning Curriculum. Available www.hunter.cuny.edu/socialwork/nrcfcpp.

National Resource Center for Foster Care and Permanency Planning. (2003). Concurrent planning: Strategies for implementation. Web conference.

National Resource Center for Foster Care and Permanency Planning. (2004, September). Findings from the initial Child and Family Service Reviews 2001–2004. New York: Author. Available: www.hunter.cuny.edu/socwork/nrcfcpp.

Nelson, K. (1992). Fostering homeless children and their parents too: The emergence of whole family care. *Child Welfare, 71*(6), 575–584.

Nelson, K., Landsman, M., & Deutelbaum, W. (1990). Three models of family-centered placement prevention services. *Child Welfare, 69*(1), 3–21.

Netting, F. E., Kettner, P. M., & McMurtry, S. L. (1998). *Social work macro practice.* New York: Longman.

Newton, R. R., Litrownik, A. J., & Landsverk, J. A. (2000). Children and youth in foster care: Disentangling the relationship between problem behaviors and number of placements. *Child Abuse and Neglect, 24*(10), 1363–1374.

Nowicki, S., & Duke, M. (1992). *Helping the child who doesn't fit in.* Atlanta, GA: Peachtree Publishers.

Oko, J. (2006). Evaluating alternative approaches to social work: A critical review of the strengths perspective. *Families in Society, 87*(4), 601–611.

Ortega, R., Guillean, C., & Najera, L. (1996). *Latinos and child welfare/latinos y el bienestar del niño, voces de la comunidad.* Ann Arbor, MI: University of Michigan.

Oyserman, D., Benbenishty, R., & Ben-Rabi, D. (1992). Characteristics of children and their families at entry into foster care. *Child Psychiatry and Human Development, 22*(3), 199–211.

Palmer, S. (1990). Group treatment of foster children to reduce separation conflict associated with placement breakdown. *Child Welfare, 69*(3), 227–238.

Palmer, S. (1997). Training workers to include families in child placement. *Community Alternatives: The International Journal of Family Care, 9*(1), 49–70.

Pardeck, J., & Pardeck, J. (1987, May–June). Bibliotherapy for children in foster care and adoption. *Child Welfare, 66*(3), 269–278.

Pecora, P., Whittaker, J., Maluccio, A., Barth, R., & Plotnick, R. (2000). *The child welfare challenge.* New York: Walter de Gruyter.

Pennell, J., & Anderson, G. (Eds.). (2005). *Widening the circle: The practice and evaluation of family group conferencing with children, youths, and their families.* Washington, DC: NASW Press.

Phillips, M., Shyne, A., Sherman, E., & Haring, B. (1971). *Factors associated with placement decisions in child welfare.* New York: Child Welfare League of America.

Phillips, S., McMillen, C., Sparks, J., & Ueberle, M. (1997). Concrete strategies for sensitizing youth-serving agencies to the needs of gay, lesbian, and other sexual minority youths. *Child Welfare, 76*(3), 393–409.

Pike, V., Downs, S. W., Emlen, A., Downs, G., & Case, D. (1977). *Permanent planning for children in foster care* (No. OHDS 77-30124). Washington, DC: U.S. Department of Health, Education and Welfare.

Pine, B., Krieger, R., & Maluccio, A. (Eds.). (1993). *Together again: Family reunification in foster care.* Washington, DC: Child Welfare League of America.

Pine, B., Spath, R., & Gosteli, S. (2005). Defining and achieving family reunification. In G. P., Mallon & P. M. Hess (Eds.), *Child welfare for the 21st century: A handbook of practices, policies and programs.* New York: Columbia University Press.

Pizzigati, K. (1998). Safety and permanence: New federal law reemphasizes both. *Children's Voice, 7*(3), 12–13.

Proch, K., & Howard, J. (1986). Parental visiting of children in foster care. *Social Work, 31*(3), 178–181.

Quinn, T. L. (2002, November–December). Sexual orientation and gender identity: An administrative approach to diversity. *Child Welfare, 81*(6), 913–928.

Ragg, D. M., Patrick, D., & Ziefert, M. (2006). Slamming the closet door: Working with gay and lesbian youth in care. *Child Welfare, 2*(85), 243–266.

Ratterman, D., Dodson, D., & Hardin, M. (1987). *Reasonable efforts to prevent foster care placement: A guide to implementation.* Washington, DC: American Bar Association.

Raychaba, B. (1989). *We got a life sentence: Young people's response to sexual abuse.* Ottawa: National Youth in Care Network.

Redding, R. E., Fried, C., & Britner, P. A. (2000). Predictors of placement outcomes in treatment foster care: Implications for foster parent selection and service delivery. *Journal of Child and Family Studies, 9*(4), 425–447.

Reddy, L., & Pfeiffer, S. (1997). Effectiveness of treatment foster care with children and adolescence: A review of outcome studies. *Journal of American Academy of Child and Adolescent Psychiatry, 36*(5), 581–588.

Report of Select Senate Committee to visit charitable and penal institutions. (1857). (New York Senate Document No. 8). Reprinted in S. P. Breckinridge (1927). *Public welfare administration in the United States: Select documents.* Chicago: University of Chicago Press.

Represent: The voice of youth in care. (2006, September). New York: Youth Communication/New York Center, Inc.

Rhodes, K. W., Orme, J. G., & Buehler, C. (2001, March). A comparison of family foster parents who quit, consider quitting, and plan to continue fostering. *Social Service Review,* 84–114.

Rice, D., & McFadden, E. J. (1988, May–June). A forum for foster children. *Child Welfare, 67*(3), 231–243.

Ricketts, W. (1991). *Lesbians and gay men as foster parents.* Portland, ME: University of Southern Maine, National Child Welfare Resource Center.

Roberts, D. (2002). *Shattered bonds: The color of child welfare.* New York: Basic Books.

Rockymore, M. (2006, April). *The role of the caseworkers in identifying, developing and supporting strengths in African American families involved in child protection services.* St. Paul, MN: Minnesota Department of Human Services.

Rutter, M. (1985). Resilience in the face of adversity: Protective factors and resistance to psychiatric disorder. *British Journal of Psychiatry, 147,* 598–611.

Ryan, P., McFadden, E. J., & Warren, B. (1981). Foster families: A resource for helping parents. In A. Maluccio and P. Sinanoglu. (Eds.), *The Challenge of Partnership* (pp. 189–199). New York: Child Welfare League of America.

Saltzburg, S. (2005). Co-constructing adolescence for gay and lesbian youth and their families. In G.P. Mallon & P.M. Hess, (Eds.), *Child welfare for the 21st century: A handbook of practices, policies and programs.* New York: Columbia University Press.

Saunders, E., Nelson, K., & Landsman, M. (1993). Racial inequality and child neglect: Findings in a metropolitan area. *Child Welfare, 72*(4), 341–354.

Schene, P. (2001). *Implementing concurrent planning: A handbook for child welfare administrators.* Portland, ME: University of Southern Maine, National Resource Center for Organizational Improvement.

Schene, P. (2005, May). *Comprehensive family assessment guidelines for child welfare.* New York: National Resource Center for Family Centered Practice and Permanency Planning.

Schneiderman, M., Connors, M., Fribourg, A., Gries, L., & Gonzales, M. (1998). Mental health services for children in out-of-home care. *Child Welfare, 77*(1), 29–40.

Semidei, J., Radel, L. F., & Nolan, C. (2001, March–April). Substance abuse and child welfare: Clear linkages and promising responses. *Child Welfare, 80*(2), 109–128.

Shlonsky, A. R., & Berrick, J. D. (2001, March). Assessing and promoting quality in kin and nonkin foster care. *Social Service Review,* 60–83.

Shostack, A. L. (1997). *Group homes for teenagers: A practical guide.* Washington, DC: CWLA Press.

Sibbison, V. H. (2000). *Evaluation of the families together project.* Washington, DC: St. Christopher-Ottilie Services for Children and Families Welfare Research.

Slingerland, W. (1919). *Child placing in families.* New York: Russell Sage Foundation.

Staff, I., & Fein, E. (1992). Together or separate: A study of siblings in foster care. *Child Welfare, 71*(3), 257–270.

Staff, I., & Fein, E. (1995). Stability and change: Initial findings in a study of treatment foster care placements. *Children and Youth Services Review, 17*(3), 379–389.

Stein, T. (1998). *The social welfare of women and children with HIV and AIDS.* New York: Oxford University Press.

Stein, T. J. (2000, November–December). The Adoption and Safe Families Act: Creating a false dichotomy between parents' and children's rights. *Families in Society, 81*(6).

Stein, T., & Gambrill, E. (1977). Facilitating decision-making in foster care: The Alameda project. *Social Service Review, 51*(3), 502–513.

Stein, T., Gambrill, E., & Wiltse, K. (1974). Foster care: The use of contracts. *Public Welfare, 32*(4), 20–25.

Stein, T., & Rzepnicki, T. (1984). *Decision-making in child welfare services: Intake and planning.* Boston: Kluwer-Nijhoff.

Stokes, J., & Strothman, L. (1996). The use of bonding studies in child welfare permanency planning. *Child and Adolescent Social Work Journal, 13*(4), 347–367.

Stone, H. (1987). *Ready, set, go: An agency guide to independent living.* Washington, DC: Child Welfare League of America.

Suchman, N., Mayes, L., Conti, J., Slade, A., & Rounsaville, B. (2004). Rethinking parenting interventions for drug-dependent mothers: From behavior management to fostering emotional bonds. *Journal of Substance Abuse Treatment, 27*(3), 179–185.

Tatara, T. (1993). *Characteristics of children in substitute and adoptive care.* Washington, DC: American Public Welfare Association, VCIS.

Taylor-Brown, S., & Garcia, A. (1995). Social workers and HIV-affected families: Is the profession prepared? *Social Work, 40*(1), 14–15.

Ten Broeck, E., & Barth, R. (1986). Learning the hard way: A pilot permanency planning program. *Child Welfare, 65,* 281–294.

Terling-Watt, T. (2001). Permanency in kinship care: An exploration of disruption rates and factors associated with placement disruption. *Children & Youth Services Review, 23*(2), 111–126.

Terpstra, J. (1997). Child welfare, from there to where. Unpublished paper.

Terpstra, J., & McFadden, E. J. (1993, Spring). Looking backward, looking forward: New directions in foster care. *Community Alternatives, 5*(1), 115–133.

Testa, M. F. (2004). When children cannot return home: Adoption and guardianship. *In The Future of Children: Children, Families, and Foster Care, 14*(1), 115–130.

Testa, M. F., & Miller, J. (2005). Evolution of private guardianship as a child welfare choice. In G. P., Mallon & P. M. Hess (Eds.), *Child welfare for the 21st century: A handbook of practices, policies and programs.* New York: Columbia University Press.

Testa, M. F., & Rolock, N. (1999, January–February). Professional foster care: A future worth pursuing? *Child Welfare, 78*(1), 108–124.

The Pew Charitable Trusts. (2007). Time for reform: Support relatives in providing foster care and permanent families for children. Philadelphia, PA: Author. Available at: www.kidsarewaiting.org.

Thoennes, N. (1996). Foster care review: Reducing delay and expense in the juvenile court. Alexandria, VA: State Justice Institute.

Thomlison, B. (1997). Risk and protective factors in child maltreatment. In M. Fraser (Ed.), *Risk and resilience in childhood.* Washington, DC: National Association of Social Workers Press.

Thompson, C. L., & Rudolph, L. B. (2000). *Counseling children* (5th ed.) Belmont, CA: Wadsworth, Brooks/Cole Counseling.

Thurston, H. S. (1930). *The dependent child.* New York: Columbia University Press.

Tourse, P., & Gunderson, L. (1988). Adopting and fostering children with AIDS: Policies in progress. *Children Today, 17,* 15–19.

Tower-Crosson, C. (2007*). Exploring child welfare: A practice perspective.* Boston: Pearson Education.

Trozzi, M., & Massimini, K. (1999). *Talking with children about loss: Words, strategies, and wisdom to help children cope with death, divorce, and other difficult times.* New York: The Berkley Publishing Group.

Twigg, R. (1995). Coping with loss: How foster parents' children cope with foster care. *Community Alternatives: The International Journal of Family Care, 7*(1), 1–14.

U.S. Department of Health and Human Services. (1999, November). *Title IV-E independent living programs: A decade in review.* Washington, DC: Author.

U.S. Department of Health and Human Services. (2000). *Rethinking child welfare practice under the Adoption and Safe Families Act of 1997: A Resource guide.* Washington, DC: U.S. Government Printing Office.

U.S. Department of Health and Human Services. (2001). *National standards for culturally and linguistically appropriate services in health care: Final report 2001.* Washington, DC: Author.

U.S. Department of Health and Human Services. (2005). *Child welfare outcomes 2002: Annual report.* Washington, DC: Administration for Children, Youth, and Families, Children's Bureau. Available: www.acf.hhs.gov/programs/cb/publications/cwo02/cwo02.pdf.

U.S. Department of Health and Human Services, Administration for Children, Youth and Families (2003). *National survey of child and adolescent well-being (NSCAW). Wave 1: Child Protective Services Report.* Washington, DC: DHHS.

U.S. Department of Health and Human Services, Children's Bureau. (2005). *CFSR 50 state report: 2005 Report to congress.* Washington, DC: Author.

U.S. General Accounting Office. (1989). *Foster parents: Recruiting and preservice training practices and evaluation.* Washington, D.C.: Author.

U.S. General Accounting Office. (1991). *Foster care: Children's experiences linked to various factors; better data needed.* (HRD-91-64). Washington, DC: Author.

Wald, M., & Martinez, T. (2003). *Connected by 25: Improving the life chances of the country's most vulnerable youth.* Available: from http://www.hewlett.org.

Walker, C., Zangrillo, P., & Smith, J. (1991). *Parental drug abuse and African American children in foster care: Issues and study findings.* Washington, DC: National Black Child Development Institute.

Walsh, J., & Walsh, R. (1990). *Quality care for tough kids.* Washington, DC: Child Welfare League of America.

Walton, E., Fraser, M., Lewis, R., Pecora, P., & Walton, W. (1993). In-home family-focused reunification: An experimental study. *Child Welfare, 72*(5), 473–487.

Weil, M., Karls, J. M., & J. M. Karls and Associates. (1985). Case *management in human service practice: A systematic approach to mobilizing resources for clients.* San Francisco: Jossey-Bass Publishers.

Weinberg, A., & Katz, L. (1998). Low and social work in partnership for permanency: The Adoption and Safe Families Act and the role of concurrent planning. *Children's Legal Rights Journal. 18*(4), 2–23.

Weinstein, E. A. (1960). *The self-image of the foster child.* New York: Russell Sage Foundation.

Wheeler, M. M. (2007). Fundamentals of drug treatment courts. Presented at Paving the Road to Recovery and Reunification: Courts, Child Welfare, and Treatment Partners. April 4, 2007. Lansing, MI.

Whittaker, J. K. (1987). Group care for children. In A. Minahan (Ed.), *Encyclopedia of social work* (18th ed.) (pp. 672–682). Silver Spring, MD: National Association of Social Workers.

Wightman, M. (1991). Criteria for placement decisions with cocaine-exposed infants. *Child Welfare, 70*(6) 653–663.

Wilber, S., Ryan, C., & Marksamer, J. (2006). *Serving LGBT youth in out-of-home care: CWLA best practice guidelines.* Washington, DC: Child Welfare League of America.

Wodrich, D. L. (1997). *Children's psychological testing* (3rd ed.). Baltimore, MD: Paul H. Brookes Publishing.

Wood, L., Herring, A. E., & Hunt, R. (1989). *On their own: The needs of youth in transition.* Elizabeth, NJ: Association for the Advancement of the Mentally Handicapped.

Wooden, K. (1976). *Weeping in the playtime of others.* New York: McGraw-Hill.

Woronoff, R., & Mallon, G. P. (2006, March/April). LGBTQ youth in child welfare. *Child Welfare, 85*(2), 341–360.

Wulczyn, F. (2004). Family reunification. *In The Future of Children: Children, Families, and Foster Care, 14*(1), 115–130.

Young, N. (2007). It's Monday morning: What do we do now? Presented by S. Gardner at paving the Road to Recovery and Reunification: Courts, Child Welfare, and Treatment Partners. April 4, 2007. Lansing, MI.

Zambrana, R., & Dorrington, C. (1998). Economic and social vulnerability of Latino children and families by subgroup: Implications for child welfare. *Child Welfare, 77*(1), 5–27.

Zetlin, A. G., Weinberg, L. A., & Kimm, C. (2005). Helping social workers address the educational needs of foster children. *Child Abuse & Neglect, 29*, 811–823.

Zuravin, S., Benedict, M., & Somerfield, M. (1993). Child maltreatment in family foster care. *American Journal of Orthopsychiatry, 63*(4), 589–596.

Zuravin, S., & DePanfilis, D. (1997). Factors affecting foster care placement of children receiving child protective services. *Social Work Research, 21*(1), 34–42.

Statutes, Administrative Rules, and Children's Bureau Interpretative Policies

Accreditation of Agencies and Approval of Persons Under the Intercountry Adoption Act of 2000 (IAA). 04/01/06 Edition. 22 CRF Chapter 1, Part 96.

Title IV of the Social Security Act, 42 U.S.C. Section 422 et. seq.

The following public laws amended sections of Title IV of the Social Security Act.

The Adam Walsh Child Protection and Safety Act of 2006, P.L. 109-248, amends 42 U.S.C. Sections 671(a) (20), 671(a) (20) (B).

The Adoption Assistance and Child Welfare Act of 1980, P.L. 96-272

The Adoption and Safe Families Act of 1997, P.L. 105-89 amending 42 U.S.C. Sections 601 et seq., 622b, 629 et seq., 653, 670-679, 671 at5, 675(5)(E), 677(a)(2)A, 675(1), 1320a-9.

The Child and Family Services Improvement Act of 2006, P.L. 109-288, amends 42 U.S.C. 620-628b,622(b), 629b(a)(8), 629b(b)(2), 629d, 629e(c), 629f(b), 629f(b)(3), 629g, 629g(a), 629g(b)(3), and 629(i).

The Deficit Reduction Act of 2005, P.L. 109-171, amending 42 U.S.C. Sections 429h©, 622(b), 629f(a), 629 h, 629H(a), 629h(b), 671, 672, 672a, 673(a)(2), and 674(a)(3).

The Indian Child Welfare Act of 1978, P.L. 95-608, 25 U.S.C. Sections 1901 – 1963.

The John Chaffee Foster Care Independence Act of 1999, P.L. 106-169 amending 42 USC Sections 671a, 673b, 674(a)(4), 675, 677, and 139a(a)(10)(A)(ii).

The Keeping Children and Families Safe Act of 2003, P.L. 108-36, amending 42 U.S.C. Sections 670, 5101, 5104(b), 5104(c)(1), 5105, 5105(a), 5105(b), 5106(a), 5106a(a), 5106a(b), 5106a(c), 5106(b), 5105(c), 5106c(c), 5106d, 5111, 5113, 5114, 5116a, 5116b, 5116d, 5116e(a), 5116f, 5116g(3), 5116h, and 5116h(1).

The Multiethnic Placement Act of 1994 and Interethnic Placement Provisions of 1996, P.L. 103-382 as amended by P.L. 104-188, Section 1808 amending 42 U.S.C. Sections 622, 671(a)(18), 674(d), 1996 b, 1996(h), and 5115a.

The Personal Responsibility and Work Opportunity Reconciliation Act of 1996, P.L. 104-193.

The Safe and Timely Interstate Placement of Foster Children Act of 2006, P. L. 109-239

Children's Bureau Policies

Children's Bureau (2006, December). Child and Family Services Reviews Procedures Manual. Available at www.acf.hhs.gov/programs/cbcwmonitoring/tools_guide/index.htm

Children's Bureau, (2007). Child Welfare policy manual, section 4: MEPA/IEP. Available at www.acf.hhs.gov/programs/cb/laws_policies/laws/cwpm.

The following policy issuances of the Children's Bureau are available at www.acf.hhs.gov/programs/cb/laws_policies/laws/cwpm.

❖ ACYF-IM-CB-97-04: The Small Business Job Protection Act of 1996, Interethnic Adoption, and Multiethnic Placement Act.

❖ ACYF-CB-PI-07-04: Issued February 21, 2007. Title IV-E State Plan Amendment—The Tax Relief and Health Care Act of 2006 (Public Law (P.L.) 109-432)

❖ ACYF-CB-PI-07-02: Issued February 22.2007. Court Improvement Program Requirements of the Safe and Timely Interstate Placement of Foster Children Act of 2006)

❖ ACYF-CB-PI-07-02: Issued January 23, 2007. Title IV-E State Plane Amendments—New Legislation.

❖ ACYF-CB-IM 06-05: Issued: December 7, 2006. The Child and Family Services Improvement Act of 2006 (Public Law (P.L.) 109-288).

❖ ACYF-CB- IM 06-04: Issued: September 1, 2006. New Legislation - The Adam Walsh Child Protection and Safety Act of 2006 (Public Law (P.L.) 109-248).)

❖ ACYF-CB- IM 06-03: Issued: August 11, 2006. New Legislation—The Safe and Timely Interstate Placement of Foster Children Act of 2006 (Public Law (P.L.) 109-239). (

❖ ACYF-CB- IM 06-02: Issued: June 9, 2006. New Legislation—The Deficit Reduction Act of 2005.

❖ ACYF-CB- IM 06-01: Issued: January 17, 2006. New Legislation—Public Law 109-113, the Fair Access Foster Care Act of 2005.

Families by Adoption

In every child who is born, under no matter what circumstances, and of no matter what parents, the potentiality of the human race is born again and in him, too, once more, and each of us, our terrific responsibility towards human life.

—*James Agee*

Bandele. (Follow me home.)

—*Swahili saying*

CHAPTER OUTLINE

CASE EXAMPLE:
Helping an Older Child Use Adoption

This case shows how a social worker, using an approach emphasizing continuity of family relationships, helped a child with a history of traumatic experiences move successfully through the adoption process. She supported him as he worked through his conflicting loyalty toward his birth family and his adoptive family, and his hesitancy to trust a new relationship after experiencing earlier rejection.

Ms. Franklin, an adoption specialist, met Grant when he was 10 years old and living temporarily in a residential center where he had gone after his adoption of one year had disrupted. Her responsibility was to help Grant, if possible, to move into a new adoptive placement.

The first task was to get to know Grant well. She learned that he had entered the child welfare system at age 7, along with his older brother, Oliver. Their mother had been unable to manage the boys, who were often truant and were causing problems in the community. She had abandoned them at the child welfare agency and later voluntarily relinquished her rights. Their father was a gambler and involved in other illegal activities; during a period of time when the boys were in his care he had exposed them to "nightlife" and had not met their basic needs. He too relinquished his sons voluntarily.

Grant was originally placed in foster care with a single, middle-aged woman who had raised her own family. After a year, she adopted Grant. Initially, things went well, but Oliver, who had not wanted to be adopted and was living elsewhere, began to exert a strong influence on Grant. He let Grant know that "this is not your real family; I'm your real family." The more the adoptive mom put pressure on Grant to distance himself from Oliver, the more Grant felt a conflict of loyalties. His behavior began to reflect the conflict he was feeling and the adoptive mother decided she could not cope. So the adoption disrupted, and Grant was placed in the residential center. He had been there for several months when Ms. Franklin met him.

After assessing Grant's needs, Ms. Franklin felt he needed a home with a strong father figure because he had had conflicts with two mothers. The family she found consisted of Mr. and Mrs. Robinson and their three children. Grant would be one of the middle children. Because Grant was an average student, Ms. Franklin was interested that the Robinsons did not put undue pressure on the children to excel in school but did expect the children to be conscientious students. Mr. Robinson had a steady job as a laborer, and Mrs. Robinson was a practical nurse. Ms. Franklin thought that this family would provide structure and guidance, and that Grant could meet their expectations.

The mother had a strong spiritual base and was active in church. Strong family networks on both sides, whose members were supportive of the placement, welcomed Grant as a cousin and grandson.

Because of Grant's previous experiences, Ms. Franklin and the Robinsons decided that Grant would feel less pressure if the placement started as foster care, which could develop into an adoption later if both sides wanted it.

Ms. Franklin visited the home twice a month for the next year to provide support and information about resources. During that time, Grant and the Robinsons, parents and children, decided to formalize the arrangement through adoption.

This decision made the adoption very real to Grant and he began to act out his anxiety over the upcoming change in his status. He started to cut classes at school and forged signatures to cover up his truancy. No matter what the parents did to establish consequences, Grant seemed unaffected. They began to question whether Grant wanted the adoption. Oliver reappeared at this time and encouraged Grant to refuse adoption. Also, at this time, Grant learned of his birth mother's whereabouts and visited her.

Ms. Franklin knew that finalizing an adoption can be very stressful for older children, since it raises concerns they have over their earlier experiences. She had to help the family and Grant work through this difficult period so they would not rush into a decision during a time of crisis.

She went back over Grant's life history with the Robinsons and discussed how the earlier losses of a family might affect his attitude. She pointed out that both the birth mother and the previous adoptive mother had reneged on a commitment, so Grant was perhaps afraid that that would happen again once the adoption was finalized. She encouraged them to help Grant explore his feelings, and Grant was able to express that he was afraid of what his brother would say about the adoption.

Ms. Franklin helped the family develop several strategies to deal with the confusion everyone was feeling. One strategy was that the adoptive father, who had been from the first an involved and available parent, became more involved with Grant. He told Grant about some incidents from his own school days and how he had tried to resolve them, and took extra time to share activities with him. Another strategy was to keep an open line with the school to avoid an escalation of the crisis by having Grant suspended or expelled. The adoptive parents worked out an arrangement with the counselor and teachers so they all could work on Grant's truancy as a team.

To deal with the influence of Oliver, Mrs. Robinson spoke with him personally and reassured him that he would not lose his brother, and that he would be welcome in her home. She also let him know that the family loved Grant, wanted to take care of him, and would not harm him. She reassured him that they were not denigrating Grant's birth family. Mrs. Robinson also met Grant's birth mother and exchanged information with her. The Robinsons let her and Grant know that it was fine for them to stay in touch with each other. Grant himself was able to come to a decision that he wanted to live in the Robinson family. He seemed to understand that the new family would not replace his earlier family but could meet his current needs.

This period of uncertainty also gave the Robinsons a chance to clarify their own feelings about making Grant a permanent member of the family. After weathering this period, they came to believe even more strongly that "this is our kid."

After the adoption was finalized, Ms. Franklin gradually cut back her involvement with the family. She let them know that they were in charge and that the agency trusted them to take full responsibility for Grant's welfare. She continued to be a resource for information on services, and she assured them that she would be available to help them manage a crisis. She also worked to help Grant transfer his trust from the adoption worker to the adoptive parents. Although Grant is now grown, he still stays in touch with Ms. Franklin occasionally. He graduated from high school and is doing well.

THE CHANGING WORLD OF ADOPTION

Adoption is a social and a legal process in which the parent–child relationship is established between persons not related by birth. By this means, a child born to one set of parents becomes, legally and socially, the child of other parents and a member of another family, and assumes the same rights and duties as those between children and their biological parents. Adoption is a life-long process of benefits to and adjustments by all members of the adoptive triad—the adopted person, the birth parents, and the adoptive parents. The complex legal framework for adoption reflects its importance to the families affected; it is the most drastic state intervention into families, as it creates new families from those not related by blood.

Adoption has become one of the most dynamic arenas of child welfare practice. Change is occurring rapidly on all fronts, bringing controversy and uncertainty in its wake (Pertman, 2006; Groza, Houlihan, & Wood, 2005). From being primarily a service matching white, healthy infants with traditional white middle-class families, adoption now is challenging long-held assumptions about the appropriate composition of families. Ideas about the qualities of people who might become adoptive parents are rapidly expanding. Senior citizens, persons with AIDS, gay and lesbian couples, single adults, relatives, and people of a different race ethnicity or culture from the adopted child are among the groups who are seeking to become adoptive parents and are publicly challenging traditional, untested assumptions about who should become a parent.

In contrast to earlier years when adoptive children were mainly healthy infants, today, almost any child in need of a permanent home is considered a candidate for adoption, regardless of age, disability, or national origin. Many of these children are older and have lived with their biological parents or with foster parents, making the adoptive experience quite different from that of an adopted infant.

The role of biological parents in the adoption process is also changing. Biological parents may want a part in deciding who adopts their child and may wish some kind of ongoing connection to the child and adoptive family. The rights of biological fathers as well as mothers now must be considered in freeing children for adoption. The policy framework for adoption is more complicated than in earlier years. There is disagreement about who should handle adoptions, and there are also special issues that arise in international adoption.

A vivid example of how the concept of adoption has expanded to include adults and children who, until recently, would not have been considered a "family," is the story of Nasdijj, a migrant worker and adoptive father. "My 12-year-old Navajo son had AIDS. I knew he did when I adopted him last year. . . . I have wiped the tears of such children before. The disturbed and the vulnerable. The throwaways. . . . I was one of them, too. . . . I have been a migrant worker all my life. . . . This summer, I drifted with my son from Michigan to Florida, picking oranges, cherries, anything, as long as the farm boss paid me. . . . You are thinking, This man should not have had a child. But I did" (Nasdijj, 2001).

As adoption has expanded to involve many different types of family situations, the public has become increasingly aware of adoption. A national survey of adoption attitudes in 2002 showed that most Americans support adoption (94 percent of those surveyed) and have had either a family member or a close friend involved in adoption (64 percent). Given the rapid pace of change in adoption, it is not surprising that large numbers of Americans express confusion about adoption, with concerns about such issues as how adopted children turn out compared to birth children, and about the perceived costs of adoption. The survey found some attitudinal differences between races: Hispanics and African Americans were somewhat more likely than white respondents to state that they would seriously consider adopting a child (32 percent, 23 percent, and 16 percent, respectively) (Evan B. Donaldson Adoption Institute, 2002b).

The following section, briefly outlining the historical development of adoption, will help to explain the social and economic changes in this country and developments in our understanding of family dynamics that have impelled the transformations occurring in adoption policy and practice.

HISTORICAL DEVELOPMENT

The adoption of children dates back to antiquity. References to adoption can be found in the Bible and in legal codes of the Chinese, Hindus, Babylonians, Romans, and ancient Egyptians. Its purpose has varied considerably by country and by period—for example, to make possible the continuance of family religious traditions, to provide an heir, to overcome difficulties in recognizing an out-of-wedlock child, or, more recently, to provide permanent homes for children in need of them.

Early Adoption Practices in the United States

The nature and social purpose of adoption as it is conceived today in many countries began to emerge in the United States during the latter part of the nineteenth century. Up to that time, inheritance had run through the history of adoptions so much more prominently than any other factor that its importance can hardly be overestimated (Witmer et al., 1963). In 1851, Massachusetts was the first state to enact an adoptive statute in line with present concepts of the purpose of adoption. The Massachusetts law required a "joint petition by the adopting parents to the probate judge and the written consent of the child's parents, if living, or of his guardian or next of kin if the parents were deceased. The judge if satisfied that the adoption was 'fit and proper' was to enter the adoption decree" (Abbott, 1938, pp. 164–165). The state's new adoption statutes put adoptive status on a firmer legal ground by giving a state some control in adoptive situations before a contest arose, and they secured permanent status for the child in a new family as well as a right to an equitable share of the adoptive parent's estate.

Infant Adoptions

During the first half of the twentieth century, statutes reflected interest in secrecy, confidentiality, anonymity, and the sealing of records (Carp, 1995; 1998). Originally, these practices "were not designed to preserve anonymity between biological parents and adopters, but to shield the adoption proceedings from public scrutiny. These statutes barred all persons from inspecting the files and records on adoption except for the parties to the adoption and their attorneys" (Hollinger, 1991, p. 13). However, from the 1920s through the 1940s, states progressively amended their statutes to deny access of the records to everyone except on "a judicial finding of 'good cause'" (Hollinger, 1991, p. 13). The identities of the birth parents were to remain secret; the original birth certificate was sealed and a new one issued at the time the adoption was finalized (Sokoloff, 1993, p. 22).

During the early decades of the twentieth century, adoption became more and more popular, especially for infertile couples wishing to adopt infants. Previously, adoption was relatively rare, due in part to concern about "bad blood" associated with waifs and foundlings. Two developments that began to change the general reluctance to adopt were the wider availability of infant formula, making adoption of newborns more feasible, and the growing view that children were more profoundly influenced by environment than by heredity (Sokoloff, 1993).

After World War I, demand for infants grew rapidly, prompting the growth of black market adoptions by unregulated "baby brokers." In response, many states amended their statutes to require social investigations and a court hearing before a judge to finalize the adoption. During the 1920s, many specialized adoption agencies were founded to offer professional adoption services. Adoption services were used almost entirely by white couples to adopt white babies; adoption for children of other races rarely occurred through formal agency auspices and was more apt to be done informally, within the extended family network.

Social workers, supported by physicians, defined an "adoptable" child as one who was nearly perfect in health and development and, as far as could be determined by extended observation and examination, one who posed minimal risk to the adopting adults. Well into the middle of the twentieth century, infants released for adoption by their biological mothers did not go immediately after birth to adoptive parents. The newborn infant was usually placed first in a foster home for a three- to six-month period of observation. During this time, infants received physical examinations and intelligence testing. Many social workers made fine distinctions from the psychological report as to the intellectual qualities that should be sought in the infant's adoptive family. Eventually it was acknowledged that a careful "matching" of intellectual abilities or physical characteristics between parents and children, even were this possible, was no guarantee of a successful adoption.

By the 1940s, agencies were faced with having many more adoptive parent applicants than children to offer, a condition that influenced them to develop procedures to restrict the number of applicants. "Matching" of socioeconomic and religious background was common. Agencies placed restrictions on the age and financial status of the applicants, even though they acknowledged that many of the applicants they rejected would make good parents (Michaels, 1947).

The mismatch between the numbers of those desirous of adopting healthy, white infants and the supply available for adoption has increased in recent times. The rate at which women relinquish their infants for adoption has declined dramatically, from about 20 percent in 1982 to about 3 percent in 1995, the latest date compiled through the National Survey of Family Growth. The 2000 Survey data has not been compiled.

The decrease of infants available for adoption can be attributed to a number of social developments of the 1960s: increasingly available, effective contraception; the rise in the abortion rate after abortion was legalized in 1973; and the increasing acceptability of single mothers keeping their infants rather than placing them out for adoption (Dukette, 1984). Families interested in adopting infants turned to transracial adoption and increasingly to international adoption. In addition, "as advances in technology have permitted, couples have sought help through alternative means of reproduction including artificial insemination by donor, in vitro fertilization, embryo transfer, and most recently, surrogate parenting" (Sokoloff, 1993, p. 23).

Today, adoption of infants is often handled through private agencies or through *independent adoption,* the term for adoption outside of agency auspices, usually by individual professionals (doctors, lawyers, and social workers). This development has raised concern that private individuals, who stand to gain financially from adoption, may not be in the best position to help a pregnant woman make a decision to relinquish her child for adoption or to assess adoptive parents.

Adoption Today: Adoption of Children from the Child Welfare System

At the same time that adoptive parents were unable to find infants, another trend was creating a different kind of mismatch: the increasing number of children without permanent families who were thought to be "unadoptable," particularly older children; children of color; and those with medical, emotional, or other handicapping conditions. Several developments led to an increase in the number of these children available for adoption. The abuse and neglect reporting laws, implemented in the 1960s and 1970s, resulted in many more abused and neglected children entering the child welfare system.

Furthermore, civil unrest and disasters in many countries led to increased numbers of orphans available for adoption.

By the 1990s, adoption had split into three practice arenas: adoption of children with special needs or children from the public child welfare system, adoption of healthy infants, and intercountry adoptions, including healthy infants and children with special needs and orphans.

In 2005, the Children's Bureau began to change its terminology from "special needs" to "children adopted from the child welfare system" in an effort to remove the stigma associated with the "special needs" label as well as to acknowledge that many of the children adopted from the child welfare system do not have medical, emotional, or other handicapping conditions; but rather, are children who are older or members of sibling groups that should be adopted together.

Adoption Today: The Cooperative Adoption Movement

In the 1970s and 1980s, *closed* (or *confidential*) adoption began to give way to a new *open* (or *cooperative*) adoption model. The notion that confidentiality was preferable for all three members of the adoptive triad—birth parents, adoptive parents, and children—came into question through the changes that have occurred in adoption during the last half of the twentieth century. As fewer infants became available for adoption, the birth mother found more leverage in the process of relinquishment and preferences about adoptive parents. Agencies learned that mothers might be less concerned with confidentiality than with helping to select the adoptive parents and with maintaining some kind of connection with the child after the adoption. Adults who had been adopted as infants, for their part, began assertively seeking to have their sealed records opened and demanded the right to know about their biological origins.

The movement to place children with special needs or children from the child welfare system in adoption changed adoption practice dramatically. If older, these children have memories of their birth parents and siblings, and their foster, adoptive, and birth parents often have met one another. Adoptive applicants of children of color and of children with special needs expressed the need for a shared partnership with the agency regarding selection and matching processes, leading to a trend toward open sharing of information with the prospective adoptive applicants so they could make an informed decision. Kinship adoption has become increasingly used as a permanent plan for children exiting foster care.

Many adoption agencies today have revised their traditional practices toward varying degrees of "openness" in the adoptive process. These changes take the form of planned communication between the adoptive parents and the biological parents prior to finalization of the adoption. All the parents may have face-to-face meetings before the birth of the child, at agreement for placement, or at various times after the birth of the child. The range of information that is exchanged may include ethnic and religious backgrounds, level of education, aspects of personality and interest, physical characteristics, genetic background, or other matters of common interest. These options are arrived at when birth parents and adoptive parents, with the help of an agency social worker, have agreed on the extent of "openness" in the present and future (Etter, 1997; Grotevant & McRoy, 1998).

State statutes vary on the enforceability of postadoption contact agreements. Some allow written and enforceable contact agreements, some are silent on the issue, some limit enforceability to stepparent adoptions, and some specifically state that they are not enforceable (Child Welfare Information Gateway, 2005).

SOME ADOPTION FACTS AND PATTERNS

No aspect of child welfare practice has yielded such a short supply of accurate statistics as adoption. The U.S. government has collected comprehensive national data at various times, but has not done so since 1975.

Some progress has been made in the collection of data. The U.S. Department of State records data for "immigrant orphan visas," that is, intercountry adoptions. The federal government also requires states to submit data on the children adopted from foster care as part of the Adoption and Foster Care Analysis and Reporting System (AFCARS). However, there is no national system for recording stepparent adoptions, relative adoptions not involving a public child welfare agency, or private adoptions of U.S. citizens, even though all adoptions are processed by the courts (McFarland, 2003).

For the first time in decennial census history, the U.S. Census Bureau's Census 2000 Questionnaire included "adopted son/daughter" as a category for relationship to householder. Of the 83.7 million children counted in Census 2000, approximately 2.1 million were adopted. However, the number derived from this census is not totally accurate because the question asks for the relationship to "householder." If the adopted child is the adopted child of someone other than the householder, then the child would not be counted as "adopted son/daughter," but as "other," "grandchild," or "nonrelated." AFCARS preliminary estimates as of September 2006 reported 51,000 children adopted with public involvement in 2005. In the past 10 years, the number of children adopted from the child welfare system ranged from a low of 25,693 in 1995 to a high of 52,881 in 2002. Even with these increases, 118,009 children were waiting to be adopted at the end of 2005 (Children's Bureau, 2006). The U.S. Department of State reported 20,679 children adopted from other countries in 2006, down from 22,739 adopted in 2005.

Agency and Independent Placements

In the earlier years of adoption as a social service, voluntary agencies arranged the majority of agency adoptions. This pattern has changed. As public agencies have assumed increasing responsibility for social services to children, public child and family services agencies and their private agency partners have substantially extended their adoption services, particularly for children adopted from the child welfare system.

Placements by private individuals, termed *independent,* are of three types. *Direct placements* are those made by legal parents to someone known to them. Sometimes parents may gradually and informally relinquish more and more of their responsibilities for a child to a family friend or neighbor, and eventually adoption takes place. These placements are arranged within the state's legal framework and tend to work out satisfactorily for the child. Direct placements of this kind are legal except in three states (Child Welfare Information Gateway, 2006).

Intermediary placements not for profit are arranged by a third person who is usually not seeking profit and may be well intentioned. Usually the adopting parents are unknown to the birth parents initially, although they may become acquainted if the adoption has some degree of "openness." An exchange of money may take place—for example, a standard fee for legal services or payment of the mother's medical or other living expenses during pregnancy—but the money exchanged is not disproportionate to real expenses and the placement is not motivated by a desire for profit. Such adoptions are legal in all but three states. A danger in this kind of independent placement is that the dividing line between paying legitimate expenses and paying for a child may be hard to distinguish and may facilitate "black market" adoptions (Hardin & Shalleck, 1984; Sullivan, 1998).

Intermediary placements for profit put children at great risk. These children are sold for adoption on the black market—that is, children are moved for profit, often across state lines. The intermediary in these instances usually charges what the traffic will bear. Sometimes these operations are carried out in connection with abortion counseling services, by which vulnerable women or young adolescents are identified—those ambivalent about abortion or too far along in pregnancy for termination, or those who appear likely to give up the idea of abortion for an assurance of profit. In all instances of black market placement, the best interests of the child are given little or no consideration; the profit motive is primary. Such placements are illegal in all states, making it difficult to obtain accurate figures on the incidence. Reports suggest that such illegal placements are increasing because of the current shortage of white infants for adoption.

UNDERLYING PRINCIPLES OF THE AGENCY ADOPTIVE PROCESS

The social work profession relies on certain principles or generalizations in planning and extending adoption services. These are similar to guidelines for foster care but reflect greater attention to the permanency in the new parent–child relationship (National Association of Social Workers, 2002).

1. If a child has no long-term home and is legally free of parental ties (or could become so), society bears responsibility for action in his or her behalf; it is not a private matter. The formation of a new family unit, once an original one is broken, carries social responsibility and requires social and legal safeguards.

2. In most instances, such homeless children should be provided with family life. Children of all ages need affection, security, continuity in relationships, and other kinds of care and guidance that are most feasibly and effectively provided within the family setting.

3. When adoption is contemplated, society has a responsibility to give protection and service to three parties: the child, the biological parents, and the adopting parents. The child must be guarded against unnecessary loss of the biological parents and protected by the selection of new parents who give evidence that they can reasonably be expected to fulfill parental responsibilities. The child's first parents merit society's early help so they can use their strengths to establish and maintain a satisfactory home. When they cannot do so, they require protection from hurried decisions made under duress and sympathetic attention as individuals facing a critical life experience. Adoptive parents are entitled to counseling or guidance that may enhance the formation of a healthy parent–child relationship and an adequate assumption of parental duties.

4. Early placement of children who need adoption is desirable. Earlier placements generally are less complicated to carry out and offer a greater chance for success.

5. Adoptive parents are of first importance to the child. The social worker's primary task is to assess and enhance the applicants' capacities for parenthood, and enable them to assess and understand their own readiness to be parents of a particular child.

6. Despite the many basic similarities between biological parenthood and adoptive parenthood, and the fundamental needs shared by all children, adopting is different from having children by birth. All adoptive parents face the necessity of accepting the child's background and the adopted child's curiosity about her or his origins.

7. For the healthy development of their identity, children must be told that they are adopted and be helped to understand the concept of adoption. This prescription is universally endorsed by social agencies. Adult adoptees need access to information about their biological parents and siblings.

8. Children lacking their own permanent homes constitute the primary service group in an adoption program. Although understanding help is offered to birth parents and adoptive applicants, children and their need for family must be paramount in planning and extending adoption services. Social workers are increasingly committed to children who need permanent homes but who are denied them because they have certain less "marketable" characteristics.

9. Adoption services must be linked to other community social services and offered in ways that reflect cognizance of community attitudes and resources.

The Experience of Adoption

The Birth Parents

The Evan B. Donaldson Adoption Institute published a study in 2006 that showed significant changes in the profile of parents who choose adoption. While historically, birthmothers were unwed teens, today only 25 percent are teens. Most are in their early to mid-twenties, have other children, and have completed high school. Approximately 90 percent choose and meet the adoptive parents. Many seek open adoptions and include written postadoption contact agreements with the adoption, although these agreements cannot include return of the child if breached. Those who maintain contact seem less conflicted and more at peace with their decisions (Evan B. Donaldson Adoption Institute, 2006b).

Agencies offering counseling to these young women, and sometimes to the prospective fathers and other family members, follow the general social work precepts of client self-determination and nonjudgmental attitudes. The decision on whether to place a child for adoption is fateful for the birth parents, and they need an environment in which they can make a voluntary and informed choice.

Agency services to help birth parents plan for the child should be comprehensive. They should be available to everyone in the community. In agencies operating from the principles presented previously, the parents are informed of all options available to them in a nonjudgmental setting. They also receive information on all relevant community resources and are helped in accessing those resources. They receive a clear statement of their legal rights and responsibilities, and information on the legal process of relinquishment. Should they decide on adoption, the agency helps them through the relinquishment process and, very importantly, offers counseling and support to them as they cope with the grief, feelings of loss, and emotional conflicts that are inevitably aroused by permanent relinquishment of parental rights (Gritter, 1997; Evan B. Donaldson Adoption Institute, 2006b).

> *The transfer of parental rights of a child should not be accepted until the birth parents have considered all alternatives, are sure of their decision, and are emotionally prepared to transfer these rights.* (E. Jean Emery, former director of the Child Welfare League of America Adoption Program, in Emery, 1993, p. 141)

Caseworkers counseling birth parents need to communicate that the final decision is the parents' and at the same time help them face the reality of their situation and reflect on what will be in the best interests of the child. Some parents, through their young age, drug use, economic situation, lack of support from family, or other reasons, are unlikely to be able to provide a minimally sufficient standard of care for the child. The reality of an infant's incessant demands for care and the level of commitment he or she requires from competent caregivers need to be presented in concrete terms. Parents may be helped to see that in their current life situation they are unable to provide for the child the type of care that they would like him or her to receive, and that relinquishment in such circumstances is an act of responsible parenting. Parents who face possible involuntary termination of parental rights in court may be helped to relinquish voluntarily, an option that preserves their dignity and sense of control. Under Adoption and Safe Families Act (ASFA), a parent whose rights to a previous child have been involuntarily terminated is in jeopardy of losing rights to later born children as a matter of course, whereas if the parent voluntarily relinquishes rights, he or she is not exposed to this future loss.

With changing laws regarding privacy in adoption, it is important that agencies give complete and accurate information to birth parents concerning the limits to confidentiality of the adoption as well as their options regarding future exchanges of information with the child and the adoptive parents. Agencies vary widely in their policies regarding openness, with some arranging ongoing, personal contact between all parties in the adoption and others providing nonidentifying information only as necessary; most agencies fall between the two ends of the spectrum.

There is controversy on whether openness in adoption helps or hinders birth parents to resolve their grief over the loss of their child. Proponents of confidential adoption suggest that openness hinders this resolution: "The increased knowledge and contact available through open adoption may encourage birth parents to avoid experiencing the loss, to postpone or prolong the separation and grieving process. Ongoing contact may serve as a continuous reminder of the loss, or as a stimulus for the fantasy that relinquishing a child is not really a loss at all" (Byrd, 1988, p. 20).

An opposing view is taken by those believing that openness promotes the resolution of grief, pointing out that loss of a child through relinquishment is different from loss through death. In death, "one can be certain that the lost person will never be encountered in earthly form again. In adoption, a parent knows that somewhere out there the child who has been relinquished still exists" (Watson, 1988, p. 27; Evan B. Donaldson Adoption Institute, 2006b). Watson (1988) takes the position that "any attempt to make the adoption relinquishment a clean and total break denies the possibility of further contact and restricts the grief process from following its natural sequence. Openness, on the other hand, accepts the possibility of ongoing or subsequent contact and allows the relinquishing parent to face the real loss, the loss of the role of nurturing parent" (p. 27).

McRoy, Grotevant, and Ayers-Lopez (1994) interviewed 720 individuals, including 169 birth mothers, between 1987 and 1992 to ascertain their experiences with adoption. Those interviewed represented the full spectrum of adoption openness, including confidential adoptions, mediated adoptions, and adoptions with ongoing contact between birth mothers and children. The researchers found that mothers who were in adoptions in which information was shared with the adoptive parents generally felt positive about the experience. One mother stated: "Once she [the child] gets older, she won't think I just totally abandoned her, I didn't just give her up. She's gonna know I just did what I thought was best. . . . I didn't back out. . . . I'm just glad we keep in touch. It will help me I guess later, because I know she's gonna one day look me up" (p. 9). Some mothers expressed concern about ongoing contact with the child. For example, one mother with ongoing, mediated contact said: "I'm not sure how it will affect my other children. I haven't told them about Kerry. I'm not ready for them to know that I had a child as a teenager. I may have to stop seeing my birthchild when she gets old enough to ask to see my other children" (p. 9).

Whatever its policy on openness, the adoption agency has an obligation to remain available to parents whenever requested to do so, including after the adoption is finalized. A continuum of agency services may provide intermediary aids such as exchange of updated information with the adoptive family, open-ended support group meetings, individual or family problem-solving counseling, and counseling and go-between services in the event that contact of birth parent and child comes about through a "search."

The Child

Agencies have an obligation to arrange adoptions for children that are in their best interest. To this end, agencies undertake assessments of the child to ascertain his or her needs and attempt to find adoptive parents who are likely to meet those needs. They work to arrange adoptions as quickly as possible so that children are not left in the limbo of being without any family. Using strategies appropriate to the child's age, agencies also prepare children for adoption and support them through the placement process and afterward.

The adoption worker undertakes a sensitive assessment of the child's readiness for adoption. Most children will benefit from adoption with well-prepared, appropriate adoptive parents. However, older children may experience loyalty conflicts or fantasies about the future ability of the birth parent to care for them, which may hinder their ability to form new family relationships. Other children have been so severely traumatized by earlier experiences of harmful or inadequate parenting that they are not able to make an emotional attachment to a family. Information on the child's physical, social, cognitive, and emotional functioning, academic progress and school adjustment, and the kind of emotional traumas that he or she has experienced are important for assessment (McNamara, 1994; Edelstein, 1995). In making a thorough assessment of the child's readiness to use adoption, workers collect information from a variety of sources. Reports from teachers, previous foster parents, birth parents, and others who have known the child are very helpful. The child's view of these experiences must also be considered (Brown, 1989).

Life books have become a popular way to help older children make the transition to adoption. They consist of materials that help the child understand the narrative sequence of his or her life, such as photographs, school records, birth certificates, letters, and other memorabilia. Foster parents, birth parents, and workers can contribute valuable items to life books. Worksheets are available to help older children organize and make sense of their experiences of separation, loss, and attachment through a journey that may have included placements with foster families as well as birth parents and relatives (Schroen, no date).

In the case example at the beginning of this chapter, the caseworker, Ms. Franklin, helped Grant to prepare for adoption in several ways. She collected extensive information about his past, including his birth family, the circumstances of his relinquishment, and his previous, failed adoptive placement. Analysis of the information led her to an assessment that Grant needed a home with a father, because he had experienced rejection from two mothers, and that he needed adults with realistic expectations for school achievement. Then she set out to find an adoptive family who would meet these criteria.

Once Grant was placed, she helped him and the adoptive family address Grant's loyalty conflicts by introducing the possibility that, to some extent, the birth family could be included in his new life as an adopted son, and by helping him see that the adoptive family "would not replace the birth family" but could provide him with the home and nurturing he needed now. She also helped the adoptive family to see that Grant's acting out was not a rejection of them or of the adoption, but was a reaction to the earlier family breakups.

The Adoptive Family

In contrast to earlier years, the process of selecting adoptive parents has become more open, engaging the applicants themselves much more in the process.

Today, agencies actively recruit adoptive parents for special needs children rather than wait for prospective families to approach the agency. Families interested in adoption are treated from the start as potential partners with the agency in the work of caring for children. Lakin (1992) described the change in perception: "Agencies began to see adoptive parents as resources to be taught the skills necessary to meet the needs of these children, rather than to be ruled out if they did not meet certain age, income, housing, or other arbitrary criteria established to handle the supply and demand issues faced when couples approached the agency for healthy European American infants" (p. 4). When foster parents seek to adopt children in their care, they are given preference as the adoptive parent. More and more, in part because of concurrent planning and the understanding of the child's need for stability, foster home and adoptive home recruitment for children in the child welfare system are conducted as one integrated process.

Prospective adoptive parents are given much more information than in the past on the child's background. The current trend is toward full disclosure. The matching of a child to the home is no longer simply a worker decision. Rather, responsibility for the decision is shared with the adoptive parents, who will ultimately have full responsibility for the child. Drenda Lakin, former director of the National Resource Center on Special Needs Adoption, now known as the National Child Welfare Resource Center for Adoption explained:

> The worker does not abdicate responsibility. The worker has experiences, skills and knowledge to share with the family. It is the worker's job to share the child's history completely, explaining what happened, how the child may have interpreted what happened, and how earlier experiences are likely to affect the future. . . . No one can predict the future, but the worker can help the prospective adoptive parents anticipate challenges. . . . The worker can help the family develop plans to handle these anticipated challenges or identify those challenges they feel they cannot handle. (*Lakin, 1994*)

For adoptive parents, the issue of openness in adoption is related somewhat to the age of the child. Older children usually have memories of their birth families and possibly foster families as well. If the adoptive parents were also the child's foster family or are relatives, it is quite likely that they have a great deal of information about the birth parents and may know them well. The decision about how much contact there will be between the two families needs to be resolved sensitively and with the help of a skilled agency worker, in light of the individual circumstances of the case. Only a few states have laws enforcing postadoption visitation agreements. In the case example that introduced this chapter, the worker supported the adoptive mother's decision to meet with the birth mother and brother to help her adopted child resolve his loyalty conflicts over leaving the birth family for the adoptive one.

Approximately twenty-two states have laws enforcing postadoption visitation agreements if the court had found postadoption contacts to be in the child's best interests and had entered an order for postadoption contact prior to or concurrent with the adoption order (Child Welfare Information Gateway, 2005).

THE LEGAL FRAMEWORK FOR ADOPTION

The legal process of adoption is regulated by a myriad of state, federal, and international laws. For the most part, adoption law, like other laws dealing with families and children, is a state rather than a federal matter. The adoption laws in the states are not uniform and have not been applied consistently in the courts. Federal legislation exists in some areas, particularly the Indian Child Welfare Act, regarding the adoption of Native American children; federal immigration and naturalization laws affecting international adoptions; and the Adoption and Safe Families Act of 1997, providing for federal subsidies for families adopting special needs children. Other federal laws affect social security and taxes as they relate to adoptive families. A number of U.S. Supreme Court decisions have implications for adoption law. (See Chapter 1.) Depending on the legislation in a particular state, jurisdiction over adoption may be vested in juvenile courts, probate courts, or family courts within a district or circuit court system. The complexity of laws and jurisdictions has created great variation over even the most basic legal procedures such as obtaining parental consent and ensuring confidentiality. Hollinger (1993) identified the legal framework for several related areas of adoption: parental consent or termination of parental rights, serving the child's best interests in making an adoptive placement, confidentiality, and permanence of adoption.

Individual state laws and federal laws can be accessed and compared at the U.S. Department of Health and Human Services' Child Welfare Information Gateway web site listed at the end of this chapter.

Parental Consent or Termination of Parental Rights

An essential condition for adoption is the consent of the biological parents or a judicial termination of parental rights so that the child is legally free for adoption. Courts will not grant adoption petitions unless the rights of the biological parents have been terminated either by consent or through involuntary termination, based on a finding that they have failed to exercise their parental responsibilities. This requirement is based on traditions of U.S. law that give primacy to parental autonomy and privacy in rearing their children.

Parental rights are not dependent on marital status. The U.S. Supreme Court has indicated that unmarried fathers who have established a parental relationship with their child have rights that cannot be terminated without clear and convincing evidence of unfitness. (See Chapters 1 and 9.)

A number of areas of uncertainty currently exist regarding parental consent, which may call into question whether a particular child is in fact "free" for adoption. For example, do the rights of the birth mother to relinquish her child and of the child to remain with adoptive parents outweigh the rights of a birth father who has been unjustly thwarted in exercising parental duties through the actions of the birth mother or adoptive parents? Once consent has been given, should it be revocable, and if so, for what length of time? Another area of uncertainty concerns which parents have the right to consent to or block the child's adoption when the child has been created through artificial insemination or surrogate parenting.

Frequently a state statute specifies that when children to be adopted are of a certain age, perhaps 10, 12, or 14, their consent must also be given to the adoption. Children even younger than this age may have the opportunity to express their wishes. Should the children's wishes override those of the birth parent or agency (Child Welfare Information Gateway, 2006c)?

Serving the Child's Best Interests

There is agreement that the prospective adopters should be suitable parents and that the primary purpose of adoption is to provide children with permanent homes rather than to provide parents with adopted children. Traditionally, this has been accomplished by requiring that a social agency make the placement, except in adoptions by close relatives, or, if the adoption is done outside an agency, that the agency at least be involved to the extent of completing a home study of the adoptive family. Whether the adoption is arranged by an agency or independently, the completion of a home study and the judge's consideration of it are essential to adoption practice.

It is of current concern that the proportion of nonrelative adoptions arranged independently of a licensed child placing agency has increased. Where placements are made outside licensed adoption agencies, there is concern that the door is open for unscrupulous or misguided third parties to cooperate with or influence a mother to place her child for adoption. The third party may be a lawyer who stands to profit through a fee for legal adoption services even though he or she may technically stand free of the charge of procuring an adoption for profit.

Confidentiality

Adoptive parents have all the same rights to family privacy and freedom from state interference that biologically created families have. Traditionally, this principle of totally and irrevocably transferring parental rights and responsibilities from birth to adoptive parents has been reflected in the practices of sealing adoption records and issuing new birth certificates following the issuance of adoption decrees. With current recognition that children in the adoptive triad remain linked in fundamental ways to both birth and adoptive families, traditional practices in these areas are changing. Since the 1970s, most states have required that agencies share with adoptive parents all nonidentifying information that is "reasonably available" to them about the child they are adopting. The statutes in these states also provide for the release of nonidentifying information to adoptees who request it after they reach adulthood.

Regarding confidentiality of adoptive records, there is general agreement that the records should be kept separate and withheld from public inspection, and that persons and agencies having a legitimate interest in the case should be able to have access to them. However, there is little agreement on how much access they should have or under what circumstances.

A particularly controversial issue has been the release of identifying information, that is information that may lead to positive identification of the birth parents/relatives or the adopted person. Within the area of adoption of children from the child welfare system, this is increasingly becoming less of an issue, since the majority of children adopted from that system are adopted by foster parents and relatives who have had contact with the birth family and have case record information that identifies the birth family. In the area of infant adoptions, this issue remains controversial. However, since the availability of infants is decreasing and the desire of birth mothers, in particular, to choose the adoptive parents and maintain varying degrees of "openness" after the adoption is increasing, the confidentiality walls are breaking down.

Many states have implemented central adoption registries with which birth families can register their interest in being or not being contacted by a child (adult adoptee) they either voluntarily released for adoption or from whom parental rights were terminated. These registries are useful in the search process.

In addition, approximately thirty-five states allow release of identifying information to biological siblings of an adopted person (Child Welfare Information Gateway, 2006b).

POSTADOPTION SERVICES

Postadoption services have developed in recognition that "normally, adoptive families from time to time will need help with some of the complex changes in their lives. Such difficulties do not represent failure or a serious problem—only an understandable part of a special life situation" (Hartman, 1984, p. 2). Adoptive parents, particularly those of children with special needs, have found that mental health professionals did not always understand the unique needs of their family or their child. Adoption agencies, in response, have developed ongoing postadoption services that continue to support the adoption after finalization. These programs vary widely in design, but tend to be voluntary, be preventive as well as rehabilitative, make use of support groups with and without professional input, and offer specialized, intensive services if the placement is at risk of disruption (Festinger, 1996; Kramer & Houston, 1998; Kreisher, 2002; Barth, Gibbs, & Siebenaler, 2001). Although postadoption services were originally established mainly to prevent disruption of placements made from foster care, many postadoption service providers offer services to "all comers," including families who adopted infants or those with children from another country (Barth, Gibbs, & Siebenaler, 2001). To date, there have been no rigorous evaluation studies of the effects of postadoption services and the extent to which they might reduce adoption disruption, especially of children adopted from foster care. Recent research on the experiences of adoptive parents suggests that many parents find ongoing services to be helpful and would like to have them more widely available (Festinger, 1996; Freundlich & Wright, 2003).

The Child Welfare League of America conducted a study of its membership to determine the prevalence and types of postadoption services. It found that 95 percent of the agencies provided postadoption services. The most common services were support groups, crisis intervention, advocacy, adoption search, family therapy, mental health treatment, and respite care. Approximately half the agencies reported that these services were funded with state or county child welfare contracts and the other half use a combination of private donations, foundation grants, and other government funding such as public assistance, Medicaid, and state mental health funds (Mack, 2006).

CASE STUDY:
The Jenkins Siblings: An Example of Postadoption Services

The following case illustrates several of the central issues in adoption that characterize the development of adoptive families and also the postadoption services offered by the agency caseworker.

Ms. Phillips first met the three Jenkins brothers when Antoine was 4, Samuel was 3, and Kareem was 2. They had been in the child welfare system for two years, having been picked up by the police because of the mother's absence from the home. The mother was a teenager who had a history of neglect. All the boys had different fathers. The mother continued to have five more children, all of whom were removed from her care shortly after birth because of her inability to provide a minimally acceptable level of care.

While in the child welfare system, both Antoine and Samuel had had six or more separate foster placements; Kareem had been in one foster home. The foster mother who eventually took all three boys was in her early sixties, and the agency decided that she was too old to adopt them. They were placed in an adoptive home but were removed soon after when the agency discovered that the parents were using extreme physical discipline and not meeting the children's medical needs. Antoine had scoliosis. Samuel was a failure-to-thrive baby and was discovered to have a learning disability. Among them, they had a number of other developmental and medical problems as well.

Ms. Phillips found an adoptive parent for the boys—a single, middle-aged mother, Ms. Martin, who had two teenage sons at home and two older sons who had left the home. The sons were all helpful with the young adoptive brothers; they were gentle with them and took the responsibility of socializing them to the family.

Unfortunately, the placement got off to a bad start when on the first day, the boys destroyed the bedroom that the adoptive mother had prepared for them.

Ms. Phillips worked closely with the adoptive mother. She helped her plan activities and devise strategies to manage the boys' behavior and set limits for them. Ms. Martin was a grandmother but she had to learn how to be a mother of young children all over again. Samuel required a great deal of medical attention. All the children needed help in school. Samuel needed special education and Kareem needed to be admitted to an early intervention program. The adoptive mother needed coaching on how to deal with the medical and educational systems, because the problems of these children were very different from the ones she had experienced with her own children. Even with Ms. Phillips's help, she had difficulty organizing a medical schedule and maintaining collaboration with the schools.

Ms. Phillips began to wonder if this home was an appropriate setting for these children. Because the placement was still officially a foster home, she started looking for a new adoptive family. However, very few families expressed interest in three sibling boys, all of whom had special medical and educational needs. Finally, another family did come forward who seemed appropriate.

The advent of this new family seemed to mobilize Ms. Martin and helped her to clarify that she really wanted these children. Ms. Phillips had to make an agonizing choice: whether to place the children with the new family, who had a proven track record as capable adoptive parents, or whether to continue to work to strengthen the current placement and avoid another separation for the boys. To help her decide, Ms. Phillips worked with Ms. Martin to explore in detail her strengths and to understand where the gaps were. After this process, both Ms. Phillips and Ms. Martin came to the decision that she would be able to meet the needs of the children.

At about this time, Antoine had surgery for scoliosis. Ms. Martin, his adoptive mother, rose to the occasion and became aware of how much she had bonded with this boy. She organized her schedule and the family's so they could help Antoine. Ms. Phillips felt that she showed commitment to the children and decided to proceed with the adoption.

Ms. Phillips also worked to help the boys recover their past. They had been in so many foster homes that much of their history was missing. The adoptive mother developed a relationship with the foster mother who had had all three of them; the foster mother became a "grandma" for the boys. This foster mother was now caring for the younger siblings of the boys, born after they had gone into care. She had pictures to share of the boys when they were very young and knew more about the birth family than was contained in the agency's records. She arranged for the boys to visit their siblings who were in her care.

Antoine, Samuel, and Kareem are now 9, 8, and 7 and are doing well. The adoptive mother calls occasionally to let Ms. Phillips know how they are faring.

Dynamics in Adoptive Family Development

Child welfare practice was long in acknowledging that most adoptive families are different from other families in at least three ways: Adoptive parents go through a unique process, often without the kinds of supports and sanctions that accrue to biological parents; adopted children come into the family by means of a unique set of circumstances; and family dynamics are affected differently by adoption than by childbirth (Bourguignon & Watson, 1987; Silin, 1996; National Adoption Information Clearinghouse, 2006c).

These differences between adoptive and biological families are apparent when the central issues of adoption are considered. Lakin (1992) identified the following themes that characterize the adoption experience: entitlement; unmatched expectations; separation, loss, and grief; bonding and attachment; and identity formation.

Entitlement is a process that occurs before and during the time the child enters the family. It refers to the sense of the adoptive parent and child that they have a "right" to each other. Legal entitlement is granted with a court decree, but emotional entitlement is more complex and may take more time to appear. Until it develops, adoptive parents and children may hold back on their commitment to each other. In the Jenkins case, the entitlement issues are illustrated dramatically. The adoptive mother, who had been struggling with three special needs brothers, found when Antoine had surgery that she had become more attached to Antoine than she had realized. She told the social worker that she became aware that "This is my kid" when she saw him in the hospital. Recognizing that she had "claimed" the boys, she mobilized resources effectively to help him recover.

When adoptive children enter the family, both the parents and the children may be confronted with a discrepancy between the *expectations* they had and the reality of the situation. This can be especially troublesome for adoptive parents at the beginning of the placement. In the Jenkins case, the adoptive mother experienced disillusionment when the carefully prepared bedroom was trashed by the boys during their first day in the home. The process of giving up one's expectations and accepting other, alternative sources of satisfaction may take a long time. Another source of stress can occur around adapting to changed *patterns of everyday life.* Birth children may feel resentful about having to develop new family roles and modifying their family routines. Older adoptive children may resist adapting to the family's life patterns.

Feelings of *loss* are pervasive in adoption. Adopted children wonder, "Why did my parent give me up?" Infertile adoptive parents may need to grieve the loss of children they will never have. Before children and parents can make a commitment to the adoptive relationship, they must have resolved, to some extent, these earlier losses (Gritter, 1997).

Attachment refers to an emotional connectedness between two people. Infants and children who are denied the opportunity to form attachments with consistent, nurturing parental figures may not learn how to make meaningful attachments. Symptoms commonly seen in children with attachment problems are in the areas of conscience development, impulse control, self-esteem, interpersonal interactions, expression and recognition of their own and others' feelings, and a variety of developmental difficulties (Fahlberg, 1991; Lakin, 1992; Levy & Orleans, 1998). The Jenkins siblings had experienced many losses in their young lives. Learning more about their past and having contact with their siblings who were in another home helped them resolve some of their feelings about having been given up by their mother and by other families, so that they could invest emotionally in their new adoptive family.

Forming one's sense of self as a unique and valuable individual with boundaries is an essential developmental task of adolescence and beyond. *Identity* is rooted in the family history, nurtured through the natural processes of development, and shaped by individual and family dynamics (Lakin, 1992; Quinton, Rushton, Dance, & Mayes, 1998). Adopted children may feel that something is wrong with them or their birth parents would not have given them up, which lowers their self-esteem and affects their evolving sense of personal identity. An important step for some adopted children is to learn about their birth family and to incorporate that heritage into their sense of self. Incorporating the adoption into one's sense of self is a process that may go on well into young adulthood. Adolescent and young adult adoptees may benefit from support groups to process their evolving sense of personal identity (Grotevant, 1997; Brodzinsky, Smith, & Brodzinsky, 1998).

Survival Behavior or Coping Strategies

When adoptive families need help, it is essential to arrive at a good understanding of the nature of the problem, based on a thorough assessment of the situation. In addition to gathering information on the child and each adoptive parent, the social worker needs to clarify his or her own expectations about families. Families may have characteristics that are highly functional for adopting older children who have behavioral difficulties, but these same characteristics may not match the worker's unexamined expectations about "ideal" families. When working cross-culturally, social workers must be particularly aware of their own culture and how it may influence their interpretation of the family dynamics (Bourguignon & Watson, 1987; Lakin, 1992).

With older children, the problem may revolve around the child's "survival behaviors," which are rooted in earlier, traumatic experiences. For some children, the main issue is that they have "unfinished business" with their earlier family; they may experience loyalty conflicts or unresolved grief. For others, the problem may be difficulty in forming attachments to caring adults. A goal of the intervention in these situations is to increase the parents' competence and reduce anxiety by helping them understand the child's behavior in terms of the child's past experiences, and to show them strategies for how to anticipate the child's reactions to particular situations and then prepare appropriate responses. For the child, the goals are to help him or her feel secure and to establish trust with the adoptive family, and then help the child mourn past losses so that he or she can make a commitment to the present (Lakin, 1992).

It is not uncommon for postadoption services to occur during a crisis, when the family is not sure that it will actually stay together. Adoptive parents may be angry at the child, at themselves for perceived failure, and at the agency, which the family may see as not having fully disclosed information about the child. Child welfare workers may blame themselves for having made the placement. Experience has shown that successful crisis intervention with adoptive families should be quick and responsive, with clear lines of communication between family and worker, so that the family can reach help whenever it is needed. At the same time, although the help should be timely and supportive, it is important that the worker not make decisions for the family or "overreact" and move the child precipitously. The caseworker's role is to guide and support the family as it, including the child, makes decisions and takes actions to resolve its crisis.

Adoption Disruption and Dissolution

Adoption is designed to be permanent, that is, to last until the child is legally emancipated. However, sometimes this is not the case. Two terms are used to identify situations in which adoptions are not permanent: disruption and dissolution. Disruption refers to situations in which the adoption ends before it is legally finalized, whereas dissolution refers to situations in which the adoption ends after it is legally finalized. Currently, there is no accurate national data system that reports disruption and dissolution rates. The AFCARS system, previously discussed, has data elements to record this information for children in the child welfare system. However, to date, this data has not been accurately reported. Furthermore, there is no recording of adoption disruptions or dissolutions that do not result in the child being placed in the public child welfare system, specifically intercountry adoption disruptions or dissolutions. Disruption and dissolution have been correlated to the child's age, placement history, behavioral history, the adoptive parents' expectations, and the depth and breadth of information shared at placement (Festinger, 2005; Evan B. Donaldson Adoption Institute, 2004).

A number of factors affect the success of special needs adoption placements. The older the child, particularly past age 7 or 8, the more likely it is that the adoption will disrupt. Some studies show that boys are slightly more susceptible to having disrupted adoptions than girls. Developmental and serious medical disabilities do not appear to be major factors in disruption. However, emotional disabilities are strong predictors, especially aggressive, acting-out behavior. Other behaviors that place a child at risk for disruption are sexual acting out (a characteristic of children who have been sexually abused), stealing, vandalizing, threatening or attempting suicide, and wetting or soiling (Rosenthal, 1993; Logan, Morrall, & Chambers, 1998; Smith, Howard, & Monroe, 1998).

Various dimensions of adoptive family life can reduce or increase the risk of disruption. Families in which the adoptive parents expect and are prepared to accept behavioral and emotional problems resulting from the stress the child already has experienced and who can be flexible in family roles and rules have a better chance of succeeding than others. Unpredicted events in family life can severely affect the chance of disruption—for example, marital stress, financial difficulties, or serious illness of an adoptive parent or of another family member that brings long-term demands on the adoptive family. In such instances, if the new family stability has not yet been established or is tentative, the risk of disruption is keen (Rosenthal & Groza, 1992; Groza, 1996; Child Welfare Information Gateway, 2004).

Adoptions by former foster parents are less likely to disrupt than those by new families, a finding that underscores the importance of thoroughly familiarizing the prospective adoptive parent with the child's situation. Research and the reports of adoptive parents have consistently shown that providing adequate background information on the child is an extremely important task that agencies must undertake to increase the chances that an adoption will be successful.

An adoption disruption does not necessarily result in continuing impermanence for the child. Many of these children are placed later in other adoptive homes, as the example of Grant, in the case study at the beginning of this chapter, shows. Pursuing homes for children through adoption requires that agencies be ready to take risks, so some disruptions are to be expected (Festinger, 2005).

Searches and Reunions

Some of the complex identity issues that adopted children must resolve are now receiving more attention as adult adoptees in greater numbers have sought access to sealed court records or have returned to adoption agencies for information about their origins. Among adult adoptees who embark on a search of their past, some want only information—for example, the personal, social, or physical characteristics of their biological parents. They may believe such information will add to an understanding of themselves and their sense of identity. Practical considerations, such as obtaining security clearance for a job or obtaining medical history, may also cause adopted persons to seek more information about themselves.

Other adult adoptees want to locate their birth parents, meet them, and attempt to establish a relationship with them. Initially, agencies thought that only people who had unsatisfactory experiences in adoption wanted to seek out their birth parents. However, it is now recognized that many people from successful adoptions return to agencies to initiate a search. Despite confidentiality laws and regulations, most adult adoptees are successful in their efforts to seek out information on their past. Caseworkers should have information about the various regional and national networks for adoption searches. Some agencies offer intermediary services, contacting the birth mother to see if she wishes a reunion with her adult child who has initiated a search.

The following case vignette illustrates the way an agency helped a young man initiate a search for his birth family.

Ramon was 19 and in an agency-sponsored independent living situation when he telephoned the agency that had placed him for adoption when he was 3 years old. His relationship with his adoptive parents became conflictual as he grew older, and he was eventually placed in a residential setting. He now was interested in learning about his birth family and particularly about two siblings, a brother and a sister, whom he had heard were a part of his original family. He wanted to know if they had also been adopted and if he could find them. The agency representative made an appointment to see him, and, after checking the records, was able to give him information about his birth family. He actually had three younger siblings, two of whom had been adopted by one family; the youngest child had remained with the mother. Ramon was overwhelmed to meet the agency worker who had actually arranged the adoption. Through an intermediary, who contacted the other siblings and the mother, Ramon was able to reconnect with his family of origin.

Caseworkers have an important supportive role in helping adult adoptees or birth parents who are seeking reunions. Those searching may need help in preparing for the myriad of emotions they face as they undertake the search process. Persons searching often need assistance in creating realistic expectations about the type of relationship they envision once a reunion is effected. Searchers need to be aware that the person being found may have very different feelings from those of the searcher over the prospect of personal contact. A very real aspect of a successful reunion is that those involved are faced with negotiating a relationship with a stranger with whom they have a genetic tie, a bond, past issues to resolve, and current lives that are not usually congruent (Bourguignon & Watson, 1987).

ADOPTION OF CHILDREN FROM THE PUBLIC CHILD WELFARE SYSTEM

The term *special needs adoption* refers to children who require special efforts to be placed in adoptive homes. They may have physical, mental, or emotional disabilities, but their primary shared characteristic is that they are wards of the public child welfare system and need planning services to be placed in permanent homes. Special agency services are needed to recruit, train, and support families who undertake adoption of these children (Neeley-Bertram, 2000).

Children Who Wait

Of great concern to child welfare policymakers are the large number of children in foster care who will never return home and require a permanent plan that will give them a stable family life and sense of belonging that will last throughout their childhood. These children are dependent on large, public child welfare bureaucracies and their private agency partners for their day-to-day maintenance and for planning their future. Caring and planning for these children is a serious, major public responsibility of both the federal and state governments. The number of children in foster care in need of an adoptive home is quite large, estimated at 114,000 at the end of 2005. In that year, 51,300 were actually placed in adoption. The majority of these adoptions were with the children's foster parents (61 percent). Kinship adoption, or adoption by relatives, accounted for 25 percent, and 15 percent were adopted by nonrelative, new adoptive parents (Children's Bureau, 2006).

"Children who wait" share characteristics that may make adoption planning particularly challenging: They tend to be older (62 percent over age 5), to have been in foster care for a relatively long time (average forty-four months), to be of minority ethnicity (36 percent African American, 15 percent Hispanic), and are slightly more likely to be male (Children's Bureau, 2006). In addition, many of these children have behavioral problems that increase the complexity of planning for them. The drug epidemic has been a factor in bringing many into the public child welfare system, with the result that the children may have fetal damage due to the drug use of their mothers when pregnant, they may be infected with the HIV virus or have AIDS, and most have had early life experiences that have left them impaired emotionally, physically, and mentally.

Overcoming Barriers to Timely Adoption

Nationally, 85 percent of the children adopted from the child welfare system were adopted by their relative or foster parent. This percentage has been relatively constant since the mid- 1980s (Children's Bureau, 2006).

In 1997, the U.S. Congress passed and President Clinton signed into law the Adoption and Safe Families Act, designed to expedite the progress of foster children who cannot return home into adoptive placements. Two key provisions of the Act are an Adoption Incentive Program that rewards states for increasing the number of adoptions, and a provision that promotes the termination of parental rights after children have been in care for a specified period. Implementation of the Act has resulted in overcoming identified barriers to adoption. For example, many states have started to do "concurrent planning," which means that they may plan to place a child for adoption or with a legal guardian at the same time that they are making "reasonable efforts" to reunify the child with his or her parents (Children's Defense Fund, 1997). Thus, concurrent planning provides for the simultaneous planning of both reunification services and, as a contingency, the preparation of an alternative permanent plan if reunification should fail (Katz, Spoonemore, & Robinson, 1994). The concern with this innovation is that parents will feel that they are being betrayed by a process that, on the one hand, ostensibly is attempting to help them become reunified with their children while, at the same time, is moving ahead with termination of parental rights. This ethical dilemma can be avoided to some extent if the agency explains to the biological family from the beginning that the two planning processes are proceeding at the same time, while communicating the hope and expectation that family reunification is the plan of choice if possible. See Chapter 9 for a discussion and a case example of concurrent planning.

Another approach to reducing delays caused by the termination of parental rights process is "mediated adoption." Mediation procedures, involving the biological parents, the agency, attorneys for all parties, including the child, and the courts, are used instead of the traditional adversarial process to achieve termination of parental rights with abusive parents within a reasonable period. Although new, mediation programs hold promise to make the termination process both quicker and more humane to the parents, who do not undergo the public humiliation of a formal court procedure, in which all their shortcomings and failures are introduced as evidence (Heath, 1998).

The Act has had the result of speeding up adoption for many children. According to Maza's (2001) analysis, older children defined as those 9 years and older, remain the greatest challenge in the effort to move children into timely adoptions. Although the large, public child welfare bureaucracies have made progress in moving children into adoption, too many children continue to wait for a long time for a permanent home. The movement to streamline the process, while retaining respect for the orderly legal safeguards of parental rights and for carefully matching the child's needs with the strengths of a possible adoptive family, continues to require close attention.

Despite these efforts, at the end of 2005, approximately 114,000 children whose parental rights had been terminated were waiting to be adopted from the child welfare system. The mean number of months they had been in continuous foster care was 41.6, or about 3.5 years. Forty-two (42 percent) of these children had been in continuous foster care for over three years (Children's Bureau, 2006). Figure 10.1 shows the number of children placed for adoption and the number of children waiting for adoption from 1998 to 2005.

There are basically two prerequisites for adoption: parental rights must be terminated and there must be suitable adoptive parents acceptable to the child who is to be adopted. ASFA has successfully achieved the termination of parental rights prerequisite, as evidenced by the increasing number of children in the child welfare system who are waiting to be adopted after termination of parental rights.

Adoptive placement of children from the child welfare system across state lines received additional support with the passage of the Safe and Timely Interstate Placement of Foster Children Act of 2006. States are now required to consider both in-state and out-of-state options when making permanency plans and conducting permanency planning hearings. In addition, they are required to complete and return a report of the results of family home studies requested by other states within sixty days of the request (P.L. 109-239; ACYF-CB-PI-07-02).

As to the suitable adoptive parents, great challenges remain despite significant expenditures of resources to recruit adoptive parents for waiting children. Katz (2005) found that only 6 percent of prospective adoptive parents who make an initial call to an adoption agency in response to a recruitment effort actually complete the home study. The barriers include differences in the child characteristics desired by the parents and the children available for adoption, difficulty accessing the agency, and frustration with the adoption study process. The study found:

❖ callers had difficulty reaching a knowledgeable person at the agency,
❖ callers felt that the agency's emphasis was on weeding out applicants,
❖ callers felt that their emotional needs were not addressed in the initial contact,
❖ applicants were not given complete and accurate information about the process, and
❖ applicants were given negative descriptions of the children available for adoption. (Katz, 2005)

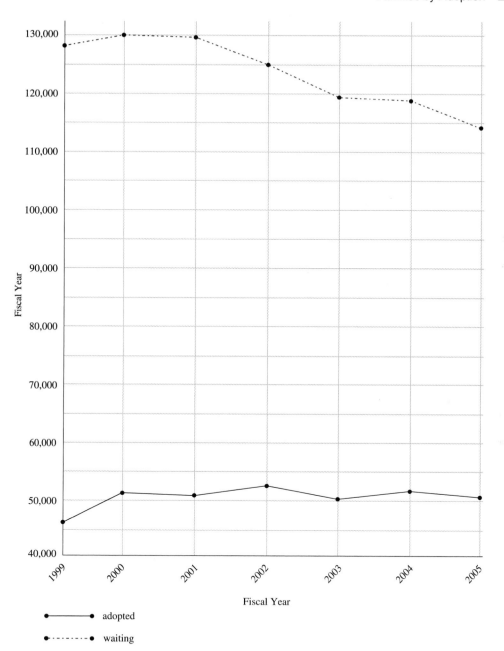

Figure 10.1 *The Child Welfare System: Children Adopted and Children Waiting to be Adopted 1999–2005*

Sources: U.S. Department of Health and Human Services, Children's Bureau. (2006). *The AFCARS Report # 13, September 2006.*
Adoptions of Children with Public Child Welfare Agency Involvement By State, FY 1995–FY 2004.
Children in the Public Foster Care System Waiting to be Adopted, Fiscal Years 1999–2004.

The answer to achieving a waiting pool of prospective adoptive parents interested in adopting the waiting children is to eliminate the barriers identified by those who took the first step toward adoption. An Urban Institute study addressed the question: What can be done to improve the recruitment process? It found that while interest among women is high (36 percent), few take action to pursue that interest (10 percent). However, interest among Hispanic and African American women has increased and the percentage of the interested taking action has not decreased. This bodes well for children in the child welfare system, the majority of whom are Hispanic or Black. This study offered the following suggestions for improving the recruitment process: shift the message from awareness to action, channel interest toward foster care adoption, use targeted recruitment to focus on groups most likely to adopt the waiting children, develop a consumer-friendly process, use available resources to develop new recruitment strategies, and test the effectiveness of strategies taken (Katz, 2005).

Adoption Subsidies

In 1980, U.S. Congress passed legislation (the Adoption Assistance and Child Welfare Act) that for the first time provided federal funds for adoption subsidies and Medicaid insurance for special needs children. The subsidies are particularly helpful in allowing many foster placements to achieve permanent legal status through adoption, because they make it possible for the foster parents to give up foster payments in return for adoption subsidy and Medicaid.

In addition to federal financial subsidies, most states provide state subsidies for those children who are not eligible for the federally financed subsidies. In child welfare adoptions, the use of subsidies is very common—89 percent of the children adopted in 2005 received a subsidy—although some subsidies are set at a very low rate and are intended mainly to establish Medicaid eligibility (Children's Bureau, 2006). States vary in setting subsidy rates, with some providing only basic support and others including special services needed by children with handicapping conditions. States also vary in the kind of documentation required to obtain subsidy.

The adoption subsidy program is growing rapidly, as more and more special needs children are placed in adoption. To date, little research has been done to demonstrate the ways that subsidies support families, but anecdotal evidence from workers and adoptive parents suggests that subsidies are vital to the adoption of children with special needs, and that the current level of subsidy is not meeting the needs of many adoptive families (Barth, Gibbs, & Siebenaler, 2001). Even though current needs are not being met with adoption subsidy, it is a very expensive program and is getting more expensive each year. The rate of entry into the program far exceeds the rate of exit, which occurs when the adopted child reaches maturity and is eligible for other disability support programs. Escalating costs raise concern about the future costs of the program (Wulczyn & Hislop, 2002; Gibbs, Dalberth, Berkman, & Weitzenkamp, 2006).

Adoption Resource Exchanges

A development in adoption practice designed to increase the likelihood of permanent homes for children who need them is that of national or regional "clearinghouses," by which agencies can cooperate more effectively in the location and use of adoption resources. Agencies that have few contacts outside their own locality tend to be limited in the range of prospective adopters and children to be adopted. For some children with very challenging needs, it is useful to have a very broad-based recruitment strategy to identify the "one in a million" family whose caregiving interests and abilities match the child's needs. See the web site AdoptUSKids, whose

URL is listed at the end of this chapter, for a view of the use of the Internet in adoption resource exchanges.

Kinship Adoption

Since 1997, states have been required to give preference to placing a child with a relative if the child required out-of-home care (42 U.S.C. 671(a) (19)). Further, one of the ASFA exceptions to filing for termination of parental rights is where the child is placed with a suitable relative and the placement is expected to be permanent (42 U.S.C. 671 (a) (18)).

Maza's (2006) analysis of the AFCARS data from 1998 to 2004 showed that relative placements increased from 15 percent to 24 percent in that period. Between 2000 and 2004, the percentage of children adopted by relatives averaged 34 percent for Hispanic children; 24 percent for African American children, and 18 percent for white children (Maza, 2006). Kinship care has become established as a sound placement choice for children in the child welfare system who cannot be reunited with their biological parents. Kinship placements promote family continuity, attachment to caregivers, and sense of belonging. The child adopted by kin has access to family history, a variety of familiar relationships, and a shared biological and cultural heritage. Questions of identity are more easily resolved within the context of family. Remaining within the extended family network reduces the effects of separation on children and minimizes the risk of "foster care drift" with multiple placements.

Questions have arisen about whether permanent placement with relatives requires legalized, formal adoption, or whether some other legal status might be more appropriate to provide an approved legal status to this family form. Children in kinship care are less likely to be adopted than children who are in nonrelative foster care settings. Although kinship caregivers usually express a commitment to and sense of permanency with the child, they may not see the need for adoption of someone with whom they already have an existing relationship (Thornton, 1991; Hegar & Scannapieco, 1994; Williams & Satterfield, 2000). See Chapter 8 for a discussion of the policy and legal issues in kinship care.

CASE STUDY

The following case example illustrates positive aspects of kinship adoption and demonstrates the importance of examining the extended kinship network for permanency options.

Jametta and Kemal, ages 3 and 5, respectively, had been placed with their grandmother when their mother had left them unattended and they were found by a Child Protective Services (CPS) worker in a filthy apartment with no food and no electricity. Their mother had been in a crack house for several days. Although substance abuse treatment services had been offered to their mother, she continued to use drugs. On several earlier occasions she had left the children alone when she was high.

Supports were offered to the grandmother to assist her in working with the children. They had a variety of needs for developmental services, including speech therapy for Kemal's elective mutism and a play group for socialization. Ms. Jones, the grandmother, also lacked day care so that she could continue employment, and needed beds and dressers for the children, which the agency helped her to obtain. With support from the kinship care worker, the children had responded well to their grandmother's nurturing and the wraparound supports put in place.

When it became evident that Keisha, the children's mother, had not responded to treatment for her addiction and was unable to stabilize her living situation, a permanency planning hearing was held. The plan was for termination of parental rights followed by adoption planning. Ms. Jones was distraught, as she felt that her health problems (arthritis and a heart condition) might preclude her from raising the children to adulthood, but she was insistent that the children should not be placed for adoption outside the family.

The kinship care worker met with Ms. Jones to set up a family group meeting to plan for the children. They contacted Ms. Jones's sister, known to the family as Auntie Grace. Auntie Grace was the family communicator, who had the names and addresses of the kinship network, and was a central figure in "holding the family together." With the help of Auntie Grace, the kinship care worker and Ms. Jones invited a number of members from the kinship network and the pastor of their church to a family meeting. At the meeting, which was held in the social hall of the church, ten extended family members met to plan for the children. The social worker explained the family situation and the need of Jametta and Kemal for a permanent home. She commended Ms. Jones for the excellent care given to the children while the agency had tried to work with their mother toward reunification. Pastor Robertson then led the entire group in a prayer, asking for a blessing on the children and their deliberations about the future plans for the children. From this meeting, two families—one, a cousin and her husband; the other, an aunt who had several adolescent children—volunteered interest in providing a long-term home for the children.

Following the family group meeting, the kinship care worker visited and studied both families as possible kinship adoption resources. The cousin and her husband were childless and eager to take the children. However, they had serious concerns about possible interference from the children's mother. The aunt, a resourceful single parent, was not concerned about dealing with the children's mother, but had reservations about being able to provide adequately for the children as she was feeling financially stretched by the needs of her own teenagers. Both homes seemed suitable to the kinship worker. She reconvened another meeting in which the grandmother, the mother, and the two prospective adoptive families discussed the next steps. They arrived at a mutually satisfactory solution. The children would be placed with the cousin and her husband after a series of family visits by the grandmother and the children. Both the grandmother and the aunt's family would be involved in supporting the adoptive placement with respite care, family outings, and setting boundaries with the children's mother. If the children and their mother wanted to see each other, visits would occur at the aunt's home with the grandmother present. They made it clear to the mother that she was not to try to visit at the adoptive home and that she would not see the children if she were high. The children's mother was pleased that the children would remain within the family and gave them a positive message about the adoptive plan.

ADOPTION OF CHILDREN OF COLOR

The development of policy for the adoption of children of color has been characterized by debate and controversy. Until the middle of the twentieth century, children of color were generally ignored in adoption policy and practice, and very few were part of the formal adoption system. Beginning in the 1950s and 1960s, with the civil rights movement, the needs of children of color for child welfare services began to be recognized. Transracial adoption became an accepted practice for the placement needs of children of color. Attitudes concerning the importance of racial and cultural identity brought this practice into disfavor, and from the 1970s until 1994, the favored approach was same-race adoption. However, controversy continued, as many believed that children were being denied permanent homes because homes of the same race could not be found, while white homes were waiting and available to these children. These children tended to remain in foster care indefinitely. The Multiethnic Placement Act (MEPA) passed by the U.S. Congress in 1994 and amended in 1997, has resolved the issue, at least temporarily, in favor of expediting permanency for children by prohibiting the delay of adoption for reasons of race of the child or adoptive parent. See Chapter 8 for a discussion of MEPA and Interethnic Placement Provisions (IEP). The tumultuous history of racial issues in adoption has varied with different ethnic and cultural groups. Examination of the events and issues of adoption of African American, Native American, and Latino children will elucidate some key themes and value conflicts in this area of child welfare practice.

African American Children

Traditionally, African American families have informally adopted children in their kin networks. The absorption of children who cannot live with their own parents into extended family systems has been a major strength of African American families (Hill, 1972; Prater, 1992). It has offered security and status as a member of a family to large numbers of children who otherwise would have been completely destitute.

No formal protections were available to children needing homes under slavery. After emancipation, very few formal adoption services were available to African American children. Until the 1970s, adoption agencies served mainly white, middle-class families. African American parents seeking to adopt tended not to use these services, due to both explicit and subtle practices of exclusion (Neal & Stumph, 1993).

Transracial adoption of children of color with white families occurred in the 1960s and 1970s, inspired primarily by the shortage of healthy white infants and by social activism emanating from the civil rights movement. The number of children adopted transracially was large; by 1972, about 10,000 African American children had been placed in white homes. More than one-third of all adopted African American children experienced transracial adoption (Klemesrud, 1972). Social workers, although not unanimous in their approval, for the most part seemed to endorse the practice as a means of providing homes for children who were otherwise likely to grow up in foster homes and institutions.

In the early 1970s, however, the climate of opinion about the appropriateness of transracial adoption began to change sharply as communities of color stressed the importance of racial and cultural identity. At its 1972 meeting, the National Association of Black Social Workers came out "in vehement opposition" to the practice of placing African American children with white families. Transracial placements were termed "a growing threat to the preservation of the black family" (Fraser, 1972). The practice of transracial placement of African American children fell off sharply and in some agencies virtually ended.

A major concern of those who opposed transracial adoption was that as children became adolescents they would face severe identity problems and that they would be vulnerable to attacks on their self-respect because they wouldn't have learned coping mechanisms to deal with racism in the larger society. A number of studies have addressed these concerns (Courtney, 1997). Some studies have tracked adopted children over time into adulthood, since they were first transracially adopted in the 1960s and 1970s (Feigelman & Silverman, 1984; Shireman, 1988; Simon, Alstein, & Melli, 1994). Other studies have used a retrospective design, collecting data during adolescence or young adulthood on children transracially adopted at a young age (McRoy & Zurcher, 1983). Rozenthal and Groze (1992) conducted a large-scale study of adopted children of color with special needs and compared those adopted inracially and transracially. The results of all these studies are quite similar. They show that, overall, there are no significant differences in outcomes of children adopted transracially from those adopted inracially. However, McRoy and Zurcher (1983) found that transracially adopted children may experience conflict over their racial identity and prefer Caucasian friends, while Rozenthal and Groze (1992) found that African American, inracial adoptive parents were somewhat more likely to report that the adoption's impact was very positive (58 percent) than were white, inracial parents (41 percent) or transracial adoptive parents (53 percent). Overall, the results of thirty years of research on this issue support both the viability of transracial adoption and the advantages of inracial adoption for African American children.

The Child Welfare League of America, in its Standards for Adoption Services, has reflected changing attitudes about transracial adoption in American society. The 1968 version of the standards stated that "racial background in itself should not determine the selection of the home for a child. It should not be assumed . . . that difficulties will necessarily arise if adoptive parents are of different racial origin" (p. 34). In 1972, the standard was amended to "it is preferable to place children in families of their own racial background." In 1988, the standards were again amended in an effort to recognize both the preference of minorities for inracial placements and the need for decisions that would not deny a child an adoptive home when one is needed. "Children in need of adoption have a right to be placed into a family that reflects their ethnicity or race. Children should not have their adoption denied or significantly delayed, however, when adoptive parents of other ethnic or racial groups are available" (p. 34). Today, with the policy instituted in the Multiethnic Placement Act, as amended by the Interethnic Placement Provisions, the adoption field is once again charged with finding homes that meet children's needs without consideration of race of the child or the potential adoptive parents unless there has been an individualized assessment that race matters for a particular child or the child has the legal right to consent to his or her adoption and chooses not to be adopted by persons of a different race (Children's Bureau, 2007).

Native American Children

Similarly to the situation with African American children, transracial adoption of Native American children occurred in the 1950s and 1960s. In the late 1950s, the Bureau of Indian Affairs and the Child Welfare League of America sponsored the Indian Adoption Project to find inracial and transracial homes for Native American children needing adoptive placement. About 400 children were placed, mainly transracially, during these years (Silverman, 1993).

By the 1970s, it was estimated that a quarter of all Native American children were not living with their families but were in boarding schools or foster or adoptive homes (Johnson, 1981). This was felt to be a great loss to Native American children of their cultural heritage and of their attachments and connections to family and tribe, and gave impetus to the passage of the Indian Child Welfare Act (ICWA) of 1978. This federal legislation was intended to restore and preserve Native American families as well as recognize the sovereignty of federally recognized tribes to establish laws governing their members.

The ICWA reaffirmed the right of tribal courts to assume jurisdiction over the placement of Native American children. Preference must be given to adoptive placements that are (1) a member of the child's extended family, (2) other members of the Native American child's tribe, or (3) other Native American families. Compliance with federal law has been enhanced over the past thirty years by the establishment of child welfare programs on many reservations. Large, urban child welfare agencies may have on staff a person whose function is to liaison with Native American jurisdictions when Native American children come into the child welfare system, and to facilitate placing the child under the jurisdiction of Native American courts, if the Native American court so chooses. The adoption of Native American children is unaffected by the Adoption and Safe Families Act, prohibiting the use of race as a factor in selecting adoptive homes. For the adoption of Native American children, the policies laid out in the ICWA continue to prevail. MEPA and IEP does not apply to the adoption of Native American children who meet the definition of "Indian Child" as laid out in the ICWA.

See Chapter 8 for a detailed discussion of ICWA.

Hispanic/Latino Children

For many years, Hispanic/Latino children who needed substitute care were "matched" not by placement with families of Latino culture but along color lines; dark-skinned Latino children with African American families and lighter-skinned children with white families. About 15 percent of children adopted each year are Latino, yet little research has been conducted to understand their needs in adoption or the extent to which they are being placed in Latino families. The evidence that is available suggests that many Latino children are adopted by white families (Gilles & Kroll, 1991; Benson, Sharma, & Roehlkepartain, 1994; Children's Bureau, 2006).

The Latino community has expressed concern about interethnic placement of Mexican American children with non–Mexican American parents. A survey of over 1,000 persons with Hispanic surnames in California revealed that around half of those surveyed agreed with one or more of the following statements: "(1) the child may have an ethnic identity conflict, (2) the child may forget his or her Latino background, (3) the child's participation in Latino cultural events may be limited, and (4) the child may not acquire the skills to cope with racism" (Bausch & Serpe, 1997, p. 136).

Elba Montalvo (1994), executive director of the Committee for Hispanic Children and Families, identified a need for more Latino adoptive homes. She pointed out that Latinos are not monolithic; the major Spanish-speaking groups in the United States are Mexican American, Puerto Rican, and Cuban. These groups differ from one another culturally in many ways. She recommends the following to increase cultural competency in placement of Latino children.

❖ Welcome Latino families into adoption agencies with posters and handouts conveying the message "Bienvenidos Latinos." Recruitment efforts should make use of radio, particularly Spanish language stations. All written materials should be conceptualized and written in Spanish first, then translated into English.
❖ Hire Spanish-speaking staff, with attention to cultural congruence with the various Spanish-speaking groups in the area.
❖ Place Latino children, in order of preference: with relatives, with someone of his or her culture (i.e., Puerto Rican children in a Puerto Rican home), with a family of another Latino background.

❖ If a non-Latino home must be used, it should be evaluated for the family's ability to help the child learn about Latino culture and have contact with other Latinos.

❖ We agree with other child advocates that it is preferable to provide a child the opportunity of a loving permanent home of any race or cultural background than to allow him or her to grow up without a permanent home and parents who care. (pp. 1–5)

Strengthening Transracial Placements

Today, policy and practice in adoption of children of color takes a two-pronged approach, working both to strengthen multiethnic placements and to develop innovative programs to reach out to communities of color regarding adoption of same-race children. The focus is on finding adoptive homes of any race for children who need them (Lakin & Malone, 2001).

In 1994, Congress reversed two decades of public policy that discouraged multiethnic placements with the passage of the Multiethnic Placement Act, which was made stronger by amendments in 1997. The current law prohibits public or private agencies receiving federal funds from delaying or denying adoption on the basis of race, color, or national origin of the child or the foster or adoptive parent.

Race, culture, and ethnicity are frequently used interchangeably. However, they are not the same. It is important to have clear definitions of these terms. The United States uses a social definition of race. In general, a person's race is determined by how they define themselves or by how others define them. Traditionally, skin color and "ancestor's blood" have been the defining characteristics for determining race.

The U.S. Office of Management and Budget (OMB) issued standards for all federal agencies and departments to use in gathering and reporting race. The accepted racial classifications are:

American Indian or Alaska Native: A person having origins in any of the original people of North or South America (including Central America) and who maintains tribal affiliation or community attachment.

Asian: A person having origins in any of the original people of the Far East, Southeast Asia, or the Indian subcontinent, including; Cambodia, China, India, Japan, Korea, Malaysia, Pakistan, Philippine Islands, Thailand, and Vietnam.

Black or African American: A person having origins in any of the black racial groups of Africa.

Caucasian: A person having origins in any of the original people of Europe, the Middle East, or North Africa.

Native Hawaiian or Other Pacific Islander: A person having origins in any of the original people of Hawaii, Guam, Samoa, or other Pacific Islands.

Multiracial: A person with parentage from more than one of the previously stated racial classifications.

Ethnicity is defined as a group with common heritage: values, rituals, traditions, racial, national, tribal, religious, linguistic, and cultural origin or background. The OMB standards identify only Hispanic or Latino as a distinctive ethnic group. A Hispanic or Latino person is someone who has origins in Mexico, Puerto Rico, Cuba, Central or South America, or a person of other Spanish cultural origin, regardless of race. The Census Bureau permits other ethnicities to be identified. The Children's Bureau collects ethnic data for Hispanics of any race and African Americans who are black. Persons who are Caucasian whose families originate in Africa are included as Caucasian (U.S. Office of Management and Budget, 1997; U.S. Census Bureau, 2000; U.S. Department of Health and Human Services, 2006).

Culture is defined as "integrated patterns of human behavior seen in the thoughts, customs, and manners of interacting, languages, practices, and beliefs of particular racial, ethnic, religious, or social or political groups" (Cross, 1988). Although some aspects of culture are dynamic, changing from generation to generation, other aspects remain relatively constant across generations.

Thus in the context of our discussion:

Transracial adoption is the adoption of a child of one race by a parent or parents of another race. For example, an Asian American child who is adopted by African American parents.

Transcultural adoption is the adoption of a child of one culture by a parent or parents of another culture. For example, adoption of a child from China by Caucasian parents from the United States is both transracial and transcultural, whereas adoption of a Caucasian child from Russia by Caucasian American parents would be transcultural but not transracial.

Transethnic adoption is the adoption of a child of one ethnicity by a parent or parents of another ethnicity. For example, adoption of a Polish American child by Mexican American parents.

Same-race adoption is the adoption of a child by a parent or parents who share the same race as the child. For example, adoption of a Native Hawaiian child by Native Hawaiian parents.

Transracial adoption is not a new phenomenon in the United States. The first recorded transracial adoption was in 1948 in Minneapolis, Minnesota. Transracial adoptions continued through the 1950s and 1960s but came to an abrupt standstill in the 1970s with the National Association of Black Social Workers' position statement opposing the placement of black children with parents of any other race, the Child Welfare League of America adopting the position that "race matching" was preferable in adoptions, and the passage of the Indian Child Welfare Act of 1978. Public child welfare adoption practice in the 1970s through the 1990s generally deferred to these positions. Transracial adoptive placements were considered as a "last resort." However, the increasing number of African American children awaiting adoption, even after significant efforts by African American agencies to effect their adoptive placement, and the advocacy of foster parent/adoptive parent organizations in the 1980s, led to the passage of the Multiethnic Placement Act in 1994 and its amendment by the Interethnic Placement Provisions of 1996 (Mallon & Hess, 2005; Lee, 2003; de Haymes & Simon, 2003; Park & Green, 2000; Patton, 2000; Crumbley, 1999; Hollingsworth, 1998; Child Welfare League of America, 1972; National Association of Black Social Workers, 1972).

Each child is a unique individual who enters into and ages in the adoption process in his or her own way. In addition, each child experiences his or her birth or adoptive family, siblings, community, and society differently. Thus, the most important advice to be given in all childrearing is to *focus on the child*. This encourages open exchange of information and individually tailored support from the perspective of the child's experience and not a generally assumed perspective or opinion. For example, it is generally assumed that all black children's hair care needs are different from that of their white adoptive parents. This is not always true. A parent of a black child needs to assess the hair care needs of the individual child, gain knowledge of the specific hair care needs, and learn the skills and methods necessary to provide proper care or have those needs attended to by someone who does.

There are many issues that could be discussed in the context of transracial adoption. The most germane are the issues of race and ethnicity. First, *culture is not the same as race or ethnicity*, although it is frequently used as a proxy for both. Culture cannot be defined by specifying race or ethnicity. People of the same race and ethnicity are not homogeneous in their cultural beliefs and practices. Furthermore, to the extent that it is learned through experience and teaching, children who are adopted from the child welfare system may or may not have a specific cultural identity rooted in their ancestral birth families. Many have been placed in foster care at birth or at a young age—thus, they never experience the ancestral culture in a memorable way. It is important for adoptive parents to recognize that while these children may not have experienced the cultural practices of their ancestral families or birth families, as they seek to develop their sense of self-identity they will be curious to know what might have been the practices. They have also experienced the culture(s) of their substitute caregivers (related or nonrelated). Thus, the caseworker and the adoptive family should gather thorough family history about the customs, manners of interacting, languages, practices, and beliefs of the child's ancestral family to share with the child as well as that of the substitute caregivers prior to the adoption. To the extent that it is safe to do so, maintaining relationships with the ancestral family and the substitute caregivers is a way of validating the child's past and supporting his or her present and future cultural development.

On the other hand, a child who is placed in foster care at school age or older has experienced a specific birth family culture. The caseworker and the adoptive parent should talk with the child, members of the ancestral family, and members of substitute caregiving families to gather pertinent information. It is important to note that all cultural values or practices do not have to be maintained or accepted. For example, an intergenerational history of child abuse and neglect is not acceptable. In moving the child away from unacceptable practices, the challenge to the caseworker and the adoptive parent is to show the child a different way of parent–child interaction, while not denigrating the child's ancestral family or foster parents. Remember, the child was part of that family and that family experience will remain part of him or her throughout life. For example, after having heard from the child that physical punishment was used in the ancestral family, it is sufficient to explain the adoptive family's disciplinary practices to the child in this way: "In our family, we do not hit children for misbehavior. We choose to explain why the behavior is not acceptable and take away privileges." The older the child is at the time of the adoption, the more he or she has experienced and perhaps integrated certain cultural practices. This needs to be acknowledged and, to the extent possible and practicable, supported by the adopted family as the child learns the new customs, practices, and norms of the adoptive family.

Ethnicity is important in that it helps the child define where he or she came from and incorporates that as part of his or her self-identity. Generally, this is defined in the geographical homes of the ancestors; for example, Mexican American, Puerto Rican American, Irish American, German American, Polish American, French American, or African American. Ethnicity needs to be identified and understood by the child and the parents because it is important in American society. People are interested in knowing family origins. The genogram is a staple of child welfare practice. In addition to basic identifying information, it should include racial and ethnic data and medical information to identify potential genetic predispositions to illnesses. A child should be told his or her ethnic heritage and be provided with opportunities to explore information about experiences of peoples of his or her ethnicity prior to coming to the United States, after immigration, and contemporaneously. Again, this exploration should be broad because not all people of the same ethnicity have experienced and are experiencing adapting to the American culture in the same way. Likewise, if the child's and parents' ethnicities are different, he or she should be provided with opportunities to explore the parents' ethnicities so that he or she feels included in the family.

Race is far more challenging to the caseworker and adoptive parent. Race does matter in the United States! Reviewing our history, it will probably matter for generations to come. Irrespective of laws passed, a child who does not have the same skin color as the persons parenting him or her will experience actions daily by others that reinforce the racial difference and the fact that he or she is adopted. Despite the best efforts of adoptive parents to create a "race neutral" environment, the nature of American society does not support that approach once the child leaves the walls of the home (Hill, 2006; McRoy, 2005). Thus, the discussion with adoptive parents of children of a different race or ethnicity should begin with: "While you may not have any concerns about the racial difference, people in your family, your community, and society in general will raise the issue at some point with your child. It is better that you understand the issues and educate your child on them before the child experiences the first incident of bias or discrimination because of his or her racial difference."

Much of the research on the effects of transracial adoption on children and adoptive families has centered on international adoptions. For the most part, the limited research on American children adopted transracially has relied on adoptive parent statements of their impressions of their adopted child's adjustment to the adoption. Most of this research has focused on black or biracial (with at least one black parent) children who are adopted by Caucasian parents. There has been no research on Caucasian children who are adopted by non-Caucasian parents. The existing body of research has found that children who are adopted by parents of different races or ethnicities adjust as well as children who are adopted by same race or ethnicity parents on measures of self-esteem, racial and ethnic identity, academic achievement, familial relationships, problem behaviors, and coping mechanisms. These studies have been and remain subjects of significant criticism because of methodological weaknesses. Methodological weaknesses identified in the research to date include small sample sizes, inadequate comparison groups, inappropriate or inadequate outcome measures, adoptive parent perception reporting as source for the child's adjustment, too few adoptees included, and interpretive inconsistencies (McRoy, 2005; Lee, 2003; Finley, 2002; Burrow and Finley, 2001; Park and Green, 2000; Hollingsworth, 1998; Johnson, Shireman, & Watson, 1987). Clearly, comprehensive, well-designed research is still needed to inform our practice.

However, looking at the existing body of research, clinical summaries, and writings in which transracially adopted children speak out about their adoption experience and its impact on their development, areas for caseworkers and adoptive parents to address prior to and during the adoption process can be identified. Children and their parents report a need to have more information and support in handling issues involving race and racism. Children are reticent to raise concerns about racial incidents in school or the community with their parents. Children feel isolated or not fully accepted in families, schools, and communities where they are the only child or one of few children of their race or ethnicity. Children are constantly confronted with the fact that they are adopted and "don't really belong."

Parents want to raise all their children in the same way. Parents often feel unaccepted by the communities to which their children are tied racially or ethnically. Parents feel that the agency should provide more information on the issues of transracial adoption before the adoption. Parents want to be connected with other parents who have adopted transracially (Trenka, Oparah, & Shin, 2006; Merz & Hightower, 2005; Weinberg, Waldman, van Dulmen, & Scarr, 2004; de Haymes & Simon, 2003; Lee, 2003: Steinberg & Hall, 2003; Patton, 2000; Eldridge, 1999; Crumbley, 1999).

Vonk (2001) suggested three areas of knowledge and competence needed by caseworkers and adoptive parents.

❖ racial awareness—sensitivity to racism and discrimination
❖ multicultural planning—developing opportunities for the child to learn about and participate in practices and customs of his or her race and birth ethnicity
❖ survival skills—preparing children to cope with racism

Caseworkers should be prepared to provide adoptive parents and children with information and resources that will assist them in developing the level of knowledge and skills necessary to ensure that the child reaches maximum cognitive, social, and emotional development and has an integrated sense of self, including ancestral and adoptive family cultures.

Prior to adopting a child of a different race, caseworkers need to ensure that parents

❖ Read a broad sampling of reference materials concerning race and ethnicity in the United States and understand the impact and implications of our racial history and current racial issues as they consider adopting a child of a different race.
❖ Read reference materials and general information of the racial and ethnic group history, culture, foods, practices, and customs of the child who is being considered for adoption. However, do not accept a generalized stereotype of any race or ethnic group, that is, all black people like grits.
❖ Read magazines and books authored by persons of different races and ethnicities.
❖ Develop personal relationships with persons of different races and ethnicities who could be mentors and friends with you and your children.
❖ Take parenting classes specific to raising a child of color in a racist world or raising a Caucasian child in a black or Hispanic family and community. Learn how to recognize racism; how to support a child of a different race in developing positive racial and ethnic identity; learn coping strategies for you, the family, and the adopted child to use in dealing with institutional racism and individual racism; and how to recognize and combat their own racism.
❖ Consider adopting sibling groups or more than one child of the same race or ethnicity so that the child is never "the only one" in the family.
❖ Talk with other families who have adopted transracially to get a better understanding of the realities of day-to-day parenting a child of a different race.
❖ Carefully examine where they live and socialize: family, friends, neighbors, schools, church, libraries, parks, and community events and ask: What factors would make a child of a different race feel included or excluded in this environment?
❖ Learn the child's spoken language if different from their own.
❖ Put themselves in the child's shoes and ask: How would I feel being adopted into this family and this community if I was of a different race?

When considering a specific child for adoption, the caseworker and parents need to:

❖ Acknowledge that race matters in the United States.
❖ Talk with the child at a level the child can understand about the racial or ethnic differences between the potential adoptive parents and give him or her several

opportunities to state how he or she truly feels about being adopted by persons of a different race.

❖ Be open and honest with the child about the potential adoptive family, the community in which they live, and the school that he or she would attend and ask how he or she would feel being a part of this community.

❖ Ask the child, depending on his or her age, what he or she would need from the adoptive parents to feel comfortable in a different race family and community.

❖ Tell the child whether the adoptive parents are willing to continue to include past relationships in the child's life after the adoption.

❖ Tell the child whether the adoptive parents are willing to exclude family members or friends from his or her life if those persons do not totally accept the child.

Living day-to-day with a child of a different race or ethnicity requires the parents to

❖ Make sure to expose the child to his or her cultural and ethnic customs on an equal basis with those of the child's race or ethnicity.

❖ Talk about race, racism, and discrimination as a normal part of daily conversation and do not wait for the child to bring up issues related to race, racism, or discrimination.

❖ Learn how to respond to incidents based on the child's race and teach the child the roots of such behaviors and how to respond to such incidents.

❖ Acknowledge and support the child's exploration of where he or she came from.

❖ Talk with the child in the language that he or she is comfortable speaking and hearing.

> *How do we help each other? For those of you who are white and whose children carry our color and the warmth of the sun in their genes, I believe we as black people can be of help . . . as you seek to give your children of color answers about their heritage, answers about the craziness of our world in relation to color.* (Sidney Duncan, director and founder, Homes for Black Children, 1988)

While the controversy over transracial adoption continues, substantial efforts have been made to increase the number of same-race adoptive families available to children that are consistent with the "diligent recruitment" provisions of MEPA/IEP discussed previously. Despite these efforts, 114,000 children were waiting to be adopted at the end of 2005. The racial and ethnic composition of these children was 40 percent white, 36 percent black, and 14 percent Hispanic (Children's Bureau, 2006).

INTERCOUNTRY ADOPTIONS

Although U.S. families have adopted children from other countries in significant numbers since World War II, recently the number of adoptions has increased dramatically, as the forces of globalization affect more and more aspects of American life.

Between 1990 and 2006, U.S. citizens adopted over 247,225 children from other countries. International adoptions have more than tripled since 1991. In 2006, 20,679 foreign-born children were adopted by U.S. citizens. Of those, almost 80 percent were adopted from China (6,493) Guatemala

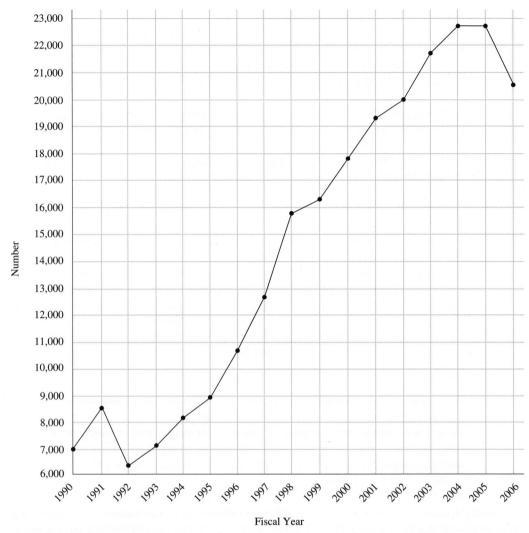

Figure 10.2 *Immigrant Visas Issued to Orphans Adopted by United States Citizens 1990–2006*

Source: U.S. Department of State (February 13, 2007). Available: http://www.travel.state.gov/family/adoption/stats_451.html.

(4,135) Russia (3,706) South Korea (1,376), and Ethiopia (732) (U.S. Department of State, 2007). Figure 10.2 shows the trends in intercountry adoptions by U.S. citizens for 1990 to 2006.

On December 21, 2006, the China Center for Adoption Affairs (CCAA) officially notified the U.S. Embassy in Beijing of new rules for intercountry adoption from China. These rules went into effect May 1, 2007. Among other things, they ban single-parent adoption. Couples must be married at least two years, unless previously divorced. If either party was previously divorced, the couple must be married for at least five years. Both must be between the ages of 35 and 45 years, with no medical or emotional problems. Neither party can be disabled, obese, or taking psychotropic medications. They must have a net worth of at least \$80,000, and have a high school diploma or vocational training equivalent to a high school diploma. At least one must be employed and earning at least \$10,000 per member of the household, including the child to be adopted. They must be between the ages of 30 and 50, unless adopting a child with birth abnormalities. In that case, they can be between 30 and 55 years. They can have no more than five children, including the child to be adopted, and the youngest child must be no less than one year. Neither may have a criminal history; they must behave honorably, have good moral character, and be law-abiding. Neither should have any history of domestic violence, sex abuse, abandonment or abuse of children, or use of illegal narcotics or any medication for mental illness that can cause addiction. There must be a ten-year sobriety period if they have a history of alcohol abuse. They must have an understanding of what adoption is and the expectations to provide a warm family for the child and to meet the child's needs for his or her proper development. They must also have an understanding of intercountry adoption and be fully prepared for the potential risks associated with adoption such as potential diseases, developmental delays, and postplacement maladjustment (The China Center of Adoption Affairs, 2006).

With these restrictions, it is expected that the number of Chinese children adopted by foreigners will decrease. There was a 1,413 child decrease from 2005 to 2006 in adoptions of Chinese children by U.S. citizens.

In addition, the Convention on Protection of Children and Co-operation in Respect of Intercountry Adoption (commonly called The Hague Convention on Intercountry Adoption) was adopted on May 29, 1993. As of February 2007, seventy-one countries have signed the Convention. This Convention ensures that the fundamental rights of children, their birth families, and their country of origin are protected. It requires the child's country of origin to certify:

- ❖ The child is adoptable.
- ❖ There is no possibility of adoption in the country of origin.
- ❖ Intercountry adoption is in the best interests of the child.
- ❖ The persons whose consent for the adoption is required have freely given that consent in writing in accordance with the laws of the country of origin.
- ❖ The consent was not induced by payment or compensation of any kind.
- ❖ The mother gave her consent after the child was born.
- ❖ The child, if of sufficient age and maturity, has been counseled.
- ❖ The child, if required, freely consents to the adoption.
- ❖ The child has not been induced by compensation or payment for his/her consent.

In addition, the receiving country must certify that

- ❖ The prospective adoptive parents have been determined eligible for adoption and suited to adopt the child.
- ❖ The prospective adoptive parents have been counseled as necessary.
- ❖ The child is or will be authorized to enter and permanently reside in the country. (The Hague Convention on Intercountry Adoption, 1993, Articles 4 and 5)

The Child Citizenship Act of 2000 and the Intercountry Adoption Act of 2000 provide additional supports to persons who wish to adopt children from abroad. The Child Citizenship Act provides U.S. citizenship to any child under the age of 18 years who lives in the legal and physical custody of a U.S. parent for whom the adoption has been finalized as of February 27, 2001.

The Intercountry Adoption Act provides for implementation of the Convention and improves the ability of the federal government to assist U.S. citizens seeking to adopt children from abroad and residents from other countries who are signers of the Convention seeking to adopt children from the United States.

The United States published requirements for adoption agencies and adoptive parents to implement the Hague Convention in February 2006, which became effective November 1, 2006. These rules are applicable to U.S. children being adopted by non-U.S. citizens as well as non-U.S. children being adopted by U.S. citizens. They require, among other things:

- ❖ accreditation and oversight of the agency processing the adoption;
- ❖ documentation of child's history and certification that the child is eligible for adoption;
- ❖ documentation of efforts to place the child within his or her own country;
- ❖ preparation and transmission of adoptive home study by U.S. authorized/foreign authorized entity prepared in accordance with the requirements of the receiving country; and
- ❖ preparation and training of adoptive parents on topics including long-term implications of multicultural adoptions; how children may react to being taken from familiar surroundings; how institutionalization affects children; attachment disorders and other emotional problems the children may have experienced; ways in which malnutrition, environmental toxins, maternal substance abuse, and other risk factors may affect children; and information about the adoption process specific to the child's country of origin. (22 CFR Part 96)

Of the children adopted by U.S. citizens in 2006, 58 percent came from countries that have joined the Convention. Guatemala and Russia, two of the countries sending many adopted children to the United States, have signed, but not ratified the Convention. The United States will not be able to approve adoptions from any country who does not comply with the Convention within three months of when the United States deposits its ratification instrument with the Hague Permanent Bureau. Both Guatemala and Russia recently began reexamining their adoption processes with the intent of meeting the Convention requirements. South Korea, the fourth largest sender of children, has not signed the Convention (U.S. Department of State, 2007).

Agency reports suggest that, to some extent, intercountry adoptions are a means for matching the "surplus" of white homes in the United States seeking to adopt with the corresponding "surplus" of orphaned, nonmarital children in other countries for whom no families are available. Other factors contributing to intercountry adoptions include the mobility of families around the world; the greater ease of communication between countries; the continuing large numbers of American servicemen stationed abroad, many of whom seek to adopt children during their residence in another country or who father children out of wedlock with no means to care for them; and a humanitarian concern by many persons for the plight of refugee and other homeless children, many of whom are grossly neglected or discriminated against in their own country because of illegitimacy or mixed racial background.

> *[During] the summer of 1997, Carole and I traveled to Bosnia-Herzegovina as part of a humanitarian relief mission. I'll never forget standing in a small Sarajevo orphanage, surrounded by a dozen babies produced by*

rapes amid bombs and the nastiness of war. I was melted with compassion for these small lives. Who would love them? If I could, I'd have scooped up all of them my arms could hold to bring them home that day. (John Towriss, CNN journalist, 2001)

The legal adoption of children from other countries requires compliance with laws in two or more countries. Islamic countries prohibit all adoption, foreign and domestic. Other countries prohibit or severely restrict international adoption. Many countries require that foreign adoptions follow the same procedures as domestic adoptions, which may necessitate that the adoptive parents come to the country to be screened. The United States has immigration rules that must be satisfied; and each state also has procedures governing adoption. The bureaucratic complexities are a significant barrier to international adoption, though adopters who work through established international adoption agencies may find that the procedures are no more complicated than those for domestic adoption. It may, however, be more expensive.

The latest data on the costs of adoption reports that the cost varies from $0 to over $40,000 per child. Adoption of children from the U.S. child welfare system is the least costly, ranging from $0 to $2,500. Private adoption costs range from $5,000 to over $40,000. Intercountry adoptions ranged fro $7,000 to over $40,000. Tax credits are available to help defray the costs of adoption as well as financial subsides for children who are adopted from the child welfare system (Child Welfare Information Gateway, 2004).

Geographical distances and national boundaries create additional hazards to an adoption service. Sociolegal aspects of intercountry adoptions require special attention to parental consent, the child's status in matters of guardianship, citizenship, birth certificate, and assurance that the adoption is legally valid in both countries. With the recent explosion of interest in intercountry adoption, numerous service providers have emerged in many countries. The number of U.S. agencies involved in intercountry adoption is fluctuating.

With the U.S. ratification of the Hague Convention, stricter standards will be instituted with respect to providers of intercountry adoption services. Each must be approved by a designated accrediting entity (22 CFR Ch 1, Section 96.12). This accreditation process is expected to have significant positive impact on the ethical practice of intercountry adoption, the information provided about the child, and the education and preparation of potential adoptive parents on issues of transcultural placement, impact of group care on children's socio-emotional development, and physical health concerns.

Despite the tremendous difficulties faced by some adoptive parents and their adopted children from abroad, research shows that, overall, children fare well in international adoption. A 1994 study compared 199 Asian adoptees with 579 white adopted children and small numbers of American children adopted transracially. The sample of families was randomly selected from the records of forty-five public and private adoption agencies in Colorado, Illinois, Minnesota, and Wisconsin. The study participants, including adopted children who were adolescents at the time the study was conducted and their adoptive parents, completed extensive and confidential survey instruments containing a wide range of psychological and family measures. The study compared the Asian adoptions with same-race adoptions in regard to identity, attachment, family, and psychological health. The findings indicate that the Asian adopted adolescents were doing as well as their white counterparts in same-race families. In the important and controversial dimension of racial identity, 79 percent of the Asian children reported that "my parents want me to be proud of my racial background," and 66 percent stated that their parents actively try to promote racial pride. The study also found that most (80 percent) of the Asian children agreed with the statement that "I get along equally well with people of my own racial background and people of other racial backgrounds" (Benson et al., 1994, pp. 97–111). Other studies have also shown mainly positive outcomes for children of international adoptions, a surprisingly optimistic result considering that many of these children had negative experiences prior to adoption that might have been expected to affect their later adjustment (Tizard, 1991).

An important issue in intercountry adoption is the relation of the adopted child, and the host family, to the child's culture and country of origin (Benson et al., 1994). In earlier years, the emphasis was on assimilating the child into the culture of the United States and downplaying cultural or ethnic differences. Today, best practice suggests the importance of building connections for the child with the original home's culture (Trenka, Oparah, & Shin, 2006). A well-developed program exists in some areas that offers summer "culture camps" to Korean adoptees, which may include group trips to South Korea. One mother, who sent her adopted daughter to Korea for a summer, explained, "Adoptive children face a lot of challenges. . . . Some of the questions that need to be answered are: who am I, where do I come from, what's my place in this world? I don't know how adoptive children can grow up to feel good about themselves without knowing their birth culture" (Zhao, 2002).

> *We really want Youjing to learn the language, . . . We want her to look Chinese and feel Chinese.* *(Paula Grande, intercountry adoptive mother, explaining why she placed her child in a school in which most of the students are children of Chinese immigrants; Zhao, 2002)*

TRENDS AND ISSUES

Gay/Lesbian Adoptive Parents

To what extent should sexual orientation of prospective adoptive parents be a factor in approving the home for adoption? This question is being asked with increasing frequency across the country in adoption agencies, courts, and state legislatures, and among gay/lesbian advocacy groups and individuals. They are arriving at very different answers. The debate concerns two somewhat separate but related types of adoption: stepparent adoption, now often referred to as "second parent adoption," in which the biological parent's partner legally adopts the child and thereby becomes legally the child's second parent; and adoption by other adults, such as occurs frequently in the adoption of children with special needs. Three states ban gay/lesbian adoption, seven permit them by law or court ruling, and elsewhere the status of such adoptions varies considerably (Goode, 2002). Social welfare agencies tend not to have formal policies on eligibility for adoptive parenthood of gay and lesbian adults, but there is usually a climate of opinion in the agency that favors or disfavors such applicants (Brooks & Goldberg, 2001; Brodzinsky, Patterson, & Vaziri, 2002). Depending on the laws of the state and the attitudes and policies of the adoption agency staff, gay and lesbian applicants may encounter a variety of responses to their request for approval as adoptive parents. They may find acceptance and help or they may have their application summarily rejected. They are quite likely to find the agency "overscrutinizing" their applications (Brooks & Goldberg, 2001). Some agencies suggest that gay/lesbian applicants hide their sexual orientation during the home study process. In some states, only one adult in the couple relationship may apply to become the adoptive parent, leaving the other partner with no legal rights to the child. In this situation, should the legal parent die or separate from the partner, the partner may have no legal means of maintaining a relationship with the child, even if he or she has filled the role of parent for a long period. Gay/lesbian adoptive applicants may find that they are considered qualified to adopt a child with multiple special needs, but would not be considered for one who would be easier to place. In short, policy and practice in regard to gay/lesbian adoptive parenthood is characterized by reliance on unexamined biases, expediency, and muddled half-measures, and has increased the risks of separation and instability in family relationships for children.

There is widespread belief that same-sex orientation and lifestyle disqualify people from receiving state sanction as parents, which occurs when the state approves an adoption. Concern may center on moral issues, but there is also genuine confusion over the effects on children of being raised in same-sex households. Those opposed to gay/lesbian adoptive parents express worries that the children may develop confused gender identities, or that they will be "recruited" into a same-sex lifestyle. There is concern that special needs children, who may already feel marginalized in society, will feel even more ostracized if their parents have a "deviant" lifestyle and will be subject to harsh taunts from their peers. Some people believe that gay/lesbian relationships are inherently unstable and may exacerbate the lack of permanency in the lives of the children they adopt.

These concerns and beliefs have not been tested by rigorous research on gay/lesbian *adoptive* families. However, an emerging body of research on gay/lesbian families has not found a difference in child adjustment or outcomes from heterosexual families (Wainwright, Russell, & Patterson, 2004; Anderson, Amlie, & Ytteroy, 2002). Recently, the American Academy of Pediatrics, citing the findings of two decades of research on this subject, issued a policy statement endorsing the adoption of children by the biological parent's partner (second parent adoption). The Academy said that such adoptions were in the best interests of the child, giving him or her the same safeguards that children have in families with opposite-sex parents. An important protection in second parent adoption is that, even if the biological parent leaves or dies, the child's ongoing relationship with the other parenting figure is ensured.

Increasingly, agencies are seeing gay/lesbian adoptive applicants as a potential resource for hard-to-place children, noting their financial security and their interest in caring for and raising children even though they may not have children of their own. Other strengths noted include strong family and friend networks, psychological stability, resourcefulness, and sensitivity to "difference," which can help them understand and cope with the challenges of parenting special needs children (Brodzinsky, Patterson, Vaziri, 2002). In their qualitative study of agency attitudes toward gay/lesbian adoption, Brooks and Goldberg (2001) suggest that agencies help these adoptive parents develop strategies for acknowledging and explaining differences to their adoptive children and for preparing the children for expressions of discrimination and scorn. They also recommend further rigorous research on the question, "How does the degree to which gay and lesbian parents are open about their sexual orientation affect the adjustment of adopted and foster children?" (p. 155). The issue becomes, then, not a question of the inherent suitability of gay/lesbian adoptive parents, but the coping strategies for dealing with discrimination and the extent to which the couple have an accepting and open environment in which to raise children.

The Evan B. Donaldson Adoption Institute is currently engaged in a research project designed to inform the debate. Thus far, it has completed reviews of the issues, existing laws, practices, policies, and research. Several court cases have been decided over the past five years that support gay/lesbian adoptions. An ABC poll conducted in 2002 found 47 percent of the respondents approved of adoption by same-sex couples, 42 percent opposed it, and 80 percent thought it should be decided on a case-by-case basis (Evan B. Donaldson Adoption Institute, 2006a).

Open Adoption: Continuing Contact after Adoption

The past three decades have seen the emergence of a controversy around the "search" phenomenon and the development of "openness" in present-day adoption practice. One result has been a recognition that the adoption experience has dimensions that were not acknowledged in closed adoption practice. The interest in various degrees of openness is in sharp contrast to the traditional viewpoint that normal well-adjusted individuals, although adopted, would not need nor want to know about their birth parents; the adoptive parents, the ones who raised them and brought them to maturity, would be sufficient. But we have learned that adoptees may at some point want access to a wider range of information that will give them a better understanding of themselves. These adoptees are not motivated by idle curiosity; they have specific questions related to their personal identity. Most searches stem from a lack of needed information (Gritter, 1997).

There is considerable acknowledgment that for birth parents and adoptive parents who freely and fully agree to ongoing contact, open adoption has the potential to bring about genuinely satisfying relationships for all concerned (Baran & Pannor, 1993). At the same time, questions have been raised as to the problems open adoption can bring and the need for various degrees of openness, and for some birth parents and adoptive parents, availability of some degree of closed adoption. Fears about too-rapid policy changes include these: Some families have more than one adopted child; what will it mean in family relationships if one has continuing contact with the birth mother and another does not? What of the risk of birth parents dropping out of the child's life after contacts have been in place? Young birth parents, however conscientiously they try to make the right decisions affecting their child at the time of adoptive planning, cannot foresee or judge future demands on their yet undeveloped capacities and the opportunities or disappointments that may follow. How will the task of helping children to understand the concept of adoption be further complicated by an active role of the birth mother in the child's life? Clearly the problem of role ambiguity is a serious and unresolved one in open adoption (McRoy, Grotevart, & White, 1988).

Some professionals have observed that in discussions of open adoption, few benefits to the adopting parents are mentioned. There are concerns that because of a deeply felt need for a child, and the stated or unstated requirement in open adoption to satisfy the needs of the birth parents, the adoptive applicants may agree too quickly to proposed arrangements that may be to the detriment of their own needs and right to privacy.

There are repeated suggestions in the literature that adopting parents and birth parents should be allowed to choose participation in either open or closed adoption. The degree of acceptable and workable openness in any adoption plan is a highly individual matter, reason enough for caution about making drastic policy changes before research has been done.

As the adoption landscape has shifted from infant adoptions to the adoption of children from the child welfare systems of the United States and other countries, the issues surrounding open adoptions have shifted somewhat from the birthparents' interests to the children's interests in knowing and maintaining contact with siblings and other relatives and with ancestral cultures.

A growing openness discussion centers on "donor dads" and the children they "father." Donor dads are those who donate to sperm banks with the expectation that their identities will not be revealed. However, recently, these men and the children they fathered are beginning to question the strict confidentiality of the arrangements. These children, like adopted children, want to know where they come from. There is also concern that siblings through sperm donations may unknowingly become romantic partners; so there is a push to provide some nonidentifying information, such as nonlinked donor numbers, to their mothers so that they may inform the children.

Adoption of Older Children and Adolescents

Children in the child welfare system who are older than 9 years are categorized as "older." Of the 114,000 children waiting for adoption at the end of 2005, 47 percent were 9 years or older. Effecting adoptive placements for these children becomes more difficult as the child ages if he or she is not adopted by his or her current relative or nonrelative foster parent. Several initiatives have been undertaken by the Children's Bureau through the AdoptUSKids to recruit adoptive homes and provide supports and encouragement to current caregivers to adopt these children.

Paternal Relative Adoptions: Sibling Splits

Public policy has focused on engaging fathers and their families as placement options for children entering or exiting the child welfare system. Many children in the child welfare systems have siblings who may have the same mother but different fathers or the same fathers but different mothers. This creates a challenge for the child welfare system in seeking out relatives and making placements in the child's best interests. Many times, it is important for the siblings to be placed together, especially when adopted; but relatives of a child's sibling who are not his or her relatives may not be willing to adopt or foster that child. What does the system do? As the next round of Child and Family Services Reviews are completed, we should have a clearer understanding of the extent to which this problem is arising, the resolutions, and their impact on all the siblings.

Chapter Summary

Adoption is a social and legal process whereby the parent–child relationship is established between persons not so related at birth. By this means, a child born to one set of parents becomes, legally and socially, the child of other parents and a member of another family, and assumes the same rights and duties as those between children and their biological parents.

Adoption of children is an ancient practice, whose original purpose was to provide an heir for a family. In the United States, adoption became common in the twentieth century, to resolve the problem of out-of-wedlock pregnancies and to meet the demands of infertile couples for a child. More recently, the adoption of infants has declined, as abortion and contraception options have become available, and single parenthood has become more economically feasible and socially acceptable. At the same time, the adoption of children formerly considered unadoptable, including older children and those with special needs, has become more common. Today, adoption practice has split into two arenas, with private agencies and third parties such as lawyers handling most of the adoptions of healthy infants and children from other countries, and public agencies maintaining responsibility for the placement of special needs children who have become free for adoption after entering the child welfare system.

Adoption practice today faces many changes. During the past 40 years, the secrecy that surrounded both the legal and social aspects of adoption has been challenged by an increasing number of public child welfare system adoptions and adult adoptees, who demand as a birthright information about their biological origins. Searching for biological family members separated by adoption has become common. Many agencies are now practicing various levels of openness in adoption, in which some measure of contact is maintained between the biological family and the adoptive family.

Protecting the right of unmarried fathers to be involved in adoption planning has required adjustments in adoption practice. As a result of U.S. Supreme Court decisions in the 1970s, the rights of unmarried fathers to their children cannot be disregarded in adoption planning. A problem arises when a father is not informed of his paternity until after the child has been adopted and then challenges the adoption. States have developed legislation to try to protect the rights of fathers while also ensuring the stability of the adoption.

Permanency planning, the policy of moving children out of long-term foster care and into permanent homes, has increased the number of older and special needs children who require adoption planning. This movement has challenged the child welfare system in several ways. Many children have waited for a long time in the child welfare system before being placed in a permanent, adoptive home, because of numerous delays in the system. Recently, new legislation, the Adoption and Safe Families Act, amendments to the Multiethnic Placement Act, and the Interstate Placement of Foster Children Act have reduced barriers to the timely adoption of children in the child welfare system. Increased recruitment efforts for adoptive parents in communities of color and more attention to kinship adoption have provided additional adoption resources.

In response to the challenges presented by the troubled histories of many children adopted after years in the child welfare system, postadoption services to children and families have expanded and developed a specialized knowledge base. Understanding children's survival behavior and accepting that children may have ambivalent feelings about permanently separating from their biological family and becoming attached to a new family, have helped social workers and adoptive parents better meet the needs of adopted children. Inevitably, some of the placements of older, emotionally troubled children break down, requiring agencies to develop sensitive practices to help the child recover from the disruption and move on to another placement.

Kinship adoption and intercountry adoption have been parts of the adoption arena for many years, but are taking on increased functions and visibility.

FOR STUDY AND DISCUSSION
STUDY AND DISCUSSION QUESTIONS

1. Watch a movie with an adoption theme, such as *Secrets and Lies* or *Raising Isaiah*. Identify ways in which the movie illustrates and expands concepts in this chapter, such as transracial adoption, open adoption, postadoption services, and psychosocial adjustment to adoption.

2. Review the section on postadoption services and then answer the questions: Are there issues in adoptive family development so specific that they must be dealt with only by specialists in adoption? Or can they be adequately addressed by generalist family and individual therapists?

3. Prepare a presentation on some aspect of intercountry adoption. Possible topics include laws and administrative rules governing intercountry adoption; the experiences of children and their adoptive families in the finding, matching, and meeting of one another; and innovative programs to connect children adopted from other countries with their country of origin. Based on your research, make recommendations on ways that intercountry adoption could be improved to better meet the needs of children.

4. What position do you take on the issue of transracial placement as an alternative adoption practice? State your reasoning on the question and compare it with that of others.

5. Consider and debate with others what you see as the benefits and the risks to open adoptions. On the assumption that some degree of "openness" in adoption practice is here to stay, state and describe a flexible policy that could best serve the needs and preferences of the three parties to the adoption triad.

6. Discover whether innovative programs exist in your area to recruit adoptive parents for special needs children. How are they working? Do they offer ongoing support to the family after the adoption?

7. Interview a family involved in kinship adoption. What kinds of supports and resources do they need from the child welfare agency? Do they have needs different from those of nonrelative adopters?

8. Read the novels *The Bean Tree* and *Pigs in Heaven* by Barbara Kingsolver, and analyze them in terms of the Indian Child Welfare Act. In what ways does the ICWA affect the adopted child, the biological mother, the adoptive mother, and the tribal nation involved?

Internet Sites

Adopt U.S. Kids. A national database of children awaiting adoption and families approved to adopt. It is an initiative of the U.S. Children's Bureau and is operated by the Adoption Exchange Association.
www.AdoptUSKids.org

Child Welfare Information Gateway. Established by the U.S. Children's Bureau, this web site provides access, information, and resources on all areas of child welare.
www.childwelfare.org

Evan B. Donaldson Adoption Institute. This organization provides up-to-date information on research, policy, and practice in adoption.
www.adoptioninstitute.org

National Center for Adoption Law and Policy. The Center, located at Capital University Law School, has the goal of providing a single online resource for child welfare and adoption law information.
www.adoptionlawsite.org

National Data Analysis System. This system integrates national child welfare data from many sources.
http://ndas.cwla.org

National Resource Center for Child Welfare Adoption. The Center was established by the U.S. Children's Bureau to assist states, tribes, and other federally funded entities in adoption programs.
www.nrcadoption.org

North American Council on Adoptable Children. The Council was founded in 1974 by adoptive parents. It is committed to meeting the needs of waiting children and the families who adopt them. www.nacac.org

U.S. Department of State. This web site provides information on adoption laws and practices in all countries. The U.S. Department of State administers the Hague Convention on Intercountry Adoptions. www.state/gov/family/adoption or www.travel.state.gov/family/adoption/intercountry

References

Abbott, G. (1938). *The child and the state, vol. 1.* Chicago: University of Chicago Press.

Alexander, C., & Curtis, C. M. (1996). A review of empirical research involving the transracial adoption of African American children. *Journal of Black Psychology, 22,* 223–235.

Andersson, N., Amlie, C., & Ytteroy, E. A, (2002). Outcomes for children of lesbian or gay parents: A review of studies from 1978 to 2000. *Scandinavian Journal of Psychology, 43,* 335–351.

Baden, A. (2001, August) Psychological adjustment of transracial adoptees: Applying the cultural-racial identity model. Proceedings of 109th Annual Convention of American Psychological Association, San Francisco, CA.

Baran, A., & Pannor, R. (1993). Perspectives on open adoption. *The Future of Children, 3*(1), 119–124 (a publication of the Center for the Future of Children, the David and Lucile Packard Foundation).

Barth, R. P., Gibbs, D. A., & Siebenaler, K. (2001). *Assessing the field of postadoption services: Family needs, program models, and evaluation issues.* U.S. Department of Health and Human Services. Available: http://aspe.hhs.gov/hsp/PASS/lit-rev-01.htm [2002, April 12].

Barth, R. P., & Miller, J. M. (2000). Building effective post-adoption services: What is the empirical foundation? *Family Relations, 49*(4), 447–455.

Bartholet, E. (1999). *Nobody's children: abuse and neglect, foster drift, and the adoption alternative.* Boston: Beacon Press.

Bausch, R. S., & Serpe, R. T. (1997). Negative outcomes of interethnic adoption of Mexican American children. *Social Work, 42*(2), 136–143.

Benson, P. L., Sharma, A. R., & Roehlkepartain, E. C. (1994). *Growing up adopted: A portrait of adolescents and their families.* Minneapolis, MN: Search Institute.

Billinsgley, A., & Giovannoni, J. M. (1972). *Children of the storm: Black children and American child welfare.* New York: Harcourt Brace Jovanovich.

Bourguignon, J. P., & Watson, K. W. (1987). *After adoption: A manual for professionals working with adoptive families.* Post-Placement Post-Legal Adoption Services Project for Special Needs Children and Their Families: Federal Grant #90-CKO-02871. Chicago: Illinois Department of Children and Family Services.

Bradley, C., & Hawkins-Leon, C. G. (2002). The transracial adoption debate: Counseling and legal implications. *Journal of Counseling and Development, 80* (4), 433–441.

Brodzinsky, D. M., Patterson, C. J., & Vaziri, M. (2002). Adoption agency perspectives on lesbian and gay prospective parents: A national study. *Adoption Quarterly, 5*(3), 5–23.

Brodzinsky, D. M., Smith, D. W., & Brodzinsky, A. B. (1998). *Children's adjustment to adoption. Developmental and clinical issues.* Thousand Oaks, CA: Sage Publications.

Brooks, D., & Barth, R. P. (1999). Adult transracial and inracial adoptees: Effects of race, gender, adoptive family structure, and placement history on adjustment outcomes. *American Journal of Orthopsychiatry, 69*(2), 87–99.

Brooks, D., & Goldberg, S. (2001). Gay and lesbian adoptive and foster care placements: Can they meet the needs of waiting children? *Social Work, 46*(2), 147–157.

Brown, S. L. (1989). *Profile: Permanency planning assessment for children with developmental disabilities and special health needs.* Southfield, MI: Spaulding for Children.

Burrow, A. L., & Finley, G. E. (2001). Issues in transracial adoption and foster care. *Adoption Quarterly*, 5, 1–4.

Burrow, A. L., & Finley, G. E. (2004). Transracial, same-race adoptions, and the need for multiple measures of adolescent adjustment. *American Journal of Orthopsychiatry*, 74(4), 577–583.

Byrd, A. D. (1988). The case for confidential adoption. *Public Welfare, 46*(4), 20–23.

Carp, E. W. (1995). Adoption and disclosure of family information: A historical perspective. *Child Welfare, 74*(1), 217–239.

Carp, E. W. (1998). *Family matters: Secrecy and disclosure in the history of adoption.* Cambridge, MA: Harvard University Press.

Casey Family Services. (2003). Strengthening families and communities: Creative strategies for financing post-adoption services. Available: http://www.caseyfamilyservices.org/pdf/casey _pafinance.pdf.

Child Welfare Information Gateway. (1994). *Transracial and transcultural adoption.* Washington, DC: U.S. Department of Health and Human Services.

Child Welfare Information Gateway. (2004, June). *Costs of adopting.* Washington, DC: U.S. Department of Health and Human Services

Child Welfare Information Gateway. (2005, December). *Postadoption contact agreements between birth and adoptive families.* Washington, DC: U.S. Department of Health and Human Services.

Child Welfare Information Gateway. (2006a, February). *Adoption disruption and dissolution: numbers and trends.* Washington, DC: U.S. Department of Health and Human Services.

Child Welfare Information Gateway. (2006b, January). *Access to adoption records.* Washington, DC: U.S. Department of Health and Human Services.

Child Welfare Information Gateway. (2006c, February). *Who may adopt, be adopted, or place a child for adoption?* Washington, DC: U.S. Department of Health and Human Services.

Child Welfare League of America. (1968, 1972, 1988). *Standards for adoption services.* New York: Child Welfare League of America Press.

Child Welfare League of America. (1994). *Kinship care: A natural bridge.* Washington, DC: Child Welfare League of America Press.

Children's Bureau. (2006). The AFCARS Report: Preliminary FY 2005 estimates as of September 2006 (B). Available: www.acf.hhs .gov/programs/cb/stats_research/afears/tar/re-port13. htm [2007, January 2]

Children's Bureau. (2007). Child Welfare Policy Manual, Section. MEPA/IEP. Available at www.acf.hhs.gov/;zee/programs/cb/Aws_poli cies/laws/cwpm.

Children's Defense Fund. (1997, November). Summary of the Adoption and Safe Families Act of 1997. Available: www.childrensdefense. org/safestart.

Cooper, L., & Cates, P. (2006*). Too high a price: The case against restricting gay parenting.* New York: American Civil Liberties Foundation.

Courtney, M. E. (1997). The politics and realities of transracial adoption. *Child Welfare, 76*(6), 749–779.

Cross, T. L. (1988). Services to minority populations: Cultural competence continuum. *Focal Point, 3*(1), 1–4.

Crumbley, J. (1999). *Transracial adoption and foster care: Practice issues for professionals.* Washington, DC: CWLA Press.

Curtis, C. M., & Alexander, R. (1996). The Multiethnic Placement Act: Implications for social work practice. *Child and Adolescent Social Work Journal, 13*(5), 401–410.

de Haymes, M. V., & Simon, S. (2003). Transracial adoption: Families identify issues and needed support services. *Child Welfare, 82*(2), 251–272.

Dukette, R. (1984). Value issues in present-day adoption. *Child Welfare, 63*(3), 233–244.

Edelstein, S. B. (1995). *Children with prenatal alcohol and/or other drug exposure: Weighing the risks of adoption.* Washington, DC: Child Welfare League of America Press.

Eldridge, S. (1999). *Twenty things adopted kids wish their adoptive parents knew.* New York: Dell Publishing.

Emery, L. J. (1993). The case for agency adoption. *The Future of Children, 3*(1), 139–145.

Etter, J. A. (1997). *A cooperative adoption workbook.* Washington, DC: Child Welfare League of America.

Evan B. Donaldson Adoption Institute. (2002, June). *National adoption attitudes survey: Research report.* Dave Thomas Foundation for Adoption and the Evan B. Donaldson Adoption Institute. Available: www.adoptioninstitute.org/survey/

Evan B. Donaldson Adoption Institute. (2004). *What's working for children: A policy study of adoption stability and termination.* Available: http://www. adoptioninstitute.org/publications/Disruption_Report.pdf.

Evan B. Donaldson Adoption Institute. (2006a, March). *Expanding resources for children: Is adoption by gays and lesbians part of the answer for boys and girls who need homes?* Available: http://www.adoptioninstitute.org/publications.

Evan B. Donaldson Adoption Institute. (2006b, November). *Safeguarding the rights and wellbeing of birth parents.* Available: http://www.adoptioninstitute.org/publications.

Evan B. Donaldson Adoption Institute. (no date). International adoption facts. Available: www.adoptioninstitute.org/FactOverview/international-print.

Fahlberg, V. (1991). *A child's journey through placement.* Indianapolis: Perspectives Press.

Feigelman, W., & Silverman, A. R. (1984). The long-term effects of transracial adoption. *Social Service Review, 58,* 588–602.

Festinger, T. (1996). *After adoption: A study of placement stability and parents' service needs.* New York: New York University, Ehrenkranz School of Social Work.

Festinger, T. (2005). *Adoption disruption: Rates, correlates and service needs.* In G.P. Mallon & P. Hess (Eds.), *Child welfare for the 21st century: A handbook of Practices, policies, and programs.* (pp. 452–468). New York: Columbia University Press.

Finley, G. E. (2002). The best interest of the child and the eye of the beholder. [Review of the book, *Abandoned children*]. *Contemporary Psychology, 47,* 629–631.

Fraser, C. G. (1972, April 10). Blacks condemn mixed adoptions. *New York Times.*

Freundlich, M. (2000). *The role of race, culture, and national origin in adoption.* Washington, DC: The Child Welfare League of America.

Freundlich, M., & Wright, L. (2003). *Post-permanency services.* Washington, DC: Casey Family Programs.

Gibbs, D. A., Dalberth, B. T., Berkman, N. D., & Weitzenkamp, D. (2006). Determinants of adoption subsidies. *Adoption Quarterly, 9*(2/3), 63–80.

Gilles, T., & Kroll, J. (1991). *Barriers to same race placement.* St. Paul, MN: North American Council on Adoptable Children.

Goode, E. (2002, February 4). Group backs gays who seek to adopt a partner's child. *New York Times,* p. A1, 21.

Gray, D. D. (2002). *Attaching in adoption: Practical tools for today's parents.* Indianapolis, IN: Perspectives Press.

Green, R. K., Malm, C., & Katz, J. (2004). A study to inform the recruitment and retention of general applicant adoptive parents. *Adoption Quarterly, 7*(4), 1–27.

Gritter, J. L. (1997). *The spirit of open adoption.* Washington, DC: Child Welfare League of America Press.

Grotevant, H. D. (1997). Coming to terms with adoption: The construction of identity from adolescence into adulthood. *Adoption Quarterly, 1*(1), 3–28.

Grotevant, H. D. (2000). Openness in adoption: Research with the adoption kinship network. *Adoption Quarterly, 4*(1) 445–465.

Grotevant, H. D., & McRoy, R. G. (1998). *Openness in adoption: Exploring family connections.* Thousand Oaks, CA: Sage.

Groza, V. (1996). *Successful adoptive families.* Westport, CT: Praeger.

Groza, V., Houlihan, L., & Wood, Z. B. (2005). Overview of adoption. In G.P. Mallon & P. Hess (Eds.), *Child welfare for the 21st century: A handbook of practices, policies and programs.* New York: Columbia University Press.

Hague Convention on Intercountry Adoption. (1993). Articles 4 and 5. Available: www.travel.state.gov/family/adoption/haguecon-vention.

Hansen, M. E., & Simon. (2004). Transracial placement in adoptions with public agency involvement: What can we learn from the AFCARS data? *Adoption Quarterly, 8*(2), 45–56.

Hardin, M. A., & Shalleck, A. (1984). Children living apart from their parents. In R. M. Horowitz & H. A. Davidson (Eds.), *Legal rights of children* (pp. 353–421). Colorado Springs: McGraw-Hill.

Harris, H. L. (1997). *Racial identity issues in transracial adoptees.* Unpublished presentation at First Annual Conference on Culture-Centered Human Services, University of Alabama at Birmingham, School of Education, Birmingham, Alabama.

Hartman, A. (1979). *Finding families: An ecological approach to family assessment in adoption.* Beverly Hills, CA: Sage.

Hartman, A. (1984). *Working with adoptive families beyond placement.* New York: Child Welfare League of America.

Heath, T. (1998, August). Qualitative analysis of private mediation: Benefits for families in public child welfare agencies. *Children and Youth Services Review, 20*(7), 605–627.

Hegar, R., & Scannapieco, M. (1994). From family duty to family policy: The evolution of kinship care. *Child Welfare, 74*(1), 200–216.

Hegar, R. L., & Scannapieco, M. (2005). Kinship care. In G.P. Mallon & P. M. Hess (Eds.), *Child welfare for the 21st century: A handbook of practices, policies and programs.* New York: Columbia University Press.

Hill, R. (1972). *The strengths of black families.* New York: Emerson Hall.

Hill, R. (2006). Synthesis of the research on disproportionality in child welfare: An update. Seattle, WA: Casey-CSSP alliance for Racial Equity in the Child Welfare System.

Hollinger, J. H. (1991). *Adoption law and practice.* New York: Matthew Bender.

Hollinger, J. H. (1993). Adoption law. *The Future of Children, 3*(1), 43–61.

Hollinger, J. H., & the ABA Center on Children and the Law National Resource Center. (1998). *A guide to the Multiethnic Placement Act of 1994 as amended by the Interethnic Provisions of 1996.* Washington, DC: American Bar Association.

Hollingsworth, L. D. (1998). Promoting same-race adoption for children of color. *Social Work, 43*(2), 104–116.

Howard, J. A., Smith, S. L., & Oppenheim, E. (2002). *Sustaining adoptive families: A qualitative study of public post-adoption services.* Washington, DC: American Public Humane Services Association.

Indian Child Welfare Act of 1978, P.L. 95-608, 25 U.S.C. Section 1901.

Johnson, B. (1981). The Indian Child Welfare Act of 1978: Implications for practice. *Chlid Welfare, 60*(7), 435–446.

Johnson, P. R., Shireman, J. F., Watson, K. W. (1987). Transracial adoption and the development of Black identity at age eight. *Child Welfare, 66,* 45–55.

Jones, C. (1993, October 24). Role of race in adoptions: Old debate is being reborn. *New York Times,* p. 1.

Katz, J. (2005). *Listening to parents: Overcoming barriers to the adoption of children from foster care.* New York: Evan B. Donaldson Adoption Institute.

Katz, L., Spoonemore, N., & Robinson, C. (1994). *Concurrent planning: From permanency planning to permanency action.* Seattle: Lutheran Social Services of Washington and Idaho.

Klemesrud, J. (1972, April 12). Furor over whites adopting blacks. *New York Times.*

Kramer, L., & Houston, D. (1998). Supporting families as they adopt children with special needs. *Family Relations, 47,* 423–432.

Kreisher, K. (2002, November–December). Supporting loving families: After the adoption. *Children's Voice.* Available: www.cwla.org/articles/cv0211supporting.htm [2003, January 8].

Krieder, R. M. (2003). *Adopted children and stepchildren, 2000: Census 2000 Special Reports.* Washington, DC: U.S. Census Bureau.

Lakin, D. (1992). *Empowering adoptive families: Issues in post adoption services.* Southfield, MI: National Resource Center for Special Needs Adoption; and Baltimore: Baltimore City Department of Social Services.

Lakin, D. (1994). Personal communication. Southfield, Michigan.

Lakin, D., & Malone, S. (2001). Recruiting resource families. *The Roundtable: Journal of the National Resource Center for Special Needs Adoption, 15*(2), 1–3.

Lee, R. M. (2003). The transracial adoption paradox: History, research, and counseling implications of cultural socialization. *The Counseling Psychologist, 31*(6), 711–744.

Leung, P., Erich, S., & Kanenberg, H. (2005). A comparison of family functioning in gay/lesbian, heterosexual and special needs adoptions. *Children and Youth Services Review, 27*, 1031–1044.

Levy, T., & Orleans, M. (1998). *Attachment, trauma, and healing: Understanding and treating attachment disorders in children and families.* Washington, DC: Child Welfare League of America.

Logan, F. A., Morrall, P. M. E., & Chambers, H. (1998, May–June). Identification of risk factors for psychological disturbance in adopted children. *Child Abuse Review, 7*(3), 154–164.

Mack, K. (2006). *Survey examines postadoption services among private agencies.* Available: http://cwla.org.

Mallon, G. P., & Hess, P. M. (2005). *Child welfare for the 21st century: A handbook of practices, policies, and programs.* New York, NY: Columbia University Press.

Maza, P. (2001). The age factor in adoption. *The Roundtable: Journal of the National Resource Center for Special Needs Adoption, 16*(1), 1–3.

Maza, P. (2002). Inter-state placement: Impact on time to permanency for children in the public foster care system. *Permanency Planning Today, 2*, 10–11.

Maza, P. (2005, October). *Adoption Data Update.* Presented at the National Association of State Adoption Programs meeting, Washington, DC.

Maza, P. (2006). Patterns of relative adoption. *The Roundtable, 20*(1), 1–3.

McFarland, M. C. (2003). *Finding permanent homes for foster children: Issues raised in kinship care.* Washington, DC: The Urban Institute.

McNamara, J. (Ed.). (1994). *Sexually reactive children in adoption and foster care.* Greensboro, NC: Family Resources.

McRoy, R. G. (2005). Overrepresentation of children and youth of color in foster care. In G. P. Mallon & P. M. Hess (Eds.), *Child welfare for the 21st century: A handbook of practices,*

policies, and programs. (pp. 623–634). New York: Columbia University Press.

McRoy, R. G., Grotevant, H. D., & Ayers-Lopez, S. (1994). *Changing practices in adoption.* Austin, TX: The Hogg Foundation for Mental Health, University of Texas.

McRoy, R. G., Grotevant, H. D., & White, K. L. (1988). *Openness in adoption: New practices, new issues.* New York: Praeger.

McRoy, R. G., & Zurcher, L. A. (1983). *Transracial and inracial adoptees. The adolescent years.* Springfield, IL: Charles C. Thomas.

Merz, H., & Hightower, M. (2005). *Knowing who you are: Helping youth in care develop their racial and ethnic identity.* Baltimore, MA: Casey Family Programs.

Michaels, R. (1947). Casework considerations in rejecting the adoption application. *Journal of Social Casework, 28*(10), 370–375.

Montalvo, E. (1994). Against all odds: The challenges faced by Latino families and children in the United States. *The Roundtable: Journal of the National Resource Center for Special Needs Adoption, 8*(2), 1–5.

Multiethnic Placement Act of 1994, P.L. 103-382, as amended by the Interethnic Placement Provisions of 1996 in the Small Business Job Protection Act of 1996, P.L. 104-188, 42 USC 622 et seq.

Nasdijj. (2001, September 16). Migrant father. *New York Times Magazine,* p. 80.

National Association of Black Social Workers. (1972). Resolution opposing the practice of placing African-American children in need of adoptive homes with Caucasian parents. Washington, DC: Author.

Neal, L., & Stumph, A. (1993). *Transracial adoptive parenting: A black/white community issue.* Bronx, NY: Haskett-Neal Publications.

National Association of Social Workers. (2002, March). Revised public and professional policies: Foster care and adoption/public child welfare. *NASW News,* 7–8.

Neeley-Bertram, D. (2000). Making the connection: Are adoption matching parties good for kids? *Children's Voice, 9*(6), 16–18.

Park, S., & Green, C. E. (2000). Is transracial adoption in the best interest of ethnic minority children? Questions concerning legal and scientific interpretations of a child's best interests. *Adoption Quarterly, 3*(4), 5–35.

Patton, S. (2000). *Transracial adoption in contemporary America.* New York: New York University Press.

Pertman, A. (2006 revised). *Adoption nation: How the adoption revolution is transforming America.* New York: Basic Books.

Prater, G. S. (1992). Child welfare and African-American families. In N. A. Cohen (Ed.), *Child welfare: A multicultural focus.* Boston: Allyn & Bacon.

Proch, K. (1981). Foster parents as preferred adoptive parents: Practice implications. *Child Welfare, 60*(9), 617–626.

Quinton, D., Rushton, A., Dance, C., & Mayes, D. (1998). *Joining new families: A study of adoption and fostering in middle childhood.* New York: John Wiley.

Rosenthal, J. A. (1993). Outcomes of adoption of children with special needs. *The Future of Children, 3*(1), 77–88 (a publication of the Center for the Future of Children, the David and Lucile Packard Foundation).

Rosenthal, J. A., & Groze, V. K. (1992). *Special-needs adoption: A study of intact families.* New York: Praeger.

Schroen, S. (no date). *Here I am: A lifebook kit for use with children with developmental disabilities.* Southfield, MI: Spaulding for Children.

Shireman, J. F. (1988). *Growing up adopted: An examination of major issues.* Chicago: Chicago Child Care Society.

Silin, M. W. (1996). The vicissitudes of adoption for parents and children. *Child and Adolescent Social Work Journal, 13*(3), 255–269.

Silverman, A. R. (1993). Outcomes of transracial adoption. *The Future of Children, 3*(1), 104–118 (a publication of the Center for the Future of Children, the David and Lucile Packard Foundation).

Silverman, J. F., & Johnson, P. R. (1986). A longitudinal study of black adoptions: Single parent, transracial, and traditional. *Social Work, 31,* 172–178.

Simon, A., Alstein, H., & Melli, M. S. (1994). *The case for transracial adoption.* Washington, DC: American University Press.

Smith, S. L. (2005). *Safeguarding interstate adoptions: The interstate compact on the placement of children.* New York: Evan B. Donaldson Adoption Institute.

Smith, S. L., Howard, J. A., & Monroe, A. D. (1998). An analysis of child behavior problems in adoptions in difficulty. *Journal of Social Service Research, 24*(1–2): 61–84.

Sokoloff, B. Z. (1993). Antecedents of American adoption. *The Future of Children, 3*(1), 17–25 (a publication of the Center for the Future of Children, the David and Lucille Packard Foundation).

Steinberg, G., & Hall, B. (2003). *What is transracial adoption?* Warren, NJ: EMK Press.

Stolley, K. S. (1993). Statistics on adoption in the United States. *The Future of Children. 3*(1), 26–42.

Sullivan, A. (1998). *Adoption and privatization.* Washington, DC: Child Welfare League of America.

Tasker, F. L. (2005). Lesbian mothers, gay fathers, and their children: A review. *Journal of Developmental and Behavioral Pediatrics, 26*(3), 224–240.

The China Center on Adoption Affairs. (2006). Available at www.travel.state.gov/family/adoption/intercountry.

Thornton, J. (1991). Permanency planning for children in kinship foster homes. *Child Welfare, 70*(5), 593–601.

Tizard, B. (1991). Intercountry adoption: A review of the evidence. *Journal of Child Psychology and Psychiatry, 32*(5), 43–56.

Trenka, J. J., Oparah, J. C., & Shin, S. Y. (2006). *Outsiders within: Writing on transracial adoption.* Cambridge, MA: South End Press.

U.S. Census Bureau. (2003). Adopted children and stepchildren: Census 2000 Special reports. Washington, DC: U.S. Department of Commerce, U.S. Census Bureau.

U.S. Census Bureau, Population Division (2000, April 12) *Racial and ethnic classifications used in Census 2000 and beyond.* Special Population Staff. Available: http://www,census.gov/ population/www/socdemo/race/racefactcb. html.

U.S. Department of Health and Human Services. (1997, June 5). ACYF-IM-CB-97-04. Washington, DC: Author.

U.S. Department of Health and Human Services. (2006 Edition). *AFCARS Data Elements*, 45 CFR 1355, Appendices A and B. Washington, DC: Author. Available: http//www.gpo.gov/AARA/cfr/index

U.S. Department of Health and Human Services, Administration for Children & Families. (2006 September). *The AFCARS Report. Preliminary FY 2005 Estimates as of September 2006 (13)*. Available: http://www. acf.hhs.gov/programs/cb/ stats_research/afcars/tar/report13.htm.

U.S. Department of State. (2007). Immigrant VISAS issued to orphans coming to the U.S.: Top countries of origin. Available at http://www. travel.state.gov/family/adoption/stats_451html.

U.S. General Accounting Office, HEHS Division. (1998). *Foster care implementation of the Multiethnic Placement Act poses difficult challenges.* Washington, DC: U.S. Government Printing Office.

U. S. Government Accountability Office. (2005). *Better data and evaluation could improve processes and program for adopting children with special needs.* Washington, DC: U.S. Government Accountability Office.

U.S. Immigration and Naturalization Service. (1991). *Statistical yearbook of the Immigration and Naturalization Service, 1991.* Washington, DC: U.S. Government Printing Office.

U.S. Office of Management and Budget. (1997). *Standards for classifications of federal data on race and ethnicity.* 45 CFR 1355, Appendix A. Washington DC: U.S. Government Printing Office.

U.S. Office of Management and Budget. (2000, March 9). OMB Bulletin No. 00-02. *Guidance on aggregation and allocation of data on race for use in civil rights monitoring and enforcement.* Washington DC: U.S. Government Printing Office.

U.S. Senate Committee on Children and Youth. (1975). Hearings before the Subcommittee on Labor and Public Welfare. *Adoption and foster care.* Washington, DC: U.S. Senate, 94th Congress, First Session.

Urban Institute. (2005). *Foster care adoption in the United States: An analysis of the interest in adoption and a review of state recruitment strategies.* Washington, DC: The Urban Institute.

Vick, C. (1995, Winter). The 1994 Uniform Adoption Act: The wrong model for positive change. *Adoptalk*, 4–5.

Vonk, M. E. (2001). Cultural competence for transracial adoptive parents. *Social Work, 46*(3), 246–255.

Wainwright, J., Russell, S. T., & Patterson, C. J. (2004). Psychological adjustment, school outcomes, and romantic relationships of adolescents with same-sex partners. *Child Development 75*(6), 1886–1898.

Watson, K. W. (1988). The case for open adoption. *Public Welfare, 46*(4), 24–28.

Weinberg, R. A., Waldman, I., van Dulmen, M. H. M., & Scarr, S. (2004). The Minnesota transracial adoption study: Parent reports of psychological adjustment at late adolescence. *Adoption Quarterly, 8*(2), 27–44.

Williams, M., & Satterfield, M. (2000). Kinship care: Is adoption the best option? *Children's Voice, 9*(6), 20–22.

Witmer, H., Herzog, E., Weinstein, E. A., & Sullivan, M. E. (1963). *Independent adoptions: A follow-up study.* New York: Russell Sage Foundation.

Wulczyn, F., & Hislop, K. (2002). *Growth in the adoption population.* Chapin Hall Center for Children. University of Chicago. Available: http://aspe.hhs.gov/hsp/fostercare-issueso2/adoptin/index.htm.

Zhao, Y. (2002, April 9). Immersed in 2 worlds, new and old. *New York Times*, p. A27.

Juvenile Delinquents

The Community's Dilemma

But the Constitution does not mandate elimination of all differences in the treatment of juveniles.

—Schall v. Martin, 1984, p. 269

CASE EXAMPLE

Peter is 15 years old. He became a temporary ward of the court when he was 4 years old. His mother had repeatedly beaten him with an extension cord. The last time he was beaten, he ran out of the house and into the street. His mother, in a drunken stupor, chased after him with the extension cord in her hands. Neighbors kept him from her and called the police. After being taken to the hospital, he was placed in a foster home. Over the next two years, his mother visited twice. When the foster parents sought to adopt him after he had been with them for two years, the agency told them that they were working on placing him with an aunt. The foster parents questioned this plan, because no family member had visited the child and he had not mentioned an aunt. The agency told the foster parents that it had located the aunt in another state. A home study had been completed and she would be coming to meet Peter in the next month. The aunt came and took Peter home with her.

Peter began to wet the bed immediately. The aunt thought he was having some initial adjustment problems, so attempted to console him when it happened. About eight months into the placement, he began to urinate on and hit other children at home and at school. The aunt became worried. The school social worker recommended that she get counseling for him. He was seen by the child guidance agency for two years. The urinating behavior stopped and the hitting behaviors were significantly reduced. Services were terminated.

At 10 years of age, Peter stole a bicycle from a garage. His aunt made him return it, spanked him with a belt, and told him he would not be allowed to play outside for a week. The next day, Peter told the teacher that his aunt had beaten him with a belt and he did not want to go back to her house. The teacher called child protective services. Child protective services talked with Peter and the aunt. Both confirmed that the aunt had hit him with a belt. The aunt said she would just as soon he not come back to her house because he had been a constant problem since he was placed with her. He was placed in a shelter.

The home state was contacted to arrange for Peter's return. After two weeks, a worker came to pick him up and took him to a shelter in the home state. The agency sought a foster home placement. As they were preparing to move him to a foster home, the shelter reported that he had been found having sexual intercourse with an 8-year-old girl in the shelter. The agency told the prospective foster parents of this incident, and they declined to have him placed in the home because they had younger children. He remained in the shelter for six months and was eventually placed in a small group home for children with sexually aggressive behaviors. He remained in this placement for two years.

Peter had to leave the group home because it could keep children only until their twelfth birthday. He moved from one group home to another. A fight with another youth that Peter had allegedly started precipitated each move. No delinquency charges were filed in any of these incidents. He is now in the juvenile detention facility charged with forcible rape of a 12-year-old girl.

This case example highlights an issue of great concern in child welfare, that children who originally come to the attention of the child welfare system because of neglect, abuse, or abandonment later appear in the juvenile justice system (Kelley, Thornberry, & Smith,

1997). Their reappearance as juvenile delinquents suggests that the earlier interventions of the child welfare system were not successful in reversing the negative effects of their maltreatment.

Jonson-Reid and Barth (2000) conducted an exploratory study of the school-aged children who had been in the California child abuse and neglect foster care system to determine their rate of entry into the California juvenile justice system. A sample of approximately 79,139 children who had been in foster care during the period 1970 to 1984 was drawn. Only 0.75 percent, or 590, of these children later entered state juvenile justice services. However, the significant findings regarding these children are informative with respect to improvements in foster care policy and service delivery. Children most likely to enter the juvenile justice system had been

- ❖ reunited with their families following their first entry into foster care;
- ❖ had spent more time in reunification than in foster care;
- ❖ had multiple foster care entries; and
- ❖ had their first foster care entry between the ages of 11 and 14 years.

In addition, African American and Hispanic children who were reunited with their families were more likely to enter juvenile justice services than were white children (Jonson-Reid & Barth, 2000). Jonson-Reid and Barth (2000) stated

> Reunification rates are considered a positive indicator of child welfare agency performance. . . . If certain home and neighborhood environments are not conducive to healthy development, however, then policy makers and practitioners must weigh these factors in the prioritization of the best interests of the child. (*p. 512*)

Perhaps the conclusion is not to question the value of reunification as a policy preference, but to address the intensity of after-care services for families reuniting after foster care, particularly those with adolescent children, as well as comprehensive community development services to remove the challenges in the communities where these families must live. Irrespective, these findings do suggest that we need to explore the nature of services provided to early adolescents during foster care placement in particular.

JUVENILE OFFENDER CATEGORIES

Juvenile delinquency policy and practice addresses two distinctly different categories of juvenile offenders: the juvenile who commits an act that violates a criminal statute, and the juvenile who commits an act that violates a law or ordinance designed to regulate his or her behavior because of his or her age or status.

Within the first category of delinquents, those who commit violations of criminal statutes, there are two subgroups. The first are those who commit violent crimes, including murder, forcible rape, robbery, and aggravated assault. These are the juvenile offenses that receive the most media attention and public discussion. Yet these offenses accounted for less than 5 percent of all juvenile offenses reported in 1999. For example, the total number of violent crimes by juveniles reported (103,900) was much less than the number of juvenile runaways (150,700) (Snyder, 2000). Despite the relatively small number of violent juvenile offenders, the failure of the juvenile justice system to effectively address them sparked the "adult crime–adult time" movement, which holds that the juvenile who commits certain categories of offenses should be tried and sentenced as an adult.

The second subgroup of delinquents who commit violations of criminal statutes, are minors whose offenses include property crimes such as burglary, larceny-theft, motor vehicle theft, arson, receiving or possessing stolen property, embezzlement, fraud, drug manufacture, possession, or sale, and the nonviolent personal crimes such as sexual offenses and nonaggravated assault.

Within the second category of delinquents are those who commit acts that are deemed status offenses, such as truancy from home, truancy from school, failure to obey the reasonable commands of the parent or guardian, and violating curfew. In some states, these juveniles are called children in need of supervision, persons in need of services, status offenders, or wayward minors. A status offense is an act that is an offense only when committed by a juvenile. A continuing controversy among policy makers is whether status offenders should be removed from juvenile court jurisdiction and their problems dealt with by noncoercive, community-based services. Those who hold this view are concerned that the traditional responsibility of the family to control children's misbehavior is being seriously weakened by a too-ready transfer of responsibility to bureaucratic discretion. There is also concern that the juvenile justice system is being forced to treat delinquents and status offenders alike, without distinction for their different statuses, in an increasingly adversarial and bureaucratic context (Howell, 1997).

This chapter explores the historical development of a separate system of justice for juveniles, the current trend toward treating juveniles who commit the more serious offenses in the adult criminal system, the risk factors for delinquency, and the range of prevention and treatment strategies used to address the multiple problems of juvenile delinquents and their families.

SCOPE OF THE PROBLEM

The data inform us that, despite negative publicity, relatively few children come before the juvenile court. Of the 33.5 million youths aged 10 to 17 in the United States in 2003, only 2.2 million, or less than 7 percent, were arrested for delinquent acts, including status offenses. Violent crimes (murder, forcible rape, robbery, and aggravated assault) accounted for 4 percent of all juvenile arrests. The ages of youths at the time of arrest for all crimes were as follows: 68 percent were 16 to 17 years of age and 32 percent were less than 15 years of age. The racial composition was 71 percent white, 27 percent black, 1 percent Native American, and 2 percent Asian. Males make up about 71 percent of all delinquency arrests (Snyder & Sickmund, 2006).

Juvenile arrests for violent offences in 2004 were the lowest since 1987. Arrests for property crimes were the lowest since 1975. The 2004 arrest rates were the tenth consecutive year of decline (Snyder 2006).

Butts (1997) completed an analysis of the arrests and juvenile court dispositions for crimes committed by juveniles under the age of 15 years in response to the perception that younger juveniles are committing more serious offenses and in increasing numbers. This perception is, in part, the basis for the push to lower the age at which juveniles can be tried as adults and for more serious punishment for juvenile offenders. They concluded:

> This study suggests that today's serious and violent juvenile offenders are not significantly younger than those of 10 or 15 years ago. Yet many juvenile justice professionals, as well as the public, would assert the opposite. What explains this discrepancy? The authors of this study believe several factors are at work.

First, overall growth in the number of violent juvenile offenders has drawn increased attention to the problem of young offenders in general. . . . Second, the nature of delinquency cases involving juveniles age 12 or younger has changed. Person offenses, which once constituted 16% of the total court cases for this age group, now constitute 25%. . . . Third, delinquency caseloads have doubled nationwide since 1970. . . . Fourth, justice professionals tend to accumulate memories of exceptional cases. . . . Finally, the news media have increased their reporting of crime, especially violent crimes by the very young. . . . The growing publicity about these cases may suggest to the public that they are occurring more frequently, even if juvenile crime trends indicate otherwise. (*p. 11*)

The Office of Juvenile Justice and Delinquency Prevention in the U.S. Department of Justice is the best source of data on juvenile crime and research and programming. Its most recent comprehensive report, *Juvenile Offenders and Victims: 2006 National Report,* provides the following trend data:

❖ The juvenile crime arrest rate decreased 18 percent between 1994 and 2003 (Snyder & Sickmund, 2006, p. 127).

❖ The number of murders by juveniles decreased 68 percent. About 80 percent of the overall decline is attributable to a drop in the number of nonfamily member murders and a drop in the minority on minority murders (Snyder & Sickmund, 2006, p. 127).

❖ The juvenile convicted of murder was likely to be a codefendant with an adult in 56 percent of the murders (Snyder & Sickmund, 2006, p. 66).

❖ The victims of juvenile murderers were predominately family members and acquaintances (63 percent) as opposed to strangers (37 percent) (Snyder & Sickmund, 2006, p. 66).

❖ Juvenile murderers used a gun in 69 percent of all murders (Snyder & Sickmund, 2006, p. 66).

❖ The disparity in violent crime arrests for black and white juveniles declined from 6 to 1 in 1980 to 4 to 1 in 2004 (Snyder, 2006).

❖ While male arrests decreased in all serious offense categories, female arrests increased. Thirty percent of juvenile offenses were committed by females. Females accounted for 31 percent of the simple assaults, 29 percent of drug abuse, 33 percent of disorderly conduct, and 69 percent of driving under the influence offenses (Snyder, 2006).

❖ While white juveniles continue to be arrested for the majority of violent crimes (52 percent) and property crimes (69 percent), black juveniles continue to be overrepresented in the arrest data. While comprising only 17 percent of the general population, 46 percent of black juvenile arrest rates are for violent crimes and 28 percent are for property crimes (Snyder, 2006).

❖ School-related crime is growing in significance. In the 2003 Youth Risk Behavior Survey (YRBS) conducted by the Centers for Disease Control, 33 percent of the youth respondents reported that they had been in a fight at school during the past 12 months. Of those, 4 percent required medical treatment for injuries suffered. In addition, 30 percent reported that they had had property stolen or vandalized, 5 percent reported that they missed at least 1 day of school because they felt unsafe at school or going to school, 6 percent carried a weapon to school, and 9 percent were threatened or injured with a weapon at school. Overall, the reported percentages are down for fighting, injuries requiring medical treatment, carrying a weapon to school, and property theft or vandalism. They are up for missing school because of feeling unsafe. They are unchanged for threatened or injured with a weapon (Snyder & Sickmund, 2006, pp. 73–74). A 2000 survey of public school principles found 18 percent reporting gang activity in their schools (Snyder & Sickmund, 2006, p. 82).

❖ Violent crimes committed by juveniles peak in the hour immediately after school ends (Snyder & Sickmund, 2006, p. 85).

The disposition of juveniles arrested were 21 percent handled within law enforcement, 70 percent referred to juvenile courts, and 9 percent referred to adult criminal courts. There had been a decreasing trend in the proportion of cases involving juveniles waived to adult courts between 1993 through 2001. However, in 2002 there was a 13 percent increase in cases waived (Stahl, 2006). This number does not include the total number of juveniles prosecuted in the adult system. Those filed in the adult system under prosecutorial discretion or legislative exclusion are not included in this count. There are no reliable data sources for these cases.

In 2002, according to Stahl (2006), 1.6 million delinquency cases were handled by the juvenile courts. Approximately 67 percent were adjudicated delinquent. Of those, 62 percent were placed on formal probation and 23 percent were placed in residential facilities. These data are estimates based on information supplied by 2,100 jurisdictions to the National Juvenile Court Data Archive. These reporting jurisdictions represent approximately 75 percent of the juvenile population. Within these jurisdictions, 7,100 juvenile cases were waived to the adult criminal justice system—less than one-half percent of all juveniles charged. Of those waived, 41 percent were for offenses against persons, 36 percent were for property offenses, and 14 percent were for drug law violations. Fifty-eight percent were less than 16 years of age, 67 percent were white, 33 percent were black, 26 percent were female, and 74 percent were male (Stahl, 2006).

HISTORICAL DEVELOPMENT OF JUVENILE DELINQUENCY SERVICES

From Adult Criminal Court to Juvenile Court

Historically, juveniles over the age of 7 years—the age recognized under common law as the age at which one could form criminal intent—who committed crimes enjoyed no special privileges due to their age. They were arrested, detained, tried, and sentenced in the same manner as an adult would be for the same crime. The Society for the Reformation of Juvenile Delinquents (the Society), organized in 1823, called for removing juveniles from adult jails. Their organizers saw this removal as a way to save these youth from the negative influences of adult criminals. Their basic belief was that prisons did not reform adult criminals, and by exposing juvenile offenders to adult criminals, the juveniles would most likely develop into better criminals (Finestone, 1976).

In 1825, the Society opened the New York House of Refuge, designed to provide an environment that would ensure the positive development of youth by focusing on meeting their basic needs, instilling in them the value of work, providing education, and overseeing their moral development. Finestone (1976) commented, "So certain were its founders of the righteousness of their mission that they showed little concern with the civil rights of the children they institutionalized: admissions included homeless children and convicted juvenile offenders indiscriminately" (p. 7).

Nonetheless, this movement caught on and spread throughout the United States (Dean & Reppucci, 1974). During the period from 1825 until the founding of the juvenile court system at the end of the century, these reform, industrial, or training schools (as they were known in various localities) continued to increase in number. Unfortunately they became sources of constant scandals rather than the incubators of positive youth development as first envisioned. They were overcrowded, used excessive disciplinary methods, experienced significant violence, and provided a custodial rather than a treatment environment (Howell, 1997).

Charles Lording Brace at the New York Children's Aid Society challenged the institutionalization of children and youth in reform schools. He promoted relocating children from the inner cities to families in the Midwest and West. (See Chapter 8.) Concurrently, Jane Addams, Julia Lathrop, and Lucy Flower were undertaking a movement in Chicago to establish settlement houses to address the impact of increasing urbanization and poverty on families and children. They chose to work with the family and child within the neighborhood. Both initiatives focused on helping the child develop within the context of a family environment rather than an institutional one.

Out of this grew the interest of the Chicago Women's Club in improving the conditions of juveniles who were institutionalized. Their work resulted in the establishment of the first juvenile court. Their vision was that this court would treat those who committed delinquent acts as children in need of firm direction and support, not as criminals deserving of punishment. The judge was given full discretion to determine what was the best course of intervention for the child, with the input of social workers and others. It is interesting to note that the Illinois statute, while precluding placing juveniles in adult prisons and providing for alternatives in dispositions such as family placement and probation, did not preclude placing them in the same reform schools that were the source of significant scandal at the time (Jacobs, 1997).

A complete discussion of the juvenile court's operation and the subsequent attacks on it is described in Chapter 5. The reader is reminded that the challenge to the juvenile courts' operations was that its "benevolence" often took precedence over the due process rights of the juvenile. These attacks on the juvenile court system operation emanated out of its informal, individualized handling of juvenile delinquency matters. Specifically, the U.S. Supreme Court decisions *In re Gault* and *Kent v. United States,* decided in 1966, marked the beginning of the juveniles' right to due process (Kramer, 2000). What had been designed as a benevolent system to handle child abuse, neglect, and delinquency and to protect children from the trauma of the adult legal system was found to be constitutionally deficient.

In the *Kent* case, the law of the District of Columbia provided that a person 16 years of age or older charged with an offense that would be a felony if committed by an adult could be waived to the adult court for trial after a full investigation by the juvenile judge. Kent, who was charged with robbery, rape, and breaking and entering, was waived. He challenged the waiver on the grounds that he was not afforded a hearing, no reasons for the waiver were provided to him, and his lawyer was denied access to his records. The Court held that under the due process clause, a juvenile was entitled to a hearing, full access to records and reports used by the court in arriving at its decision, and a statement of the reason for the juvenile court's decision (*Kent v. United States,* 1966).

Gault was a 15-year-old Arizona teenager charged with making a lewd telephone call to a neighbor. He was on probation at the time of the call. He was arrested without notification to his parents, detained, not provided counsel, and never afforded a formal hearing. He was found delinquent and committed to the state training school until the age of majority. He challenged the proceedings. The Court, in reversing the decision of the Arizona Supreme Court, established the due process requirements for juvenile delinquency hearings: (1) notice of sufficient detail to mount a defense; (2) right to be represented by counsel and, if necessary, right to court appointed and paid counsel if child and parents could not afford counsel; (3) privilege against self-incrimination; and (4) right to review evidence and cross-examine witnesses. Justice Fortas made two statements in this decision that challenged the basic foundation of the juvenile court system and signaled the scope of constitutional protections for juveniles:

> . . . neither the Fourteenth Amendment nor the Bill of Rights is for adults alone. (*In re Gault, 1967, p. 13*);

and

> . . . juvenile court history has again demonstrated that unbridled discretion, however benevolently motivated, is frequently a poor substitute for principle and procedure. (*Ibid., p. 18*)

Subsequent U.S. Supreme Court decisions went on to place the rights of juveniles in the juvenile court system on par with the rights granted adults in the criminal system in most respects. The Court held that the standard of proof in a delinquency case is "beyond a reasonable doubt," the same standard required in adult criminal proceedings (*In re Winship,* 1970). It held that a transfer to adult court for prosecution after an adjudication of delinquency in the juvenile court violates the Fifth Amendment protection against double jeopardy (*Breed v. Jones,* 1975).

The Supreme Court has not required that the juvenile court operate like the adult criminal courts in all respects. It has supported variations in the treatment of juveniles in the juvenile court system. In *McKeiver v. Pennsylvania* (1971) it held that the fundamental fairness standard in fact-finding procedures for juvenile proceedings as developed by *Gault* and *Winship* did not require a jury trial. The 1984 *Schall v. Martin* decision, in which the Supreme Court upheld a New York statute that provided for pretrial detention, reflects the continuing balancing of juvenile rights and differential treatment provided by the juvenile courts. The Court stated:

> There is no doubt that the Due Process Clause is applicable in juvenile proceedings. "The problem," we have stressed, "is to ascertain the precise impact of the due process requirement upon such proceedings. . . ." We have held that certain basic constitutional protections enjoyed by adults accused of crimes also apply to juveniles. . . . But the Constitution does not mandate elimination of all differences in the treatment of juveniles. . . . The State has "a *parens patriae* interest in preserving and promoting the welfare of the child," . . . which makes a juvenile proceeding fundamentally different from an adult criminal trial. We have tried, therefore, to strike a balance—to respect the "informality" and "flexibility" that characterize juvenile proceedings, . . . and yet ensure that such proceedings comport with the "fundamental fairness" demanded by the Due Process Clause. (*p. 263*)

The issue of whether the imposition of the death penalty on a juvenile violates the U.S. Constitution's Eighth Amendment cruel and unusual punishment protections has been before the U.S. Supreme Court four times. In 1988, the Court held that the imposition of the death penalty on juvenile less than 16 years of age at the time of the offense violated the Constitution (*Thompson v. Oklahoma*, 1988). In 1989 and 2002, it held that the imposition of the death penalty on a juvenile who commits the offense when they are 16 or 17 years of age did not violate the Constitution (*Stanford v. Kentucky*, 1989; *In re Kevin Nigel Stanford*, 2002). However, in March 2005, the Court reversed itself and held that the Eighth and Fourteenth Amendments forbid the imposition of the death penalty on offenders who were under the age of 18 years when they committed the crime. Its rationale for the change was basically that a national consensus had developed to support this decision (*Roper v. Simmons*, 2005).

In summary, then, for juveniles charged with delinquent or criminal offenses, the Court has clearly established that they must be afforded due process rights equal to those afforded adults and that the states can, provided the fundamental fairness tests are met, maintain some flexibility and informality in its juvenile court processes to ensure the benevolent treatment of juveniles.

Federal Government Leadership

The federal government began an active involvement in juvenile justice policy in the 1960s. As is the norm, it established policies and influenced state action, acceptance, and implementation of these policies by linking federal funding to adoption and implementation of the federal policies.

The White House Conference on Children and Youth of 1960 was followed by the 1961 establishment of the Crime Committee on Juvenile Delinquency and Youth Crime. The Crime Committee combined the efforts of several federal departments to focus on delinquency prevention projects. The Juvenile Delinquency and Youth Offenses Control Act of 1961 funded demonstration projects for delinquency prevention.

The Juvenile Delinquency Prevention and Control Act of 1968, which was renamed the Juvenile Delinquency Prevention Act in 1971, provided federal support to states for delinquency services.

In 1974, the Juvenile Justice and Delinquency Prevention Act (JJDPA) signaled the beginning of a new era in juvenile justice policy reform at the federal level. This Act was the result of several reports articulating juvenile court failures, namely lack of due process for juveniles before the court, crowded training schools, excessive use of detention of children in jails, increasing juvenile crime rates, and ineffective interventions (Empey & Stafford, 1991). The Act called for, among other things, diversion of minor offenders from the juvenile court, separation of juvenile offenders from adult offenders in detention, the removal of status offenders from secure detention facilities and the establishment of nonsecure alternatives for them, and the establishment of the Office of Juvenile Justice and Delinquency Prevention (OJJDP). The Act was especially significant in that it required compliance with these provisions as a condition for states to receive federal funding (Howell, 1997, p. 33).

Over the course of the thirty years since its initial passage, the Act has been amended several times. These amendments have provided exceptions to some of the original mandates and expanded others. For example, the adult–juvenile separation mandate progressed from total sight and sound separation to total removal of juveniles from adult jails to delineation of specific instances in which juveniles can be detained with adults. In addition, status offenders can be ordered into secure facilities if there is sufficient evidence to show that they have violated a court order and secure detention is found to be the only way to contain them. This option can be used for a limited period of time. The 1988 amendment called for states to pursue reductions in the disproportionate representation of minorities in the system. This provision was made a mandate in 1992 (Howell, 1997). We will address this issue in more detail later in this chapter.

Monitoring reports suggest that all eligible states and territories are participating, with fifty-five of the fifty-seven governmental bodies in full compliance with the mandates. Howell (1997) states, "These accomplishments are unprecedented in the history of federal social legislation. . . . Excepting the creation of reform schools and juvenile courts, these are the most significant changes in the history of juvenile justice in the United States" (p. 38). The reasons he gives for this success are

- ❖ professionals and advocacy organizations joined together
- ❖ required infrastructure to monitor compliance at the state level
- ❖ prevention and intervention program focus
- ❖ Department of Justice legal support for compliance
- ❖ JJDP Act's promotion of progressive programming (pp. 39–41)

Back to the Criminal Court

Despite the successes of the Juvenile Justice and Delinquency Prevention Act and the Office of Juvenile and Delinquency Prevention in administering it, the juvenile justice system is being challenged with the "just deserts" or "adult crime–adult time" punishment approach. This approach rests on the assumption that the juvenile court system has not been effective in deterring juvenile crime nor correcting juvenile offenders' behaviors. Clearly the data support that conclusion and have been used by those who wish to eliminate the juvenile court system. According to the proposed reform, juveniles would be adjudicated by the criminal courts and incarcerated in adult prisons if the crimes were serious enough. Howell (1997) notes: "Once again, punishing the offense rather than the offender is the object of current crime policy" (p. 23).

RISK FACTORS FOR DELINQUENCY

Many factors contribute to delinquency. Hawkins and Catalano (1992) have summarized the research findings from longitudinal studies that have identified risk factors within the community, the family, the school, and the individual that contribute to adolescent problem behaviors of substance abuse, delinquency, teenage pregnancy, school dropout, and violence. Figure 11.1 summarizes those risk factors and the adolescent problem behaviors likely to result from those risk factors.

This conceptualization of the risk factors of delinquency has influenced the development of a model of delinquency prevention and intervention called Communities That Care, which is being implemented in many communities. Essentially, the conceptualization and model suggest the following (Hawkins & Catalano, 1992; Howell, 1995):

- ❖ The greater the number of exposures to risks, the higher the likelihood of the juvenile engaging in the undesired behaviors.
- ❖ Because risks are found in multiple domains, multiple strategies must be used concurrently to reduce the risks.
- ❖ There is consistency in risk factors across races and cultures, although the levels of risk vary.
- ❖ Some common risk factors are predictive of the different problem behaviors, which indicates implementation of prevention strategies that can address multiple problems.
- ❖ Protective factors can reduce the impact of exposure to risk factors.
- ❖ Communities have a significant number of resources that can provide the protective factors.

Figure 11.1 *Communities That Care: Risk Factors for Adolescent Problem Behaviors*

Risk Factors	Adolescent Problem Behaviors				
	Substance Abuse	Delinquency	Teen Pregnancy	School Drop-Out	Violence
Community					
Availability of drugs	✓				
Availability of firearms		✓			✓
Community law and norms favorable toward drug use, firearms, and crime	✓	✓			✓
Media portrayals of violence					✓
Transitions and mobility	✓	✓		✓	
Low neighborhood attachment and community disorganization	✓	✓			✓
Extreme economic deprivation	✓	✓	✓	✓	✓
Family					
Family history of the problem behavior	✓	✓	✓	✓	✓
Family management problems	✓	✓	✓	✓	✓
Family conflict	✓	✓	✓	✓	✓
Favorable parental attitudes and involvement in the behavior	✓	✓			✓
School					
Early and persistent antisocial behavior	✓	✓	✓	✓	✓
Academic failure in elementary school	✓	✓	✓	✓	✓
Lack of commitment to school	✓	✓	✓	✓	✓
Individual/Peer					
Alienation and rebelliousness	✓	✓		✓	
Friends who engage in a problem behavior	✓	✓	✓	✓	✓
Favorable attitudes toward the problem behavior	✓	✓	✓	✓	
Early initiation of the problem behavior	✓	✓	✓	✓	✓
Constitutional factors	✓	✓			✓

Source: DRP, Inc. (1994), *Risk and Resource Assessment.* San Francisco, CA: Jossey-Bass. © 1996–1997, Developmental Resource and Research Programs, Inc., www.DRP.org. All rights reserved.

❖ Communities must take charge of the prevention and intervention of juvenile delinquency by engagement in a strategic process that identifies the risks and resources within the community and targets intervention with specific programs that have been proven to be effective in reducing or eliminating the identified risks.

The OJJDP Program of Research on the Causes and Correlates of Delinquency began three longitudinal studies in 1987 to "develop a firm, scientific understanding of the origins of delinquency." These studies are located in Denver (Colorado), Pittsburg (Pennsylvania), and Rochester (New York). They include information on over 4,000 youth aged 7 through 30, male and female, black, white, and Hispanic. These studies have and continue to examine specific risk factors within the individual, family, school, and community that contribute to delinquency. Interestingly, while these studies have provided data that supports a model of three distinct pathways to serious and violent offending, noted in Figure 11.2, much of the data needed to develop the "firm, scientific understanding of the origins of delinquency" is inconclusive. That is, the findings from the longitudinal studies cannot document that the presence of a given risk factor will lead to or result in delinquent behaviors for youth in the general population. They can document that the majority, though not all, youth arrested for delinquent offenses do have a combination of risk factors and, for many of those arrested, the more serious and violent the offense, the more risk factors present and the longer the duration of those risk factors (Thornberry, Huizinga, & Loeber, 2004; Thornberry & Krohn, 2003). The question remaining is: Given the same risk factors, why do some youth engage in delinquent

Figure 11.2   *Developmental Pathways to Serious and Violent Offending*

❖   The Authority Conflict Pathway starts with stubborn behavior before age 12 and progresses to defiance and then to authority avoidance (e.g., truancy).

❖   The Covert Pathway starts with minor covert acts before age 15 and progresses to property damage and then to moderate and then to serious delinquency.

❖   The Overt Pathway starts with minor aggression and progresses to physical fighting and then to more severe violence (no minimum age is associated with this pathway).

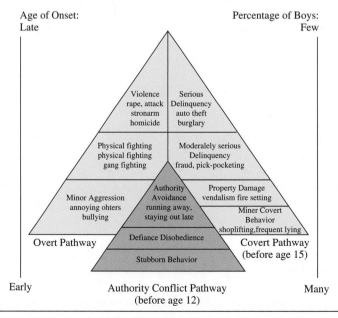

Source: Thornberry, T. P., Huizinga, D., & Loeber, R. (2004). The causes and correlates studies: Findings and policy implications, *Juvenile Justice, IX*(1) 5–6. Available: www.ojp.usdoj.gov/ojjdp.

acts and some do not? The identification of resiliency factors has not been thoroughly examined. The results from that research will provide much to inform delinquency prevention and delinquency intervention programming.

JUVENILE DELINQUENCY PREVENTION AND INTERVENTION STRATEGIES

In the past twenty years, the concepts of "graduated sanctions," "balanced and restorative justice," and "adult crime–adult time" have become the guiding philosophies in juvenile justice policy and practice. It is expected that they will remain so for the foreseeable future. All rest on the principle that juveniles should be held accountable for their antisocial or criminal behaviors. Shepherd (1999) stated

> In sum, the trends of the past decade have all been in the direction of transforming the juvenile court from an institution that still resembled the rehabilitative model envisioned by the founders at the turn of the twentieth century into a criminalized institution that more closely resembled the adult criminal court disdained by the founders. (p. 599)

Graduated sanctions in juvenile justice means that a juvenile receives some "punishment" for each adjudicated offense. The nature and severity of the sanction is determined by the nature of the offense and the juvenile's offense history. For example, a juvenile with no prior juvenile offense record steals a CD and is adjudicated. An appropriate sanction would be to pay for the CD and apologize to the owner. Three months later, he steals another CD. An appropriate sanction would be to pay for the CD, apologize to the owner, and perform ten hours of community services. Another juvenile robs an elderly woman at gunpoint. This is his first offense. Given the nature of the offense and the vulnerability of the victim, an appropriate sanction would be more severe, such as detention until trial and, after adjudication, secure residential placement as well as supervised community services.

Balanced and restorative justice means that the juvenile is held accountable for his behavior and has a responsibility not only to repair the harm caused the victim through restitution but also to repair the harm caused the community through constructive community service. It encourages victim and community engagement in the rehabilitation process for the juvenile. The second offense sanction for stealing a CD in the earlier example and the first offense sanction for armed robbery in the example above are applications of balanced and restorative justice concepts.

Adult crime–adult time means that juveniles, of certain ages with reasoning capacities, who are convicted of committing violent offenses, differently defined in state statutes, should experience the same punishments that adults would experience for the same offenses. The assumption is that the offenses are so reprehensible and the success of the juvenile system in preventing future crimes by violent offenders so low, that protection of the community dictates severe punishment.

Practices developed under graduated sanctions and the balanced and restorative justice philosophies have provided an opportunity for the juvenile court and the juvenile justice system to demonstrate that rehabilitation and community protection can coexist. Shepherd (1999) stated

> Since youth are developmentally different from each other, the correction of juvenile delinquents through services that are expressly designed to treat their behaviors and problems in an individualized fashion is best capable of preventing future offending. (p. 601)

Juvenile delinquency prevention and intervention strategies developed and implemented over the last thirty years with federal funding assistance include parenting training, early education, school behavior management, conflict resolution and violence prevention, mentoring, intensive family preservation services, gang prevention, recreation and leisure activities, vocational training, community services, policing strategies, out-of-home placement continuum, and incarceration. All these strategies have been shown to be effective with some juveniles and not with others.

The three sections that follow present the research findings for the types of interventions that work to prevent and treat juvenile delinquency. The discussion is divided into prevention and early intervention strategies effective with status offenders, with nonchronic offenders, and with chronic or serious juvenile offenders. A chronic or serious offender is one who commits four or more crimes and/or who commits at least one violent offense (Butts, 1997).

Prevention and Intervention with Status Offenders

Status offenses are acts that are only an offense because of the juvenile's age; they would not be offenses if committed by an adult. Examples of status offenses are truancy from home, truancy from school, failure to obey the reasonable commands of the parent or guardian, violating curfew, and underaged drinking. In some states, juveniles who commit these acts are also classified as juvenile delinquents. In other states, these juveniles are called children in need of supervision, persons in need of services, status offenders, or wayward minors (Kramer, 2000).

Data collection variations preclude accurate national estimates at this time. A sample-based profile for 1985 to 2002 found adjudications for status offenses were distributed as follows: 34 percent were for truancy, 30 percent were for underage drinking, 19 percent were for runaways, and 17 percent were for incorrigibility or ungovernability. Females accounted for 42 percent of the status offense cases adjudicated. Females were most likely to be adjudicated for running away from home and truancy whereas males were most likely to be adjudicated for liquor offenses and incorrigibility. White youth represented 77 percent of all youth adjudicated for status offenses. Approximately 9 percent of status offenders were held in detention. The majority of these youth had been charged with running away from home (Snyder & Sickmund, 2006; Stahl et al., 2005).

A continuing controversy among policymakers is whether status offenders should be removed from juvenile court jurisdiction and their problems dealt with by noncoercive community-based services. "It has been urged that only juveniles whose acts would result in criminal prosecutions if they were adults be handled in the juvenile justice system and that status offenders should be kept from contact with the juvenile justice system and cared for by alternative agencies" (Simonsen, 1991, p. 449).

The issue of jurisdiction over status offenders is complicated by research findings on the question of whether status offenders are more similar to than different from delinquent youth. So far, the weight of evidence strongly suggests that youth tend to be concurrently involved in both delinquent and status offense behavior. Such findings imply that it is not possible at this time to differentiate involvement in status offenses from involvement in delinquency, at least in less serious delinquency. "There seem to be two major categories of illegal involvement . . . one is petty illegal behavior which includes status offenses and less serious delinquency, and the other is serious delinquency" (Weis, Sakumato, Sederstrom, & Seiss, 1980, p. 99; OJJDPS, 1997).

Such findings suggest that the juvenile justice system should treat the two categories of petty and serious offenders differently. Some recommend that jurisdiction over status offenders, as well as over less serious delinquents, should be restricted or perhaps abandoned. Appropriate dispositional decisions by the court and treatment alternatives in the community for status offenders and for less seriously delinquent youth may well be the same (Weis, et al., 1980).

As the juvenile court approached its one hundredth anniversary, youth policy planners questioned whether any quasi-legal means of regulating childhood can take the place of the family as the primary source of nurture and support for the child. The juvenile justice system, many contend, has been vested with overwhelming and sometimes quite unrealistic expectations. Its institutional limitations must be acknowledged and efforts made to reeducate the public about the responsibilities the family and the community must accept, particularly in relation to children in need of supervision (Smith, Berkman, Fraser, & Sutton, 1980, p. 160; Schwartz & Orlando, 1991; Ayers, 1997).

For the most part, status offenders commit no offenses except against themselves. Their actions are often a response to neglect, abuse, alcohol and substance abuse, or other family dysfunctions, but they are treated as if they were guilty of some very serious wrongdoing. Some of them do come within the province of the delinquency system; however, their offense is more likely to be running away, truancy, substance abuse, or being ungovernable or incorrigible. Children who run away from home, foster homes, or residential placements, for the most part, can cite credible reasons. Some understand that their lives would be in danger if they did not run away. Many have been rejected by their families and thrown out of their homes. Unhappily, many have had bad experiences with social welfare agencies and other would-be helpers who wished to help but unwittingly made matters worse. In such cases, the activities of these children should be seen as urgent signals to look into the causes. For some advocates this suggests that the family or the child welfare agency is not the caring and supporting environment that others contend, and, in those situations in which the parental actions do not rise to the level of abuse or neglect under the statute, status offenders should have a quasi-legal system to protect children from the actions of their parents.

Arguments cited in support of removing status offenders from the legal system usually focus on the misapplication of judicial power and the injustice that often results when the punishment is out of proportion to the offense—for example, truancy or being on the streets after curfew. The proponents of policy change also cite the harm done to youths by the stigma of having participated in the judicial process. They maintain as well that the juvenile justice system clearly lacks the capability to resolve individual behavior problems typical of minors in need of supervision. On the other hand, juvenile court judges in many states strongly oppose the proposal to remove status offenders from their authority. In their view, there is no other system with any control power over the juvenile. Further, they cite the fact that over 40 percent of all status offender cases are brought to juvenile courts by parents or persons acting in *loco parentis* (Snyder & Sickmund, 2006; Stahl, 2006).

The status offender problem is persistent despite the efforts of the National Institute of Juvenile Justice and Delinquency Prevention (NIJJDP) and the various states to improve the handling of minors in need of supervision. An assessment by the NIJJDP of the current state of knowledge concerning status offenders found that they continue to be involved in a significant portion of juvenile arrests, intake and court procedures, and detention homes and other institutional placements. Wide variation in state status offense legislation exists, negating any assumption that decisions are being made on uniform principles and procedures. Dealing with noncriminal adolescent behavior is a significant issue in most states (Smith, et al., 1980; Kramer, 1994; Jacobs, 1995; supp. 1997; Howell, 1997).

The status offender is generally first treated as a nonchronic offender with respect to dispositional alternatives. However, a disproportionate number of status offenders receive detention or residential placement because of family refusal to have them in the home. Juveniles who have multiple status offenses—particularly those who run away from home or foster care placements, are truant from school, or are incorrigible—challenge current intervention options. The future success of reducing the number of status offenders in the courts appears to lie with early intervention programs involving parents and children and early intervention with academic difficulties.

To assist local communities in addressing the truancy issue and to support early intervention services in truancy cases, the OJJDP, in cooperation with the National Center for School Engagement, developed the *Toolkit for Creating Your Own Truancy Reduction Program*. The *Toolkit* provides a comprehensive review of the issues, the risk factors, the legal requirements of the No Child Left Behind statute related to supporting school attendance, and provides direction for developing effective interventions, promising programs, and funding sources to assist program development and evaluation (Office of Juvenile Justice and Delinquency Prevention, 2007a).

Prevention and Early Intervention with Nonchronic Offenders

The objective of prevention and early intervention programs is to reduce risk factors, increase protective factors, and achieve prosocial behavior. While no intervention has proven to be completely successful with all children and youth, in the last twenty years, many programs have been implemented that are designed to reduce the number of youth who engage in delinquent behaviors and/or reduce the number of youth who have been adjudicated delinquent who commit subsequent offenses (recidivate). The prevention programs are aimed at populations identified as at-risk because of the presence of risk factors discussed above. Early intervention programs are aimed at children who have had a nonserious offense contact with the police or who have exhibited problem behaviors that, if not corrected, could lead to delinquent behaviors.

Parenting Programs. Provide parents with developmental information, so that they are better able to direct the behaviors of their child and themselves in relation to the child. Most focus on both parent and child factors. For example, a program provides education and training for the mother's employment as well as information of developmental needs of the child and modeling parental approaches to problem behaviors. These programs have proven successful for general prevention in at-risk populations and with the nonchronic status offender and nonviolent offender.

Early Education Programs. Academic achievement or lack thereof is a significant risk factor for problem behaviors. Early education programs focus on providing the child with a head start cognitively and socially. If children enter school ready to learn and knowing how to interact with others in a socially appropriate, nonaggressive way, they are more likely to succeed. These programs are targeted to at-risk populations.

Early Elementary School Programs. Focus additional training on social development for children identified as at risk because they engage in antisocial behaviors. In addition, many school districts provide general health promotion instruction for all children to encourage positive development. Mentoring and after-school leisure and recreation programs are added interventions.

Middle and High School Programs. Focus specifically on substance abuse education and alternatives; sex education; gang prevention; social conduct and peer relations, for example, peer mediation and counseling. Mentoring and after-school leisure and education programs continue in importance.

Specific Interventions. Focus on juveniles who have committed nonserious offenses. They are designed to specifically address the underlying issues that precipitated the offense with the expectation of "turning the juvenile around." Interventions include mental health counseling, substance abuse treatment, teen issues groups focused on providing general awareness and alternative approaches, intensive family preservation services, placement outside the parental home if that environment is found to contribute to the youth's problem behaviors, remedial education, vocational training, and supported employment.

Intervention with Chronic or Serious Juvenile Offenders

As stated previously, although the number of chronic or serious juvenile offenders is relatively small, they have been and continue to be the focus of both the public's and the policymakers' discourse. Although the person crimes arrest rates decreased, 24 percent of the 2004 delinquency caseload was adjudicated for person offenses, up from 19 percent in 1985. In addition, approximately 9,400 juveniles were waived to adult courts for serious offenses. This shifting in caseload composition necessitates a reexamination of the service continuum for serious offenders and expanded exploration of community-based alternatives (OJJDP, 2007b; Ziedenberg, 2006).

In 1993, OJJDP proposed a graduated sanctions model to address this issue. Specifically, this model combines treatment and rehabilitation with reasonable, fair, humane, and appropriate sanctions, and offers a continuum of care consisting of diverse programs. The continuum includes the following:

❖ immediate sanctions within the community for first-time, nonviolent offenders
❖ intermediate sanctions within the community for more serious offenders
❖ secure care programs for the most violent offenders
❖ after-care programs that provide high levels of social control and treatment services (Howell, 1995)

In implementing the graduated sanctions philosophy over the last ten years, practitioners have focused on risk assessments and interventions based on the juvenile's likelihood to reoffend based on the risk assessments. It is too early in the process to provide conclusive statements as to the effectiveness of this approach. To support graduated sanctions philosophy, several new program interventions have been added to the traditional group homes or institutions/training schools. They include boot camps, wilderness/survival programs, intensive community supervision, work-study-home detention, and individual mentoring. These programs are designed to give immediately more severe consequences to the youth with the hope that the youth will see that all behaviors have consequences (graduated sanctions). Some commentators suggest that the system was out of control because juveniles did not see any immediate consequences for their behaviors and continued to escalate until they had to be incarcerated because of the nature of the offenses. If the behaviors receive progressively more severe consequences, then escalation might not occur (Torbet, et al., 1996). The prevention and early intervention programs discussed earlier are critical to the continued decrease in the number of youth who commit serious or violent offenses because early antisocial behavior is generally documented in case histories of youth who commit these acts. Increasingly, interventions at the later childhood years are recognizing the need for multidimensional, integrated interventions instead of simply targeting the children and youth with school-based programs (Wasserman & Miller, 1998). No comprehensive evaluation has been completed on the effectiveness of the graduated sanctions philosophy.

THE FEMALE JUVENILE OFFENDER

Females accounted for 30 percent of the juvenile arrests in 2004 and 27 percent (approximately 450,000) of the delinquency cases handled by juvenile courts in 2004. Of the charged offenses, females accounted for 30 percent of the person offenses, 27 percent of the property offense, 20 percent of drug law violations, and 28 percent of the public order offenses (disorderly conduct, weapons offenses, liquor law violations, etc.) (OJJDP, 2007b). In 2004, approximately 142,000 charges involving females were adjudicated. Some charges noted previously had not been adjudicated as of the end of the 2004 reporting period (Stahl, Finnegan, & Kang, 2007).

Clearly, the juvenile justice system remains male offender dominated. However, it is concerning to policymakers and practitioners that the female offender proportionate share of delinquency cases rose from 19 percent in 1991 to 27 percent in 2004. Furthermore, female offenders are committing more serious, violent crimes, as noted previously. Aggravated assault is up 84 percent, homicides are up 58 percent, and forcible rape is up 63 percent (Snyder & Sickmund, 2006). It is unclear whether these changes reflect an increase in delinquent behavior by females or whether it reflects a change in the systems' response to their behaviors.

The research to date does not inform us as to why this trend has developed and continues (Snyder & Sickmund, 2006). From these data, it is clear that female offenders are found within all categories of offenders: status offenders, nonchronic offenders, and serious or chronic offenders.

In the 1996 edition of this text, we stated that juvenile delinquency in the United States is largely a male phenomenon: "Males under the age of 18 account for the overwhelming majority of arrests, the bulk of the referrals to juvenile courts, and the largest proportion of young people in detention centers and training schools across the country." Nevertheless, large numbers of girls enter the juvenile justice system each year, and some are inappropriately sent into institutions because few if any community-based programs have been provided for delinquent females. For the most part, these girls have been confined because of relatively minor delinquent acts. Follow-up studies have not produced clear evidence that locking girls into institutions has been helpful to them in any clear way. Instead, it appears that "most young female offenders can be managed and treated in their own community without compromising public safety." Nevertheless, troubled and delinquent girls continue to be neglected amid policy-maker preoccupation and public concern about violent juvenile crime, primarily committed by male adolescents (Schwartz & Orlando, 1991).

In the 2000 edition of this text, we stated that a 1996 study by Poe-Yamagata and Butts, *Female Offenders in the Juvenile Justice System,* found that juvenile female arrests for violent crimes increased 131 percent compared to juvenile male arrests for violent crimes, which increased by 66 percent between 1986 and 1995. Furthermore, juvenile female arrests for property crimes increased 38 percent while juvenile male arrests for property crimes increased only 1 percent. With these increases, females accounted for 20 percent of the juvenile violent crime arrest growth and 89 percent of the growth in property crime arrests. Since that report was issued, NCJJ has issued these additional findings:

❖ 702,200 juvenile females were arrested in 1995.
❖ By 1995, the ratio of male to female arrests for violent crimes was 6 to 1 and for property crimes was 3 to 1, down from 8 to 1 and 4 to 1, respectively, in 1986.
❖ The female proportion of all juvenile court cases increased from 19 percent to 21 percent between 1985 and 1995.

❖ In 1994 delinquency cases involving females were less likely to be adjudicated once petitioned (52 percent versus 56 percent), and females whose cases were processed formally were more likely to receive probation and less likely to be in detention or out-of-home placement. (National Center for Juvenile Justice, 1997)

The potential for change is contained in the Juvenile Justice and Delinquency Prevention Act (JJDPA). Federal funds are available for developing alternative programs for juvenile offenders. The act states specifically that assistance must be made available to "all disadvantaged youth, including . . . females." Young female offenders have some special needs that, for the most part, are not addressed in the juvenile justice system. They are frequently victims of sexual abuse and can see only one way to safety—to run away. In such instances they soon learn that there is no safety for them on the street. Access to crisis intervention services, shelter care, day treatment, therapeutic foster care, independent living arrangements, and, not to be overlooked, access to continued education are much needed.

The 1992 reauthorization of the JJDPA required states to include

An analysis of gender specific services for the prevention and treatment of juvenile delinquency, including the types of such services available and the need for such services for females; and a plan for providing needed gender-specific services for the prevention and treatment of juvenile delinquency.

The negative trending of female offender data, as well as the desire to assist states in meeting the requirements of the 1992 amendment to the JJDPA, led to a comprehensive report, *Juvenile Female Offenders: A Status of the States Report* (Maniglia, 1998). After a thorough review of national and state efforts, the author concludes

When the entire range of services is available for young women and when each individual program is developed with the young women's critical needs in mind, the system is more likely to be able to provide appropriate and effective placements, no matter what a young woman's level of involvement. (*p. 38*)

The report identifies the following "elements of a female continuum":

1. *Prevention services:* including services such as prenatal care for pregnant women, early childhood education, family living skills, comprehensive health and sexuality information, education, career development and life skills, and parenting skills.
2. *Early intervention and diversion services:* including gender-specific counseling; education; substance abuse education and intervention if necessary; skills in assertiveness in handling everyday life challenges such as domestic violence and abuse; alternatives to family placement: shelters, group homes, respite residential placements; and single gender support groups.
3. *Juvenile justice intervention services:* including all female treatment homes; specialized homes depending on her needs; staff-secure halfway houses or residential facilities with range of intervention services for nonchronic, nonviolent offenders; secure facilities

with range of intervention services for chronic or violent offenders; transition services; and after-care reintegration.

The report concludes

Although States have put forth a deliberate effort, the goal established by Congress to develop and adopt policies that prohibit gender bias and ensure that female youth have access to a full range of services remains a challenge. Policymakers, service providers and juvenile justice professionals have begun to realize the need for change in providing services to girls. What is required now is the commitment to evaluating services that work and implementing the necessary policies to warrant provision of effective programs for this too often ignored population. (*Ibid., p. 58*)

After an aborted attempt in 2001 to establish a researcher–practitioner study group to develop sound, theoretical foundations to guide development of strategies to effectively address female delinquency, OJJDP was successful in establishing the Girls Study Group in 2004. The goal of the group is to "develop a sound theoretical and empirical foundation to guide future development, testing, and dissemination of strategies to effectively prevent and reduce girls' involvement in delinquency and violence and to reduce the consequences of such involvement" (Allen-Hagen, 2004). To date, the Group has identified and conducted an evaluation of the effectiveness of girl only programs based on the stringent guidelines of the *What Works Repository*. It found that none of the eighteen evaluated could be classified as effective and only four could be classified as promising. Of the sixty-two programs identified, none met the effectiveness requirements for experimental research design, external replication, and evaluation, demonstrating significant and sustained effects. These results speak to the need to fund research, replication, and evaluation of gender-specific delinquency prevention and intervention programs (Zahn, 2007).

The Girls Study Group holds promise to help understand the causes and correlates of female delinquency and how the delinquency risk factors discussed previously may or may not be significant to female delinquency trajectories. Furthermore, knowledge of effective programming and services that are specific for the female offender should be forthcoming. Policymakers and practitioners know that the female offender has different trajectories toward delinquency, is differentially impacted by the common risk factors discussed earlier, has some risk factors that differ from the male offender, and requires different interventions that acknowledge differences in gender development and social context. Hopefully by the next edition of this book, we will have the empirical data to support this "knowledge" and will have implemented research methodologies and evaluation of programs that better inform policy and practice strategies—sixteen years is long enough! The reader is directed to the Girls Study Group web site, http://girlsstudygroup .rti.org, for contemporaneous reports on its findings and efforts.

TRENDS AND ISSUES

Although the juvenile justice system has changed greatly since passage of the Juvenile Justice and Delinquency Prevention Act in 1974, the issues that have plagued it since the early 1970s continue to remain of concern. Specifically, the nation's provisions for juvenile offenders have not yet resolved the following issues: overrepresentation of minorities; alternatives to the use of secure detention;

school violence; death penalty for juveniles; and the community's readiness to support alternative programs. These concerns reflect the increasing severity of mental health and substance abuse problems of juvenile offenders.

Overrepresentation of Minorities

Overrepresentation means that a particular racial or ethnic group is represented in a greater percentage in the juvenile justice system than it is represented in the general population. For example, if black youth are 15 percent of the general youth population and they are 25 percent of the juvenile justice system population, they are overrepresented in the juvenile justice system. However, if they were only 12 percent of the juvenile justice system population, they would be underrepresented.

The issue of overrepresentation of minorities in the juvenile justice system was first brought to national attention in 1988. Since that time, the JJDPA required states to address the issue of reducing *minority confinement* in the juvenile justice system to receive Formula Grant Program funds. The 2002 JJDPA amendments expanded this requirement to address the issue of reducing *minority contact* with the juvenile justice system. In 2006, OJJDP issued the third edition of *DMC Technical Assistance Manual* (Hsia, 2007).

Minorities include Blacks, Hispanics, Native Americans, Asians, and Pacific Islanders. Table 11.1 shows percentage, by race, of juveniles arrested, adjudicated, not adjudicated, and waived in relation to their percentage of the total juvenile population. In addition, while there was a 10 percent decline in the percentage of minority juveniles in custody between 1997 to 2003, they still comprised 61 percent of the "confined" or "in-custody" juvenile population with Blacks accounting for 38 percent and Hispanics accounting for 19 percent (Snyder & Sickmund, 2006).

Table 11.1 *Arrest, Adjudication, and Waiver by Race*

Count	Percent of Population 2004	Percent of Juveniles Arrested	Percent of All Juveniles Adjudicated	Percent of All Juveniles Not Adjudicated	Percent of All Juveniles Waived
White	78	60	65	67	55
Black	17	37	32	30	42
American Indian	1	1	1.7	1.5	2
Asian/Pacific Islander	4	2	1.5	1.4	.9
Total	100	100	100.2	99.9	99.9

Sources: Stahl, A., Finnegan, T., & Kang, W. (2007). *Easy access to juvenile court statistics: 1985–2004.* Available: http://ojjdp.ncjrs.gov/ojstatbb/ezajcs/.
Snyder, H. N., & Sickmund, M. (2006, March). *Juvenile offenders and victims: 2006 national report.* available: http://ojjdp.ncjrs.gov.

The data supports that Blacks continue to be overrepresented at all points in the juvenile justice system. Despite addressing this concern for almost twenty years, we cannot provide a definitive explanation for the persistent minority overrepresentation at every stage of the juvenile justice system (Snyder & Sigmund, 2006). A recent study found that, compared to white youth who commit the same type of offense, they are more likely to be arrested and less likely to be released while awaiting trial. A Florida study found that "Florida courts were three times as likely to transfer an African-American or Native American charged with delinquency to adult court than they were to transfer his or her white counterpart. The impact on African Americans was particularly disproportionate, and they were far more likely to be sentenced to detention by a juvenile court" (American Bar Association, 1993, p. 62).

As stated previously, a 1992 amendment to the Juvenile Justice and Delinquency Prevention Act requires states to reduce the number of minority youth in detention, but the federal government has not enforced this provision in the law. The ABA Presidential Working Group on the Unmet Legal Needs of Children and Their Families (American Bar Association, 1993) recommended that communities develop culturally sensitive training for police and judges and increase the representation of minority staff at the juvenile court. They also recommended that effective grievance procedures be instituted for situations in which the police use excessive force or other situations relating to ethnic, racial, or gender bias.

In 2000, the Office of Juvenile Justice and Delinquency Prevention reported that African American juveniles, who comprised 15 percent of the juvenile population in 1996, accounted for 28 percent of all juvenile arrests, 58 percent of murder arrests, 45 percent of forcible rape arrests, 60 percent of robbery arrests, 42 percent of aggravated assault arrests, 38 percent of motor vehicle theft arrests, 42 percent of fraud arrests, and 77 percent of gambling arrests. Additionally minority youth, including African Americans, Hispanics, Asian/ Pacific Islanders, and Native Americans, who were 32 percent of the youth population in 1996, made up 68 percent of the detention center population on the day in time chosen. Further, they represented 68 percent of the juveniles in public long-term facilities (Snyder & Sickmund, 2000).

Despite addressing this concern for over twenty years, we cannot provide a definitive explanation. Research to date has presented inconsistent findings. Since 1970, research has focused on the effects of race, race and gender, and race and family status on decisions at all stages of the juvenile justice system. The findings have been inconsistent (Leiber & Mack, 2003, p. 35). Recent data analyses and studies show that blacks' overrepresentation in the juvenile justice system was greater in 1996 than in 1987. Overrepresentation occurs at all stages of the juvenile justice system: referrals to juvenile court, detention, adjudication, probation, and residential placement (Snyder & Sickmund, 2000).

Leiber (2002) conducted an analysis of state and federal efforts based on compliance reports submitted to OJJDP. He concluded that OJJDP's weak enforcement of the 1992 JJDPA requirement that the states reduce disproportionate minority youth confinement (DMC) and its lack of direction to the states produced identification and assessment reports fraught with weaknesses and incapable of generalization. Within the last two years, OJJDP has taken a more active role and Leiber (2002) submits,

> OJJDP has begun to address these deficiencies and the benefits of these efforts may result in a greater number of states becoming more committed to DMC and information to better inform strategies to reduce the disproportionate representation of minority youth in our juvenile justice system. (p. 6)

Leiber and Mack (2003) argue that race alone may not be the determining factor for overrepresentation of minority youth in the juvenile justice system. They suggest that race, gender, and family considerations must be evaluated in combination to discern the reason for the overrepresentation. Research studies had examined each of these variables independently; none had attempted to examine the interactional effects. Leiber and Mack (2003) took a random sample of cases in four Iowa jurisdictions over a twelve-year period, 1980 to 1991. They concluded, "Being African American interacts very little with gender and family status to influence juvenile justice outcomes . . ."(p. 58).

In the 2002 Formula Grant applications from forty-six states, the District of Columbia, and four territories, states identified the following contributing factors to DMC:

❖ *Juvenile justice system:* Racial stereotyping and cultural insensitivity, lack of alternatives to detention and incarceration, misuse of discretionary authority in implementing laws and policies, lack of culturally and linguistically appropriate services

❖ *Educational System:* Lack of educational resources in schools in minority neighborhoods, failure of the schools to engage minority students and their families, high dropout rates for minority students

❖ *Socioeconomic conditions:* Poverty, substance abuse, high unemployment, high crime rates in minority neighborhoods, more serious crimes committed by minority youth

❖ *Family conditions:* Family disintegration, diminished traditional family values, single-parent households, parental substance abuse, poor supervision

To address these factors, states reported taking or planning to take the following actions:

❖ develop more community-based prevention, intervention, and diversion programs.

❖ conduct cultural sensitivity trainings.

❖ develop linguistically competent informational materials and staff.

❖ empower communities to monitor the problem.

❖ use standardized screening instruments.

❖ strengthen state leadership on the issue.

❖ improve juvenile justice information systems for collection of reliable data.

❖ Create legislation mandating cultural competency, prosecutorial standards, experimental programs, and annual reports to the legislature.

OJJDP identified the following remaining challenges:

❖ eighteen states have not completed identification of factors contributing to DMC,

❖ inadequate data systems to collect and track the data required,

❖ lack of ongoing evaluation of intervention efforts and data-driven modifications,

❖ inadequate system change strategies, and

❖ lack of institutionalization of mechanisms to assess and respond to DMC issues.

(Hsia, Bridges, & McHale, 2004)

This remains a complex issue requiring focused, objective attention from researchers, policy-makers, practitioners, youth, their families, and communities to solve. Unfortunately, issues involving race rarely are approached with "objectivity" in the United States.

Alternatives to the Use of Secure Detention

Criteria established by the National Council on Crime and Delinquency for admission of children and youth into secure detention emphasize that detention should not be used "unless failure to do so would be likely to place the child or the community in danger" (Pappenfort & Young, 1980, p. 99). In all jurisdictions, courts are faced at times with children who, after arrest or some other form of intake, cannot be returned home. In such instances, secure detention is often misused. The reasons given in justification are numerous: (1) A child's psychiatric and neurological problems require attention, and no alternative to detention is available. (2) Neglected and dependent children are sometimes classified as children in need of supervision and detained, pointing up in another way the common characteristics of status offenders and other children before the court. (3) Some youth must be detained to prevent the chance of their committing a delinquent act or engaging in incorrigible behavior while awaiting adjudication. (4) Some children go into secure detention only because there is no other place for them to stay. (5) Some children who present little or no danger to themselves or the community go into detention so that they can be readily referred into services that otherwise would not be available to them (Pappenfort & Young, 1980).

Many jurisdictions are attempting to avoid inappropriate use of detention by developing strict criteria for its use, by reviewing early the detention decisions by a juvenile court judge, and by developing nonresidential and residential alternatives. Home detention is one such alternative. Youths are released to their parents to await court hearings with supervision by a youth worker attached to the court's probation department (Howell, 1997). Residential group homes also are used as alternatives to detention and are frequently directed toward runaway children, a type of status offender generally considered to be troublesome to deal with effectively. Another alternative to detention is found in some jurisdictions in which foster parents are paid an annual salary to make their homes available for youths on a short-term basis. The foster parent role is to provide care and supervision as well as companionship to troubled youth awaiting court hearings (Austin, Johnson, Weitzer, 2005).

The Annie E. Casey Foundation supported the Juvenile Detention Alternatives Initiative in Sacramento County, California, Cook County, Illinois, and Multnomah County, Oregon, from 1993 through 1997. Two other sites, New York City and Milwaukee, Wisconsin, terminated involvement quite early in the project. The Initiative's objectives were to reduce unnecessary or inappropriate detentions; to minimize the number of youth who do reoffend pending adjudication or fail to appear for court hearings; to redirect public funds to reform strategies; and to improve conditions of confinement (Annie E. Casey Foundation, 2003). Preliminary results show that detention admissions dropped in all three counties until 1997, when they went up in all counties. Youth failure to appear at court hearings decreased and youth arrested again before trial remained the same. In addition, courts reduced their case processing times.

These results occurred by

❖ specifying the offenses for which detention would be required, typically the violent, person offenses, and those that would be subject to review using a risk assessment tool for alternative assignment. This was a necessary prerequisite to calm the anxieties of both the law enforcement/juvenile justice professionals as well as the community. Judge William Hibbler, presiding judge of Cook County Juvenile Court, said

> With everybody out there talking about how we need to lock more kids up, you don't want to go around wearing a button that says, "I'm for detention alternatives." You need an educational process to let people know that this is not a crazy idea. (*Stanfield, 2000, p. 9*)

❖ developing alternatives: including house arrest with electronic monitoring bracelets; day and evening reporting centers; graduated sanctions, that is, violate and automatically given detention; nonsecure foster and group home placements.

❖ developing comprehensive, collaborative approaches with law enforcement, education, mental health, and substance abuse programs.

Casey Foundation funding for the projects ended in 1999. All the projects were continued. The lessons learned from these projects have been shared with many other jurisdictions. It is expected that many more jurisdictions will see reductions in unnecessary and inappropriate detentions over the next five years. The repeat status offender is presenting ongoing challenges to alternatives to detention. Many jurisdictions are using an approach of warning them at disposition that they will be placed in detention if they absent themselves from home or community placement, fail to attend school, or use liquor or drugs. It is too early to determine whether this approach will reduce the number of repeat status offenders who are detained in secure facilities.

Risk classification and risk assessment instruments that predict the likelihood of recidivism or commission of another crime have been found to be useful to courts in determining appropriate alternatives to secure detention. As these instruments are refined and their use increases, coupled with increasing costs and overcrowding in juvenile detention facilities, development and use of alternatives that ensure public safety and youth presence at court hearings will increase (Gottfredson & Snyder, 2005).

School Violence

Because of several high-profile cases, attention to school violence issues increased tremendously. Fatal crimes against students occurring on school property, at school events, or going to and from school are relatively rare. Approximately 54.9 million students were enrolled in prekindergarten through twelfth grade in the 2004–2005 school year. There were twenty-eight school-associated deaths reported—twenty-one homicides and seven suicides for students aged 5 to 18 years. In addition, there were 863,000 thefts, 476,000 simple assaults, and 107,000 serious violent crimes (rape, sexual assault, robbery, and aggravated assault) of students aged of 12 to 18. Primary and high schools reported lower rates of thefts and violent crimes than middle schools (Dinkes, Cataldi, Kena, & Baum, 2006).

The rate of crime against students at school declined 53 percent for theft and 42 percent for all violent crime from 1992 through 2004. There were 33 thefts per 1,000 students and 22 violent crimes per 1,000 students in 2004. In all years, the rate of violent crime was lower when students were at school than when they were not (U.S. Department of Education, 2006).

Bullying and use of hate-related words continue to be growing issues in the school environment. In 2005, 28 percent of students aged 12 to 18 reported being bullied at school, 11 percent reported use of hate words against them, and 33 percent reported hate-related graffiti at school (Dinkes, et al., 2006).

Student use of alcohol (43 percent of students consumed alcohol and 4 percent consumed alcohol on school premises) and illegal substances (23 percent used marijuana and 5 percent used marijuana on school property) is alarming although use on school premises is rather small (Dinkes, et al., 2006).

Reported threats and physical attacks on teachers is rather low (7 percent). These reports varied by location, with 10 percent of urban teachers reporting threats and 5 percent reporting physical attacks; these numbers were 6 percent and 3 percent for teachers in urban fringe schools and 5 percent and 3 percent for teachers in rural schools. Elementary school teachers were more likely than secondary school teachers to report being physically attacked by students (4 versus 2 percent) (Dinkes, et al., 2006).

Pollack and Sundermann (2001), citing a 2000 report from the U.S. Department of Education and the U.S. Department of Justice, state: "Although some may perceive schools as dangerous, schools remain the safest place for a child to be" (p. 14). They suggest that creating safe schools includes having comprehensive prevention and intervention strategies; an emergency response plan; a positive, respectful environment; partnerships with law enforcement, mental health, and social services; and encouraging parental and community involvement. While the incidence of violence at schools or school-related events is comparatively small, schools are seen as a natural site to educate children in alternatives to violence.

Community Readiness to Support Alternative Programs

The term *community-based* implies an intention to enable troubled youth to retain their ties to persons in the community, to move about and communicate freely within the community, and to experience some degree of acceptance from others in the community. Yet community residents often object to plans for alternative programs. Such proposals, especially for residential programs, often bring prompt and vigorous opposition on the assumption that the kind of youth served would be a danger to the surrounding neighborhood. Somewhat paradoxically, professional interests and federal guidelines that favor community-based alternatives came at a time when many citizens were expressing intense fear about delinquency and crime, and state legislatures were enacting more restrictive laws affecting the handling of law offenders generally. Those statements are as accurate today as when stated by citizens in 1996. There is some hope of community support, as evidenced by the expansion of diversion and early intervention programs for less serious offenders. But, as to the serious and chronic offender, community support for community-based alternatives does not exist (Howell, 1995, 1997).

CHAPTER SUMMARY

This chapter has focused on juvenile delinquency. The chapter gives voice to juveniles involved in delinquent activities and discusses delinquency within the scope of child welfare and family services. Historically, U.S. society has addressed these youth separately from abused, neglected, and abandoned youth. Increasingly, society is seeing that they are the same or that some children in the same family carry abuse or neglect labels while others carry juvenile delinquent labels. If society is to develop effective child, family, and community interventions to prevent and treat child abuse, neglect, and delinquency, we must begin to look at children and families holistically.

The November, 2002, Amendments to the Juvenile Justice and Delinquency Prevention Act recognize the interconnection between the child welfare and the juvenile justice systems. States are required to implement policies across systems to ensure sharing of case information necessary for treatment planning and services, and require case plans and review policies and procedures for federally funded (Title IV-E) delinquency cases similar to those required for abuse and neglect under Title IV-E.

This chapter provided an overview of the scope of the problem, the types of offenses committed by juveniles, the processing of juveniles in the juvenile court and criminal court systems, some persistent issues, and some promising interventions.

FOR STUDY AND DISCUSSION
STUDY AND DISCUSSION QUESTIONS

1. Explain and evaluate the aims of the juvenile justice system. How do they differ from those of the adult corrections system?

2. Give arguments to support either the traditional benevolent-rehabilitative model of the juvenile court or a model based on constitutional guarantees of due process and legal justice.

3. Obtain a copy of the juvenile court act in your state or some other. Evaluate it in these terms:

    a. What is the expressed intent of the act? How well does this intent reflect a modern juvenile court philosophy?

    b. Compare its definitions of classes of children who come under its jurisdiction to the categories discussed in this chapter.

    c. What indications are there in the statute that the child's and parent's constitutional rights shall be respected?

    d. How adequate are the act's provisions in regard to personnel and services of the court?

4. What are some of the principal differences between children and youth who are (a) neglected or abused, (b) delinquent, or (c) guilty of a status offense? What are some of their similarities?

5. How would you design an "ideal" juvenile delinquency program? What would be its features? Why? How could stigma be averted?

6. What would you do to minimize minority overrepresentation? What services would be unique for girls and why?

7. Review the data discussed in the Scope of the Problem section. Is delinquent behavior as serious as the media projects? Explain your answer.

8. Develop a truancy reduction program for your school district usng the *Toolkit*.

Internet Sites

ABA Center on Children and the Law. This Center, a program of the American Bar Association, aims to improve children's lives through advances in law, justice, knowledge, practice, and public policy.
www.abanet.org/child/home.html

Girls Study Group. This web site offers specific information on girls in the juvenile justice system. The Study Group is comprised of researchers from several universities, governmental units, and juvenile justice practitioners.
http://girlsstudygroup.rti.org

National Center for Juvenile Justice. The Center is a resource for independent and original research on topics related directly and indirectly to the field of juvenile justice. It is the research division of the National Council of Juvenile and Family Court Judges.
www.ncjj.org

National Center for School Engagement. This Center provides extensive research and program guidance on school engagement issues.
www.schoolengagement.org or
www.truancyprevention.org

National Council of Juvenile and Family Court Judges, Inc. The Council's mission to improve courts and systems practice and raise awareness of the core issues that touch the lives of many of our nation's children and families.
www.ncjfcj.org/

Office of Juvenile Justice and Delinquency Prevention (OJJDP). Located within the U.S. Department of Justice, OJJDP is responsible for administering Federal policies and funding for the juvenile justice system. It is the most comprehensive web site for information on juvenile delinquency and for links to other credible web sites. The Disproportionate Minority Contact program locate within OJJDP can be accessed directly at http://ojjdp.ncjrs.gov/dmc/index.html.
http://ojjdp.ncjrs.org

U.S. Department of Education, Office of Safe and Drug-Free Schools. This Office administers federal mandates and funding. It maintains extensive information on prevalence of the problems and promising interventions regarding drugs and schools.
www.ed.gov/osdfs

References

Acoca, L. (1999 October). Investing in Girls: A 21st century strategy. *Juvenile Justice, VI* (1), 3–13. Washington, DC: OJJDP.

Allen-Hagen, B. (2004, September). *Overview of OJJDP girls study group program requirements.* Washington, DC: U.S. Department of Justice, Office of Justice Programs, Office of Juvenile Justice and Delinquency Prevention. Available: www.ojp.usdoj.gov/ojjdp.

American Bar Association. (1993). *Unmet legal needs of children and their families.* Chicago: American Bar Association.

Annie E. Casey Foundation. (2003). *Juvenile detention initiatives.* Available: www.aecf.org/programs.

Austin, J., Johnson, K. D., & Weitzer, R. (2005, September). *Alternatives to the secure detention and confinement of juvenile offenders.* Washington, DC: U.S. Department of Justice, Office of Justice Programs, Office of Juvenile Justice and Delinquency Prevention. Available: www.ojp.usdoj.gov/ojjdp.

Ayers, W. (1997). *A kind and just parent: The children of the juvenile court.* Boston: Beacon Press.

Bazemore, G. (2001). Young people, trouble, and crime: Restorative justice as a normative theory of informal social control and social support. *Youth and Society, 33*(2), 199–226. Thousand Oaks, CA: Sage.

Behrman, R. E. (Ed.). (2002, Summer–Fall). *Children, youth and gun violence. The Future of Children, 12*(2).

Breckenridge, S., & Abbott, E. (1912). *The delinquent child and the home.* New York: Russell Sage Foundation.

Breed v. Jones, 421 U.S. 519 (1975).

Butts, J., & Mears, D. P. (2001). Reviving juvenile justice in a get-tough era. *Youth and Society, 33*(2), 169–198. Thousand Oaks, CA: Sage.

Butts, J. A. (1997, April). Prosecuting juveniles in criminal court. *National Center for Juvenile Justice in brief vol. 1* (No. 4). Pittsburgh, PA: National Center for Juvenile Justice.

Dean, C. W., & Reppucci, N. D. (1974). Juvenile correctional instructions. In D. Glasser (Ed.), *Handbook of criminology* (pp. 865–894). Chicago, IL: Rand-McNally.

Dinkes, R., Cataldi, E. F., Kena, G., & Baum, K. (2006, December). *Indicators of school crime and safety: 2006.* U.S. Departments of Education and Justice. Washington, DC: U.S. Government Printing Office.

Egley, A., & Ritz, C. E. (2006, April). *Highlights of the 2004 national youth gang survey.* Washington, DC: U.S. Department of Justice, Office of Justice Programs, Office of Juvenile Justice and Delinquency Prevention. Available: www.ojp.usdoj.gov/ojjdp.

Empey, L. T., & Stafford, M. C. (1991). *American delinquency: Its meaning and construction* (3rd ed.). Belmont, CA: Wadsworth.

Finestone, H. (1976). *Victims of change.* Westport, CT: Greenwood.

Finkelhor, D., Cross, T. P., & Cantor, E. N. (2005, December). *How the justice system responds to juvenile victims: A comprehensive model.* Washington, DC: U.S. Department of Justice, Office of Justice Programs, Office of Juvenile Justice and Delinquency Prevention. Available: www.ojp.usdoj.gov/ojjdp.

Flexner, B., & Baldwin, R. N. (1914). *Juvenile courts and probation.* New York: Century.

Flowers, R. B. (2002). *Kids who commit adult crimes.* Binghamton, NY: Haworth.

Gottfredson, D. M. (Ed.). (2000). *Juvenile justice with eyes wide open: Methods for improving information for juvenile justice.* Pittsburgh, PA: National Center for Juvenile Justice.

Gottfredson, D. M., & Snyder, H. N. (2005, July). *The mathematics of risk classification: Changing data into valid instruments for juvenile courts.* Washington, DC: U.S. Department of Justice, Office of Justice Programs, Office of Juvenile Justice and Delinquency Prevention. Available: www.ojp.usdoj.gov/ojjdp.

Grisso, T., & Underwood, L. (2004, December). *Screening and assessing mental health and substance use disorders among youth in the juvenile justice system: A resource guide for practitioners.* Washington, DC: U.S. Department of Justice, Office of Justice Programs, Office of Juvenile Justice and Delinquency Prevention. Available: www.ojp. usdoj.gov/ojjdp.

Hawkins, J. D., & Catalano, R. F. (1992). *Communities that care.* San Francisco: Jossey-Bass.

Heide, K. M. (1999). *Young killers: The challenge of juvenile homicide.* Thousand Oaks, CA: Sage.

Howell, J. C. (1995). *Guide for implementing the comprehensive strategy for serious, violent, and chronic juvenile offenders.* Washington, DC: Office of Juvenile Justice and Delinquency Prevention.

Howell, J. C. (1997). *Juvenile justice and youth policy.* Thousand Oaks, CA: Sage.

Hsia, H.M. (2007). *A disproportionate minority contact (DMC) chronology: 1988 to date.* Washington, DC: U.S. Department of Justice, Office of Justice Programs, Office of Juvenile Justice and Delinquency Prevention. Available: http://ojjdp/ncjrs.gov/dmc.

Hsia, H. M., Bridges, G. S., & McHale, R. (2004, September). *Disproportionate minority confinement: 2002 update.* Washington, DC: U.S. Department of Justice, Office of Justice Programs, Office of Juvenile Justice and Delinquency Prevention. Available: www.ojp.usdoj.gov/ojjdp.

In re Gault, 387 U.S. 1 (1967).

In re Kevin Nigel Stanford, 537 U.S. _____ (2002).

In re Winship, 397 U.S. 358 (1970).

Jacobs, T. A. (1995, supp. 1997). *Children and the law: Rights and obligations.* St. Paul, MN: West.

Jonson-Reid, M., & Barth, R. P. (2000). From placement to prison: The path to adolescent incarceration from child welfare supervised foster or group care. *Children and Youth Services Review, 22*(7), 493–516.

Kelley, B. T., Thornberry, T. P., & Smith, C. A. (1997, August). *In the wake of childhood maltreatment.* Washington, DC: Office of Juvenile Justice and Delinquency Prevention.

Kelly, B. T., Huizinga, D., Thornberry, T. P., & Loeber, R. (1997, June). *Epidemiology of serious violence.* Washington, DC: Office of Juvenile Justice and Delinquency Prevention.

Kendall, J. R. (2007). *Families in need of critical assistance. Legislation and policy aiding youth who engage in noncriminal misbehavior.* Washington, DC: American Bar Association Center on Children and the Law.

Kent v. United States, 383 U.S. 541 (1966).

Kramer, D. T. (1994, supp. 2000). *Legal rights of children* (2nd ed.). Colorado Springs: Shepards/McGraw Hill.

Kuffer, D. A. (2004). Death penalty for juveniles: Has a national consensus been reached? A look at the modern legal history of the juvenile death penalty. *Children's Legal Rights Journal, 24*(2), 12–21.

Leiber, M. J. (2002). State responses to disproportionate minority youth confinement. *The Prevention Report, 2002* (1). Iowa City, IA: The National Resource Center for Family Centered Practice.

Leiber, M. J., & Mack, K. Y. (2003). The individual and joint effects of race, gender, and family status on juvenile justice decision making. *Journal of Research in Crime and Delinquency, 40*(1), 34–70. Thousand Oaks, CA: Sage.

Livsey, S. (2006, November). *Juvenile delinquency probation caseload, 1985–2002.* Washington, DC: U.S. Department of Justice, Office of Justice Programs, Office of Juvenile Justice and Delinquency Prevention. Available: www. ojp. usdoj. gov/ ojjdp.

Loeber, R., & Farrington, D. P. (Eds.). (1998). *Serious and violent offenders: Risk factors and successful interventions.* Thousand Oaks, CA: Sage.

Maniglia, R. (1998). *Juvenile female offenders: A status of the states report.* Washington, DC: Office of Juvenile Justice and Delinquency Prevention.

Mankey, J., Baca, P., Rondenell, B. S., Webb, M., & McHugh, J. D. (2006, October). *Guidelines for juvenile information sharing.* Washington, DC: U.S. Department of Justice, Office of Justice Programs, Office of Juvenile Justice and Delinquency Prevention. Available: www. ojp. usdoj.gov/ojjdp.

McKeiver v. Pennsylvania, 403 U.S. 538 (1971).

Mihalic, S., Fagan, A., Irwin, K., Ballard, D., & Elliott, D. (2004, July). *Blueprints for violence prevention.* Washington, DC: U.S. Department of Justice, Office of Justice Programs, Office of Juvenile Justice and Delinquency Prevention. Available: www. ojp. usdoj.gov/ojjdp.

Miner, M. H. (2002). Factors associated with recidivism in juveniles: an analysis of serious juvenile sex offenders. *Journal of Research in Crime and Delinquency, 39*(4), 421–436. Thousand Oaks, CA: Sage.

Muck, R., Zempolich, K. A., Titus, J. C., Fishman, M., Godley, M. D., & Schwebel, R. (2001). An overview of the effectiveness of adolescent substance abuse treatment models. *Youth and Society, 33*(2), 143–168. Thousand Oaks, CA: Sage.

National Center for Juvenile Justice. (2000). *NCJJ in brief.* Pittsburgh, PA: National Center for Juvenile Justice.

Office of Juvenile Justice and Delinquency Prevention. (1997). *Juvenile offenders and victims: 1997 update on violence: Statistics summary.* Pittsburgh, PA: National Center for Juvenile Justice.

Office of Juvenile Justice and Delinquency Prevention. (2007a, February). *A toolkit for creating your own truancy reduction program.* Washington, DC: U.S. Department of Justice, Office of Justice Programs, Office of Juvenile Justice and Delinquency Prevention. Available: www.ojp.usdoj.gov/ojjdp.

Office of Juvenile Justice and Delinquency Prevention. (2007b). *OJJDP Statistical Briefing Book.* Available: http://ojjdp.ncjrs.gov/ojstatbb/court/qa06206.qaDate=2004.

Pappenfort, D. M., & Young, T. W. (1980, December). *Use of secure detention for juveniles and alternatives to its use: A national study of juvenile detention.* Office of Juvenile Justice and Delinquency Prevention. Washington, DC: U.S. Government Printing Office.

Poe-Yamagata, E. (1997, March). *Detention and delinquency cases, 1985–1995* (Office of

Juvenile Justice and Delinquency Prevention Fact Sheet #56). Washington, DC: Office of Juvenile Justice and Delinquency Prevention.

Poe-Yamagata, E. (1997, February). Female participation in delinquent behavior is on the rise. *NCJJ in Brief, 1*(2). Pittsburgh, PA: National Center for Juvenile Justice.

Poe-Yamagata, E., & Butts, J. A. (1996). *Female offenders in the juvenile justice system.* Washington, DC: U.S. Department of Justice, Office of Juvenile Justice and Delinquency Prevention.

Pollack, I., & Sundermann, C. (2001). Creating safe schools: A comprehensive approach. *Juvenile Justice, 7*(1), 13–20.

Reaves, B. A. (2006, July). *Violent felons in large urban counties.* Washington, DC: U.S. Department of Justice, Office of Justice Programs, Office of Juvenile Justice and Delinquency Prevention. Available: www.ojp.usdoj.gov/ojjdp.

Reitsma-Street, M. (2004). Radical pragmatism: Prevention and intervention with girls in conflict with the law. *Children & Youth Services Review, 26*(2), 119–137.

Roper v. Simmons, 543, U.S. 1 (2005).

Saltzman, A., & Proch, K. (1990). *Law in social work practice.* Chicago: Nelson-Hall.

Scalia, J. (1997, January). *Juvenile delinquents in the federal criminal justice system.* Washington, DC: Office of Juvenile Justice and Delinquency Prevention.

Schall v. Martin, 467 U.S. 253 (1984).

Schwartz, I., & Orlando, F. (1991). *Programming for young women in the juvenile justice system.* Ann Arbor: University of Michigan, Center for the Study of Youth Policy.

Shepherd, R. E., Jr. (1999). The child grows up: The juvenile justice system enters its second century. *Family Law Quarterly, 33*(3), 589–605.

Sickmund, M. (2003). *Juveniles in corrections.* Washington, DC: Office of Juvenile Justice and Delinquency Prevention.

Sickmund, M. (2006, June). *Juvenile residential facility census, 2002: Selected findings.* Washington, DC: U.S. Department of Justice, Office of Justice Programs, Office of Juvenile Justice and Delinquency Prevention. Available: www.ojp.usdoj.gov/ojjdp.

Siegel, J. A., & Williams, L. M. (2003). The relationship between child sexual abuse and female delinquency and crime: A prospective study. *Journal of Research in Crime and Delinquency, 40*(1), 71–94.

Simonsen, C. (1991). *Status offenders: An attempt to clarify the system. Juvenile justice in America.* New York: Macmillan.

Skowyra, K., & Cocozza, J. J. (2006, June). *A blueprint for change: Improving the system response to youth with mental health needs involved with the juvenile justice system.* Delmar, NY: National Center for Mental Health and Juvenile Justice. Available: www.ncmhjj.com.

Small, M., & Tetrick, K. D. (2001). School violence: An overview. *Juvenile Justice, 7*(1), 3–12.

Smith, C. P., Berkman, D. J., Fraser, W. M., & Sutton, J. (1980). *Jurisdiction and the elusive status offender: A comparison of involvement in delinquent behavior and status offenses.* U.S. Department of Justice, Law Enforcement Assistance Administration, Office of Juvenile Justice and Delinquency Prevention. Washington, DC: U.S. Government Printing Office.

Snyder, H. N. (2000, December). *Juvenile arrests 1999.* Washington DC: Office of Juvenile Justice and Delinquency Prevention.

Snyder, H. N. (2006, December). *Juvenile arrests 2004.* Washington, DC: U.S. Department of Justice, Office of Justice Programs, Office of Juvenile Justice and Delinquency Prevention. Available: www.ojp.usdoj.gov/ojjdp.

Snyder, H. N., & Sickmund, M. (2000). *Juvenile offenders and victims 1999 national report.* Washington, DC: Office of Juvenile Justice and Delinquency Prevention.

Snyder, H. N., & Sickmund, M. (2006, March). *Juvenile offenders and victims: 2006 national report.* Washington, DC: U.S. Department of Justice, Office of Justice Programs, Office of Juvenile Justice and Delinquency Prevention. Available: www.ojp. usdoj.gov/ojjdp.

Stahl, A., Finnegan, T., & Kang, W. (2004). *Easy access to juvenile court statistics 1985–2004.* Available: http:ojjdp.ncjrs.gov/ojstatbb/ezajcs.

Stahl, A. L. (2006, November). *Delinquency cases in juvenile court, 2002.* Washington, DC: U.S. Department of Justice, Office of

Justice Programs, Office of Juvenile Justice and Delinquency Prevention. Available: www.ojp.usdoj.gov/ojjdp.

Stahl, A. L., Puzzanchera, C., Sladky, A., Finnegan, T. A., Tierney, N., & Snyder, H. N. (2005, December). *Juvenile court statistics 2001–2002.* Pittsburg, PA: National Center for Juvenile Justice.

Stanfield, R. (2000). *Pathways to juvenile detention reform: The JDAI story: building a better juvenile detention system.* Baltimore, MD: Annie E. Casey Foundation. Available: www.aecf.org/publications/pdfs/pathways8.pdf.

Stanford v. Kentucky, 482 U.S. 361 (1989).

Teplin, L. A., Abram, K. M., McClelland, G. M., Mericle, A. A., Dulcan, M. K. & Washburn, J. J. (2006, April). *Psychiatric disorders of youth in detention.* Washington, DC: U.S. Department of Justice, Office of Justice Programs, Office of Juvenile Justice and Delinquency Prevention. Available: www.ojp.usdoj.gov/ojjdp.

Thompson v. Oklahoma, 487 U.S. 815 (1988).

Thornberry, T. P., Huizinga, D., & Loeber, R. (2004, September). The causes and correlates studies: Findings and policy implications. *Juvenile Justice, IX*(1), 3–19.

Thornberry, T. P., & Krohn, M. D. (2003). *Taking stock of delinquency: An overview of findings from contemporary longitudinal studies.* New York: Kluwer/Plenum Publishers.

Torbet, P. et al. (1996). *State responses to serious and violent juvenile crime.* Washington, DC: Office of Juvenile Justice and Delinquency Prevention.

U.S. Department of Education, National Center for Education Statistics. (2006). *The condition of education 2006.* NCES 2006-071. Washington, DC: U.S. Government Printing Office.

Wasserman, G., Ko, S., & McReynolds, L. (2004, August). Assessing the mental health status of youth in juvenile justice settings. *Juvenile Justice Bulletin, 8*, 1–7.

Wasserman, G. A., & Miller, L. S. (1998). The prevention of serious and violent juvenile offending. In R. Loeber & D. P. Farrington (Eds.), *Serious and violent juvenile offenders: Risk factors and successful interventions.* Thousand Oaks, CA: Sage.

Weis, J. G., Sakumato, K., Sederstrom, J., & Seiss, C. (1980). *Reports of the national juvenile justice assessment centers: Jurisdiction and the elusive status offender: A comparison of involvement in delinquent behavior and status offenses.* U.S. Department of Justice, Law Enforcement Assistance Administration, Office of Juvenile Justice and Delinquency Prevention. Washington, DC: U.S. Government Printing Office.

Zahn, M. A. (2007). Girls Study Group. Presented at National Juvenile Justice Networking Forum, June 14, 2007 in Washington, DC: Available: http://girlsstudygroup.rti.org.

Zavlek, S. (2005, August). *Planning community-based facilities for violent juvenile offenders as part of a system of graduated sanctions.* Washington, DC: U.S. Department of Justice, Office of Justice Programs, Office of Juvenile Justice and Delinquency Prevention. Available: www.ojp.usdoj.gov/ojjdp.

Ziedenberg, J. (2006, December). *Models for change: Building momentum for juvenile justice reform.* Washington, DC: Justice Policy Institute. Available: www.justicepolicy.org.

CHAPTER 12

Professional Responsibilities

Ethics and Advocacy

Vision without action is merely a dream. Action without vision just passes the time. Vision with action can change the world.

—Joel Arthur Barker, The Power of Vision

CHAPTER OUTLINE

Susan Smith is a child welfare worker for the Big County Children's Services Agency (BCCSA). She has worked in child welfare for two years since receiving her MSW from Big State University. She has had approximately eight days of program-specific training and attended a one-day conference on permanency planning since employment. She is a member of the National Association of Social Workers (NASW). She began employment in BCCSA in the protective services program and moved into the foster care program approximately six months ago.

Last week Susan received the Blue case. There are three children, Mary (4 years old), Michael (2 years old), and Joseph (2 weeks old). The case came to protective services on a complaint from the hospital that Joseph was born drug addicted. The protective services worker recommended that a petition be filed and all children be removed from the home.

Susan's initial assessment, based on the materials in the files, was that the children should not have been removed from the home. The case file stated that the mother denied using cocaine on an ongoing basis. She stated that she went to a party about two weeks before Joseph's birth and smoked cocaine for the first time. Susan confronted the protective services worker in the staff lunchroom and they engaged in a loud, heated argument about their different assessments of the case. Her final statement to the protective services worker was "You are so ignorant! I'm going to bring this case to the attention of the administration. You ought to be fired."

Susan proceeded to tell her supervisor that this was the third case that she had received from this protective services worker. In all three cases, there had been inadequate documentation to justify a removal under the agency's policies. It appeared to her that this protective services worker and her supervisor did not accept the agency's family preservation policies and were intentionally harming children and families because of this bias. She stated that, in one of the cases, after she gave her testimony, the judge stated that BCCSA administration needed to "do something" with this worker and supervisor. She forgot to pass the information on to administration at the time.

Susan is concerned that other workers might not be as vigilant as she in defending families against the misjudgments of this worker. She wants administration to intervene so that no family has to suffer the trauma of separation due to worker bias, inadequate and incomplete investigations, and the general incompetence of the worker.

After this communication with her supervisor, Susan interviewed the mother. She told the mother that the file did not contain sufficient documentation to warrant removal of the children from the home. Susan told her that she wanted to work with her to get the children returned as soon as possible. To help her determine the approach to presenting her recommendation, Susan asked Ms. Blue to tell her everything she needed to know about the one instance of drug use. Ms. Blue stated that she had used cocaine during the entire pregnancy and that she had used cocaine for about three years. The downstairs neighbor would check on them several times a day and would take Mary and Michael to her flat when she found Ms. Blue too high to care for them. The neighbor had called protective services once when she did not come home for two days, but Ms. Blue arrived before protective services came out, and the neighbor had called protective services back and told them she made a mistake.

Ms. Blue had been in a substance abuse treatment program, but services were terminated because she had received the full thirty days of services for which she was eligible under Medicaid. Ms. Blue stated that she loved her children and that she knew it was stupid to continue to use cocaine while she was pregnant. She knew it was stupid to deny to the protective services worker that she was an ongoing user, but she did so because she knew the protective services worker was against her from the beginning.

Ms. Blue said she would like the children returned to her as soon as possible and she would do whatever Susan required because she felt Susan understood her. Susan became concerned and asked her to talk more about her drug use. As the story unfolded, Susan told Ms. Blue that she would have to reconsider her recommendation due to Ms. Blue's admissions of long-term and continuing drug use. Susan needed to discuss the matter with her supervisor. Ms. Blue became enraged that Susan would "worm her way into her confidence with false promises." She asked Susan to leave immediately.

Case Commentary

While Susan Smith seems to have the right credentials for child welfare practice—several years of child welfare experience, the appropriate advanced degree, membership in a professional organization, and some training—she has apparently had a lapse in judgment and then committed an ethical violation in the course of her work on the Blue case. One wonders why her credentials did not better prepare Susan in the area of sensitivity to ethical practice. The most obvious ethical violation was her public criticism of a colleague. But the lapse in judgment was potentially more problematic. Without having interviewed the new client, Susan decided, based only on materials in the file, that the children should not have been removed from the home. This placed her in the awkward position of appearing to promise to return the children from foster care soon. On discovering that the parent did have a long-standing history of substance abuse, Susan had to reevaluate her earlier position, which was now completely invalidated by her new knowledge.

In all likelihood Susan is a conscientious professional who would be shocked and upset to think that she had violated part of the NASW Code of Ethics and that she did not use sound professional judgment in her interactions with her client. If she is as busy as most foster care workers are, she may not even have time to reflect on her actions. Yet if she is to develop her professional potential, it is imperative that she understand the implications of her actions. Failure to do so could result in damaged relationships with clients, an ethics complaint, or even, at some point, litigation. Child welfare workers operate under difficult conditions. Many are not as well prepared as Susan.

This chapter addresses several issues that on the surface appear disparate: professional responsibility, liability and malpractice, confidentiality and privileges, forensic interviewing, risk management and duty to warn, the client's right to treatment in a managed care environment, testimony, and advocacy. The common thread is the social work profession's mission, ethics, and values. "The primary mission of the social work profession is to enhance human well-being and help meet the basic human needs of all people, with particular attention to the needs and empowerment of people who are vulnerable, oppressed, and living in poverty" (National Association of Social Workers, 1999, p. 1).

Child welfare practice presents many ethical dilemmas. These dilemmas result from the challenges of serving multiple clients—parents and children—in multiple organizational environments (public and private child welfare, mental health, substance abuse agencies, schools, hospitals, mental health facilities, and juvenile and family courts) subject to multiple legal and regulatory requirements that are not consistent and/or compatible. In previous chapters, we have discussed legal and regulatory issues. In this chapter, we raise and discuss several common dilemmas within the context of the NASW Code of Ethics (the Code). The Code is liberally cited and case examples are used to help you recognize some of the dilemmas and the alternate considerations. Reamer (1995) stated "there is no precise formula available for resolving ethical dilemmas. Reasonable thoughtful social workers can disagree about the ethical principles and criteria that ought to guide ethical decisions in any given case" (p. 64). He suggested a seven-step process in resolving these dilemmas.

1. Identify the ethical issues and the conflicts.
2. Identify individuals, groups, and organizations who might be affected by the decision.
3. Identify all courses of action and benefits and harms to each party.
4. Examine the reasons supporting or negating a particular course of action.
5. Consult with supervisors, administrators, and attorneys.
6. Decide and document how you came to that decision.
7. Monitor impact of decision. (Ibid., pp. 64–65)

PROFESSIONAL RESPONSIBILITY

Professional responsibility is an ominous term. It embraces the concept that a person who has attained the education and training necessary for entry into a profession has a responsibility to maintain the integrity of that profession. The integrity of the profession is maintained if its individual members are accountable to the general public for individual execution of the values and standards that the profession has established for itself or that have been established by various state statutes and regulatory schemes.

A major concern of the social work profession is that the majority of child welfare caseworkers are not professional social workers. That is, they do not hold professional degrees in social work although they carry out social work functions. Most states now require social workers to be licensed or certified. However, most also permit exemptions to licensure or certification for persons engaged in public child welfare casework (Association of Social Work Boards, 2007). One of NASW'S legislative advocacy agenda items during the current federal legislative session is to promote "legislative proposals to create a well-trained, competent, and stable child welfare workforce and to protect and improve federal child welfare training programs" (NASW).

Ethics in the context of our discussion is defined as the function of the social worker–client relationship and the responsibilities that inhere because of that relationship.

National Association of Social Workers Code of Ethics

The National Association of Social Workers (NASW) is the largest professional organization of social workers in the United States. It adopted its first code of ethics in 1960 (Reamer, 1995). There have been several revisions, the latest in 1999. Codes of ethics are adopted by professional organizations to establish norms and standards for the operation of the profession. If the professions themselves adopt these norms and standards, then it is less likely that outside administrative organizations will find the need to do so. In addition, these codes provide objective criteria for adjudicating misconduct (Reamer, 1995). Operationally, they are not as black and white as this might lead you to believe. The NASW Code of Ethics has been revised several times since its original adoption in 1960. Those revisions have occurred in response to developments in the profession and in the NASW. In this chapter, we use the latest revision, adopted in 1999.

The Code sets out the mission, values, ethical principles, and ethical standards for social work professionals in the United States. Other countries have different codes, which reflect the interplay of the social work profession within the context of their societies. The Code identifies six purposes to be served: to identify the core values of the profession; to provide a summary of the core values and standards to guide practice; to assist in resolving professional conflicts or ethical uncertainties; to provide notice to the general public of the expectations of the profession; to socialize new practitioners to the profession; and to give standards by which the profession can regulate itself (NASW, 1999).

The challenge to the professional is found in this statement:

> The Code offers a set of values, principles, and standards to guide decision making and conduct when ethical issues arise. It does not provide a set of rules that prescribe how social workers should act in all situations. Specific application of the Code must take into account the context in which it is being considered and the possibility of conflicts among the Code's values, principles, and standards. *(NASW, 1999, pp. 2–3)*

Space does not permit us to discuss all the principles and standards stated in the Code. We discuss only those principles that raise ethical dilemmas for child welfare practitioners most often: that social workers should respect the inherent dignity and worth of the person; that social workers should recognize the central importance of human relationships; that social workers should behave in a trustworthy manner; that social workers should practice within their areas of competence, and develop and enhance their professional expertise; and that social workers should challenge social injustice.

It should be noted that NASW has an established procedure for dealing with alleged violations of the Code of Ethics. The *NASW Procedures for Professional Review* was last updated in July 2005. The goals are to

- ❖ protect the public,
- ❖ protect the member, and
- ❖ protect the profession.

The *Procedures* provide the option of mediation or adjudication. The process is a shared responsibility of the Office of Ethics and Professional Review and the individual NASW state chapters. In general, the approach is intended to be constructive and educative, not punitive (NASW, 2005).

Professional Malpractice and Liability

Malpractice is the failure to meet the standards of the profession in the provision of professional services. A person is held legally responsible for the consequences of his or her actions or inactions if the suing party has sufficient evidence to prove all of the following factors.

❖ The person against whom the suit is brought owed the suing party a duty.

❖ The person breached that duty.

❖ The person's breach was unreasonable—that is, a reasonable person of like education and training, under the same or similar circumstances, would not have acted in the same way.

❖ The suing person suffered injury or damages.

❖ The breach was the proximate cause of the injury or damages.

In child welfare practice, federal and state laws, administrative policies, rules, and regulations create duties, case decisions, and standards adopted by the profession. Previous chapters addressed the duties created in decisional and statutory law and administrative policies, rules, and regulations. Such issues as who can consent to entry into the home, interviewing children without parental permission, visual inspections of children's bodies, medical examinations without parental permission, failure to adequately monitor care provided in parental homes after abuse or neglect has been found, failure to adequately monitor care provided in foster homes and institutions, and failure to ensure permanency have been litigated. In this chapter we focus on the ethical duties created by the Code. The question becomes whether the social worker's behaviors were within the ethical standards of the profession.

The first section of the Code of Ethics addresses the ethical responsibility for competent practice. This may feel problematic to child welfare workers, who often feel overwhelmed by the responsibilities of being entrusted with decisions that can affect children's lives. Like Susan Smith in the case study at the beginning of this chapter, child welfare social workers may have the right credentials but still have difficulty learning the fine points of child welfare practice. Code Section 1.04 states

(a) Social workers should provide services and represent themselves as competent only within the boundaries of their education, training, license, certification, consultation received, supervised experience, or other relevant experience.

(b) Social workers should provide services in substantive areas or use intervention techniques or approaches that are new to them only after engaging in appropriate study, training, consultation, and supervision from people who are competent in those interventions or techniques.

(c) When generally recognized standards do not exist with respect to an emerging area of practice, social workers should exercise careful judgment and take responsible steps (including appropriate education, research, training, consultation, and supervision) to ensure the competency of their work and to protect clients from harm. *(NASW, 1999, pp. 8–9)**

---

*Copyright 1996, National Association of Social Workers, Inc.

Section 4.01 states

   (a) Social workers should accept responsibility or employment only on the basis of existing competence or the intention to acquire the necessary competence.

   (b) Social workers should strive to become and remain proficient in professional practice and the performance of professional functions. Social workers should critically examine and keep current with emerging knowledge relevant to social work. Social workers should routinely review the professional literature and participate in continuing education relevant to social work practice and social work ethics.

   (c) Social workers should base practice on recognized knowledge, including empirically based knowledge, relevant to social work and social work ethics. *(NASW, 1999, p. 22)*

Child welfare, as a field of practice, is one of the most complex in the field of social work. Its complexity lies in the multiplicity of the knowledge base and intervention techniques required, as well as the ever-changing public attitudes that translate into federal and state policies. Child welfare practitioners, as a whole, do not hold degrees in social work, yet are characterized as social workers or caseworkers in the minds of the general public. Those who have degrees in social work frequently are in need of supplemental education and training specific to child welfare practice. The demands on child welfare workers are such that frequently they lack the time to engage in the further education and training necessary. Thus the dilemma.

Liability is based in state laws, policies, and procedures applied to the facts of the individual case. Therefore, we cannot conclusively say that committing this act will yield this result. In fact, every action that a child welfare worker takes could result in a lawsuit. However, a review of case decisions has found that there are certain actions in child welfare work with great risk for legal action. Many of these areas were first identified in 1991 but assigned lower risk levels because of the lack of case law on them (American Bar Association, 1991). The areas at high risk for legal action include

❖   failure to report suspected child abuse or neglect by mandated reporters;

❖   failure to adequately investigate a child protective services report and the child dies or suffers severe physical injury proximate in time to the report;

❖   failure to adequately protect a child from harm in foster care (placements unsuitable to meet child's needs, not meeting agency home visitation standards, failure to conduct criminal record checks of all members of the household);

❖   failure to remove a child from the home and the child dies or suffers severe physical injury proximate in time to the report;

❖   failure to provide all known information about the child's conditions or behaviors, which could result in harm to the child or others in the home;

❖   failure to provide all known information about the child's conditions or behaviors to adoptive parents.

Child welfare practice is, for the most part, an involuntary service. Even when there is no court intervention, the parents' general belief is that they must do what the worker and the agency expects or risk having their children removed from their custody. It is the rare parent who comes to a child protection agency requesting assistance. Many parents seek assistance from mental health agencies or juvenile or family courts when their children are exhibiting behavioral difficulties.

Some receive this assistance and some do not or do not receive it in the manner necessary to resolve the difficulties. The latter group generally receives involuntary services through the abuse or neglect or delinquency systems. The involuntary nature of the system, coupled with the dual client problem, raises many ethical issues. Code Section 1.03 states

    (a) Social workers should provide services to clients only in the context of a professional relationship based, when appropriate, on valid informed consent. Social workers should use clear and understandable language to inform clients of the purpose of the services, risks related to the services, limits to services because of the requirements of a third-party payer, relevant costs, reasonable alternatives, clients' right to refuse or withdraw consent, and the time frame covered by the consent. Social workers should provide clients with an opportunity to ask questions. . . .

    (b) . . .

    (c) In instances when clients lack the capacity to provide informed consent, social workers should protect clients' interests by seeking permission from an appropriate third party, informing clients consistent with the clients' level of understanding. In such instances social workers should seek to ensure that the third party acts in a manner consistent with clients' wishes and interests. Social workers should take reasonable steps to enhance such clients' ability to give informed consent.

    (d) In instances when the clients are receiving services involuntarily, social workers should provide information about the nature and extent of services and about the extent of clients' right to refuse service.

    (e) . . .

    (f) Social workers should obtain clients' informed consent before audiotaping or videotaping clients or permitting observation of services to clients by a third party. *(NASW, 1999, pp. 7–8)*

In general, children lack the capacity to give informed consent. In most cases, it is the role of the parent or guardian to give consent on behalf of the child. In child welfare practice, however, the interests of the parent and child may conflict. Should the social worker inform the parent that he or she will request court intervention in those situations in which, in the social worker's judgment, the parent's decision is not in the child's best interests? Should the social worker inform the parent that he or she will report statements made by the client to the court? What does the social worker tell the child client? Consider this case situation.

David, an autistic child with extremely self-injurious behaviors, has not been helped by a number of behavioral programs designed to control head banging and self-mutilation. An expert that the parents consulted independently recommends that the child be sent out of state to a private treatment setting that uses electric shocks as a deterrent to the behavior. This treatment center claims outstanding results in reduction of self-injurious behavior and maintenance of the non-self-injurious state, through an ongoing program of intermittent shocks when the child first begins to display the undesired behavior.

Understandably, the parents feel quite desperate. They have stated to you that their marriage is in jeopardy due to the stress from this child. The mother is not willing to have the child placed in group care or an institutional setting. The father is stating that his wife's constant preoccupation with David's needs is damaging the well-being of their other two children. Jenny, the younger sister, appears depressed. Donny, the eldest child, has been failing in school. Clearly the whole family is in a lot of pain. Their minister has counseled them to take the advice of the expert, who seems to be highly regarded within their denomination.

In order to be admitted to the program, the family must be recommended by their minister and by a child and family therapist. They plead with you to make the referral for them. They believe it is David's last chance, and the family's last chance to remain intact.

Confidentiality and Privileges

Confidentiality and *privilege* are frequently used interchangably, but they do not mean the same thing. *Confidentiality* refers to the statements made by a client with the expectation that they will not be shared with persons other than those to whom they are spoken unless the client authorizes otherwise. *Privilege* refers to confidential communications that are protected by statute from being disclosed in legal proceedings. The rationale for privilege statutes is that confidentiality is necessary to ensure and establish a trusting relationship so that the client divulges information necessary in the intervention process that he or she might not otherwise divulge if he or she thought the information might be passed on to someone else without her or his knowledge or consent (Gothard, 1995).

Child welfare communications may or may not be privileged, depending on individual state statutes and the specific evidence contained in the confidential communication. Even where states provide for social worker–client privilege, there are generally exceptions to absolute privilege— that is, disclosure only with client consent—that provide that confidential information can be disclosed by order of the court under certain circumstances delineated in the statutes. Remember that the confidence and the privilege belong to the client and not the professional. While the professional can state that the communication is confidential and/or privileged, the client is the one who must assert the privilege—that is, consent or not consent to the release of the information—and in the final analysis, the court will determine if it should overrule the client's decision not to consent.

You should review the privilege statute for the state(s) in which you are currently practicing or intend to practice.

The Code provides direction and dilemma on this issue. Section 1.07 states

(a) Social workers should respect clients' right to privacy. Social workers should not solicit private information from clients unless it is essential to providing services or conducting social work evaluation or research. Once private information is shared, standards of confidentiality apply.

(b) Social workers may disclose confidential information when appropriate with valid consent from a client or a person legally authorized to consent on behalf of a client.

(c) Social workers should protect the confidentiality of all information obtained in the course of professional service, except for compelling professional reasons. The general expectation that social workers will keep information confidential does not apply when disclosure is necessary to prevent serious, foreseeable, and imminent harm to a client or other identifiable person or when laws or regulations require disclosure without a client's consent. In all instances, social workers should disclose the least amount of confidential information necessary to achieve the desired purpose; only information that is directly relevant to the purpose for which the disclosure is made should be revealed.

(d) ...

(e) Social workers should discuss with clients and other interested parties the nature of confidentiality and limitations of clients' right to confidentiality. Social workers should review with clients circumstances where confidential information may be requested and where disclosure of confidential information may be legally required. This discussion should occur as soon as possible in the social worker–client relationship and as needed throughout the course of the relationship.

(f) . . .

(g) . . .

(h) . . .

(i) Social workers should not disclose confidential information in any setting unless privacy can be ensured. Social workers should not discuss confidential information in public or semipublic areas such as hallways, waiting rooms, elevators, and restaurants.

(j) Social workers should protect the confidentiality of clients during legal proceedings to the extent permitted by law. When a court of law or other legally authorized body orders social workers to disclose confidential or privileged information without a client's consent and such disclosure could cause harm to the client, social workers should request that the court withdraw the order or limit the order as narrowly as possible or maintain the records under seal, unavailable for public inspection.

(k) Social workers should protect the confidentiality of clients when responding to requests from members of the media.

(l) Social workers should protect the confidentiality of clients' written and electronic records and other sensitive information. Social workers should take reasonable steps to ensure that clients' records are stored in a secure location and that clients' records are not available to others who are not authorized to have access.

(m) . . .

(n) . . .

(o) . . .

(p) Social workers should not disclose identifying information when discussing clients for teaching or training purposes unless the client has consented to disclosure of confidential information.

(q) Social workers should not disclose identifying information when discussing clients with consultants unless the client has consented to disclosure of confidential information or there is a compelling need for such disclosure. *(NASW, 1999, pp. 10–12)*

Section 1.08 states

(a) Social workers should provide clients with reasonable access to records concerning the clients. . . . Social workers should limit clients' access to their records, or portions of their records, only in exceptional circumstances when there is compelling evidence that such access would cause serious harm to the client. Both clients' requests and the rationale for withholding some or all of the record should be documented in the clients' files.

(b) When providing clients with access to their records, social workers should take steps to protect the confidentiality of other individuals identified or discussed in such records. *(NASW, 1999, p. 12)*

Section 3.04 states

    (a) Social workers should take reasonable steps to ensure that documentation in records is accurate and reflects the services provided.

    (b) Social workers should include sufficient and timely documentation in records to facilitate the delivery of services and to ensure continuity of services provided to clients in the future.

    (c) Social workers' documentation should protect clients' privacy to the extent that is possible and appropriate and should include only information that is directly relevant to the delivery of services. *(NASW, 1999, p. 20)*

The Code encourages protection of client's privacy while at the same time acknowledging that there are instances in which the client's privacy must give way to the sharing of the information with or without client consent. In child welfare practice, there are many instances in which the confidentiality of clients may be compromised. For example, when a child with HIV is placed in a foster home, the foster parents will need to know about the child's medical condition in order to work as part of a health care team. Or if a parent, believing that he has a confidential relationship with a child welfare worker, confides in the worker that he did indeed molest his child, this information could be used in criminal proceedings against that parent.

Under the law, social workers are required to report abuse and neglect. Yet in doing so, the social worker may face angry accusations of betrayal from a parent or other client who dared to trust. Social workers also have an affirmative responsibility to act to prevent murder or suicide. It is important in all professional relationships to discuss the limits of confidentiality when first engaging a client.

Child Client Confidentiality.   The ever-present question for the child welfare practitioner is what information provided by the child the social worker may share and with whom. The social worker also faces the dilemma of needing to confirm the child's information without revealing the source. Consider the following case situation.

> Hank, age 13, was in a residential treatment setting. His foster care worker was making a routine visit to monitor Hank's progress, when Hank confided that he was being "beat up" by other youths in the program who made fun of him and harassed him after lights out. Hank said he had a secret that he would only share if his worker promised not to tell anyone. Janice, his worker said, "I won't tell anyone unless it is absolutely necessary to protect you." After some hesitation, Hank confided that he couldn't take it any more and had developed a plan to commit suicide.
>
> Janice moved quickly to inform child care staff and Hank's therapist of the suicide threat and to put necessary precautions in place. Hank was very angry and told Janice he couldn't trust her any more. Janice reminded him that she had said she would not tell anyone unless it was necessary to protect Hank. "Hank, this time it was necessary. It could have been a matter of life and death. Your well-being is my first concern."

Working with Other Professionals

Child welfare practice involves engagement with many different professionals. Given the diversity of professionals, it is not atypical for professional disagreements to arise. Code Section 2.01

provides guidance to the social worker on how to handle referrals and the disagreements that may result from these referrals. It states

> (b) Social workers should avoid unwarranted negative criticism of colleagues in communications with clients or with other professionals. *(NASW, 1999, p. 15)*

Section 2.04 states

> (a) Social workers should not exploit clients in disputes with colleagues or engage clients in any inappropriate discussion of conflicts between social workers and their colleagues. *(Ibid., p. 16)*

Section 2.06 states

> (a) Social workers should refer clients to other professionals when the other professionals' specialized knowledge or expertise is needed to serve clients fully or when social workers believe that they are not being effective or making reasonable progress with clients and that additional service is required.
>
> (b) Social workers who refer clients to other professionals should take appropriate steps to facilitate an orderly transfer of responsibility. Social workers who refer clients to other professionals should disclose, with clients' consent, all pertinent information to the new service providers. *(Ibid., p. 17)*

Self Care: Preventing Compassion Fatigue, Burnout, or Vicarious Traumatization

Compassion fatigue, burnout, or vicarious traumatization refers to the "burden that helping professionals feel from overexposure to clients' traumatic events. It is believed to result from the constant empathy, caring, and emotional investment that helping professionals put into their work in order to be genuine and empathic to clients" (Strom-Gottfried & Mowbray, 2006, p. 12). It is ultimately manifested in feelings of anger; sadness; helplessness; physical, emotional, and spiritual exhaustion; apathy; and general discontent with self and others. The term, *compassion fatigue,* was first noted in the literature in 1992 in reference to the experiences of nurses who were faced with dying patients. It is no less significant and relevant to child welfare caseworkers who on a daily basis must confront situations in which children have been hurt (Brohl, 2004; National Child Welfare Resource Center for Family-Centered Practice, 2004; Azar, 2000).

Caseworkers want to immediately take away the pain and make everything right for the children. Too often, we cannot remove the pain. Too often, it takes far longer than we would like to get the help that the child and family needs. Too often, we feel like we don't know what to do next. We have no one to talk with regarding how the situation is affecting us and "feel like we are going to lose it." Our professional and personal responsibility is to take care of ourselves so that we do not reach this point (Strom-Gottfried & Mowbray, 2006). In point of fact, the *NASW Standards for Palliative & End of Life Care* (2004) recognizes this concern and promotes self-care and self-knowledge to avoid the detrimental effects of compassion fatigue.

The literature suggests that the following steps are helpful in mitigating the trauma of child welfare work on the professionals involved: prepare and train staff for the situations they are likely to encounter; anticipate possible traumatic reactions to children who are killed or severely physically harmed; promote self-care activities for staff; and create an organizational climate that recognizes signs of compassion fatigue, offers early supportive help, and normalizes the feelings associated with compassion fatigue. While these suggestions are directed at the organization, the caseworker is equally responsible and accountable for his or her self-care. An effective child welfare worker's mantra is, "If I am not good to me, I cannot be good to anyone else." Because the demands of the job always exceed the time devoted, it is important that caseworkers engage in "responsible selfishness" to prevent compassion fatigue. Take time off! Develop and utilize a specific protocol each day for leaving the issues of the day behind when you leave the office. Engage in an enjoyable activity each day. Reframe the issues that concern you. Ask for help (Strom-Gottfried & Mowbray, 2006; Brohl, 2004; National Child Welfare Resource Center for Family-Centered Practice, 2004; Azar, 2000).

SPECIAL ISSUES IN CHILD WELFARE PRACTICE

Treatment in a Managed Care Environment

Managed care is gaining momentum in child welfare practice. It became a standard in mental health and substance abuse services during the 1990s. For many of the parents, and increasingly for many of the children, these services are critical to successful outcomes in child welfare. Historically, the lack of availability of appropriate mental health and substance abuse services in the appropriate "dosage" have been identified as barriers to permanency for children in out-of-home care and as underlying conditions for referrals to children's protective services and juvenile justice services. Managed care practice exacerbates the problem (Field, 1996; Kowal, 1996; Institute for Human Services Management, 1996; U.S. General Accounting Office, 1998; Stroul, Pires, Armstrong, & Meyers, 1998).

In addition, managed care potentially raises ethical dilemmas for the social worker. Section 1.16 of the Code states

> (a) Social workers should terminate services to clients and professional relationships with them when such services and relationships are no longer required or no longer serve the clients' needs or interests.
>
> (b) Social workers should take reasonable steps to avoid abandoning clients who are still in need of services. Social workers should withdraw services precipitously only under unusual circumstances, giving careful consideration to all factors in the situation and taking care to minimize possible adverse effects. Social workers should assist in making appropriate arrangements for continuation of services when necessary. *(NASW, 1999, pp. 14–15)*

Given the complexity of child welfare cases, it is highly unlikely that they will be conducive to a managed care model that limits the number of sessions provided or the period in which service eligibility exists. Several states are experimenting with the concept of managed care in the child welfare environment to determine its applicability to child welfare practice and any necessary modifications to the model for implementation to child welfare practice (National Community Mental Healthcare Council, 1997).

A related ethical problem is raised within the policy and financing context demonstrated in the following case situation.

> You are employed by a foster care agency to provide treatment for abused and neglected children and adolescents. You have been working with an 8-year-old girl who, after six months of treatment, has begun to trust you enough to disclose sexual abuse by both her

parents. She has been placed in a kinship care situation with an aunt, who is due to receive guardianship as a permanence plan. (Parental rights were terminated earlier.) Because the permanence plan is about to be completed, the agency is preparing to close the case. The agency's service contract, which funds you, provides funding for treatment of foster children. It does not, however, provide funds for children in guardianship situations. This means that you as therapist will no longer be funded to provide treatment. Thus you have been advised by agency management to terminate treatment within the next two weeks.

You have seen the child's reaction as she began to play out sexual abuse themes. You can honestly describe the child as having been in a state of terror at that time. You are also aware of her dissociative episodes and are beginning to speculate as to whether the child may have a multiple personality disorder. You are of course concerned about the possible potential of the child to perpetrate against other children. You have strong clinical indications that it is essential for you to continue treatment at this critical point.

You have suggested that the agency continue the child's foster care status so as not to disrupt treatment. The agency management is not willing to do so, as such an action would violate their funding contract by prolonging foster care when a permanence option was available. Your supervisor suggests that the aunt could take the child to the local community mental health agency, or even that she could bring the child to your agency's private-pay family counseling branch, and pay the sliding scale fee herself. The problem as you see it is that changing therapists at this point would jeopardize the child's progress in treatment at the most critical point, when the child's defenses are down and she has just started to trust.

The supervisor has suggested tactfully to you that you may perhaps be emotionally overinvolved with the child, as you are having problems "letting go." The supervisor is also concerned that if you press your point with the aunt she may be reluctant to assume guardianship. She feels her niece is "a normal kid who just needs a lot of love." You think that to terminate prematurely for reasons related to agency funding patterns constitutes the ethical violation of client abandonment.

Child welfare practice is inherently a process of risk evaluation and risk taking. Advocates have long argued that to be effective, child welfare practitioners need to have a comprehensive knowledge and skills base coupled with a range of supportive resources and interventions that could be utilized, based on their comprehensive initial assessment and continuous reassessment of the family, its individuals and its environment. Managed care is a system based on the principle that the majority of cases and conditions fall within a prescriptive intervention that can be delivered in a certain period or number of sessions. Child welfare policy has advanced the concept of permanency through the adoption of specific time frames, although not absolute time frames, for returning the child to the home or termination of parental rights. This policy is based on research addressing the child's needs for stability in relationships, not on research on the effectiveness of service delivery systems in meeting the complex needs of multiproblem child welfare cases.

Duty to Warn and Report

All states now have statutes that require certain professionals to warn third parties, generally through law enforcement agencies, of threats to their physical safety made by clients receiving treatment from the professional if the professional believes the client has the intent and means to carry out (Dickson, 1995). In addition, all states require social workers, as well as other specifically identified professionals, to report instances of suspected child abuse and neglect (National Clearinghouse on Child Abuse and Neglect Information, 1998). Code Section 1.07 (e) states

> Social workers should discuss with clients and other interested parties the nature of confidentiality and limitations of clients' right to confidentiality. Social workers should review with clients the circumstances where confidential information may be legally required. This discussion should occur as soon as possible in the social worker–client relationship and as needed throughout the course of the relationship. *(NASW, 1999, p. 11)*

Forensic Social Work Practice

Child welfare matters, including juvenile delinquency, frequently result in court intervention. *Forensic* means "belonging to or connected with a court" (Black, 1992). Juvenile court procedures have changed substantially since their inception as a court of benevolent and discretionary decision making. Court decisions, discussed in Chapter 1, have resulted in greater formalities in the decision-making processes to ensure constitutional safeguards for children, juveniles, and their parents. These formalities have resulted in the need to conduct child welfare investigations in ways that preserve the evidence and limit the attack by opposing attorneys on the child welfare worker's methodology in the collection of the evidence.

The goal of a forensic interview with a child "is to obtain a statement from the child, in a developmentally-sensitive, unbiased and truthseeking manner, that will support accurate and fair decision-making in the criminal justice and child welfare systems" (Michigan Governor's Task Force on Children's Justice, 1998, p. 1). The process of forensic interviewing has been discussed in Chapter 4. Here we are concerned with the ethical dilemmas raised when you know that you are interviewing to gather information for use in a legal proceeding. Section 1.07 of the Code states

> (a) Social workers should inform clients, to the extent possible, about the disclosure of confidential information and the potential consequences, when feasible before the disclosure is made. This applies whether social workers disclose confidential information on the basis of a legal requirement or client consent. . . .
>
> (b) Social workers should discuss with clients and other interested parties the nature of confidentiality and limitations of clients' right to confidentiality. Social workers should review with clients circumstances where confidential information might be legally required. This discussion should occur as soon as possible in the social worker–client relationship and as needed throughout the course of the relationship. . . .
>
> (c) Social workers should protect confidentiality of clients during legal proceedings to the extent permitted by law. When a court of law or other legally authorized body orders social workers to disclose confidential or privileged information without a client's consent and such disclosure could cause harm to the client, social workers should request that the court withdraw the order or limit the order as narrowly as possible or maintain the records under seal, unavailable for public inspection. *(NASW, 1999, pp. 10–11)*

The dilemma is that, by informing the client of the possible uses and consequences of disclosures in advance of those disclosures, you limit the information available for assessment and intervention. This could result in improper intervention and decision making. On the other hand, if you do not inform the client in advance, you are not complying with your ethical duty.

Testifying in Administrative and Judicial Proceedings

The principles of testifying were discussed in Chapter 6. Here the focus is the dilemmas raised by Section 1.7 (j) of the Code:

> Social workers should protect confidentiality of clients during legal proceedings to the extent permitted by law. When a court of law or other legally authorized body orders social workers to disclose confidential or privileged information without a client's consent and such disclosure could cause harm to the client, social workers should request that the court withdraw the order or limit the order as narrowly as possible or maintain the records under seal, unavailable for public inspection. *(NASW, 1999, p. 11)*

How do the terms *to the extent permitted by law* and *could cause harm to the client* apply in child welfare practice? The social worker is engaged with the child and family to carry out a public function, that is, the protection of vulnerable children and/or the protection of society from the actions of wayward or delinquent children. Which client do you protect—the adult or the child? Perhaps even society is your client. Whose interests are paramount? Should you consider the potential harms to yourself and your agency? The child welfare worker must be aware of federal laws, such as strict confidentiality with respect to federally funded recipients of substance abuse services, that supercede state laws with respect to what information the court can order divulged.

CHILD ADVOCACY

The history of the social work profession is rich with initiatives focused on advocacy for the poor and vulnerable. Over the years, the profession has shifted focus to individual, group and community practice and, in the view of some commentators, has lost sight of its roots in social reform (Fink, Anderson, & Conover, 1968; Bailey & Brake, 1975; Richan, 1991; Netting, Kettner, & McMurtry, 1998; Chambers, 2000; Haynes & Mickelson, 2000). While advocacy efforts for some disadvantaged groups may have diminished, it is clear that child advocacy efforts continue to grow and achieve significant gains at the federal, state, and local levels (Ness, Pizzigati, & Stuck, 2002).

Responsibility for Advancing Social and Economic Justice

The social worker's ethical responsibility to engage in advocacy efforts is delineated in Section 6 of the Code. The responsibilities are broad-based and rooted in the concept of advancing social and economic justice. Section 6.01 states

> Social workers should promote the general welfare of society, from local to global levels, and the development of people, their communities, and their environments. Social workers should advocate for living conditions conducive to the fulfillment of basic human needs and should promote social, economic, political, and cultural values and institutions that are compatible with the realization of social justice. *(NASW, 1999, pp. 26–27)*

Section 6.02 states, "Social workers should facilitate informed participation by the public in shaping social policies and institutions" (Ibid., p. 27). Section 6.04 states

(a) Social workers should engage in social and political action that seeks to ensure that all people have equal access to the resources, employment, services, and opportunities they require to meet their basic human needs and to develop fully. Social workers should be aware of the impact of the political arena on practice and should advocate for changes in policy and legislation to improve social conditions in order to meet basic human needs and promote social justice.

(b) Social workers should act to expand choice and opportunity for all people, with special regard for vulnerable, disadvantaged, oppressed, and exploited people and groups. *(NASW, 1999, p. 27)*

Many child welfare workers and supervisors are intimidated by the mention of "advocacy." They think that it involves skills beyond their grasp. They have no idea about where to start once the advocacy involves more than advocating for a particular client for a particular service or benefit from a particular agency responsible for providing that service. However, as you can see from Box 12.1, clinical practice and case/policy practice and advocacy share common general problem-solving steps: definition of the problem; data collection and analysis; choosing an appropriate intervention; continuous reevaluation and modification of the chosen interventions based on new information or changed circumstances; and finally goal attainment. Certainly, the individual techniques used will vary. We will discuss techniques and skills useful at all levels of child advocacy in the rest of the chapter. We want to assure the reader that these techniques and skills are within the grasp of each reader through building on and adapting micro skills.

Box 12.1

Comparison of Clinical Practice and Policy Practice/Advocacy Steps

Clinical Practice Steps	Policy Practice/Advocacy Steps
1. Get client's view of problem	1. How does society define the problem? How does the advocacy group define the problem? What are the points of differences in the definitions?
2. Collect data to confirm client's definition or revise it (psychosocial history)	2. Complete needs assessment (scope of problem; who is affected; current policies and programs; regulations)
3. Diagnose or assess	3. Identify appropriate site of intervention (legislative, executive, or judicial) and stage (policy formulation, implementation, or evaluation)
4. Develop treatment plan	4. Develop intervention strategy options
5. Execute treatment plan	5. Execute chosen strategy
6. Evaluate and modify treatment plan	6. Evaluate and modify chosen strategies
7. Achieve desired outcome	7. Achieve desired outcome

Source: Adapted from K. S. Haynes and J. S. Mickelson (2000), *Affecting change: Social workers in the political arena* (Boston: Allyn and Bacon).

Advocacy in the Local and Global Context

"Think globally, act locally" should be the mantra of the child welfare advocate. All children, irrespective of geographic, political, and cultural origins are entitled to adequate nurturance to ensure the maximization of their emotional, cognitive, social, moral, and spiritual development. What this nurturance looks like varies from place to place, but the essential end is that all children are free from abuse or neglect at the hands of their immediate caretakers as well as their governments and are provided care and nurturance to guarantee survival and development in all domains.

The United Nations' Convention on the Rights of the Child has fifty-four articles specific to the rights children all over the world should be ensured by their governments. The following summarizes the major rights identified in those articles. Children shall have the right to

> ❖ care and protection necessary for his or her well-being including life, survival, and development.
> ❖ know and be cared for by their parents and the right to live with their parents absent a judicial determination that separation is in the best interests of the child.
> ❖ maintain contact with their parents, if separated, even across political jurisdictions.
> ❖ freedom of thought, expression, conscience, and religion, and to voice opinions and desires freely if capable of forming their own views and to have their views given weight in accordance with age and maturity.
> ❖ receive care and services in facilities and from programs that meet minimum standards in the areas of health, safety, and staff competency and sufficiency.
> ❖ respect given to the responsibilities and rights of their parents, extended family, and community in caring for them.
> ❖ a name, a nationality, a registered birth, and a right to preserve this identity as well as ethnic, religious, cultural, and linguistic background.
> ❖ intercountry adoption only if the child cannot be placed in a foster or adoptive home in his or her country of origin.
> ❖ special care for any disabilities and access to education, training, health care services, rehabilitation services, preparation for employment, and recreation opportunities in a manner conducive to achieving full potential.
> ❖ access facilities for primary health care, illness treatment, and rehabilitative health care.
> ❖ a standard of living adequate to physical, mental, spiritual, moral, and social development.
> ❖ compulsory, free primary education in a humane environment.
> ❖ be protected against economic exploitation and from performing hazardous work, drug trafficking, and sexual prostitution including pornographic performances.
> ❖ be free from torture, degrading treatment, and unlawful detention.
> ❖ not be required to engage in armed conflicts if they are 15 years of age or younger.

The Convention is the one document that all advocates can look to as the organizing framework for global advocacy. As of this writing, all 197 member nations except Somalia have signed it, acceded to it, or ratified it. A signature implies intent to comply with its assurances and to refrain from taking any action that might undermine the intent of the Convention. An accession or ratification is the agreement to be legally bound by it. The United States signed the document in February 1995, but as of this writing, it has not ratified it. Until ratification, the United States is not legally bound to adhere to the terms (Office of the United Nations High Commissioner for Human Rights, Retrieved 02/21/2007).

Clearly, none of those signatory states has met the prescribed standards. Therefore, much global advocacy is necessary. The complexity of actual advocacy in a country—and in some countries a region—other than that of the advocate's residence is beyond the scope of this text. However, that does not preclude all child advocates from

❖ voicing concern over the plight of children in other countries,
❖ providing support to the advocates in those countries attempting to secure the rights their governments' promised their children upon signing the Convention, and
❖ encouraging our government to use our resources of influence and affluence to influence how those governments treat their children.

Further, we must remain mindful that the United States, despite its influence and affluence, does not ensure that every child has adequate economic support, nutrition, health care, education, behavioral/mental health services, family support services, protective services, out-of-home care services, independent living services, or permanency and adoption services. In advocating for and securing universal services for all of our children, we can demonstrate to other nations and advocate that it is possible to ensure that all children and their families have the supports they need to reach adulthood with maximum capabilities for citizenship and personal fulfillment.

What Is Advocacy?

In 1981, the Child Welfare League of America defined child advocacy as "the process of sensitizing individuals and groups to the unmet needs of children and to society's obligation to provide positive response to these needs" (p. ix). This definition emphasizes the educational role inherent in all advocacy efforts. But the League also recognized the definitional dilemma by stating: "Whether one talks in terms of advocacy, or influencing public social policy, or engaging in social action or promoting institutional change makes no essential difference" (p. 1). It is interesting to note that persons who viewed advocacy as a large part of their work defined it as "intervention on behalf of a client or client groups with an unresponsive system" (Epstein, 1981, p. 8). Mickelson (1995) has advanced the following definition: "In social work, advocacy can be defined as the act of directly representing, defending, intervening, supporting, or recommending a course of action on behalf of one or more individuals, groups, or communities with the goal of securing or retaining social justice" (NASW, 1999, p. 95).

Jansson (1999) differentiates policy practice and policy advocacy. Policy practice includes efforts to change policies at all levels and stages of policy development and implementation, whereas policy advocacy is a specific policy practice common to the social work profession in that it is directed toward helping the powerless and disenfranchised individual or group by securing benefits and services (Jansson, 1999, pp. 10–11).

While case and class advocacy are the two broadest conceptual categories of child advocacy, this text discusses case, class, and policy advocacy as three distinct types of child advocacy. This is done because in the context of the child welfare worker's and supervisor's experience, they are more accustomed to case advocacy being done for individual clients within their agency or with another agency to obtain a service for the individual; class advocacy being done for a group of named individual clients within the context of their agency or other administrative agencies or through litigation in the courts; and policy advocacy being done to change public policy on behalf of a targeted service population within the context of the political arena.

Historical Background. The practice of child advocacy takes different forms as the needs of children and the organizational environments responding to those needs change. Present-day child advocacy has its origins in 1899 with the juvenile court movement, the 1910 White House Conference on Children, and the establishment in 1912 of the Children's Bureau at the federal level. Among the forces that helped to produce interest in child advocacy in more recent times were the new visibility given to

❖ poverty and delinquency in the 1960s and the government programs intended to reduce the number of children and families living under seriously inadequate economic conditions;

❖ child protection, the protection of juvenile offenders, and permanency for children in foster care in the 1970s;

❖ family preservation, family reunification, and getting tough on juveniles who commit serious offenses in the 1980s;

❖ child safety as the "paramount concern" over family preservation or reunification; permanency through adoption for children in out-of-home care; expanding the adult crime–adult time approach to juvenile offenders; and "work, not welfare" in the 1990s extending into the 2000s.

From the Mobilization for Youth project came the concept of "client advocacy," defined as intervention "on behalf of a client with a public agency to secure an entitlement or right which has been obscured or denied" (Cloward & Elman, 1967, p. 267). In later sections, this type of advocacy is called "case advocacy." Mobilization for Youth was an inner-city youth project developed by a multidisciplinary social agency on New York City's Lower East Side. Its focus was on the need for broad social, economic, and institutional reform. Delinquency was viewed as the result of a lack of congruence between a young person's aspirations and opportunities. A range of services was offered—employment, legal, educational, psychological, and social. The community action programs under the Economic Opportunity Act were largely modeled on the Mobilization for Youth experience. The "War on Poverty" launched by the Economic Opportunity Act produced the principle of "maximum feasible participation" on the part of clients affected by the new antipoverty programs, challenged the conventional and sometimes complacent service delivery methods, and persistently questioned the processes that led to institutional decisions about poor families and children.

Another set of influences that moved the idea of child advocacy forward came from attention to problems in public school education. The 1960s brought a stream of studies, evaluations, and opinions with provocative titles such as *How Children Fail, Death at an Early Age,* and *Crisis in the Classroom,* about inadequate educational facilities and the failure of the schools to educate children, especially children of the poor and children with special needs—for example, children who are physically and mentally handicapped and children in need of bilingual education (Holt, 1964; Kozol, 1967; Silberman, 1971). Out of the controversy came attempts to create new approaches to education by modifying school conditions and practices.

Successful demonstrations in the late 1960s of the gains to be made for children through the use of the judicial system constituted another influence on the development of the child advocacy movement. The *Kent* and *Gault* decisions affirmed due process rights of juveniles alleged to be delinquent. A significant court case in Pennsylvania questioned the constitutionality of school policies that resulted in the exclusion of handicapped children (*Pennsylvania Association,* 1971). Similar suits followed and eventually played an important part in congressional enactment of the Education for All Handicapped Children Act of 1975. Another major litigation challenged conditions in juvenile correctional institutions and resulted not only in an order for changes in such institutions but also in the creation of a community-based system of alternative forms of care and treatment (*Morales v. Thurman,* 1974). These and other demonstrations of ways in which litigation can be used to advance child rights not only led to change in service procedures and methods but also helped to establish important principles inherent in the concept and practice of child advocacy.

Another development that began in the 1960s was also related to the emergence of interest in child advocacy. Ralph Nader's consumer advocacy efforts have been focused on the obligations of corporations to respond to consumer interests and on the failure of government regulatory authorities to monitor the activities of industry adequately. Knitzer (1976) pointed out that unlike the participatory model of antipoverty activists, Nader's strategies are "overtly elitist, both in choice of staff and in the processes by which issues are selected" (p. 207). Nevertheless, she acknowledged, Nader and his staff have been highly successful in researching and focusing attention on systemic problems—an accomplishment that has not been lost on proponents of child advocacy.

Illustrations of avant-garde child advocacy programs are found in the records of the U.S. Children's Bureau in the years between the progressive era and the enactment of the Social Security Act in 1935 and in the contemporary Children's Defense Fund. In each instance, far-thinking and daring women committed to social justice for women, children, and young families are credited with successful leadership. Julia Lathrop was the first and Grace Abbott the second chief of the Children's Bureau; Marian Wright Edelman is the founder and president of the Children's Defense Fund. All three have records that encompass the following:

- ❖ effective definition of problems that require social action
- ❖ development and maintenance of diverse constituencies
- ❖ building and supporting coalitions
- ❖ conceptualizing and implementing systematic studies of the problem and the forces affecting it
- ❖ disseminating findings in strategic forums
- ❖ astutely recognizing political factors that control the targeted problem
- ❖ applying sound judgment as to where and when pressure can be effective

Children's Defense Fund. Following the new surge of advocacy in the 1960s, attempts were made to develop national child advocacy organizations, most of which had limited success (Steiner, 1976). One that has survived as an effective and dynamic advocacy unit is the Children's Defense Fund (CDF), a nonprofit organization committed to long-range systematic advocacy to bring about reforms in behalf of children. Marian Wright Edelman, who founded the organization in 1973 and has provided its leadership since then, is recognized as a dynamic and highly effective advocate for children in the complex and competitive arena in which social policies and legislation are influenced.

Carefully defined goals in relation to children and their unmet needs seemed to Edelman an effective focus for broadening the base and building a coalition for social change. Edelman sought to cut through race and class barriers by addressing the needs of children throughout the country.

> *What scares me is that today people don't have the sense that they can struggle and change things. In the sixties, in Mississippi, it just never occurred to us that we weren't going to win. We always had the feeling that there was something we could do, and that there was hope. (Marian Wright Edelman—Tomkins, 1989, p. 74)*

The CDF set out to protect effective programs already in existence and work for new programs that would emphasize parental involvement and community change. The selection of targets for reform activity was made on the premise that effective advocacy must be specialized, not global, in its approach to change, and that the issues should be ones that affect large numbers of children; that are easily understood by the public; that are subject to attacks at local, state, and federal levels; and that give promise of being affected by a combination of strategies. The early issues the CDF chose to pursue included the following:

❖ the exclusion of children from school
❖ classification and treatment of children with special needs
❖ the use of children in medical (particularly drug) research and experimentation
❖ the child's right to privacy in the face of computerization and data banks
❖ reform of the juvenile justice system
❖ child development and child care
❖ children in foster care (Beck & Butler, 1974)

Over time, CDF has broadened its areas of interests to include other issues such as child neglect and abuse, children's health care, early education/Head Start, homelessness, poverty, youth violence, and teenage pregnancy and parenting. The wide dissemination of findings from CDF studies by means of publications, testimony before congressional committees, and presentations in a variety of public forums has been highly effective in securing interest and action for change.

On the assumption that some groups that may not support a general effort may come together around a children's issue that affects their special interests, the CDF relies on specialized coalition building as a primary strategy. Issues for reform activity are selected not only for their importance to children and families but also for their potential for building coalitions and constituencies. Other specialized strategies and activities include litigation, drafting and pushing legislation, monitoring administrative agencies, providing public education, and organizing local groups who work with children and offering them technical support.

Case, Class, and Policy Advocacy

The types of situations and issues that indicate the need for child advocacy have been discussed in each chapter of this book: poverty, poor nutrition, inadequate housing, homelessness, lack of proper health care, and the failure to provide educational programs that succeed in preparing young people for the basic skills that are required for entry into the world of work. Specific to the field of child welfare are issues of the application of due process guarantees in the juvenile courts; the definitions of child abuse and neglect; the meanings of reasonable efforts, permanency, family preservation, and child protection; the jailing or secure detention of youth prior to adjudication; sexism and racism in the dispositional decisions of child welfare agencies and the courts; the provision of legal representation for children and parents in adjudications directly affecting them; and the question of the scope of constitutional protections for children.

Advocacy on behalf of children is needed now as much as it has been in the past. All of these situations, and others as well, call attention to the necessity of monitoring legislative, administrative, and budgetary processes and, at times, the professional behavior of persons charged by society to act on behalf of children. The approach to advocacy for a specific issue can include techniques focused on resolution of the issue for an individual client (case advocacy) or techniques focused on resolution of the issue for all persons now affected or who may be affected in the future (class advocacy). Class advocacy can be undertaken within agencies (the administrative/executive level), through litigation (the judicial level), or through the political process in the form of policy change (the legislative level). Because of the potential impact of policy advocacy on child welfare service delivery, it will be discussed separately from class advocacy occurring in the context of litigation or named individuals currently harmed by an existing policy or practice. Through elaboration of the facts in the case example presented at the beginning of this chapter, we will illustrate how you might undertake case, class, and policy advocacy.

Case Advocacy.   Case advocacy is focused on an individual child in order to bring about resolution of some barrier to the child's receiving a needed service or concrete benefit. A child may need a service that is not available in the community, or is in such short supply as to be unavailable to this particular child. Sometimes the service exists, but parents do not know how to find and use it, and sometimes children are denied service without any defensible rationale. In other instances, services may be given, but in a form that is seriously inadequate or inappropriate. In situations such as these, someone directly concerned usually initiates advocacy action for the child—a social worker or other professional, or a paraprofessional, such as a health aide or teacher's aide.

Other situations that invite case advocacy are readily illustrated—a child is unfairly detained in jail; a child is inappropriately or unfairly placed outside the mainstream of the school learning structure; a child is denied an adoptive home because no one in the foster care system has initiated or followed through on a positively oriented review of his or her suitability for adoption; or a child is repeatedly suspended from school without a hearing by school personnel to determine whether the child is persisting in the offending behavior for reasons over which he or she has little or no control.

Class Advocacy.   If these individual case advocacy issues appear over time to involve the same policy, practice, or agency, then the effective advocate will shift to class advocacy techniques. This approach is more efficient when the problem is widespread, in that class advocacy maximizes the current benefit to all children who should receive the benefit or who should not be subjected to the sanction. When successful, it results in changes in policies, practices, or agency administration. For example, the advocate may involve a citizen's group in examining the conditions that lead to children being held in the community's jails, or, with a group of parents, the advocate may endeavor to bring change in school practices in relation to suspensions or placement of children in special education classes. These actions may not be adversarial nor require legal action. Rather, they may be aimed at supporting school or court personnel in the development of corrective measures to advance generally approved goals for children.

If there is a need for litigation, Rule 23 of the Federal Rules of Civil Procedure (2007) provides that a class action can be advanced if these four conditions exist:

❖ The class membership is so numerous that to join all members in the court action is impracticable.
❖ There are questions of law or fact common to the class.
❖ Claims of the representative members are typical of the claims of the class.
❖ The representative members will fairly and adequately protect the interests of the class.

Action on behalf of a class of persons is done primarily for the purpose of efficiency. Progress on a case-by-case basis takes too long and does not necessarily bring change for others. Nor does case advocacy provide the political leverage that helps to bring change for children generally in related problem areas.

Thirty-two states have been involved in class action litigation involving the child welfare system between 1995 and 2005. In all but two cases, the states were ordered or agreed to make substantial changes to their child welfare systems on issues such as provision of services to meet the identified needs of children and their families; establishing and achieving permanency goals; protective services reporting, intake and investigation; staffing issues including caseload size, staff training, development, supervision, and accountability; organization of the service delivery system; placement issues including recruitment of foster homes, securing appropriate residential treatment services, matching the child's needs with the caregiver's capacities, relative placement preferences, and support; adoption; and judicial reforms. Children's Rights, an advocacy group, based in New York City has been instrumental in advancing the majority of the class actions in collaboration with law firms located in each of the states. The general consensus is that these actions have led to many improvements in the states. However, no system has yet to fully achieve the desired outcomes. Many are still operating under consent decrees or settlement agreements (Kosanovich, Joseph, & Hasbargen, 2005).

Policy Advocacy. When these organization's practices are inconsistent with governmental policies, then case or class advocacy through administrative processes or litigation are appropriate strategies. However, when these organizations are constrained by policies or practices imposed by governmental units and these policies or practices are inconsistent with the service needs of the targeted client population, then policy advocacy is the appropriate level of advocacy.

Policy is defined as

> statements that prescribe courses of action in organizations. They govern the internal functioning of organizations, their external relations, and the way they attain their goals. They are codified in documentary form and facilitate standardized decision-making. *(Midgley, Tracy, & Livermore, 2000, p. 3)*

Public policy, also called social policy, is all the policies of government that define its responsibilities to its citizens and its citizens' responsibilities to their government and one another. As we have discussed throughout, public child welfare as we know it today is driven by federal and state policies in the form of statutes/public laws, administrative rules and regulations, and judicial decisions interpreting those statutes/public laws or administrative rules and regulations. Public policies are not stagnant. The major child welfare legislations summarized in Chapter 1 and discussed in Chapters 7–11 have been amended several times since original passage of the enabling legislations. These amendments occur because some group or groups, typically external to the government itself, determine that the current policies are not achieving the desired goals or the current policies are no longer desirable within the value or knowledge context of the group or society. This is policy advocacy. To simplify the distinction, case and class advocacy, as discussed above, always involve attempts to resolve policy implementation disputes for named individuals. Policy advocacy focuses on advocacy for a particular approach to an issue that affects unnamed children and their families now alive and yet to be born.

Nevertheless, efficiency and political leverage are by no means the central reason for child advocacy. Protecting the rights of the child is the central purpose of all child advocacy efforts. Although for child advocacy to be successful individual needs must often be grouped and classified, the needs and the rights of the individual are the heart of advocacy at any level and for any group of persons. Case, class, and policy advocacy are inseparably related.

Common Assumptions. Writing from the perspective of the highly effective advocacy programs of the Children's Defense Fund, Knitzer (1976) identified some underlying assumptions common to all forms of advocacy.

1. Advocacy assumes that people have, or ought to have, certain basic rights.
2. Advocacy assumes that rights are enforceable by statutes, administration, or judicial procedures.
3. Advocacy efforts are focused on institutional failures that produce or aggravate individual problems.
4. Advocacy is inherently political.
5. Advocacy is most effective when it is focused on specific issues.
6. Advocacy is different from the provision of direct services. (p. 205)

Child advocacy, then, is primarily concerned with seeing that existing organizations and services work for children.

Components of Child Advocacy

Child advocacy projects vary in significant ways. Within the diversity, however, there appear to be features that are fundamental to all projects: auspices, sanction for intervention, and target selection, and basic tasks, strategies, and techniques.

Auspices. The question of auspices for a child advocacy program is a significant one. Auspices determine certain basic characteristics of a project: who authorizes it, who pays for it, and who runs it.

Early debate about who should authorize and fund child advocacy centered on the question of whether child advocacy should be separate from any governmental system to avoid the inhibitions that might result from risks in challenging high-level officials. But private funding can also pose constraints. In practice, the necessity of locating and competing for funds has meant that both public and private funds have been used for child advocacy projects.

As child advocacy has developed, advocacy projects have come to include these types, classified according to their auspices:

❖ Projects authorized and paid for by a governmental body made up of citizens. These projects are mandated by local, county, state, or federal governments. For example, if the state elects to receive federal funding for child abuse and neglect, foster care, and adoption programming, it is required to establish and staff Citizen Review Panels, Children's Justice Act Task Forces, and Juvenile Justice Task Forces to oversee the state's policies and practices in the areas of children's protective services, foster care, adoption, and juvenile delinquency/juvenile justice.

❖ Projects authorized and operated within a governmental body, often at the state level, with staff members who are employees of government. For example, the federally mandated State Protection and Advocacy organization is mandated to provide advocacy services for persons with mental illnesses, emotional disturbances, and developmental disabilities.

❖ Projects independent of government and funded by private foundations, by memberships, or by individual contributions; for example, the Children's Defense Fund and the National Association of Child Advocates.

The auspices of a project can be a crucial determinant of what can be undertaken and accomplished. But, as Knitzer (1976) pointed out, any advocacy effort involves risks, and important as the auspices are, the energy, commitment, and political know-how of the advocates are equally important.

Who Is the Advocate?   The question of who is best equipped to be an advocate for children continues to be debated. Some have argued for a more limited role for professionals. In fact, the renewed interest in child advocacy was largely based on a mistrust of professionals and the organizations they operate. The fear was that professionally directed advocacy efforts would be weighted more toward professional self-interest than toward the needs of children. This has led to a demand for a significant degree of citizen and paraprofessional participation in advocacy projects.

In many cases, an effective advocacy effort involves multiple groups of professionals, scholars, citizens, and the youth themselves. Many advocacy efforts are complex, requiring a variety of roles to be filled, depending on the situation. Successful child advocacy programs have employed, in various configurations, different kinds of personnel, including college students, social scientists, parents, citizens, lawyers, and other professionals. There is obviously not a single answer. What is most clear, however, is that the welfare of children is best served when increased numbers of people from all stations of life become actively involved.

Sanction for the Right to Intervene.   Child advocacy requires sanction. Responsible child advocacy means that persons who attempt to intervene in society's institutions must be sure that their assertive or adversarial stance is justified.

In view of all that has been said about the injustice to children and the unmet needs for social services, one may well question why individuals should be required to justify their right to try to improve the status of children. But when an advocacy group decides that an individual agency or institution is not responding adequately to the children for whom it carries responsibility, then that advocacy group is usually attempting to bring about some significant change in an institution or agency, such as making the target agency more flexible in its approach to child needs, increasing budget allocations, undertaking new programs, or reassigning control of programs.

But on what basis can child advocates establish their right to intervene? Kahn, Kamerman, and McGowan (1972) gave the following guidelines for validating the right to advocate.

1. A sanction for child advocacy exists when children have justifiable rights, that is, "legislatively specified benefits for which administrative discretion is quite circumscribed and which can be adjudicated in the courts when administrative agencies do not deliver." In such instances there is a clear-cut entitlement to a benefit or a specific service, such as survivors' benefits under Social Security, or an appropriate educational program in the least-restrictive environment for a handicapped child. In such cases, the child advocate's sanction to act is clear-cut. Other instances in which the right to advocate is easily recognized include those where there is strong indication that some children or families are being treated differently from others in a similar situation, perhaps because agencies and personnel are ignoring their own policies and procedures or are acting carelessly or in a discriminatory way. For example, the right to advocate is clear if a children's agency mandated by law to receive and investigate all reports of child abuse and neglect attempts to manage a heavy workload by deciding to respond to reports of neglect only when those reports carry an indication of physical abuse as well, or if a juvenile court makes sure that middle- and upper-income parents are present and informed of their right to counsel when hearings affecting them and their children are held, but fails to do the same for parents who are very poor.

2. A sanction for child advocacy exists when the effort is intended to expand the boundaries of legally governed child rights. For example, it is generally held that the parent–child relationship remains intact, with parental rights primary, unless serious abuse, neglect, or unfitness on the part of parents is established. But a question arises as to whether continued state intervention is justified if it is merely an exchange of governmental neglect for parental neglect. If a child's parents make the difficult but often necessary decision to institutionalize their child and only a simple regime of enforced custodial care is given—not treatment that is appropriate and adequate in light of present knowledge—then the issue of a right to treatment emerges.

   In situations like these, advocates for children may choose to work for an extension of child rights beyond what is already clearly established in law. Sometimes the sanction to do so rests on a series of lower court decisions or inconclusive actions, or simply on statements of some authoritative body that has spoken out on the issue.

3. A sanction for child advocacy may exist even when no specific right or statement of principle appears in law. The right to intervene may be validated in a number of ways, which Kahn et al. (1972) identified:

   (a) Available professional knowledge and expertise about dangers to child development may provide backing for child advocacy.

   (b) The joining of knowledge and values may bring about agreement on a "social minimum" that finds support in professional and community norms and thus gives validity to the child advocacy effort.

   (c) Sometimes groups such as parents of disadvantaged or handicapped children articulate their own needs, and in doing so provide a sanction for child advocacy. Even though this sanction rests on self-definition and personal experience, it is often enough for advocacy to proceed.

   (d) Sometimes the view people have of society, social justice, and acceptable priorities in the use of resources leads them to study social indicators of the status of children and to collect data about families and children in relation to such critical factors as school attendance and achievement, health and illness, and nutrition. Their analysis of such data then becomes a sanction for child advocacy. *(pp. 70–75)*

Selecting the Target for Advocacy. The target for advocacy is the system or organization that is the locus of the service or disservice to the child(ren) or their family(ies). In some child advocacy projects, the target is only one system—for example, the school system. The individual caseworker or supervisor and the advocacy group attempt to deal with a range of school situations whereby children or families are affected, such as suspension, corporal punishment, education for children with disabilities, and the use of drugs for control of pupil behavior. Other projects may at various times attack issues involving a number of agencies or institutions. Often a project that starts out with only one organization or system as the target begins to uncover negative effects of other organizations or systems on children, and so its advocacy efforts are expanded. For example, dealing with advocacy issues in a public school often raises questions about the mental health system, and attention to the mental health system may lead in turn to concern about the juvenile justice system. Further, advocacy initiatives that begin as case or named-class advocacy frequently lead to policy advocacy concurrently or subsequently.

Tasks, Strategies, and Techniques. All advocates, irrespective of the type or level of advocacy undertaken, use four basic skills:

❖ analytical,
❖ political,
❖ interactional, and
❖ value clarification or ethical reasoning.

Analytical skills are needed to gather, synthesize, and evaluate the interrelationship of various data elements central to the issue under review and to develop alternative action strategies or recommendations. Political skills are needed to develop feasible action strategies, to help identify people of influence to assist in advancing the message, and to help develop political strategies. Interactional skills are needed to develop and facilitate networks and coalitions to assist in realizing the advocacy goal. Value clarification or ethical reasoning skills are needed to ensure that the means taken to realize the advocacy goal are not inconsistent with the goal itself or higher principles are not compromised to achieve the end (Jansson, 1999). Maryann Mahaffey, a social worker and president of the Detroit City Council, said

> A social worker brings to the political process something that's unique, that no one else has. . . . What the social worker brings is a value system that, if implemented, along with the skills, makes the difference. *(Haynes & Mickelson, 2000, p. 40)*

Advocates use a range of specific techniques—suggestion, negotiation, education, consensus building, persuasion, pressure, demands, confrontation, legal action, legislative testimony, pickets, providing data for media exposes, and the like—in case, class, and policy advocacy projects.

Child advocacy sometimes is an adversarial process, but, as Knitzer (1976) reminds us, "it is also a problem solving process that requires keen attention to problem definition and analysis" (p. 208). There are four major tasks for all advocacy projects:

1. fact-finding,
2. development of strategies to secure remedies or solutions,
3. implementation of the strategies, and
4. monitoring for results.

Once a constituency is settled on, whether that constituency be an individual child or a group of children sharing a similar condition such as mental illness, teenage parenthood, being adrift in foster care, waiting for a permanent home, or being subjected to given corporal punishment at school, then the advocate or advocacy group must turn its energies to fact-finding. Both client-centered and organization-centered or system-centered data that are relevant to the need for advocacy must be collected, organized, studied, and assessed—data such as the identified characteristics, needs, and legal rights of clients; societal and institutional perceptions of the client group; the responsibilities and resources of the organization or system; the location of the sources of power in the organization or system; and the nature of the decision-making process in the organization or system.

Gaps in services and obstacles to the utilization of services must be identified, such as barriers posed by insufficient or inappropriate allocation of staff resources, untrained staff, or failure to develop alternative practices—for example, alternatives to the use of secure detention for juvenile status offenders. The problem that is causing the trouble—the difficulty in the child–environment transactions—must be documented and analyzed before remedies can be developed and effective intervention can take place. Frequently this procedure requires becoming informed on substantive matters that affect the workings of the target organization or system; the nature of law and the judicial process; the knowledge about foster care that has been verified through research; the curriculum content of a public school program and what school administrators and teachers consider to be major curriculum issues; or the organization's or system's sources of funding and the legal constraints on its budgeting processes.

Political factors that affect or control the situation of concern must be assessed. These could include the positions taken earlier by key persons in the organization or system target or the points at which pressure is likely to be effective or to intensify resistance.

Once the problem has been defined and analyzed, then comes attention to what Knitzer terms "the heart of advocacy," that is, *the development of strategies and remedies.* "Without attention to strategies and remedies, fact-finding alone would be nothing more than an exposé" (Knitzer, 1976, p. 308). The advocate may rely on a single strategy or a range of interventions.

You have essentially asked and answered these questions during fact-finding:

> ❖ What specific service do I want this organization or system to provide for my child?
> ❖ If I cannot get this service, what service would be acceptable?
> ❖ Does this organization have a mandate to provide this desired or acceptable service?
> ❖ Does my child meet the eligibility criteria for this service as stated in the organization's policies?

Having determined that the organization is mandated to provide the service to children with conditions like your child has, the next step is to get the organization to provide the service. The strategy to do this may be benign or adversarial. A benign strategy is recommended when you know that the organization's mandate is to provide the desired or acceptable service. In some situations, the organization's policies include an internal dispute resolution or appeal process to a caseworker's decision. If the organization has such a policy, follow it!

An adversarial strategy, particularly if it involves administrative tribunals or courts, can take many years to resolve the conflict. However, even in a benign strategy, there is adversity if there has been a prior contact and services have been denied or the organization is overwhelmed by the volume of children needing the service and encourages screeners to apply narrow readings of the organization's policies to individual referrals. In this situation, you would confirm the decision with the person making the decision, attempt to understand the basis for their decision, provide additional information as necessary, discuss your understanding of the organization's policies as applied to your child's situation, and, if you cannot resolve the matter with him or her, advise that you wish to speak with the supervisor. Then you or your superiors convey the same message to people in that organization at progressively higher levels within the organization until you get the desired or acceptable service, or you have talked with the top person in the organization with no positive response. It is at this point—a final decision from the organization has been received—that an external adversarial strategy is pursued. This can be administrative or judicial in nature. For example, during fact-finding you identified the organization's source of funding, so you contact the funder requesting assistance in resolving the matter, or your agency or an advocacy organization files a lawsuit on behalf of the child alleging that the agency denied services to a child who met the eligibility criteria for services as stated in the agency's policies. Another increasingly useful strategy in situations in which organizations or systems are failing to meet their responsibilities is the media exposé. This will be discussed in more detail in the policy advocacy example that follows. The critical component in benign or adversarial strategies is that the advocate has facts and documentation that support the advocate's position. Enthusiasm, compassion, and a sense of mission are not enough. Box 12.2 summarizes the essential steps in a case advocacy project. See this chapter's Internet Sites and References sections for references on advocacy skills.

While case advocacy, class advocacy, and policy advocacy share many of the same steps as those stated in Box 12.2, class advocacy projects on behalf of named individuals and public policy advocacy projects include strategies infrequently used in individual case advocacy

Box 12.2

Steps in Case/Class Advocacy

1. Identify the specific child or children with the unmet need.
2. Define the specific problem to be resolved.
3. Determine the desired and acceptable resolutions.
4. Identify the barrier(s) to accomplishing your objective policy, practice/procedure, or person.
5. Determine who has the authority to eliminate the barrier(s)—start with the lowest person in the chain of command.
6. Assess options in approaching authority—who has the greatest potential to get them to agree to your position?
7. Implement approach strategy.
8. If unsuccessful, proceed through chain of command until final decision is received.
9. If no internal resolution, evaluate litigation option on behalf of an individual child or on behalf of a group of children who have similar unmet needs.

Source: Content adapted from Jansson, 1999; Chambers, 2000; Haynes & Mickelson, 2000; Mather & Lager, 2000; Midgley, Tracy, & Livermore, 2000.

projects. The primary strategy of all such projects is the development of coalitions of different groups of people, sometimes quite diverse, who have an interest in the problem or the proposed remedy. Steiner (1976) emphasized the significance of involving groups with a self-interest and joining them with social altruists as a driving force in the children's cause. As an example, he cited the national school lunch program. A powerful coalition of political forces came together to produce a greatly expanded national school lunch program. Lobbyists for agricultural interests and congressmen from rural states wanted to maintain an outlet for surplus farm products. Welfare-oriented congresspersons were responsive to the nutritional problems of children in poor families. The school lunch program was a convenience for middle-income groups, and the middle-income subsidy it provided was popular with some lawmakers in Washington, DC. Lobbyists for various nutrition groups and others interested in children's learning problems saw hungry children as unable to learn at school. Proponents of the War on Poverty viewed school lunches as an acceptable relief program. The American School Food Services Association, an association that exists in all fifty states, had a self-interest in an expanded universal program rather than one for poor children only. The association is made up of school lunch directors, supervisors, and line workers, and their organizational intent is to maintain job opportunities and improve wages and working conditions. A group of social altruists—an ad hoc Committee on School Lunch Participation—made up of five women's organizations, each with a religious orientation, set out to learn why relatively few children were participating in the school lunch program and why it was failing to meet the needs of poor children. As a result of their inquiry, they came out on the side of a universal program. An expanded program also had the support of another lobby, the Children's Foundation, an antihunger organization made up of social altruists and functioning independently of governmental funds. The result was a social benefit that is almost universally available in schools. Aside from public education itself, Steiner noted, no social welfare program provides public benefits to more children than the national school lunch program (Steiner, 1976).

As important as coalition building is, so is the *maintenance of coalitions*. Keeping a coalition together can be difficult and sometimes impossible, particularly when advocacy efforts at the peak of their consensus and influence meet powerful opposition.

A strategy that has been used successfully by advocacy groups as a way to increase the cadre of advocates and give them a self-interest in bringing about reform is to *reach out to and co-opt groups of volunteers*. "The volunteer-as-participant invariably becomes the volunteer-as-partisan" (Steiner, 1976, p. 249).

Box 12.3 summarizes the steps in policy advocacy. Box 12.4 summarizes the steps in developing a movement to effect policy change when it is necessary to develop interest in an issue to expand the number of participants in the coalition or to get people of influence to support your position with the legislative body.

Most policy advocacy occurs in the political arena. To be effective in that arena, child advocates must understand the difference between educating a legislator about a specific issue and lobbying for the introduction, passage, or defeat of a specific bill pending before the legislature. Education is permissible without limitations whereas lobbying is not. Lobby is "an attempt to influence legislation at the local, state, or federal level" (Internal Revenue Code, 26 CFR Section 1.501 (c) (3)-1(c) (3)). Many child advocates employed in private, nonprofit organizations and governmental units believe that they cannot engage in any lobbying activities. That is incorrect. Nonprofit organizations and their employees can lobby, but with restrictions as to what funds may or may not be used and how much of the organization's total resources, cash and in kind, can be

Box 12.3

Steps in Policy Advocacy

1. Define the problem.
2. Establish your desired outcomes—remember that policymaking is a compromise process—know when to hold them and when to fold them.
3. Identify other organizations and individuals who have an interest in the issue and share your concerns and desired outcomes with them.
4. Establish a coalition of individuals and organizations willing to pursue policy advocacy consistent with your values, principles, and objectives/outcomes.
5. Identify the policymaking branch and people within it who have the authority to change policies/programs to achieve the desired outcomes: legislative, executive, or judicial.
6. Determine the formal/informal systems for decision making in the appropriate policymaking branch.
7. Determine what actions will persuade public policymakers to implement changes (the strategy).
   ❖ Documentation
   ❖ Testimony
   ❖ Expert witnesses
   ❖ Written communications
   ❖ Face-to-face communications
   ❖ Client empowerment
8. Develop an advocacy plan acceptable to all coalition members including desired outcomes, strategies, and techniques.
9. Implement the advocacy plan with continued reassessment and modification until you achieve your desired objectives.
10. Achieve your advocacy objective and establish a monitoring system to ensure implementation.

Source: Content adapted from Jansson, 1999; Chambers, 2000; Haynes & Mickelson, 2000; Midgley, Tracy, & Livermore, 2000.

used. Prior to engaging in lobbying activities, the advocate, if employed by a nonprofit organization or governmental unit, must review his or her organization's policies on lobbying.

A child advocate working in the political arena on a consistent basis must have technical knowledge about government structures, budgeting, legislatures, and official program and policy guidelines as well as skills in political negotiation. It is not enough to know how to reach and influence major officials: The advocate must also be well informed on substantive issues. These advocates are generally from advocacy organizations with full-time staff for this purpose, such as the Child Welfare League of America, Children's Defense Fund, and National Association of Child Advocates. A child advocate who becomes active with a legislative body around a specific issue or pending legislation generally does so to provide information through letters and written or oral testimony. Haynes' and Mickelson's book, *Affecting Change: Social Workers in the Political Arena,* Fourth Edition, is an excellent resource for practical tips on legislative letter writing (campaigns or individual efforts) and testimony (oral and written).

Box 12.4

Steps in Developing a Movement to Effect Policy Change

1. Identify one or two people who share your interest, establish a leadership structure, define the problem, and establish desired outcomes.
2. Develop awareness of the need or problem by completing thoroughly researched policy briefs with executive summaries no longer than three pages.
3. Distribute the executive summary to targeted individuals or groups that have similar advocacy or policy interests. Tell them a policy brief is available if they wish more detail. Ask for their perspectives on the issue.
4. Utilize frequent and persistent contact, written and verbal, to educate these individuals and groups on the importance of the issue to children and to their overall concerns.
5. Increase presentation of issue to more groups, organizations, and individuals to increase awareness as well as expand options for potential solutions and advocacy strategies.
6. Encourage open discussion of the issue and mediate conflicts as the various solutions and strategies emerge.
7. Use fact-finding to resolve conflicts as well as to analyze potential strategies and solutions and develop a compromise position.
8. Use print and broadcast media to bring the issue and possible resolutions to the attention of the general public.
9. Continue with steps 4–10 listed in Box 12.3, Steps in Policy Advocacy.

Source: Content adapted from Jansson, 1999; Chambers, 2000; Haynes & Mickelson, 2000; Midgley, Tracy, & Livermore, 2000.

Another important part of successful advocacy is *monitoring*—maintaining contact with persons in a position to watch over the conduct of those who serve children. Monitoring, or follow-through, is essential if advocacy is to be more than a one-time exposé. Monitoring is a way to assure continuous community awareness and presence. It is particularly important in class action litigation in order to make sure that the process of implementing court decisions gets under way. It has also been used successfully in assuring that federal agencies implement legislation or that state agencies observe federal program guidelines.

CASE STUDY:
Using Different Advocacy Strategies and Skills.

This case example will highlight advocacy at the case, class, and policy levels. Due to space limitations, it will not demonstrate each step in the processes nor every skill. It is designed primarily to show how these different levels of advocacy are interrelated and how a single caseworker carrying out her day-to-day case management responsibilities can be the conduit for system change. Further, it demonstrates that child advocacy in child welfare includes parent advocacy. The case is intentionally designed to raise issues for disagreement and discussion. Disagreement, discussion, and compromise are the hallmarks of most advocacy projects. As we all know, there are no easy answers nor is there one resolution to any given set of facts in child welfare. This case is also designed to raise ethical considerations; for example: Should an employee request a court order mandating that her employer provide a needed service for a client?

The Blue case, discussed at the beginning of this chapter, was brought to the attention of children's protective services because 2-week-old Joseph was born drug addicted. There are two other children, aged 4 and 2 years. All children are in foster care. The mother, Ms. Blue, admitted to using cocaine during her entire pregnancy and for about three years overall. She reported that her neighbor took care of the children when Ms. Blue was too high to do so. She also reported that she had been in a substance abuse treatment program, but services were terminated because she had received the full thirty days of services for which she was eligible under Medicaid. Let us look at this case from three advocacy approaches: case, class, and policy advocacy. Our goal in this case is to return these children safely to their mother as soon as possible.

Common to all the approaches is fact-finding. Considering the facts necessary for a case advocacy approach, you know that there are three children under the age of 5 years and a mother who admits to ongoing substance abuse. Further, you know that she is sometimes too high to care for the children. Based on your knowledge of substance abuse and child development, you know that children of these ages require constant adult supervision and attention and that the use of cocaine inhibits the ability of Ms. Blue to meet these needs. Ms. Blue told you that a neighbor took care of the children when she was too high to do so. You need to verify that with the neighbor. You need to know how she knows when Ms. Blue is too high. You need to know her level of commitment to caring for these children on an ongoing basis because we know that substance abuse is an addiction subject to relapse at any time. You need to determine Ms. Blue's behaviors toward the children when she is and is not on drugs. You need to know what substance abuse services are available to Ms. Blue and the cost for those services. The results of your fact-finding follow:

❖ The neighbor, Mrs. Green, who lives in the downstairs flat, is an older woman who is retired with income from Social Security and a pension. She owns the house and has rented to Ms. Blue for about five years. She reported that she had checked in on Ms. Blue two or three times a day while she was pregnant. She reported that Ms. Blue was really too high "maybe twenty times in nine months." Prior to Ms. Blue's pregnancy, she would check in with her if she heard a lot of noise from the children or saw Ms. Blue come home "looking funny." In addition, she saw Ms. Blue and the children most afternoons on the porch or in the backyard. Sometimes Mrs. Green would be gardening while the children were playing outside. She had previously taken care of the older children while their mother was receiving in-patient substance abuse services. Further, she took care of the older children most afternoons while their mother was pregnant. Mrs. Green said that she had told the protective services worker that she was willing to be licensed as a foster parent for the children when the worker came to remove the older children from the mother's home after the baby was born. She remains committed to helping Ms. Blue and the children "in whatever way she can."

❖ Ms. Blue has had no previous reports of child abuse or neglect. Despite the fact that Ms. Blue said she had used drugs for about three years, the 2-year-old child was not born addicted to drugs based on the hospital birth records. You confirmed that Ms. Blue completed a thirty-day in-patient drug treatment program and was discharged because her Medicaid would pay for only thirty days. You were told that people with private insurance generally remain in the program for sixty days. She was placed on a waiting list for community-based services at discharge, has been on the waiting list for four months, and "probably would be in services in a month or so" according to the substance abuse treatment agency.

❖ During a visit, you observe Mrs. Green and Ms. Blue interacting with the children and with one another. Mary, the 4-year-old, easily goes back and forth between her mother and Mrs. Green to show off her drawings and to get help building a Lego toy. Michael, the 2-year-old, after some quiet play with the trucks, throws one at Mary. His mother comes over and tells him "don't throw things." About a half hour later, he runs around the room, falls over a truck, and lies on the floor crying. Mrs. Green goes to him, picks him up, sits in the rocking chair and rocks him, saying, "Is Granny's baby tired? Let's rest." Michael calms down. Joseph, the baby, wakes up. Ms. Blue checks his diaper, asks Mary to bring his bottle, and then sits beside Mrs. Green and starts feeding the baby.

How do these facts help your decision? You know that Mrs. Green is supportive and has been for the entire period Ms. Blue has lived upstairs. You know the children have a bond with her. It appears that Mrs. Green and Ms. Blue have a good relationship with one another and have a coparenting relationship with the children. You know that Ms. Blue was honest about her substance abuse treatment and is willing to continue with community-based services when "her turn comes up." From this, you conclude that there is no serious risk of harm to the children if they are returned home now. The supervisor is a little concerned because of the length of time the mother has used drugs and the lack of information as to when, why, and with whom she uses; but says to go ahead with the recommendation at the court hearing. The judge orders the children returned to the mother only if Mrs. Green agrees to provide daily contact with Ms. Blue and the children. Mrs. Green and Ms. Blue readily agreed to this stipulation. Further, the judge ordered weekly visits by the worker to include face-to-face contacts with all the children, the mother, and Mrs. Green. Finally, he orders the agency to get Ms. Blue into substance abuse treatment services this week because he is "tired of all these families waiting for months to get service." He wants you back in court next Tuesday to report that the order has been carried out.

Now your challenges begin. You have both a case advocacy and a potential class advocacy issue. The case advocacy issue is getting Ms. Blue into a substance abuse treatment program in one week when she is not scheduled to enter services for "a month or so." The judge, in his order and comments, identified a potential class advocacy issue: the long delay in getting parents of children in foster care into drug treatment services. You know that this issue is real because on your caseload alone you have five parents on waiting lists for substance abuse treatment services. This problem has been raised at staff meetings for the last year, and the supervisor says that higher-ups are meeting with the substance abuse agency to try to get more services. To your knowledge, this is the first time the judge has ordered the agency to get the parent services immediately.

You go to your supervisor and show her the order. She directs you to contact the substance abuse treatment agency and report that you have a court order requiring you to get Ms. Blue into services by next Monday. She takes a copy and says she would bring the matter to the attention of her superiors.

You contact the substance abuse treatment agency. You are told that there is no possible way Ms. Blue can get into services next week. There are thirty people on the waiting list before her. The court ordered your agency not the treatment agency to get her into services. You say that the only agency you can refer to is this agency because it is the central screening agency for all substance abuse services in the county. The screener says that is true, but she cannot make a decision to move someone up on the waiting list. You ask her for the name of the person who could make that decision. She gives you the name and phone number of her supervisor, Mrs. Yellow. You call her and leave a voice mail message. You tell your supervisor, and she says to keep her informed. She has shared the order with her supervisor, who, in turn, sent it to your legal affairs office. Your supervisor says, "This might be just what we need to bring this problem to a head." You are thinking about standing before the judge next Tuesday and the perspiration starts.

You get no call back before the end of the day, so you call Mrs. Yellow again. Her voice mail message now says she is out of the office until Thursday. Your supervisor is gone for the day. You have a sleepless night. The next morning, you contact the screener again and ask for someone above her supervisor. She gives you Mr. Brown's name and phone number. You call and leave a message in his voice mail. You then tell your supervisor the new developments. Also, you let her know that you have to replace a teen today, and it will take all day because you are moving him to a residential facility across the state. Your anxiety is high. She sees it and says she will follow up with Mr. Brown. You go. You have another sleepless night.

You return to the office hoping to see a message from your supervisor telling you that the problem is resolved. There is no message. Your supervisor, along with all the managers, is in a meeting out of the building until noon. You call Mr. Brown. He tells you quite angrily that he told your supervisor yesterday that he would have to discuss the matter with the agency's executive director because granting an exception in this case could lead this judge to order all the parents of children in foster care to be serviced by his agency immediately, which would create total chaos. You thank him. You remain anxious.

You call Ms. Blue to let her know the status. She says she is scared the judge will take the kids away from her if she is not in a program by next Tuesday. She says she talked to some women who were in the residential program with her. They meet at the church down the street from her each day—just them, no professionals—to support each other. She could join their group. Would that work? You tell her that you are not sure, but to go ahead and attend their meetings and ask if some of them would come to the hearing next Tuesday. You will talk with your supervisor about it this afternoon.

Your supervisor finally gets to the office. You tell her what has happened. She says you made a good decision in telling Ms. Blue to go ahead with the voluntary group because things did not look hopeful with the substance abuse treatment agency. Later that day, her supervisor tells her that there is a meeting of the executive directors of your agency and the substance abuse agency this afternoon. You get no feedback from the meeting by the end of the day. You rest a little better knowing that the executives had met and it is no longer just your problem.

It is Friday at last! You go to court on another case before the same judge. You hope he does not ask about Ms. Blue's situation. He does not, but he does order the agency to get the mother in this case into drug treatment within a week. You are on the treadmill again!! You immediately tell your supervisor. She had good news about Ms. Blue. She is to start in the program on Monday. However, she thinks this new order will upset the executives. It appears that you are the only worker who has been getting these orders. Are you asking for them? You tell her that you would have to be out of your mind to bring this kind of stress on yourself. You become quite upset that she would even ask the question. You tell the other workers what happened with your supervisor. They say they will start asking the judges to give them the specific orders on their cases that have been waiting for substance abuse and mental health services for long periods. They say: "It is about time somebody does something about this problem. The executives have known about it for years and done nothing. It is unfair to the children, their mothers, and the workers!!!" The movement begins.

You call Ms. Blue to tell her where to go to begin services on Monday. She tells you she will go. She will also continue with the self-help group and will bring two of them to the court hearing on Tuesday. Mrs. Green will take care of the children while she is gone.

At the hearing on Tuesday, you and Ms. Blue report that she is in substance abuse treatment. She talks about the self-help group. The judge listens to one of the women from the group and tells you that these self-help options should be considered by your agency instead of just letting the mothers stay on waiting lists indefinitely. He commends you and Ms. Blue for your creativity. He could see this approach as very cost effective and helpful to parents after agency services end to reduce relapses. He says he knows his orders have created quite a stir in both agencies because they have requested a meeting with all the judges to discuss the problem. He hopes this signals a reexamination of how the systems are structured so that children, families, and workers have an easier time getting the services that so many families need in order for the children to safely return home. Your opinion of him begins to change!

You immediately report to your supervisor. She appears troubled by the judge's comments. She tells you that you both must meet with the executive director tomorrow to discuss why you are the only one getting these orders. You are anxious and angry. You go back to your desk and see copies of five other court orders that other workers have gotten on their cases. These orders required your agency to start substance abuse or mental health treatment services for these mothers within seven to ten days. The anxiety and anger eases as you think, "I am not in this alone."

Over the course of the next two months, the executives of child welfare, substance abuse, and mental health and the judges meet and develop a plan accepted by all to increase the responsiveness of all systems to the children and parents served by the child welfare system whether under court order or not. This plan is shared with the workers. It looks as though the system will be more responsive. A group of workers met after reviewing the plan in detail. They discovered in reviewing the plan that there were federal funding

> requirements that mandated mental health and substance abuse services be provided and that priority be given to families with children in out-of-home care. These requirements had been in place for years. They concluded that they needed to work together on an ongoing basis to make sure that they knew what the regulations were and that they monitored their agency's implementation of the regulations on an ongoing basis. They had had too many sleepless nights and anxious days trying to get needed services that should have been readily available for children and families.

TRENDS AND ISSUES

Media attention to problems of children, youth, and their families will continue to play a significant role in elevating the needs of children to public exposure, discussion, and debate. Television, newspapers, opinion journals, popular magazines, and films publicize in different ways the problems of poverty, teenage pregnancy, juvenile crime, youth drug use and sales, increased HIV infection and AIDS in children and adolescents, multiple foster care placements, sibling separations, adoption drift (legally available children languishing in foster care because adoptive homes are not available), inadequate mental health services, and homelessness. Much of the publicity has drawn attention to the inadequacies of the child welfare system, among others. Currently, and historically, media publicity often focuses on the inadequacies of the systems and individuals charged with the responsibility to provide services to these children. Effective use of these media stories as advocacy tools requires, in the author's opinion, less defensiveness on the part of the systems and individuals attacked and greater readiness to objectively analyze the weaknesses and strengths of the system and make constructive changes. The College of Journalism at the University of Maryland has established the Casey Journalism Center for Children and Families as a national resource for journalists who cover children and their parents. It promotes careful and thorough examination of issues by reporters and supports this with conferences that expose journalists to national policy and research experts on a range of issues affecting disadvantaged children. This type of engagement promotes, within the journalism profession as a whole, reporting that provides more "good news" stories in which the systems or individuals are effective and more evidence based, specific target stories in which the systems or individuals are ineffective (Casey Journalism Center on Children and Families).

Federal and state legislation on behalf of children does not come easily. The 1990s saw continued shrinking of resources and a concomitant increase in competition for those that are available. This trend continues. Without doubt, many decisions in the next decade will be reached on the basis of finances. In such a milieu, the need for case, class, and policy advocacy on behalf of children (illustrated repeatedly throughout this text) will be critical. An essential piece of advocacy in the 2000s will be data. Outcome data on organizations and programs currently serving the population will be a requisite to enter the executive and legislative hallways. Once in the doors, advocates must clearly articulate how their proposals will enhance those outcomes. Suggesting and monitoring legislation, building coalitions, testifying in Congress and state capitals, securing and maintaining presence on executive agency policymaking and advisory committees, and becoming active in political campaigns will be necessary. Parents, youth, and other citizens need encouragement to express their views about the status of child and family life, the risks they see, and the changes they want in order to strengthen and maintain strong family life and maximum opportunity for children and youth.

The qualifications and training of child welfare workers continues to receive public scrutiny. Most child welfare workers are not professionally trained in social work. Few receive the depth and breadth of in-service or on-the-job training and supervision necessary to effectively manage the responsibilities of their positions. Many professionally trained social workers do not have child welfare–specific expertise. This presents challenges to the profession as well as to the individual worker. The community as a whole views all child welfare workers as "social workers." Bad practice is attributed to the profession, irrespective of the training of the child welfare worker involved. The National Association of Social Workers has undertaken the professionalization of child welfare workers as a strategy to alleviate the current situation (National Association of Social Workers, 2002). Legal judgments or settlements in individual cases or class actions against systems involving "bad practice" as well as the potential sanctions for not meeting the federal expectations under the Child and Family Services Review have encouraged many states to attend to issues of workforce development and system changes designed to facilitate compliance with existing mandates.

CHAPTER SUMMARY

In discussing professional responsibility, this chapter has provided a broad set of issues to consider as you undertake child welfare practice: confidentiality and privacy, liability and malpractice, confidentiality and privileges, forensic interviewing, risk management and duty to warn, clients' rights to treatment in a managed care environment, testimony, and advocacy. Its purpose was to show the range of responsibilities attributed to the professional and the dilemmas inherent in these responsibilities. Many of the dilemmas have no conclusive answer that the child welfare worker can rely on in every case. Decisions require balancing interests and consequences as applied to the current case situation. On the other hand, some are clearly resolved by statutory requirements that supercede ethical principles and standards, such as reporting suspected child abuse or neglect. A methodology has been provided to assist the worker in resolving the dilemmas and pursuing change for children through case, class, and policy advocacy.

FOR STUDY AND DISCUSSION
STUDY AND DISCUSSION QUESTIONS

1. Apply Reamer's seven steps for resolving ethical dilemmas to the following case situation. Kevin, age 16, has run away from his adoptive home. You have been working with the adoptive parents and Kevin concerning his adjustment to the family's expectations (he was adopted two years ago), his poor academic performance and acting-out behaviors in school (he was recently expelled for bringing a knife to school), and his sometimes explosive anger. You have identified several critical issues in your individual work with Kevin. He has never processed his grief over the termination of parental rights prior to his adoption. He yearns to find his birth family and has threatened to run away to look for them. He is frightened of some of the other male students at his high school and has verbalized that they might do "terrible things" to him, although he refuses to say more on the topic. His self-esteem is, as Kevin himself says, "so down in the pits it couldn't be lower." Kevin's perception is that he will never fit into his adoptive family because they are "so good and so religious."

You are awakened from a deep sleep at 2 A.M. by your agency on-call service. Kevin is in crisis and needs to talk to you immediately. You call the number given. Kevin is so upset that the conversation is disjointed and rambling, and it takes your best skills to keep him talking and get the facts: Kevin ran away in search of his birth parents, whom he could not locate. He is calling from the home of his (biological) uncle. While at his uncle's house he used some drugs (he does not specify what) and allowed his uncle to have anal intercourse with him, hoping to please his uncle so that he could find out what happened to his parents. He has been having what he describes as "flashbacks" about "nasty things that I did when I was a kid." He is afraid that he is gay and is in a panic. He wants to meet with you to talk, but will not do it unless you promise that you will not tell his adoptive parents you have had contact with him. If you try to contact his parents (or the police) he says he will either run away and never come back, or kill himself. He will not tell you where his uncle's house is or what his uncle's name is. He offers to come to your house to see you now or to meet you in some place away from the agency in the morning.

2. Which should take precedence when the needs of the child, the family, the agency, or society in general are in conflict? Are we ever justified in violating the law to help a client?

3. Joe is a 10-year-old child who entered foster care after his mother had broken his arm for the third time. He wants to go home with his mother. Does he have a right to self-determination? Why or why not? How do you explain your answer to him?

4. Joan is the 8-year-old daughter of the mayor of Big City. She has been referred to you by her teacher because she appears unusually anxious. Joan told you that her father has been rubbing the inside of her leg next to her vagina each night since school started. She thinks he should not be doing this and she wants to tell her mother, but she does not want her mother to get mad at her. You tell her that her father should not be doing this and you will help her. You report this to your supervisor and tell her that you will make the mandated report to the child protective services agency. She tells you not to make the report. She will make the report after she has discussed the situation with "administration." What do you say?

5. How can children and youth be given an opportunity to help define the problems and issues that are advocated in their behalf?

6. Methodically apply the advocacy steps outlined in this chapter to the case example given. Identify from that process the knowns and unknowns or places in which additional facts must be gathered and alternative strategies devised.

7. Select a problem facing a group of children or youth in your state or community. Apply the steps of advocacy described in this chapter to the problem.

8. Debate the merits of a variety of persons acting as children's advocates. Include lawyers, social workers, college students, parents, and teachers. A list of qualifications for advocates should emanate from such a discussion.

9. Discuss the limits on the extent to which agency child welfare workers can act as advocates for children on their caseloads and children not on their caseloads who are served by the agency.

10. Responsibility for the neglect of today's youth is broadly shared. Discuss ways in which society could reshape its attitudes and priorities to help children and youth with their problems.

Internet Sites

The following Internet sites provide excellent information to support advocacy efforts. Expanded descriptions are provided only for sites that were not described in other chapters. In addition, readers should consult the listings of Internet sites in other chapters for specific topics.

Administration for Children & Families, Children's Bureau
www.acf.dhhs.gov/programs

American Academy of Pediatrics.
www.aap.org.

American Public Human Services Association.
www.apwa.org.

Annie E. Casey Foundation.
www.aecf.org.

Casey Journalism Center on Children & Families.
www.cjc.umd.edu

Center for Law and Social Policy.
www.epn.org/clasp.html

Child Trends.
www.childtrends.org

Child Welfare Leagus of America.
www.cula.org

Child Welfare Information Gateway.
www.childwelfare.gov

Children's Defense Fund.
www.childrensdefense.org

Children's Rights, Inc. A New York based advocacy organization for abused and neglected children utilizing class action litigation as a source of change.
www.childrensrights.org.

Children, Youth and Family Education and Research Network.
www.cyfernet.mes.umn.edu/index.html

Families & Work Institute.
www.familiesandworkinst.org

Family Life Development Center.
http://child.cornell.edu/fldc.home.html

Federal Interagency Forum on Child and Family Statistics.
www.childstats.gov

First Gov. This is the website access for all agencies and departments of the Federal government. It provides access to all the national clearinghouses and resource centers on mental health, substance abuse, as well as the child welfare national resource centers.
http://firstgov.gov

Girls Study Group.
http://girlsstudygroup.rti.org

Kids Count.
www.aecf.org

National Association of Child Advocates.
www.childadvocacy.org

National Association of Social Workers.
www.naswdc.org

National Center for Children in Poverty.
www.cpmcnet.columbia.edu/dept/nccp

National Child Welfare Resource Center on Legal and Judicial Issues.
www.abanet.org/child/rclji

National Child Welfare Resource Center for Organizational Improvement.
www.muskie.usm.maine.edu/helpkids

National Center on Substance Abuse and Child Welfare (NCSACW).
www.ncsacw.samhsa.gov.

National Resource Center for Child Welfare Adoption.
www.nrcadoption.org

National Center for Adoption Law and Policy.
www.adoptionlawsite.org

National Center for School Engagements.
www.schoolengagement.org or
www.ttuancyprevention.org

National Data Analysis System.
http://ndas.cwla.org

North American Council on Adoptable Children.
www.nacac.org

Office of Juvenile Justice and Delinquency Prevention (OJJDP).
http://ojjdp.ncjrs.org

Race Matters Consortium.
www.racemattersconsortium.org

U.S. Department of State.
www.state/gov/family/adoption or
www.travel.state.gov/family/adoption/
intercountry

U.S. Department of Education, Office of Safe and Drug-Free Schools.
www.ed.gov/osdfs

U.S. Government Accountability Office (GAO). Until 2004, this office was known as the General Accounting Office (GAO). The GAO provides an accurate, fair, and balanced picture of federal programs and policies that are working well and acknowledges progress and improvements. GAO regularly consults with lawmakers and agency heads on ways to make government work better, from adopting best practices to consolidating or eliminating redundant federal programs.
www.gao.gov.

References

American Bar Association. (1991). *Liability in child welfare and protection work.* Chicago: Author.

Association of Social Work Boards (2007). Retrieved 02/22/2007 www.aswb.org. Social work laws & regulations online comparison guide.

Azar, S. T. (2000, May). Preventing burnout in professionals and paraprofessionals who work with child abuse and neglect cases: A cognitive behavioral approach to supervision. *Journal of Clinical Psychology*, 643–663.

Bailey, R., & Brake, M. (Eds.). (1975). In *Introduction: Social work in the welfare state.* New York: Pantheon Books.

Beck, R., & Butler, J. (1974). An interview with Marian Wright Edelman. *Harvard Educational Review, 44(1),* 1–12.

Black, H. C. (1992). *Black's law dictionary* (8th ed.). St Paul, MN: West.

Brohl, K. (2004). The new miracle workers: overcoming contemporary challenges in child welfare work. In *Understanding and preventing worker burnout.* (pp. 141–157). Washington, DC: Child Welfare League of America.

Casey Journalism Center on Children and Families. Retrieved February 21, 2007 from http://www.cjc.umd.edu.

Chambers, D. E. (2000). *Social policy and social programs: A method for the practical public policy analyst* (3rd ed.). Boston: Allyn & Bacon.

Child Welfare League of America. (1981). *Statement on child advocacy.* New York: Author.

Cloward, R. A., & Elman, R. M. (1967). The storefront on Stanton Street: Advocacy in the ghetto. In G. Brager & F. P. Purcell (Eds.), *Community action against poverty.* New Haven, CT: College and University Press.

Dickson, D. T. (1995). *Law in the health and human services—A guide for social workers, psychologists, psychiatrists and related professionals.* New York: Free Press.

Epstein, I. (1981, Summer). Advocates on advocacy: An exploratory study. *Social Work Research & Abstracts.*

Federal Rules of Civil Procedure (2007). Retrieved 06/27/2007 from www.supreme courtus.gov/court order/frcv07pdf

Field, T. (1996, Summer). Managed care and child wefare—Will it work? In *Public Welfare.* Washington, DC: American Public Welfare Association.

Fink, A. E., Anderson, C. W., & Conover, M. B. (1968). *The field of social work.* New York: Holt, Rinehart and Winston.

Gambrill, E. (1999). Evidence-based practice: An alternative to authority-based practice. *Families in Society, 80,* 341–50.

Gambrill, E. (2001). Social work: An authority-based profession. *Research on Social Work Practice, 11,* 166–175.

Gothard, S. (1995). Legal issues: Confidentiality and privileged communication. In *Encyclopedia of social work, vol. 2* (19th ed.) (pp. 1579–1584). Washington, DC: National Association of Social Workers.

Gustavson, N., & Maceration, A. E. (2002). Death and the child welfare worker. *Children and Youth Services Review, 24,* 903–915.

Haynes K. S., & Mickelson, J. S. (2000). *Affecting change: social workers in the political arena.* (4th ed.). Boston: Allyn & Bacon.

Holt, J. (1964). *How children fail.* New York: Pitman. Institute for Human Services Management (1996). *Managed care and child welfare: Are they compatible? Design issues in managed care for child welfare.* Bethesda, MD: Author.

Internal Revenue Code, 26 CFR § 1, 501(c) (3).

Institute for Human Services Management. (1996). *Managed care and child welfare: Are they compatible? Design issues in managed care for child welfare.* Bethesda, MD: Author.

Jansson, B. S. (1999). *Becoming an effective policy advocate: from policy practice to social justice* (3rd ed.). Pacific Grove, CA: Brooks/Cole.

Kahn, A. J., Kamerman, S. B., & McGowan, B. G. (1972). *Child advocacy: Report of a national baseline study.* Washington, DC: U.S. Children's Bureau.

Knitzer, J. E. (1976). Child advocacy: A perspective. *American Journal of Orthopsychiatry, 46(2),* 200–216.

Kosanovich, A., Joseph, R. M., & Hasbargen, K. (2005). *Child welfare consent decrees: Analysis of thirty-five court actions from 1995 to 2005.* Washington, DC: Child Welfare League of America and ABA Center on Children and the Law.

Kowal, L. W. (1996). *Keeping the focus on kids: Outcomes, ethics and partnerships in a managed care environment.* Paper presented at the American Humane Association's roundtable in Vail, Colorado.

Kozol, J. (1967). *Death at an early age.* Boston: Houghton Mifflin.

Mather, J. H., & Lager, P. (2000). *A unifying model of practice.* Belmont, CA: Brooks/Cole.

McNeill, T. (2006, April). Evidence-based practice in an age of relativism: Toward a model for practice. *Social Work, 51*(2), 147–156.

Meier, A. (2000). Offering social support via the Internet: A case study for an online support group for social workers. *Journal of Technology in Human Services, 17*(2/3), 237–266.

Menon, G. M., & Miller-Cribbs, J. (2002). Online social work practice: Issues and guidelines for the profession. *Advances in Social Work, 3*(2), 104–116.

Michigan Governor's Task Force on Children's Justice and Family Independence Agency. (1998). *Forensic interviewing protocol.* Lansing, MI: Family Independence Agency.

Mickelson, J. S. (1995). Advocacy. In *Encyclopedia of Social Work, vol. 1* (19th ed.) (pp. 95–100). Washington, DC: NASW Press.

Midgley, J., Tracy, M. B., & Livermore, M. (2000). *The handbook of social policy.* Thousand Oaks, CA: Sage.

Milner, V. (2004). The new frontier of social work: Using respect, empathy, curiosity and time. *Social Work Review, 16*(3), 38–43.

Morales v. Thurman, 380 F. Supp. 53E. D. Tex. (1974).

National Association of Social Workers. (1999). *Code of ethics.* Washington, DC: Author.

National Association of Social Workers. (2002). *Social work speaks.* Washington, DC: NASW Press.

National Association of Social Workers. (2004). *NASW standards for palliative and end of life care.* Washington, DC: Author.

National Association of Social Workers. (2005, July). *NASW procedures for professional review.* Washington, DC: Author.

National Association of Social Workers. Legislative agenda. Retrieved from website, http://www.naswdc.org/advocacy/childwelfare 02/22/2007.

National Association of Social Workers and Association of Social Work Boards. (2006). *NASW and ASWB standards for technology in social work practice.* Washington, DC: Authors.

National Child Welfare Resource Center for Family-Centered Practice. (2004, Winter). *Best practice/next practice: Family-centered child welfare: Mental health in child welfare: A focus on caregivers.* Washington, DC: Department of Health and Human Services.

National Clearinghouse on Child Abuse and Neglect Information. (1998). *State statute series.* Washington, DC: Author.

National Community Mental Healthcare Council. (1997). *Child welfare and managed care briefing.* Rockville, MD: Author.

Ness, M., Pizzigati, K., & Stuck, E. (2002). *A child advocacy primer: Experience and advice from service providers, board leaders, and consumers.* Washington, DC: Child Welfare League of America.

Netting, F. E., Kettner, P. M., & McMurtry, S. L. (1998). *Social work macro practice* (2nd ed). New York: Addison Wesley Longman.

Office of the United Nations High Commissioner for Human Rights. *Signatures and Ratifications of the Convention on the Rights of the Child.* Retrieved February 21, 2007 from http://www.ohchr.org/english/countries/ratification/11.htm.

Parker-Oliver, D., & Demiris, G. (2006, April). Social work informatics: A new specialty. *Social Work, 51*(2), 127–134.

Paul, J. L. (1977). *Child advocacy within the system.* Syracuse, NY: Syracuse University Press.

Pennsylvania Association for Retarded Citizens v. Commonwealth of Pennsylvania, 334 F. Supp. 1257, E.D. Pa. (1971).

Reamer, F. G. (1995). *Social work values and ethics.* New York: Columbia University Press.

Reamer, F. G. (2003). *Social work malpractice and liability: Strategies for prevention* (2nd ed.). New York: Columbia University Press.

Reamer, F. G. (2006). Nontraditional and unorthodox interventions in social work: Ethical and legal implications. *Families in Society, 87*(2), 191–197.

Richan, W. C. (1991*). Lobbying for social change.* New York: Haworth.

Rule 23 Federal Rules of Civil Procedure.

Rosen. A., & Proctor. E. K. (2003). *Practice guidelines and the challenge of effective practice.* In A. Rosen & E. K. Proctor (Eds.), *Developing practice guidelines for social work intervention: Issues, methods, and research agenda* (pp. 1–16). New York: Columbia University Press.

Silberman, C. E (1971). *Crisis in the classroom.* New York: Random House.

Specht, H., & Courtney, M. E. (1994). *Unfaithful angels: How social work has abandoned its mission.* New York: Free Press.

Steiner, G. Y. (1976). *The children's cause.* Washington, DC: The Brookings Institution.

Stoesen, L. (2004, April). Technology is focus of new initiative. *NASW News.* Washington, DC: NASW Press.

Strom-Gottfried, K., & Mowbray, N. D. (2006). Who heals the helper? Facilitating the social worker's grief. *Families in Society, 87*(1), 9–15.

Stroul, B. A., Pires, S. A., Armstrong, M. I., & Meyers, J. C. (1998). The impact of managed care on mental health services for children and their families. *The future of children: Children and managed mental health care, 8*(2).

Tompkins, C. (1989, March 27). Profiles: Marian Wright Edelman: A sense of urgency. *New Yorker,* 48–50.

United States Government General Accounting Office. (1998). *Child welfare: Early experiences implementing a managed care approach.* HEHS-99-8. Washington, DC: U.S. Government Printing Office.